THE HOWARD HUGHES HOAX

HOAX

CON MEN, CORRUPTION AND THE FAKE BURIAL OF A BILLIONAIRE

REVIEWS: *The HOWARD HUGHES HOAX*
****

I do not profess to be expert in all the medical arts. However, in consideration of my knowledge of endocrinology, (toxicology) it appears to me that the lab-tests, evident in Mr. Clotfelter's book *"The Howard Hughes Hoax,"* are not indicative of renal failure being the sole cause of death of the corpse, believed to be "Howard Hughes," autopsied at the Methodist Hospital, Houston, Texas, in 1976.

Furthermore it was apparent to me, as it would be to most in the medical arts, that the destruction of the ribcage, breastplate, clavicle, and spinal bone tissues (as described in numerous news articles concerning Howard Hughes and his 1946 XF-11 test plane crash into Beverly Hills, Calif.) could not have healed to the extent of being non-evidential in the Methodist Hospital "HH" corpse autopsied 30 years later.

> DR. ROLAND MD
> ANESTHESIOLOGIST

The thesis begins too fantastic to be true. The implausible begins to appear possible, then even probable. An impressive compilation of supporting exhibits makes a compelling case.

> STEPHEN H. RODGERS
> ATTORNEY AT LAW

As a follow-up to his earlier work (*The Price of Their Souls*), Mr. Clotfelter's exquisitely researched work (*The Howard Hughes Hoax*) captures the essence of conspiracy to mislead the public and camouflage the truth about Howard Hughes's death. In doing so, Mr. Clotfelter unfurls a treasure trove of background material which makes his analysis and conclusions both thought provoking and compelling.

> ALAN R. BRADFORD M.S.

As far as insights into the medical side of Mr. Hughes's life, I have one major remark. Pathological evidence of identity usually would have to pertain to the skeletal system. His collarbone fracture, regardless of surgery or close reduced, *would leave evidence.* If an x-ray of the remains depicted a healed or unhealed fracture identity could be confirmed. If the collarbone appears anatomic (without irregularity) more cause for DNA testing could be argued.

> DR. CASEY MD
> PODIATRIST

Other publications by
Charles R. Clotfelter

Price of Their Souls
The Truth About Howard Hughes and Those Who Betrayed Him

We Aquatus

THE HOWARD HUGHES HOAX

CON MEN, CORRUPTION AND THE FAKE
BURIAL OF A BILLIONAIRE

THE CONTINUING INVESTIGATION INTO:
"The Truth about Howard Hughes and Those Who Betrayed Him"

A Documentary by Charles R. Clotfelter

Area 51 Publications

THE HOWARD HUGHES HOAX

CON MEN, CORRUPTION AND THE FAKE BURIAL OF A BILLIONAIRE

Published by Area 51 Publications
www.area51publications.com

The HOWARD HUGHES HOAX © 2021 by Charles R. Clotfelter 1st ed.
Book Jacket Design by: Anton Tielemans
Author Photographed by: Kelly Viers-Milburn
Interior Design: Dr. Donna Raymond PharmD
Proofing: Jo A. Wilkins
Editor: Sophia Falke

Clotfelter, Charles R.
The Howard Hughes Hoax: Con Men, Corruption And The Fake Burial Of A Billionaire.
Charles R. Clotfelter. — 1st ed.
p. cm.
ISBN-: 978-1-892584-01-4 Trade paperback
ISBN-: 978-1-892584-00-7 Hardback

1. Biography & Autobiography / Rich & Famous.
2. True Crime / Con Artists, Hoaxes & Deceptions.
3. True Crime / Murder / General.

Printed in the United States of America

10 9 8 7 6 5 4 3 2 1

Aside from minor speculation this book is a factual documentary. The investigative work done, and the revelations herein, is quite possibly the last chance to vindicate the most brilliant industrialist of the 20th Century. Not a perfect man, none of us are, he was genuine, good, and a better man than most.

To the memory of
Howard Robard Hughes, Jr.

Acknowledgement

Writing a book and correlating its contents is not the finality. In publishing, there are many necessary components.

Special thanks to:

Chief Laurence "Russ" Russell for his knowledge and numerous contributions within the book. Keven Towe for his knowledge of computers and his willingness to help whenever needed. Prakit Dechasit, my stepson, forever present when my computer was having indigestion. Anton Tielemans, graphic designer, for the book's cover and creative suggestions thereon. Jo A. Wilkins for her knowledge of publishing and guidance. Dr. Donna Raymond PharmD for her great job of interior design and partial editing. Sophia E. Falke for the book's editing and its Introduction.

For reviews and observations by:

Dr. Roland MD

Stephen Rodgers Attorney at Law

Alan R. Bradford MS

Dr. Casey MD

THE TRUTH ABOUT HOWARD

Write a book to right a wrong
Perhaps few there are to believe
Then will come those who say
"He seeks to deceive!"
Those degenerate men of ill-gotten gain
With their political powers renowned
Marshaling up a malevolent force bray:
"Drive it underground!"

But it's too late! For you shall know
What is true and what's a lie
There's a division within this world
Encountered by and by
Those mostly of the good
Who'll look you in the eye
And those who'll travel Hell's dark realms
When it comes their time to die.

A boy came once into this world
In his youth shy and withdrawn
Later to tread upon life's path
Brilliant, aware and strong
His mother passed at too young an age
His father died soon after
Leaving him a hollow lad
Devoid of joy and laughter

At his parents' graves he must have made
A promise to them both
"We shall not lose the name of Hughes"
To Heaven he sent the note
Know you this! In these current days

When we take to the air and fly
The Hughes name flies there with us
In the hardware or the drive

Howard took many a chance
Lesser men would not have taken
In peril he would leave the earth
Testing his own creations
He flew them fast and flew them far
Oft risking his life alone

Several times he crashed his craft
Or barely made it home
Did capricious Fates exact a debt?
From the man in his power bird?
"Oh Hell!" within that airborne craft
A sickening sound was heard!
With no one there but Howard
To know what had occurred

As if Shiva's hand grasped the plane's right wing
And pressed it toward the earth
With nerves of steel he gripped controls
Preparing for the worst
Going down, up came the ground
Were there others there beneath?
Could he save them and himself?
His thoughts a shroud of grief

Confined within the derelict
He flew it to the end
Did he ask God for one more chance
A miracle to send?
Is prayer once granted a debt to pay?
None can know save God

Did Howard keep his desperate vow
Once pulled from that plane's crushed pod?
What can we know of heavenly realms?
What's taken or forgiven?
A broken man at a future time
Was this Howard's price for living?

Yes! Howard died a broken man
Though not the way they said
To have his true condition known in life
Would he rather have been dead?
They said he died a sick old fool
A hypochondriac was he
Consuming vast arrays of drugs
To set psychosis free

Did he take drugs? Of course he did!
With pain he daily reckoned
Slowly crushed within himself
Minute to minute stricken
Did Howard take drugs recreationally?

He took them to stay alive!
Those who would say other than this
Would be a devil's lie!
Did Howard die in seventy-six?
As chroniclers had believed
Most likely he died in sixty-five
In agony, alone and aggrieved

I'm honor-bound to write this book
Though it saddens me to do it
Could justice be served another way?
I prayed God to point me to it
From the universal God to me
There came no verbose answer

Yet a whisper deep within me urged
"Try to heal this cancer"

When first we come into this world
We gain the gift of sight
What molds us in the passing years
Is to learn what's wrong or right
If we've seen grave injustice done
Attempting not to make it right
Better were we not born at all
Having never seen the light

Heaven and Hell wait high and low
When a father gives up his son
Was it for a sacred cause?
Or for iniquity was it done?
Should the tale a father's son must tell
Be shallow and unfounded
Cast him away into the Pit
Bewildered and astounded!

Should you read on and agree with me
Through knowledge or persuasion
We must set our conscience free
And form a close liaison
I have faith in acts of God
Of being aided if we try
Even if it's just we two
We'll be allies you and I

Table of Contents

Table of Contents
Continued

INTRODUCTION

It was my honor to edit this book, *The Howard Hughes Hoax: Con Men, Corruption, and the Fake Burial of a Billionaire*, by Charles Clotfelter. When I suggested to Charles that it would help the reader if he added an Introduction to explain why he wrote this documentary, the purpose of certain stories and history lessons, and a little about his writing style, he asked me if I would write the Introduction. I jumped at the chance, because I believe this work needs to be shared with the world.

As Charles Clotfelter mentions in the Forward, this book exposes one of the greatest hoaxes of the twentieth century and uncovers how a small group of cunning, larcenous men and women conspired to line their own pockets and fool an entire world.

If you are of a certain age, you will remember Howard R. Hughes, Jr. Depending on which news report you saw, movie you watched, or biography you read, you may think of him as eccentric, reclusive, secretive, private, brilliant, innovative, wealthy beyond measure, generous, or an addict. What I learned from editing this book is that much of what we think we know about Howard Hughes is carefully crafted fabrication and illusion intended to defraud a vulnerable man and deceive a gullible public. If this were a movie (and I hope someday it will be), it would be filled with intrigue, conspiracy, cover ups, incompetence, lies, tragedy, and premeditated murder made to look like accidents.

Do we have your attention? This book makes some serious allegations, and it's about to name names and provide evidence to support these claims. But first I want to tell you why Charles wrote this book and why he cares that the world knows the truth about Howard Hughes.

In Chapter II, Charles tells the story of how a sick young man named Charles was helped by a man named Howard. It was 1964 and took place in Mexico. Charles Clotfelter, the author of this book, is that Charles, and he was 24 years old. He didn't realize that the kind man who helped him in his time of need was the famous Howard Hughes. He also didn't realize that the holographic (handwritten) document that Howard put in his backpack might well have been a codicil to Hughes's will.

Charles didn't think much more about his interaction with Howard until after he moved to Las Vegas, Nevada, and happened upon a portrait of Howard R. Hughes at the University of Nevada, Las Vegas. This jogged Charles's memory of that chance meeting so many years prior, and it got him curious because the portrait of a tall, straight man was much different from the crippled Howard he had met. It triggered a memory of Howard's description of crashing his plane in Beverly Hills, the damage it did to his body, and how the doctors had told him he would die within a year. So, Charles began to research who and what Howard Hughes was. The more Charles uncovered, the more he experienced disbelief and dismay over the many negative, derogatory descriptions portrayed of Howard Hughes in the news, in books and movies.

I asked Charles why he cared so much that the world might have the wrong picture of Howard Hughes. The answer moved me. "For one, the man that I spent two days with back in 1964 was a man of integrity, kindness, and honor. I base this opinion on the open and honest conversations we had and his willingness to help a stranded young fellow." Charles continued to describe how what is said about Howard Hughes from 1965 to 1976 is based on lies and deceit. He believes Howard's act of kindness in 1964 may have saved his life. Charles wants to repay Howard's kindness by exposing the hoax perpetrated by his inner circle of high-level employees and restoring Howard R. Hughes's legacy.

In this book you will find that Charles sometimes writes in the present tense even though the event occurred many years ago. He does this to bring you more intimately into the narration. And even though he presents a great deal of factual documentation from which you can draw your own conclusions, he sometimes lets his opinion of certain people show through by giving them less-than-positive nick names. And yes, sometimes he thinks the evidence is so blatantly obvious, he lets his incredulity that anyone would miss the truth show with less-than-positive side comments. In short, Charles can be a little sarcastic at times. And yes, he is prone at times to using colloquialisms. That's just the way he talks. Within the text, Charles differentiates between the living Howard Hughes and the doppelgangers and forgers by using quotation marks (" ") around the "Hughes" name. You will find the quotation marks appearing most often for the years after 1965, when the real Howard R. Hughes, Jr. died. You will also discover that Charles can be repetitious. He does that intentionally to make it easier for you to find the documentation included in this book and remember its relevance and why it is important.

In Chapter I, Charles tells the story from his childhood when he encountered a dog fight and discovered the power and tenacity of the bulldog. He tells the story as a prelude to his introduction of Laurence M. Russell, a retired law enforcement officer, whose "bulldog" diligence and tenacity unearthed much of the documentation you will find in this book. In later chapters he also offers mini history lessons to provide context and support for the hypotheses and speculations presented.

In short, Charles's intent is to present a compelling story drawn from history and (until now) little known facts, mix in a little educated speculation, and pay tribute to a great man who deserves to be honored and have the truth of his life and contributions known to the world.

Sophia E. Falke
Speaker, Coach, and Author

FOREWORD

What is the measure of a man? The question is not original and is most likely as old as history itself. If one said a man's measure is determined by the size of his bank account, this misses the mark in the eyes of the truly intelligent. Legions are those who grew exceedingly wealthy because of what they usurped from others; yet it is wrong to say, "All wealthy men are unscrupulous." Then there are those who would say that the man of greatest stature is he who can subjugate all others to his ideologies; however, this idea is also false. There are honorable men who may contribute little to the society of man, but they do so to the best of their abilities and there is a great need for them within the productive societies of men. Yet, although the honorable man is well accepted in his community and none need fear or have reason to shun him, the man who has achieved great wealth because of his diligence, intelligence, and ability to organize great projects is the greatest of us all. Why? Because *all men are not created equal*. The truth within the human condition is simply this: No man or woman has the same fingerprints, the same genetic code, the same morality, the exact same beliefs, are benevolent or evil to the same degree, or have the same drive or intellectual ability to remember, plan, or think creatively.

Many are misled by politicians who unscrupulously preach the ideology of "all men are created equal" to inflate the egos of the populace. They are pandering for the people's votes. However, the idea of true equality (as in "the same as") is pure fiction. *All men are created <u>unequal</u> and are unequal regardless of their ethnicity*; this is the real truth. The meaning of equality within the preamble of the laws that govern us was – and is – necessary to firmly establish that <u>all citizens</u> of the United States *are to be equal before the law*. Many would believe that equality before the law is the "Will of God" or that "all men are equal in the eyes of God." However, the statement that "all men are created equal," welded together our forefathers against a common foe, and this is a given. We had a war to fight to free ourselves from an overbearing monarchy; we wanted to be free men, not subjects. Our forefathers were willing to gamble their fortunes, lives, and sacred honor for the greater good. Hence, we have the freedom and prosperity we now enjoy in this great republic known as the United States of America. In the words of John Adams, "The very definition of a republic is '*an empire of laws and not of men.*'"

This book is mainly about a man named Howard Robard Hughes, Jr. – a man who did not seek to subjugate others or to deprive them of their substance in any way. He was simply a man with great ideas and a bit of wealth with which to bring them to fruition. His companies became pioneers in the movie industry, aeronautics, electronics, and military weaponry. Within the pages of this book you will learn the true greatness of a man who oversaw an empire which generated massive employment for many thousands of people. He was a fair and honorable man, mostly admired and willingly worked for. The portrayals of a Hughes who became a drug addicted, xenophobic recluse are totally false! This misleading and abusive publicity surfaced only after 1965 – the year in which he actually died. This adverse propaganda about Hughes was necessary so his once trusted inner-circle and their minions could steal what was not rightfully theirs.

Within this book you will not only learn about the greatest hoax of the twentieth century, you will also discover to what lengths his renegade lieutenants would go after his death to gorge and enrich themselves at the trough of Hughes's vast fortune. In order to gain their illicit wealth and power, they needed to destroy his legacy, degrade him, and portray him as a decadent, sorry man.

The deceit began when Hughes dropped out of public view after 1954. The propaganda was that he disappeared because of mental illness or drugs. That is a lie; and within the pages of this book, you will discover the actual reasons for his withdrawal. It is likely that if we had the same problems to deal with as Howard did, we would have evaded society as well. Was he a man without faults? None of us are. Was the degree of his faults objectionable? No, not really. Was he a better man than most? I believe the answer is simply, "Yes."

Charles R. Clotfelter

THE HOWARD HUGHES HOAX

CON MEN, CORRUPTION AND THE FAKE BURIAL OF A BILLIONAIRE

THE CONTINUING INVESTIGATION INTO:
"The Truth about Howard Hughes and Those Who Betrayed Him"

CHAPTER I

COURAGE WITH INTENT

It was many years ago. So long ago that Charlie was amazed he could remember an incident with dogs that so fascinated him in his youth.

Never much of a crowd pleaser as a child, with one or maybe no friend, the boy would often wander far afield on weekends, *seldom* arriving back home in time for dinner – an inconsideration which greatly displeased his mother. The boy never wanted to intentionally cause his mother grief, but the constant tug of adventure seemed an uncontrollable genetic trait within him. When he left the front door of his house on a weekend morning, any idea of scheduling went out the back door. Unrestrained desire for adventure is often not good in a child, *especially* one less than ten. However, the tangible rewards often discovered by the boy were "golden" to his inquisitive mind.

The landscape in San Diego, California, was sparsely populated in the 1940s. Saturday had arrived, and Charlie was gone for the day. After hiking for an hour, the boy delighted in finding himself among rolling hills and grassy meadows – just the environment where amazement could be kindled by the observation of wild creatures in their natural habitats.

The late spring day was relatively mild, with sparse clouds in a bright blue sky. A cool breeze tugged gently at the boy's blond hair as he neared the crest of a hill. From the other side, voices of anguish and antagonism soon became audible. Charlie quickly discerned that the voices were of boys, perhaps older boys. *What was causing the excitement in the field beyond?* Curiosity prodded him as he hurried to the hilltop. Below were four boys and two dogs.

At a glance, it was difficult to discern what was taking place. Walking down the slope of the hill toward the commotion, Charlie viewed the hostile, larger dog as it danced about snapping at, then closing in and slashing the body of its squat, smaller adversary. The little dog was obviously suffering the abuse of the larger, but always managed to position itself between its antagonist and the youngest of the boys. Charlie soon realized to whom the small dog belonged, as the younger pleaded tearfully with an older boy to call off his dog. The older boys continued to cheer on the large dog as it snarled, snapped, and lacerated its smaller short-legged opponent.

To side with the younger boy, Charlie looked about for a heavy stick with which to even the odds. Finding only a nearby rock, he picked it up and continued toward the commotion. Bracing to throw his rock at the larger dog, he hesitated as an incredible thing took place. The larger dog closed in, perhaps for a kill, when suddenly, with amazing swiftness for such a squat little fellow, the smaller dog leapt up and sank a wide bite into the throat of the larger. Bracing firmly, the larger dog frantically tried to shake loose the smaller, which held its grip and swayed like a pendulum beneath the larger dog's neck. Within a minute the larger dog was on the ground. Now, with the younger boy pulling desperately at the mid-section of his dog and an older boy pulling at the hind legs of the larger dog, they tried to separate the two. Their efforts were futile. Even when the other boys pitched in, the biter and the bitten could not be separated. The larger dog's fight for conquest had now become a fight for life. All too soon the large dog was laying on its side thrashing about to no avail. Eventually the large dog's flailing was replaced by trembling, then stillness, as its eyes glazed over. In all of six minutes the large dog was dead, suffocated, its windpipe crushed. Now it was the older boy who cried as he looked about and picked up a rock, clearly meant for the little champion. Charlie threw the rock he held at the older boy's head. It landed, causing the boy to drop his rock and pace about in pain holding his head. By this time, the smaller dog had released its grip and ambled over to his owner who, now sitting cross-legged, joyfully cradled his bloodied victor in welcoming arms. The other two boys looked like they were about to go after the young boy and his dog but saw that Charlie had picked up the rock their friend had dropped and, perhaps thinking him to be pretty good in the art of rock-tossing, had second thoughts about taking him on. Perhaps they also thought of what that little dog might do to a leg if further provoked. So, they picked up the dead dog and headed off, followed by its owner, still in tears, still holding his head.

Charlie's new friend and his dog found a pond nearby. They washed the blood, as best they could, from the dog's body. The younger boy took off his shirt and used it to dry the excess water and blood from his happy vanquisher. Badly lacerated and obviously still in pain, the boy's dog nevertheless vigorously wagged his little stump of a tail in a show of affection for his young master.

When Charlie asked the boy where he had gotten such an amazing little dog, the boy told him his father had gotten it at the pound when just a puppy. Father and son had agreed on the name of "Billy" for the new family addition, thinking this to be an appropriate name for the little Bulldog. Billy would prove to be a friendly and docile companion over the years – up until now, when he believed duty called him to the defense of his master. Later that day both father and son would be discussing the heretofore unknown attributes of the household pet with the veterinarian as he stitched up Billy's numerous wounds.

Charlie had never forgotten the intelligence, bravery, and determination of that amazing little dog, which had waited for the larger dog's mistake and then intuitively made its move, holding its vital grip until the last tremors of life had left the body of its much larger opponent.

It would grip Charlie's mind in later years that had the astrologers of old known of Bulldogs, they most certainly would have incorporated this creature into their discipline. Perhaps the Bulldog would have replaced the Ram or Lion in their charts as a symbol of courage, tenacity, and determination.

We will come back to the concept of bulldog personalities later, but prudence now deems that we recap previous happenings in this continuing investigation into *The Howard Hughes Hoax: Con Men, Corruption, and the Fake Burial of a Billionaire. The Continuing Investigation Into: "The Truth About Howard Hughes and Those Who Betrayed Him"*. We will then move into current investigative events which will amaze even the most skeptical of readers.

CHAPTER II

RECAP: *THE PRICE OF THEIR SOULS*

This chapter recaps information found in Charles Clotfelter's first book, *The Price of Their Souls*, published in 2012. The summary below is necessary to introduce the previous investigations to those who have not yet read that book and to refresh the episodes in the minds of those who have. This book expands and deepens our understanding of the hoax perpetrated against Howard Hughes, one of the great innovators and industrialists of the twentieth century. This in-depth investigation is possible because of the research, expertise, and insights of Laurence M. Russell, beginning with Chapter III: "The Bulldog."

Who was that fellow they buried in the Hughes family plot in 1976?

In 1964 a young man named Charles finds himself sick with dysentery and stranded without funds in the bottom of Mexico. His father wires him 50 dollars, and he begins his 3,000-mile trek back to the United States. Because he is so sick, he believes he needs to get back stateside quickly since a bout with another illness, perhaps even the flu, together with his current dysentery could do him in. Because of various mitigating circumstances, he believes his quickest exit from Mexico would be to hitchhike – not really the safest or wisest of decisions.

Just north of Ciudad Hidalgo, Charlie catches a ride with a man who is terribly bent and deformed. To drive his van, he must look *through* the steering wheel rather than over it as most people do. Once in the van, Charlie reaches toward the driver in a friendly gesture to shake hands and introduce himself. The fellow refuses Charlie's gesture, claiming that the shaking of hands is *"the best way in the world to transmit disease."*

After an extended period of silence, the man introduces himself as *Howard*, and Charlie notices that Howard's *large brown felt hat* seems to accent his personality. Charlie explains that he is trying to reach Oaxaca where he can readily board a northbound train back to the States. Howard responds, "I believe I can get you most of the way there."

In their journey together, Howard and Charlie talk about many things. But the portion of the conversation which remains to this day vividly etched in Charlie's memory is when, after an extended period of silence, Howard explains, *"I wasn't always like this you know."* Of course, Charlie didn't know but was soon to find out that Howard had been **a non-military test pilot and had crashed a plane into the Beverly Hills area of California.** Howard explains that he had sustained multiple injuries, especially to his back, and that, *"At first the doctors thought I would be okay, but they were wrong!"* Howard further shares that, *"Eventually my spinal column began to collapse, and I became as you see me now."* Howard tells Charlie, *"Because of the collapsing vertebrae, the top part of my body is now crushing my internal organs and eventually they will cease to function."* After a brief pause Howard continues, *"The doctors have only given me eight months to live."* Charlie is greatly saddened by this information. Silence ensues. Charlie, although not meaning to be rude but weakened by his own illness, unintentionally doses off.

Charlie is awakened by the van rocking its way over several potholes in a driveway leading into a small motel. Howard tells Charlie, *"You can sleep in my van, but only if you promise not to go through my personal things."* Charlie is grateful and promises.

Charlie sleeps sporadically in Howard's van but vaguely remembers, as if in a dream, someone opening the driver's side of the van and putting something into his backpack upon which Charlie had rested his head. The next day Howard explains to Charlie, *"I put a letter in your backpack last night while you were sleeping. It won't mean much to you now, but will later, so don't lose it."* Charlie is a bit concerned that Howard had been able to place a letter in his backpack while he slept but dismisses it as an idiosyncrasy of his benefactor. Howard, more than true to his word, drops Charlie at a train station in or near Oaxaca.

Once on the northbound train, Charlie looks in his backpack for medicine to help control his dysentery, when he comes across the letter Howard had left him. Charlie removes the letter from its plain white envelope and notices it is well-written, almost as if done by a calligraphist. But he quickly returns it to its envelope and stuffs it back into his backpack. Charlie heads for the restroom where he relieves the now liquid contents of his bowels – one of many trips he will make on his journey north. Exhausted from the episode, he finds his way back to his seat and drifts off to sleep, forgetting about the letter.

Charlie eventually reaches Snow, Oklahoma, where his father owned a ranch at the time. The day after his arrival at the ranch, his stepmother Ricki goes through his backpack and finds Howard's letter. She gives the letter to Charlie's father who holds it up in his left hand and asks, "Son, is this your letter?"

Having nearly forgotten about Howard's letter Charlie asks, "What is it dad?"

His father explains, "Ricki found it in your backpack while looking to wash your clothes."

At this point Ricki walks up to Charlie's father and says, "George, I believe it's a will." Charlie doesn't believe this and doesn't want to go into an explanation of what he feels to be a personal relationship between Howard and himself. He does not discuss the fellow's medical problems with his dad and stepmother. Charlie dismisses the letter as non-consequential and eventually loses track of it – never having read it.

Charlie's father had opted to retire from the Navy in 1964 and raise cattle in a state where the land was poor. Traditionally where the land is poor – as most of Oklahoma is – the people are poor, but his father had his military retirement to live on and had saved up a bit of money while in the service. **Charlie returns to Oklahoma after 1976.**

He is proud of his father's accomplishments and presumes that his dad has literally pulled himself up by his boot straps, buying a 1,400-acre ranch out of receivership near Wardville, Oklahoma, while still owning the 360-acre starter ranch in Snow, free and clear. Immediately Charlie sees that his Dad is extremely successful with more than a million dollars in state-of-the-art farm equipment and blooded Brangus cattle, which he sells mostly for breeding purposes. "All this in 10 years?" Charlie asks himself. But all is not well in paradise. Charlie discovers his dad is no longer the father he once knew; it appears that wealth has changed his dad.

Charlie meets his wife and starts a family in Oklahoma. However, he realizes he no longer belongs there and relocates his family to the up-and-coming metropolis of Las Vegas, Nevada. Once settled in Las Vegas, Charlie needs some dental work done and, upon the advice of a friend, goes to a dental school on West Charleston across from University Medical Center hospital. As he enters the front area of the building, where the school is located, he notices a large portrait of a man standing near a plane who looks much like the Howard he had known in Mexico. Memories come flooding back as Charlie remembers **Howard, the non-military test pilot,** who had generously helped him get back stateside in that long-ago time.

All but hypnotized by the portrait, he remembers the similar facial features. Even the hat is the very same brown felt type hat that his friend Howard had worn those many years ago in Mexico. But the fellow in the portrait is straight and tall, whereas the Howard Charlie had met in Mexico had been appallingly bent and misshapen. Then Charlie remembers that Howard had told him how he was terribly injured in a plane wreck in the Beverly Hills area of California. Feeling a bit disturbed and not noticing the small plaque on the wall near the portrait, Charlie asks in several offices for the identity of the man in the portrait and soon learns that the portrait is indeed that of his long-ago friend Howard – **Howard Hughes!?**

Although Charlie is working 12 hours a day driving a cab, he is fascinated by what he has discovered and begins research into the life and times of Howard Hughes. The following is what he learns. Please see bracketed numbers [ ] within the text of this book that send you to the Appendix B, "Endnotes." There you will find the books referred to, along with page numbers.

MELVIN DUMMAR

A movie production by Linson/Phillips/Demme, written by Bo Goldman and directed by Jonathan Demme, was of great interest. It was a takeoff on a book written by Melvin Dummar, the fellow who was the subject of the infamous "Mormon Will" scam.

A synopsis of the *Melvin and Howard* storyline: Young Melvin just happens to be doing some night driving somewhere out of Gabbs, near Tonopah, Nevada. He pulls off the main drag to "make a little rain" [his words]. As depicted in the film *Melvin and Howard*, Howard Hughes had been enthusiastically riding a dirt bike, joyfully jumping dirt mounds in the area earlier that day. He crashes, suffering serious injuries. (All of this is speculative, of course.) Howard lies out in the desert for several hours and into the night until he is discovered by "rain-making" Melvin. [1]

Note: (Tonopah was the little town where Howard Hughes and Jean Peters got married in 1957…well, maybe.)

There's another take on the story as to why Howard just happened to be found in such a remote area by Melvin. This myth speculated that Howard had been visiting a nearby bordello and, upon leaving, was attacked by ruffians, beaten, robbed, and left to die beside the roadway. Now there's some juicy, degrading, speculation, which supposes that this wealthy man who had his pick of the most beautiful starlets in Hollywood, in past years, had degraded himself to whore-mongering in such a remote area. With his money, the real Howard Hughes could have had anything, or anyone flown in from anywhere in the world, and delivered to his abode atop the Desert Inn Hotel, if, indeed, that was ever his residence.

In any event, back to the movie. Melvin loads "Howard Hughes" into his pickup and they head off to Las Vegas, leaving Howard's dirt bike behind. Melvin really wants to take Howard to a hospital, but Howard refuses. The implications here are that if Melvin had not found him in the desert, Howard would have died; therefore, Melvin is attributed with saving Howard's life. He drops Howard off behind the Sands Hotel. Howard asks Melvin for some small change and says goodbye. Melvin drives off and gets on with his life.

Eight years later, Melvin has "stepped up" in the world. He and his new wife own a gas station in Willard, Utah. A stranger comes into Melvin's station. There's some small talk and the stranger buys a pack of cigarettes. When Melvin isn't looking, the mysterious stranger drops an envelope on Melvin's desk and leaves. As the stranger and his driver depart, the stranger discards the cigarettes. This implies that the stranger didn't really want the cigarettes because he was of the Mormon faith, didn't smoke, and was merely doing a good deed by dropping off Melvin's envelope. Melvin finds the envelope, which instructs him to take it to David O. McKay, Prophet of the Mormon Church at the time the will was written. However, Melvin cannot restrain himself, his curiosity gets the better of him, and he steams open the envelope. Lo and behold, there is the holographic (hand-written) Last Will and Testament of Howard R. Hughes, Jr. Melvin reads the document and discovers that the good deed he'd done eight years earlier has returned to him $156 million-fold. *Wow!* But it does seem strange that the Good Samaritan who delivered the will to Melvin at his little gas station had selected Melvin to be the courier for the billion-dollar document. Why did he not simply deliver the will to the Mormon Church Prophet to whom it was addressed?

1. When being questioned by the Court, Dummar lies twelve times under oath. He denies having taken the document to the Mormon Church offices. When forensic work concerning the document is done by a crime lab, a telling discovery is made. Dummar's latent palm print is found on the will's envelope. Upon being confronted with the evidence, Melvin is placed under tighter scrutiny and confesses that *he did* deliver the document to the Mormon Church offices.

2. When first questioned as to whether he knew the contents of the envelope, he claims not to have known. Later he confesses to having steamed open the envelope and to reading its contents. Therefore, he *did* in fact know the document had designated him as a beneficiary of Hughes's bequest to the tune of $156 million.

3. Melvin fails several polygraph tests!

Strangely enough, there was a lot of controversy about whether the so-called "Mormon Will" was an authentic document, despite the numerous misspelled words and sloppiness of the handwriting. Dummar still hoped to pull off the scam. He and his attorney took another run at it in November of 2006 in the U.S. District Court of Judge Bruce Jenkins, Utah. The case was not reopened.

The Dummar case was a good source of circumstantial information, not because it was truthful on Dummar's behalf, but because someone must have "spilled the beans" about what happened to a fellow named Charles in Mexico in 1964. There are simply too many coincidences in Dummar's story.

1. Dummar claims to have found Howard Hughes in the Nevada desert in January of 1968 and gives Hughes a ride to his destination. [2]

2. Hughes gives Charles a ride in Mexico in late 1964 and tells Charles that "the doctors have only given me eight months to live."

3. The year when Howard gives Charles a ride in Mexico and the year in which Dummar supposedly gives Hughes a ride to Las Vegas, are coincidentally close (within 38 months.)

4. Dummar's story about Hughes and Charles's involvement with Hughes <u>both begin</u>

along roadways. Howard gives Charles a ride to his destination. Dummar gives Howard a ride to his destination.

5. Howard gives Charles a *holographic* will (or similar document.) Howard supposedly includes Dummar in a *holographic* will. [3]

6. Howard had said to Charles, "I hope I spelled your name right." The "Mormon Will" has Dummar's name spelled "DuMar."

The six "coincidences" above are indeed unusual. Are you a person who doesn't believe in coincidences? It's hard for most of us to believe in even two coincidences, let alone *six*! Someone here is a liar with inside information; and Melvin Dummar, in a court of law and under oath, lied many times.

Interesting notes:

1. The "Mormon Will", which claims to be a Last Will and Testament of Howard Hughes, has his name spelled out on the last of three pages "Howard R. Hughes, Jr." Whereas Charles's document had only "H.H." at the bottom of a single sheet.

2. The "Mormon Will" was written on legal-length yellow-lined sheets, according to several news reports at the time. (The lines and paper color did not show up on the Xeroxed copies found in the FBI files. Sometimes this was the case with older Xerox machines. The copiers simply did not pick up paper color or blue lines.) Charles's letter was written on clear white paper. The paper was nearly, or was in fact, translucent and unlined. The handwriting was neat and orderly.

3. It was, and still is, believed by many that Howard Hughes lived until 1976. Allegedly, after 1965, he had written numerous directives on yellow legal pads. Therefore, to make the "Mormon Will" appear authentic, the forgers had no alternative but to forge the "Mormon Will" from documents which were themselves forgeries. They also used the same type of paper stock. (Cursive analysis to come later in Chapter VI.)

4. It's not surprising that the "Mormon Will" forgers would misspell the last name of Howard's nephew - "Lommis" instead of Lummis. [4] As you will see later, the "Mormon Will" was one of the poorest attempts to defraud in the history of the FBI.

5. The letter Howard gave Charles in 1964 in Mexico was written on clear white, quality stock paper, neatly spaced, and appeared to have been written with the expertise of a calligraphist.

Imagine the revelation when evidence was found from Hughes's aide John Holmes concerning Hughes's writing of his will. Even earlier than this was a memorandum to his personal aide Howard Eckersley wherein Howard confided that he had written a *holographic* will. Charles may well have held what they described in his hand in 1964 – or perhaps a codicil. The document was not signed with a full signature, only "H.H." at the bottom of a single sheet. It was disconcerting to find that although Donald Barlett and James Steele entered the Holmes and Eckersley information in their book *EMPIRE*, they appeared hesitant to believe it. "Hughes probably never wrote a holographic will" they claimed. You may be assured that Howard Eckersley and John Holmes had, in this instance, told the exact truth (though either Holmes, the "Hughes" caretaker, or Barlett and Steele in their book *Empire,* seem to have gotten their dates mixed up.) [5]

Given the above testimony from John Holmes and Howard Eckersley, the obvious presumption is that Marvin Dummar never talked to either one of these guys. Had he and his accomplices done so, they would have at least striven for better grammar, spelling, and neatness! [6]

In his book *Bashful Billionaire*, Albert Gerber's research indicates that Howard had been a perfectionist in the writing of letters, with no allowances for erasing, smudging, or error. [7]

The most glaring conclusion of all is that Melvin Dummar obviously knew something about Hughes's predisposition to holographic wills. Where did he get these nuggets of knowledge? Most wills are typewritten, so why *not* falsify a typewritten will?

Taking into consideration the above scenario, there are several questions begging for answers:

1. Was Charlie's document merely a *guidance* document which would lead him to a more in-depth will? After all, Howard did not sign his name to Charlie's document. Only the letters "H.H." appeared at the bottom.

2. Could Howard's true final will and testament have been entrusted to the Council of the Twelve of the Mormon Church during the time of David O. McKay? Markers seem to point in that direction.

3. Did one, or several, of the Council members accidentally, or intentionally, leak the information, hence kicking off the Melvin Dummar scam?

4. Was the reason for Charles *not* being contacted by the Mormon Church because of the amounts of money involved? They would need to be certain as to whom the funds belonged.

5. Did prudence deem that they would have to wait for Charles to show up with the guidance document (e.g., a codicil)?

6. Do the archives of the Mormon Church contain information that Hughes, in fact, died in 1965? Throughout his life Howard Hughes did not appear to be a half-way sort of fellow. Being as close to death as he was in 1964, one may be assured he would have immediately contacted the custodians of his will as to any changes.

7. Was the whole "Mormon Will" scam concocted to dilute any testimony Charles might give as to having met Howard in Mexico in 1964?

The document given to Charles, by Howard, was probably more of a guidance document than it was a complete will. Was the Mormon Church also named in Howard's final will? Howard was not a smoker and drank little. Obviously, he had an abiding respect for those of the Mormon faith, believing them to be clean, honorable, and benevolent in their works. The Fathers of the Mormon Church (The Counsel of Twelve) must be of exemplary character to achieve those most honored positions. Were these the only men Howard could turn to in the end? Were they the men he believed he could trust with sensitive information, *without* revealing his disfigured physiology for the world to see? Was the Mormon Church, Jean Peters, and Charles the only ones Howard deemed worthy to be his beneficiaries?

It's probable that Hughes's lieutenants Bill Gay, Nadine Henley, and Chester Davis had been planning ahead. Perhaps they were not completely sure that they held the only copy of Charles' letter from Howard (owing to the deal made with Charles's father and stepmother). Once the "Mormon Will" was identified as fraudulent, wouldn't Charles's claim to the letter by Howard Hughes that Charlie once held, or even a copy thereof, also be immediately labeled a fake?

In Chapter VI, you will learn that virtually all those *collective* exemplars *erroneously* used as *known* exemplars by Rosemont, Inc. and others, *were written after* 1965 and *could not* have been written in the same hand as the Hughes document *written in 1964* that Charles once carried. Charlie's Hughes document was in the *true* handwriting of Howard Hughes.

An interesting development would be to find that the Mormon Church still holds and controls a substantial amount of the Hughes estate. After all, from whom would the deceptive Melvin Dummar expect to get his $156 million had U.S. District Court Judge Bruce Jenkins reopened the case in November of 2006 and Dummar prevailed?

CLIFFORD IRVING AND "BAHAMIAN HOWARD"

In 1972 Clifford Irving attempted to defraud the publishing house of McGraw-Hill. (Clifford claimed to be Howard Hughes's personal biographer.) The craziness of Howard Hughes is a foregone conclusion of Irving's. In confidence, with his co-conspirator, Clifford labeled Hughes "a lunatic hermit," obviously buying into the myths about the man.

If the movie or the book *"The Hoax"* is halfway correct about the fraudulent procedures used and the results obtained, then this engenders immense speculation. It's a given that Clifford Irving is a good writer, but making a living as a professional forger is probably an unlikely conclusion to draw. That he could write extensive documentation that looked like other letters, *supposedly written by Hughes,* and produce a tape recording that sounded like Hughes's voice is also intriguing. This begs the question: if Clifford Irving could masquerade as Hughes and nearly pull off a million-dollar scam, why would it *not* be possible that others could be successful when *hundreds of millions of dollars* were at stake? After all, a piece of that kind of money, in those years, would have been almost anyone's price. Likely, those "others" had already embezzled millions with which to fund their schemes. Soon to learn, you will be amazed at how this happened. In any event, as Irving's "sting" ambles along toward transparency, Journalist Gladwin Hill is still a believer and does not want to lose the book.

* * *

Chester Davis, attorney for Summa, Inc. (powerhouse of the Hughes empire) denounced Irving's claim. Naturally, he would. He knows that the real Howard Hughes was dead in 1965. To confirm Irving's fraudulence, a conference call was set up supposedly between Howard Hughes, Gladwin Hill, and various members of the press. ("Howard Hughes" was supposedly in the Bahamas at the time – with no Bahamian Visa and no American Passport.) [9] Once "set up" by Chester Davis, "Bahamian Howard" came on the line and began to talk randomly about his exploits, as if reading from a script. After a while, wherein most were assured it was Hughes's voice they were hearing, "Hughes" denied any knowledge of Clifford Irving *or* a biography about himself being done by Clifford Irving. Gladwin Hill and the reporters present were not yet 100 percent convinced. They had prepared test questions they would ask of "Hughes" to be assured of the authenticity of the person speaking. (Irving had been adamant in his insistence that he *was* Hughes's biographer.) Surprise! Surprise! "Bahamian Hughes" *could not correctly answer five out of seven questions* posed by the reporters and Gladwin Hill. (The questions were non-technical.) A most glaring lapse of memory was that "Bahamian Howard" could not even remember General Harold George.

Harold George had managed Hughes Aircraft Company as it transformed from being a hobby to an important defense contractor. The General had run Howard's pet company for ten years but stepped up the effort in his last two years, building it from 78 planes and 1,800 men into an Air Transport Command of 4,000 planes and 330,000 men! [10] General George left Hughes Aircraft for a while but was later persuaded by Hughes *personally* to come back on board in 1947. He then ran the company until 1953. The General built the electronics department of Hughes Aircraft into one of the *finest* electronics laboratories in the world, closing out the competition against such heavies as Westinghouse and General Electric. [11] In the conference call, "Bahamian Howard" had said, "He never worked for *me*, did he? I don't remember General George ever working for me?" He couldn't remember that "for luck" Hughes's co-pilot's wife had stuck a wad of gum on the tail of the Lockheed-14 prior to its circumnavigating the globe? [12] At the sendoff news podium prior to boarding the plane, the real Howard

Hughes had stated, "I will never forget Harry's wife's faith in us." But "Bahamian Howard" even went so far as to say, "No, I don't recall, and it must have happened without my knowledge?" [13] During the development of the Constellation airplane, which was a huge project for the *real* Hughes, he had the assistance of a professional pilot and personal friend named Martin. "Bahamian Howard" couldn't remember the fellow's first name or what he had done during the enterprise, even when the reporter *gave* him the man's last name!

But in the end, all were convinced that nothing was very out of character in the interview. [14] Is something missing here? In *Empire*, Barlett and Steele tried to explain away "Hughes's" lack of memory. It was a lame try. That Howard had only "a cold relationship with machinery and *no* relationship with people" is a stretch as well. "Hughes" was supposedly 66 years old at the time of the McGraw-Hill conference call. When one considers the brilliant industrialist, Howard Hughes had been for so many years of his life, it's simply *not believable* that at age 66 he would have had a memory that had gone off-center so quickly. The conspirators would have you believe it was the drugs.

Let's get *real* here. Few 66-year-old prodigies, which Howard Hughes *definitely* was, have the above-mentioned lapse of memory – unless, of course, they're *dead* already.

* * *

Strangely, the outrageous successes of the Hughes Aircraft electronics division under General Harold George only vaguely appeared in *Empire*. However, in *Bashful Billionaire*, Mr. Gerber was quite specific. "The electronics division had been a shining jewel of rewarding accomplishments in Hughes's industrial realm. This portion of his industrial complex employed more than a *thousand* physicists, electronic engineers and mathematicians, as well as other high-grade professional technicians." There's simply no way *in hell* that the real Howard Hughes could possibly have forgotten General Harold George! [15]

In the movie, *The Hoax,* Irving turns up some information on Howard's (earlier than 1965) escape location, "The Salina Cruz Hotel"—a resort in the Juchitán Mountains of Mexico, a part of Mexico that Howard might have taken Charles through. Perhaps it was the city of Juchitán where Charles had boarded the northbound train? Perhaps Howard didn't take Charles all the way to Oaxaca, but that they had been in that area of Mexico – another coincidence surfaces.

Poor ol' Irving went to jail for hoaxing a biography on Howard Hughes. The big-time hoaxer-pirates were probably having a celebration knowing their manipulative charade had become more indisputable than ever. Isn't it amazing that the more ridiculous the lies told by Irving became, the more readily people were willing to believe them? (However, this was small potatoes when compared with the lies and wealth Bob Maheu, Bill Gay, Nadine Henley, and Chester Davis got away with.)

It's a given that there was plenty of money already pilfered from the Hughes estate in offshore accounts at the time. Bill, Bob, Nadine, and Chester were probably ready to skip off to Switzerland if the scam went sour. There was no extradition from Switzerland in those years – or even today – not even for murder.

[**Note:** Gay, Henley, and Davis were Howard Hughes's chief lieutenants before 1965 and up until 1977, except for Maheu, who joined the Summa, Inc. top echelon *after* 1965. But he was fired in 1970 after having been out maneuvered by Gay, Henley, and Davis.]

There must be some way Irving, or his son could collect damages when the full truth about Howard Hughes comes to light (perhaps with the publishing of this book). Irving guessed 100 percent correctly that Howard Hughes would never make a public appearance to denounce him, and Hughes never did. Irving thought it was because Howard didn't want to be served papers for an appearance at the T.W.A. hearings which had resurfaced. At one point in his trial, Irving speculated that Hughes was dead. "Ya-got-ta' hand it to that guy, he almost smoked-em out!" That, right there, would have been worth millions, had a follow-through investigation ensued.

At the beginning of the movie *The Hoax,* there is the statement that, "This movie is based on actual events." This statement was true regarding Clifford Irving, but certainly not completely true regarding Howard Hughes – and most certainly not the least bit true regarding Hughes's activities, after 1965.

In Martin Scorsese's movie, ***The Aviator***, Howard is portrayed as insane much of the time. Is it not interesting that by the mid-1950s, Howard's companies were generating $1.4 million *per day* and employing 50,000 people? [33] Is it not remarkable that although he was never seen or photographed in public since 1954, Howard Hughes regained control of T.W.A. and eventually the stock sold for $86.00 per share? (Finality of this sale was April 11, 1966 after years of massive litigation, although the lawsuits particulars dragged on into the 1970s.) This is the same stock he had paid $12.00 per share for in 1940. The transaction turned Howard a handsome profit of $460 million. [34] Is that *crazy* or what!? Although the real Howard Hughes was, most likely, dead by May 3, 1966, when the T.W.A. stock sale finalized. Unquestionably, it was he who earlier had laid the plans for this commendable success. Howard gained controlling interest in Atlas Mfg. and 66 percent of North-East Airlines between December 4, 1961 and December 18, 1962. If these were the antics of a crazy man, we should all want to be *this crazy.*

By April of 1967, the Hughes companies began to spin out of control under the same *alleged* stewardship as was in place prior to 1965. One may suppose that Howard's lieutenants had taken a little time to get their tennie-boots on. They took a run at the fortune; and from 1967 into 1976, Summa's losses alone would total $131 million! Something seems to be missing here. From *January 1, 1966* through *September 30, 1976*, Summa, Inc. generated *liquid* assets of $715 million from the sale of T.W.A. and the Hughes Oil Tool Division. By March of 1977, total liquid assets of Summa were $94 million? [35] An *idiot*, blind in one eye, and unable to see out of the other, could see something wrong with that picture! The above-mentioned dead-loss scenario took place under the guidance of that brilliant quadrumvirate of Bill Gay, Bob Maheu,

Nadine Henley, and Chester Davis. Yep! Those four puppies were real golden retrievers, especially if it was someone else's gold.

Thanks to the information uncovered by James Phelan, (*Howard Hughes: The Hidden Years*), it was thought that a Hollywood actor named *Brooks Randall* was walking in Howard's shoes. Randall worked for the Hughes Corporation as a "double" under the supervision of – you guessed it – *Bob Maheu*! [41] It was thought that perhaps Brooks found himself gainfully employed for ten years after 1965? The thought earlier was that he had been the drug addict that everyone was led to believe was Howard Hughes. (More current information, regarding Randall, comes to light later in this book.)

An incident also uncovered by **James Phelan** in ***Hughes: The Hidden Years*** concerned one Mell Stewart. Mell believed himself to be Hughes's personal aide when they vacated the Desert Inn and moved "Hughes" to Mexico. He was first instructed by Romaine Street Headquarters to "gather up all the glass bottles in the penthouse, especially the ones that 'Hughes's painkilling drugs had come in, put them in a gunny sack, smash them with a hammer, and bury them far out into the desert." But soon enough this order was superseded. Mell was instructed to pack the bottles into boxes and deliver them to the Romaine Street Headquarters in California. [42] What might "Sleuth Marlow" deduce from this event? Well, let's guess. *Somebody else's fingerprints other than Howard Hughes's were on all those bottles*? Strangely enough, in their book, *Empire*, Donald Barlett and James Steele's *shallow* mention of Mell Stewart was mostly that Mell was a bit of a problem child. His job was that of "barber" and "reluctant enema specialist" for "Hughes" (heavy on the enema specialist.) [43] Mell is painted by Barlett and Steele, as pretty much *last* in the pecking order of "Hughes's" caretakers. They completely overlooked Mell's testimony regarding the collecting of the glass bottles at the Desert Inn and what was to be done with them. These important orders came directly from Romaine Street Headquarters. What do you think? A bit peculiar, yes?

Maheu reached his pinnacle of glory at the top of the Summa, Inc. pecking order *after* 1965, when *allegedly* he became "Howard's" right-hand man. The documented incidents set forth below occurred *after* 1965.

Maheu gets a $520,000 annual retainer with Hughes Corporation. [44] That's about *five million* per year in today's inflated dollars, but it just wasn't enough. He got into trouble with the I.R.S. Eventually he ends up with a $150,000 interest-free loan. Hank Greenspun (Las Vegas *Sun*) had been loaned $4 million by Hughes ToolCo, Inc. The four "mil" was in addition to a $500,000 *prepaid* advertising contract, together with another $500,000 *gratuity*!?[45] (Shameful, shabby bookkeeping, Nadine!) Looks like Greenspun, a "pillar" of the Las Vegas community, also had his finger in the pie. That's why Hank Greenspun didn't mind lending a paltry $150,000 to his friend, Bob Maheu, the good ol' boy who'd set up the deals. [46]

Did the "Mob" still run Las Vegas back in those days? My! My! That "Howard Hughes" was a real nice guy. With a nice guy like "Howard" around, who needed those high interest bank loans? Greenspun had important things to do with his borrowed money. He'd been indicted by a federal grand jury for inciting the murder of a United States Senator. Senator Joseph McCarthy was a bit too hard on communists for Greenspun's tastes. [47] Should we guess at Greenspun's political affiliations? Wait a *minute* – didn't Howard Hughes *and* Senator McCarthy *both hate Communists*!? [48] [49]

All the while, millions of Hughes's Summa, Inc. dollars were being lost in Nevada mining investments, but it's a small wonder. Instead of Maheu doing his job and overseeing Johnny Meier, who was out buying all those worthless mining claims for "Hughes," Bobbie, now back on his feet, was out buying a yacht and refurbishing his cabin at Mt. Charleston, Nevada. And in between work and play, he still found time to buy and remodel his penthouse at the Balboa Bay Club in Newport Beach, California. Maheu really liked things big and luxurious. He built a French Colonial mansion on the Desert Inn Golf Course at a sum equivalent to $20 million in today's inflated dollars. But it's okay, "Howard" said Bob could spend the money. [50] Oh, I almost forgot! Maheu also bought a $500,000 dollar mansion in Bel Air, California, for his son, (that's over 5 million in today's soft currency) for which he also had a 4-foot by 6-foot dog house built, complete with peak shake-type roof to match that of the ornate mansion. (The dog house's motif had been a special request by Bob's son, Peter.) [51] Ever wonder what a mansion in Bel Air, California, might cost today? Unlike most people, Magic-Man Maheu had no financial worries because he worked for such a kind and understanding boss. He often used Howard's money to bail out financially distressed companies in which he was a stockholder. [52] The truth is that Howard was *dead* in those days, but the pirate propagandists had him labeled as a live, reclusive, crazy, drug addict.

Considering that a "half a mil" in the Seventies was worth a whole lot more than it is today, that Bobby Maheu was a real spendthrift. It's no wonder Gay, Henley, and Davis got testy and decided to toss him out of the club. [53] Who knows? Bobby was probably on the "naughty-mat" anyway for *not* paying closer attention to John H. Meier.

Johnnie was the "bag-man" who skipped off to Canada with millions. That's right, folks, *millions* from all those worthless Nevada mining claims that Hughes *supposedly* bought after 1965 – worthless mines whose original owners "kicked back" substantial sums under the table. [54] You can view John Meier's photo in Exhibit 212-L. Never was it truer that "a picture speaks a thousand words." John Meier had been a good friend of Bill Gay, so embezzlement was to be expected. After all, Johnny was instrumental in laundering $9.5 million through a computerized credit reporting company. The company was known as "Hughes Dynamics" but was unknown to Howard Hughes even though it was Howard's money that seeded the operation. The phantom company was set up by – you guessed it – Bill Gay. [55] [56]

Apparently when the bony finger of rightful accusation was pointed at Maheu, it was time to kill the sacrificial lamb. Johnny got the ax; but by that time, John Meier was safe in Canada with his embezzled millions, so what the heck? John Meier was a fun guy to be with. It was assumed that Johnny had a doctorate degree in something. In any event, he was referred to as "Dr. Meier," though in truth he had little or no education above a high school diploma. [57] This prince of a fellow, John Herbert Meier, eventually became recognized as an out-and-out con artist. [58] We might not find him to have been quite as *secretively* unsanitary as Bob Maheu, Bill Gay, Nadine Henley, or Chester Davis, but all five were most certainly dirty birds of a feather. Bobby, Billy, Chester, and Nadine undoubtedly intended to profit handsomely from Johnnie, but they had not wanted to be swindled out of their embezzled share, by con-artist Meier, when they brought him into the fold. [59]

Eventually, Bob Maheu began to make up his own rules, i.e. he was *not* playing ball according to the game plan set up by Gay, Henley, and Davis. The original three conspirators created a conspiracy within a conspiracy and were successful in firing Bobby. Now out of the loop, Maheu was madder than hell because, you see, he knew the truth! He was a key player in the scam to bilk the Hughes estate, but he couldn't say or do anything about it without incriminating himself. Bob Maheu and Hank Greenspun were pissed. They certainly didn't want Gay, Henley, and Davis to remove the imposter "Hughes" from Las Vegas. They started working hard trying to figure a way to snatch back the reins of the Hughes empire. [60]

In the beginning, Maheu must have been a big help to Gay, Henley, and Davis when it came to "laundering" all the ill-gotten gain they'd embezzled from the Hughes companies. Maheu's "goodfella" friend, Salvatore "Sam" Giancana (professional money launderer for the Mob) must have been helpful in that department. [61] Maheu stepped up later, during the "Mormon Will" scam and declared that Melvin Dummar was "onto something" with the holographic document he'd turned up. Bobby knew that in the *phony* will, he was among the *key* men who would divide up *one-eighth* of the liquid assets in the Hughes estate – a whopping $300 million! (This was a conservative estimate at the time, but it was probably considerably more.) Could Maheu have schooled Melvin Dummar in the writing of that phony will? What about Gay, Henley, and Davis? Did they *not* want to "wake a sleeping dragon?" Did they know that something was being held in the Mormon Church's Archives, a true will, a document wherein they were *not* named? Oh, hell no! They weren't going to throw in with Bobby. The "Mormon Will" was too sloppy a sting for them to get involved with. Besides, if they could continue to breathe life into Howard's corpse via an imposter, they had a constant *cash-cow* anyway. Why complicate things? But Maheu had been kicked out of the club and had nothing to lose! Even Noah Dietrick (an earlier lieutenant of Howard Hughes) weighed in on the Dummar con. "It's his handwriting and his signature. It's not just similar, it's the real thing." But then Hughes fired Noah in 1957. [62] Noah must have figured on getting a substantial piece of the action (Noah Dietrick had been named in the "Mormon Will" as its executor), so ol' slimy Noah gave Melvin Dummar money and an attorney.

After Howard's death in 1965, the Gay-Henley-Davis-Maheu quadrumvirate were in full control and wanted to make sure that no one started snooping around. With a spider's patience, they had waited for Howard's demise. Deviously, they had planned their treachery over the several years prior and at long last, their dark desires were fulfilled. Upon Hughes dying his painfully tragic death, the fraudulent foursomes instigated their grandiose scheme. One of their first tricks out of the bag in July of 1966 was to form Rosemont Enterprises, Inc. [70] [71] Though quasi-legal at best, Rosemont, Inc. claimed to have sole control over all of Howard's letters, photos and biographic material. Maynard E. Montrose was Director and Vice-President of Hughes ToolCo, Inc. at the time. Montrose appears to be another player in this drama, along with Chester Davis who was Secretary-Treasurer and its attorney as well. [72] These important clues were also glossed over by Barlett and Steele as Maynard E. Montrose is hardly ever mentioned in their book *Empire*. [73] On page 368, he's merely "Monty Montrose." In the index, he's simply "Montrose, M. E." [74] *Nothing* appears in *Empire* about Rosemont Enterprises, Inc., including *the date it was formed or who put it together?*

Nevertheless, Rosemont Enterprises, Inc. was successful in its purpose. However, as the structure began to weaken, due to legal pressure, the bandits began to leak misinformation to satisfy the multitudes. They implied that Howard Hughes was *physically and psychologically* unable to properly manage his business dealings. Hence, by warping the truth, there was no mystery to inquisitive minds as to why the Hughes's industries went into the toilet after 1965. The truth was that Howard was no longer in control – *not* because he had become a pitiful, reclusive, drug addict, but because he was *dead*! What's puzzling here is that all the evidence of fraud, deceit, and embezzlement would have been obvious to any law enforcement agency willing to swear out the warrants and do the shallowest of investigations, so why wasn't that done? Did all that money frighten away the inquisitive? Was the grandiosity of the treachery simply too vast? Could they not see the proverbial forest for the trees? Was it simply because the Hughes's lieutenants cleverly hid the sting in plain sight? Did law enforcement simply not know when or *where* to start a detailed investigation? The reasons, most probably, were all the above.

Note: There are documented indications that even earlier than 1965, Howard's lieutenants were committing larceny, such as the activity of Chester Davis on September 6, 1962. (As mentioned above, he was also the attorney who set up Rosemont Enterprises, Inc.) Hughes's signature was forged on documents pertaining to a deposition regarding the T.W.A. lawsuit. The paper was served on Hughes ToolCo, Inc. A lieutenant at the Romaine Street Headquarters forged Howard's signature and Chester Davis used the *forged* signature to receive documents supposedly on Howard's behalf. The forgery was exposed! [75] The question begging here is how many other times had Howard's signature been forged? The con artists getting caught in 1962 was, as this book will soon expose, the tip of an exceptionally large iceberg. When the day arrives and everyone knows that Howard Hughes died in 1965, there will be sundry forgeries found that were used to get kickbacks from clients and siphon off money from Hughes's bank accounts. With all that *tax-free* money hidden and undeserved, it will then be obvious that Gay, Henley, Davis, and Maheu, using Howard's money, had extremely deep pockets. Nevertheless, Howard never received service for the T.W.A. deposition and earned $500 million on the T.W.A. deal in the end. [76] It's unfortunate that Howard was no longer alive to appreciate his well-calculated victory. Obviously, he had been attentively aware and lucid concerning his business dealings up to the very end of his life. *Not* giving a deposition had worked to his advantage, as he must have known it would; and his deformity was kept concealed. Not long before his demise in 1965, Howard must have realized that Davis, Montrose, Gay, and others were acting illegally and against his wishes concerning his industries and, in addition to this activity, they had nearly exposed his unhappy deformity. Nevertheless, Howard had "cast the die" for victory in the T.W.A. lawsuit and his companies reaped the rewards. (More on Rosemont Enterprises, Inc. in Chapter IX; the documents are "in hand" now.)

Let us again take up the subject about Howard Hughes having a double to stand-in for him prior to 1965. An actor would have done whatever Hughes, or his lieutenants asked of him. [78] This activity apparently continued after Howard died in 1965. (Photo Exhibits and further in-depth research in Chapter VII: Doppelgangers)

It's a sound bet that somebody was doubling as Howard Hughes. Let's suppose that during this fellow's tenure as the imposter "Hughes," he liked to "get high" and watch movies. After all, he was the actor of the century. At times he must have been despondent that so few knew of his expertise. He couldn't tell anyone or he'd lose his cushy job, access to his abundant supplies of drugs, and perhaps his life!

Living must have been easy for the pretender in the beginning. The imposter Hughes could ask anything, and it would be granted. If he wanted ice cream, he got ice cream. If he wanted drugs, he got drugs. Eventually the Hughes double became too addicted to care about anything except drugs. It's not difficult for a drug addict to give up his social life. A hard-core addict *has no social life* – none of any significance anyway. The imposter would continue to play the role of Hughes, but his requirements would be that those in the know would keep him well supplied with narcotics and necessities. If they didn't, the imposter would blow the whistle on the whole scam. They couldn't just kill him because who could they have gotten to replace him? If they did find another passable double, what would they need to contend with there? "The devil they knew" was better than the devil they didn't know, so the conspirators kept the imposter Hughes pumped up and flying high to the very end.

When any of the "Hughes" caregivers got sick, they were immediately flown back to the States for proper medical attention; [79] but for the Hughes imposter, this was not to be. [80] Gay and the boys could take no chances of being exposed. Bill Gay and his minions were squeezing the turnip for its last drop of blood.

So now it's 1976. The conspirators have an appallingly sick imposter pumped full of codeine and unconscious for nigh-on 24 hours – virtually on the borderline between life and death. [81] Dr. Lawrence Chaffin, a personal physician getting paid big bucks, is at the imposter's bedside; but he just can't figure out what to do. He calls in Dr. Victor Montemayor, a Mexican doctor, who takes one look at the appallingly sick wretch in the bed and is *astonished*! "What the hell's going on here?" he asked. "Get this man to a hospital in the United States!" Dr. Montemayor believed the man could be saved with proper medical care. [82] Apparently Dr. Chaffin had hoped that Dr. Montemayor would say, "This man will not make it through the night." Then Chaffin could give the *coup de grace* injections as soon as Montemayor was out of sight. But with Dr. Montemayor's conviction that "the man can be saved with proper medical care," the game plan had to change.

Dr. Chaffin called Romaine Street and told them the bad news. The imposter Hughes must be killed before or during the flight back to the States, but the caretakers must make it look like they were trying to save him. In any event, Howard's double took his last ride in 1976. The payback from his addictions and neglect had taken its toll. His failing health and emaciated body could take no more, making it an easy task to kill him. They couldn't take the pretender back to a stateside hospital *alive* because this would have created opportunities where the imposter's identity would be exposed. (It wasn't Brooks Randall, more on this is documented later in Chapter VII: "Howard Hughes's Doppelgangers.") By removing the possibility that the Hughes imposter could have recuperated in a stateside hospital, all the conspirators needed to do was fabricate the fingerprints or bribe a technician to replace the imposter Hughes's fingerprints with ones that had been taken from the authentic Hughes back in 1965, [83] (by Bob Maheu?)

Mexican lab results and later the *autopsy* at Methodist Hospital of imposter Hughes's kidneys, indicated chronic renal disease. [84] But the Mexican lab technicians lied, so the imposter Hughes's doctors would remain conveniently unsuspicious of *that* ongoing development. If the best medical care money can buy (and we know the Hughes empire was green with it) gets a fellow this type of care, it's not just scary, it's *criminal*! Their patient's emotional confusion, swollen face, bad breath, bladder retention, fatigue, nausea, edema, constipation or diarrhea, back pain, electrolyte imbalance, and toxic blood must have made it a *tiny-bit* obvious that something was amiss. We thought the big bucks bought the best doctors, but then I guess even *little* mistakes can be made every now and then? All the while kidney machines (for cleansing the blood) were readily available at the Howard Hughes Medical Institute in Florida. [85]

Connecting the above information, we have "Acapulco Hughes" *with more things wrong than most dead people* and all the nasty symptoms imaginable. *Not only* is he being allowed drug overdoses, but he's aided by his employees in dissolving the codeine phosphate tablets into solution, drawing the "junk" into syringes, and shooting it up!?

When Dr. Wilbur Thain, one of "Hughes's" personal physicians (who also happens to be Bill Gay's brother-in-law) went to trial, Dr. Forest S. Tennant (Professor of Public Health at University of California Los Angeles who headed up one of California's largest drug abuse treatment programs) testified that the Hughes autopsy indicated (and pharmacologists and pathologist agreed) that *lethal doses of codeine had been administered six to eight hours prior to death.* [86] But Dr. Chaffin and aides (Myler, Waldron, and Holmes) who were with the Hughes imposter, maintained that "Hughes"

21

had been unconscious for <u>twenty-four hours</u>. [87] One is left in wonderment as to who it was that did all the tablet dissolving, syringe-loading, poking, and squeezing! *Wow!* That guy was one tough junkie! He must have been a real disappointment to Bill Gay, Nadine Henley, Chester Davis, and their minions. They were wishing the guy would just hurry up and die! After all, there was a lot of heavy lifting to do, what with the carrying away those huge piles of money from the Hughes empire. They were itching to get on with the show. No doubt Gay and the others believed they could still control the Hughes empire without the troublesome double. Even if they lost control, they probably had millions in offshore accounts to fall back on. (Dr. Wilbur Thain's activities are further unveiled in Chapter XIII.)

So, it's 1976 and the imposter Hughes is close to heaven on an airplane headed to Houston, accompanied by fiends, and possibly getting more injected drinks loaded with codeine. Eventually he gives up the ghost, someone substitutes the real Hughes's prints from 1965, the autopsy at Methodist Hospital is skewed, and the grifter staff of seven (Gay, Davis, Henley, and now Montrose, Holmes, Myler, and Eckersley) continue to bilk the Hughes estate. (Montrose, Holmes, Myler and Eckersley got to join the club when their services or confidentiality were required.) It seems that Gordon Margulis and Mell Stewart (caregivers to the imposter Hughes) suspected that, just maybe, they were caring for a doppelganger. The information they gave James Phelan for his book *Howard Hughes: The Hidden Years* indicates they felt something was amiss.

Note: Upon leaving Nicaragua sometime in the Seventies, the "Hughes" entourage relocated to Vancouver, British Columbia, caregiver Gordon Margulis gave his remembrance of his boss liking a particularly large room where he could look out of a picture window at a nearby bay. "This is nice, 'Hughes' had said," enjoying a view of the nearby harbor. But Gordon maintained that the senior aides (Holmes, Waldron, and Myler?) "didn't like that one bit." They told Gordon to "get him away from the window and into his bedroom!" [88] Apparently Gordon didn't like the idea of shuffling the man, he believed to be Hughes, off into his traditionally dismal, small, stark abyss, especially since the view was obviously giving his boss a small measure of pleasure. But what's a boss to do when the senior employees are directing the show? Unfortunately, James Phelan didn't ask Gordon who the senior aides were at the time. Research has indicated that it was John Holmes, and Clarence Waldron. (See Exhibits 179-D and E.)

Something else to consider: If the senior aides were that much in control, as per above, why didn't they see to it that their boss was taken to a stateside hospital when he later became severely ill? "Acapulco H.H." in Mexico couldn't possibly have put up much resistance to John Holmes, Clarence Waldron, Drs. Chaffin and Thain, who were "caring" for him at that time.

Another likely probability that comes to mind is: What was all that moving from place to place in such a short period of time about anyway? Bob Maheu, who had supposedly been Hughes's right-hand man, was fired in December of 1970. [89] *Immediately* thereafter, "H.H." was vacated from the Desert Inn in Nevada. The "Hughes" entourage secretly relocated to the Bahamas where they remained from 1970 to 1972. But when Gay, Henley, and Davis had to reveal the location of "Hughes" to rid themselves of the Clifford Irving fiasco, *Maheu now knew where they were*! Maheu must have thought, "By golly they *did* take 'H.H.' to Nassau in the Bahamas (later to Freeport) and they didn't stay at the Emerald Beach Hotel, but the Nassau Beach Hotel instead." (It's kind of like a felon, having escaped from prison, rents an apartment next to a Police Station. Who could have guessed it?) It would be to Maheu's advantage to get "H.H." back to the States where he would have better maneuverability. Maheu quickly sent a team of private investigators to the Bahamas who stirred up Bahamian trouble. [90] (Supposedly "Hughes" and his aides didn't have American passports, visas, or work permits and "the entourage had to sneak out of the Bahamas quickly to avoid criminal prosecution?") Charles, having been in the Bahamas in 1964, and worked there as well, found that his work permit was *easily* obtained. It's highly unlikely that "Hughes" and staff were obligated to leave the Bahamas for lack of proper papers, especially if you consider the amount of money they were spending. A simple explanation to Immigrations as to the need for specialized care (and a little cash on the side) would easily have solved any problems. (Well, that's all that would have been needed if "Hughes" had been willing to sign off on his immigration visa, get photographed, and be fingerprinted – thirty minutes required at most. Why was this not done?)

"Hughes" and his staff temporarily relocated to Florida (No, *not* to the Howard Hughes Medical Institute in Miami!). They then traveled to Managua, Nicaragua (Feb. 1972 to Mar. 1972), then to Vancouver, Canada (Mar. 1972 to Aug. 1972), back to Managua, Nicaragua (Aug. 1972 to Dec. 1972), then to London, England (Dec. 1972 to Dec. 1974), then to Freeport, in the Bahamas (1974 to Feb. 1976), and finally to Acapulco, Mexico (Feb. 1976 to Apr. 1976).[91] All that moving around couldn't have had anything to do with better business leveraging, so there's no explanation there. Changing residences for medical reasons? That doesn't work either or they would have gone to and stayed at the Howard Hughes Medical Institute in Florida. Do you think that Gay, Henley, and Davis could have been keeping one step ahead of Maheu? This "Hughes" was accustomed to taking orders from Bob Maheu. He had worked with Maheu in the beginning of his tenure with the Hughes empire. Now what do you suppose might have happened if Maheu had somehow gotten that fellow off to the side and threatened him with the loss of his cushy job and drugs if he wasn't willing to play ball according to Maheu's game plan? The answers are quite simple. The shoe would have been on the other foot and Maheu would have been successful in snatching back the reins of the Hughes empire. And then, with a reversal of fortune, Gay, Henley, and Davis could have done little about it without being incriminated for conspiracy and fraud! Remember, it was the senior aides while they were in Vancouver, who were controlling the activity of "Hughes." According to Gordon Margulis, he was instructed by the senior aides to "get him away from the window and into his bedroom!" The senior aides, in turn, were controlled by Bill Gay, Nadene Henley, and Chester Davis. **Note**: John Holmes gave testimony that Howard had confided in him regarding the writing of a holographic will earlier then 1965. Was this a slip-up? Did this, along with other knowledge, lead to a confrontation with Gay, Henley, and Davis? (Holmes became a member of the Summa Board in 1973, one of the most powerful positions in the Hughes organization. Holmes was another fellow who originally had been brought on board by Bill Gay.) [92] Did Holmes know too much? Did he give evidence that he had sufficiently "covered his butt" and, if so, did the original pirates have no alternative but to invite him into the fold?

One-time soap salesman John Holmes was a smoker and *not* a Mormon. He began his career with Hughes Corporation as a lowly aide, but Holmes somehow found favor with Bill Gay, a Mormon, who must have found cigarettes offensive. In any event, Holmes eventually ended up as "Hughes's" chief narcotics courier. [93] Hey! Didn't that "Hughes" they flew up from Mexico have a *bunch* of codeine pumped into his body? Heavens! Wasn't "Candy Man" Holmes on the plane that flew "Hughes" back to the States? [94] Do you think that Holmes could have been the only "caretaker" on hand, along with Dr. Lawrence Chaffin and Thain, in those six to eight hours prior to "Hughes's" death? Heavens! Why wasn't Donald Barlett and James Steele's "*Empire*" clearer in these matters?

Note: Levar Beebe Myler started off in the lowly position of chauffeur for the Hughes companies. He eventually got appointed by Bill Gay *as personal aide to Howard Hughes in the late 1950s.* [95] This was after 1954 when Howard began his disappearing scenario (i.e., no photos, no visuals, etc.) [96] But surprise, surprise! In 1972, Wizard Beebe finds himself one of the directors of Summa, immediately receiving a big fat salary and who knew what else under the table. [97] He became one of the main cogs running a multi-billion-dollar operation with the educational experience garnered in one year of college (well...maybe) and expertise as a machinist. Will wonders never cease? All this even *after* caregiver Myler allowed "Hughes" to fall while he was helping him to the toilet. [98] (This negligent incident was also *not* mentioned in the book *Empire*. Hence, another little clue neatly glossed over.) Myler knew something and he, like Holmes, must have "covered his butt" well. You will discover, later in the book, that those boys *knew* the man they had cared for was a *phony*. No doubt this knowledge necessitated confidentiality – at a price – from the original four con artists!

Another note of interest here (although perhaps a bit redundant) is that in 1966, Maheu (ex-FBI and notorious for his relationships with gangland Capone types) had a "bug" planted in the hotel suite of comedian Dan Rowan. *Supposedly* Maheu was freelancing for the CIA at the time and was doing a favor for his *money laundering* friend Sam Giancana. However, the Florida private detective Maheu hired to do the job, wanted to have a little fun while in Vegas. He left the radio receiving device unattended in the neighboring room. The device was found by a fastidious maid and reported to the police. The Florida detective was arrested for invasion of privacy and implicated Maheu before "goodfella" John Rosselli could post bond. [99] As an example of how "things change," in July of 1976 Juicy-Johnny Rosselli ended up in a steel barrel afloat somewhere off the coast of Florida. [100] For a "connected" fellow, it must have been a great disappointment. But with all that Hughes money free for the taking, things can go bad anytime, anywhere.

In the interests of heightened awareness and in hopes the reader will not construe it as paranoia, it's of concern that Donald Barlett and James Steele in their book *Empire* came up with an enormous amount of well documented material for their book in a minimal amount of time. Where did they get it from and what about their downplaying and omitting critical information?

Furthermore, concerning the Clifford Irving fraud, Barlett and Steele's lame attempt to explain "Bahamian Howard's" terrible lack of memory needs to be noted. They appeared to be oblivious to the possibility that the fellow, talking on the telephone to Gladwin Hill and the reporters, could have been an imposter.

As cited above Maynard Montrose is hardly more than a name mentioned in *Empire*, and Rosemont Enterprises, Inc. is not mentioned at all, even though it was formed in 1966 (after 1964 when Charles had met Howard in Mexico and after 1965 when the real Hughes died.) The main players being Maynard "Monty" Montrose and Chester Davis. [102] Its purpose was specifically to control the Hughes biographical material, inclusive of letters, photos and all other biographical material concerning Howard Hughes. Rosemont, Inc. had been to court, on various Hughes issues, *numerous* times.

Cited above is the testimony of Howard's aides, Eckersley and Holmes regarding Howard's writing of a holographic will. Barlett and Steele politely call them both liars. "Hughes probably never composed a holographic will." [103]

When most wills are typed, why do you suppose Melvin Dummar and accomplices came up with a fraudulent holographic will? The answer is that there were others, and eventually Charles knew a holographic will was out there somewhere. There is no other reasonable explanation. Oh my, the sins of omissions and partial truths can be rewarding!

Was the information for *Empire* hastily gathered and released by Will Lummis in a roundabout way after 1976? Could it have been Will Lummis who provided the information and finances for Barlett and Steele, *withholding* choice bits of knowledge? (The court named Will Lummis chairman of Summa Corporation in 1976. Summa, as you will remember, was the powerhouse of all Hughes's companies.)

After 1965, Gay, Henley, Maheu, Davis, and Montrose were getting real sensitive regarding information about Howard Hughes, yet no one ever wondered why. From 1976 on, no matter how evident the neglect, no matter how clear the autopsy evidence, no matter how obvious the lies, the fraud and deceptions, the only punishment that all the players received was a slap on the wrist. One can only suppose that the public, judges, and attorneys swallowed the phony bait that Howard was alive until 1976. All were led to believe that Howard was nothing more than a derelict drug addict who had done all these terrible things to himself and the Hughes's industries. In this book, the evidence gathered *does not* support this propaganda.

After the death of his parents, Howard had bitter disputes with both his father's *and* his mother's sides of the family. The bitterness between Howard's uncle Rupert

Hughes and his aunt Annette Lummis is well documented. [104] That Howard ever saw any of their offspring (i.e., Willie Lummis) as "adorable" is speculative at best. [105] Nevertheless, Will Lummis gets into the driver's seat of the Summa Corporation on May 11, 1976 by judicial decree. (As a practicing attorney, he was probably a little more astute in business matters than chauffeur Beebe Myler or soap salesman John Holmes.) Perhaps this was a move the bandits had not anticipated happening so soon. Will Lummis found the Hughes estate to be a financial nightmare! Gay and his co-conspirators had been walking away with the proverbial candy store *for ten years!!!* [106] Will quickly realizes what's been happening.

Lummis was a cool cookie. He appointed Mickey West and William Rankin to the Board of the Summa Corporation. At the time "Hughes" had *allegedly* died in 1976, the Board of Directors was comprised of Bill Gay, Chester Davis, Nadine Henley, Levar Myler, and John Holmes. (All of the Hughes industries took their orders from Summa, Inc.) It's obvious that Mickey West and William Rankin got the goods on what was going down in Summa, Inc. Will Lummis then held *all* the cards. However, Gay and his cohorts could well have believed they still had an angle. They could have shown Will Lummis a single-page copy of a letter, or perhaps an original written in longhand by none other than *the real* Howard Hughes, Jr. It was a codicil to Howard's *holographic* final will – or a "guidance" document to a final will. Will Lummis quickly realized that none of the nefarious five or any Lummis were to be in line for the rewards specified in the document. Gay and his co-conspirators explained to Will Lummis that the letter was procured from a man and his wife in Oklahoma. It was either a holographic will or a holographic codicil giving directions to a full and final will in safekeeping somewhere. As an attorney, Will Lummis knew all about wills – it's even his name. Will is invited to "belly up to the bar" under the presumption that he will join with the others in the further swindling of the Hughes estate.

Though there are instructions in the document revealed to Will Lummis(e.g., "the bearer must deliver it to a certain location ten to twelve month hence") it's identified on its surface only by "H.H." at the bottom of the page. Will either recognized the handwriting as authentic or had it researched and found it to *indeed* be a legitimate guidance document and/or a last will. Whatever it instructed the bearer to do, or whatever of the Hughes estate it left the bearer and others, was decisive.

The original tribunal (Bill Gay, Nadine Henley, and Chester Davis) probably tried to make a deal with Will Lummis. But Will, having expertise as an attorney, probably had other plans. You know those "hot-blooded" attorneys, they don't play nice. Will Lummis may well have informed the trio, "Screw you guys, I'm clean, you're dirty. I'm going to exercise the power in the Hughes estate given me by decree. I'm taking control and if you don't like it – or tell anyone my cousin was dead in 1965 – I'll personally see that the whole damn bunch of you go to jail for conspiracy, fraud, and murder one!" (Will had seen the grotesque condition of the imposter corpse which had been flown up from Mexico and had taken into consideration the vast amounts of codeine pumped into the doppelganger's body.) Will *clearly* saw what had been done and, most probably, reinforced his promises with, "I'll deny to my dying day that I ever saw the letter you're carrying or that we ever had this discussion!"

Will Lummis most probably, informed the *iniquitous seven* that they would eventually (though slowly) be fired and lightly prosecuted for gross mismanagement. Will promises the seven that he will not press for out-and-out conspiracy, fraud, or murder. His thinking was most likely motivated by the possibility that someone could turn state's evidence to get a lighter sentence. That would mean the truth would come out, and a Hughes holographic will could be found. Most certainly, Will wanted to hang onto the good thing that had found him. As a result, the original tribunal and their minions got to keep their ill-gotten gains squirreled away in various offshore accounts.

On March 16, 1978, a federal grand jury returned an indictment against "Hughes's" doctors, Norman Crane and Wilbur Thain, and aide John Holmes on a charge that they unlawfully supplied Howard Hughes with narcotics. Nothing much came of it except judicial hearings. Dr. Wilbur S. Thain, Bill Gay's brother in-law who supplied "Howard Hughes" with abundant and, eventually, lethal quantities of drugs for two or more years until "Hughes" died in 1976, was also found innocent. (More on this in Chapter XIII)

Wilbur Thain was the same doctor who had been hard pressed to leave a party in the Bahamas to attend to his dying employer in Mexico in 1976. When he finally showed up, he set about shredding documents for nearly two hours instead of tending to his patient. [107] (The shredding was probably suggested by Dr. Thain's brother-in-law, Summa C.E.O. Bill Gay.) Later, feeling satisfied with the shredding, Thain went in and injected the *comatose* "H.H." He then informed Dr. Chaffin and the aides, "It will take a while for the medication to work." [108] Well, he was *right on* with that statement. The injections didn't kill "H.H." immediately, but the fellow was dead before the plane arrived in Houston. [109] What *was* that nasty stuff? It appears that lethal amounts of toxin were already awash in the man's body before Dr. Wilbur finally got on the job. When the imposter refused to die, did he get more of the ambrosial fluid pumped into his body *in route* to Houston? That junkie must have been tough as leather. On top of dealing with renal failure, dehydration, starvation, and toxic blood, he was awash with codeine. For Heaven's sakes! How did that miserable wretch of a man get all those pieces of needles in his arms and in such hard to reach places? [110] Did Chaffin and Holmes hold him down while Thain anxiously injected syringe after syringe into the imposter's thin arms or did they take turns? [111]

What about Dr. Lawrence Chaffin who testified that "there never was any legitimate medical purpose for giving him ("Hughes") codeine," and that "He took the drugs because he wanted them." [112] Dr. Chaffin must have made "Hughes" *real-happy* on that flight from Acapulco to Houston. How did Chaffin fare in the courtroom? Well, he plea-bargained his way out of it!

Consider:

The above partial synopsis of *The Price of Their Souls* was fashioned in several instances on a speculative basis. However, it fits well with the factual exhibits inclusive in this book.

Soon you, the reader, will find that the 1976 date when Howard Hughes *supposedly* died, is erroneous. The date when he really died makes it impossible that he ever aspired to take up residency in the Desert Inn Las Vegas, Nevada. But Bob Maheu kept busy collecting data and *supposedly* forwarded it to "Hughes." Eventually Hughes was awarded a gaming license for his Desert Inn lease – a gaming license for which he never provided any personal information, had a photograph taken, was fingerprinted, or made a personal appearance. It's a good guess that "Howard Hughes" was the first and last man in history to enjoy such privileges from the State of Nevada. This gratuity was supposedly granted because Howard had agreed to donate to the University of Nevada Medical School in Reno. [113] Well now, could it have been kickback money at work again. Everyone was so happy to have a dead man's money; it makes you wonder why they didn't go down to Houston and dance on his grave in 1976. Oh well, the real Hughes wasn't there to enjoy the festivities anyway. A grisly summation is that even *a dead man* can be awarded a gaming license in Nevada if there's enough money to be had.

What became of Dr. Vern Mason, the doctor who Hughes had said "saved his life" after the XF-11 crash in Beverly Hills? Mason was a man Howard trusted, a personal friend who would later head up the Howard Hughes Medical Institute in Miami, Florida. He was a man who knew the *real* extent of Howard's injuries. Dr. Mason died in November 1965. [114] Well now, isn't *that* a coincidence – right on schedule? It would have been difficult to set up Rosemont Enterprises, Inc. in 1965, with that guy still around. (Yet another important clue glossed over by Barlett and Steele in *Empire*.) Davis and Gay finally weaseled their way in as the Medical Institute's directors. Millions were there to be had. One could certainly suppose that both held self-awarded MDs in "*Con-ology*." [115]

Was Mason an honorable man – a man of principle? Did he know of Howard's impending death? Did he calculate the progression and make the final diagnosis that Howard had but a limited time to live? Was he going to check in on his friend in Mexico toward the end, unaware that he would be *checking out himself* with a little help from fiends? After all, Dr. Mason was not about to go along with a ploy by Noah Dietrich to have Howard committed to an institution back in 1958. [116] Dr. Mason knew the truth about Howard's spine-warping injury. Noah's plan was to try to get Dr. Vern Mason in on the scam. But alas, the devious plan was conveyed to Hughes, *probably by Mason.* (Dr. Mason's profile, Exhibit 65-A.) When Vern's profile was uncovered it was just the way one would expect it to be. It's hard to imagine a finer fellow than Dr. Vern Mason.

Let's not forget attorney Richard Gray, partner in the law firm of Andrews, Kurth & Gray, who represented the supposed "Howard Hughes" in many Las Vegas business deals. What if Gray suspected – or knew – of the reality of the scams? Remember all those bogus mining claims? Poor Richard died of a heart attack at the ripe old age of forty-nine. That's 49 on May 7, 1975 – only 10 months before a dead "Hughes" was flown up from Acapulco. Richard met his demise in an airplane as well. [117] Did he know too much? Barlett and Steele didn't say. It seems just a little too convenient. If the conspirators had already decided to kill "Hughes," and Gray knew it, perhaps he wanted more money to keep his mouth shut. Or perhaps Gray just pissed off someone who liked to kill people – someone who didn't like his politics [118] or someone who didn't like paying interest on a $4 million-dollar loan. And, of course, all this happened after 1965. [119] (Hank Greenspun?)

"Hughes" *supposedly* had a dispute with attorney Raymond A. Cook (after 1965). Cook had exercised control over the Howard Hughes Medical Institute (H.H.M.I.) a few years before. There were millions of dollars tied up there. Ray and his wife "accidentally" got in the way of a bus on August 9, 1975 [120] – just five months before "Acapulco Hughes's" timely demise in 1976 and two months after Richard Gray' death. Although Cook resigned from the H.H.M.I. in 1970, did he know too much? Did he resign out of disgust after being badgered by Bill Gay and Chester Davis? Or was his and his family's lives threatened when he stumbled across information left behind by Dr. Vern Mason? Looks like it's coming together here. I wonder if that bus driver who "accidentally" smashed into Cook's car managed to survive. How many witnesses were there? All too soon Gay and Davis were running the show at the medical institute. [121]

Bob Maheu's "goodfella" connections Johnnie Rosselli and "Sam" Giancana also met their *timely* demise within a year of each other. [122] Now let's all count on our fingers – from 1975 to 1976, Cook, Gray, Rosselli, Giancana, and a hypothetical "Howard Hughes" all shake hands with the Grim Reaper? Well, Sleuth Marlow, that's five people solidly connected in some way to the Hughes empire and all dead within 14 months!? My goodness, will coincidences never cease? You know, it appears that Bill Gay and the "in crowd" figured that "*these guys know too much—they want too much! We'd better get 'The Cleaner' in the field.*" Johnnie Rosselli's and "Sam" Giancana's supposed involvement in a plot to kill Castro certainly seems like a BS cover story. [123] I suppose there's a possibility that they might have taken the money for the job and then reneged on the deal. But what we do know about Johnnie and Sam is that they were *professional killers*. To a thinking man's mind, they were "snuffed" by *someone they knew* – someone who led them around with a suitcase full of money -- because no one else could have gotten close enough. What do *you* think, Sleuth Marlow?

The information presented in the following chapters makes it quite clear that the fellow they brought up from Mexico in 1976 was an imposter. That fellow had *lethal* amounts of codeine pumped into his body. Where had they gotten all those drugs? The word "prcmcditation" comes to mind. Indications found in "Hughes" literature (after 1965) indicates that the "Hughes" aides had been warehousing the stuff! [124] It was horrific to see the x-rays of all those broken needles in the imposter's arms in hard to reach places. [125] The weak, emaciated Hughes imposter must have been terrified; he probably lapsed into unconsciousness many times as they filled and injected syringe after syringe into his emaciated body, keeping him perpetually "stoned." It would have been impossible for him to escape on his own because he hadn't walked in three years after breaking his hip in London!

Two years later, pathologist Jack Titus at Methodist Hospital, Houston, who had led the autopsy on the *supposed* "Hughes" corpse, admitted in Dr. Thain's trial that he'd made "a little mistake." (He probably figured the heat was on and he wanted to get away from the flame.) Titus confessed that the blood levels of codeine were *1,000 times greater than he had originally thought*. (The good doctor didn't know the difference between *milligrams* and *micrograms*? [126] Where did *he* go to school?) It's no wonder Bill Gay and his fellow conspirators, along with Annette and Will Lummis, wanted the corpse cremated! [127] Also considering that one-half to two-thirds of a dose of codeine is dispelled from the body within six to eight hours and dissipation is complete within twenty-four, how the hell did Holmes, Thain, and Chaffin escape complicity in the death of the imposter? How obvious can it be that they pumped him full of the junk either immediately before or after they shuffled him onto the plane? It certainly seems reasonable – even to the most naïve – that Dr. Titus (lead doctor at Methodist Hospital Autopsy) could have been on the "take." Did he then get cold feet under oath because he realized that (a) the corpse had not been cremated, (b) x-ray records and blood samples from the XF-11 crash could be accessed and compared, and (c) *he could become complicit in first degree murder*? [128] [129]

The above scenarios are supported with the factual exhibits in this book. However, you may be assured that the target was scarcely missed in the first book. How many coincidences do we need to determine that things are erroneous with the contemporary saga of Howard Hughes?

In any event it's now 1977:
1. Will Lummis is in control of the Hughes estate. [131]
2. The infamous seven eventually quit and depart with a reprimand.
3. The doctors and aides who pushed the drugs, had the best of attorneys. Eventually they also got "whitewashed" in the courtroom.
4. The Hughes Companies once more begin to show multi-million-dollar profits [132]

Postscript:

After meeting and traveling with Howard Hughes in 1964, it would take Charles many years – including three and a half years of intense research – to garner a reasonable and factual understanding of the true saga of Howard R. Hughes, Jr. When they met in 1964, Charles knew him only as Howard. At the time, Charles was unaware of Howard Hughes's world-changing exploits. Perhaps it would have been better in 1964 if Howard had given Charles a better upfront understanding of his life.

But then there's the overwhelming possibility that Charles may well have become a target earlier than he did. In contemplation, Charles realized that *had he delivered the document* given him by Howard in Mexico, *he and the document may have come to an immediate end*. When Charles met Howard in 1964 Mexico, he noted that Howard gave the appearance of a man who cared little for the accolade's others had bestowed upon him. He never mentioned even one of them. It would be later that Charles would see Hughes as an intellectually gifted man who had done great things, enriching the lives of many with cutting edge technologies still used extensively in today's aerospace industries.

Let not his memory be tarnished! He did fantastic things for which he rightfully deserves recognition. His last years, as a physically broken man are lamentable, to say the least. That he wished *not* to be in the limelight is perfectly understandable; you would have understood, as Charles did, had you known him then. Although physically unpleasant to the eye, his mind was crystal clear. His brilliance extended unto the last days of his life, as evidenced by how well he managed his empire from afar. It was only after his death in 1965 that his life's work fell into disarray.

What now follows is less speculation and more laboriously gathered factual supportive materials. At times, the reader will find information brought forward again that has previously been covered. This is purposeful for the sake of perspective, clarification, and to explain additional information which dovetails into the dialogue. Hence, speculation morphs into revelation.

Years ago, there was a popular television serial called *Dragnet*. Sergeant Joe Friday was the police detective who solved many a crime and successfully put numerous bad guys behind bars. Few reading this book will remember that series; it was a long time ago. However, Joe solved many of the criminal mysteries through his excellent ability to successfully interrogate his suspects. Often when Detective Friday encountered a suspect or person of interest who might be privy to the information he needed, Sergeant Friday would begin the discourse with, "We are interested in the facts Sir/Mam nothing but the facts." In this book *"The HOWARD HUGHES HOAX: CON MEN, CORRUPTION AND THE FAKE BURIAL OF A BILLIONAIRE"* that is *exactly* what you are going to get – *less* speculation, *more* facts!

CHAPTER III

LAURENCE M. RUSSELL
Former Special Investigator U.S. Postal Service.
Former United States Department of Justice Consultant, El Salvador.
Former Fraud Detective, (Several California Localities.)
Former California Chief of Police, (Several California Localities.)
(Now Retired)

"RUSS"
"THE BULLDOG"

It was a chilly day in January when he stepped into the tailor shop. Charles thought it to be just a normal day, thinking him to be the usual customer, like the thousands of others who had come and gone before. Charles seldom remembered the names of the many who had come in to get their clothes altered. Remembering names was never his strong point. This customer was different. After changing into the pants to be hemmed and standing on the stage where Charles's wife would assess his needs, this special customer eventually returned to the counter, where Charles began filling out the claim ticket:

"What's your name sir?"

"Russ."

"Your phone number?" etc.…

Glancing to his left Russ noticed on display the book *The Price of Their Souls* that Charles had written.

"This is a book about Howard Hughes?" he queried, recognizing the photo on its front.

"Yes."

"Do you know the author?"

"Yes."

"You must think quite highly of him if you're selling his books"

"He's not such a bad fellow."

"He lives here in Henderson?"

"Yes."

"How did you meet him?"

"I 'R' him."

"Oh. Well, I was once a postal inspector in the California bay area. At the time, I had been involved in the Clifford Irving scandal concerning Howard Hughes."

Charles was riveted.

"Hughes died in 1976, didn't he?"

"No, he died in 1965."

"Are you sure of that?"

"Yes"

"All available information indicates that he died in 1976."

"I know. I also know that the Howard Hughes's legacy after 1965, was the greatest hoax of the 20th century."

"Did you know the man?"

"I knew him in 1964. He told me, at that time, 'the doctors have only given me eight months to live.'"

"I see on the book's cover that your name is Charles; you go by Charles?"

"Charlie."

"Well Charlie, are you saying they buried an imposter thinking that person to be Howard Hughes?"

"Yes." Charlie answered while thinking, *"This fellow asks a lot of questions."*

"I guess you know that the only way your claim is going to get validated is if there's enough information available to exhume the imposter's body and do some DNA testing?"

"I believe there is enough information. I was hoping that law enforcement would 'throw in' with me by now. But to date, that hasn't happened, although several strange things have happened which I think may be related to my exposé. The motive for the Hughes Hoax," continued Charles, "is twofold and, quite clearly, 'power' and 'money.' Of course, money is power. I strongly suspect that Howard knew, in later years, that his lieutenants were 'knocking down' the cash register – kickbacks, selling contracts, and whatnot. They probably had real deep pockets even before Howard died in 1965. I suspect Hughes knew this as he left them no 'golden parachutes.' Read my book and you will understand *why* he hid himself away after 1954. He was not the drug addicted recluse they portrayed him to be. But then, how else could the poor management of Summa Inc., powerhouse of the Hughes Industries, after 1965 have been explained away? This degenerative portrayal of Hughes after 1965 allowed the pirates to embezzle hundreds of millions, and it would not look atypical. The badly run empire was not because the king had lost his mind, etc. The real reason was that the captain was no longer at the helm. He was dead."

Russ listened attentively; and when Charlie had finished, paused a moment and asked, "Would you like me to help you with some investigative work?"

"Yes."

Charles liked this guy Russ.

The cliché "you can't tell a book by its cover" was certainly the case with Laurence "Russ" Russell. At first Glance, one would see Russ as a congenial fellow who might help a little old lady cross a busy street and then go about his business never to think twice of it. That's what most good men would do. But that he would be willing to help Charles, and not even question Charles's involvement with Howard Hughes in earlier years, seemed a bit strange – until Charles got to know him better. Russ would prove to be an affable fellow that few, if any, of us would chance to meet in our lifetimes. After several lunches and in-depth conversations, Charles could well determine that Russ had indeed been a U.S. Postal Inspector, as well as having been involved in many other aspects of law enforcement. He took part in numerous high-profile investigations, two glaring examples being the Clifford Irving and Pattie Hurst scandals. Later he would show Charles documentation concerning these cases. Charlie was quick to recognize that Russ would be an asset to the yet-to-be-done investigative work concerning Howard Hughes. When Charles inquired as to payment for his services, Russ responded with, "Don't worry about that Charlie." Yes, Charles *liked* Russ.

As it would turn out, Charles's new friend Russ was not the sort to believe or disbelieve any claim with a glimpse at its facade. If a fellow was fortunate to have Russ as a friend, he would be willing to help you out, but during the investigative work, if he perceived you to be lying, that would be the end of his contributions, perhaps the end of the friendship as well.

Born in Brooklyn, New York, in 1946, Russ had been a child prodigy on the violin. Early on, with near clairvoyance, his Mother believed that there was a greatness wasting away within her son. She got him a violin, signed him up for lessons, and oversaw his attendance. At six years of age Russ, had well-mastered the use of a 3/4 sized instrument – not a toy by any stretch of the imagination. His instructor during these formative years was a Mrs. Chamberlin. Russ took lessons from Mrs. Chamberlin for several years and either never knew or soon forgot her first name. However, he did remember her as a "hard-ass woman." She instructed him well and made him practice; his mother took over on the home front.

When Russ was ten years old, the Hampton Theater Symphony came to town and was having tryouts for various positions. Russ pleaded with his mother to let him give it a try, perhaps hopeful for a reprieve from Mrs. Chamberlin's demanding tutelage. His mother gave in, perhaps thinking the tryouts to be for a diminutive musical group of no great importance. The tryouts were held in the auditorium of the nearby high school. Russ and his parents soon discovered the magnitude of the full-blown symphony ensemble. Russ remembered that most of the other hopefuls were much older than he and dwarfed him as thcy stood about talking to one another, paying him little attention. There were smirks and muffled laughter when the ten-year-old was called to the podium. Russ was asked to play some Tchaikovsky and Beethoven from sheet music on the stand before him. He had never played either piece before. After he finished, silence prevailed in the room, and the conductor asked Russ's mother and father to keep their son nearby. Young Russ had been a bit intimidated by "the big people" that were also trying out for the open positions. After the tryouts, ninety percent of the hopefuls were excused, leaving him and five others. The conductor approached Russ and said, "I want to hear you play another piece." The selection was from the stage play of *Guys and Dolls*. When Russ finished, the conductor, obviously impressed, said, "We want to keep you around." From that day forward Russ became, not just another violinist in the orchestra, but *"first chair"* violinist who soon found himself playing music from the stage plays of *South Pacific*, *Guys and Dolls*, *Camelot*, *Hall of the Mountain King*, and many others. However, like most young boys, Russ enjoyed playing sports. His love of football often caused injury to his fingers, and his endeavors in this pursuit soon began to overshadow his gift as a violinist, much to the disappointment of his mother.

Russ finished High School and continued on to college, graduating from Montgomery Junior College, Maryland, with an associate's degree in 1967, the University of Kentucky, Lexington, with a bachelor's degree in 1969, then graduate school at American University in Washington, D.C. (majoring in Law Enforcement which consisted of evidence, organized crime, Constitutional law and etc.), and Virginia Polytechnic Institute in Blacksburg. Russ got a full-time job as a U.S. Postal Inspector in California. While there, he tried his skills at teaching, including a course in forensic science at Santa Rosa Junior College, California, in 1972. Classifying and the "lifting" of fingerprints were part of the course. However, working full time as a U.S. Postal Inspector is a laborious job when done properly, so Russ was compelled to give up his teaching job. He didn't want it to interfere with his main occupation of catching bad guys – those who misused the mail for fraudulent activities. Two of the many cases Russ worked, in his *eleven years* as an inspector, were those of Clifford Irving and Pattie Hurst, both considered high profile.

When considering the above narration, it's important to remember that as federal agents, federal postal inspectors' collar more bad guys per case load than do agents of the Federal Bureau of Investigation (FBI.) From this job Russ went on to work for the San José Police Department, starting out as a beat cop. He soon moved into the job of detective and undercover officer, rising to the rank of sergeant. After eleven years at the San José Police Department, he left to take his first appointment as Chief of Police in the town of San Juan Batista, California. San Juan Batista is located south of Gilroy and San José. (For you theater buffs, San Juan Batista is the town where they filmed the blockbuster movie *Vertigo* with James Stewart and Kim Novak.) Russ later served as Chief for the Coalinga and Parlier police departments in central California. He then retired.

In their many conversations over lunches together, Russ would talk to Charles about various cases of interest he'd worked on and solved. Several of these cases, narrated below, need little dramatization as they are fascinating in their utter reality.

True to his word, Russ turned up many documents concerning Howard Hughes to help Charles in his investigations. He even went to the Glenwood Cemetery in Houston, Texas, to examine the Hughes burial plot and expressed his suspicions to Captain Ready of the Houston, Texas police department.

As you have already read in this book and will see throughout, Charles correlated Russ's investigative work with information found in his previous book, *The Price of Their Souls*, thus reinforcing and clarifying that previous exposé. Be assured that the evidence uncovered by Russ and used in *this* book *is not* hearsay or opinion. Most of the information that follows could be used in a court of law for verification purposes.

It wasn't long before Charles began to understand the depths of his new friend Russ. Drawing upon his extensive expertise in law enforcement, Russ knew what information was needed in a case, where to find it, and how to get it. If Russ took on a project and it was possible to resolve it, he would do so! This unique determination to *hang on* and investigate all aspects of a case earned Russ the nickname of "The Bulldog" among his fellow officers. Russ proved often to be a bad guy's worst nightmare.

The following are examples of cases in which Russ was involved. Russ's proficiency as postal inspector, beat cop, detective, sergeant and chief of police in both large and small cities goes unquestioned.

THE CASE WHEREIN "GAY" DOESN'T ALWAYS MEAN HAPPY
OR
NOT A GAY DAY IN SAN JOSÉ

In 1986 a "gay" fellow who worked for a large computer firm over in Silicon Valley, California, was murdered in his upscale condominium. The San José police department was on the job and so was Russ. The condo had been burglarized, and the crime scene team were there for two full days. They processed the entire place for fingerprints and turned up a few. However, since none of the fingerprint owners had been previously fingerprinted, the police didn't know to whom they belonged. The police had been diligent but could not find additional prints that might identify a close friend of a felonious nature. There were not a lot of extraneous prints since the maid, who cleaned weekly, was very meticulous. That made the print lifted off a light bulb even more significant. However, it could not be processed at the time as its owner had never been "fingered" before. The police considered three probabilities regarding this suspect's print. Perhaps he loosened the bulb because he intended to wait for his victim in the dark; perhaps he was focused on burglarizing when the victim showed up unexpectedly and expediency was required; or perhaps he just wanted to darken the condo while burglarizing it. In any event, the print was put into a fingerprint identity instrument in San José but produced no suspect. The department then carried the print up to San Francisco Police Department and ran it through that data base – again, no match. At that point, the trail of evidence appeared to be stone cold. However, the state-of-the-art fingerprinting apparatus used in San Francisco stored all prints put into it. Two weeks later a fellow was arrested for drunk and disorderly conduct in San Francisco. *Now* they had a match for the light bulb print. The San Francisco Police Department had already let the bad boy out of jail before the print "hit." But now they had an address so Russ could go with a team to arrest the suspect. Once again in custody, the police wanted to question the suspect further, since it appeared that there may have been more than just one person in on the crime. However, the suspect hung himself in his jail cell before they could gather more information.

THE LONGIVITY OF A TOUCH
OR
CREAM GOES BAD

Postal Inspector Russell received a stolen treasury check, three-to-four years old, which had been forged and passed. The check was turned over to the forensic laboratory, which found a nice crisp, clean *latent fingerprint*. In making the comparison, they found that it belonged to a guitar player in an old rock group called The Cream. Russ and several other agents went over at 5:00 a.m. to arrest the fellow who was living on a houseboat in Sausalito. The suspect and friends had been out on a gig into the wee hours of the morning. It was an easy bust, and they pulled the suspect right off the boat.

There are those who believe "all men are created equal," but a biological reality is, among other things, that their fingerprints *are not*. Unfortunately, for the team Cream fellow, he did some time for the crime in federal prison. There is no statute of limitations on a forged treasury check. We will go in-depth into latent fingerprint longevity later in this book.

BLONDE STRIKES AGAIN AND AGAIN
– AND AGAIN – AND AGAIN – ETC....

In most major cities, after a short series of successful robberies, prolific robbery suspects are given "pseudonyms" or nicknames by the police. The objective is to tie each criminal to their particular M.O. or, more specifically, a demographic or physical characteristic. Hence the thief who has a nose-ring becomes simply "Nose-Ring" or a suspect who has a tattoo on his ear becomes "Ear-Paint" etc. ("M.O." is a short for "modus operandi" or method of operation.)

Such was the situation back in 1983. Detective Russell had worked a series of gas station holdups (robberies with weapons displayed.) As a night detective, Russ was often assigned to robberies committed during his shift. These could include Blockbuster Video stores, persons walking down the street, Kentucky Fried Chicken and other restaurants and, of course, gas station holdups, etc.

However, one particular string of robberies in Detective Russell's estimation, merited closer attention. The M.O. of the perpetuator was *nearly identical* during 17 gas station holdups. The suspect told the gas station attendant to take all money from the cash drawer, bag it, and hand it over. With the gun at his back, the attendant was then forced to walk to the men's room where he was struck on the head with the suspect's gun. He was left on the floor of the stall with the warning, "Don't leave or try to call the police or anyone else."

Daytime Robbery Detectives gave the suspect the initial nickname of "Stoner" due to his gaunt appearance, perhaps caused by drugs. Later this description was changed to "Blonde" because of his flowing dirty blond hair as described by his victims.

Blonde traveled far and wide to find isolated gas stations to hold up. Detective Russell, in turn, had been compelled several times to travel to these remote locations for investigative follow-up. On the night of March 14, 1968, Blonde struck a Union 76 gas station some 15 miles south of central downtown. Upon Detective Russell's arrival he found the attendant (victim) sad and worried about what his boss would think or do. The miserable and lonely guy had received little emotional support from the patrol officers who had taken the initial report.

With no other cases or crimes in the works pending his arrival, Detective Russell had more time than usual to investigate this gas station holdup. Serious but friendly, Russ wrote down everything the victim told him, taking every opportunity to put the attendant at ease. Russ took many photographs because he was, as all detectives should be, categorically thorough.

Systematic, nearly to a fault, Detective Russell had his own M.O. for follow-up, which encompassed a time-consuming walk-through of the crime scene with the victim guiding the way. Along the way the victim would sometimes recall suspect actions or behaviors which he had failed to recall when giving the initial report to the patrol officers. Russ made careful notes of these mannerisms and behaviors, which would eventually help to identify and arrest the suspect.

The Union 76 gas station attendant recalled several new things during the walk-through. Russ's questioning encompassed everything from the attendant's initial encounter with the suspect forward. From the cash drawer, with gun at his back, the attendant was told to walk to the men's room. Once there, he was struck across the forehead with the suspect's gun and violently pushed into an open stall. The attendant fell to the floor next to the toilet.

Detective Russell walked alongside the attendant in the men's room, carefully studying the characteristics and strategy of the suspect as described by the attendant. He asked the attendant to slowly describe everything that had occurred in that restroom. The attendant's story varied little from that given to the responding patrol officers. However, in Russ's estimation, certain questions had not been asked which needed answers. Having investigated numerous crime-scenes, Detective Russell knew there was more to the story.

Russ asked the attendant to re-enact what he could recall, down to the suspect closing the bathroom stall just before leaving. Russ told the attendant *not to touch anything* in the process. Nearing the end of the walk-through, without touching the stall door, the victim showed Russ how the suspect had reached over the stall door from the outside and pulled it closed.

With the robbery walk-through completed, Russ went to his car and returned with a full fingerprint kit which he always carried. He processed the inside of the stall door where the suspect had placed his hand. Almost immediately a partial handprint of the suspect appeared, containing nearly all portions of four fingers. Russ used lifting tape to procure and save the displayed fingerprints. The gas station attendant exhibited surprise and happiness in the fingerprint discovery.

Detective Russell reported back to headquarters and submitted the lifted finger-prints to the Crime Laboratory. Two days later Daytime Robbery Detective James Cook called Russell at home and advised him that the lifted fingerprints of Blonde matched those of a *known* suspect. However, initial efforts to locate him were unsuc-cessful. About three months later Russell received another call asking if he would like to go to Eugene, Oregon, to pick up his fingerprinted suspect, who was in temporary custody relative to a different crime committed in that city.

Blonde never struck again, and Detective Russell sometimes wondered what he looked like without his long hair. This is one felon who was put away for a long-long-long time. No long hair there.

SERENDIPITY – ONE OUT OF THREE

Serendipity can mean chance, fate or destiny, or the faculty of finding valuable things not sought for. In the case cited below, the name Serendipity meant: "tell the investors we booked three, delivered one. Tell-em the turnout was bad and keep *all* the money!"

The Serendipity Singers were quite a hit in their time with several gold records to their credit. As we all know, the limelight fades fast for singing groups. But there are those who will always love them and pay top dollar for concert tickets. What is not apparent to many of their fans is that these groups are indebted to – *and their names are owned by* – those who created the popularity that moved them up the ladder of success.

Sending fraudulent correspondence through the mail and collecting money and not delivering the product falls within the jurisdiction of the federal postal inspectors. This was the criminal goings-on of The Serendipity Singer's *management* in 1976. Russ was asked to investigate. He found that investors, investing in shows of actors and famous people, were getting ripped-off! The fraudulent management company was taking the investors' money and lying about events which never took place, maintaining that profits had been minimal or that the band was a no-show, etc. Apparently, the shows where The Serendipity Singers were to perform were the ones most abused, and it was around them that Russ built his case. Most of the actors and famous people whose names were used didn't know they had been contracted for by the Serendipity Management Group. Among those victimized were Bob Hope, John Davidson, Buck Owens, and The Smothers Brothers.

In each case, after much of the fraud had been uncovered, Russ's job entailed contacting the famous person or their agent. In the case of Bob Hope, Russ interviewed him twice at his home in Toluca Lake, California. After getting statements from these famous people, Russ closed in on the fraudulent theater group in Napa, California. He found it was run by a father/son team who were embezzling investors' money derived from "ghost bookings."

Russ contacted The Serendipity Singers and sat down with each to get their stories. During the interviews, Russ asked them if anything else had happened during their association with the management team. One of the singers replied, "Do you know about our accident in Houston?" She then went on to relate on how they had done a concert, after which they were on a freeway and their driver had taken an off-ramp near their destination. Their bus was hit head-on by a driver going up the ramp the wrong way. The nasty collision landed the whole group in the hospital. Injuries were numerous, but fortunately nonlife threatening. All received invoices from the hospital, and the group told the hospital to send the bills to their father/son theatrical management group, and they would pay. Management had filed a lawsuit against the driver responsible and there was insurance on the bus as well. The Singers were required to visit their management team of "Crook & Theft," that had prepared their insurance documentation. Each of the singers certified to X-amount of injuries on their documents, which they then gave back to the Theatrical Management Group. Only one of the seven singers took a photocopy of his document. Eventually in the courtroom on investor-fraud and mail-fraud, Management would also be charged with insurance fraud concerning the Houston accident. Russ could prove that the pages the singers had signed had been altered. For instance, if one of the singers had signed a document to settle for $8,000, which Management said the insurance companies were willing to pay, the true amount, the insurance companies had been willing to pay was $18,000. Management simply ran the agreement document through the typewriter, one more time, adding a one in front of the eight. Management kept $10,000 and cut a check of only $8,000 for the entertainer. The fellow who had photocopied his claim was the hero of the day by providing the proof. Russ turned the papers over to his department analyst who then illustrated the scam in the courtroom. Both father and son did serious time.

Russ was never a fellow to let grass grow beneath his feet. He once had an ambition to make on an average of one felony bust a night for a month while working for the San José Police Department and was successful at it. It would be interesting to explain just how this was done However, it's time to get on with the Howard Hughes information uncovered by our talented super-sleuth Laurence "Russ" Russell.

The analysis of *fingerprints and cursive writing,* by Agent Russell, has been in-depth and compelling and proves the fallacy of many documents and fingerprints contained thereon – or <u>not</u> on. These are documents used <u>erroneously</u> by the Federal Bureau of Investigation, the United States Postal Service investigations, Clifford Irving, Rosemont Enterprises, Inc., the Melvin Dummar "Mormon Will" scam, etc.

Chapters IV through VII contain references to pertinent substantiating documentation that are made *often* for clarification purposes. These chapters are *crucial* in this multifaceted investigation.

CHAPTER IV

A QUESTION OF CREDIBILITY

Contrary to popular propaganda, there were many who, at the time, did not accept that the corpse flown into Houston, Texas, in 1976, was that of the real Howard Hughes, Jr. There were also those earlier than 1976 who suspected felony to be afoot. When viewing the documents and credentials of these non-believing individuals, it would be difficult to label them as "conspiracy theorists." (We have entered enquiry Exhibits of one Mae Brussell, an investigative reporter, for contrast.) Although none had first-hand knowledge about Hughes, they believed many things to be dubious. And quite frankly, they were mystified. There were many within their ranks – customs agents, postal inspectors, etc. – who after 1965, viewed a waning Hughes with a jaundiced-eye. You will soon see that these letters are of importance and should have garnered closer scrutiny. The federal folks believed these letters of inquiry (as per Exhibits below) to be evidential enough to keep in their files. There were numerous redactions within the FBI files before their release to Russ on a FOIA (Freedom of Information Act request). However, enough was retained to provide a substantial volume of pertinent information. The following letters are from both internal federal agency communications and from the outside citizens to the federal agencies. Enough of these inquiries were released and used without over emphasis to set the trend for this continuing investigation.

Please keep in mind that federal officials <u>do not</u> go to extremes to waste valuable manpower and crime lab time because they're bored with their jobs. That's the quickest way to *lose* their gainful employment. Although customs officials are paid to be suspicious, there must be sufficient validating information to support further investigation, rather than suspicion alone. Crucial observations must be made by customs agents to arouse their suspicion. For example, unusual body language of persons attempting to block the signing of necessary documents from the eyes of the agents. One person feigning a signature, or a close-in follower signs his signature and another's as well. Persons passing through customs intently eyeing or furtively glancing at the agents, etc.

Also, regarding latent fingerprints, the customs agent must be near certain that the latent prints sent off to the lab were left on the sheet by the fellow in question. There may be other prints on the document, but the near exact location of *where* the document was pressed by the fellow in question and his having touched it and held it to the table while signing is vital. Even if prints overlap, there will most likely be enough of a partial print to indicate to whom it belongs. If the print is not that person's, this would be indicated in the lab report. Chapter V concerns itself with fingerprints. In this Chapter IV, we are primarily concerned with suspect activities concerning "Howard Hughes."

EXHIBITS FOUND IN FBI FILE 1222257-95-HQ-179917

Exhibit 1: File Page 1:

Envelope containing questioned documents, sent off to the federal latent print examiner.

Note: To be sure all pertinent latent prints on document were captured, <u>four (4) photos</u> had been taken.

Exhibit 2: File Page 2:

Prints determined to be those of Howard Hughes are noted.

Note: Agents are trained to consider all areas held or pressed by the person in question. (Original prints were obviously of better quality then what appears below. Xerox equipment was not as good in bygone years and after several Xerox copies, documents often lost their "crispness.")

Exhibit 3: File Page 17:

Questionable "Hughes" signature on Customs I.D. card - Canada. Agents pick up on unusual activity regarding a private plane passenger purported to be Howard Hughes.

Note: Customs concerns obviously motivated *by more than* mild suspicion.

Exhibit 4: File Page 18:

Canadian Customs wants more than just a cursive writing examination. They want latent fingerprints examined as well, believing "something to be wrong with the picture."

Note: You will find more in-depth understanding of "latent fingerprints" in Chapter V.

Exhibit 5: File Page 15:

Canadian Private Aircraft Inspection Report, purportedly signed by Howard Hughes.

Notes:
   a) All passengers printed their names, except "Hughes" and one other fellow (line 6 and 7). Printing or signing appears to have been acceptable to customs agents.
   b) Except for a "Hughes" signature on line 7, all *printing* on lines 7 and 8 appears to have been done by Howard Eckersley. Did Customs also take note that Eckersley had signed "Hughes's" signature as well? Consider this: <u>all passengers must sign or print his own name</u>. Therefore, if Eckersley, who printed his own name, had forged a *printed* Hughes name, *a forgery would have been obvious.* It appears that Eckersley forged a signature for

"Hughes," because they did not have the real Hughes to print or sign his name. Then Eckersley printed his own name and the rest of the information required on lines 6 and 7 – in the belief that this would be acceptable? It wasn't.

c) Howard Eckersley traveled with the Hughes entourage as it bounced a sickly "Hughes" from Nevada to the Bahamas, Canada, England, Nicaragua, back to the Bahamas, and lastly to Acapulco, Mexico. It is curious that Eckersley was also the internal notary for Summa, Inc. – having notarized many documents *supposedly* signed by Howard Hughes. One was a Power of Attorney for Richard Gray (dead at an early age), which gave Gray control of the Hughes Nevada operations, including purchasing of precious metal mines (in which there were precious little of the valued metals), hotels, airport properties, thousands of acres of undeveloped land, etc. Is it not reasonable to presume that Eckersley waxed prolific in the forging of a "Hughes" signatures early on, for lack of a genuine living Hughes? Could he *also have forged a Hughes signature on Richard Gray's Power of Attorney?* (More on Richard Gray in Chapter X.)

Exhibit 6: File Page 20:
Expanded analytical procedure done by FBI.

Exhibit 7: File Page 22:
Identity of Hughes's signature inconclusive – printing after Hughes's signature indicates, most probably, that it was done by one person.

Exhibit 8: File Page 24:
None of the latent fingerprints found on the document were those of Howard Hughes, even though the fellow <u>alleged</u> to be Hughes held it and pressed down upon the document when signing?

EXHIBITS FOUND IN FBI FILE 12222-0-62-HQ-99801

Exhibit 9: File Page 66:
a) "Howard Hughes" arrives in Las Vegas, Nevada, just prior to Thanksgiving Day, 1966.
b) Resides on the 9th floor of the Desert Inn Hotel, never goes anywhere, and is seen only by his caretakers.
c) "Hughes" buys four hotels with casinos and <u>never</u> submits a proper fingerprint card (A print card from FBI file number 2 702 851, *which had been taken years before*, was sent in with Hughes's superficial information, but no original "inked" Hughes prints accompanied this.) Background history, photos, etc. were never properly submitted. Hughes <u>never</u> makes a personal

appearance before the gaming commission. He gets permits anyway – a first and last for Las Vegas since the Mob operated there in the good ol' days. Last of 3rd paragraph on following page: "*Agent cannot guarantee, in any way, that prints submitted were those of Howard Hughes*," identification record appears to be *bogus* as well.

d) Hughes purchases other properties including two airports in Clark County, Nevada. (No records could be found, news articles, etc. of Hughes visiting any properties prior to or after purchasing them.) This is a strange way for a billionaire with a lifetime of acquisitions to behave.

Exhibit 10: File Page 67:

a) Gaming commission is concerned with issuing gaming licenses for Hughes Hotels, no one has ever seen Hughes personally, including Governor Laxalt, and they question, "Is there a live Howard Hughes?"

b) 1st paragraph, lines 10 and 11. "…even though everything appears to be 100% above board." What? They have no valid fingerprints, no current photos. They have never even seen or spoken with "Hughes?" and everything appears to be 100% above board?

c) 1st paragraph, lines 15, 16 and 17. Concern that a "great 'hoax' could be being perpetrated on the state officials"? Oh, my goodness and *wow!* Whatever brought someone to *that* conclusion?

d) 2nd paragraph, lines 5 and 6. Richard Gray comes into play.

e) 2nd paragraph. The Nevada Gaming Commission wants one of their men to "have a confrontation" with Howard Hughes. Richard Gray loses his composure and states that, "Mr. Hughes would probably withdraw from active participation in gaming in the state of Nevada." My, my – is that anyway for a businessman to react, losing millions in profits, because someone wants a short interview with him? Oh heck, we must keep in mind that Howard Hughes was a crazy, xenophobic, drug addicted recluse. Oh yeah, that *must* have been the reason!

f) Last paragraph. Richard Gray has a Power of Attorney signed by "Hughes" on 12/13/67. That's real close to 1965, soon after Rosemont Enterprises came into play. (Much more on Rosemont in Chapter IX.)

Exhibit 11: File Page 68:

Top of page. "The fingerprint record furnished to the gaming authorities *could not* be positively identified as that of Howard Hughes." How strange?

a) First paragraph. Hughes holds and signs document, but leaves nary a *latent* fingerprint behind?

b) Second paragraph. That guy "Hughes" is just plain "nuts" - he just doesn't have *any* fingerprints?

Exhibit 12: File Page 69:

Now you federal guys be nice and do not do anything *officially* to upset the apple cart. We just want to be sure you are dealing with a real Howard Hughes. Sounds a bit abstruse, but what do you think?

Exhibit 13: File Page 79:

Anonymous communication to Mr. Jack Anderson of the FBI that raises valid questions.
    a) The letter is pretty accurate regarding what was going down in Las Vegas with "Hughes." Final paragraph concerning Jean Peters Hughes is pretty much "spot on." There is more on Jean Peters later.

Exhibit 14-A: File page 90 and Exhibits 14-B and 14-C from Allen Gerber's book *Bashful Billionaire*, pages 258 and 259:

"Bahamian Howard" (the supposed "Hughes" who just could not remember who General Harold George was?) cedes power to Bill Gay and Chester Davis and states, via a questionable example, that he has terminated Robert Maheu. Unusual, don't you think, for a billionaire industrialist who has been a "hands on" sort of fellow since he was 19 years of age? Maheu was supposedly "Hughes's right-hand man." (Letter was later determined to be bogus by the FBI.)

Exhibit 15: File page 91:

Governor Laxalt is now assured that "Hughes" is alive and well. "Hughes" supposedly tells Laxalt that he intends to return to Nevada to "live the rest of his life." (Of course, he never did. A sickly "Hughes" got bounced around the world, getting his hip broken in London, his arm dislocated in the Bahamas, and finally, died in his jet as it flew him to Houston, Texas, from Acapulco, Mexico. (Worthy of remembering here is that Howard Hughes <u>owned</u> a hospital in Miami, Florida. Strange that after 1965, "Hughes" was *never* taken there for *anything* medical.
    a) Mentions a document purportedly signed by "Howard Hughes" personally. I wonder if that one was also "notarized" by Eckersley?
    b) Maheu's "bombshell"? Of course, he has an "ace in the hole" – he knows the truth about Hughes. But the bombshell Maheu promises (a forged document to fire him) stops short of completion when FBI Agent Appel finds two other forged "Hughes" signatures. Maheu apparently realizes that the FBI might uncover the whole scam – a con where, in the beginning, he was a major player. He backs off.

Exhibit 16: File page 92:

Document supposedly signed by "Hughes" to oust Maheu, <u>is a forgery</u>. Former Bureau document examiner Charles Appel <u>also</u> picks up on <u>yet another</u> forged Hughes signature occurring in *approximately 1964 or 1965?* Document examiner claims that this could be "the most monumental steal attempt in American history." The above-referenced dates of *1964* and *1965* are extremely important to this case.

a) It appears that Gay and Davis still have the upper hand. With the advent of Agent Appel's discovery that other forged signatures occurred in 1964 and 1965, Maheu knows that the whole scam could come "undone" and he *also* could be implicated. This appears to be the point where Maheu begins to back away from the hope of once more regaining control of doppelganger "Hughes" and whoever the cursive "Hughes" might be. This was his only chance to snatch back the reins of power and begin, once more, to pilfer more wealth from the Hughes empire.

Exhibit 17: File page 93: [FBI official's name redacted]
a) Telephone call to Gov. Laxalt from "Hughes" not believed.
b) Serious doubt as to Hughes's whereabouts, competence, and wellbeing.
c) "Gay – Davis faction will have no alternative but to relinquish control and depart Nevada in a hurry"? The Gay – Davis faction didn't relinquish control; but under their supervision, the "Hughes" aides did leave Las Vegas in a hurry, taking "Hughes" with them.
d) Difficult to believe that senior officials in the FBI are prone to idle speculation; evidence is reasonably conclusive.

Exhibit 18-A: File Page 107:
Maheu is not to be trusted; but the information he divulges about Raymond Holliday is correct. Holliday (CEO of Hughes ToolCo, Inc.) knew things were not right. More in-depth information concerning Holliday later.

Exhibit 18-B:
Indication here is that Raymond Holliday was much more than "just a friend" of Hughes; he was instrumental and trusted by Hughes in many major undertakings. Exhibit 18-B is a lead-in document to the monumental Trans World Airlines (TWA) lawsuit wherein Holliday, together with Hughes's tool company, Toolco, Inc., and Howard Hughes, were defendants. When one speaks of Howard Hughes's trusted friends, Raymond Holliday and Dr. Vern Mason are prime examples.

Exhibit 18-C:
Evidence of the complexity of the TWA lawsuit and Raymond Holliday's importance in bringing it to fruition in the absence of Howard Hughes. Hughes *trusted* Holliday.

Exhibit 18-D:
TWA lawsuit is finally won in the Appellant Court, in totality, by Raymond Holiday, Hughes ToolCo, Inc., and Howard Hughes.

EXHIBITS FOUND IN FBI FILE 1222257-0-32-HO-278

Exhibit 19: File page 53:
   a) Many redacted names.
   b) <u>A question of switched fingerprints and misidentification.</u> (bottom paragraph)

EXHIBITS FOUND IN FBI FILE 1222257-0-62-HO-99801

Exhibit 20: File page 74:
   Many redactions. Is Howard Hughes "dead or alive?" letter to J. Edger Hoover FBI, from a man of importance.

Exhibit 21: File page 78:
   Designation cover letter to Jack Anderson, FBI.

Exhibit 22: File page 79:
   Anonymous source – many questions – all of them professionally researched.
   a) Bottom of page – <u>Jean Peters Hughes never did appear with Hughes in court.</u> Later started a lawsuit for money promised but never received.

Exhibit 23: File page 80:
   Mafia connection suspected.

Exhibit 24: File page 81:
   There is truth in this postscript, "Howard Hughes was never a fellow to deal with corrupt persons." But being dead earlier in 1965, **not** 1976, he would not have had a say in the types of people Bob Maheu, Chester Davis, Bill Gay, and Nadine Henley brought into the "pilfer party" *after* 1965. There is substance here. Bob Maheu, Johnnie Roselli, and Sam Giancana are all birds of the same feather and all Mafia linked. Johnnie and Sam were brought into the "Hughes" fold by Bob Maheu. Maheu was brought in by Bill Gay. Earlier than 1965 the real Howard Hughes was never known to associate with criminal entities.

Exhibit 25: File page 171:
   A person from San Antonio, Texas, who has grave concerns for a Texas Native Son. It certainly appears that the federal folks dropped the ball regarding Howard Hughes. They could have done more to uncover the truth on many occasions and, although they came incredibly close to doing just that, for one reason or another, they never followed through. Why is that?

Exhibit 26: File page 206:

Mae Brussel was a conspiracy theorist in tune with the mindset of the times. She certainly knew how to ask the questions. She must have rocked the federal boat on numerous occasions. Her letter was a keeper for the feds.

Exhibit 27: File page 207:

They kept copies in several locations – apparently for future reference. Unfortunately for Mae no further information was forthcoming (no FOIAs in those years).

The analysis above is extensive and to the point. However, all the above will be readily conclusive when reading excerpts from FBI files themselves. Exhibits follow the overview below.

OVERVIEW

Concerning Exhibit 22: FBI file overview, page 79, bottom of page:

Jean Peters Hughes never did appear with Hughes in court. Later she started a lawsuit for money promised, but never received. Apparently, "Howard's" "ex" Jean got the payoff she expected, so she went quiet. Her "marriage" to Hughes delivered extraordinarily little gossip fodder for the press, other than the idea that Hughes may have been a bit eccentric. So, let us take a possibility to the edge of a cliff and hopefully *not go over* the side.

JEAN PETERS

- Born October 15, 1926 - Died October 13, 2000.
- A stanch Republican, she donated her time and money to Dwight D. Eisenhower, Richard Nixon, and Ronald Reagan. She voted for George Bush in October of 2000 via absentee ballot.
- Entered the Theater Industry at 21 years of age, having won a Miss Ohio State beauty contest. Along with the prizes was a Fox Screen Test.
- Was signed onto a 7-year contract with Fox and ascended to immediate stardom in
- *Captain from Castile* in 1947.
- Had been noticed by Howard Hughes in 1946 on Catalina Island where she partied with war hero Audie Murphy. Ditching Murphy for Hughes, she and Hughes become close in their relationship.
- At the time, Hughes owned RKO Studios; and he and Jean see each other often. They view movies in his screening room.
- When Hughes crashed his XF-11 Test-Plane, Jean Peters was one of the select few he allowed to his bedside. His aunt Annette and nephew Will Lummis were turned away.

MOVIES WITH JEAN PETERS

1947—*Captain from Castile*
1951—*Anne of the Indies*
1952—*Viva Zapata*
1953—*Pick-up on South Street*
1953—*Niagara*
1954—*Three Coins in the Fountain*
1954—*Apache*
1954—*Broken Lance*
1955—*A Man Called Peter*

- She was suspended from her studio after *A Man Called Peter* for refusing other films and "loan outs."
- In 1954 she married Texas oil man and Lockheed plane executive Stuart Cramer, III. The marriage lasted 33 days. According to Cramer, she had bouts with depression and a drinking problem as well.
- In 1957 Peters Marries Hughes in the ever-so-small town of Tonopah, Nevada. Peters uses the alias of "Marian Evans" and Hughes uses "G.A. Johnson." There were no bridesmaids at the wedding. Peters' mother and sister were not in attendance. The Preacher who married them is still a mystery. There was no direct news coverage at the time and only speculation as to why all the secrecy and intrigue. So, a little more speculation would suggest that there was something about Howard Hughes he didn't wish to become common knowledge. Hughes had begun his disappearing act in 1954 – no photos and no face-to-face meetings. Communication with anyone was done by telephone or facsimile. Noah Dietrick, a Hughes attorney, had begun a coup d'état in 1957 to have Hughes deemed incompetent and committed to an institution. Dietrick cited Hughes's inaccessibility as reason for concern and an indication of mental illness. When Hughes marries Jean Peters, it throws a monkey-wrench into the machinery of the Dietrick ploy. It seems that Dietrick was stopped cold when forced to consider Jean's support and friendship with Dwight D. Eisenhower and other powerful political figures. Hughes retaliates against Dietrick and almost immediately fires him in 1958. Hughes continues his isolation from the social and business mainstream, never meets with anyone, does not allow photos, and is never seen in public with Jean or anyone else.

When Jean Peters first divorced Hughes in 1967, no courtroom activity occurred, and no settlement or alimony money was apparent at the time. However, later she sues for a reward promised. (An out-of-court settlement gets Jean her reward.)

So, what was the purpose of all the mystery surrounding an inaccessible Hughes and his marriage to Peters – the supposed "secret wedding" that just about everyone knew about? It could only have been one of two probabilities: 1) Howard was losing his mind or 2) his body was beginning to change because of injuries sustained in the 1946

XF-11 crash in the Beverly Hills area, and he did not want his deformation to be seen. Let us consider possibility 2. Why? Earlier, but most specifically, between the years of 1958 and 1965, the Hughes Industries were growing dynamically in wealth and contracts. Although Hughes was an absentee landlord after 1954, he ran his businesses well from afar via telephone and facsimile. It was only *after* 1965 that things began to go badly in the Hughes empire.

In 1966 Peters sues for divorce, opts for, and is granted a $70,000 a-year settlement. This is *not* alimony. The understanding is that she will get this reward no matter what path life takes her down. ($70,000 in 1966 is equivalent to approximately $800,000 in today's inflated currency.) The conditions of this award are that Peters must sign non-disclosure agreements, which means she cannot divulge any personal information about Howard Hughes or their lives together. (Ominous years 1965 and 1966. Things concerning Hughes began to become peculiar.)

By 1971 cash flow is running thin for Peters. Except for bit parts after 1955, she has not worked seriously for 15 years. She wants the money promised in 1966, and the Hughes Industries (Summa, Inc.) have been stonewalling. The reward is finally granted in 1971 when Peters *threatens* to take Howard Hughes "personally" into court. Howard Hughes *was never* in the courtroom with Jean Peters, or in any other courtroom *after* 1954.

Let's try for a different perspective on what could have been going down in 1957, 1958 and beyond:

Hughes was a fellow who liked well the ladies of his life. In his youth, Hollywood was his cornucopia, and he easily could have had any single starlet of his choosing. Howard was rich, good looking, a gentleman, and active in the theater industry. It has been well documented that when Hughes was attracted to one lady or the other, it was flowers often, jewelry that could garner the envy of a princess, and dining in the finest restaurants. It has been said that Howard's preparation for the main course, which the woman knew would eventually be her, would often leave them mystified as to when he would get to the point. Nothing forced or rushed, Howard was noted as the finest gentlemen. You may be assured that Jean Peters was no exception to his amorous thoughtfulness. Peters not only benefitted greatly in her theatrical career from her association with Hughes, but it most certainly appears that they had bonded as well. It's difficult to imagine either of them as celibate. Isn't this what we always secretly suspected and now know about the theater industry? When Hughes crashed his XF-11 test plane into Beverly Hills, Peters was one of the few he allowed to his hospital bedside.

Time "rocks along" and Hughes came to realize that his injuries, sustained in the XF-11 crash were worse than he and his doctors had first anticipated. His spine had been severely injured and, instead of repairing itself, began to gradually disintegrate. This development forces him to realize that not only would his physique become badly deformed, but that it would eventually bring him to an earlier death. The unnatural folding of his upper torso would ultimately press down upon his vital organs and they would cease to function. Hughes decides not to be in the limelight when these unsightly events become evident. He wants no pity, so he disappears into Mexico where he can still effectively run his empire from afar by telephone and facsimile. This was all he now had to make his life worthwhile. His secret was well kept until the end. It's possible that not even his lieutenants knew of his unfortunate dilemma.

However, Noah Dietrick, one of his lieutenants, was a shark that smelled blood. He attempts to take advantage of a bad situation and tries to form a coup' within the Hughes Industries. Dietrick claims that "Hughes is mentally ill because of his self-isolation and should be removed from his life's work and confined to an institution." He attempts to get Dr. Vern Mason, Hughes's personal physician and CEO of the Howard Hughes Medical Institute, Miami, in on the plot. The coup' fails. Now Hughes has *more* of a dilemma to deal with than just his health. Dietrick may eventually try again, citing ever-growing military contracts. Hughes does not want to be forced out into the open for the world to see his unsightly and progressive medical disability. He decides that a marriage, preferably to Jean Peters, would resolve his quandary.

With the advent of the Hughes-Peters wedding, Noah Dietrick knows he has no path. If he tries to force Hughes into court on a mental disability ploy, he will have Jean Peters, intricately connected to the political landscape, to deal with. If Jean called in her "markers," Detrick would be dead in the water. Howard will never see the inside of a courtroom with Dietrick, and Dietrick knows it. Noah quits the scheme.

EXHIBIT 1

FBI FILE 1222257-95-HQ-179917-1—PAGE 1

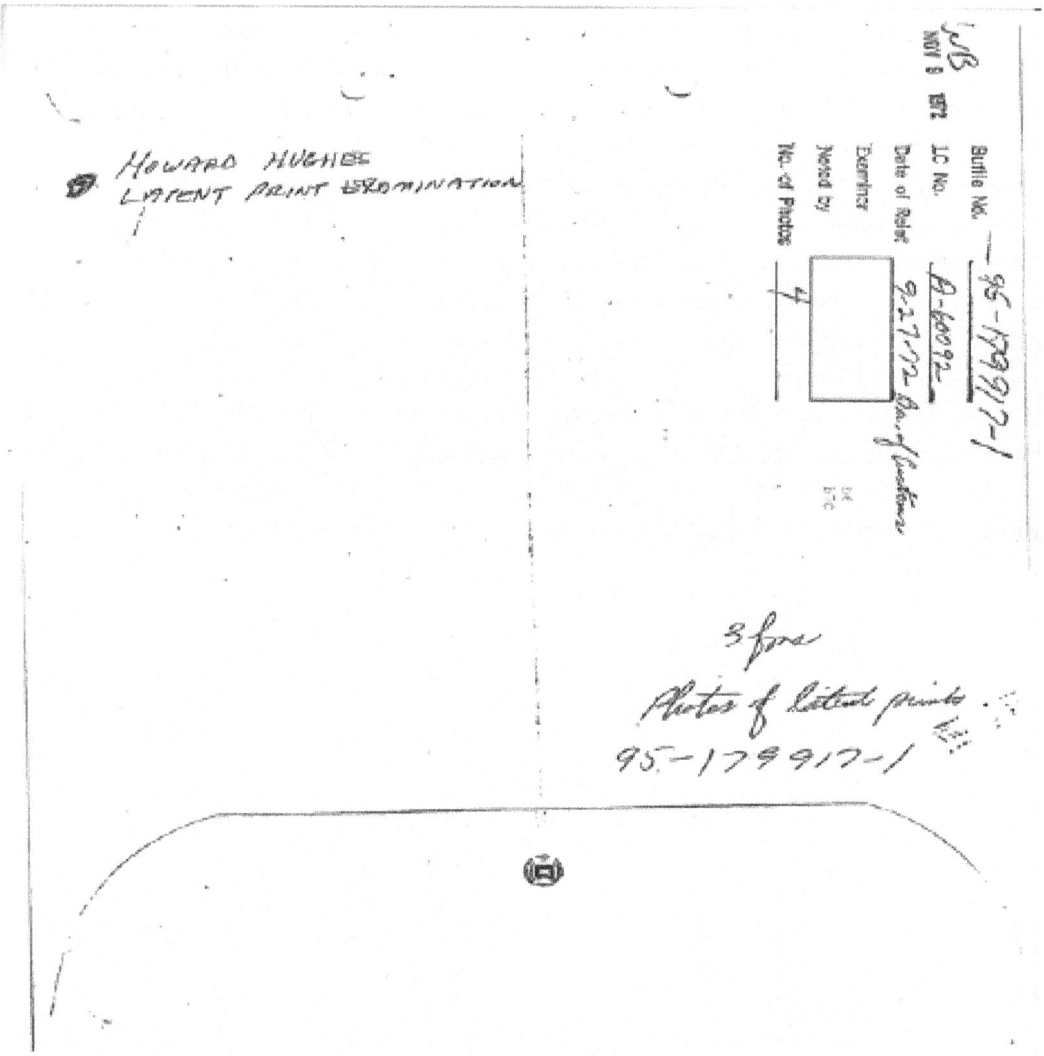
HOWARD HUGHES
LATENT PRINT EXAMINATION

NOV 8 1972
Bufile No. 95-179917-1
LC No. A-6092
Date of Rec'd 9-27-72 Bur. of Customs
Examiner
Noted by
No. of Photos 4

Photos of latent prints
95-179917-1

EXHIBIT 2

FBI FILE 1222257-95-HQ-179917-1—PAGE 2 (LATENT PRINT LOCATION)

FILE PAGE 2 EXEMPLAR 2

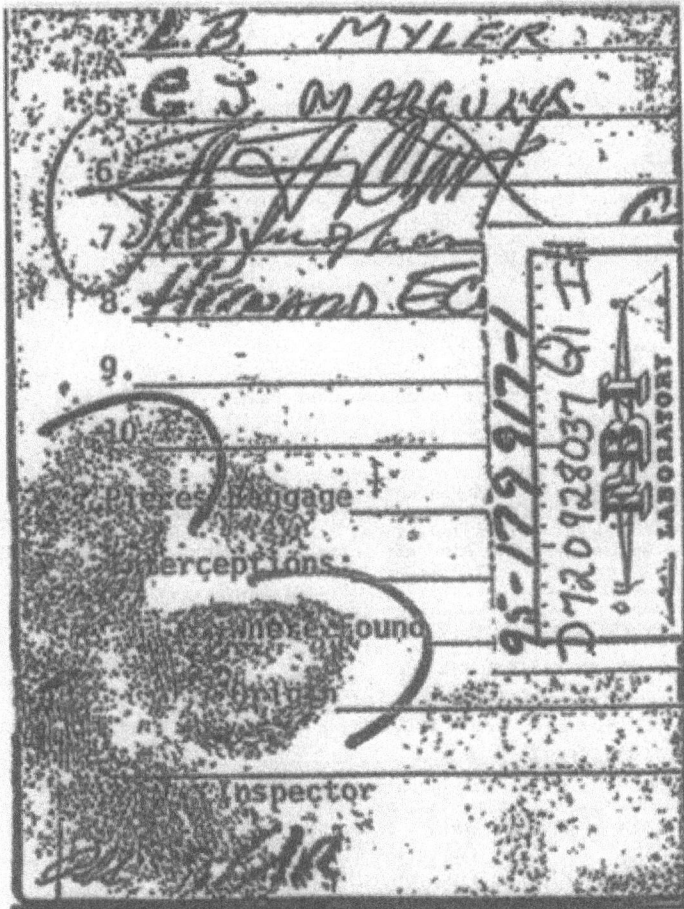

EXHIBIT 3

FBI FILE 1222257-95-HQ-179917-1—PAGE 17

THE DEPARTMENT OF THE TREASURY

BUREAU OF CUSTOMS

WASHINGTON, D.C.

SEP 2 7 1972

REFER TO
INV.20.010

720928037

The Honorable
L. Patrick Gray III
Acting Director
Federal Bureau of Investigation
Department of Justice
Washington, D. C. 20530

Attention: Mr. Ivan W. Conrad, Assistant Director

Re: Howard Hughes
D.O.B.: 12/24/05

Dear Sir:

This will confirm the telephone conversation on September 22, 1972, between Mr. Norman T. Buselmeier, of my staff, and Mr. Ivan W. Conrad concerning Mr. Howard Hughes.

On August 29, 1972, aircraft number N123H arrived at El Paso, Texas, en route from Vancouver, B.C. Canada, to Managua, Nicaragua. One of the passengers was purported to be Howard Hughes. This individual signed line number 7 of the Customs Private Aircraft Inspection Report as "H. Hughes."

This office is conducting an official investigation in an attempt to establish whether or not the person referred to above was Howard Hughes. In this regard, I am forwarding to you the original of the referenced document in an envelope marked Exhibit Q-1.

A facsimile of the original document is also attached for your examination prior to handling the original. This document has not been previously examined.

In furtherance of our investigation, you are requested to compare the signature on line number 7 of Exhibit Q-1 with any known standards of the signature of Howard Hughes to determine if he was actually the author of the questioned writing.

95-179917

18 SEP 29 1972

ST-106

REPLY TO: COMMISSIONER OF CUSTOMS, WASHINGTON, D.C. 20226

EXHIBIT 4

FBI FILE 1222257-95-HQ-179917-1—PAGE 18

2

It is also requested that an attempt be made to develop any latent fingerprints which exist on Exhibit Q-1 and compare such prints with the actual fingerprints of Howard Hughes.

Please return the original document with your reply to the Commissioner of Customs, Office of Investigations.

Thank you very much for your assistance in this investigation.

Sincerely yours,

Harold F. Smith

Assistant Commissioner
Office of Investigations

EXHIBIT 5

FBI FILE 1222257-95-HQ-179917-1—PAGE 15
Aircraft Inspection Report With Questionable "Hughes" Signature (Line-7)

FILE PAGE 15 EXEMPLAR 5

VI-RC-69 PRIVATE AIRCRAFT INSPECTION REPORT AIR-4-IC

Plane No N123H Make ____ Model ____

Nationality USA Color W & Gold

Pilot R. J. GERCEVICH License No. 1091371

Address 1040 EUCLID SANTA MONICA CALIF.

Owner HILTON HOTEL INC

Address 720 S. MICHIGAN CHICAGO, ILL.

Departure from U. S. SANTA MONICA Date 8-28 Time 5:15 PM

U. S. Arrival Time 1125 Last Foreign Port VANCOUVER Hour 0800

Foreign Ports Visited ____

Time Inspection Requested ____

Inspector Travel Time ____ Waiting ____ Inspection ____

	Name of Passengers	Address	Citizenship
1	R. S. BROWN	Co PILOT	USA Sylmar, CALIF
2.	L. F COLLIN	FLT ENG	USA HAWTHORNE CALIF.
3.	J. H. RICKARD	2063 N 220 E. PROVO	U.S.A.
4.	L.B. MYLER	4897 S. NANILSON S.L.	USA
5.	C. J. MARGULIS	4000 SAN JOAQUIN. LAS VEGAS	USA.
6.	[illegible signature]	508 E ST. S.L.	USA
7.	H. Hughes	GULF BLDG HOUSTON	USA
8.	HOWARD ECKERSLEY	5472 ~~~~ Rd, 2374 LAURA KAY Dr S.L.	USA
9			
10.			

Pieces Baggage ____ Cargo Yes ____ No ____

Interceptions: ____

Where Found ____

Origin ____

Inspector Service Date

(1st Rev. - Jan. 1972)

Adl. W.A.R.

D720928037 Q1 IH

FBI

EXHIBIT 6

FBI FILE 1222257-95-HQ-179917-1—PAGE 20
Expanded Analitical Early Hughes and "H.H." Signatures – Customs – Canada

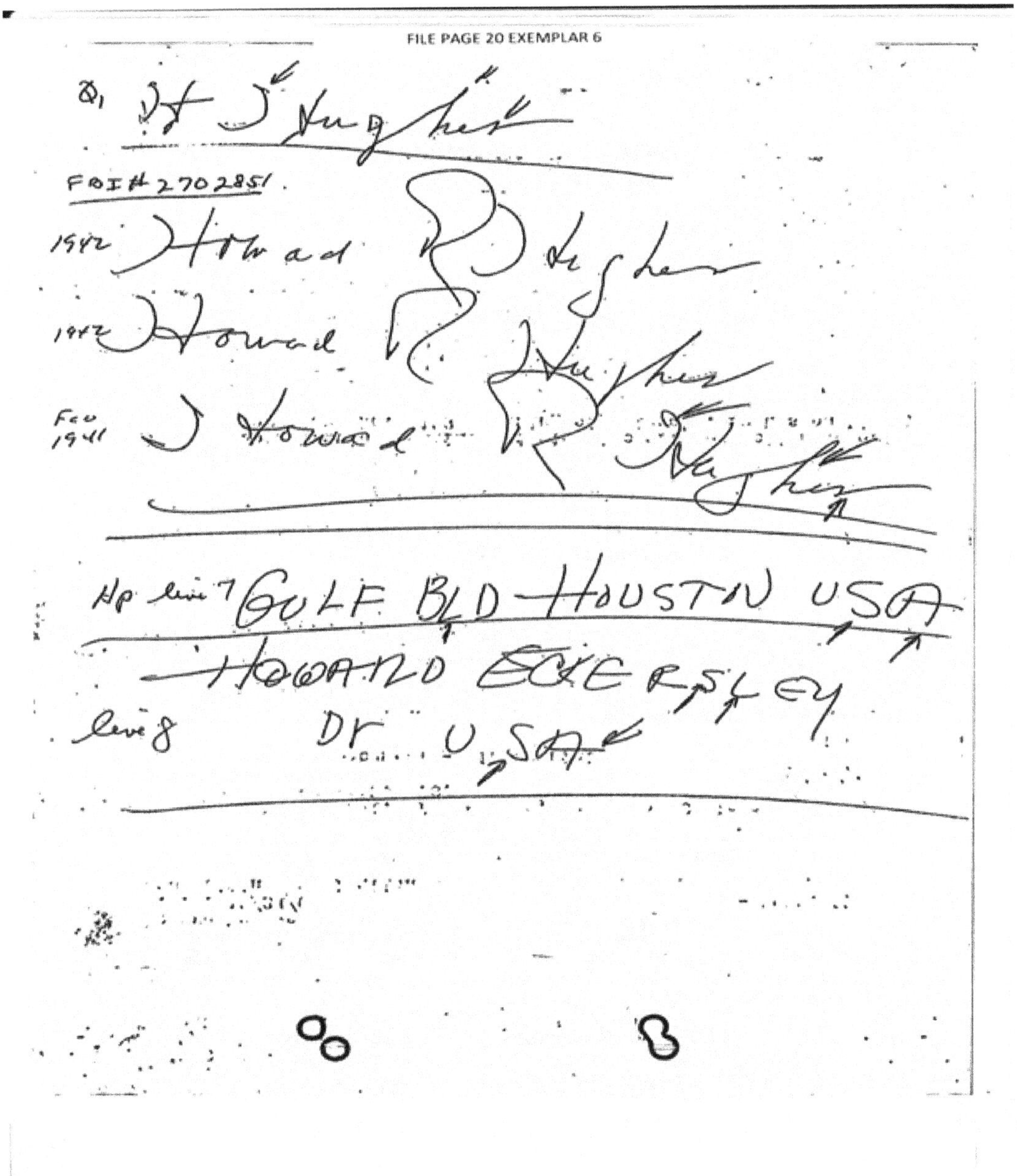
FILE PAGE 20 EXEMPLAR 6

FBI# 2702851

1942

1942

Feb 1941

GULF BLD HOUSTN USA

HOWARD ECKERSLEY

DR USA

EXHIBIT 7

FBI FILE 1222257-95-HQ-179917-1—PAGE 22

2-1 (Rev. 5-1972)

REPORT
of the
FBI
LABORATORY

FEDERAL BUREAU OF INVESTIGATION
WASHINGTON, D. C. 20535

1 – Mr. Devine
1 – Mr. Gillham

To: Commissioner
Bureau of Customs
Department of the Treasury
Washington, D. C. 20226

October 2, 1972

Attention: Mr. Norman T. Busolmeier

L. Patrick Gray
L. Patrick Gray, III
Acting Director

Re: Howard Hughes,
D.O.B. 12/24/05;
Handwriting Examination

YOUR NO. **INV.20.010**
REC-70
FBI FILE NO. 95-179917-1

Examination requested by: Addressee

LAB. NO. D-720920037 IH

Reference: Letter dated 9/27/72

Examination requested: Document - Fingerprint

Q1 Form bearing heading "Private Aircraft Inspection Report"
for Plane No. N123H bearing signature "H. Hughes" on
Line 7

Result of examination:

Due to the limited nature of the questioned
signature on Q1 and because of the differences in time in
the preparation of the questioned signature and available
known signatures, a definite conclusion could not be reached
whether the questioned signature on Q1 was prepared by
HOWARD ROBARD HUGHES, whose available known handwriting
consists of signatures appearing on fingerprint cards.

It is noted that a few hand printing characteristics
in common were noted in the hand printing after the Hughes
signature on Line 7 and the hand printing on Line 8 of Q1
indicating the possibility that one person may have prepared
this hand printing.

Q1 has been photographed and is returned herewith.
A separate report is being furnished on the requested
fingerprint examination of Q1.

1 - Bufile (62-99801)
1 - Bufile (87-119739)
Enclosure

Felt
Mohr
Rosen
Bates
Bishop
Callahan
Campbell
Casper
Cleveland
Conrad
Dalbey
Marshall
Miller, E.S.
Ponder
Soyars
Walters
Tele. Room
Mr. Kinley
Mr. Armst.
Ms. Herwig
Mrs. Neenan

ENCLOSER

MAIL ROOM ☐   TELETYPE UNIT ☐

EXHIBIT 8

FBI FILE 1222257-95-HQ-179917-1—PAGE 24

1-336 (Rev. 5-24-72)

FEDERAL BUREAU OF INVESTIGATION
Washington, D. C. 20537

REPORT
of the
IDENTIFICATION DIVISION
LATENT FINGERPRINT SECTION

YOUR FILE NO.
FBI FILE NO.
LATENT CASE NO. A-60092

October 2, 1972

TO: Mr. Myles J. Ambrose
Commissioner
Bureau of Customs
U. S. Department of the Treasury
Washington, D. C. 20226

Attention: Mr. Harold F. Smith
Assistant Commissioner
Office of Investigations

RE: HOWARD HUGHES
LATENT PRINT EXAMINATION

REFERENCE: Letter September 27, 1972
EXAMINATION REQUESTED BY: Addressee
SPECIMENS: Q1, private aircraft inspection report

The listed Q specimen is described in the Laboratory report, which is being furnished separately and will include the disposition of Q1.

Three latent fingerprints of value for identification purposes were developed on Q1.

The latent prints are not identical with the fingerprints of Howard Robard Hughes, born December 24, 1905, in Houston Texas, FBI #2702851.

Photographs of the latent prints have been prepared
(Continued on next page)

L. Patrick Gray, III, Acting Director

THIS REPORT IS FURNISHED FOR OFFICIAL USE ONLY

61

EXHIBIT 9

FBI FILE 1222257-0-62-HQ-99801—PAGE 66

Note: Lab Cursive at page bottom: "We should have absolutely nothing to do with this."

OPTIONAL FORM NO. 10
MAY 1962 EDITION
GSA GEN. REG. NO. 27

UNITED STATES GOVERNMENT

Memorandum

Mr. Tolson
Mr. DeLoach
Mr. Mohr
Mr. Bishop
Mr. Casper
Mr. Callahan
Mr. Conrad
Mr. Felt
Mr. Gale
Mr. Rosen
Mr. Sullivan
Mr. Tavel
Mr. Trotter
Tele. Room
Miss Holmes
Miss Gandy

TO : DIRECTOR, FBI   DATE: 12/14/67
      (PERSONAL ATTN: ASST. DIR. I. W. CONRAD)

FROM : SAC, LAS VEGAS

SUBJECT: HOWARD R. HUGHES
         REQUEST FOR LABORATORY
         AND FINGERPRINT EXAMINATION

Re my phone call to Section Chief W. D. GRIFFITH
today.

As the Bureau is aware, HOWARD R. HUGHES came to Las
Vegas to establish residence just prior to Thanksgiving, 1966.
He has resided in absolute seclusion on the 9th floor of the
Desert Inn Hotel since his arrival in Las Vegas. As has been
publicly stated, he has purchased three major hotels on the
Las Vegas "Strip" and a fourth hotel of lesser stature. He has
also purchased two airports and many acres of land in addition
to thousands of acres which he has owned for many years in
Clark County.

In connection with HOWARD HUGHES' ownership of the
various hotels in Las Vegas, he has been licensed as the sole
owner and operator of these hotels by the Nevada state gaming
authorities who have dispensed with their normal procedures of
requiring an applicant for a gaming license to appear before the
Gaming Control Board and Gaming Commission and to submit fingerprints and detailed background information regarding personal
history and financial responsibility.

In connection with the normal fingerprint requirement
officials of the Nevada Gaming Commission had previously requested
that I obtain a fingerprint record from the Identification Division,
if possible, without the submission of a current fingerprint card.
Based on background information the Identification Division furnished me a fingerprint record which appeared to be that of
HOWARD R. HUGHES which has FBI Number 2 702 851. Since neither
fingerprints nor an identifying number, which is indexed in the
Identification file, accompanied the request from Las Vegas the

REC-32   62- 97801-7   6 JAN 3 1968

② - Bureau (Enc. - 1) (RM)
1 - Las Vegas
DWE:jp
(3)

We should have absolutely nothing to do with this.

SENT DIRECTOR   12-18-67

Buy U.S. Savings Bonds Regularly on the Payroll Savings Plan

EXHIBIT 10

FBI FILE 1222257-0-62-HQ-99801—PAGE 67

LV

Identification Division could not guarantee in any manner that this record positively concerned HOWARD R. HUGHES. This was stamped on the Identification Record which was furnished to the gaming authorities.

On 12/13/67, [   ] of the Nevada Gaming Commission, personally called on me and informed me that on 12/11/67, a conference was held at Carson City, Nevada, which was attended by the members of the Gaming Commission, the Gaming Control Board, and Governor PAUL LAXALT of the State of Nevada. [   ] stated that it was the unanimous consensus of this entire group that some effort should be made to enable the Nevada state authorities to know for certain that HOWARD HUGHES actually is alive and that they are actually licensing a "live individual." [   ] stated that even though everything appears to be 100% above board in connection with the purchase and licensing of the various hotels to HOWARD HUGHES, no one, including the Governor of the State of Nevada, has ever personally seen, talked with or discussed any licensing matters with HOWARD HUGHES personally. He stated that there is grave concern among the Nevada gaming authorities and Governor LAXALT that a great "hoax" could be being perpetrated on the state officials and for this reason some effort should be made to determine whether HOWARD HUGHES is actually in Las Vegas and is, in fact, dealing with state officials.

[   ] stated that in initial negotiations with HOWARD HUGHES representatives it was pointed out that it appeared that the gaming authorities or at least one individual should have a confrontation with HOWARD HUGHES. [   ] stated Attorney RICHARD GRAY of the Hughes Tool Company had handled most of the matters before the gaming authorities and when Mr. GRAY was asked if this would be possible [   ] stated that Mr. GRAY lost his composure and indicated that if the gaming authorities would require this then Mr. HUGHES would probably withdraw from active participation in gaming in the State of Nevada. [   ] stated at that time no further effort was made to pursue a course of a personal meeting with HOWARD HUGHES.

[   ] brought with him on 12/13/67, the original of a Power of Attorney to RICHARD GRAY purportedly made and signed by HOWARD R. HUGHES. This Power of Attorney is an official record of the Gaming Control Board. [   ] requested that, if possible, the Nevada gaming authorities and Governor PAUL LAXALT desired that the FBI, in a most confidential nature, attempt to do

- 2 -

EXHIBIT 11

FBI FILE 1222257-0-62-HQ-99801—PAGE 68

LV

a handwriting comparison of the signature of HOWARD R. HUGHES
appearing on the Power of Attorney with his signatures appearing
on fingerprint cards which it is hoped are contained in the files
of the Identification Division. It was pointed out to ☐
and he was aware of the situation that the fingerprint record
furnished to the gaming authorities could not positively be identified as those of HOWARD R. HUGHES. It was also pointed out to
☐ that the fingerprint cards indicated on this record
were quite old, having been taken in 1936 and 1942. ☐
neverthe less desired that, if possible, this comparison be made.

At the time ☐ handed me the Power of Attorney
I suggested to him that perhaps a fingerprint of HOWARD HUGHES
might be on the document which he handed to me. This had not
entered ☐ mind and as soon as I told him of this
possibility he also requested that an effort be made to lift a
latent fingerprint of HOWARD HUGHES off this document. ☐
stated he regretted this document had not been preserved for fingerprints and that it had been handled by many persons connected with
this matter. He stated he would still appreciate it if an effort
could be made to obtain a fingerprint of HOWARD HUGHES from this
document. ☐ stated he would not put any restriction
on the treating of the document for the attempt to obtain a latent
other than a request that it be readable when it is returned to him.

As the Bureau can observe, the Nevada gaming authorities
have been placed in a difficult position due to the idiosyncrasies
of HOWARD HUGHES and the fact that he has lead the life of a recluse
since coming to Nevada. The authorities do not want to jeopardize
their relations with the HOWARD HUGHES authorities since they feel
HUGHES' interest and activities in the State of Nevada have been
beneficial, particularly in cleaning up many of the hotel-casinos
formerly dominated and controlled by organized crime.

Governor PAUL LAXALT has had a conference with the Director
and I have been instructed since Governor LAXALT took office to
brief him on matters of interest to the State of Nevada from the
organized crime standpoint. The Bureau has also given me permission
to include ☐ of the Nevada Gaming
Commission, in these briefings.

In view of the highly confidential request ☐
also requested that this matter be handled personally by me and
that the results of any examination be furnished directly to me
rather than the gaming authorities. ☐ stated that the

- 3 -

EXHIBIT 12

FBI FILE 1222257-0-62-HQ-99801—PAGE 69

LV

Nevada gaming authorities do not desire to do anything of an official nature with the results of this examination other than to satisfy in their own minds that HOWARD HUGHES exists and that they are dealing with him.

EXHIBIT 13

FBI FILE 1222257-0-62-HQ-99801—PAGE 79

October 24, 1970

Mr. Jack Anderson
Washington Merry Go Round
Washington, D. C.

Dear Mr. Anderson:

Here is a debatable question for someone: "Is Howard Hughes dead or alive?" Perhaps you can start the fire and let the Federal Bureau of Investigation make the final determination. Believe me, this is not based on idle gossip.

After listening to your debate with Governor Laxalt, I decided to contact you because of your apparent fearlessness. Bearing directly on the present administration, the Nevada law has certainly been circumvented by Governor Laxalt, Frank Johnson and the gaming commission in granting licenses to Hughes without the customary finger-printing, personal interviews and the like before making their approvals. This was never done and they never asked for photographs such as other must furnish. Furthermore, the Hughes licenses were granted in a few days while other applicants mus wait weeks or months. Mr. Johnson stated publicly the board granted the Hughes licenses immediately as he was so well known. How could they be sure he was alive or in Nevada?

The tough Clark County Sheriff made the same exception and let the Hughes licenses slide through without investigation, personal contact or fingerprints. Recently, the Washoe County Sheriff did likewise. How much money was passed along for these exceptional favors? How would Laxalt have answered this question? His brother, John, in Las Vegas was broke when the governor took office. How could he buy a TV station as you stated, or part of one?

A few months ago, Mrs. Howard Hughes showed up in Hollywood with the announcement she would file suit for divorce against her industrialist Husband and that they had agreed on a financial settlement. No such action has ever been filed in any state and none is expected. You cannot file against a dead man. Even if she does file, he would not be required to appear but an attorney or two might be asking for trouble. Conclusion of the public: "She was probably given a big sum of money and told to keep her mouth shut, or else."

EXHIBIT 14-A

FBI FILE 1222257-0-62-HQ-99801—PAGE 90

FEDERAL BUREAU OF INVESTIGATION
COMMUNICATIONS SECTION

DEC 8 1970

TELETYPE

NR 006 LV PLAIN

110 PM URGENT 12-8-70 DLB

TO DIRECTOR ATTN: ASSISTANT DIRECTOR A. ROSEN.

FROM LAS VEGAS (62-582) 4P

Mr. Tolson
Mr. Sullivan
Mr. Mohr
Mr. Bishop
Mr. Brennan C.D.
Mr. Callahan
Mr. Casper
Mr. Conrad
Mr. Felt
Mr. Gale
Mr. Rosen
Mr. Tavel
Mr. Walters
Mr. Soyars
Tele. Room
Miss Holmes
Miss Gandy

HOWARD HUGHES, INFORMATION CONCERNING.

REMYTELS DECEMBER ONE, FOUR, FIVE, AND SIX LAST AND TELCALL TO BUREAU TODAY.

POWER STRUGGLE FOR REPRESENTATION OF HUGHES' NEVADA INTERESTS BETWEEN CHESTER DAVIS - FRANK W. GAY (HUGHES TOOL CO.) AND ROBERT MAHEU (HUGHES NEVADA OPERATIONS) CONTINUES. LOCAL, NATIONAL, AND NUMEROUS FOREIGN PRESS REPRESENTATIVES AGGRES- SIVELY PURSUING INTERESTS OF NEWS MEDIA IN LAS VEGAS.

DURING PM OF DECEMBER SEVEN LAST GOVERNOR PAUL LAXALT ANNOUNCED TO THE PRESS THAT HE AND CLARK COUNTY DISTRICT ATTORNEY GEORGE FRANKLIN HAD TELEPHONE CONVERSATION WITH HUGHES EARLIER IN DAY. TELEPHONE CALL REPORTEDLY EMANATED FROM THE BAHAMAS AND LAXALT RELATED THAT HUGHES HAD TOLD HIM THAT HE HAD AUTHORIZED TAKE-OVER OF HUGHES NEVADA OPERATIONS BY DAVIS AND GAY AND HAD IN FACT TERMINATED ROBERT MAHEU AND JACK HOOPER. GOVERNOR LAXALT

END PAGE ONE

REC-35 62-99801-16
EX-113

DEC 16 1970

XEROX
DEC 23 1970

66 DEC 29 1970

MR. SULLIVAN FOR THE DIRECTOR

NATIONAL ARCHIVES
DATE 1/26/95 EDWARD T. Morgan

EXHIBIT 14-B

Page 258 From Allen Gerber's book *Bashful Billionaire*

talked about landing space ships on the moon and performing other electronic miracles, and to the practical-minded, cigar-smoking general it all sounded like science-fiction.

But Hughes could be most persuasive when he wanted to. General George, tempted with an offer of $50,000 a year and an exciting new venture, could resist no longer and agreed to go to work for Hughes Aircraft. Hughes added Charles B. Thornton of the Ford Motor Company, and his old friend, Lieutenant-General Ira Eaker, to the Management Section. To handle the technical side of the operation he hired two brilliant scientists—Dr. Simon Ramo of the California Institute of Technology and Dr. Dean Wooldridge of Bell Telephone's Research Department. These two gifted men were given the broadest latitude in hiring the people they needed and in deciding on projects to be developed.

With his team of experts assembled, Hughes set about obtaining government contracts in the electronics field. His earliest efforts involved a missile-guidance system and an airplane radar system. The radar project was an effort to combine airborne radar, a Sperry gunsight, and an electronic computer in such fashion that, without visual contact, an air-gunner could shoot at an enemy plane. The missile-guidance system was intended to permit an aircraft to launch an air-to-air missile at another aircraft and then to guide it after launching.

The government did not at first take the electronics venture seriously. Ramo and Wooldridge, however, began to develop a really promising electronic fire-control device. One test after another was successful and it looked like the diligent scientists were about to solve the problem. Simultaneously the Air Force became concerned because it lacked an interceptor device for the air defense of the United States—one which would function reliably in bad weather.

The desires of the Air Force and the work of Ramo and Wooldridge coincided, and late in 1948 Hughes Aircraft signed a contract to develop an all-weather fire-control unit for installation in the Lockheed F-94. This contract, involving $8 million, was comparatively small but, as General George said, it turned out to be Hughes Aircraft's "dress re-

EXHIBIT 14-C

From Allen Gerber's Book *Bashful Billionaire*

hearsal for mobilization." Not long after, the Korean fighting broke out, and orders for military equipment flooded the industry. Hughes Aircraft became the sole source of supply for the fire-control systems of all interceptors—North American Aviation's F-86, Northrop's F-89 and F-94, and even the Navy's McDonnell Aircraft F-2H4.

Up to the Korean conflict most of the industrial giants of America had left this type of electronics manufacturing to small outfits like Hughes Aircraft. However, in 1950 the Air Force sponsored a design competition for an electronic fire-and-navigational control system to be used in the F-102 Supersonic Interceptor. This newly developed fighter plane would become a mainstay of the American defensive and offensive systems, and production of its electronic firing and navigational systems would involve millions of dollars.

More than twenty companies competed for the design award, including General Electric, Westinghouse, and organizations new to the field who were seeking to diversify. Hughes Aircraft exhibited remarkable ingenuity in winning this competition and shutting out the major American corporations. The company acquired a near-monopoly on the Air Force's sophisticated electronics requirements, especially in the fire and navigational control fields.

Delivery figures indicate the rapid rise of the company. In 1949 Hughes Aircraft delivered $8,600,000 in equipment. This rose the following year to $151 million and approached $200 million by 1953.

Hughes was delighted with the turn of events. He gave his people at Hughes Aircraft carte blanche in ordering equipment and personnel, with the result that the Culver City establishment in the mid-1950's had one of the finest electronics laboratory facilities in the world and employed some of the best brains in the industry.

Over a thousand physicists, electronics engineers, mathematicians, and other high-grade professional technicians worked for Hughes Aircraft. An incomplete roster would include the names of Dr. Ralph P. Johnson, formerly Deputy Director of Research of the Atomic Energy Commission; Dr.

EXHIBIT 15

FBI FILE 1222257-0-62-HQ-99801—PAGE 91

PAGE TWO

INDICATED HE WAS NOW ASSURED THAT HUGHES WAS ALIVE, WELL, AND HAD
VALIDLY AUTHORIZED CHANGE OF REPRESENTATION. LAXALT FURTHER
COMMENTED THAT HUGHES HAD TOLD HIM HE INTENDED TO RETURN TO
NEVADA TO "LIVE THE REST OF HIS LIFE". DA FRANKLIN CONFIRMED THAT
HUGHES TOLD HIM AND LAXALT HE WAS IN FINE PHYSICAL CONDITION.

FOLLOWING THE GOVERNOR'S NEWS RELEASE THE MAHEU FACTION MADE
A PRESS RELEASE INDICATING THEY WOULD NOT RELINQUISH CONTROL UNTIL
LEGALLY ORDERED TO DO SO, BUT MADE NO OPEN CHALLENGE OF THE
VERACITY OF THE GOVERNOR'S RELEASE.

FURNISHED THE FOLLOWING INFORMATION
TO SAC LAS VEGAS TODAY. THE MAHEU FACTION PLANS TO INITIATE A
"BOMBSHELL" IN THE MATTER THIS AM. HE STATED THE ENTIRE CASE OF
THE DAVIS - GAY FACTION IS BASED UPON A DOCUMENT PURPORTEDLY SIGNED
BY HOWARD HUGHES PERSONALLY, WHICH AUTHORIZED THIS FACTION TO TAKE
COMMAND OF THE HUGHES NEVADA OPERATION. HE POINTED OUT THAT THE
END PAGE TWO

EXHIBIT 16

FBI FILE 1222257-0-62-HQ-99801—PAGE 92

PAGE THREE

DAVIS - GAY FACTION HAVE FAILED TO PRODUCE THIS DOCUMENT UNTIL
FORCED TO DO SO LATE LAST NIGHT IN CONNECTION WITH A LEGAL
PLEADING THEY ARE PURSUING TO HAVE THE RESTRAINING ORDER WHICH
WAS ISSUED AGAINST THEM DISMISSED. THE DOCUMENT ITSELF WAS FLOWN
TO WASHINGTON, D.C., LAST NIGHT AND EXAMINED BY CHARLES APPEL,
FORMER BUREAU DOCUMENT EXAMINER. [   ] STATED APPEL FOUND
HUGHES' SIGNATURE TO BE A FORGERY AND WILL TESTIFY TO SAME CON-
CLUSION. [   ] INDICATED HE FEELS PROOF OF THIS FORGERY WILL
SURFACE WHAT HE AND OTHERS CONSIDER TO BE THE "MOST MONUMENTAL
STEAL ATTEMPT IN AMERICAN HISTORY".

[   ] ALSO ADVISED THAT HE IS AWARE THAT DAVIS, AS GENERAL
COUNSEL FOR HUGHES AND AS HIS LEGAL REPRESENTATIVE IN THE TWA
SUIT AGAINST HUGHES, PRODUCED A PURPORTED SIGNATURE BY HOWARD
HUGHES WHICH WAS ALSO DETERMINED TO BE A FORGERY. THIS OCCURED
IN APPROXIMATELY NINETEEN SIXTY-FOUR OR SIXTY-FIVE IN THE SOUTHERN
DISTRICT OF NEW YORK. NO PROSECUTIVE ACTION WAS TAKEN AT THAT TIME
AGAINST DAVIS OR HIS GROUP INASMUCH AS THE POINT BECAME MOOT DUE
END PAGE THREE

EXHIBIT 17

FBI FILE 1222257-0-62-HQ-99801—PAGE 93

PAGE FOUR

TO THE DIRECTION THE SUIT THEREAFTER TOOK. THE BUREAU WILL RECALL THAT THE JUDGEMENT AGAINST HUGHES WITH ACCRUED INTEREST AMOUNTS TO APPROXIMATELY TWO HUNDRED MILLION DOLLARS AND IS CURRENTLY UNDER APPEAL.

[ ] STATED HE DOES NOT BELIEVE THAT THE TELEPHONE CALL REPORTED BY GOVERNOR LAXALT WAS FROM HOWARD HUGHES AND THERE IS SERIOUS DOUBT IN HIS MIND AS TO HUGHES' WHEREABOUTS, COMPETENCY, AND PHYSICAL WELL-BEING. [ ] SPECULATED THAT WHEN THE FORGERY IS OFFICALLY ANNOUNCED AND ACCEPTED, THE DAVIS-GAY FACTION WILL HAVE NO ALTERNATIVE EXCEPT TO RELINQUISH CONTROL AND DEPART NEVADA IN A HURRY.

ABOVE FURNISHED FOR INFORMATION. NO INQUIRY OF ANY KIND BEING CONDUCTED OR COMMENTS BEING MADE IN THIS MATTER BY LAS VEGAS OFFICE, HOWEVER, INFORMATION OF POSSIBLE PERTINENCE TO BUREAU INTERESTS BEING ACCEPTED.

END

EBM FBI WA CLR

C-MR. ROSEN

EXHIBIT 18-A

FBI FILE 1222257-0-62-HQ-99801—PAGE 107

PAGE FOUR

    MAHEU ALSO ADVISES EXECUTIVE VICE PRES AND DIRECTOR OF HUGHES TOOL CO., RAYMOND M. HOLLIDAY, WHO IS PERHAPS ONE OF HUGHES CLOSEST PERSONAL CONTACTS IN PAST, HAS RESIGNED FOR REASON HE BELIEVES DAVIS - GAY TAKE-OVER IS NOT WITH HUGHES VALID CONSENT OR AUTHORITY.

    ABOVE FURNISHED BUREAU FOR INFORMATION. NO INQUIRY BEING CONDUCTED OR COMMENTS BEING FURNISHED IN THIS MATTER BUT INFORMATION OF PERTINENCE TO BUREAU INTERESTS BEING ACCEPTED.
END
LRC FBI WASH DC

4

MORE IN-DEPTH LOOK AT THE HUGHES/HOLLIDAY RELATIONSHIP

Let's take this idea of Raymond Holliday being *"perhaps* one of Hughes closest personal contacts" a few steps further. He was considerably more than just *that*, as per Exhibits below. He, not Chester Davis, was the front man for one of the largest lawsuits that Howard Hughes would successfully wage to secure total control of Trans World Airlines, Inc.

The legal proceedings against Howard Hughes by TWA, Inc. began in June of 1961 and dragged on in the courtroom for 10 years, culminating in a <u>final</u> decision favorable to Hughes in <u>September 1971</u>. As indicated in documents below, Holliday had been deemed by Hughes, to be his confidant in this massive financial undertaking. Raymond Holliday (CEO of Hughes ToolCo, Inc.) was the only Hughes employee that Hughes trusted to carry out his wishes – not Bill Gay, not Chester Davis, not Robert Maheu, and definitely not Nadine Henley.

Keeping in mind that a lawsuit of this magnitude takes on a life of its own when its filed and may last for a number of years after the death of one of its defendants. It was Holliday who carried the ball into the end zone. Holliday was *more* than just "a close personal contact." It was Holliday only who could talk directly with Hughes from the early 1960s forward to 1965. Shortly after the TWA lawsuit was finalized, Hughes Industries (now renamed Summa, Inc.) sold the Hughes Tool Company. (ToolCo, Inc.). Millions of dollars from that sale, would eventually vanish.

EXHIBIT 18-B

449 F.2d 51

1971 Trade Cases P 73,690

TRANS WORLD AIRLINES, INC., Plaintiff-Appellant,
v.
Howard R. HUGHES, Defendant, and Hughes Tool Company
and
Raymond M. Holliday, Defendants–Appellants.

Nos. 883, 834, Dockets 34902, 35114.

United States Court of Appeals,
Second Circuit.

Argued May 7, 1971.
Decided Sept. 1, 1971.

James V. Hayes, New York City (Ralstone R. Irvine, Mahlon F. Perkins, Jr., New York City, David A. Wier, of counsel; Donovan, Leisure, Newton & Irvine, Davis & Cox, New York City, on the brief), for defendants-appellants.

Dudley B. Tenney, New York City (Paul W. Williams, Immanuel Kohn, Marshall H. Cox, Jr., Abraham P. Ordover, Lawrence C. Browne, Michael P. Tierney, New York City of counsel; Cahill, Gordon, Sonnett, Reindel & Ohl, New York City, on the brief), for plaintiff-appellant.

Before SMITH, KAUFMAN and HAYS, Circuit Judges.

IRVING R. KAUFMAN, Circuit Judge:

We are presented in this case with cross-appeals from a final judgment entered April 14, 1970, premised upon a previous default judgment, in favor of plaintiff Trans World Airlines, Inc. (TWA) against defendants-appellants Hughes Tool Company and its chief financial officer, Raymond M. Holliday (Toolco), which, the district court tells us, 312 F.Supp. 478, at 480, is some thirty times greater than the next highest monetary award ever entered.

The extraordinary aspect of this complex litigation is in large measure

EXHIBIT 18-C

attributable to the elusiveness of Howard R. Hughes, progenitor and sole owner of Toolco, protagonist in its operations, in a sense the central character of this litigation as well, and yet not a party to this appeal because Hughes himself, although named as a defendant in TWA's complaint, could not be located for service of process.

I.

Since the facts in this litigation have been set forth in detail in many prior reported decisions, see 214 F.Supp. 106 (S.D.N.Y.1963), 32 F.R.D. 604 (S.D.N.Y.1963); 332 F.2d 602 (2d Cir. 1964); 38 F.R.D. 499 (S.D.N.Y.1965); 308 F.Supp. 679 (S.D.N.Y.1969); 312 F.Supp. 478 (S.D.N.Y.1970), in the interest of avoiding unconscionable length of this opinion, we will limit our own initial statement to a brief resume of the tortuous history of the case, sufficient to permit a meaningful statement of the issues raised.

More than a decade ago, by a complaint dated June 30, 1961, TWA filed its complaint in this action charging Toolco and Hughes with violations of the Clayton and Sherman Acts, 15 U.S.C. Secs. 1, 2, 11, and 18, as well as with a claim, for which pendent jurisdiction was asserted, alleging malicious and willful injury to the business of TWA.

Convoluted and protracted pre-trial maneuvers culminated in the failure of Toolco to produce Hughes for a deposition scheduled by court order to be taken on February 11, 1963. As a result of Hughes's confessed unwillingness to appear, as well as the nonproduction by Toolco of certain papers and documents whose disclosure to plaintiff had also been required by court order, the Rule 2 judge assigned to the action (Rule 2, General Rules for the Southern and Eastern Districts of New York), Judge Metzner, on May 3, 1963 filed two orders. One entered the default against Toolco and granted TWA's motion to increase the ad damnum clause of its complaint from $105,000,000 to $135,000,000, after trebling. In the second order Judge Metzner also found Toolco in default with respect to five counterclaims that Toolco had asserted against TWA and several additional defendants. Judge Metzner dismissed these counterclaims and also granted TWA's motion for summary judgment on a sixth counterclaim.

We granted leave to take an interlocutory appeal from the former order, after Judge Metzner had certified that an appeal was appropriate under 28 U.S.C. Sec. 1292(b). But we limited our review to considering whether the district court's jurisdiction over the antitrust action was ousted because primary jurisdiction lay with the Civil Aeronautics Board, which had approved various

EXHIBIT 18-D

steps by which Toolco gradually assumed virtually complete control of TWA, holding about 78% of its stock at the time the complaint was filed, and whether certain of the CAB orders associated with those grants of approval constituted a good defense to TWA's action. The interlocutory appeal was consolidated with defendants' parallel appeal as of right from Judge Metzner's dismissal of the counterclaims. A panel of this court ultimately ruled that the district court did properly assert its jurisdiction and that the CAB orders did not constitute blanket approval of the claims in the complaint and hence were not a defense to TWA's action. In the appeal on the counterclaims, the orders of the district court were affirmed with one exception, not relevant here (determining that the CAB had exclusive jurisdiction over one of the dismissed counterclaims). 332 F.2d 602, cert. granted, 379 U.S. 912, 85 S.Ct. 261, 265, 13 L.Ed.2d 184 (1964), cert. dismissed as improvidently granted, 380 U.S. 248, 249, 85 S.Ct. 934, 13 L.Ed.2d 817, 818 (1965).

7   Judge Metzner's ruling adjudging Toolco in default necessitated an extensive hearing to determine damages. Herbert Brownell, Esq.,[1] appointed Special Master for this purpose, conducted hearings between May 2, 1966, and April 9, 1968. On September 1, 1968, in a thorough report, the Master awarded TWA trebled damages of $137,611,435.95. Both sides filed objections. On December 23, 1969, Judge Metzner adopted Brownell's report in all respects, 308 F.Supp. 679, and then in a subsequent opinion awarded attorneys fees of $7.5 million and assessed costs in the amount of $336,705.12. 312 F.Supp. 478. On April 14, 1970, the district court entered its final judgment, with 6% interest to run from that date, in the sum-impressive even by space age and inflationary standards-of $145,448,141.07.[2]

II.

A. Toolco Appeal

8   The first thrust of the Toolco appeal is directed at the default judgment itself and primarily concerns issues that were not the focus of the damage hearing before Special Master Brownell. The broad question pressed by Toolco is whether TWA is entitled to recover any amount whatever on the record before us, regardless of the adequacy of its proof of damages. Toolco contends (discussed in part III below) that the default judgment was improperly entered against it, in violation of its due process rights, and should be vacated; that (part IV) even if the default judgment is valid, the judgment does not justify assessing damages against Toolco for any antitrust violations, since in Toolco's view the evidence in the record conclusively refutes the possibility that any such violations could have occurred; and that (part V) even if the default

EXHIBIT 19

FBI FILE 1222257-0-32-HO-278—PAGE 53

OPTIONAL FORM NO. 10
JULY 1973 EDITION
GSA FPMR (41 CFR) 101-11.6

UNITED STATES GOVERNMENT

Memorandum

TO   : FILE (32-278)   DATE: 11/2/76

FROM   : SAC ROBERT RUSS FRANCK

SUBJECT: HOWARD R. HUGHES
         IDENTIFICATION MATTER

        On 11/2/76, [ ] a Contributing
Editor for Texas Monthly Magazine, came to the office and
advised me that he was working on a story about HOWARD HUGHES
for his magazine. He inquired as to what I could tell him
about the fingerprint identification of HUGHES, and I told
him that Dr. JOSEPH JACHIMCZYK, Chief Medical Examiner of
Harris County, had requested FBI Identification Division
assistance in comparing the prints taken April 6, 1976,
in the morgue of the Methodist Hospital, Houston, Texas,
with known prints of HUGHES on file in Washington, D. C.

        I related to [ ] that following examination
of the prints taken from the deceased male at Methodist
Hospital, I issued a press release (serial 6), 4/7/76,
to the effect that the prints were found to be identical
with those of HUGHES on file with this Bureau. I related
to [ ] also that we had had a Latent Fingerprint
Examiner come to Houston from Washington to make a tentative
identification and, thereafter, he returned to Washington with
the fingerprints of the deceased male and made a formal report
to Dr. JACHIMCZYK dated 4/9/76, attesting to the prints being
of one and the same person.

        [ ] advised me that he has already talked to
Dr. JACHIMCZYK and HORACE TUCKER, who works for Dr. JACHIMCZYK,
and who physically took the prints from the deceased male and
was attempting to write his story to determine whether HUGHES
was, in fact, dead. He inquired as to whether the prints
could have been switched to effect any misidentification of
HUGHES, and I told him I could make no comment concerning
that in that all the FBI did was to take prints furnished
to us by the Medical Examiner's Office and compare them with
known prints of HOWARD HUGHES. [ ] thanked me for
my taking the time to talk to him.

ACTION: None - for information.

RRF/cb1
(1)

Buy U.S. Savings Bonds Regularly on the Payroll Savings Plan

b6
b7C

b6
b7C

b6
b7C

32-278-20

EXHIBIT 20

FBI FILE 1222257-0-62-HO-99801—PAGE 74

April 17, 1970

Mr. J. Edgar Hoover, Director
Federal Bureau of Investigation
Washingron, D.C.

Dear Mr. Hoover:

My associates have long been questioning the fact that
Howard Hughes, the multi-millionaire, is still alive.
Can you tell me if you know for a fact that he still lives?

My associates and I feel that you, above all, would know,
if anyone does.

Respectfully,

b6
b7C

New Orleans, La.   70139

REC 94   62-99801-9

b6
b7C

1   APR 27 1970

CORRESPONDENCE

ack/nml
Lee: ELN
4-23-70
24

EXHIBIT 21

FBI FILE 1222257-0-62-HO-99801—PAGE 78

DO-6   OFFICE OF DIRECTOR
FEDERAL BUREAU OF INVESTIGATION
UNITED STATES DEPARTMENT OF JUSTICE
October 27, 1970

Attached copy of letter to Mr. Jack
Anderson, Washington, D.C. was
sent to the Director by an
anonymous source from Reno,
Nevada.

wmc

MR. TOLSON
MR. SULLIVAN
MR. MOHR
MR. BISHOP
MR. BRENNAN, C.D.
MR. CALLAHAN
MR. CASPER
MR. CONRAD
MR. FELT
MR. GALE
MR. ROSEN
MR. TAVEL
MR. WALTERS
MR. SOYARS
MR. JONES
TELE. ROOM
MISS HOLMES
MRS. METCALF
MISS GANDY

EXHIBIT 22

FBI FILE 1222257-0-62-HO-99801—PAGE 79

Mr. Tolson
Mr. Sullivan
Mr. Mohr
Mr. Bishop
Mr. Brennan C.D.
Mr. Callahan
Mr. Casper
Mr. Conrad
Mr. Felt
Mr. Gale
Mr. Rosen
Mr. Tavel
Mr. Walters
Mr. Soyars
Tele. Room
Miss Holmes
Miss Gandy

October 24, 1970

Mr. Jack Anderson
Washington Merry Go Round
Washington, D. C.

Dear Mr. Anderson:

Here is a debatable question for someone: "Is Howard Hughes dead or alive?" Perhaps you can start the fire and let the Federal Bureau of Investigation make the final determination. Believe me, this is not based on idle gossip.

After listening to your debate with Governor Laxalt, I decided to contact you because of your apparent fearlessness. Bearing directly on the present administration, the Nevada law has certainly been circumvented by Governor Laxalt, Frank Johnson and the gaming commission in granting licenses to Hughes without the customary finger-printing, personal interviews and the like before making their approvals. This was never done and they never asked for photographs such as other must furnish. Furthermore, the Hughes licenses were granted in a few days while other applicants mus wait weeks or months. Mr. Johnson stated publicly the board granted the Hughes licenses immediately as he was so well known. How could they be sure he was alive or in Nevada?

The tough Clark County Sheriff made the same exception and let the Hughes licenses slide through without investigation, personal contact or fingerprints. Recently, the Washoe County Sheriff did likewise. How much money was passed along for these exceptional favors? How would Laxalt have answered this question? His brother, John, in Las Vegas was broke when the governor took office. How could he buy a TV station as you stated, or part of one?

A few months ago, Mrs. Howard Hughes showed up in Hollywood with the announcement she would file suit for divorce against her industrialist Husband and that they had agreed on a financial settlement. No such action has ever been filed in any state and none is expected. You cannot file against a dead man. Even if she does file, he would not be required to appear but an attorney or two might be asking for trouble. Conclusion of the public: "She was probably given a big sum of money and told to keep her mouth shut, or else."

62-99801-10

REC 85

18 OCT 29 1970

60 NOV 6 1970

ANONYMOUS COMMUNICATIONS KEEP ENVELOPE ATTACHED

UNRECORDED COPY FILED IN 94-62600-1

EXHIBIT 23

FBI FILE 1222257-0-62-HO-99801—PAGE 80

It is well-know Mr. Hughes was an eccentric during his years in public life. After his complete withdrawal from society, particularly after he allegedly took up residence atop the Desert Inn Hotel in Las Vegas, what a perfect target he became for the Mafia, or any organization of gangsters.

Since Hughes had no relatives to inquire about his welfare, only his wife was in the way. Sheer fright could keep her quiet. In this day-and-age of drugs, hypnotic control and ill-designed brain washing it would be a simple matter to effect a complete take-over of the billion dollarorganisations, together with Mr. Hughes and his wife. Who remained to ask question about him? Who could prove anything?

A couple of months ago, it was announced Hughes purchased a home somewhere in the Sierra Mountains in the Lake Tahoe area but nothing more was heard of it. Perhaps it will be used as a hideaway for some of his "friends".

About four months ago, I saw a picture in some cheap magazine like The Enquirer, purported to be of Howard Hughes taking a sunbath beside his pool with a burly bodyguard standing nearby. If this is a legitimate photograph, it would lead to the belief Hughes is alive but it would be no proof of his being a free man in full possession of all his faculties. The bodyguard may have been there to be sure he did not go anywhere.

This letter is written from a purely humanitarian purpose with the thought in mind it may help man who is beyond helping himself. Perhaps I should add that not a single person in Las Vegas, including Mr. Mayhew, his attorneys or top officials have ever seen Howard Hughes. Nor have they talked to him on the telephone. Orders simply come to them from "upstairs". Who is in charge "uptairs"? No one has that answer.

I am not involved in politics in any way and who is elected governor does not concern me. But I do believe Laxalt and Johnson were wrong in licensing Hughes without a usual, careful examination. It was certainly a violation of the rules and regulations to do so. You could bring this out without tipping your hand on the Hughes rumors until Mr. Hoover does some investigating. The City of Las Vegas, the Sheriff of Clark County and other did likewise.

Please treat this letter as confidential information.

Good luck

cc: Mr. Edgar J. Hoover, Director
Federal Bureau of Investigation

EXHIBIT 24

FBI FILE 1222257-0-62-HO-99801—PAGE 81

P.S. As an afterthought which may be helpful is that many of
the managers and front men for the Hughes clubs are questionable
characters who may be traced to the Mafia. As you may learn
the Bally slot machines are used exclusively in all the clubs.
This company had or has Mafia connections. Howard Hughes was
never a man to deal with corrupt persons so who is behind the
throne "upstairs"?

EXHIBIT 25

FBI FILE 1222257-0-62-HO-99801—PAGE 171

TRUE COPY

San Antonio, Tex. 78214
January 27, 1972

Dear Mr. Hoover:

Please investigate the where bouts of Mr. Howard Hughes.

And please see him for your self, don't take messages from any other person.

See that he is not intimidated or held captive by the people who manage his business.

It is my personal opinion that he has been slain by his hirelings. The people are entitled to know the truth, is he alive?

Or is he an invalid and prisoner? No sane man would leave the world in such impossible doubttas has been perpertrated on the American public, if he could help it. I blame The Hughes Tool Co. If he just wants to be a recluse, that is perfectly fine. But find out if he does want to be un-approachable.

I don't believe it for one moment, and this has become more frightening thamone of the Hitchcock hair raisers. What is Federal Bureau of Investigation for? If not to protect the citizens of America, even if they are Billionaires or shoe shine boys.

EX-102
What kind of don't care people have we become? if we just sit by Idly and wonder what is going on? REC-6 62-99801-37

Please do something about this poor man, and let the people know, clear away the mystery. Once and for all. FEB 3 1972

Sincerely

"Private Citizen who cares"

TRUE COPY

84

EXHIBIT 26

FBI FILE 1222257-0-62-HO-99801—PAGE 206

MAE BRUSSELL
25620 Via Crotalo
Carmel, California 93921
408/624-9103

April 9,1976

Dear Mr.Kelley,
For the past twelve years, I have researched various conspiracies committed inside the USA by Federal employees and agents.
The Howard Hughes case tops them all because of it's lasting affect upon our society for generations to come. *Deceased*

Will you please provide me with the following information.
Dr.Joseph W.Jackimcyzk took fingerprints from the body in Houstan, Texas, that was allegedly Howard Hughes.

1)Who was present with Dr.Joseph W.Jackimcyzk when this print was taken?
2)How many persons were in the room when the print was taken?
3)Do you have their names?   *Howard Robard Hughes*
4)What country was Dr.S.Jackimcyzk born in?
5)What time did he enter the United States?
6.How long has he been at the hospital in Houston?

The Fingerprints arrived in the FBI office in Washington,D.C.
1)HOW MANY AGENTS EXAMINED THEM?
2)do you have their names?May I have them,or the documents?
3.How long have they been with the FBI.
4.Would you allow non-government experts on fingerprints to come to the FBI offices to confirm your findings?

The fingerprints of Howard Hughes alledly matched a Hughes application "in the 1930's".
1.Would you provide the exact date on the application?

Somebody was impersonating Howard Hughes,signing his name in Mexico, which was a forgery.If they didnt have power of attorney,are you going to presecute for this?
If persons inside the Howard Hughes empire come forth and prove that he did,indeed,pass away several years ago....will your witnesses,Dr.L.Jackimcyzk and the FBI agent in DC who identified the prints as Hughes be prosecuted?

No more Watergates,Mr.Kelley.
Please answer these for me.
Sincerely, *Mae Brussell*

EX-115
REC57 *62- 99801-50*
3 APR 22 1976
CORRESPONDENCE

"WHY WAS MARTHA MITCHELL KIDNAPPED?"
THE REALIST, issue 93
August 1972
$1.00 copy

"THE SENATE SELECT COMMITTEE
IS PART OF THE WATERGATE COVER-UP"
THE REALIST, issue 95
August 1973
$1.00 copy

"WHY WAS PATRICIA HEARST KIDNAPPED? or
HOW DO YOU TELL A CIA ESPIONAGE PLOT FROM
A RADICAL GUERILLA, TERRORIST ARMY?"
THE REALIST, issue 98   July 1974 $1.00 copy

FEMINIST PARTY MEDIA WORKSHOP AWARD — MAY, 1974

EXHIBIT 27

FBI FILE 1222257-0-62-HO-99801—PAGE 207

A

REC-59 62-99801-51

EX-115

PERS-REC'D UNIT

May 13, 1976

Ms. Mae Brussell
25620 Via Crotalo
Carmel, California 93921

Dear Ms. Brussell:

In response to your letter of April 25th, with enclosures, regarding the recent fingerprint identification of Mr. Howard Hughes, this is to advise that all information we are able to provide you was contained in my letter of April 21st.

I regret that we are unable to be of further assistance in this matter.

Sincerely yours,

C. M. Kelley
Clarence M. Kelley
Director

1 - Houston - Enclosures   (3)
1 - San Francisco - Enclosures   (3)
1 - Mr. Ash - Enclosures   (3)
   Attention:

b6
b7C

NOTE: Assistance for this response was provided by the Identification Division. Bufiles did not reflect any derogatory information regarding correspondent.
JMG:rgj   (6)

MAILED 10

MAY 13 1976
FBI

APPROVED:
Assoc. Dir.
Dep.-AD Adm.
Dep-AD Inv.
Asst. Dir.
Admin.

Comp. Syst.
Ext. Affairs
Gen. Inv.
Ident.
Inspection
Intell.

Laboratory
Legal Coun.
Plan. & Eval.
Rec. Mgmt.
Spec. Inv.
Training

Assoc. Dir.
Dep. AD Adm.
Dep. AD Inv.
Asst. Dir.
Admin.
Comp. Syst.
Ext. Affairs
Files & Com.
Gen. Inv.
Ident.
Inspection
Intell.
Laboratory
Legal Coun.
Plan. & Eval.
Spec. Inv.
Training
Telephone Rm.
Director Sec'y

55 JUN1 1976   MAIL ROOM ☐   TELETYPE UNIT ☐

GPO 1975 O - 594-190

CHAPTER V

FINGERPRINTS

(Forensics, Longevity of Latent Prints, Print Cards properly and improperly used, etc.)

Fingerprints should be the <u>first things collected, at the beginning of any autopsy,</u> or when investigating any criminal activity. The identity of the person laying on the "slab," be they a suspected criminal, innocent victim, or a John/Jane Doe, goes a long way in solving *any* mystery. Numerous crimes have been solved by fingerprint examination alone when little other circumstantial evidence could be found. (See examples in Chapter III.) Of course, the reasoning behind any such fingerprint examination is that law enforcement is reasonably sure they have their man/woman when prints, collected at a crime scene, match those of a previously convicted criminal or any others in their data base. Why? *Everyone has fingerprints peculiar to him/her alone,* and they are *never* the same as anyone else's. It is greatly suspected that in the entire world there can never be found two individuals with the exact same prints; even identical twins (mirror twins) who may look alike in every respect, will *not* have the same prints.

One often hears in the courtroom, when eyewitnesses to a crime cannot be found, that "the evidence is circumstantial." Do not be deceived into believing that simply because evidence is *circumstantial* that it cannot be binding in criminal cases. Many a felon are now doing hard time because of it.

WHAT ARE LATENT FINGERPRINTS?

Our man Russ sported many hats in law-enforcement down through the years; several were in detective positions where he excelled in utilizing fingerprints. Of course, this is extremely important when looking for bad guys and many were arrested due to his diligence. Russ had even taught a college class in fingerprint technology while working as a Federal Postal Inspector. But he gave it up when it started to interfere with what he enjoyed doing most – catching bad guys.

Whenever we touch a glass object, any painted object, a door handle, or the door itself, a sheet of paper, a light bulb, etc. we leave behind *a residue* because of the slightly acidic-oily nature of the human body. Exacting techniques have been developed over the years (probably beginning as early as the 1920s) with which these "latent" prints can be lifted off various surfaces. These are often submitted in a court of law as *circumstantial* evidence. However, there are *rare* situations where a person may touch an object and not leave a print. For example, wearing gloves. However, when a latent print *is* left behind, it has an *amazingly long-lasting life span.*

Below we have illustrated various exhibits of correspondence with a retired, but extremely astute, lady skilled in the art of fingerprint technology. She is someone that Russ greatly depended upon at times during his career. Russ created a lasting friendship with this lady criminalist who has graciously aided us in solving this case. (Her name and e-mail are confidential. She is retired and desires to remain anonymous.)

One of the major problems to solve was how did a corpse that most believed to be that of a deceased "Howard Hughes," become identified as such at the Methodist Hospital in Houston, Texas? The evidence uncovered is convincing and beyond a reasonable doubt, that the body buried in the Hughes Plot in Houston, is *not* the body of Howard R. Hughes, Jr.

One of the many deceptive tactics used in identifying the corpse flown into Houston were *erroneous* fingerprints. High profile autopsy files, such as those of Howard Hughes, should be closely guarded. A qualified interested party (via subpoena) may get copies of an autopsy file, but it would be considered a criminal act to remove (or in effect, steal) the file from the hospital or coroner's lab wherein it resides. So, it is certainly strange that the "H.H." autopsy files *disappeared from both the Methodist Hospital and Coroner's Office in Houston.* It appears that there were those, of a nefarious nature, who simply did not want the information in the "Hughes" autopsy report to be available to someone who might ask, "Is the body buried in the Hughes family plot really the body of Howard R. Hughes, Jr.?"

However, Mr. "Super-Snoop Russ" was able to recover copies of the Methodist Hospital autopsy files of "Howard Hughes," which he discovered in the possession of a Dr. Forrest S. Tennant. (One of the doctors called to testify in 1976 <u>concerning drug use</u> in the "Hughes" autopsy findings.) Dr. Tennant now resides in California.

Below are documents found in both the FBI files and the Methodist Hospital Hughes autopsy file. (Russ's take on the findings starts below the first group of exhibits.) Upon investigating these autopsy files, many possibilities emerged to explain the disappearance of the originals. One may certainly conclude they were <u>not</u> accidently misplaced. Many unusual aspects of the "Hughes" autopsy at Methodist Hospital, Houston, will be brought to light in Chapter XI and XII. For now, the main concern is with fingerprints.

The evidence used to make this part of the case are copies of blank fingerprint cards, so you can understand how *easy* it is to correctly fill out the cards and take prints by those skilled in the art. Exhibits of print cards *properly* used are displayed as well. Also, legitimate prints of Howard Hughes, with proper identifying factors, are presented as examples. More than a few curiosities in the "H.H." Methodist Hospital autopsy files were found, as well as curiosities in the "H.H." FBI files. And last, but certainly not least, is clarification of *fingerprint procedures that should have been used at Methodist Hospital in 1976 and were not.* In this Chapter the glaring question is raised as to *why* proper procedures in the submission of "H.H." prints *were not used?* Also strange is that between the years of 1965 and 1976, <u>no</u> legitimate H.H. "inked" prints (on proper standard cards) were ever used for the identification of Howard Hughes. The Methodist Hospital identity of the "H.H." corpse flown into Houston, Texas in 1976 is <u>clearly suspect!</u>

SHORT OUTLINE OF FINGERPRINT CRITERIA USED:

A. Correspondence exhibits stating latent print longevity between two professionals skilled in the art. (Exhibits 28, 29, 30, 31-A, 31-B) When knowing what to look for, one may go online and find additional information regarding longevity of latent fingerprints. (Exhibit 31-B)

B. Exhibits of blank print cards. If you peruse them closely, you will see but *minor* differences in information required for proper processing. (Exhibits 32 and 33. Exhibit 34 is the back of 33.)

C. Exhibits of cards on which <u>properly</u> inked prints were taken and information <u>properly</u> entered. Exhibit 35: Howard R. Hughes – National Defense Program (front of fingerprint card), page 4. Exhibit 36: Howard R. Hughes prints (back of fingerprint card), page 5. See Exhibit 37-A as example of prints properly taken.

D. Russ's analysis of prints taken in "Howard Hughes" autopsy at Methodist Hospital Houston, Texas, follows the exhibits below.

The several question and answer responses below have been labeled "Exhibits" and their information inserted into the Exhibit Index for easy reference. Latent fingerprints and their use in the criminal justice system are never done randomly or without investigative intent.

For clarification purposes, the forty-year-old latent Nazi fingerprint discussed below belonged to a wanted war criminal named Valerian Trifa. He had posed as a Romanian Archbishop here in the United States. His print was found on a post card, not an ID (identification) card.

In a series of e-mails (name and e-mail address redacted at her request since she's retired) a criminalist, who had worked for over 30 years for the Postal Inspector Laboratory in California, told Russ the following in response to specific questions.

EXHIBIT 28

Q: If an article is wrapped in cellophane, handled multiple times, and then put in a freezer for an extended period of time, would there still be a way to recover "fingerprints" from that cellophane? *A fellow in my city of Henderson asked me about this in connection with a "suspicious death" case he and I are working on. Thanks much for any response you can provide.*

A: There is no way to tell whether you would get fingerprints on the cellophane until you try. I would use super-glue fumes. Some prints may survive, at least on the inside surface.

EXHIBIT 29

Q: Can fingerprints be developed from decade old paper?

A: I have known of hundred-year-old prints being developed with ninhydrin. It depends on several factors, like storage conditions, and the amount of material in the original deposit. The oldest one that went to court was a print developed on a Nazi ID card. That print was developed in the 1990s. Put a pan of warm water in the tank with the superglue - moisture helps the process.

- **Note**: Ninhydrin is the name given to a chemical combination, developed by the Postal Inspector Crime Laboratory in the 1960s. It comes in both spray and full liquid form. Once primarily used to develop fingerprints on paper, it has since been expanded to be used to develop fingerprints on an assortment of materials. Ninhydrin is a chemical combination which can be purchased over the counter from firms offering criminal identification instruments. It compares very favorably to the use of super-glue but reacts much quicker to fingerprints developed on paper products. Heated Superglue is used to develop fingerprints on hard objects such as door frames, guns, and bullets, as well as car interiors.

- **Note:** The art of fingerprint analysis can be a bit mysterious at times. It's a fallacy to believe that all people have or leave fingerprints. Crime-scene technicians rarely discuss this trait. Medically, there can be those who lack fingerprints because they are born with fingers lacking depth in their print ridges. Occupationally, fingerprint ridges may be worn down because of handling abrasive materials such as bank tellers counting large quantities of money, bricklayers, etc. And finally, we have criminals who have either worn gloves or removed their prints with an acid wash. However, given the above, it's believed that these groups only comprise three percent of the population and that most persons (97 percent) can leave fingerprints at a crime scene or in connection with a civil case where fingerprints need to or can be developed.

Notes Above by L. "Russ" Russell

EXHIBIT 30

Q: Are there any new gas processing techniques, out there, I don't know about?

A: I don't know of any new gas processing. But I have been out of the fingerprint business a long time. I do know it is a bad idea to get forensic information from (redacted.) They are factually challenged, to keep it politically correct. The hundred-year-old prints previously mentioned, developed with ninhydrin, depended on several factors like storage conditions and amount of material in the original deposit. The oldest one that went to court was a print developed on a Nazi id card that was developed in the 90s. There are some ways of reprocessing documents, but chances of success are very low. Well, for anybody but you. You have the best Karma I have ever seen. Your wild ideas seem to work out.

- **Note**: Further research indicates *it was not an ID card* the Nazi print was found on, *but a postcard* belonging to the former Nazi war criminal (last name "Trifa") posing as a Romanian Archbishop in the United States.

EXHIBIT 31-A

Russ parts with his long-standing friend and Criminalist:

Many thanks for answering my inquiry about fingerprints. Thanks for that information on the Nazi fingerprints. It sure gives us somewhere to start. A fellow in Utah presented a 3-page "Will" allegedly written and signed by Howard Hughes. Only problem is that none of the pages has a single finger or palm print on them. Envelope has a print outside – that of the "presenter" guy in Utah.

Good lead on that Nazi print info. Thanks very much.

In my last year's we were using Super Glue to process car interiors. I understand it is now being used to pull up prints on paper. I still would depend on ninhydrin, though. Its tried and tested.

Thanks again for being there when I have a question.

L. "Russ" Russell

EXHIBIT 31-B

Can fingerprints be found on rusty wood screws left in parking lot?

Posted on Wednesday, September 10, 2003 - 12:31 pm:

How long does fingerprints stay on a smooth surface? For instance, on metal or steal?

Posted on Saturday, September 06, 2003 - 08:59 am:

not to my knowledge but there have been a number of remarkable cases of latent prints being developed by chemicals or laser processes up to 40 years after they were deposited. check out the case of the rumanian church in the USA's archbishop who turned out to be awanted Nazi Identified by a latent print of his thumb left on a Nazi document from WW2 developed in the 1990's by laser - exact details and names escape me though. the good state of preservation probably had a lot to do with the fact that the document had been meticulously preserved for many years and lay untouched in an east german archive for so long

Posted on Saturday, September 06, 2003 - 08:48 am:

EXHIBIT 32

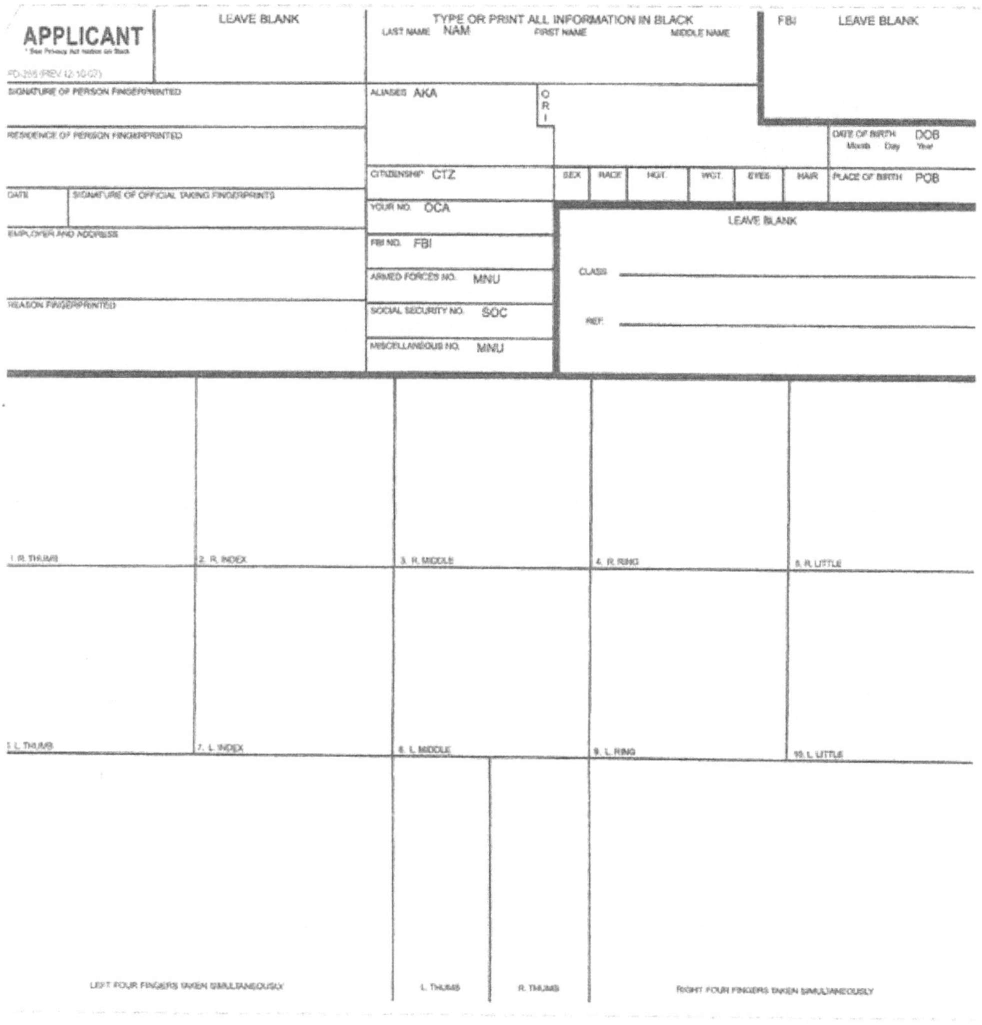

EXHIBIT 33

	LEAVE BLANK	TYPE OR PRINT ALL INFORMATION IN BLACK			FBI	LEAVE BLANK
APPLICANT COMPLETE BOTH SIDES		LAST NAME **NAM**	FIRST NAME	MIDDLE NAME		

SIGNATURE OF PERSON FINGERPRINTED

ALIASES **AKA** / MAIDEN NAME

ORI

DATE | SIGNATURE OF OFFICIAL TAKING FINGERPRINTS

DATE OF BIRTH **DOB**
MONTH   DAY   YEAR

CONTRIBUTING AGENCY AND ADDRESS

DRIVERS LICENSE NO. **DOL**

SEX | HGT. | WGT. | EYES | HAIR | PLACE OF BIRTH **POB**

YOUR NO. **OCA**

LEAVE BLANK

FBI NO. **FBI**

CLASS _____

STATE ID NO. **SID**

SOCIAL SECURITY NO. **SOC**
VOLUNTARY - FOR ID ONLY

REF _____

INFORMATION PROVIDED ON THIS FORM MAY BE COMPUTERIZED IN LOCAL, STATE AND FEDERAL FILES.

DATE FINGERPRINTS SUBMITTED

1. R. THUMB	2. R. INDEX	3. R. MIDDLE	4. R. RING	5. R. LITTLE

6. L. THUMB	7. L. INDEX	8. L. MIDDLE	9. L. RING	10. L. LITTLE

LEFT FOUR FINGERS TAKEN SIMULTANEOUSLY	L. THUMB	R. THUMB	RIGHT FOUR FINGERS TAKEN SIMULTANEOUSLY

EXHIBIT 34
(Back of Exhibit 33)

TYPE OR PRINT ALL INFORMATION

DO NOT FOLD

APPLICATION FOR EMPLOYMENT

- ☐ PEACE OFFICER (830 PC)
- ☐ CRIMINAL JUSTICE EMPLOYEE
- ☐ STATE EMPLOYEE
- ☐ CITY/COUNTY EMPLOYEE
- ☐ SCHOOL EMPLOYEE
- ☐ OTHER EMPLOYEE

☐ THIS EMPLOYMENT TITLE IS EXEMPT FROM THE PROVISION OF SECTION 432.7 OF THE CALIF. LABOR CODE PLEASE CITE STATUTE OR OTHER REASON FOR EXEMPTION

POSITION TITLE:

APPLICATION FOR LICENSE, PERMIT OR CERTIFICATION

APPLICATION FOR:

- ☐ LICENSE
- ☐ PERMIT
- ☐ CERTIFICATION
- ☐ CCW LICENSE
- ☐ OTHER (SPECIFY)

LICENSE - PERMIT - CERTIFICATION TITLE:

AGENCY AND ADDRESS:

(NOTE: TO INSURE CORRECT MAILING, THE ABOVE INFORMATION MUST BE COMPLETED)

PERSONAL INFORMATION

APPLICANT'S RESIDENCE ADDRESS:

BID-7 (5/90)

EXHIBIT 35

FBI FILE 32-HO-278—PAGE 4

NATIONAL DEFENSE PROGRAM

FEDERAL BUREAU OF INVESTIGATION, UNITED STATES DEPARTMENT OF JUSTICE
WASHINGTON, D. C.

APPLICANT

Name of contributor .... COMMANDING GENERAL S.O.S. U.S. ARMY .... City ....WASHINGTON.... State ..D. C.
(State whether Police Department, Sheriff's Office, or other official designation)

Applicant for ....Pilot....
(Specify position)

(PLEASE PASTE PHOTO HERE)
(USE OPTIONAL)

Name of company ..LOCKHEED AIRCRAFT CORP..

Date ..6-25-42..

Address ..HUGHES AIRCRAFT CO. CULVER CITY, CALIF.
3921 Yoakum, Houston, Texas

Birthplace Houston, Texas .... Citizenship ..Amer..

Age ..36.. Date of birth ..Dec 24, 1905..

Height ..6'3".. Weight ..160..

Hair ..dk. brown.. Eyes ..brown..

Complexion ..med.. Build ..med..

Scars and marks ..small scar over right eyebrow – scar right leg..

APPLICANT

IN CASE OF EMERGENCY NOTIFY: HOWARD HALL, FRIEND, HUGHES AIRCRAFT CO., CULVER CITY, CALIF.

RECORDED
OCT 1 1942
IDENT. DIV.

IMPORTANT—PLEASE INCLUDE ALL REQUESTED DATA

EXHIBIT 36

FBI FILE 32-HO-278—PAGE 5

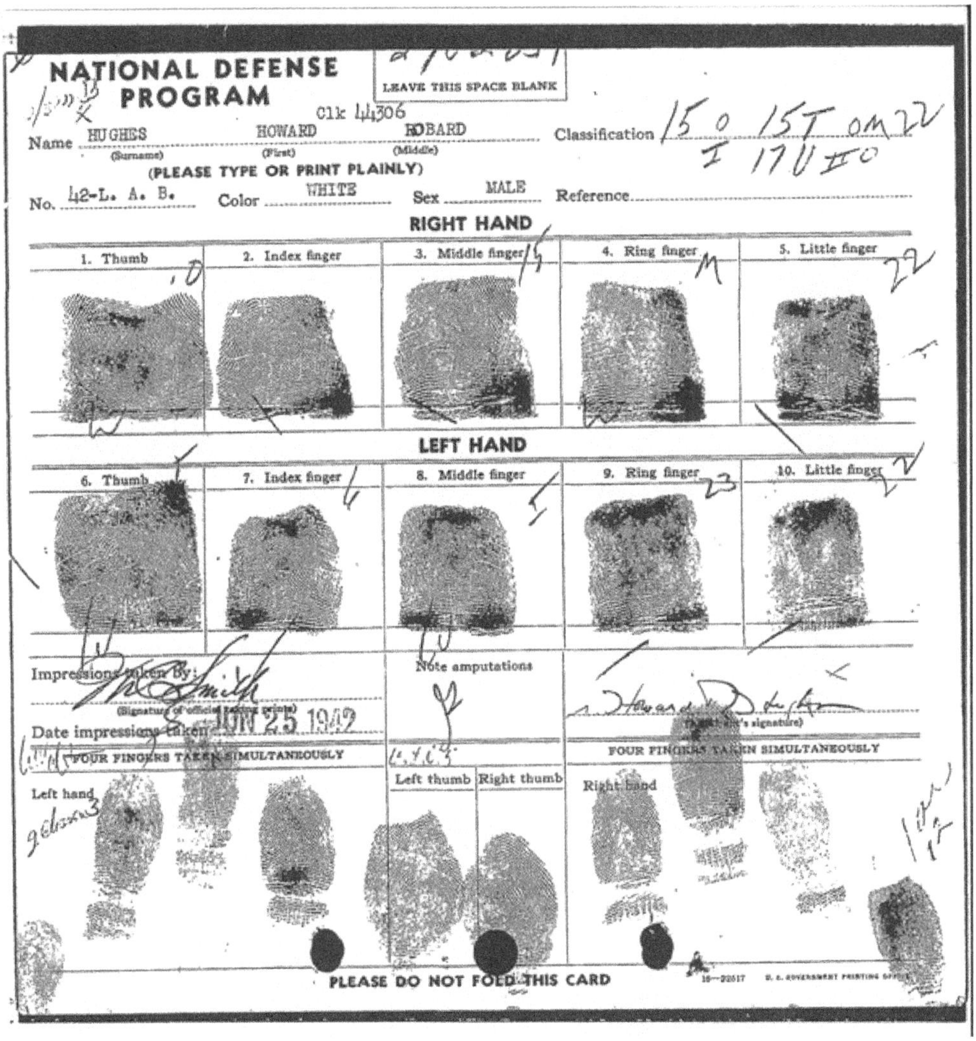

NATIONAL DEFENSE PROGRAM

LEAVE THIS SPACE BLANK

Clk 44306

Name HUGHES (Surname) HOWARD (First) ROBARD (Middle) Classification 15 0 15T OM 22 I 17U II O

(PLEASE TYPE OR PRINT PLAINLY)

No. 42-L. A. B. Color WHITE Sex MALE Reference

RIGHT HAND

1. Thumb	2. Index finger	3. Middle finger	4. Ring finger	5. Little finger

LEFT HAND

6. Thumb	7. Index finger	8. Middle finger	9. Ring finger	10. Little finger

Impressions taken by: [signature] (Signature of official taking prints)

Date impressions taken JUN 25 1942

Note amputations

(Signature)

FOUR FINGERS TAKEN SIMULTANEOUSLY

Left hand

Left thumb Right thumb

FOUR FINGERS TAKEN SIMULTANEOUSLY

Right hand

PLEASE DO NOT FOLD THIS CARD

16—22517 U. S. GOVERNMENT PRINTING OFFICE

EXHIBIT 37

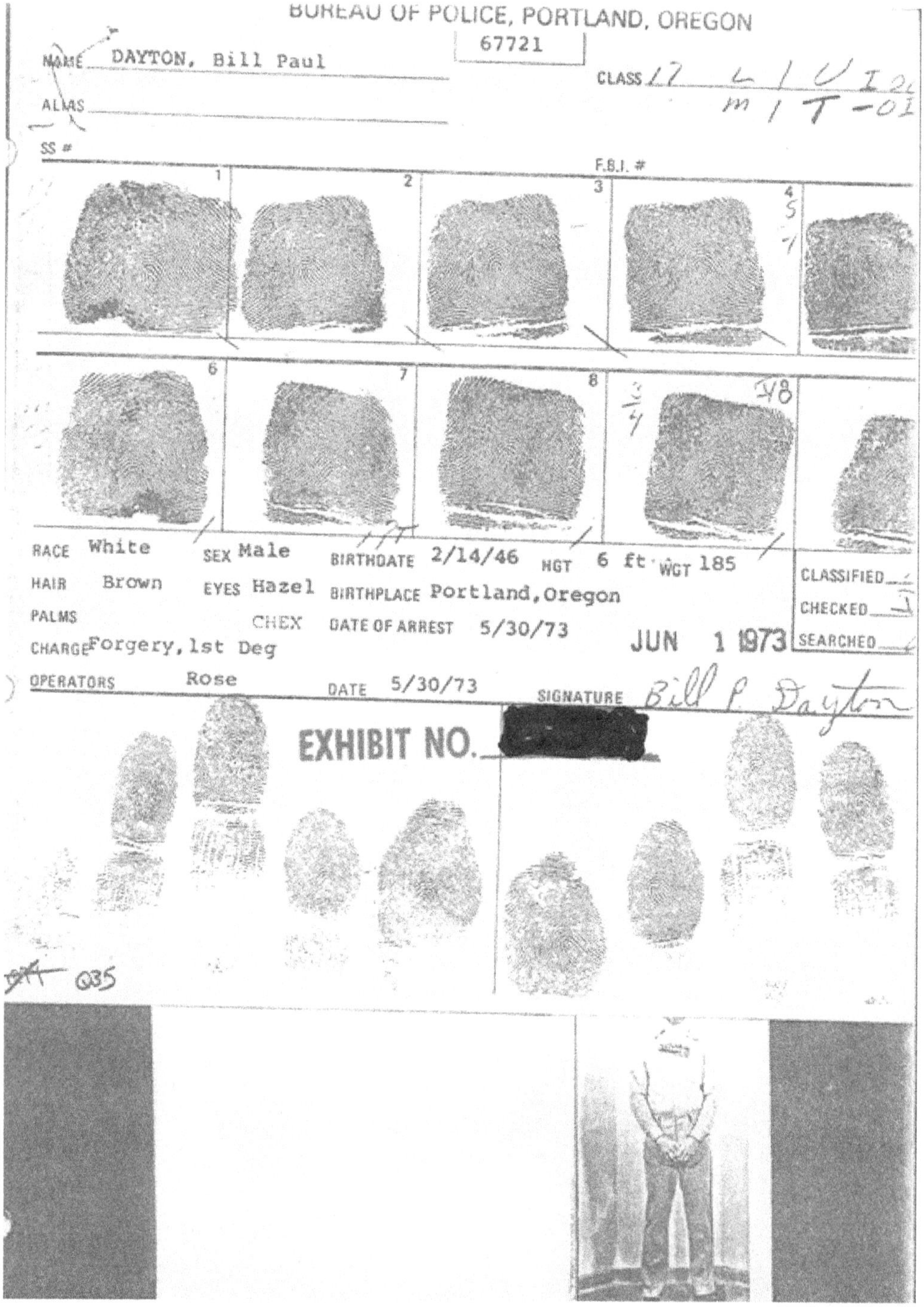

BUREAU OF POLICE, PORTLAND, OREGON

NAME DAYTON, Bill Paul   67721   CLASS

ALIAS

SS #   F.B.I. #

RACE White   SEX Male   BIRTHDATE 2/14/46   HGT 6 ft   WGT 185
HAIR Brown   EYES Hazel   BIRTHPLACE Portland, Oregon
PALMS   CHEX   DATE OF ARREST 5/30/73   JUN 1 1973
CHARGE Forgery, 1st Deg
OPERATORS Rose   DATE 5/30/73   SIGNATURE Bill P. Dayton

CLASSIFIED
CHECKED
SEARCHED

EXHIBIT NO.

Deficiencies in the Autopsy Process
(Aka: The "Fingerprinting Fiasco" of the Mexican Corpse.)
As Per L "Russ" Russell, Investigator.

EXHIBITS FOLLOW NARRATIVE:
(A.R.): Autopsy Report of "Howard Hughes."
(CAT.): Category in H.H. Autopsy File.
(32-HO-278): Location of Exhibits in FBI File.

There are three major reasons for obtaining fingerprints prior to autopsy procedures (and, in fact, fingerprinting is a required part of the autopsy protocol throughout the United States of America). Fingerprint analysis assists in identifying the body. But more importantly, identifying the body leads to further identification (confirmation of identity) through knowledge and review of known body irregularities, such as broken bones, missing organs, major scars, surgical procedures, tattoos, etc. Fingerprinting without further identification can lead to misidentification, especially when the lifted fingerprints are deficient.

Body anatomical analysis and comparisons are a vital part of the autopsy process. In Houston, Texas, this analysis did not take place at all. Whether by design or by accident, this process did not take place. But first, we will discuss the fingerprinting procedures conducted in Houston.

In the case of the Houston corpse flown from Mexico and brought to Methodist Hospital on April 5, 1976 (arriving approx. 2:20 pm), apparently fingerprinting protocol <u>was</u> religiously followed. In his book, titled *Hughes – The Private Diaries, Memos, and Letters*, author Richard Hack advised that Dr. Malcolm McGavran, chief pathologist of Methodist Hospital Pathology department, began the autopsy on April 5th by fingerprinting the corpse flown in from Mexico. Houston's medical examiner, Joseph Jachimczyk, "rejected the initial set of fingerprints that were taken as being insufficient for the purpose of identification." (Exhibit 130-F)

The corpse was (allegedly) fingerprinted a second time the next afternoon around 3:00 pm (April 6), *some 25 hours later*. These fingerprints were put on "strips of paper" and then superimposed over a blank fingerprint card (Exhibit 38), which is unsigned and incomplete in its totality. An approved Coroner's Fingerprint card utilized nationwide in 1975 by autopsy personnel *was not utilized at all*. It was these fingerprint impressions that were allegedly used later by the FBI to establish the corpse as being that of Howard Hughes.

The fingerprint technician who actually worked for Harris County Coroner's Office, Horace Tucker, showed up for work at Methodist Hospital without bringing a coroner's fingerprint card with him. He took the corpse's prints on strips of paper and then adhered those strips to a blank fingerprint card, *not a coroner's fingerprint card*, with no descriptive body data on it.

This was *incredibly sloppy and inefficient work*. Superimposing the strips containing the corpse's prints fails to lend legitimacy to the fingerprinting process conducted in Houston.

The first sets of fingerprints *(taken on April 5)* are nowhere to be found. Even if that weren't utilized or forwarded to the FBI laboratory in Washington, DC, at the very least they should have been retained within all other papers and records of the autopsy by Methodist Hospital. This act of omission is both suspicious and disturbing.

All in all, this entire process easily led to potential deceit and manipulation. And in fact, the editor of *Texas Monthly Magazine* asked the FBI (Exhibit 39) "if the prints could have been switched to affect any misidentification of Hughes." A very valid question considering the irregular fingerprint procedures conducted by Methodist Hospital personnel, with the endorsement of hospital management.

Methodist Hospital personnel relied on the body's identification by two unknown out-of-state doctors and two members of Hughes's family who had not seen or talked to Hughes in more than 21 years. Hospital personnel did no further investigation. The body was so sickened and emaciated that further identification was really needed, if not required. No state or government identification accompanied the body (driver's license, passport, pilot's license, etc.). No past confirmed body x-rays, dental records, or other hospital reports were provided to Methodist Hospital personnel—*nothing*. Methodist Hospital personnel only had the word of two doctors, two estranged relatives, and a fringe Hughes company employee to attach a name to the body.

A few days after the autopsy, the FBI provided details of their fingerprint analysis, in which they advised that the fingerprints (*allegedly* taken on April 6, 1976) matched fingerprints of Howard Hughes, which they possessed within their files. Apparently the first sets of prints taken on <u>April 5</u> were never submitted to the FBI. This raises some suspicion that someone may have <u>substituted prints that could have actually been taken some years prior</u> to the fingerprinting of this corpse to the FBI. And, in fact, the envelope (Exhibit 40-A and 40-B) bearing the fingerprint "strips of paper" was apparently opened and resealed for some reason several days after the fingerprints of the corpse were taken. One can only imagine why this envelope was opened and resealed – a most convenient method for substituting fingerprints from another individual.

As to further discussion of fingerprints, reference is now made to an FBI memorandum dated 4/12/1976, in which an unknown FBI Special Agent (name redacted, see Exhibit 41, 32) wrote that the fingerprints of the corpse were taken by Horace Tucker, an "employee of the Harris County Medical Examiner's Office," and that he took three separate sets of fingerprints, but they were put on "two strips," one bearing the right-hand finger impressions and one bearing the left-hand finger impressions. At no time was this fact listed on affidavits completed and signed by Dr. Joseph A. Jachimczyk of Memorial Hospital (Exhibit 41). In fact, when the doctor and others involved mention the taking of the corpse's fingerprints, they often allude to "fingerprint cards," (Exhibit 42-A, 42-B and 42-C) and *not* "strips of paper." Now we can see how Exhibit 38 was contrived. This Exhibit shows a fingerprint card, but the prints appear to be inserted or superimposed from another source (strips of paper with inked prints on it) and, as previously noted, this fingerprint card (Exhibit 38) contains no descriptive information of the body fingerprinted, no full signature of the body fingerprinted, and no full signature of the person who took the fingerprints. And, as it turns out, this contrived fingerprint (Exhibit 38) was used by the FBI fingerprint examiner to verify the alleged identity of Howard R. Hughes, Jr. Really?

As noticed in Exhibit 38, the fingerprint card lists no description of the deceased individual – none. And with respect to actual completion of these fingerprint cards, they are "not fully signed or dated." Some sorts of initials are found on Exhibit 38, but nothing else. This was totally improper and deficient. **Note**: Go to Exhibit 213. View a *real* coroner's fingerprint card properly annotated. Although this card was used in 1987, it is the same coroners' print cards used in 1976 when the supposed "Hughes" corps was autopsied at Methodist Hospital Houston, Texas. (This exhibit was a late comer; some information redacted for confidentiality.)

Very little credibility (or integrity) can be attached to the validity of any of these fingerprint cards. Incomplete cards, non-signed or dated cards, and even just the use of the fingerprint card itself – not from the card stock associated with the fingerprinting of autopsied bodies throughout the United States. This is a fiasco of the highest authority. And now we learned that the entire Harris County Original Autopsy file is "missing." It further appears that irregularities in the autopsy procedures have been disguised or hidden.

Exhibits 116-A and B are prints on the Clifford Irving Denial Letter which is obviously an attempt to lend credibility to this questionable document. Investigator Russell was asked what he saw in these prints, and to make a comparison of known Hughes prints found in Exhibit 36. Also, Exhibit 38 are prints of the Methodist Hospital Corpse believed to be "Howard Hughes." Russ's comparison of known Hughes prints, Exhibit 36, with Exhibit 38, follows:

"In Exhibits 116-A and B and Exhibit 38, we see what type of fingerprints are found. Trying to make an identification, as to who these fingerprints might belong, I found it virtually impossible; both sets of prints are unreadable. Furthermore, it appears that the poor quality of these prints was intentional; they are unreadable and un-comparable." (Exhibits 116-A and B and Exhibit 38 were taken *after* 1965.)

L"Russ"Russell

\

EXHIBIT 38

1976 AUTOPSY REPORT / CAT. 7, PAGE 13
METHODIST HOSPITAL HOUSTON, TEXAS.

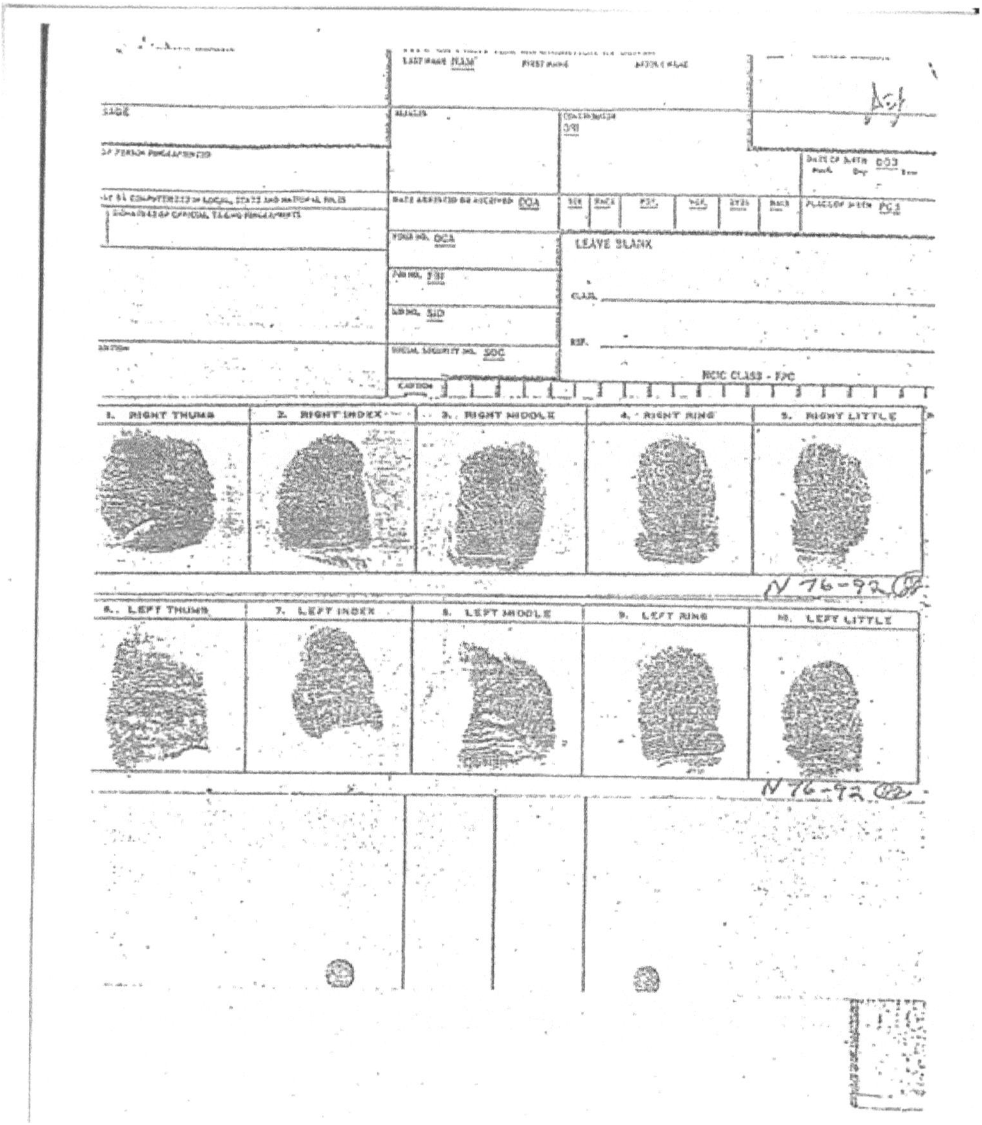

In Exhibit 130-F, we find that the first set of "H.H." prints taken by Dr. Malcolm McGavran (as per autopsy protocol) were rejected by the Houston Medical Examiner, Dr. Joseph Jachimczyk. It is difficult to believe that those prints, taken by Dr. McGavran and later discarded, could have been inferior to the unreadable and incomparable "Hughes" autopsy prints found above in Exhibit 38.

Note: Legitimate Hughes prints taken in 1942, as per Exhibit 36 are clearly readable and a comparison can easily be made.

EXHIBIT 39

FBI FILE 32-HO-278—PAGE 53

OPTIONAL, FORM NO. 10
JULY 1973 EDITION
GSA FPMR (41 CFR) 101-11.6

UNITED STATES GOVERNMENT

Memorandum

TO   : FILE (32-278)   DATE: 11/2/76

FROM : SAC ROBERT RUSS FRANCK

SUBJECT: HOWARD R. HUGHES
         IDENTIFICATION MATTER

      On 11/2/76, [   ] a Contributing Editor for Texas Monthly Magazine, came to the office and advised me that he was working on a story about HOWARD HUGHES for his magazine. He inquired as to what I could tell him about the fingerprint identification of HUGHES, and I told him that Dr. JOSEPH JACHIMCZYK, Chief Medical Examiner of Harris County, had requested FBI Identification Division assistance in comparing the prints taken April 6, 1976, in the morgue of the Methodist Hospital, Houston, Texas, with known prints of HUGHES on file in Washington, D. C.

      I related to [   ] that following examination of the prints taken from the deceased male at Methodist Hospital, I issued a press release (serial 6), 4/7/76, to the effect that the prints were found to be identical with those of HUGHES on file with this Bureau. I related to [   ] also that we had had a Latent Fingerprint Examiner come to Houston from Washington to make a tentative identification and, thereafter, he returned to Washington with the fingerprints of the deceased male and made a formal report to Dr. JACHIMCZYK dated 4/9/76, attesting to the prints being of one and the same person.

      [   ] advised me that he has already talked to Dr. JACHIMCZYK and HORACE TUCKER, who works for Dr. JACHIMCZYK, and who physically took the prints from the deceased male and was attempting to write his story to determine whether HUGHES was, in fact, dead. He inquired as to whether the prints could have been switched to effect any misidentification of HUGHES, and I told him I could make no comment concerning that in that all the FBI did was to take prints furnished to us by the Medical Examiner's Office and compare them with known prints of HOWARD HUGHES. [   ] thanked me for my taking the time to talk to him.

ACTION: None - for information.

RRF/cbl
(1)

Buy U.S. Savings Bonds Regularly on the Payroll Savings Plan

105

EXHIBIT 40-A

AUTOPSY REPORT / CAT. 7, PAGE 15

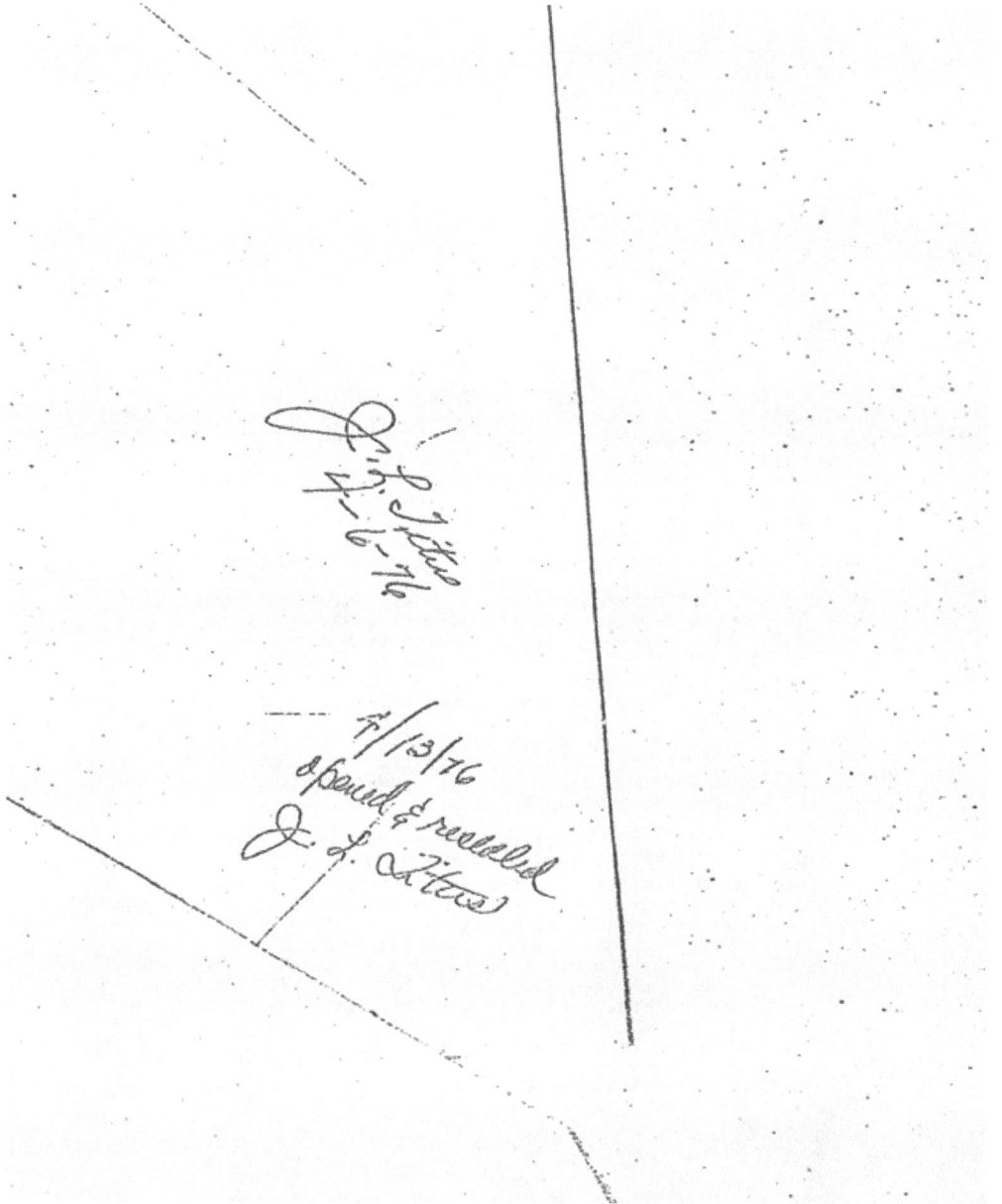

EXHIBIT 40-B

AUTOPSY REPORT / CAT. 7, PAGE 16

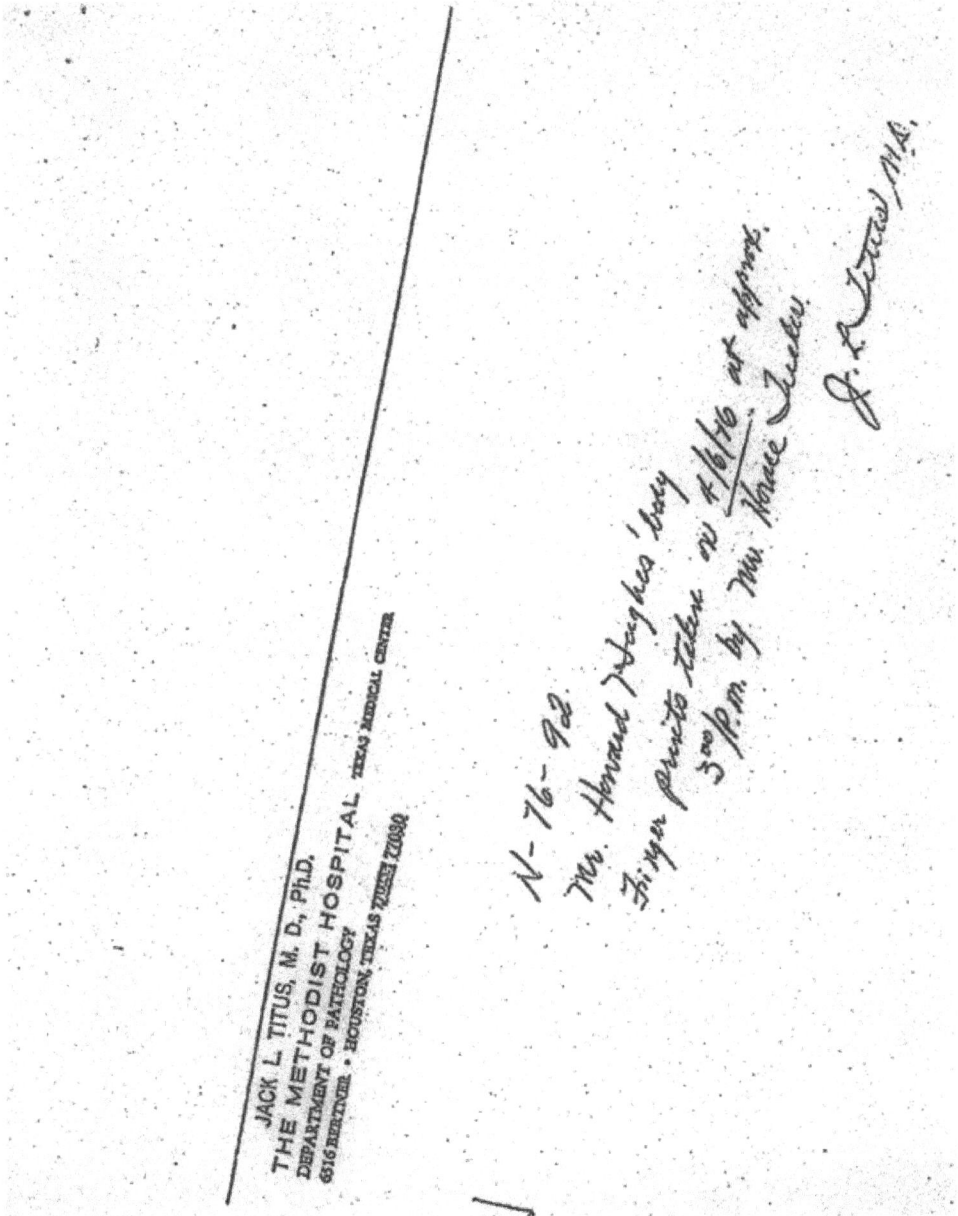

EXHIBIT 41

FBI FILE 32-HO-278—PAGE 47

FD-302 (REV. 11-27-70)

FEDERAL BUREAU OF INVESTIGATION

Date of transcription_____4/12/76_____

    Mr. HORACE G. TUCKER, Investigator, Office of
the Medical Examiner, Harris County, JOSEPH A. JACHIMCZYK,
Chief Medical Examiner, turned over to SA [   ]
at 9:35 AM, in the office of ROBERT RUSS FRANCK, Special
Agent in Charge, Houston FBI, one of three sets of inked
impressions taken by Investigator TUCKER of the deceased
subject believed to be HOWARD ROBARD HUGHES. These inked
fingerprints were in two strips, one containing the right
hand impressions and the second the left hand impressions
and each was marked on the front "N76-92", the initials
"JJ" (by Dr. JOSEPH A. JACHIMCZYK) and on the reverse side
of each was the signature "H. TUCKER 3 PM 4-6-76."

b6
b7C

    At 2:15 PM, the prints were turned over from
SA [   ] to [   ] Fingerprint Specialist
of the FBI Identification Division upon his arrival in
Houston.

b6
b7C

Interviewed on ___4/7/76___ at ___Houston, Texas___ File # ___HO 32-278 - /3___

by ___SA [   ]___ b6 b7C :jam   Date dictated ___4/7/76___

This document contains neither recommendations nor conclusions of the FBI. It is the property of the FBI and is loaned to your agency;
it and its contents are not to be distributed outside your agency.

EXHIBIT 42-A

AUTOPSY REPORT / CAT. 7, PAGE 14

Copies of the two aforementioned fingerprint cards,

bearing my initials in the upper right-hand corner, are attached.

(Signature)
James E. Jenkins
Assistant Custodian
For the Director
Federal Bureau of Investigation

Washington
District of Columbia

Before me this 9th day of April, 1976, James E. Jenkins has appeared and signed this affidavit first having sworn that the statements made therein are true.

My commission expires 11-30-78

Notary Public in and for the
District of Columbia

109

EXHIBIT 42-B

FBI FILE 62-99881-58.

UNITED STATES GOVERNMENT

Memorandum

TO : MR. MC DERMOTT

DATE: 9-8-76

FROM : R. H. Ash

SUBJECT: HOWARD ROBARD HUGHES
IDENTIFICATION MATTER

Assoc. Dir.
Dep. AD Adm.
Dep. AD Inv.
Asst. Dir.:
Adm. Serv.
Ext. Affairs
Fin. & Pers.
Gen. Inv.
Ident.
Inspection
Intell.
Laboratory
Legal Coun.
Plan. & Eval.
Rec. Mgnt.
Spec. Inv.
Training
Telephone Rm.
Director Sec'y

PURPOSE: This memorandum is to recommend we accede to a request from the Attorney General, Texas, for certified copies of fingerprint cards of Howard Hughes, which show Texas as a listed residence of Hughes.

DETAILS: On 9-7-76, Fingerprint Specialist James E. Jenkins, who effected the identification of the fingerprints obtained from Hughes' body with known prints in our files in April, 1976, received a telephone call from Bert W. Plúÿmen, Special Assistant Attorney General, Office of the Attorney General, Post Office Box 12548, Austin, Texas 78711, who requested that the Identification Division furnish certified copies of any fingerprint cards contained in the Identification Division's files showing Texas as a place of residence of Howard Robard Hughes.

A request was made in May, 1976, by an attorney acting for Noah Detrich for the FBI to conduct document and latent fingerprint examinations of one of the alleged Howard Hughes' wills. This request was referred to the Department which advised that Bureau involvement in the matter would be premature at that time. In view of the previous Departmental interest, Inspector F. B. Still contacted Scott Crampton, Assistant Attorney General, Tax Division, on 9-8-76, and apprised him of the request of the Texas authorities and the facts regarding listed addresses for Hughes in Identification Division files. Mr. Crampton stated he could see no reason not to accede to the request of the Texas Attorney General.

Instructions have been issued to prepare certified copies of two fingerprint cards for transmittal to the Office of the Attorney General of Texas. The two cards being prepared were submitted by the Federal Communications Commission (FCC), Washington, D.C., on 7-27-42, and by the Commanding General, Services of Supply, U.S. Army, Washington, D.C., on 10-1-42. The FCC card lists the address as 3921 Yoakum Boulevard, Houston, Texas, and the Army card lists two addresses: (1) Hughes' Aircraft Company, Culver City, California, and (2) 3921 Yoakum, Houston, Texas. The other two fingerprint cards for Hughes which are in file do not contain residence addresses.

REC-51 62-99807-58 21 SEP 1976

EXHIBIT 42-C

FBI FILE 62-99801-44, Case No: B-28943

FEDERAL BUREAU OF INVESTIGATION
LATENT FINGERPRINT SECTION WORK SHEET

Recorded: 4-8-76   2:18 p.m bjg   Reference No:
                                      FBI File No: 62-99801-44

Received: 4-8-76   Latent Case No: B-28943

Answer to: Dr. Joseph A. Jachimczyk, Chief Medical Examiner for Harris
           County, Room 209, 301 San Jacinto Street, Houston, Texas 77002.

Examination requested by: Addressee

Copy to: SAC, Houston

RE: HOWARD ROBARD HUGHES;
           HOUSTON, TEXAS
           IDENTIFICATION MATTER

Date of reference communication: Inked fingerprints received in Houston, Texas
Specimens: on 4-7-76 by Fingerprint Specialist

                                                                          b6
                                                                          b7C

          Two cards bearing inked fingerprints, Your #N76-92
                                        of a deceased male

Result of examination: Examination by: Jenkins
                                    Evidence noted by:

Prints f deceased male morgue #N76-92, taken by Homer G
Tucker, witnessed by Dr Jachimczyk of prts Howard Robard
Hughes, printed 6/25/42 # 42-L.A.B. application for position
of pilot, Lockheed aircraft Corp., FBI # 2702851.

Specs returned   as verified
                                                                          b6
                                                                          b7C

Examination completed 2:30 pm 4/8/76   Dictated 4/8/76

111

EXHIBIT 42-D

From Albert Gerber's Book *Bashful Billionaire*, Page 290.
"Don't call me – I'll call you."

sounded a false alarm when its battery ran down!

Publicity about the location of Hughes' secret headquarters and his inaccessibility has led to several attempts to enter the Romaine Street building illegally. No known attempt has ever succeeded.

In the 1960's some changes were made in the procedure at headquarters. Before this time, anyone who called OL 2-4500 would hear the operator reply simply by giving the phone number. Anyone asking for Hughes would be instructed to state his name, telephone number, and the nature of his business and would be informed that Mr. Hughes would be advised. A series of people then evaluated the message and made the decision about whether Hughes would be called.

In the early 1960's Hughes served notice that he was not to be called under any circumstances. His attitude, very simply, was, "Don't call me—I'll call you." Now from time to time Hughes or someone close to him does call the headquarters to check on messages. This is presently his sole contact with his empire on any formal basis.

EXHIBIT 42-E

From Albert Gerber's Book *Bashful Billionaire*

three o'clock in the morning. He remarked to Hughes that he could hardly understand how Hughes could be so alert at that hour.

"Listen for a moment," Hughes said softly.

Bautzer and Hughes sat and listened. There was no sound.

Hughes continued, "You don't hear anything, do you? No car noises, no people noises, nothing to bother you."

This, indicated Hughes, was the perfect time to concentrate —completely free from outside distractions. Hughes called it "the clean time of the night."

In spite of the large number of typists and stenographers working at 7000 Romaine Street, Howard Hughes has no personal secretary to keep track of his affairs. The person closest to filling that position is an attractive 28-year-old brunette named Mrs. Betty Patrick, who works at the Hughes Tool Company in Houston, Texas. In reality she works directly for Raymond M. Holliday, Executive Vice-President of Toolco, but she also handles phone calls coming in for the unreachable Howard Hughes, and the rerouting of his mail. She receives many calls for him, most of them from crank inventors. Her standard reply is, "I'm sorry, Mr. Hughes is not here. I don't know where he is."

Questioned on the subject, Mrs. Patrick insists that she herself has never spoken to Hughes. However, she admits that she does regularly consult Holliday by telephone on problems relating to Hughes. All such calls are made on a private "hot line" that does not go through the company switchboard.

Hughes is a firm believer in the "hot line." Because he is such an inordinate user of telephones, he has learned a great deal about them and how they work. He is always careful of tapped wires, eavesdroppers, and listening devices which might create an intelligence leak by telephone. Consequently, for a long time all of his executives have had special telephones rigged in such fashion that they do not go through the switchboard. These phones are never used for outgoing calls so that the lines can be kept open for Hughes' use. These are the instruments generally known as the "hot line."

EXHIBIT 42-F

448   EMPIRE

been hearing these stories for a year now, although never from Meier. Indeed, Meier always denied them when confronted. Usually, the tales filtered back to Las Vegas from Washington, New York, or other cities. For example, the letter Maheu received from his old friend, the Washington attorney Edward Morgan, dated August 15, 1969:

This one will give you a boot! I had lunch today with Steve McNichols, former governor of Colorado. After two or three "swacks" he told me of his great deal for the sale of a silver mine near Tonopah, Nevada. He had the top man, so he said, in the Hughes organization lined up to make the purchase—the only man who sits at Hughes' right arm. I inquired as to who this man of influence might be and learned, to my great surprise, that it was your Mr. Meyer [sic]. I suggested to Steve that I understood that a fellow named Maheu was Mr. Hughes' top man. He seemed undismayed in the certain knowledge that Mr. Meyer was *the* man who truly had Mr. Hughes' ear. According to advice from Mr. Meyer, the only thing holding up the purchase of the mine was Mr. Hughes' absorption with the Air West deal. I did not disillusion him. Where ignorance is bliss, 'tis folly to be wise. So sayeth the bard.[71]

If Maheu found this news disconcerting, he made no outward sign. The mining business proceeded apace. On September 2, Meier wrote Maheu that "the next of our options which we have outstanding expires September 20 midnight. We have an option on 69 claims in White Pine County, Nevada, near other properties we own. This particular property has silver, lead, copper, and gold on it. From 1920–40, the shipping records show that over $20 million of ore was taken out during that time; 95 percent of which was high grade silver. . . . In one area alone there was approximately 400,000 tons of ore which can be put into production immediately and have an ore value of from $12–$17 a ton. . . . The option is for $1.9 million."[72]

The option was exercised, and the acquisition completed in December. Of the $1.9 million that Hughes paid for the claims, the two owners of the properties received about $165,000. It was not an unreasonable return on their investment, considering that they had bought the claims earlier in the year for $25,000.

What happened to the remaining $1,735,000 of Hughes's money? A total of $585,000 is unaccounted for. But on December 19, two checks totaling $1,150,000 were issued by the First Security State Bank in Salt Lake City to Everd B. Van Walsum, who promptly moved the money into foreign bank accounts.

Was anyone in the Hughes organization auditing the mining expendi-

114

EXHIBIT 42-G

reasonably contemplated hijacking costs. The long and short of our position is that we are in trouble, and very serious trouble.[52]

Some weeks later, Holliday forwarded another financial report to Hughes. This one dealt with Nevada. The report showed that Hughes's Nevada properties lost $3.2 million in 1968 and $8.4 million in 1969. For the first seven months of 1970, the losses amounted to $6.8 million. "If the 1970 losses continue at the present rate," Holliday said, "it appears that the overall loss for 1970 will be on the order of $13–$14 million."[53] Considering that Hughes had invested more than $150 million in Nevada since 1967, the figures were most depressing.

Against this background, a whispering campaign began in Las Vegas. Someone whispered to Hughes that Hughes Tool and Romaine Street had given hundreds of thousands of dollars to Maheu that he was unable to account for, that Maheu was stealing. Hughes believed the whispers.

Clearly, Hughes had been swindled out of millions, and clearly, many an executive on the Hughes payroll, including Maheu, was doing quite nicely for himself at Hughes's expense. Some segments of his empire—and not only those in Las Vegas—were outrageously mismanaged.

Maheu was certainly not a financial wizard, or an especially talented business executive. Back in 1948, about a year after he resigned from the FBI, he became president and major stockholder of a company called Dairy Dream Farms, which had obtained a franchise on "a new process for canning pure cream without additives."[54] Supported by "unlimited credit," the product was on sale in twenty-two states when a company chemist determined "there was a problem with the lining of the can which caused oxidation."[55] The Food and Drug Administration was notified, and the Dairy Dream Cream recalled, plunging the company into a financial crisis. Maheu "had made so many personal loans to try to keep the [company] viable" that it was suggested he should "go through bankruptcy."[56] Rejecting the advice, he said, he eventually "paid every creditor one hundred cents on the dollar," although it took him some time.[57] Twenty years later, while directing Hughes Nevada Operations, Maheu was "almost always overdrawn at the bank," displaying "little concern for cash deficits."[58]

This fumbling in business administration or finance, however, could hardly be equated with thievery. Nor could Maheu be held accountable for the financial performance of all Hughes's Nevada properties. But he

EXHIBIT 42-H

Although Hughes was doing less work than ever, Romaine Street sent another aide, James H. Rickard, to Vancouver to join the industrialist's personal staff, bringing to six the number of male attendants now looking after Hughes around the clock. Born November 20, 1919, at Powell, Wyoming, Rickard had studied mechanical engineering and business for three years at the University of Wyoming and Montana State College, and then had compiled a checkered employment career before joining Bill Gay's band of Chevrolet drivers at Romaine Street in October of 1953. After serving as a pilot during the Second World War, Rickard was a construction worker in California, ran a drive-in movie theater in Montana that was a casualty of the state's climate—"We opened on Memorial Day and it snowed about a foot and a half two weeks later"—sold life insurance in Arizona, and finally returned to California to go to work for Hughes Productions.[29] Like so many others at Romaine Street, Rickard was hired through his Mormon connections —his brother-in-law was active in church affairs with Gay. Then in 1957, after four years as a Hughes driver, Rickard took a one-year leave of absence to try his hand at managing a logging and sawmill operation in Bozeman, Montana. That business failed, too—"The lumber market price dropped about $50 about two months after we started"— and Rickard hurried back to Romaine Street.[30]

In August of 1972, the Hughes caravan, which had already moved twice in seven months, unexpectedly pulled up stakes and returned to Nicaragua, vaguely citing Canadian taxes as the reason for leaving. On Tuesday, August 29, Hughes and his aides boarded a jet and flew back to Managua, again checking in at the Intercontinental Hotel. Nicaragua's ruler was gratified by Hughes's return. "I am very pleased that Mr. Hughes has accepted my personal invitation to once again visit with us," General Somoza said, assuming that Hughes was in Managua by his own choice. "I know that all Nicaraguans will join in extending to him our traditional hospitality."[31] The general did not see Hughes this time. Nor did Raymond Holliday, who flew to Managua only to be turned away a third time.

Hughes probably lacked the strength to be truly difficult, as he would have been in healthier days, but he nevertheless made it clear that he

CRITIQUE OF THE ABOVE FINGERPRINTING ACTIVITIES AT METHODIST HOSPITAL HOUSTON, TEXAS:

What first comes to mind concerning corpse identification by the forensic staff at Methodist Hospital? Yes, they got away with it. They hid the whole fabricated procedure in plain sight. And there you have it, plain and simple. What becomes obvious as well is that *any* credible law enforcement agent, *skilled it the art of fingerprinting*, would see the procedures used above the way Russ did, "sloppy at best, possible unlawful at worst."

Let us not move on too fast from the above analysis. Let's get into some well-supported speculation. What could really have been happening with that corpse, presumed to be Howard Hughes, and fingerprinted at Methodist Hospital, Houston?

Note: "Summa, Incorporated" is what the Hughes Industries called themselves soon after 1965 as referenced below.

A. The wealthiest man in America virtually disappears after 1954? After this date, no more "face-to-face" contacts took place <u>with *any* of his employees, relatives, or friends</u>. Nor would a photograph be taken of him. Apparently, there is a double being used. The double is taken care of by several aides, most of whom believe that double to be Howard Hughes.

B. All know that Hughes is still alive after 1954, and it is never questioned up until 1965. Hughes runs his business enterprises well from afar. He is able to accomplish this task through the skillful use of telephone and facsimile, but he never makes a public appearance as the notorious Howard Hughes *after* 1954. (See Exhibits 42-D and 42-E above.) However, his existence *is questioned numerous times after 1965*.
   Note: At this juncture we should also correlate the other evidence of Exhibits 18-A, B, and C and 42-D and E, above.

   1. Bill Gay and Chester Davis get Bob Maheu fired in 1970 with a phony document. Robert "Bob" Maheu was "the tail that waged the Summa, Inc. dog" *after 1965,* until he was fired.
   2. Bob Maheu had hoped to regain his feather-bed job as "Hughes's Right-Hand Man" after having been out-scammed by Bill Gay and Chester Davis.
   3. In Exhibit 18, Maheu throws a bone to the federal boys. He hopes, because the feds do not know "the full lay of the land," they will have conversations with Bill Gay and Chester Davis.
   4. Maheu anticipates that by putting the heat on Gay and Davis, they will be concerned that the con could be uncovered and invite him back into the fold. *It did not work.*

5. The bottom line here is that Raymond Holliday, Vice-President of Hughes ToolCo, Inc., undoubtedly had some grave concerns after 1965. Apparently, he did not feel comfortable no longer hearing directly from Hughes, by phone, as he previously had (Exhibit 42-D and 42-E.) and then having to deal with Bob Maheu. Apparently, it becomes too much when Maheu gets fired in 1970 and Bill Gay and Chester Davis take over the reins of Summa, Inc. Holliday, knowing something is terribly wrong, <u>resigns</u> as Executive Vice-President and Director of ToolCo, Inc., hence Exhibit 18-A.

C. Speculation had run wild after 1954 as to why the prodigy entrepreneur Howard Hughes so thoroughly isolates himself visually from his lieutenants, he trusts to carry out his day-to-day business decisions. Nevertheless, the Hughes's businesses do well up until 1965. Although he runs operations from a remote hidden location, <u>the Captain is still at the helm.</u>

D. Speculation turns into the realization for the Hughes lieutenants. The cat is *not* in the house; the mice have more freedom to play. Under-the-table contracts are sold, and various tax-free opportunities begin to present themselves between 1954 and 1965. The Hughes Industries higher-echelon employees begin to prosper handsomely. Soon they become mildly wealthy, but it's not enough to satisfy their illicit desires. One of the Hughes lieutenants, with a biblical name, decides to spearhead a coup. He and several of the Hughes Industries financial top feeders put their heads together and come up with a plan to have Hughes declared mentally ill and incompetent. Therefore, *he should not* be allowed to run the massive industries he has created. They want to confine him to an institution. They try to get Dr. Vern Mason, Howard's long-time friend to join them in the ploy. However, the honorable Dr. Vern *knows the truth about Hughes* and *why* he has withdrawn into isolation. Dr. Mason tells Howard about the plot and the biblically named fellow gets fired. The others back off from their immediate dreams of greater wealth, but they do not quit their dissolute desires. They wait, like spiders, for a more viable opportunity. However, Howard now knows their minds and although he may not know *all* the players in the scheme, he knows the main players who did not come forward when the ploy was conceived. With a little research, he discovers that his top echelon lieutenants have been "knocking down the cash register." He decides there will be no "golden parachutes" for those he cannot trust, and he excludes them from his will.

E. Howard Hughes is terribly sick by 1964. Injuries to his back sustained in the 1946 XF-11 crash in Beverly Hills, California, are taking their final toll. Except for two maids who took care of his needs since 1954, he has lived in solitude. Over that grueling ten-year period, his spine has gradually collapsed, and the top part of his terribly warped physique is pressing painfully down on his internal organs. Soon they will cease to function. In 1964 the doctors determine he has only eight months to live. (This diagnosis was probably given by his employee and friend Dr. Vern Mason.)

F. In <u>1965</u> Howard Hughes dies (*in a finally disclosed location*) somewhere in Mexico.

G. The Summa, Inc. trio of Nadine Henely, Chester Davis, and Bill Gay send down an Ex-FBI agent Robert "Bob" Maheu. Bob has been a *fringe* employee for several years, including a few years prior to 1954. Robert has helped the Henley, Davis, and Gay team find and use several doubles as replacements for Howard Hughes in inconsequential situations. Later, after 1965, he will provide other useful employees for the Summa, Inc. team, including an imposter "Hughes" and "Goodfellas" Johnnie Rossellini and the money laundering Salvatore Giancana.

H. Maheu finds the warped corpse of Howard Hughes and, although he is not 100 percent sure that the fellow is really Hughes, Maheu takes freshly inked fingerprints and fills out the print card in ink, as he was trained in the academy. Then following Gay, Henley, and Davis's instructions, the real Hughes is interred in Mexico. The Summa Inc. trio have somehow known that Hughes had been terribly ill for quite some time. They have planned for the death of their employer.

I. On his way back to the States, Maheu begins to realize what the Summa, Inc. "threesome" is up to. *If* the fellow he printed in Mexico is the real Howard Hughes, 1) his life could be in danger or 2) he might have a golden opportunity to be one of the main contenders in the bilking of the Hughes empire. (Perhaps Maheu was asked to destroy all evidentiary materials particular to Hughes which could link him into the Summa, Inc. trios' scheme.)

J. Maheu arrives back stateside but *does not* deliver the Hughes fingerprints immediately to the Summa, Inc. board of directors. Instead he gets copies of the prints and makes plans so that if anything were to happen to him, others – perhaps a friend or two in the FBI and various police departments – would know of the ploy hatched by Nadine, Chester and Bill. He has "covered his ass." Maheu *demands* a seat on the Summa, Inc. board of directors, *not* just as an equal to the other three, but as <u>the</u> major player. *He wants an identity as Hughes's right-hand man.* The devious deal is struck and a few months later the Hughes companies' profits, which were in the millions, begin to evaporate. The con is on. Literally overnight, Maheu has become "the tail that wags the corporate dog" and believes he has positioned himself where none can oppose him.

K. Maheu turns over the print card, as per the Summa, Inc. trio's agreement, but there is a problem: the card has been fully inked with date, Maheu's name, signature, etc. and therefore, <u>cannot be used for identity purposes</u> (in its entirety) <u>at a future date</u> without the scam to bilk the Hughes estate becoming obvious.

L. A doppelganger, once used by Hughes when he was still alive, is contacted for full-time employment. This double is chosen because the Summa, Inc. group know him to be a drug addict, and they will supply him as one of the jobs perks. Most likely he gets drugs other than codeine in the beginning, but they will ply him with codeine at the end of his usefulness. The imposter must appear, as Hughes once did, as a user of codeine. Codeine is the drug recommended by Dr. Vern Mason (Hughes's personal friend and physician) to replace the painkiller morphine, which is highly addictive.

M. Over a ten-year span, the "Hughes" doppelganger becomes increasingly more addicted to the drugs provided to him, becoming sicklier from their use. Eventually, when the double is on the cusp of death, the consortium of Hughes estate pirates must decide on how they will deal with the double's death. Even during a time when the double could have been saved, they know they cannot put him in a stateside hospital. His *true* identity would surely be discovered. He might recuperate. Someone might take his fingerprints for identification purposes. He might tell the hospital staff how poorly he had been treated for years, thereby arousing suspicion. He might spill the beans while under the influence of medication, etc.

N. The doppelganger finally reaches his end, and he will soon be dead. Thain, Chaffin, and Holmes assure the Summa trio that the double will <u>not</u> arrive in Houston *alive*. Bill Gay and Chester Davis pack their California bags and head for Houston, Texas. Bill Gay makes sure he has several carrycases full of clean cash. He wants to be sure he can *buy* those who *need* to be bought and satisfy those whose bribes have been prearranged. (At that time $500- and $1,000-dollar bills were relatively common for larger business transactions.)

O. A problem surfaces. The Hughes estate bandits *are not going to get the Hughes doubles' corpse immediately cremated*, as was their desire and that of Hughes's relatives, Annette, and Will Lummis. Somehow the Lummis duo become aware that the Mexican corpse is an imposter, and they are looking forward to jumping into those fat Hughes bank accounts. <u>But fingerprints will be taken of the Methodist Hospital Houston corpse!</u> <u>What's to be Done?</u> (See Exhibits 130-D and 130-E.)

1. The only originally inked fingerprints of Howard Hughes, in the possession of the Summa, Inc. trio, are those brought up from Mexico in 1965 by Bob Maheu.
2. The fingerprint card on which the originally inked 1965 Hughes prints reside, had been filled out in ink by Robert Maheu.
3. *This card cannot be used in its entirety* because it has Maheu's name on it, and Maheu had been *fired* several years before *by* the Summa-triad. The date is also wrong. Trying to make the card appear more contemporary would be dangerous since it must pass the FBI print analysis test. The trio carefully cut out the *prints only* strips *from the 1965 print card completed by Maheu* and affix these to a legitimate print card, which they leave blank except for two initials in the top right-hand corner. (It had been mentioned that there was a signature on the back of the blank print cards,

but no evidence was seen as such, therefore, an Exhibit cannot be presented.)

4. Several times in the FBI files, as well as in the Methodist Hospital autopsy files, it was stated that the prints taken off the "H.H." Methodist Hospital corpse had been taken on "strips of paper." Three sets were taken. To be exact, three strip-sets of the right hand and three-strip sets of the left. One set was to go into the Methodist Hospital autopsy file, one set was to go into the Harris County Coroner's Office, and one set was to be delivered to the FBI.

5. Then it was time for those carrycases of cash to come into play. Chief autopsy lead, Dr. Jack Titus, is busy trying to make an imposter corpse look like the corpse of Howard Hughes. He has invited Drs. Wilbur Thain and Lawrence Chaffin into the autopsy for briefing, but the boys *have not* done their homework (as you will see later in Chapter XI). So, we have busy little bees in the autopsy room. When investigator Horace G. Tucker, from the Harris County Medical Examiner's Office, shows up to take fingerprints from the corpse, he arrives without proper coroner print cards, but has plenty of numbered paper strips? (The previous prints taken on a legitimate print card by Dr. Malcom McGaven, when the corpse first arrived at Methodist Hospital, Houston, have been discarded.)

6. Apparently, Horace was willing to take the corpse's prints on "strips of paper," but that was as close as he wanted to get in the scam. He did *not* fill out the print cards to which the strips of paper were adhered – a clever maneuver to sidestep the scam if trouble were to develop later, i.e. "Those are *not* the prints I took!"

7. Either Tucker or Drs. Thain, Titus, or Chaffin affixed the print strips of paper to print cards (Exhibit 38.) And, as stated before, one set was designated for the Harris county autopsy file, one set was designated for the Methodist Hospital file, and one set was slipped into a manila envelope for the FBI. (Exhibits 40-A and 40-B.) Note the patchiness in Exhibit 38 where the paper strips had been attached to the print boards. But there were problems with the envelope containing the "Hughes" prints designated for the FBI. (Exhibits 40-A and 40-B) The manila envelope for the FBI must somehow have contained copies of the *imposter's prints* and not those of the *real* Howard Hughes taken by Maheu in 1965.

> a. The strips of paper on which the corpse's fingerprints appear are numbered. This shows they were cut from a legitimate print card. The supposition here can only be that Horace Tucker just happened to have numbered strips of paper for that special occasion, yet could not find a print card? By calling the board strips "strips of paper" they were able to avoid having to explain why the fingerprints were cut from a regular print card – yet it was *alluded to several times* that the prints had been taken on regular fingerprint cards. (Exhibits 41, 42-A and 42-B)
> b. Is it not strange that they affixed the strips of paper to standard fingerprint boards? So, why didn't they simply use those print boards to take the prints and fill them out properly? Of course, that would never have worked because the Methodist Hospital corpse was not the corpse of Howard Hughes; prints taken

would never have matched up with the prints on file with the FBI. Apparently someone at Methodist Hospital happened to be watching, so they were obligated to slip one of the print boards with its attached *non-Hughes print-strips* into the manila envelope intended for the FBI and stamp it with the Methodist Hospital location. (Exhibits 40-A and 40-B)

c. Now comes the final move in this fingerprint scam. Dr. Titus intercepts the manila envelope (he has a week to pull this off), opens it, retrieves the phony prints, slips in the original Hughes prints taken in 1965, and reseals it. Now, apparently after all the pertinent arrangements had been made, the envelope is ready to be passed off to Robert Frank, special agent in charge of the Houston FBI. (See Exhibit 40-A and take notice of the two dates thereon.) All federal officials, with the need to know, are notified that the prints are those of Howard Hughes *and they are,* but *they are not* the prints taken from the Methodist Hospital "H.H." corpse in 1976. All fraudulently concerned parties are satisfied, and sooner rather than later, reap the benefits of their duplicity. (You might ask, "Why not check the 'Hughes' prints located at Methodist Hospital or the Harris County Coroner's Office against legitimate prints in the FBI's files?" The answer to that question is, "Those files have been lost or destroyed!" (Russ has researched this.) Just exactly how the prints passed the scrutiny of the FBI crime lab is another drawn-out speculative ball of string, but let's let it sleep for now. As more evidence is brought forward in this literary journey, the above scenario will become clearer.

Let's finish out this Chapter on fingerprints by doing a fast forward to Exhibits 158-B, 158-C, and 158-D. It was pertinent to put these three Exhibits into Chapter XI: The Autopsy because they also deal extensively with kidney problems that this "H.H." had for a long time prior to his death. There will be more on kidney issues later. As for now, let's look at the strange, in-depth concerns that Romaine Street (Hughes headquarters) had with any glass containers which were handled by "Hughes." Exhibits 158-B, 158-C, and 158-D, found in Chapter XI, are from James Phelan's book *Howard Hughes: The Hidden Years.* The information below is as substantial as it is authentic, being "from the horse's mouth," so to speak. Were you to go to the library and check out Phelan's book, you would find on the back dustcover a photo of Phelan together with "Hughes's" aids Mell Stewart and Gordon Margulis. (Exhibit 158-D) These two aides are a direct source of the information below. When one considers Gordon Margulis's concern about his boss in Canada (when "H.H." was shuffled off to his dark, dingy room against his wishes), it's likely that Gordon and Mell were mostly on the up and up at that time in their responsibilities concerning a fellow they believed to be "Hughes."

**None Of The Pertinent Details Below Were Included In Barlett And Steele's Book
Empire Or Its Re-Publication As *Howard Hughes: His Life And Madness.***
(Same book – different title.)

In any event, let's consider the information below revealed by Gordon Margulis and
Mell Stewart and their "clean-up jobs" when the Hughes Romaine street headquarters
gave the orders for the "Hughes" entourage to vacate the Desert Inn Penthouse in Las
Vegas. The destination to a clandestine location was known only by a select few but
was unknown to Bob Maheu who had just been fired.

A. Chuck Waldron (Senior Aide) changes all the locks on the ninth floor to make certain
the secret of "Hughes's" departure was preserved as long as possible. Waldron was
brought on board by C.E.O. Bill Gay and quickly rose to the position of *Senior Aide*
and "Hughes's" private secretary after 1966. He is obedient to the Summa, Inc.
board of directors. (The idea of Waldron being a private secretary is a bit strange
since he did not even know how to type. (See the bottom of Exhibit 178-B).
1. Was "H.H." skipping out on his lease at the Desert Inn? Or was Waldron trying to
keep out the maids prior to removing evidence that could have been incriminating?
2. Was the move secret because they were traveling to a remote location where they
hoped this "H.H." would not be found by Robert Maheu? (The letter used to fire
Bob Maheu was later determined to be "bogus" by the federal boys. But *even after*
the FBI forgery determination, *it would still be used later as a known exemplar by
Rosemont Enterprises, Inc. and others*; although, in truth, it was a *questionable
exemplar.* Of course, Bob Maheu *knew* the letter was a forgery. (Exhibits 15, 16 and
17) When other Hughes's forgeries began to reveal themselves, Maheu began to
believe *it was not a good idea to lean too heavily in the forgery direction.* Perhaps
Maheu thought that someone might get off track and begin to question his real
involvement with Gay, Henley and Davis? It's like being tied together on a log over
quicksand. If one falls in, the rest go with him. Nevertheless, Maheu later stirs up
trouble when he discovers that "H.H." is squirreled away in the Bahamas.

B. Mell Stewart, Eric Bundy, Norm Love, and Fred Jayka were left behind to clean up
the small "H.H." Desert Inn Penthouse bedroom. Under directions from Romaine
Street headquarters, the aides and their activities are clearly described. (Exhibits
158-B, 158-C, and 158-D)
1. It was probably about time; the room had not been cleaned in 4 years!?
2. At first, only the aides were allowed into the room to clean it. But a supposition
could be made that it was only *after* pertinent evidence had been removed, by the
aides that the hotel maids were allowed in to finish the cleaning.
3. It's understandable that Mell Stewart would be reluctant to talk about the squalor
in that little room when there was little indication that he, or any other of the aides,
had ever cleaned it. The aides are often depicted as being shakers and movers in

the business dealings of "Hughes," but <u>after 1965</u>, it was always Bill Gay, Nadine Henley, and Chester Davis who were running the Summa, Inc. show from the Hughes Romaine Street headquarters in Los Angeles. In most cases, the aides' jobs were simply to clean up after "Hughes" and bathe and feed him. They were getting paid a bloated wage for supposedly doing this. None of those boys was a registered, or even a practical, nurse; and as for secretarial duties, none of them had a history of these skills or even knew how to type. But why should any of them care? The man was an imposter anyway, "the fix was in!"

C. Here we get to the crux of the matter: "It was Mell Stewart's job to dispose of 'Hughes's' bottles of pain-killing drugs."

1. Numerous bottles had been stacked on a wide shelf in the bedroom closet. "Stewart was astonished at the sight, *hundreds of them*." (Exhibit 158-B)

2. Given #1, you will later learn in "The Autopsy" chapters that a statement made by lead autopsy physician Jack Titus was that "it was difficult to determine if 'Hughes' was a drug addict." But this statement was *understandable* coming from a fellow who *miscalculated* the codeine, per milliliter of blood, in the Methodist Hospital "H.H." corpse. More on this later in Exhibit 127-B, 4th paragraph. Could this pretended ignorance have served his intentions to *skew* the autopsy findings?

3. Stewart's first instructions concerning the "H.H." penthouse medicine bottles was to "put them in a gunnysack, smash them with a hammer and bury the sack of smashed bottles at some remote spot far out in the desert." Then his instructions were changed. He was told to "pack the bottles in boxes and deliver them to Romaine Street headquarters." Mell and his wife made the delivery to Los Angeles, no questions asked.

4. This also raises the question as to why the empty bottles were stored in the first place? Why were they not simply disposed of after they were emptied? (Exhibit 158-B)

5. Stewart maintains that "I don't know why they wanted them, and I didn't ask." (One doesn't want to be too inquisitive when getting paid ten times more than the going rate for menial labor).

D. "Hughes" had kidney problems when he resided at the Desert Inn:

1. "Relieving himself took hours and he was too weak to sit all that time in the bathroom. He urinated into wide mouthed Mason jars. Instead of being emptied, the jars had been capped and stacked in a corner of his little room." Upon exiting the Desert Inn Penthouse, "Hughes" aides had been instructed by Romaine Street headquarters, to empty the urine from the Mason jars and <u>wash</u> and <u>destroy</u> the jars. (Three years of urine storage?)

    a. "Putting the ducks in a row," the washing of those Mason Jars had to have served some purpose for Romain Street headquarters? They could not have been planning to *recycle the jars* as the aides were instructed to destroy them *after* washing.

b.   The Howard Hughes Medical Institute (H.H.M.I.) in Miami had the latest technology in kidney treatment and kidney machines for cleansing the blood. Yet in the ten years prior to "Hughes's" death, which was attributed to renal failure, *he was never taken to H.H.M.I. for treatment?*

E.   As for spend-thrift Bob Maheu, he knew *why* he had been booted from the syndicate. For him there had to have been little mystification. His B.S. dialogue-reasoning upon discovering the news was partially correct; it wasn't Howard Hughes that fired him.

F.   The bottom-line question here is: *why all the fuss about those glass containers left behind by "Hughes" in the Desert Inn Penthouse?*

G.   Later in Exhibits 214-A, B, C, and D, we find that "Hughes's" aide Gary Lewis Ray (per his affidavit) and aide Jan Johnson were *also* sent into the "Hughes" Desert Inn Penthouse to help Mel Stewart with the clean-up of that disgusting abode. We get an even more in-depth understanding of the clean-up crews and their missions. According to Gary Ray, "In Las Vegas, we rented an eighteen-foot enclosed truck. We had received instructions from Mr. Glenn that this was a 'hush hush' project and that we were to pack the items we found and return them to Romaine Street." (Kay Glenn was a Personal Assistant to William "Bill" Gay C.E.O. of the Hughes Industries.) "We found and boxed the following items, among many others: numerous syringes, dozens of them; ampoules of some kind of medication, such as sterile water or dextrose; bottles of dextrose, saline solution, etc.; several cabinets such as one would find in a doctor's office; porcelain trays, stainless steel trays; dozens of bottles of medication; various types of pills and the like--enough bottles to fill a good-sized box, 24x24x20; numerous empty medicine bottles and empty clear bottles the size of canning jars; medical instruments and instruments which appeared to be surgical instruments; an operating or examination table; large lamp such as used in an operating or examination room; centrifuge and sterilization units; and dozens of quart jars of urine. I remember no labels or dates on the jars containing urine. We transported these boxed items to Romaine Street in Los Angeles, California as instructed by Mr. Glenn, and placed them in the back part of the building. I know that these items remained there for a relatively short period of time and then I noticed these things were no longer where we had placed them."
Gary Ray also reported that when he was later assigned to install physical security equipment at "Hughes's" location in Nassau, Bahamas, Hughes's aides told him that, "Hughes would sleep as long as eighteen to twenty hours at a time."

We could speculate as to what was going on in that Desert Inn Penthouse for a couple more pages, but we can now say that this imposter "Hughes" was knocked out for extended periods of time on drugs and *perhaps* eventually began to believe he actually *was* Howard Hughes?

Having uncovered tremendous amounts of evidence, more of which you are soon to see, has created a bit of a dilemma. This copious information found, sorted, and correlated was no easy task. Although the evidence contained in this book is extensive, it was pertinent to be selective of the material used to make the case. Therefore, it's appropriate to break from the Methodist Hospital fingerprinting fiasco, revisiting it from time-to-time as we move along further into the facts.

CHAPTER VI

FORENSIC CURSIVE WRITING ANALYSIS
Legitimate Documents, Forged Documents, and Explanations

Cursive "handwritten" documents are readily identifiable. No one's handwriting, much like their fingerprints, is the same as another's. Of course, a previous "legitimate" or "known" document must *first* be available for comparison purposes if the letter or note is to be a verifiable instrument or used for identification purposes. Typewritten documents can be readily and easily manipulated. A few forged initials or a signature, witnessed by a "bent" federal employee or notary, can easily be passed off as authentic. However, a complete and extensive *cursive will*, contract, or even a sheet of cursive music cannot. References back to this chapter from time-to-time in this documentary is essential so that eventually you, the reader, will have knowledge few possess concerning forgeries, Howard Hughes, and cursive writings in general.

Explanation of the proper identification of cursive documents:

INVESTIGATIVE CONSULTANT RUSS RUSSELL'S CURSIVE EXAMINATION AND COMMENTS AS FOLLOWS: (Handwriting Analysis "H.H." Case as of 12-28-2016)

After several years of collecting handwriting exemplars on Federal Fraud cases (conducting informal comparisons) and performing three additional years of handwriting analyses in San José, California. I was questioned and adjudged to be a Handwriting Expert in 1991 during a Grand Theft trial in Santa Clara County Superior Court.

In 2016 and 2017 Charles Clotfelter asked me to take a look at handwritten papers and signatures relating to Howard Hughes (H.H.) and his associates. In connection with a FOIA (Freedom of Information Act) request, the FBI provided us with a large portion of their H.H. file. The file, itself comprised 2,100 pages of content. Some of the materials were redacted by the FBI, while other pages were very thorough. Within that file I observed numerous documents, the authorship of which was unknown. I also reviewed copies of FBI Crime Laboratory requests (submitted to them by FBI Agents and investigators from a few State agencies) and analyzed the numerous documents submitted with those Laboratory requests. The FBI Crime Laboratory requests incorporated two distinct types: 1) Fingerprint comparisons; and 2) Handwriting analysis. My primary focus, at the time, was on the handwriting analyses requested of the FBI Crime Laboratory.

Contained within the FBI Laboratory Handwriting Analysis requests were numerous documents. By procedure it is required that a request for a laboratory handwriting analysis have, already designated, submittals of handwritten exemplars as either known (K) or questionable (Q). Known handwritten exemplars refer to documents/signatures actually witnessed being written/or signed. Credibility of the witness is ensured if that witness is a Federal Agent or employee of a Federal/State/or Municipal Government Agency. Other witnesses have much less credibility, depending upon his/her relationship to the alleged author of the handwritten document/signature.

While reviewing the documents submitted with the FBI Laboratory Handwritten Analysis requests, I observed a peculiar designation *not normally found in other formal Laboratory Handwriting Analysis requests.* My explanation is as follows: A questionable document has no other meaning or designation. It is deemed questionable because no one can attest to the authorship or authenticity. A known document cannot have any duplicity. It is either witnessed by a reliable person, or it loses its status as a known document or signature. However, in the case of several of the FBI Crime Laboratory Handwriting Analysis Requests, I noted that many submitted documents were designated as known, when their definite authorship could not be verified. In performing handwriting comparisons using those un-witnessed documents, they should have been designated as "collective exemplars," which are in a separate category from both known and questionable exemplars. Collective exemplars usually refer to writings performed over time within a business environment, which taken together may indicate the same author. Collective exemplars are not known exemplars in the pure sense of the word and should only be used in conjunction with known exemplars submitted to a Crime Laboratory for analysis.

To divert for a moment, I note that extensive research has failed to uncover many documents written by Howard Hughes, and more importantly actually witnessed by a reliable person. As previously indicated earlier in this book, as he aged, Howard Hughes was a closely guarded private person and few people were ever present when he chose to write or sign anything. In my efforts to locate true and/or reliable Howard Hughes handwriting exemplars, I had much difficulty. Other than his signatures on fingerprint cards (in 1936 and 1942), I could only locate one single Howard Hughes, Jr. handwritten document witnessed by anyone (discussed later in this report.) There are several documents purportedly written or signed by H.H., but full investigation revealed that they were actually prepared by someone else. In the case of US vs. Clifford Irving, there are letters in the file, signed in the name of H.H., but before the Federal case could be scheduled for trial, Clifford Irving admitted to forging each of the H.H. signed letters. Whether he (Irving) or someone else "forged" the documents is unknown, but through his "guilty" plea, we do know that the real H.H. did not perform any of those writings (See Exhibits 45-53, below.)

Many documents found listed as known documents, in most of the FBI Crime Laboratory Handwriting Analysis requests have the same exact trait: they have no credible witness who renders the document(s) as known rather than questionable.

As indicated above, other than H.H. signatures on three (3) Fingerprint cards (See above Exhibit 35 with FBI NDP document attached Exhibit 36);

inherently designated as a known exemplar, only one other witnessed H.H. handwritten document could be located (see below).

There is one document, found within FBI files, *but not submitted as* a known handwritten exemplar for any Crime Laboratory analysis, which merits some discussion. If this document could be positively authenticated as a witnessed known handwritten exemplar, *it would be the rarest of all known specimens said to have been written by Howard Hughes.*

On an unknown exact date, during a period of time near 1956, a waitress named Barbara Thackery, working as a cocktail waitress at the Flamingo Hotel in Las Vegas, took a "drink" order from Howard Hughes and he reinforced the verbal order by using a cocktail pad* to write down the various drinks he was ordering for himself and the three people at his table.** Although "skimpy," this pad's writings (See Attached Exhibits 43 and 44: Bar pad and Thackery affidavit) represent the largest of known H.H. handwriting specimens. Looking at the H.H. handwriting on this pad, and using it to compare to some of the documents, I came to the following conclusions:

It is reasonable to believe that the writing on the cocktail pad is authentic and written by H.H. Several of the written letters are identical to those found in his Fingerprint card signatures, and certain traits (i.e. pen lifts) are also contained within a few written words.

1. The cocktail pad writings are smooth and flowing. H.H. was known to be a well and self-educated man, and his writings would reflect a well-thought out combination of correct, grammatically spelled words, and idioms.

2. More than one other individual practiced H.H. writing characteristics and managed to send and submit forged and questionable letters, under the H.H. signature, purporting them to be those of Hughes. (Exhibits 45 thru 53 below, Harold McGraw forged letter. Exhibits 54 and 55 below, first and last page of a three-page "Chester and Bill" questionable letter, and Exhibits 56 and 57 below, first and last page of a three-page forged will.)

3. Although, in the past, Hughes had at least one, and more probably two, secretaries at his constant disposal, somehow letters and documents with dates <u>after</u> 1965, were handwritten, rather than typed and, in almost every case, the papers are believed to be "forgeries," and non-authentic in terms of H.H.;

4. Although he retained multiple attorneys for his land and business acquisitions, again correspondences relating to legal matters were handwritten after 1965, rather than typed, when H.H. was the alleged author. And, as before, these writings are believed to be "forgeries," and non-authentic in terms of H.H.

* **Note** that this cocktail pad was accompanied by an Affidavit (See attached Exhibits 43 and 44, below,) signed by the cocktail waitress, when used on an un-related 1971 civil court case in Clark County, NV. In addition, the Affidavit indicates that three named individuals witnessed H.H. writing on the cocktail pad.

** What is perplexing to me is why this "cocktail pad" handwriting is not found within any submitted FBI Crime Laboratory H.H. Handwriting Analysis Requests, especially because it appears to be the only true document authenticating Howard Hughes's writing, witnessed and contained within FBI files as an official Affidavit. Other than its appearance within FBI files, *I found no mention of the cocktail pad handwriting in any FBI report or Laboratory Analysis.*

L "Russ" Russell

EXHIBIT 43

KNOWN EXEMPLAR – BAR NOTEPAD
FBI FILE: 12222-0-87-HQ-119739 BULKY 19— PAGE 78

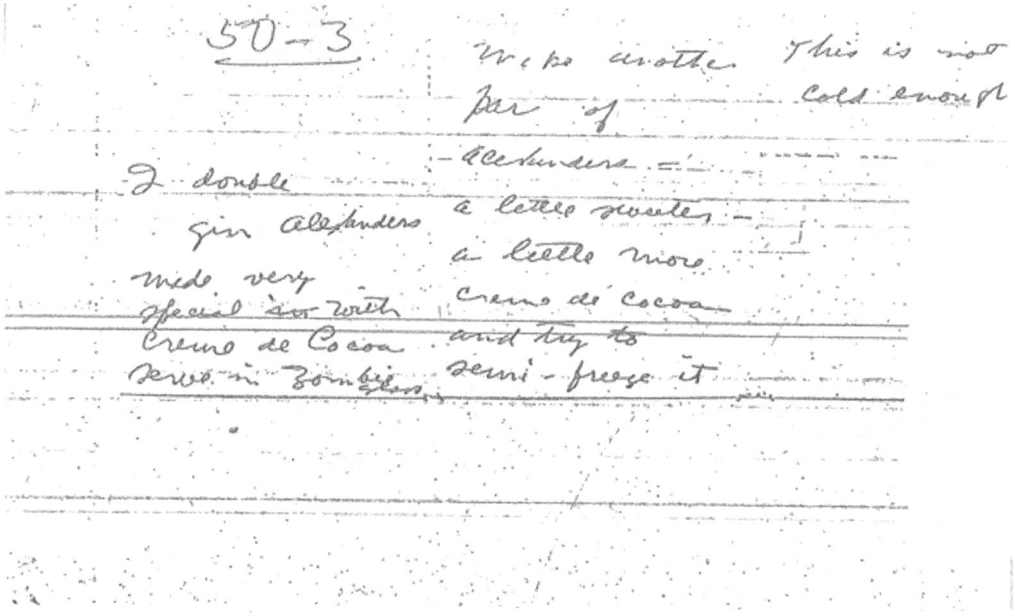
50-3

2 double
gin alexanders
made very
special ice with
Creme de Cocoa
serve in Zombie glass

Make another
pair of
alexanders –
a little sweeter –
a little more
creme de Cocoa
and try to
semi-freeze it

This is not
cold enough

EXHIBIT 44

KNOWN DOCUMENT– BAR NOTEPAD AFFIDAVIT
FBI FILE: 12222-0-87-HQ-119739 BULKY 19—PAGE 79

COUNTY OF CLARK)

> BARBARA THACKERY, being first duly sworn, deposes and says:

> That she was employed at the Flamingo Hotel during the years 1955 and 1956 as a cocktail waitress;

> That sometime during that period, the exact date she does not recall, in the course of her employment she served drinks to a party known to her to be Howard R. Hughes;

> That, in her presence, the person known to her as Howard R. Hughes wrote out directions for the drinks he ordered on a waiter's order pad;

> That the zerox copy attached to this affidavit as Exhibit "A" is a true and correct copy of the writing made by Howard R. Hughes, the original of which is retained in affiant's possession;

> That Walter Kane, Jack Dennison and May Alexander were present and can verify that Howard R. Hughes was the writer.

> Dated this 21 day of October, 1971.

Barbara Thackery
Barbara Thackery

Subscribed and sworn to before me this 21 day of October, 1971.

Shirley Miller
Notary Public in and for said County and State

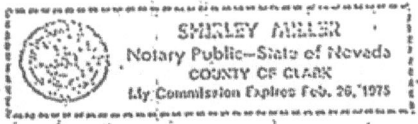

SHIRLEY MILLER
Notary Public—State of Nevada
COUNTY OF CLARK
My Commission Expires Feb. 26, 1975

EXHIBIT 45

QUESTIONABLE EXEMPLAR – HAROLD McGRAW LETTER PAGE (1 OF 9)
FBI FILE:1222257-O-87-HQ-119739-BULKY-19— PAGES 21 THROUGH 29

11-17-7[

NOV 22 1971
McGRAW-HILL BOOK CO.

Mr. Harold McGraw
McGraw Hill
New York, N.Y.

Dear Mr. McGraw –

The facts placed before me, I find astonishing. I do not understand, in the first place, why it is not possible for your publishing house in possession of a legitimate contract between myself and Mr. Clifford Irving and between yourselves and Mr. Irving, for the publication of my autobiography, cannot deal firmly and forcefully with other publishers who which are asserting fraudulent claims to the rights which I have granted to Mr. Irving and Mr.

EXHIBIT 46

QUESTIONABLE EXEMPLAR – HAROLD McGRAW LETTER PAGE (2 OF 9)
FBI FILE:1222257-O-87-HQ-119739-BULKY-19—PAGES 21 THROUGH 29

~~this~~ Irving in Turin has granted to you, without my intervention.

I have said before, and I will say again, that this Mr. Post and Mr. Eaton in no way represent me and have no rights granted by me to sell articles or books purporting to be authorized or written by me ... I have given no material whatsoever to these people and no documents, and any claim by them to the contrary is fraudulent and criminal and I am sure these people are employed by my enemies.

In the event that they or any publisher

EXHIBIT 47

**QUESTIONABLE EXEMPLAR – HAROLD McGRAW LETTER PAGE (3 OF 9)
FBI FILE:1222257-O-87-HQ-119739-BULKY-19—PAGES 21 THROUGH 29**

publish any material supposedly secured by me or authorized by me, and you can do nothing to prevent this through normal channels, I assure you - and I ask that you in turn will no assure them - that I will do all in my power, and take whatever legal steps are necessary to halt what I consider an outrage on my privacy and my painfully worked out agreement with you and Mr. Clifford Irving.

I have been made aware, although not fully to my satisfaction of McGraw Hill's apparently embarrassin

EXHIBIT 48

QUESTIONABLE EXEMPLAR – HAROLD McGRAW LETTER PAGE (4 OF 9)
FBI FILE:1222257-O-87-HQ-119739-BULKY-19— PAGES 21 THROUGH 29

position relative to
these fraudulent
representatives and
other publishers. By
that I mean, as I
said, that I do not
fully understand why
your publishing company
in conjunction with
Life Magazine cannot
without my intervention,
an intervention very
difficult for me under
the circumstances of
my health and for
other private reasons,
cannot handle this
matter by yourselves.

Be that as it may,
I am aware of the
gravity of your problem
as well as my own,
and considering
this as well as my
very deep desire
that my autobiography

EXHIBIT 49

QUESTIONABLE EXEMPLAR – HAROLD McGRAW LETTER PAGE (5 OF 9)
FBI FILE:1222257-O-87-HQ-119739-BULKY-19—PAGES 21 THROUGH 29

in Mr. Irving's possession be published as soon as possible, I will accede to your needs.

That is to say – any provisions in my agreement with Mr. Clifford Irving to the contrary notwithstanding, I, Howard R. Hughes, grant McGraw Hill and Life magazine the right to publicly announce, and at any time following your receipt of this letter, that fact that they and their licensees may and will publish my autobiography as defined in my agreements with Mr. Clifford Irving – provided that McGraw Hill's final payment to Mr. Irving under the terms of your contract with him

EXHIBIT 50

**QUESTIONABLE EXEMPLAR – HAROLD McGRAW LETTER PAGE (6 OF 9)
FBI FILE:1222257-O-87-HQ-119739-BULKY-19—PAGES 21 THROUGH 29**

is made simultaneously
with this public
announcement, and pro-
vided that payment
to me by Mr. Irving
is made immediately
thereafter, whether
this be McGraw Hills
check on cashiers
check being beside the
point.

Moreover, to assure
you of my good faith
in this matter, I ~~have~~
hereby authorize McGraw
Hill and/or Life
Magazine to take what-
ever legal steps are
necessary, in their
considered judgement,
on my behalf, or to
retain legal counsel on
my behalf, to seek an
injunction against any
material published ~~by~~
or announced for publi-

EXHIBIT 51

**QUESTIONABLE EXEMPLAR – HAROLD McGRAW LETTER PAGE (7 OF 9)
FBI FILE:1222257-O-87-HQ-119739-BULKY-19—PAGES 21 THROUGH 29**

cation by any publisher which is not one of McGraw Hill's licensees, that purports to be authorized by me or purports to be in any way, shape or form my partial or complete autobiography or memoirs or that in any way, shape or form conflicts with the publication by McGraw Hill and its licensees of my authorized autobiography, and to prosecute to the full extent of the law any perpetrators of such impostures.

I have tried to be as clear as possible in this letter and I regret that I ~~was could~~ not be more concise under the circumstances but I trust I have

EXHIBIT 52

**QUESTIONABLE EXEMPLAR – HAROLD McGRAW LETTER PAGE (8 OF 9)
FBI FILE:1222257-O-87-HQ-119739-BULKY-19—PAGES 21 THROUGH 29**

made my intentions
very clear.

I would also ask
that you provide to
me a copy of your
public announcement,
either before or after
it is made, through
Mr. Clifford Irving, as
I do not read news-
papers, and I respect-
fully request that your
announcement lean
more to the side of
dignity than sensation-
alism.

I am very sorry
that this matter has
become so complicated,
and please believe
me when I say
that I earnestly
look forward to the
successful publication
of my book in the

EXHIBIT 53

**QUESTIONABLE EXEMPLAR – HAROLD McGRAW LETTER PAGE (9 OF 9)
FBI FILE:1222257-O-87-HQ-119739-BULKY-19—PAGES 21 THROUGH 29**

very near future.
I have already given
my approval in
advance to Mr. Irving,
and I have the utmost
faith that he will
be faithful to my
wishes in his preparation
of the manuscript.

Most sincerely yours,

Howard R. Hughes

EXHIBIT 54

**QUESTIONABLE EXEMPLAR – CHESTER AND BILL - LETTER PAGE (1 OF 2)
FBI FILE:12222-57-O-95-HQ-211845-BULKY-84—PAGE 88**

Dear Chester and Bill —

I do not understand why the problem of Maheu is not yet fully settled and why this bad publicity seems to continue. It could hurt our company's valuable properties in Nevada, and also the entire state.

I believe my company is one of the biggest employers (if not the biggest in the state, and surely what damages an entity employing this many Nevadans is bad for the state itself.)

You told me that, if I called Governor Laxalt and District Attorney George Franklin, it would put an end to this problem.

I made these calls, and I do not understand why this very damaging publicity should continue merely because the properly constituted board of directors of Hughes Tool Company decided, for reasons they considered just, to terminate all relationship with Maheu and Hooper.

EXHIBIT 55

QUESTIONABLE EXEMPLAR–CHESTER AND BILL-LETTER PAGE (2 OF 2) FBI FILE:12222-57-O-95-HQ-211845-BULKY-84—PAGE 90

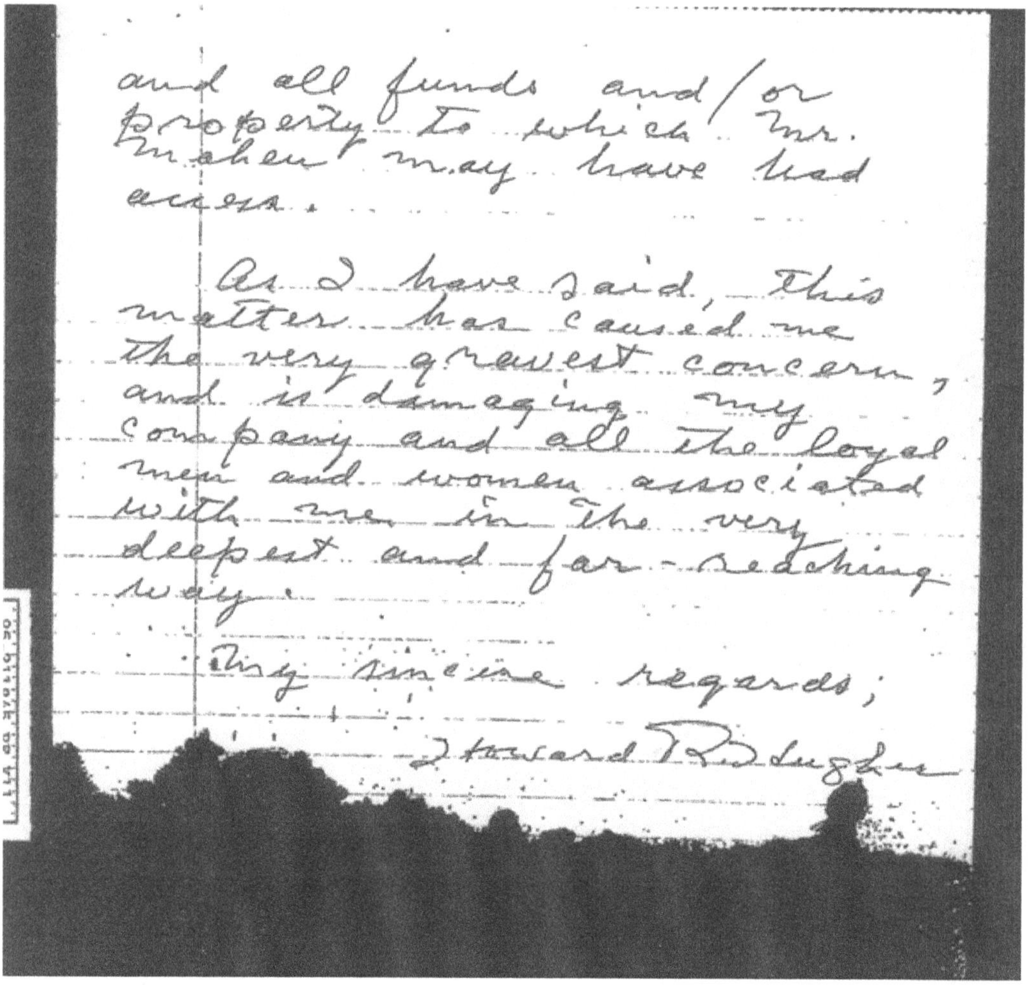

and all funds and/or property to which Mr. Maheu may have had access.

As I have said, this matter has caused me the very gravest concern, and is damaging my company and all the loyal men and women associated with me in the very deepest and far-reaching way.

My sincere regards;

Howard R. Hughes

EXHIBIT 56

FIRST PAGE OF A FORGED WILL (1 OF 2)
FBI FILE:12222-95-HQ-211845-BULKY-84—PAGE 14

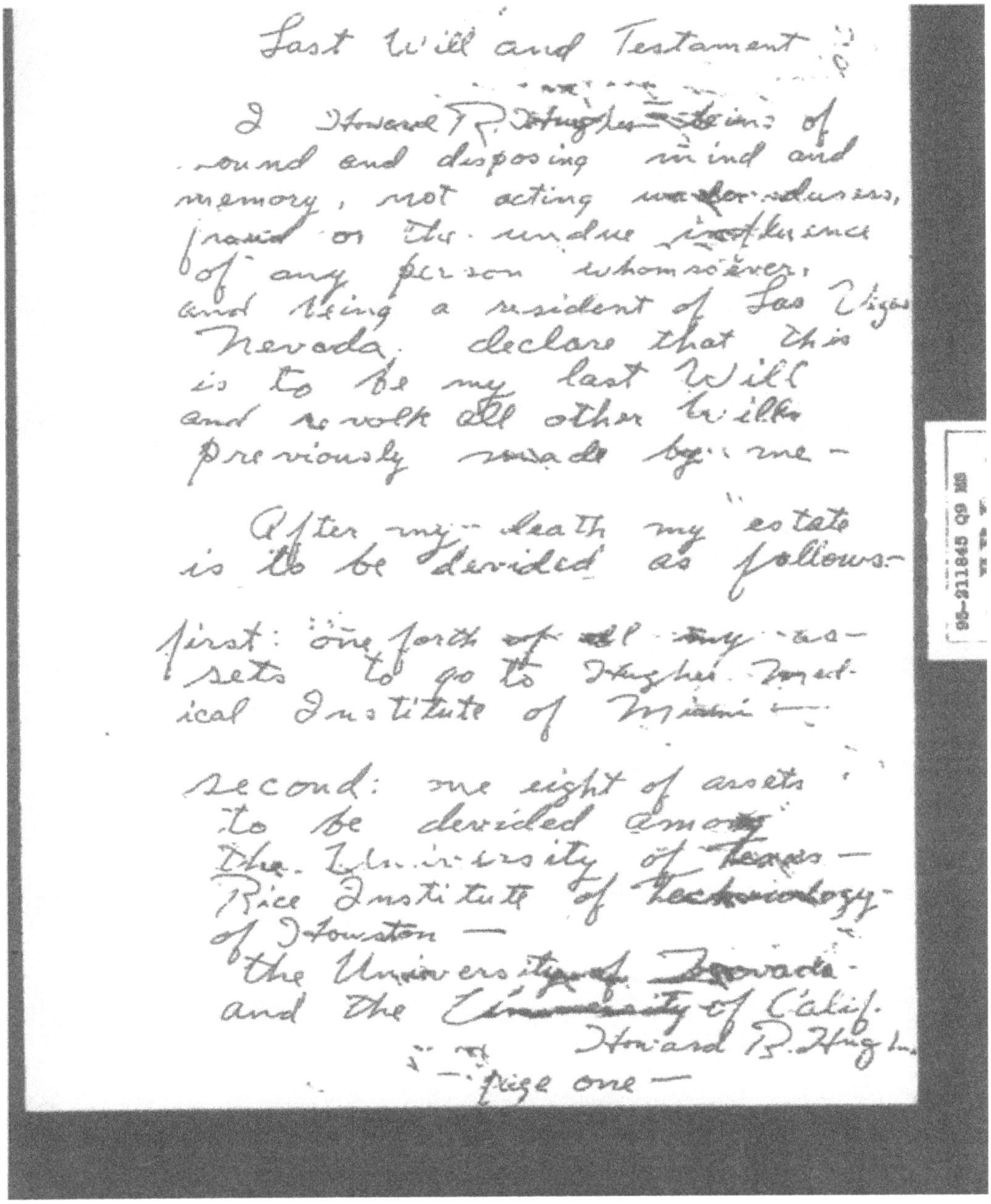
Last Will and Testament

I Howard R. Hughes being of
sound and disposing mind and
memory, not acting under duress,
fraud or the undue influence
of any person whomsoever.
and being a resident of Las Vegas
Nevada. declare that this
is to be my last Will
and revolk all other Wills
previously made by me —

After my death my estate
is to be devided as follows —

first: one forth of all my assets to go to Hughes Med-
ical Institute of Miami —

second: one eight of assets
to be devided among
the University of Texas —
Rice Institute of Technology
of Houston —
the University of Nevada
and the University of Calif.
Howard R. Hughes
— page one —

95-211845 Q9 MS

EXHIBIT 57

THIRD PAGE OF A FORGED WILL (2 OF 2)
FBI FILE:12222-95-HQ-211845-BULKY-84—PAGE 16

ninth: one sixteenth to be
devided amoung my
personal aids at the time
of my death -

tenth: one sixteenth to be
used as school scholarship
fund for entire Country -

the spruce goose is to be given
to the City of Long Beach, Calif -

the remainder of My
estate is to be devided among
the key men of the company's
I own at the time of my
death.

I appoint Noah Dietrich
as the executer of this will -

signed the 19 day of
March 1968

Howard R. Hughes

- page three -

95-211845 Q11 MS

CHAPTER VII

HOWARD HUGHES DOPPELGANGERS

Barlett and Steele, in their book *Empire* attempt to depict Howard as having "a cold relationship with machinery and none with people," perhaps in justification of their *lame* attempt to portray "Bahamian Howard" as the *real* Hughes (during the Clifford Irving conference call). How can they say that Hughes was simply lackadaisical and forgetful during the Irving conference call, when previously in *Empire* (page 142), they had lauded Howard's "prodigious memory" during the "Senator Brewster Hearings?"

Nowhere in *Empire* is it mentioned that there had been a "double" for Howard Hughes (i.e., Brooks Randell or anyone else) or that a doppelganger had ever been under the tutelage of Bob Maheu. Information collected recently and seen below in Exhibit 58 of a news article from page 60 in 32-HO-278 section 1, FBI File, indicates that there were several doubles used from time to time (with a *strong indication* that they were under the tutelage of Robert "Bob" Maheu.) As it turns out, the man investigator Russell found in his search for a "Brooks" Randell was, in reality, a "Brucks" Randell. The name "Brooks Randell" was erroneously used in so much of the Hughes literature researched that it was originally thought that the dead fellow they flew up from Acapulco, Mexico, was "Brooks." But, according to a newspaper interview with "Brucks" Randell in December, 1979 (Exhibit 58), it becomes probable that the fellow (who died in flight from Acapulco) may have been another bit actor by the name of "Vance Cooper or L. Wayne Rector." However, the research is ongoing.

Finally, to find "Brucks" Randall was indeed an achievement (thank you Russ). In checking out Brucks, Russ found him to have *an extensive criminal record* Exhibits 61-A, 61-B and Exhibit 63 below. However, this <u>would not</u> have excluded him from the job as these were the types of personnel Bob Maheu, Bill Gay, Chester Davis, and Nadine Henley most liked to do business with (for example, Mafia associates Johnnie Roselli and Sam Giancana, con man Johnnie Meier, etc.) We may eventually turn up Vance Cooper or L. Wayne Rector. (Exhibit 60-A and 60-B) One of them may well be the imposter in the Glenwood Cemetery, Houston, Texas – under eight feet of dirt, inside the <u>1,000 lb. sealed casket</u> inside that *stainless-steel vault, under that thick slab of concrete*. However, Brucks Randell's story concerning a "cryonics laboratory" (his not knowing what is now known concerning *questionable* fingerprinting and cursive writing) can only have been a best guess by a fellow who knew the personalities of those running the Hughes empire at the time. Brucks erroneously believed they planted the real Hughes corpse in Houston. It's pertinent to interject here that regarding Exhibit 62, that there was no need to have a double that could "write like Hughes" as the writings used in those many court cases <u>were not, in reality, known Hughes exemplars</u>. They most likely used a separate individual, other than the doppelganger, to forge documents. (Refresh in Chapter V1 and later in Chapter IX.)

Prior to 1965, and perhaps thereafter for a short while, Brucks Randell was simply a fellow con man, who had been used as a Hughes impersonator from time to time, and he had his suspicions about a 1976 corpse reputed to be that of Howard Hughes. The physiology of Howard Hughes, known to Charles in 1964 Mexico, could never have been stretched into the straightened dimensions of the fellow that arrived dead at the Methodist Hospital, in Houston, Texas, in 1976.

The information above and below gives a strong indication as to how Bob Maheu maneuvered himself into the driver's seat of the entire Hughes empire as "Hughes's right-hand man" by using covert knowledge and an "H.H." impersonator. It certainly seems credible now, and will seem more so later in this book, that under the guidance of Bob Maheu, the Summa, Inc. group used a double for several years before Hughes died (in 1965 *not* 1976). They then used that same imposter "Hughes" as part of a ploy to steal millions, up until the double himself died in 1976. Their control of the lookalike, and apparently the eventual enslavement of that poor soul, was achieved by using drugs. The "con" program progressed quite well for a few years as the pirates raided the Hughes companies. However, Maheu eventually became too egocentric and flamboyant a spendthrift for Bill Gay, Nadine Henley, and Chester Davis. They may have felt he would eventually blow their cover. Therefore, by devising a conspiracy within a conspiracy, they got control of the doppelganger "Hughes." They then got control of the forger (who was the writer of all those questionable documents supposedly written by Hughes), found an obliging judge, and with the use of a *forged* document got Maheu fired. Alas for Maheu, the tail no longer wagged the dog. The record shows that Maheu was madder than hell about *that* turn of events, but what could he do? If he were to tell the truth concerning the *imposter* "Hughes," he would have implicated himself in the *scam* from its beginning! (Immediately after firing Bob Maheu, the "Hughes" entourage began its multiple and secretive trips about the globe, staying far away from slick Bobby.) As for the imposter, he was probably provided with even more of the fun drugs he enjoyed, such as morphine, cocaine, heroin, etc. But it would be codeine* that the double would be pumped up with in his last few hours so that the pitiable corpse that arrived at Methodist Hospital in Houston would appear as the real Hughes. This was essential for the hoax to continue and to assure that the foxes were *not* caught in the chicken coop. The "Hughes" caretakers *must* come off as "Guardian Angels" instead of the Devils they really were.

*<u>**Note:**</u> Codeine was the drug agreed upon by Hughes and his personal friend, Doctor Vern Mason, after the XF-11 crash which had so irreparably damaged his body in 1946. Codeine was prescribed because of its less addictive nature and its ability to numb extreme pain. (Codeine is seldom the choice of addicts because it lacks the thrill of morphine, heroin, opioids, etc., although codeine does partially convert to morphine in the body.)

EXHIBIT 58

FBI FILE 32-HO-278-SECTION 1—PAGE 60
DESERT NEWS – NOVEMBER 20, 1979

A double for Hughes?

By James Bacon

HOLLYWOOD (NANA) — Howard Hughes was such a man of mystery that wild theories about his death will continue to crop up for centuries to come.

The latest one, as I reported last Friday, is that Howard Hughes did not die in Acapulco on April 5, 1976. Instead, it was Vance Cooper, a twin for Hughes who had acted as the billionaire's double since the 1940s.

That theory comes from Brucks Randell, who himself was once a double for Hughes. It is the basis of a screen treatment he sent to me and he claims he can prove every word.

"According to Randell, Hughes actually died on Nov. 16, 1970, and his body was frozen in a $100,000 cryonics lab the recluse had helped establish on a ranch he owned. When Cooper died in Acapulco, Randell asserts, Hughes' body was thawed out and was substituted for Cooper's in a Houston cemetery.

I told Brucks I thought his treatment interesting, but that I didn't believe it. I based this on several telephone conversations I had with Hughes since Nov. 12, 1970.

One, of course, was the famous televised press conference a good year later, in which Howard denounced the Clifford Irvinb book as a hoax. It was a denouncement that sent Irving to jail for claimin to have written Hughes' "autobiography."

The public saw only 20 minutes, at most, of that press conference on TV. It lasted two hours and 40 minutes. I was the only one on the panel of newsmen who knew Howard as a friend. The others were there because they represented major wire services and newspapers. A few had talked with Hughes after his famous world-circling flight of 1938.

Even before the press conference began, the late Dick Hanna put me on the phone at Howard's request.

**THE FOLLOWING EXHIBITS (59 THROUGH 61-B) ARE LETTERS OF DUE DILIGENCE
(PERTINENT ADDRESSES, E-MAILS AND PHONE NUMBERS, REDACTED FOR CONFIDENTIALITY.)**

EXHIBIT 59

Russ L. Russell

March 5, 2016

Mr. Brucks Randell
550-A Silverwood Avenue – Apt A
Upland, CA 91786

     Re: Conducting Research on Howard R. Hughes

Dear Mr. Randell:

We need your assistance.

A friend of mine, here in Henderson NV, is researching Howard R. Hughes. Several historical newspapers have mentioned your name in connection with someone who had "stood in" for Mr. Hughes on various occasions in the late 1950's-60's. Other newspaper articles mention "L. Wayne Rector," and "Vance Cooper" as individuals who performed the same role on other occasions.

If you are up to it, and can spare the time, my friend and I would very much like to talk with you regarding your knowledge of Howard Hughes. We can meet you at any place there in Upland, and would very much like to invite you to lunch or dinner during which time we can talk.

Please consider helping us in our research of Howard R. Hughes.

I look forward to your response. Your information will be very valuable to our research efforts.

Sincerely,

Russ L. Russell

EXHIBIT 60-A

Page 1

Russ L. Russell

January 23, 2017

Scott Eric Randell
1127 Brewster Drive
Pomona, CA 91767

Re: Asking Your Assistance in Interviewing Brucks Randell

Dear Mr. Randell:

We are very hopeful of your assistance and guidance on an important matter.

Several months ago I wrote to Brucks Randell, which I believe to be your father. As an associate of the late Howard Hughes we had some questions that he may be able to answer regarding Mr. Hughes. In the interim time period, we have been able to get many of our questions answered by other people acquainted with Mr. Hughes. For some reason, Mr. Brucks Randell did not respond to my letter.

Our current focus is on an individual known as "**L. Wayne Rector**." We believe that Mr. Brucks Randell has some information regarding Mr. Rector, and we just wish to ask him a couple of questions regarding that individual. We are having difficulty identifying Mr. Rector, and are hopeful that Mr. Brucks Randell possesses some information which will assist us.

I am very hopeful of your valuable assistance in arranging either a telephone call or personal visit wherein we could ask Mr. Brucks Randell a couple of questions, each regarding "**L. Wayne Rector**."

Additional Research has inferred that Brucks Randell is actually a Hollywood alias used by **Raymond Lee Black**. It would surely assist us if you could kindly confirm that information. If so, I could then shift part of my attention to the Black name, and personally advise you of my research information and success.

EXHIBIT 60-B

Page 2

Scott – I really need your help and I can assure you that information (and clarification) which I will uncover – will likewise assist you in a similar fashion.

Thank you very much, in advance, for your assistance in this matter.

Sincerely,

Russ L. Russell

Copies of this letter also mailed to:

1. Scott Eric Randell, 1429 Bonita Avenue, La Verne, CA 91750-5238
2. Scott Eric Randell, 805 Bradford Street, Pomona, CA 91767-4607
3. Scott Eric Randell, 2917 Hollander Street, Pomona, CA 91767-1529

Attachment: Copy of March 5, 2016 letter sent to Mr. Brucks Randell

EXHIBIT 61-A

FIRST PART OF RUSS LETTER

Laurence M. Russell

February 9, 2017

Archives and Records Center
222 North Hill Street, Room 212
Los Angeles, CA 90012

    Re: Research of Older Criminal case

Dear Sir/Madam:

I need some help and look to your office for advice and direction.

I am conducting some important research on a fellow who lived in Los Angeles in the 1950's.

The man was arrested and prosecuted in Los Angeles back in **1954/55** for Grand Theft, Conspiracy, and possibly another lessor crime. I am trying to locate all information regarding that 1954/55 Criminal Case.

Here's the information I know of:

    Defendant's Name: ***Raymond Lee Black***, aka *"**Brucks Randell**"*

                (most likely charged in 1954 under the <u>Randell</u> name)**

    Date of Birth: Either **June 30, 1929 or June 30, 1930**

He was charged (in March or later 1954   with at least **one felony count of Grand Theft** and **Conspiracy**, pled Guilty in 1955, and was sentenced to CA State Prison for two years (**San Quentin** is where he did his time). It is believed that he pled **"guilty"** to the charges sometime during possibly the first part of March, 1955.

This case was a little famous: It was known as the **Black Dahlia fraud case**. The Defendant solicited investments from people for a movie production that never took place.   (although someone else, unrelated, did eventually do a famous movie on the Black Dahlia case)

EXHIBIT 61-B

SECOND PART OF RUSS LETTER

I am hopeful that you can provide some help in locating this LA Superior Court criminal case file, and providing me with a copy of the **entire regular "Public Records" file for this case**.

I understand the reproduction costs are 50 cents a page. I have enclosed a blank check, made payable to Los Angeles Superior Court, "Not to exceed" $ 50 for reproduction costs.

I thank you in advance for your research and assistance in this important matter.

Please call me if you have any questions. (or email me, too).

Laurence M. Russell

EXHIBIT 62

ARIZONA REBULLIC NEWSPAPER (PHOENIX, ARIZONA)
MONDAY, JAN. 24, 1972 - PRINTED FEBRUARY 29, 2016

Ex-guard tells of hoax with Hughes

Associated Press

THOUSAND OAKS, Calif. — A man who once hired a character actor to double for Howard Hughes to fool newsmen says a similar trick may have been played on Clifford Irving, author of a purported Hughes autobiography. But Irving's attorney discounts the idea.

The man who says he hired the double — a fact confirmed by the Hughes organization — is former private detective Gerald C. Chouinard, who describes himself as the former head of Hughes' security staff.

As Hughes aged, "he wasn't as careful as he used to be," and tricksters could have learned detailed information for a purported Hughes autobiography by "bugging phones and taping conversations," Chouinard said.

Chouinard says he feels that persons close to Hughes could have hired an actor to meet with Irving and pretend he was Hughes. Chouinard said he hired actor Brucks Randell in 1957 and 1958 to impersonate Hughes.

In New York, Irving's attorney, Martin S. Ackerman, said yesterday in response to the report of a double such as Randell,

"Well, the question is, can Randell write, like Hughes, some 20 pages of writing and is he the kind of guy who would know the facts and circumstances surrounding Hughes. I cannot believe it."

But Chouinard said, "Even though I wasn't connected with Hughes the past few years, I was able to, without revealing how, keep track of him. I know just where he went, where he's been and how he's lived. It would be just impossible that Hughes has met with anybody like this writer."

A spokesman for Hughes Tool Co. confirmed that Chouinard was in charge of

Howard Hughes in 1955, at left; at right, bit actor Brucks Randell

some Hughes guards from 1950 to 1968 and at one time hired a Hughes double without the knowledge or approval of anyone in the Hughes organization.

Chouinard said he hired Randell to pose as Hughes and draw newsmen and others off the recluse's trail.

"I did this on my own incentive because I was afraid to ask Hughes' permission," Chouinard said. "At the time I felt he needed this, I was afraid he'd turn me down. We fooled the press. We fooled everybody.

"We never had to say this is Howard Hughes anywhere we went. We never

mentioned that name to anyone. We let people draw their own conclusion."

Once, he said, he and the actor rented a restaurant dining room on the condition that no one else be allowed in, then arrived with bodyguards in a chauffered limousine. Another time, he phoned a Las Vegas night club, said his friend wanted to see the show but would enter through the fire door after the lights went out, and asked that all tables near his be empty.

"Everyone just figured it was Hughes," said Chouinard. The actor, he said resembled Hughes in his younger

Warrant issued for woman in

EXHIBIT 63

Man Sentenced in Black Dahlia Film Scheme
Los Angeles Times (1923-Current File): Apr 14, 1955;
pg. 23

Man Sentenced in Black Dahlia Film Scheme

Brucks Randell, 38, Hollywood promoter who assertedly bilked several persons out of some $54,000 in an alleged scheme to produce a film of the Elizabeth (Black Dahlia) Short murder, yesterday drew two consecutive one-to-five-year sentences in State Prison.

Superior Judge Kenneth C. Newell in Pasadena imposed the sentences after rejecting a plea for clemency by Randell's attorney, Jack Hardy, who asserted that Randell hoped to make restitution.

"I doubt that Mr. Randell will be able to make restitution," said the judge, adding that the defendant did not merit special consideration in view of the fact that most of the money invested in his film venture represented the life savings of elderly persons and Randell had spent the money for his own purposes.

Randell previously had pleaded guilty to one count of grand theft and another of conspiracy to violate State corporation laws.

EXHIBIT 64-A

April 2, 1952. *United Press International* (Top Page)
November 20, 1952. *United Press International* (Bottom Page)
Also, photo section between pages 262 and 263 of the book *Empire*

After making a ringing denunciation of Communists in the movie industry to the Hollywood post of the American Legion, Hughes receives congratulations from Post Commander John D. Hone, April 2, 1952.
United Press International

Below: Trying to elude a photographer on November 20, 1952, after testifying in Los Angeles against Paul Jarrico, the screenwriter Hughes fired when he was subpoened to testify before the House Committee on Un-American Activities. *United Press International*

EXHIBIT 64-B

EXPANDED PHOTOS

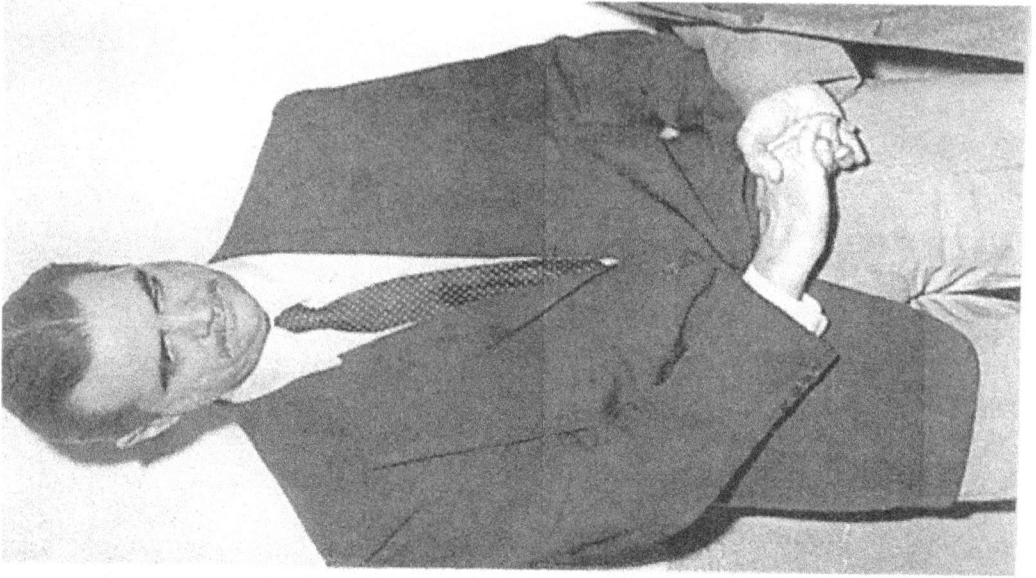

CRITIQUE ON EXHIBITS 64-A AND 64-B ABOVE

Something went wrong in the photo section above of the book *Empire* – wrong for Barlett and Steele and whoever employed them, that is. After 1976 United Press International willingly furnished the *two* photos of Howard Hughes, as per above and for the book *Empire* without closely analyzing their content. Barlett and Steele then had no alternative but to use the information and put the photos in their book. Had they *not* used the information provided, suspicions may well have arisen and the previous, and ongoing, scams could have been questioned and possibly exposed.

Of the two photos displayed in Exhibit 64-A, the top photo of "Hughes" is the "lookalike," having occurred in a less important setting (Hollywood Post of the American Legion, April 2, 1952). The bottom photo is that of the *real* Howard Hughes, taken when Hughes exited the House Committee on Un-American Activities (November 20, 1952). After viewing these two photos, Russ found an alternate source. The "cleaner" photos were then laid side-by-side into a copier and expanded. (Exhibit 64-B) This is what became apparent:

1. In the top photo "Hughes" is shaking hands. Hughes *never* shook hands with any-body. He believed that "Shaking hands is the best way in the world to transmit dis-ease." If there are any still alive who knew Howard Hughes as a friend, they would tell you this exact same thing "Howard never shook hands."

2. Because of the propaganda concerning Hughes, many believed that Hughes's refus-al to shake hands, as well as his preference for a reclusive lifestyle, were symptoms of mental illness. Of course, the Summa, Inc. thieves built on these two Hughes characteristics by citing other *supposed* aberrations of his personality. These en-hancements were categorically false. However, it allowed them the opportunity to steal with impunity and, as the money disappeared, blame the dwindling Hughes fortune on the indiscretions of a "crazy" Hughes. If you were to go to the Mayo Clinic's website, you would find articles on hygiene which talk in length about the importance of handwashing and teaching the practice to your children. As for Hughes's reclusive lifestyle, after 1954 he simply did not want to be viewed by a pitying public as his body began to bend and twist.

   a. The "shaking of hands" quote above is what Hughes had said to Charles when he refused a handshake in Old Mexico in 1964. In later years, it was remember-ing this characteristic that helped Charles identify that the Howard he had met in 1964 was the *real* Howard Hughes.

3. In the top photo, the head hair and eyebrows appear to be darker and thicker, and perhaps black, when compared to the bottom photo. The reason is that the real Howard Hughes had dark brown hair, as it seems to appear in the bottom photo. The top of the nose (in the top photo) is narrower and the eyebrows are closer together. Compare them with the bottom photo where the top of the nose is wider and, because of this, the brows are farther apart.

    a. Of course, these photos are in black and white, but even when we consider the darker skin tone in the top photo, the man's hair seems substantially darker when compared with the bottom photo.

    b. The skin color (top photo) is that of a fellow who gets out in the sun from time to time, whereas the lighter skin of Hughes in the bottom photo is that of a fellow who does not spend much time outside, or perhaps not at all. The reason for this is his physiology is beginning to change; he does not want to be seen in public.

4. The face in the bottom photo appears narrower, the top photo wider.

5. The nose appears more elongated in the top photo than in the bottom photo.

6. Nose in the top photo is wider in the nostril area than in the bottom photo.

7. The eyebrows in the top photo are straighter across. Hughes's eyebrows in the bottom photo have a curvature downwards to the sides of the eyes.

8. The chin is narrower in the top photo than in the bottom.

9. Distance between the eyebrows and hairline (bottom photo) is greater than the top. Even though these photos are better, by our source, they are still miniature when compared with the actual photos. Forensics could more readily point out the differences in these two photos if they had the originals to work with, expanding them up to life-size.

10. Charles and his wife own a tailoring shop, Newt's Tailoring in Henderson, Nevada, and the aspects below of clothing are easily picked out by them. Down through the years (15 years in the Henderson location alone), they have done all manner of men's and women's alterations. They *know* men's clothing and they know when it's right or wrong!

    a. The "Hughes" in the top photo wears a full dark suit.

b. Shoulders in the top photo (even though this fellow is wearing his coat) are considerably broader than the bottom photo. Hughes, in the bottom photo, has draped his coat over his shoulders, perhaps for coolness, even though it's November and one of the cooler months of the year. The reason for this is twofold:

1) not only is he cooler, but he is wearing an undergarment beneath his shirt to cover and help to hide what lies beneath,

2) by draping his coat over his shoulders, he has hidden a possible back brace because his physique is beginning to change, and he does not want the brace and it's covering to be obvious. In fact, this bottom photo was one of the last to have been taken of Howard Hughes before he dropped out of sight completely in 1954 and began his reclusive lifestyle.

c. Top "Hughes" wears a crisp, nicely ironed and well fitted shirt with cufflinks.

d. His shirt collar fits properly to his neck.

e. His tie is tightly tied in a small, neat, half-Windsor knot.

11. The bottom photo of Hughes was taken as he attempted to evade reporters coming out of the House Committee on Un-American Activities in 1952 only six months later than the top photo. He appears to be a bit tousled; but then, clothing-wise, he went into the committee wearing what he came out in. This would obviously be the real Hughes as it concerned screenwriter Paul Jerrico, a Hughes employee, who Hughes had fired upon receiving the committee's subpoena. This was a situation where only the *real* Hughes would have had all the answers. *This would definitely not be the job of even a well-schooled doppelganger*. In analyzing these two photos, we can be well assured that the bottom photo is that of the *real* Hughes. A doppelganger would *only* be substituted for negligible gatherings and meetings. But even this ended in 1954 when all face-to-face meetings, photos, and get-togethers with the real Hughes – or a double – stopped.

The real Howard Hughes, for all practical purposes, vanished from the limelight (if indeed the world is a stage). It's realistic to presume that Hughes's stature had already begun making its unbecoming transformation into the way Charles saw him, ten years later in 1964. It's also reasonable to believe that after all the remarkable accomplishments of his life, Hughes chose not to be visible to world, as his body began to bend and twist. Some might call it shame, others vanity, but Charles eventually saw Howard's decision as a practicality which would let him live his tragic waning years in relative peace – or at least a comparative peace with which to deal as best he could with his tragically progressive deforming body. It's entirely convincing that the *real* Howard Hughes is the fellow in the bottom photo, and he looks disheveled for reasons listed below.

a. The shirt is extra-large; the collar-size is too big. The arm sleeves are large and blousy. It would be difficult to find an extra-large shirt with the appropriate collar size for him. What necessitates the extra-large shirt is a possible body brace. (His spine is beginning to fold and soon he will no longer be able to hide it.) Therefore, the shirt must be large enough, not only to cover the brace but to cover a thick garment over it which helps to conceal the ridges of the brace. (*This is a very heavy man's shirt* and the collar size may well be 22 inches in circumference.)

b. Howard Hughes was *never* fat. Eighteen years earlier at 6 feet 3 inches tall, he only weighed 160 pounds. (See known Exhibits 35 and 36.) When one considers that a 5-foot 8-inch fellow weighing 160 pounds is *not* fat, the real Hughes in the bottom photo appears quite portly. The likely explanation is that a back brace extends downward to and over the hips and extends upward to just under the arms. Also, for this reason his shoulders seem out of proportion with the rest of his body. His pant-waist is uniformly *large* as well, which would compensate for the body hardware beneath. Soon after the bottom photo was taken (November of 1952) Howard Hughes effectually became a well-hidden "ghost."

12. In doing the above analysis, it is important to keep in mind that these photos were taken *less than seven months apart!* Some might say that both photos look alike, and they would be correct, but then isn't this the purpose of a doppelganger? If they did not look similar what would be the point? Consider this. A doppelganger, for one of the world's wealthiest men, *must* meticulously look the part! These *are not* photos of the same man and if forensics were to get a hold on the original photos, expanding them up to life size, the differences would be even *more* obvious.

Barlett and Steele's implication that "Howard Hughes probably never employed a double" seems a bit lame at this point – much like their weak explanation as to why "Bahamian Hughes" could only answer correctly *two* out of *seven* questions asked by reporters in the Clifford Irving conference call hoax?

We can no longer be assured that the book *Empire* was constructed as merely a book on the life and times of Howard Hughes. What has become obvious is that the book *Empire* has been, and continues to be, *a cover for a huge hoax which continues to this very day.*

Let's close in on the above as best we can. I will cite two incidents here and they will be valid no matter to which political party you belong. At the time this exposé is being written, the previous Secretary of State, Hillary Clinton, is in the forefront of the Democratic run for the Presidency. But for her there is most certainly broken glass in the grease intended to slide her into the White House. She used a *personal* server to negotiate government business while Secretary of State and then attempted to lie her way out of it – a definite "no-no" for any government official. (Central Intelligence Agency [CIA] Director David Petraeus was fired and almost went to prison for *far less* careless handling of government documents – and there are many others.)

When Hillary was caught, she attempted to have her private-server information cleaned instead of handing it over intact to those who wished to know why she would do such a thing in the first place. And then there was Lois Learner of the IRS, who marched out of her congressional hearing refusing to testify further while claiming "I did nothing wrong." But Lois and her employees were caught targeting groups that didn't feel right about the government spending their children and grandchildren into bankruptcy. (Do not be deluded into believing that these are just unfounded right-wing conspiracies, one would be hard pressed to make this stuff up.) Oh yeah, Learner's server got sick and crashed, losing all its information, which furthered even more concern about what the agency had been up to.

The argument to be made is that the deliberate hiding of pertinent information can be just as detrimental to the truthfulness and integrity of an individual as outright wrongdoing. *This certainly applies to the credibility of the <u>post 1965</u> portions the book "Empire", which was written as a documentary.* The book *Empire* also seems *overly demeaning* concerning here-say information attributed to Hughes. It seems that decisions were made that caused Howard Hughes to look bad at every opportunity (most especially the imposter "Hughes" *after* 1965).

As indicated earlier and to be further reiterated below, there is a vacuum of important information in the book *Empire* <u>after</u> 1965. Also, as mentioned earlier, *Empire* has been lauded as a composite of the most verifiable history of the life and times of Howard Hughes, Jr. A*nd it is* <u>however, not after 1965</u>. The re-publication of this same book as *Howard Hughes: His Life and Madness*, is *also* <u>devoid</u> of the same information which concerns us most. Why is it that *<u>only after 1965</u>* the books information goes awry? *Was there something to hide? Were there those who were paid to hide it?*

It almost seemed to be a passing thought in Barlett and Steele's *Empire* to maintain that "Hughes probably never employed a double to impersonate him." Now, why was that so important to imply? Consider this: a fellow known to Charles only as "Howard" in Old Mexico in 1964, befriends and helps him out of a perilous situation. On the following day, he informs Charles that he has put a letter in his backpack and "It won't mean much to you now, but will in the future, so don't lose it." But fortunately, or unfortunately, it becomes lost. Later in life Charles realizes that, from the characteristics of the man and the experiences that man had revealed to him, that his friend "Howard" had been none other than the reclusive billionaire Howard Robard Hughes, Jr.

There were <u>four</u> major problems to solve for Bill Gay, Chester Davis, Robert Maheu, and Nadine Henley (Hughes's *former* trusted lieutenants) so they could steal a lion's share of the Hughes estate with impunity.

FIRST PROBLEM TO SOLVE:

Knowing that Howard Hughes would soon be dead and that there was no will in which they were included and no golden parachutes provided them by Howard Hughes, the original Summa-trio of Gay, Davis, and Henley needed a way to secure the maximum amount of time possible to embezzle hundreds of millions of dollars from the Hughes estate after his death in 1965. It was imperative that they hire a fellow skilled in the art of money laundering. (They found him in Sam Giancana, mob friend of Bob Maheu.) Also, it was important to make it look like the money was misspent or lost because of a still living, but *derelict*, Howard Hughes. This included worthless mining claims, interest free loans never repaid, overpayment for ads run in a local Las Vegas newspaper, various Hughes companies losing millions of dollars both stateside and offshore, Robert Maheu arbitrarily spending millions of dollars, and, of course, God only knows what Bill Gay, Nadine Henley, and Chester Davis had embezzled and squirreled away in various offshore accounts from 1954 and forwards to 1976.

SECOND PROBLEM TO SOLVE:

That there <u>were</u> doubles used to portray Hughes is a given. Now what the Hughes estate pirates needed after 1965 was a doppelganger who could be controlled and manipulated at their discretion. To date, we propose that the double is buried in the Hughes plot, but we do not know exactly *who* the Hughes double was. Brucks Randell was not that double since he was alive in 1979 when he gave his story to the *Desert News*. (From many articles eventually found, concerning Brucks Randell, it appears obvious that Brucks had indeed been a double for Hughes and that it was newsman James Bacon of the *Desert Sun* who had the wool pulled over his eyes early on in the "Bahamian Hughes"-Irving conference call.) Also, additional information gained in various searches indicate that L. Wayne Rector and a fellow named Vance Cooper had also been used as doubles for Hughes. With what is now known, it is reasonable to believe that it's either Wayne or Vance who is buried in Hughes' family-plot in Houston, Texas.

From the information above it seems apparent that Hughes's lieutenants *did* use lookalikes as per the claims of various writers and newspaper articles, one of which was found in the FBI files. (Exhibits 58 and 62) The indication from this news clippings is that they used *several* doubles for Hughes, <u>with his knowledge,</u> prior to his death in <u>1965</u>. Also likely is that a double, used previously, was also used after the death of Howard Hughes (1965) and *up until* 1976 when the imposter died. (Exhibit 22: FBI File) If *Brucks* Randell and the others could be found after spending a lot of time looking for a *Brooks* Randell, why was it so difficult for Barlett and Steele to find and enter these observations in *their* book? They were the ones with first-hand information. Their statement in *Empire*, "There probably never was a double for Howard Hughes," is an obvious gloss over and lends credibility to the belief that it was done in compliance with whoever it was that employed them, paid them well, and provided them with the abundant Hughes documents for their publication. (Will Lummis?)

THIRD PROBLEM TO SOLVE:

Secure total control of their doppelganger accomplice from 1965 forward. How? *Drugs!*

FOURTH PROBLEM TO SOLVE:

Gather and destroy all known cursive documents written by Howard Hughes from all Hughes's domiciles and business locations from *prior* to 1965. It seems that the felonious parties involved had a great deal of money to gain if these documents were found and destroyed. There are probably papers in Hughes's handwriting still in existence. They may turn up. However, for now they are not available. (See Chapter VI.) Hence the fourth problem was solved for those who betrayed Hughes and exploited one of the world's great fortunes. They had clandestinely eliminated any true <u>legitimate</u> cursive documents to compare the forgeries with. The letter given Charles by his friend Howard <u>would have proved that the documents used by Rosemont Enterprises, Inc. in their numerous court cases were forgeries</u>. The use of questionable exemplars and phony documents in the courtroom to prove their cases against Clifford Irving, Melvin Dummar, and others was an example of gross stupidity and incompetence. We know that Clifford Irving and Melvin Dummar were frauds, yet their own *fraudulent documents* are what brought their scams into the light. It boggles the mind that <u>their own attorneys</u> didn't know the difference between a questionable and a known exemplar. (It can be safely presumed that Clifford Irving had the "Howard Hughes" document forger temporarily in his employ; but the phony bank account in Switzerland led to his downfall (more on Irving later in Chapter IX). Melvin Dummar and his "Mormon Will" scam also jumped on the wagon. He and his duplicitous crew attempted to create the phony "Mormon Will" using previous *fraudulent* writings (see Chapter VI.)

The documentation in Chapter VI proved that there were **no** <u>credible known documents</u> cursively written by Howard Hughes after 1965. This means that any documentation used by Rosemont Enterprises, Inc., or any other party, to prove *anything* truly factual concerning Howard Hughes <u>after</u> 1965 is false. This also applies to documents predating 1965, An *extensive* collective exemplar can only become such if there is are *extensive* known exemplars with which to compare it. Neither the Irving camp nor Rosemont Enterprises, Inc. had such a document. Oh, they had some Hughes signatures, which had been forged many times down through the years, and they had Barbara Thackery's bar pad (also "iffy" but just in time to be used by the Clifford Irving hoaxers). However, attorneys for Rosemont Enterprises, Inc., the Irving camp, and Melvin Dummar <u>could never reveal</u> that the exemplars used by their opposing camps were <u>unverified</u>. To do so *would have delegitimized the exemplars each were using*! It seems the judges had overlooked this as well. (Refresh with Chapter VI.)

See Exhibits 64-C and 64-D that follow from Albert Gerber's book *Bashful Billionaire* and Exhibit 64-E, James Phelan's book *Howard Hughes: The Hidden Years*. These Exhibits clearly describe Rosemont Enterprises, Inc. and who put it together when it was formed in 1965. In and out of court numerous times after 1965, Rosemont, Inc. had not used or acquired a single known cursive exemplar in Howard Hughes's handwriting. Does is seem plausible that they could not find even a tiny known exemplar written before or after 1965? Could it be that Rosemont, Inc. itself destroyed all Hughes documents it could find or that disingenuous others took on the task for financial and nefarious reasons? Howard Hughes knew how to write; he gave Charles a hand-written exemplar in 1964. There had to have been numerous other documents Hughes had cursively written through the years – documents that had been notarized by officers of various courts throughout the land. *None* of the extensive documents in the possession of Rosemont, Inc. and supposedly written by Howard Hughes were known exemplars. They were, simply, collective forgeries bandied about in numerous courtrooms by Rosemont Enterprises, Inc. as known documents. Yes, questionable documents purported to be known documents when they were nothing of the sort! Well, guess what? It's believed that there still are extensively written Howard Hughes documents in existence and, if Russ can find them, they will be entered in this case study. If Russ cannot find them, maybe it is time for the federal boys to re-evaluate what they have.

An important thing to point out here is that there is absolutely no mention of Rosemont Enterprises, Inc. in Barlett and Steele's book *Empire*. In that huge 766-page book, you will not find a single reference to Rosemont Enterprises, Inc. Only one of two things could explain this omission: 1) Their source for the abundant material included in their book failed to reveal this information, or 2) They were told to omit it!

EXHIBIT 64-C

Okay, Howard was definitely a ladies' man, and the ladies he dated had nothing less than glowing words with which to describe those encounters. However, the remarks below concerning "the girls" and "Jean Peters" infer that Hughes was alive, unfaithful, and doing business as usual. This was all untrue, except for Rosemont Enterprises, Inc. and when it was established. (1965-66, dates vary in Exhibits.)

Howard Hughes and His Biographers   321

"I don't believe it," Stuart said flatly.

Bautzer said that Goodman could have access to never-before-made-public corporate records. He listed other material that would be made available.

"How about Hughes himself?"

"Nothing doing," said Bautzer.

Nevertheless, before the two men parted Bautzer agreed that he would relay to Hughes the proposition that Hughes answer, in writing, a variety of questions. There would be three sets of questions, and finally, a face to face confrontation for a one hour interview. Everything could be discussed "except the girls."

Bautzer was firm about the girls. He explained that Jean Peters got upset when she read about the girls. Howard simply didn't want to upset her.

Stuart agreed to consult with his author. "I'll give him the opportunity because he's the one who has to gather the material. But I might as well tell you now that I'm against the offer."

"Fire your best shot," Bautzer said. "Think about it and I'll be in touch with you."

Before the two men parted Stuart happened to mention that Goodman and he had labeled the book "project X." This brought a surprised laugh from Bautzer who said that quite coincidentally, he and Hughes had named the Stuart-Goodman book "project X" and referred to it that way in phone calls and memos!

Some weeks later there was a conference in the Emerson home. Goodman had been flown from California and was Bautzer's guest at the St. Regis hotel in Manhattan. He was accompanied by his attorney. Stuart's attorney, Martin J. Scheiman, was present. Also attending was Perry Lieber, a former Hughes press agent who was still linked to the Hughes organization though serving a major film company as his full-time job.

The conference was unsuccessful. Stuart wasn't buying.

As it later turned out, Goodman was very much of a mind to sell.

Next, either Hughes or his representatives concocted a unique device to block the biography. In September, 1965, a company known as Rosemont Enterprises, Inc., was formed. The officers and directors of the new corporation consisted of three people: Maynard H. Montrose, president and a director (he was also senior vice-president of the Hughes Tool

EXHIBIT 64-D

The following is information on Rosemont Enterprises, Inc., including how it was formed, when it was formed, and by whom it was formed. It was difficult to come up with dates of Incorporation, but all dates (above and below) are within the timeframe of how long Howard told Charles he would live when they met in 1964. In late October or early November of 1964, Howard told Charles, "The Doctors have only given me eight months to live."

322   *Bashful Billionaire*

Company); Chester S. Johnson, vice-president (also a retired officer of Toolco); and Chester C. Davis, secretary-treasurer and a director (long-time attorney for Hughes personally and for Hughes Tool Company). These three individuals owned all of the stock of Rosemont.

Why "Rosemont?" There was a Rosemont Enterprises doing business in New York. A fellow named Norman Rosemont managed theatrical people, including Robert Goulet. But when Hughes wanted something, nothing could stand in his way. Rosemont sold the right to his corporate name.

The new company qualified to do business in New York and in California. In New York its office was located at 120 Broadway, which just happened to be the office of Attorney Chester C. Davis. The address of the California office was 1700 Ventura Boulevard, Encino, California. All of the furniture in the latter office was the property of Hughes Productions—a division of Hughes Tool Company which just happened to occupy a neighboring suite in the same building. All of the employees in the California office, in fact, worked for Hughes Productions. There is no question that Rosemont Enterprises, Inc., was simply a corporate tool of the Hughes empire.

The incorporation, although purporting to be dated July 2, 1965, apparently really took place in September of that year, which presented something of a legal problem because they needed a contract to predate the incorporation.

Shortly thereafter Rosemont Enterprises, Inc., entered into a contract with Howard Hughes in which Hughes purportedly granted to Rosemont Enterprises the *exclusive* right to use, publish, write, etc., the name, personality, likeness, biography, life story, and incidents relating thereto of Howard R. Hughes. The contract is dated before the company was incorporated.

The formation of the corporation and the signing of the contract were bald-faced legal maneuvers designed to allow entry into court with the statement, "Here, your Honor, I have the exclusive rights to all of the information about Howard Hughes and anybody who writes a biography is violating my contract."

In addition, there is a significant subsidiary purpose. Hughes always tried to avoid bringing legal actions on his own, because as the plaintiff he would subject himself to examination in pretrial depositions, could be made to appear in court, leave himself open to cross-examination, and in general become liable to suffer all of the personal vicissitudes of litiga-

EXHIBIT 64-E

Here we have unknowledgeable writers and newspersons busily putting words in a dead man's mouth, while Monty Montrose, Chester Davis, and Chester A. Johnson all knew that Howard Hughes never gave them the authority to form the entity known as Rosemont, Inc.

Foreword xiii

boundaries of the United States, beyond the reach of the law.

This nation deposed, in a single administration, a Vice-President and a President. But in a quarter-century it was not able to force Hughes to show up in court, give a sworn deposition, or appear before any governmental agency. No one could subpoena or arrest an invisible man.

Journalists faced a similar problem. How could one report on a man no one could see? They were impelled to try because many of his secrets affected the citizenry and their government and hence belonged in the public domain.

Hughes wanted nothing written about him that he could not control. To gratify his wish, Hughes's chief counsel, Chester Davis, invented in 1966 a contrivance called Rosemont Enterprises, Inc.

Davis maintained that Rosemont owned "sole and exclusive right to use or publish [Hughes's] name, likeness, personality, life story, or incidents therein."

"The publication of any story about Mr. Hughes," he went on, "would appear to invade such rights, even if the matters therein are assumed to be factually accurate." This was the ultimate act of secrecy and acquisition, to own and keep from others the facts of his life.

One night at dinner in Greenwich Village Davis explained this to me as "the Joe DiMaggio bat theory."

"If you are going to put out a bat with Joe DiMaggio's name on it," Davis declared, "you have to get DiMaggio's permission and pay DiMaggio a royalty."

Because books, unlike baseball bats, are protected by the First Amendment to the U.S. Constitution, Davis's contention has been rejected by every court in which Rosemont has pressed its claim. Yet Davis's firm still writes what the publishing industry has come to term the "Don't You Dare" letter. Although legally absurd, this book-aborting device is not wholly ineffective. The mere prospect of having to go to court against the well-financed Hughes attorneys discourages marginal publishers reluctant or unable to finance a court fight even though they are certain of winning it.

The core, the *sine qua non* of the Secrecy Machine in Hughes's

It is appropriate to move on now. However, more evidence concerning the above will come to light in the following chapters.

CHAPTER VIII

A SHORT CHAPTER
"BEHIND THE BLINDS"

The Price of Their Souls should have generated more activity and investigations on behalf of law enforcement than it did. The reasons it did not were fourfold:

1. The first reason is obvious. The original Summa, Inc. pirates spent millions to cloak their activities – literally brainwashing the news media and whoever else might possibly have questioned the ruse.

2. The Hughes lieutenants had to release some information or people would soon question why the Hughes companies were losing millions around the world. Tactfully they hid the scam under the public's noses using an imposter. Although they were extremely careful to keep the pretender out of sight, they discreetly leaked little nuggets of information, such as how "Hughes" went around nude much of the time, urinating in glass containers and storing them in various areas of his Desert Inn Penthouse; how he let his hair and nails grow to unsightly lengths; how he wrote strange notes as to how best to make a cheese sandwich and what kind of ice cream he liked, etc. Most were preposterous stories that, for lack of anything else, were accepted and proliferated throughout the media.

3. The conspirators had connections which allowed them to bribe a predominant news source in Las Vegas, Nevada, which other news sources relied on for information. Whatever their desires, benign or cruel, the public wanted to know about one of the world's greatest industrialists, including his exploits or downfall.

4. They may well have murdered those they could not deceive, control, or buy. Chapter X contains information on *two* known murders and *four* strong possibilities. Perhaps it's a bit too speculative to suggest that Dr. Vern Mason may have been among those mentioned in this book's Chapter X scenario, but it's certainly not outside the realm of possibility. Below is what we know:

   A. Dr. Vern Mason was Howard's personal friend and whose medical expertise Howard claimed "saved his life" after the crash of the XF-11 in Beverly Hills. Mason <u>conveniently</u> dies in 1965, allegedly from complications caused by ventricular fibrillation. At the same time, Chester Davis and "Monty" Montrose are busy setting up Rosemont Enterprises, Inc. As already mentioned, the purpose of Rosemont, Inc. was to control *all letters,* photos, and biographical material of Howard Hughes. It may be true that Howard had few friends. However, it has often been said that "he who has *many* friends has no *true* friends." Rest assured that Howard chose his friends wisely. Dr. Vern had been Howard's *personal* physician and friend since the early 1920s and, over a thirty-year time span, both he and Howard had talked many times about setting up a medical institution and the implications therein. This idea became a reality in 1954 when Vern Mason became the first chairman of the Howard Hughes Medical Institute's board in Miami, Florida – a position which he held until his death in 1965.

In looking at Dr. Vern Mason's profile below, we now know that Howard and Vern were not just friends, but the best of friends, and we can be assured that Dr. Vern was a man of principle and *not* one who would sell out a friend at any price. Vern Mason had to have known all along about Howard's debilitating physiology. It's likely Mason was the doctor who supplied Howard with various pain drugs through the years and was one of the doctors who had informed Howard that he only had eight months to live in 1964. (From the 1950s on, the slow, relentless, collapsing of Howard's spine and the crushing of his internal organs had to have been increasingly and wretchedly more painful as the weight of his upper torso continued to press down upon them. It stands to reason that Howard would have needed to increase his pain medications to have had any type of a life at all. In short, with Howard Hughes's death in 1965, Rosemont Enterprises, Inc. had the perfect opportunity to activate their scam. But if Dr. Mason had he been alive in 1965, he would have stood in the way. <u>He knew the truth about Howard</u> and would have exposed the scam! Rosemont, Inc. *could never have been created while Dr. Vern Mason was still alive.*

B. At its conception, Rosemont Enterprises, Inc. was quasi-legal at best. However, this ploy enabled Bill Gay, Chester Davis, Nadine Henley, Bob Maheu, and their minions, to slow down enquiries and even stop investigations by using threats backed by the immense wealth of the Hughes empire. Investigations were stopped cold *when clues were fresh*. Rosemont, Inc. served its purpose well, even though it was declared unlawful later. "The public had a right to know." Most interesting to Charles, of course, was that the first thing Rosemont, Inc. wanted to control were "any letters." (Much more on Rosemont Inc. later in Chapter IX.)

There were sundry problems in the gaining of information on Vern Mason; but finally, Russ discovered the "metal" of the man. (Profile and Death – Exhibits 65-A and B.) What is now known is that Dr. Mason had a distinguished track record as a physician and military man and that he retained his position as CEO of the Hughes Medical Institute until his death in 1965. (1965, an ominous year.)

EXHIBIT 65-A

PROFILE: COLONEL VERN R. MASON, MD (1889 -1965)

Vern received his B.S. from University of California, Berkeley in 1911 and M.D. Phi Bata Kappa from Johns Hopkins Medical School in 1915. He held the following positions at Johns Hopkins from 1915 to 1921: Intern, Assistant Resident Physician, Resident Physician, Assistant in Disease. The most important of his publications was a landmark article in the *Journal of the American Medical Association (JAMA)* on "Sickle Cell Anemia" (*JAMA* 1922; 79:1318-1320), in which he named the disease and described its cause. Lucy M. Ginn, RN (Ginny) married Vern in August of 1921 in Winchester, Virginia. They moved to Los Angeles, California, and he went into private practice as an internist and became a noted diagnostician. He was appointed Professor of Medicine at University of Southern California School of Medicine in 1922, where he initiated resident training at Los Angeles County Hospital. He held this position until his retirement. In 1956, he was appointed "Emeritus Clinical Professor of Medicine." Howard R. Hughes and Vern's association as physician and friend began in the early 1920s. Their discussions of a medical institute and its implications went on for thirty years before Howard decided to make it a reality in 1954. In 1955 Vern became the first Chairman of the Howard Hughes Medical Institute's Advisory Board, a position he held until his death in 1965. Vern served 20 months in the American Expeditionary Forces (AEF) in France in World War I (WWI) and 64 months in World War II (WWII) as consultant in internal medicine in the 9th Corp Area. The latter consisted of supervising the performance of all the Army hospitals in the nine western states (July 1942 through April 1945). He was assigned to the Pacific Ocean Area (April 1945 thru Sept. 1945), where he performed the same duties as in the 9th Corp Area. On September 15, 1945, he was assigned responsibility for selecting and leading a team of medical investigators to gather information of the effects of the A-bomb on Hiroshima. This investigation lasted until December 1945. From February 1946 through May 1946, he worked with the Hiroshima and Nagasaki medical team members at the Army Institute of Pathology in Washington, D.C., to generate reports requested by the military from the information they had gathered from the first use of the Atomic Bomb. The reports were not completed when he left the service in May 1946 to return to his medical practice. He received two combat stars in WWI. In WWII he was awarded three stars, a bronze star, and a Good Conduct Medal. He was wounded at Okinawa and left the service as a full Colonel.

It appears that Dr. Mason died *mysteriously* in Miami, Florida, in 1965. The word "mysteriously" is used because it's only known *when* he died and what he supposedly died of; *there are no autopsy records available, no newspaper obituaries, and no police report.* Mason's death certificate (Exhibit 65) states he died "11-16-65" and was cremated only two days later 11-18-65. We have yet to uncover evidence of a ceremony (unusual for a high-profile dignitary such as Colonel Vern Mason, MD, and CEO of the multimillion-dollar Howard Hughes Medical Institute in Miami, Florida since 1955).

Also, it should be mentioned here that when a supposed "Hughes" arrived dead in Houston, Texas, in 1976, Hughes's Aunt Anette Lummis, his Nephew Will Lummis, and the "Hughes care team," all wanted the corpse immediately cremated – no autopsy, no photos, and no fingerprints. However, this was not done due to the legality involved. (More on this in Autopsy Chapter XI.)

EXHIBIT 65-B

CERTIFICATE OF DEATH: VERNE RHEEN MASON

The first five digits of the decedent's Social Security Number has been redacted pursuant to §119.071(5), Florida Statutes.

,State Registrar

Date Issued: **December 3, 2019**
REQ: 2021080599

WARNING: THE ABOVE SIGNATURE CERTIFIES THAT THIS IS A TRUE AND CORRECT COPY OF THE OFFICIAL RECORD ON FILE IN THIS OFFICE. THIS DOCUMENT IS PRINTED OR PHOTOCOPIED ON SECURITY PAPER WITH WATERMARKS OF THE GREAT SEAL OF THE STATE OF FLORIDA. DO NOT ACCEPT WITHOUT VERIFYING THE PRESENCE OF THE WATERMARKS. THE DOCUMENT FACE CONTAINS A MULTICOLORED BACKGROUND, GOLD EMBOSSED SEAL, AND THERMOCHROMIC FL. THE BACK CONTAINS SPECIAL LINES WITH TEXT. THE DOCUMENT WILL NOT PRODUCE A COLOR COPY.

CERTIFICATION OF VITAL RECORD

CHAPTER IX

ROSEMONT ENTERPRISES, INC.

One of the most comprehensive and in-depth books ever written about the life and times of Howard Hughes was *Empire* by Donald L. Barlett and James B. Steele. (Please pardon the replication here, but it helps to clarify the case.) It was amazing how these two men managed to research, compile, and put into bookstores their exhaustive 766-page book in little more than two years after "Hughes's supposed death in 1976." (These were the days before "Print on Demand", the advanced computer technology we enjoy today.) Even more amazing is that several of the extensive FBI's files concerning Rosemont, Inc.'s legal activities in the Clifford Irving "H.H." biography hoax and the Melvin Dummar "Mormon Will" scam *are not mentioned once* in this supposedly all-encompassing documentary of Hughes. Of course, the hoaxes are but *Rosemont, Inc. is not*. And yet there are extensive articles (Bulky FBI files and legal documents – literally reams of documentation) that mention Rosemont Enterprises, Inc. Why wasn't Rosemont, Inc. mentioned?

References to sources of the information presented below are annotated in [brackets] to indicate in which appendix it appears at the end of this book.

It's important to take a *hard* look at Rosemont Enterprises, Inc., who they were, and what they did, and their amazingly successful deception regarding Howard Hughes after 1965. There were extensive FBI files regarding Rosemont, so it's surprising that Bartlett and Steele never mentioned Rosemont Enterprises, Inc. in their massive documentary *Empire*.

Initially, it was not generally known that Rosemont, Inc. had been set up in July 1965 by Chester Davis. Davis was its Attorney, Secretary, and Treasurer and Maynard E. <u>Montrose</u> was its President. (The new company's name, "Rosemont," was created by simply transposing the syllables of Montrose's name.) M. E. Montrose was also a Vice-President of Hughes ToolCo, Inc. Rosemont's singular purpose was to control all <u>letters, photos, and biographic materials</u> regarding Howard Hughes (supposedly at the behest of Howard Hughes himself). The information presented here and below are but a fraction of the lawsuit activity concerning Rosemont, Inc.

Important clues are glossed over by Barlett and Steele in *Empire*. Maynard E. Montrose is loosely mentioned in the book [Appendix B-73]. On page 368 he's merely "Monty' Montrose." In the index, he's simply "Montrose, M. E." [Appendix

B-74] Nothing appears in *Empire* about Rosemont Enterprises, Inc. – *the date it was formed, who put it together, or why it was established.* The same holds true for a re-publication of *Empire* as *Howard Hughes: His Life and Madness.*

Question: If you are now considering the possibility that *Howard Hughes did die in 1965,* would it have been possible to set up Rosemont Enterprises, Inc. while his honorable and trusted friend Dr. Vern Mason was still alive? We did not fully understand who Dr. Vern Mason was, his relationship with Hughes, or how he had died in 1965 when this investigation began. This knowledge, along with much more, was a startling slap of reality when our super-sleuth "Russ" dug up the following.

ROSEMONT ENTEPRISES, INC.
DOCUMENTS

There were *hundreds* of pages accumulated by the FBI on Howard Hughes and activities related to him. Only a small portion of these documents have been used here to make our case. (Activities involving Rosemont Enterprises, Inc. and Howard Hughes can be found in the 297-page federal file 12222-0-87-HQ-119739-BULKY-19. There were numerous other incidents that Rosemont was involved in that were not entered into this file.) Also, in the 70's and prior to that, the photocopying and keeping of archives by federal agents were not as sophisticated as they are today. Much has improved with today's advanced computer technologies.

CLIFFORD IRVING

The Clifford Irving hoax concerning Howard Hughes is probably one of the best known. In the beginning, Irving probably thought he could stir up some newsworthy activity by claiming Hughes had retained him as his biographer. After all, it would have been the coup of the century to get Howard Hughes (the mysterious and reclusive billionaire) to reveal himself and repudiate the claim. Not knowing Irving's underlying plan, we can still make an educated guess to his thinking. Let us suppose Hughes quickly countered Irving's claim before any money had changed hands. Irving was probably prepared to claim, "Who the hell was that guy who *set me up* claiming to be Howard Hughes?" Let us suppose further (and this is only supposition) that as Irving continued working on the book, Hughes still showed no signs of surfacing to deny Irving's claim.

It is possible that because almost everyone was accepting Irving's claims, Clifford became emboldened and decided to make some money off the situation. It's also possible that Irving started believing the ridiculous propaganda that was generated by the Hughes Romaine Street headquarters and the Desert Inn penthouse – that Howard Hughes was a crazy xenophobe who would never appear in-person – or in court – to make a public denial. Perhaps Irving and his accomplices even began to believe that Hughes was *dead*! It goes without saying that if Howard Hughes was thought to be dead at the time of the hoax and the Hughes lieutenants continued to claim Hughes was alive in a court of law, Rosemont, Inc. would have had to produce a live Hughes on the witness stand. Fingerprints would probably have been required for identity purposes.

Of course, none of this ever happened.

This isn't to condone Irving's actions. He and his accomplices willingly and knowingly committed fraud. It's just that the Irving hoax is nonsensical. In the beginning, it would have been simple for Hughes to write Irving a cursive letter and have it notarized by an officer of the court. The letter could then have been compared with documents that Irving had produced and previous known letters (if in hand) written by Hughes. This would have immediately stopped the Irving hoax. So why did this not take place? Also, if the real Hughes was alive, he could simply have met with Irving face-to-face to say, "Irving, you're a goddamn scammer. I want you to desist from making these false claims that you're my biographer or suffer the consequences of being sued, causing these publishing companies to be sued, and landing yourself in the slammer for fraud!" Irving would probably have backed off and that would have been the end of it.

There is a good reason why this did not occur and why it coasted along in the courtroom for such a long time. There is no doubt that Irving became "cock-sure" he could get away with his hoax. (**Note**: If the real Hughes had truly been alive and had written a notarized cursive letter to denounce Irving, this item could have been used as verification of all those other Rosemont, Inc. exemplars as well. However, *questionable* exemplars are what they were and what they will always be.) In Chapter VI, you saw a denial letter that had supposedly been written by "Hughes." However, it was not a known document and had other problems as well. More on this later.

In the beginning of this investigation, the Irving/Hughes debacle required some in-depth contemplation. How could any author profess to be the biographer of a living legendary personality that he has never personally met, talked to, or with whom he did not have a legitimate contract? You may be assured that Clifford Irving, a renowned author with numerous publications to his credit, was no fool. Clifford Irving had to have known something, but what did he know?

Note: The material below pertains primarily to Rosemont Enterprises, Inc. Monty Montrose, Chester Davis, the Osborn cursive analysis team, and activities that occurred after 1965. Extensive research has lent itself to an amazing conclusion that could never have been anticipated. The fact that no one realized what had *really* taken place during the "Rosemont, Inc. vs. Clifford Irving" saga certainly explains a lot, but it also deepens the mystery as to why the information, recently uncovered in *this* book, did not become properly correlated and made public back in 1971.

Note: The documents critiqued below were accrued by the FBI to be used if it had been determined that federal crimes were committed by Clifford Irving. Most of this documentation pertains to writing the Howard Hughes biography for which Hughes had allegedly retained Irving. Federal crimes had, in fact, occurred – mail fraud, bank fraud, forgery, etc. However, it was Rosemont Enterprises, Inc., the legal arm of the Hughes empire, that brought Clifford Irving, Melvin Dummar, (the Mormon Will scam) and others into the courtroom on numerous occasions.

EXHIBIT 66

FBI FILE 1222257-0-87-HQ-119739-BULKY-19—PAGE 1
Lead-in document begins the FBI's file – wherein Rosemont Enterprises, Inc. takes on Clifford Irving, McGraw-Hill, and others, (Our super-sleuth "Russ" Russell was part of this one as a Federal Postal Inspector.)
Note: Federal Postal Inspectors "collar" more criminals, per case load, then Federal Bureau of Investigation agents (FBI)

Date 1/27/72 Via Airtel

```
TO:        DIRECTOR, FBI

FROM:      SAC, NEW YORK  (87-0)

SUBJECT:   UNSUB, aka
           Howard R. Hughes
           MAIL FRAUD


           Re Bureau teletype, 1/26/72.

           Enclosed for the Bureau are copies of affidavits
pertinent to captioned matter.  This material is furnished
for Bureau review in event subsequent Bureau investigation
is requested.

           Copies of these documents have been furnished
to Postal authorities at New York.
```

"ENCLOSURE ON BULKY RANP"

EX-115
REC-5

87-119739-19

2 - Bureau (Encls.18) (RM)
1 - New York
HCL:ALG
  (4)

JAN 29 1972

Approved: _____ Sent _____ M Per _____
Special Agent in Charge

EXHIBIT 67

FBI FILE 1222257-0-87-HQ-119739-BULKY-19—PAGE 2

A typed letter signed by "Howard Hughes." This is unusual because of Howard's "alleged" predisposition to cursive letters <u>after 1965</u> and into the 1970s. This letter contains a bogus signature and was most likely typed and signed by Clifford Irving.

PREFACE

It was never my intention to cut along the dotted line and write a standard, polite autobiography. I believe that more lies have been printed and told about me than about any living man - therefore it is my purpose in this book to restore the balance and set the record straight forever. Several biographies of me have been published before - all of them misleading and childish. I am certain that in the future more lies and rubbish will appear. I chose to work with Clifford Irving because of his sympathy, his descernment and discretion; and, as I learned, his integrity as a human being. The story of our meetings and how my life was swallowed up and spat back at me by a tape recorder, I leave to him. I should make it clear that I do not agree with everything he has to say, either in his introduction to this book or in his notes; but I do not dispute his right to say it.

The end result of our work together was not the biography that either of us had originally planned. The book you hold in your hands is my own narrative of my life. The words - other than some of the questions which provoked them - are my own spoken words. The thoughts, opinions and recollections, the descriptions of events and personalities, are my own. I have not permitted them to be emasculated or polished because I decided, after the many interviews had been completed, that this was as close as I could get to the elusive, often painful truth. Let it stand.

I believe you will realize that I have tried very hard to tell the truth. I have lived a full life and, perhaps, what may seem a strange life - even to myself. I refuse to apologize, although I am willing now to explain as best I can. I regret much of the past, but I have little feelings of shame about it. I did, as I will relate, what I believed I had to do in order to come out whole.

Call this my autobiography. Call it my memoirs - call it what you please. It is the story of my life in my own words.

Howard Hughes

EXHIBIT 68

FBI FILE 1222257-0-87-HQ-119739-BULKY-19—PAGE 3

Ralph Graves's affidavit, *in opposition,* **comes forth in an attempt to stop Rosemont Enterprises, Inc. (Plaintiff) from obtaining a preliminary injunction to stop (Defendants) McGraw-Hill, Clifford Irving, and others, from publishing Hughes's autobiography.**

SUPREME COURT OF THE STATE OF NEW YORK

COUNTY OF NEW YORK

ROSEMONT ENTERPRISES, INC.,

                Plaintiff,

    -against-

McGRAW-HILL BOOK COMPANY, McGRAW-HILL INC., TIME INCORPORATED, DELL PUBLISHING COMPANY, INC., CLIFFORD IRVING and JOHN DOES I. THROUGH III,

                Defendants.

Index No. 800/72

AFFIDAVIT IN OPPOSITION TO MOTION FOR PRELIMINARY INJUNCTION

STATE OF NEW YORK,)
) ss.:
COUNTY OF NEW YORK,)

    RALPH GRAVES, being duly sworn, deposes and says:

    1. I am the Managing Editor of LIFE magazine ("LIFE"), a division of Time Inc., one of the defendants herein. I have held the position of Managing Editor for LIFE since June 1, 1969, and in that position am ultimately responsible for all purchases of literary properties by LIFE and for what is published by LIFE. I am personally familiar with the facts and circumstances hereinafter recited.

    2. I submit this affidavit in opposition to the motion of plaintiff Rosemont Enterprises, Inc. ("Rosemont") for a preliminary injunction and an order granting Rosemont leave to take depositions upon oral testimony, and in support of defendants' application for a protective order.

EXHIBIT 69

FBI FILE 1222257-0-87-HQ-119739-BULKY-19—PAGE 12
Last page of Ralph Graves's affidavit, Managing Editor for *LIFE Magazine,* in opposition to a motion for preliminary injunction by Rosemont Enterprises, Inc. (Pages 2 through 9 of affidavit non-inclusive – it is obvious he's an Irving believer.)

has, since the public announcement on December 7, 1971, made it necessary to permit increasing numbers of people to read the manuscript. By now, the number of people who have read or have had access to the manuscript is quite substantial. The substance of portions of that manuscript, if not the text, is already beginning to appear in the pages of competing news organizations and in the broadcasts of radio and television networks and stations. News, and the Hughes autobiography is news, is a perishable commodity. The intense effort by competing news media to learn the autobiography's content will continue and increase. If the United States Government cannot safeguard the security of its own confidential papers, surely McGraw, LIFE and Dell cannot long do so.

26. For all of these reasons I most respectfully represent that any delay in publication of the LIFE excerpts from the manuscript will substantially and irreparably injure LIFE.

Ralph Graves
Ralph Graves

[SEAL]

Sworn to before me this
19th day of January 1972.

Christopher A. Wilburn
Notary Public

CHRISTOPHER A. WILBURN
Notary Public, State of New York
No. 24-4266600
Qualified in Kings County
Certificate filed in New York County
Commission Expires March 30, 1973

EXHIBIT 70

FBI FILE 1222257-0-87-HQ-119739-BULKY-19—PAGE 21

Extensive cursive letter *allegedly* written by Howard Hughes. It strongly designates Clifford Irving as his biographer. (Page 1 of 4)

11-17-71

JR.
NOV 22 1971
McGRAW-HILL BOOK CO.

Mr. Harold McGraw
McGraw Hill
New York, N.Y.

Dear Mr. McGraw -

The facts placed before me, I find astonishing. I do not understand, in the first place, why it is not possible for your publishing house in possession of a legiti-mate contract between myself and Mr. Clifford Irving and between your-selves and Mr. Irving, for the publication of my autobiography, cannot deal firmly and force-fully with other publishers ~~who~~ which are asserting fraudulent claims to the rights which I have granted to Mr. Irving and Mr.

EXHIBIT 71-A

FBI FILE 1222257-0-87-HQ-119739-BULKY-19—PAGE 22
H.H. cursive letter. (Page 2 of 4)

~~this~~ Irving in Turn has granted to you, without my intervention.

I have said before, and I will say again, that this Mr. Post and Mr. Eaton in no way represent me and have no rights granted by me to sell articles or books purporting to be authorized or written by me. I have given no material whatsoever to these people and no documents, and any claim by them to the contrary is fraudulent and criminal. I am sure these people are employed by my enemies.

In the event that they or any publisher

EXHIBIT 71-B

FBI FILE 1222257-0-87-HQ-119739-BULKY-19—PAGE 23
H.H. cursive letter with signature. (Page 3 of 4)

should attempt to
publish any material
supposedly secured
by me or authorized
by me, and you can
do nothing to prevent
this through normal
channels, I assume
you - and I ask that
you in turn will now
assure them - that
I will do all in my
power, and take what-
ever legal steps are
necessary to halt
what I consider an
outrage on my privacy
and my painfully
worked out agreements
with you and Mr.
Clifford Irving.

I have been made
aware, although not
fully to my satisfaction
of McGraw Hills
apparently embarrassing

EXHIBIT 72

FBI FILE 1222257-0-87-HQ-119739-BULKY-19—PAGE 29
Pages 24 to 28 non-inclusive as drift is obvious. H.H. cursive letter. (Page 4 of 4)

very near future.
I have already given
my approval in
advance to Mr. Irving,
and I have the utmost
faith that he will
be faithful to my
wishes in his preparation
of the manuscript.

Most sincerely yours,

Howard R. Hughes

EXHIBIT 73

FBI FILE 1222257-0-87-HQ-119739-BULKY-19—PAGE 31
Frank McCulloch (New York Bureau Chief, Time-Life News Service) weighs in with an affidavit *in opposition* to a motion by Rosemont Enterprises, Inc. for a preliminary injunction to stop Clifford Irving, McGraw-Hill Book Company, and others.

```
SUPREME COURT OF THE STATE OF NEW YORK

COUNTY OF NEW YORK

----------------------------------------

ROSEMONT ENTERPRISES, INC.,            :
                                       :
                        Plaintiff,     :    Index No. 800/72
                                       :
        -against-                      :    AFFIDAVIT IN
                                       :    OPPOSITION TO
McGRAW-HILL BOOK COMPANY, McGRAW       :    MOTION FOR
HILL, INC., TIME INCORPORATED, DELL    :  PRELIMINARY INJUNCTION
PUBLISHING COMPANY, INC., CLIFFORD     :
IRVING and JOHN DOES I through III,    :
                                       :
                        Defendants.    :

----------------------------------------


STATE OF NEW YORK,   )
                     ) ss.:
COUNTY OF NEW YORK,  )


        FRANK McCULLOCH, being duly sworn, deposes and
says:
```

1. I am the New York Bureau Chief of Time-Life News Service, a division of Time, Inc. ("Time"), one of defendants herein. I have been employed by Time in various journalistic capacities since 1953, except during the years 1960-1963 when I was Managing Editor of the Los Angeles Times. From 1963 until 1968, I served as China and Southeast Asia Bureau Chief and as Senior Correspondent, Asia, for the Time-Life News Service. During 1968-1969, I was Washington Bureau Chief of LIFE Magazine ("LIFE"). I have been New York Bureau Chief of the Time-Life News Service since 1969.

2. I am personally familiar with the facts and circumstances hereinafter recited, and I submit this affidavit in opposition to the motion of Rosemont Enterprises,

EXHIBIT 74

FBI FILE 1222257-0-87-HQ-119739-BULKY-19—PAGE 32

It never ceases to amaze me how many people were, and still are, so willing to buy into the alleged craziness of Howard Hughes. *Prior to 1965*, Howard Hughes may well have changed his mind in business deals if, upon further research, they did not look right to him. But couldn't this have been viewed as prudence rather than craziness?

Inc. ("Rosemont"), for a preliminary injunction and an order granting Rosemont leave to take depositions upon oral testimony and in support of Time's motion for a protective order.

3. LIFE, also a division of Time, has obtained, pursuant to an agreement with McGraw-Hill, Inc. ("McGraw"), the exclusive worldwide magazine syndication rights to publish excerpts from "The Autobiography of Howard Hughes". That agreement is attached as Exhibit B to the affidavit of Ralph Graves submitted in this action.

4. I am convinced beyond any reasonable doubt as to the authenticity of the Howard Hughes autobiography. This conviction is based upon my long-standing personal familiarity with Howard Hughes, my reading of the manuscript and my interviews with Clifford Irving. My belief in the substance of Clifford Irving's story concerning his interviews with Howard Hughes and his role in the preparation of Hughes' autobiography is not shaken by the denials of that story, nor is my belief in the authenticity of the autobiography shaken by denials which I have heard from a man whom I believe to be Howard Hughes. Such actions are perfectly consistent with the Howard Hughes I knew.

5. I first met Howard Hughes in 1958 while gathering material for an article on TWA for FORTUNE Magazine. A copy of that article is attached hereto as Exhibit A. I interviewed Hughes face-to-face during the fall of that year. The interviews were cordial; Mr. Hughes seemed to take a liking to me, and the friendship which arose between us during those conversations has, insofar as I know, continued to the present day.

So here we have Mr. Frank McCulloch laying his job on the line in the belief that he *had* talked to Howard Hughes in a conference call in 1971. And now he *also* believes that Hughes had employed Clifford Irving to write his biography. However, Frank McCulloch also believes that H.H. lied in his Irving denial questionnaire and that after having second thoughts, Hughes was now trying to renege on the deal.

EXHIBIT 75

FBI FILE 12222-0-87-HQ-119739-BULKY-19—PAGE 33.

Frank McCulloch probably had telephone conversations with Howard Hughes between the years of 1958 and 1962, but with the evidence now available in this book, the conference call set up by Chester Davis in 1971 *was not* with Howard Hughes. McCulloch claimed to have spoken with Hughes in <u>1964</u> and <u>1965</u> and this also is highly probable. However, Frank also claimed that he had not spoken to Hughes <u>after 1965 up until December 1971, which was during the Clifford Irving trial.</u>

6. Howard Hughes and I had many telephone conversations concerning the publication in FORTUNE of that article. Mr. Hughes was at that time adamantly opposed to the publication of the article and exerted great pressure in an attempt to prevent its appearance. However, despite Hughes' opposition to the publication of that article, I continued, during the years 1958-1962, to engage in occasional phone calls with Howard Hughes on a variety of subjects. The last time I spoke with Howard Hughes, prior to the events of December 1971, was in 1964 or 1965. I was at that time covering the Vietnam war for the Time-Life News Service. During a visit to New York, I was asked to meet Mr. Hughes in Los Angeles, I gather to discuss the war, and I then talked briefly to him on the telephone. At the appointed time and meeting place, however, Mr. Hughes failed to appear, and I returned to Vietnam without seeing him.

7. I next spoke to a man whom I believe to have been Howard Hughes on December 14, 1971. At approximately 4:30 on the afternoon of that day, I received an unexpected telephone call from Richard Hannah of the Carl Byoir public relations agency in Los Angeles, California, and Perry Lieber, another Hughes public relations representative. Their proposition was this: Howard Hughes wanted to talk with someone he trusted concerning the controversy that had arisen with respect to his autobiography. I indicated that I would be happy to talk to Hughes and it was arranged that his attorney, Chester C. Davis, would place the call from the offices of Time.

9. The call was placed at approximately 6:00 p.m. on the evening of December 14, 1971. Present at that time

EXHIBIT 76

FBI FILE1222257-0-87-HQ-119739-BULKY-19—PAGE 33
(Conference call to discredit Clifford Irving claim.)

a) Frank McCulloch probably had telephone conversations with Howard Hughes between the years of 1958 and 1962. Based on the evidence in this book, the conference call set up by Chester Davis in 1971 *could not have been* with Howard Hughes. McCulloch claims to have spoken with Hughes in <u>1964</u> and <u>1965</u>. This is highly probable. However, Frank claims he had not spoken with Hughes <u>after 1965 until Dec. 1971</u>. "Hughes's voice fades in and out."

b) Charlie was in the Bahamas in 1964 and remembers the phone system between the Bahamas and United States was good – necessary for booking reservations for hotels and ordering food items.

Editorial Counsel of Time, Chester C. Davis and Seymour F. Mintz and E. Barrett Prettyman, Jr., of Messrs. Hogan & Hartson, a Washington law firm which I understand represents the Hughes Tool Company. After some difficulties in establishing a telephone connection, and after a few preliminary remarks to the person on the other end by Chester Davis, the phone was handed to me.

10. I believe that the voice on the phone was that of Howard Hughes. The telephone connection was bad, and the voice tended to fade in and out. Nevertheless, I immediately recognized the slightly nasal, raspy quality that I remembered from my many prior conversations with Hughes. The phrasing, pace and general plaintiveness of his speech were also as I remembered. However, I did not see the other person and under the circumstances I cannot be certain the voice at the other end of the wire was that of Howard Hughes; I will, however, refer to the voice as Hughes.

At the beginning of our conversation Hughes requested that it be off the record. However, since Mr. Davis, representing that he has full power of attorney from Mr. Hughes, elected to refer to the subject matters of this telephone conversation in his letter dated January 7, 1972, to Harold W. McGraw, Jr. (copy attached hereto as Exhibit B), and in his affirmation submitted on Rosemont's motion (see paragraph 4(b)), I feel free to reveal the contents of our discussion.

11. Hughes repeatedly denied the authenticity of

EXHIBIT 77

FBI FILE122257-0-HQ-119739-BULKY-19—PAGE 35.

The Osborns – Albert, Paul, and Russell – enter the picture. (We will delve into their contributions, in depth, later.) The most erroneous and glaring aspect of McCulloch's affidavit appears here. He believes Irving's manuscript to be authentic and that Hughes is trying to renege on the deal. (Frank reads the Irving manuscript and, 400 pages later, believes Irving.) Here "Bahamian Hughes" claims to have written the "Chester and Bill letter" and that the documents on file with the Las Vegas Gambling control Board are known documents. But <u>none of them are!</u>

met Clifford Irving. He stated that members of his staff
have been assembling and classifying materials about him
for some time but that Irving could not possibly have had
access to that material and that only Rosemont had any right
to it. Mr. Hughes also confirmed that he had written the
"Chester and Bill" letter (attached to the joint affidavit
of Albert D. Osborn, Paul A. Osborn and Russell D. Osborn
as Exhibit F; hereinafter "Osborn Aff."), and he also
assured me of the authenticity of those documents on file
in the offices of the Gambling Control Board of the State
of Nevada in which he gave his proxy and power of attorney
over his business interests in that state to Bill Gay and
Chester Davis. (These are among the documents which were
examined by the Osborns in connection with their certification of the genuineness of the Howard Hughes' signature
and handwriting on the letters, contracts and checks in the
possession of McGraw (see Osborn Aff., ¶ 10).) At the close
of our conversation it was agreed that we would talk again.
This second call, however, never took place because of
Mr. Davis' insistence as a condition for such call that
McGraw and Time produce to him the evidence justifying their
judgment that the Hughes autobiography was authentic.

12. The next evening, December 15, I read for the
first time the first half of the manuscript of "The autobiography of Howard Hughes", more than 800 typewritten pages.
I approached this reading with skepticism, especially in
view of the denials I had heard the day before from a man
whom I believed to be Hughes. To read the manuscript, however, is to be convinced of its authenticity. The style,
the pace, the earthiness of his language, the way he talks

EXHIBIT 78

FBI FILE 1222257-0-87-HQ-119739-BULKY-19—PAGE 36.

Irving convinces Frank McCulloch that the H.H. manuscript is authentic. Frank goes on to maintain that Hughes's method of doing business is that he often changes his mind on business deals. Come on Frank! Hughes was a mega-industrialist who jockeyed million-dollar deals, he had the right to change his mind if he became suspicious or the deal turned sour. Hughes managed to amass billions back when a "buck" was truly a "buck." Obviously, he was a *brilliant* businessman. However, in this Rosemont-Irving case, we have a hoax proving a hoax.

nd thinks are all reflected with great accuracy. Moreover, the manuscript reveals with intricacy and considerable detail and depth his love and commanding knowledge of airplanes and airplane performance. It recounts with detail many anecdotal incidents of which I was already aware, but does so in a manner revealing Hughes' hand in the telling, often shading the story to put him in a more favorable light than in the accounts I had heard before. After completing the manuscript I was certain, beyond any reasonable doubt, that it contained the story of Hughes' life in his own words.

13. After my reading of the manuscript, I had a lengthy meeting on approximately December 16, 1971, with Clifford Irving at the offices of McGraw. Although I was by now convinced of the authenticity of the autobiography, I was skeptical of Irving's role in its preparation. I cross-examined him in the toughest way I knew. He handled my questions well, however, and after a lengthy session with him, I came away persuaded that what he had to say was completely truthful in substance. I was particularly impressed with the specificity with which he was able to respond to my specific questions and his ability to answer quickly questions which I felt he would have been unable to anticipate.

14. I am convinced that "The Autobiography of Howard Hughes" is genuine. Moreover, I believe that Hughes' repeated denials of the genuineness of that document and his repudiation of Irving is absolutely consistent with the man I have known.

Frank McCulloch

Sworn to before me this 18th day of January 1972.

Notary Public

MURRAY COHN
Notary Public, State of New York
No. 41-5746100
Qualified in Queens County
Cert. filed in New York County
Commission Expires March 30, 1973

EXHIBIT 79

FBI FILE 1222257-0-87-HQ-119739-BULKY-19—PAGE 23
Letter to McGraw-Hill Book Company from "Hughes attorney" Chester Davis in which he threatens Harold W. McGraw, Jr. (To quote Plato, "the highest reach of injustice is to be deemed just when you are not." This typifies Chester Davis.)

<u>BY HAND</u>   January 7, 1972

Mr. Harold W. McGraw, Jr.
President
McGraw-Hill Book Company
330 West 42nd Street
New York, New York 10036

Dear Mr. McGraw:

Until now, I have proceeded on the assumption that McGraw-Hill was acting in good faith and that even though you were in error you honestly believed that you had an authorized autobiography of Howard Hughes. That assumption has now been seriously brought into question by your letter of December 23, 1971 and your continued refusal to permit us to get at the facts and reveal the identities of those responsible for this impersonation.

Even if you honestly believed prior to December 14, 1971 that you had in your possession an authorized autobiography, the telephone conversation on that date with Mr. Hughes, in which both Mr. McCulloch and I participated, should have alerted you -- at the very least -- to the possibility that you were in error. Three facts about that telephone call cannot be disputed:

1. You know that Mr. McCulloch is Chief of the News Bureau of Time and, if you are acting in good faith, you must view him as a man of honesty, integrity and high competence.

EXHIBIT 80

FBI FILE 1222257-0-87-HQ-119739-BULKY-19—PAGE 54
Here, Chester Davis has presumed too much as Frank McCulloch eventually did believe the Irving H.H. manuscript to be authentic.

January 7, 1972
Page Two

    2. Mr. McCulloch, who had personally known Mr. Hughes over an extended period of time, had traveled with him and had had conversations with him on numerous and prolonged occasions, was convinced beyond a doubt that he was speaking to Mr. Hughes.

    3. In that conversation, Mr. Hughes flatly and without caveat of any kind denied knowing Mr. Irving, denied having given Mr. Irving, McGraw-Hill or anyone other than Rosemont Enterprises authorization to publish his autobiography and denied having given information which can be used in a book based on his life-story. This was established immediately after the telephone conversation by the answers to questions put to McCulloch by Mr. Dowd and Mr. Wilson of Time, Inc. and Mr. Mintz and Mr. Prettyman of Hogan & Hartson.

    I repeat: even if this telephone call did not fully convince you that the so-called "autobiography" which you claim to possess was a fake and a fraud, it surely should have put you on notice, at the very least, that this was a real possibility. As an initial step, a reasonable party acting in good faith would have promptly tried to communicate with Mr. Hughes and would have displayed to those in a position to establish the truth <u>at least</u>

EXHIBIT 81

FBI FILE 1222257-0-87-HQ-119739-BULKY-19—PAGE 55
This sheet is critical to our case wherein Chester Davis states, *"Since 1965 Rosemont has held exclusive rights to Mr. Hughes' life story"* per document signed by H.H. *Really?*

Mr. Harold W. McGraw, Jr.
January 7, 1972
Page Three

(a) the 11-page letter which you had told the press you had received directly from Mr. Hughes authorizing the "auto-biography," and (b) the checks which you had told the press had been paid to and cashed by Mr. Hughes in connection with the publication of the "autobiography." Instead you have deliberately refused to produce any documents of any kind to authenticate the claims you have made to the press and I under-stand that you have objected to having Mr. McCulloch investigate the matter further. I simply cannot understand the basis or justification for your position.

It is incumbent upon me to give you formal notice that Rosemont Enterprises, Inc., whom I represent as legal counsel, intends to take all requisite action to preserve and protect its legal rights under its agreement with Mr. Hughes, with which you are, I believe, generally familiar. Since 1965 Rosemont has held the exclusive rights to Mr. Hughes' life-story pursuant to that agreement, which was personally signed and acknowledged by Mr. Hughes before a notary, who is available. The agreement empowers Rosemont, in addition to enforcing the rights granted to it under the agreement, to exercise all rights that Mr. Hughes may have to prevent and restrain anyone else from publishing any biography or life-story of Mr. Hughes. That agreement is available at my office for your inspection.

Since 1965

EXHIBIT 82

FBI FILE 1222257-0-87-HQ-119739-BULKY-19—PAGE 56

In this page Chester is asserting his honor and integrity. He must have been very disappointed when Frank McCulloch joined the Irving camp and eventually believed the H.H. manuscript *to be authentic.* (Remember that old Bogart movie, *Casablanca,* where the police chief claimed, "I am shocked, shocked, to find out there's gambling going on in here!" as he pockets his winnings?)

Mr. Harold W. McGraw, Jr.
January 7, 1972
Page Four

The publicity given this so-called "autobiography" has already severely injured Rosemont.

One other matter which I feel I must mention is the question you have raised as to my authority to represent Mr. Hughes in this matter. Obviously for me to purport to represent someone whom I am not authorized to represent would be the most unprofessional of conduct and a clear violation of the Canons of Ethics. I am shocked that you or your counsel would even suggest this possibility. Moreover, the conversation with Mr. McCulloch, which I arranged and in which I participated, should have dispelled any question as to my authority, particularly since Mr. Hughes clearly indicated to Mr. McCulloch that the further submission of questions and facts, and the arrangements for a further telephone conversation between Mr. Hughes and Mr. McCulloch, were to be carried out through me as an intermediary.

Nevertheless, to dispel any possible question, as a member in good standing of the Bar of the State of New York I represent to you that I have Mr. Hughes' authorization and have been acting as his attorney with respect to this particular matter as well as others. I am sure your attorneys will appreciate the significance of this representation.

EXHIBIT 83

FBI FILE 1222257-0-87-HQ-119739-BULKY-19—PAGE 57
Chester makes sure that the opposition knows he's coming. He knows that Hughes did not give Irving a deal to publish his biography because he had known the truth about Howard Hughes since 1965.

Mr. Harold W. McGraw, Jr.
January 7, 1972
Page Five

       In the event that I do not hear from you promptly to the contrary, I shall be forced to conclude that you are continuing to proceed with the publication of this fraudulent work.

                    Very truly yours,

                    Chester C. Davis

CCD:sd

xc: By Hand to the following:

    Mr. Shelton Fisher
    President and Chief Executive Officer
    McGraw-Hill, Inc.
    330 West 42nd Street
    New York, New York 10036

    Mr. Andrew Heiskell
    Chairman of the Board and
      Chief Executive Officer
    Time Incorporated
    Time & Life Building
    Rockefeller Center
    New York, New York 10020

    Mr. Garry Valk
    Publisher
    LIFE
    Time & Life Building
    Rockefeller Center
    New York, New York 10020

    Mr. George T. Delacorte
    Dell Publishing Co., Inc.
    750 Third Avenue
    New York, New York 10017

EXHIBIT 84

FBI FILE 1222257-0-87-HQ-119739-BULKY-19—PAGE 59

Here come the Osborns who have been retained by McGraw-Hill. They are the best money can buy. The fee must have been substantial since they laid their credibility on the line. (Joint affidavit by the Osborns *in opposition* to a motion for a preliminary injunction by Rosemont Enterprises, Inc. They were the *hammer* as cursive writing analysis professionals?

```
SUPREME COURT OF THE STATE OF NEW YORK
COUNTY OF NEW YORK.


ROSEMONT ENTERPRISES, INC.,
                    Plaintiff,              Index No. 800/72

    -against-                               JOINT AFFIDAVIT
McGRAW-HILL BOOK COMPANY, McGRAW-           IN OPPOSITION
HILL, INC., TIME INCORPORATED,             TO MOTION FOR
DELL PUBLISHING COMPANY, INC.,             PRELIMINARY
CLIFFORD IRVING, JOHN DOES I               INJUNCTION
THROUGH III,
                    Defendants.


STATE OF NEW YORK   )
                    ) ss.:
COUNTY OF NEW YORK  )

         ALBERT D. OSBORN, PAUL A. OSBORN, and RUSSELL D.
OSBORN, being duly sworn, each individually and jointly
depose and say:

         1.  Each of affiants is an examiner of questioned
documents, commonly known as a handwriting expert, and each
is associated with the firm of Osborn, Osborn & Osborn,
Examiners of Questioned Documents, 233 Broadway, New York,
New York 10007.  Each affiant is fully familiar with the
facts stated herein, and each submits this affidavit in
opposition to the motion of Rosemont Enterprises, Inc.
("Rosemont"), for a preliminary injunction and an order
granting Rosemont leave to take depositions upon oral
testimony.

         2.  The examination of questioned documents in-
cludes the investigation and identification of handwriting,
typewriting, erasure, ink, paper and other problems relat-
ing to documents, such examination being carried out by a
```

EXHIBIT 85

FBI FILE 1222257-0-87-HQ-119739-BULKY-19—PAGE 60
The Osborn boys are proud of themselves. Look at these credentials!

variety of scientific techniques including the use of
magnifiers, microscopes, measuring plates, lighting instruments, projectors, ultra-violet light equipment and various
photographic equipment.

3. Affiant Albert D. Osborn has been engaged in
such work on a full-time basis for over forty years. Said
affiant has lectured on the subject of questioned documents
before bar associations, law schools and the Federal Bureau
of Investigation. Said affiant has testified with respect
to questioned documents on many occasions before the courts
of this State and others, and said affiant has been appointed
pursuant to Rule 28 of the Federal Rules of Criminal Procedure, as a handwriting expert by federal district courts
located in the States of New York and Connecticut.

4. Affiant Paul A. Osborn has been engaged in
the examination of questioned documents on a full-time
basis since 1953. Said affiant has lectured on the subject
before various law schools, bar associations and banking
groups. Said affiant has testified on the subject of questioned documents on numerous occasions before the courts
of this State and others and has been qualified as an expert
in his field by the American Arbitration Society, the
National Labor Relations Board and the Insurance Department
of the State of New York.

5. Affiant Russell D. Osborn has been engaged in
the examination of questioned documents on a full-time basis
since 1954. Said affiant has testified on the subject of
questioned documents on many occasions before the courts of
this State and others.

6. Each affiant has studied and is fully

EXHIBIT 86

FBI FILE 1222257-0-87-HQ-119739-BULKY-19—PAGE 61
Leads to conclusion.

familiar with the leading books, articles and monographs relating to the examination of disputed documents, and each has participated from time to time in the preparation of such books or articles or monographs.

7. Each affiant is an active member of the American Society of Questioned Document Examiners (ASQDE) and the American Academy of Forensic Sciences (Questioned Documents Section) (AAFS). Affiant Albert D. Osborn is a past president of ASQDE and affiant Paul A. Osborn is currently vice president of that society and a past chairman of the Questioned Documents Section of AAFS.

8. The opinions set forth herein are the independent opinions of each affiant, as well as their joint opinions, and are based upon personal examination and comparison of the documents in question and/or photographs or portions thereof by each affiant working independently. Each affiant fully subscribes to the reasons stated herein in support of those opinions.

9. On December 17, 1971, prior to the commencement of this action, affiants were requested to examine, on behalf of McGraw-Hill, Inc., and Time Incorporated, various documents to determine, if possible (1) whether all the signatures "Howard Hughes", "Howard R. Hughes" and "H. R. Hughes" on those documents were or were not written by the same individual and (2) whether the continued writing in the body of certain of those documents was or was not written by the same individual.

10. In connection with this request, affiant Russell D. Osborn examined certain documents on file in the offices of the Chairman of the Gaming Control Board of the

EXHIBIT 87

FBI FILE 1222257-0-87-HQ-119739-BULKY-19—PAGE 65

Taking into consideration that Nazi latent fingerprints were use 40 years after the fact to gain a conviction (see Chapter V), why was it that neither Rosemont, Inc. nor the Irving camp ever suggested the documents presented, supposedly written by Howard Hughes, be sent to the lab for latent-print analysis? The answer is simple. <u>*Both parties knew*</u> *their documents were phony and no Hughes print would have been found on any of them!*

the signature "Howard R. Hughes", copy attached hereto as Exhibit M;

(f) original of envelope bearing the handwritten address "Mr. Harold McGraw, McGraw Hill Publishers, 330 West 42nd Street, New York, New York", copy attached hereto as Exhibit N;

(g) copy of letter of agreement dated March 4, 1971, between Howard R. Hughes and Clifford Irving, containing seven typewritten pages and bearing the signatures "Howard R. Hughes" and "Clifford Irving", copy attached hereto as Exhibit O;

(h) original of letter of addendum dated September 10, 1971, to letter of agreement dated March 4, 1971, between Howard R. Hughes and Clifford Irving, consisting of six typewritten pages and bearing the signatures "Howard R. Hughes" and "Clifford Irving", copy attached hereto as Exhibit P;

(i) original of typed preface received upon information and belief in November or December 1971, bearing the signature "Howard Hughes", copy attached hereto as Exhibit Q;

(j) original of check No. 110866, dated September 22, 1971, drawn on The Chase Manhattan Bank, N.A., cleared on October 5, 1971, and bearing the endorsement "H. R. Hughes", copy attached hereto as Exhibit R; and

(k) original of check No. 111112, dated December 12, 1971, drawn on The Chase Manhattan Bank, N.A., cleared on December 14, 1971, and bearing the endorsement "Deposit only to account of H. R. Hughes, H. R. Hughes", copy attached hereto as Exhibit S.

EXHIBIT 88

FBI FILE 1222257-0-87-HQ-119739-BULKY-19—PAGE 67

Don't you think it's *highly* unusual that Howard Hughes, who once had a battalion of secretaries to type his letters, began to wax prolific in cursive writing after l965? *Not a single document* used to disprove the Clifford Irving or Melvin Dummar scams were written prior to 1965 (except, perhaps, for a drink request on a waitress's note pad).

signatures, and of specimen and questioned letter forms and letter form combinations, prepared as illustrations for that report, and all enlarged to approximately nine times original size, are appended hereto as Appendices A and B, respectively. Said report, and its accompanying photo-graphic illustrations, do not attempt to set forth all the evidence upon which our opinion is based. They are intended rather to demonstrate the basic reasons for our conclusion that the specimen and questioned signatures and continuous writing were all written by the same individual.

    15. The essential reasoning upon which our opinion is based may be summarized as follows: Both the specimen and questioned documents reveal great speed and fluency of writing. Yet the questioned documents accurately reflect in every detail the genuine forms and habits and variations thereof which make up the basic writing identity of the author of the specimen documents. Moreover, in spite of the prodigious quantity of writing contained in the questioned documents, careful study has failed to reveal any feature which raises even the slightest question as to the common identity of all the specimen and questioned signatures and continuous writing. These basic factors, we-believe, make it impossible as a practical matter, based upon our years of experience in the field of questioned handwriting and signatures, that anyone other than the writer of the specimens could have written the questioned signatures and continuous writing.

The Speed and Freedom of the Writing

    16. Perhaps the single most important indicia of

EXHIBIT 89

FBI FILE 1222257-0-87-HQ-119739-BULKY-19—PAGE 69
It certainly appears that the Osborns used the best analytical procedures available at the time.

natural variation in pen pressure consistent with handwriting speed. The carelessness in many of the signatures is also illustrated, for example, by the capital "R" in the first signature on photograph 1, which is actually not finished. These characteristics are equally apparent in the questioned signatures contained in photographs 3 and 4 in Appendix A. The fourth signature on photograph 3, written with a felt-tipped pen, is typical of the free, rapid and careless writing which characterizes these questioned signatures. Compare, for example, the end of the first stroke of the "H" in "Howard" or the finish of the "w", where the ink line fades away to a point, indicating that the pen was in rapid motion as it came off the paper. Again, the capital "R" in this signature reveals the light upward stroke and rapidly made top and finish characteristic of all the specimen and questioned signatures.

Identity of Basic Writing Forms and Habits and Genuine Variations

18. The genuine handwriting of Howard R. Hughes is unusual not only in the distinctiveness of its developed forms and habits, but also in the great number of genuine variations thereof, all of which are a product of the great speed, freedom and carelessness of his writing and all of which constitute his basic writing identity. This combination of speed in execution and distinctiveness and unusual variation in developed forms and habits, which are revealed in the specimen writings, determine the parameters of the monumental task which would face anyone attempting to imitate the genuine writing of Howard R. Hughes. Any

EXHIBIT 90

FBI FILE 1222257-0-87-HQ-119739-BULKY-19—PAGE 73
The Osborns continue to advocate that the Irving letters were written by the same (person) hand that wrote the Chester and Bill letter, Dear Bob letter, and all the other documents that had *supposedly* been written by Hughes *earlier* than the Clifford Irving hoax.

made available to us for examination. It is most unusual to have available such an abundance of specimen and questioned material. This great abundance of writing bears signifi-cance to our opinion in two respects.

23. First, we were able to make a most complete study of the basic writing identity of the author of the specimen documents, including the many genuine variations in his forms and habits. We were then able to compare that identity with an even greater quantity of questioned writ-ings, enabling us to make a very complete and certain identification of the authorship of the questioned documents. As we have said above, these questioned writings accurately reflect the writing forms and habits and genuine variations thereof of the writer of the specimen documents and in our opinion all the specimen and questioned signatures and writing were written by the same hand.

24. Second, the sheer volume of questioned con-tinuous writing and the large number of questioned signa-tures would present a monumental task for an imitator attempt-ing to reproduce the idiosyncrasies of the writer of the specimen documents. Yet the questioned documents reflect these idiosyncrasies with great accuracy. Based on our individual and combined experience in the field of ques-tioned documents, we do not believe any imitator, however skilled and artistic, could have produced such a bulk of writings so accurately reflecting the writing identity of the writer of the specimen documents. As we have stated above, in all of the great bulk of questioned writings which we have examined there is no evidence of any element of

EXHIBIT 91

FBI FILE 1222257-0-87-HQ-119739-BULKY-19—PAGE 74

Here the Osborn trio signs off on a joint affidavit that should have sent them all, along with Frank McCulloch and Ralph Graves, looking for new lines of work. This analysis of questioned documents most likely went down in history as one of the *worst* analyses ever. But then Albert Osborn (the old man) helped to send Richard Bruno Hauptmann to the electric chair years before. (We'll get into that later.)

form or habit which is in any way inconsistent with the basic writing identity of the author of the specimen documents. It is our firm conclusion that all the signatures and continuous writing, both specimen and questioned, were written by the hand of the same man.

Albert D. Osborn

Sworn to before me this 19 day of January 1972.

Notary Public

JOHN MURPHY
Notary Public, State of New York
No. 03-8071585
Qualified in Bronx County
Certificate filed in New York County
Commission Expires March 30, 1972

Paul A. Osborn

Sworn to before me this 19 day of January 1972.

Notary Public

JOHN MURPHY
Notary Public, State of New York
No. 03-8071585
Qualified in Bronx County
Certificate filed in New York County
Commission Expires March 30, 1972

Russell D. Osborn

Sworn to before me this 19 day of January 1972.

Notary Public

JOHN MURPHY
Notary Public, State of New York
No. 03-8071585
Qualified in Bronx County
Certificate filed in New York County
Commission Expires March 30, 1972

EXHIBIT 92

FBI FILE 1222257-0-87-HQ-119739-BULKY-19—PAGE 123
Cover sheet: continued analysis of Irving's supposed H.H. documentation by the Osborns.

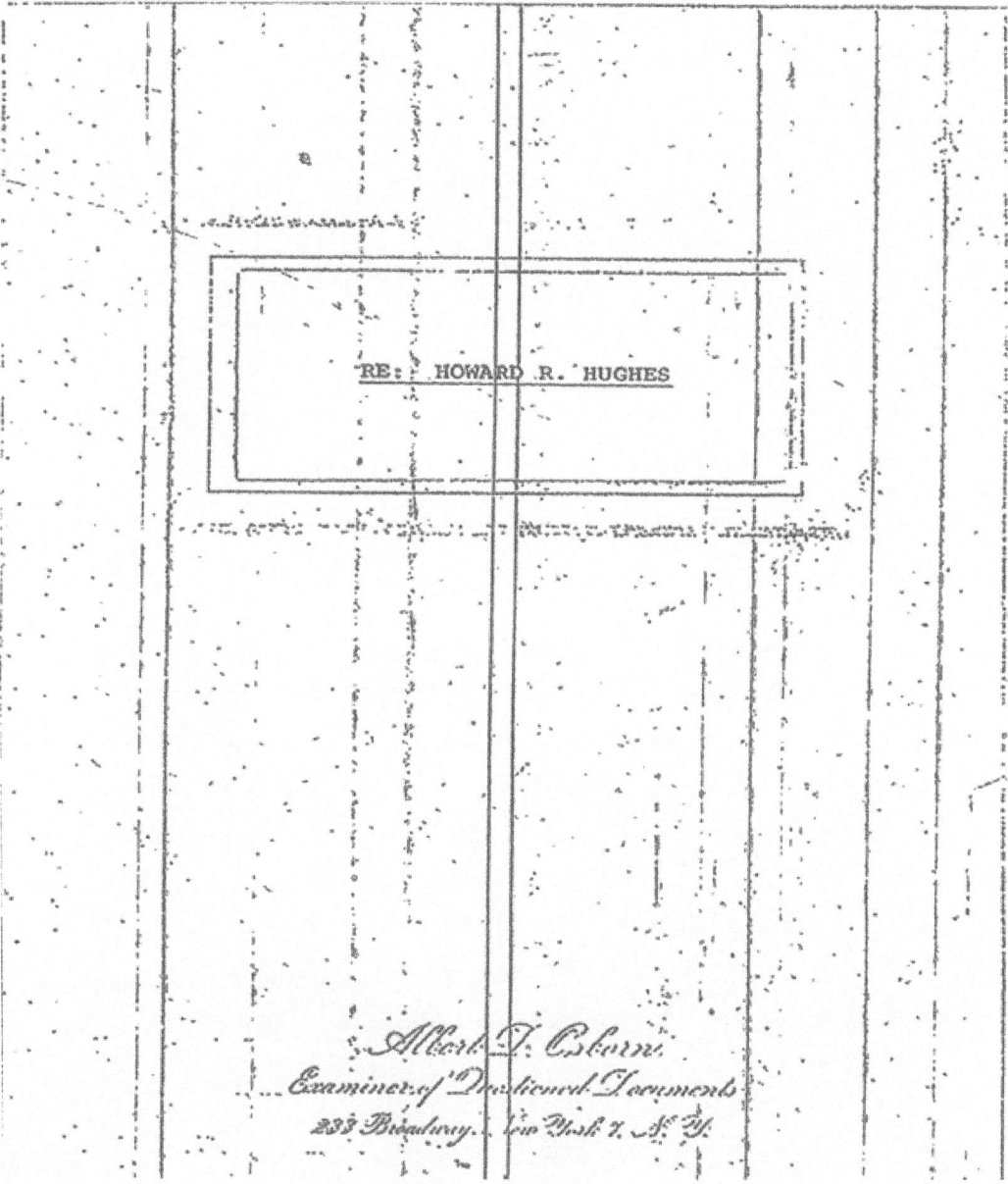

EXHIBIT 93

FBI FILE 1222257-0-87-HQ-119739-BULKY-19—PAGE 126
Problems, conclusions, and reasons for Osborn conclusions, which eventually created even more problems for them – a hoax by any other name, etc.

20. Photocopy of seven-page agreement
dated 3/4/71.

PROBLEM:

The question to be resolved, if possible, is whether all the names signed "Howard Hughes," "Howard R. Hughes" and "H. R. Hughes" on the above-listed documents were or were not written by one individual.

Furthermore, it has been requested to determine whether the continued writing on the documents submitted, where such writing is present, was or was not all written by one individual.

CONCLUSION:

The independent conclusions of the signers of this report are that the signatures "Howard R. Hughes," "Howard Hughes" and "H. R. Hughes" were all signed by one individual, being the same individual who wrote all the continued writing on the documents submitted where continued writing is present.

REASONS FOR CONCLUSION:

Reference is made to the signatures which have been submitted as having been written by Howard R. Hughes, shown in Album No. 1 in photographs 1 and 2 on the left side. On

EXHIBIT 94

FBI FILE 1222257-0-87-HQ-119739-BULKY-19—PAGE 127

Here the Osborns are absolutely convinced that signatures on McGraw-Hill checks and "deposit to the account of" were written by the same hand (person). This implies they were written by Howard Hughes.

the right side in Photographs 3 and 4 is a group of eleven signatures from ten documents which may be denied by Howard R. Hughes. The two signatures at the top of Photograph 3 "H. R. Hughes" are from the back of the McGraw-Hill check dated 12/2/71, drawn to the order of Mr. Hughes. Above the first signature on the back of this check are the handwritten words "Deposit only to the account of." These handwritten words "Deposit only to the account of" and the two signatures were all written by the same individual. An endorsement on a second check of McGraw-Hill to the order of Mr. Hughes, dated 9/22/71, is shown as the fifth signature in Photograph 3, written over the printed words "Order Swiss Credit Bank."

The two signatures at the top of Photograph 3 illustrate in part, some of the normal variations of one person's writing, found in all nineteen signatures illustrated.

One of the identities showing the same handwriting throughout all these signatures is the method of writing the capital "H," both in "Howard" and in "Hughes," as shown in the first two signatures in Photograph 1 and the third and fourth signatures in Photograph 3. However, as will be seen in these two signatures at the top of Photograph 3 on this check of 12/2/71, the wide variation in this writing is evident, for example, in the beginning of the two initials "H" on the check. The lower one begins with a loop at the top and the

EXHIBIT 95

FBI FILE 1222257-0-87-HQ-119739-BULKY-19—PAGE 137
On and on…

oval of the letter and the manner of making the letters "nd" are the same.

Naturally, when we say there is a definite connection, that does not mean that every stroke is just the same, but the habits are the same. These words "and" are not unique, but they show the further common habits in handwriting.

The next photograph, No. 7, shows a line of words at the top "you" and "your," while below are the same words in the letters to McGraw-Hill. Some of the forms are quite common, but plainly the same at the top and bottom, indicating further the same writer.

In Photograph 8, the manner of writing the beginning "t" in "to" at the top and at the bottom, where occasionally the finish of the "o" is carried up to make the "t" crossing, is the same. The manner of writing the final "t" in these words "not" also shows the same habits; occasionally a separate "t" crossing and a continuously made "t."

At the right the "th" combination of letters is clearly the same, where the "t" crossing starts with a hook at times and the finish of the "h" is abbreviated.

The last photograph in this album, No. 9, shows at the top the beginning of the endorsement on the check of 12/2/71, while below are writings submitted, presumably of

EXHIBIT 96

FBI FILE 1222257-0-87-HQ-119739-BULKY-19—PAGE 138
On and on…

Mr. Hughes. Even this short notation on the check is clearly the same writing as in these writings below, as illustrated in the style "D" in "Deposit" and "Diehl" and "Davis" and "Dear"; also in the word "to" where the "t" crossing is begun with a little hook. In the word "of," with the typical long downward stem, clearly the letter "f" is the same at the top as below.

Further, the word "the" is like the "the" below, even to the little hook at the beginning on the "t" crossing which is shown just below in the word "these" or again below in "the."

The style of final "t" in "account" and and "Deposit" follows out the habits of the writer in making these letters, as shown below in "support" and "quest."

Even the small "y" in "only" gives the impression of leaning to the right, as the right-hand side of the "y" is considerably lower than the left, plainly the same as below in "my."

Of course, in referring to these photographs showing the connection between the continued writing in the various items submitted, we have not pointed out many of the connecting features. However, with the amount of writing here in the matter submitted as being from Mr. Hughes and in the communications to McGraw-Hill, many more connections in writing habits could be pointed out.

EXHIBIT 97

FBI FILE 1222257-0-87-HQ-119739-BULKY-19—PAGE 139
The "on-and-on boys" once again sign off on another persuasive masterpiece of deception.

Certainly on what has been submitted here, the evidence is overwhelming that the signatures were all written by the same party, and the continued writing as well was also written by the same individual.

Respectfully submitted,

New York, N. Y.
January 10, 1972

EXHIBIT 98

FBI FILE 1222257-0-87-HQ-119739-BULKY-19—PAGE 140

The question that arises here is, "What if the Osborns – father and sons – were somehow convinced that Clifford Irving's Howard Hughes manuscript was authentic?" There were three reasons for including the Osborn documentation in these exhibits:

1) To question the vacuum regarding Rosemont Enterprises, Inc. in the documentaries of *Empire* and *Howard Hughes: His Life and Madness*

2) To make clear that Rosemont, Inc. was established in <u>1965</u> by Monty Montrose and Chester Davis

3) To clarify that virtually *none* of the documents used by Rosemont, Inc. as courtroom proof were valid Howard Hughes known exemplars (see Chapter VI). As it turns out, much more was found, which will be examined later.

ROSEMONT ENTERPRISES, INC. AGAINST MCGRAW-HILL BOOK COMPANY. JOINT AFFIDAVIT OF ALFRED D. OSBORN, PAUL A. OSBORN AND RUSSELL D. OSBORN.

INDEX NO. 800/72

SUPREME COURT : NEW YORK COUNTY

ROSEMONT ENTERPRISES, INC.,

Plaintiff,

-against-

McGRAW-HILL BOOK COMPANY, McGRAW-HILL, INC., TIME INCORPORATED, DELL PUBLISHING COMPANY, INC., CLIFFORD IRVING, JOHN DOES I THROUGH III,

Defendants.

JOINT AFFIDAVIT OF ALBERT D. OSBORN, PAUL A. OSBORN AND RUSSELL D. OSBORN.

CRAVATH, SWAINE & MOORE
Attorneys for Defendant Time Incorporated

ONE CHASE MANHATTAN PLAZA
NEW YORK, N. Y. 10005

EXHIBIT 99

FBI FILE 1222257-0-87-HQ-119739-BULKY-19. PAGE 207
Items #1 and #2 below can be considered known exemplars. Item #3 is not a known exemplar because there is no extensive known exemplar written by Howard Hughes with which to compare it. Item #4 cannot be considered as a known exemplar since it was notarized by an "inside" person rather than an officer of the court or a law-enforcement official. (See L. Russell's explanation in Chapter VI.)

Note: #1 and # 2 are signatures anyone can get and have been forged prolifically on documents alleged to be Hughes documents throughout the years.

RE: HOWARD R. HUGHES

— * —

DOCUMENTS SUBMITTED:

The following documents were submitted for examination:

1.   Copy of Los Angeles Police Department
Fingerprint Card No. LA-184-W-9,
dated 7/12/36, bearing the signature
"H. R. Hughes."

2.   Copy of National Defense Program
Fingerprint Card, bearing signature
"Howard R. Hughes" (undated, but
presumably made around 1940).

3.   Copy of handwritten letter starting
"Dear Chester and Bill," consisting
of three pages, signed "Howard R.
Hughes" (copy dated in margin
12/10/70).

4.   Copy of Proxy marked for identification Defendant's Proposed Exhibit
Q, dated November 14, 1970 and
notarized on the same day, signed
"Howard R. Hughes."

EXHIBIT 100

FBI FILE 1222257-0-87-HQ-119739-BULKY-19—PAGE 208

Item #9 was the best they had – Barbara Thackery's affidavit made October 21, 1971. It was a hastily written drink order on a small notepad which she and several other witnesses believed was written by Howard Hughes. We know Items #10, #11, and #12 are bogus because Clifford Irving and his co-conspiritors Richard Suskind and Edith Sommer Irving admitted to their participation in the H.H. biography hoax and went to prison for their fraud and deception.

5.   Color photograph of post card containing on the face, among others, the name "Howard R. Hughes" to Bill Schneider, Jr., Gon Del., Washington, D. C., postmarked July 21, 1938.

6.   Original letter on stationery of Howard R. Hughes, dated August 15, 1971, to "My dear Governor," consisting of two pages and signed "Howard R. Hughes."

7.   Handwritten letter on yellow scratch pad paper to Mr. John W. Diehl, Chairman, Nevada Gaming Commission, Carson City, Nevada 89701, consisting of two pages of handwriting, signed "Howard R. Hughes."

8.   Typewritten letter dated October 2, 1971 to "Dear Mr. Diehl," signed "Howard R. Hughes."

9.   Copy of writing on a waiter's order pad, presumed to have been done by Howard R. Hughes in 1955 or 1956, and witnessed by waitress Barbara Thackery according to an affidavit made October 21, 1971.

10.   Two-page handwritten letter, received December 10, 1970, to "Dear Mr. Irving," starting "Thank you for the gift of your book," which I thoroughly enjoyed reading... etc., signed "Yours truly, H. R. Hughes."

11.   Letter received January 8, 1971 consisting of one page and starting "Dear Mr. Irving: I have in hand your most recent letter...," etc., signed "H. R. Hughes."

12.   Letter received January 20, 1971, consisting of three pages and starting "Dear Mr. Irving: I thank you again for the thoughtfulness of your letter to me...," etc., signed "Sincerely yours, Howard Hughes."

EXHIBIT 101

FBI FILE 1222257-0-87-HQ-119739-BULKY-19—PAGE 209

More submittals of "supposed" documentation by the Osborns. Items #13 through #19 are all bogus. It was all a hoax, albeit an elaborate hoax. The question is, "How was it possible for Irving to somehow create the ruse and convincingly garner the Osborns' support?"

13. Handwritten letter consisting of one sheet with writing on both sides, dated 9/11/71, on the letterhead of The Beach Inn, starting "Clifford Irving-I have read and understood the terms and conditions of your contract...," etc.

14. Nine-page letter dated 11/17/71 to "Mr. Harold McGraw, McGraw Hill, New York, N. Y.," starting "Dear Mr. McGraw- The facts placed before me I find astonishing...," etc., signed "Howard R. Hughes" and stamped "Received H. W. McGraw, Jr., Nov. 22, 1971 - McGraw Hill Book Co."

15. Typewritten letter of addendum of 9/10/71 to letter agreement of 3/4/71 between Howard R. Hughes and Clifford Irving, consisting of six typewritten pages, bearing signatures "Howard R. Hughes" and "Clifford Irving."

16. Typed Preface bearing signature "Howard Hughes," undated, but received in November or December 1971.

17. Check No. 110866, dated 9/22/71, drawn on the Chase Manhattan Bank, cleared 10/5/71, endorsed "H. R. Hughes."

18. Check of Chase Manhattan Bank, No. 111112, dated 12/2/71, cleared 12/14/71, with the handwritten endorsement "Deposit only to the account of H. R. Hughes, H. R. Hughes," deposited in Swiss Credit Bank Zurich.

19. Envelope bearing the handwritten address to Mr. Harold McGraw, McGraw Hill Publishers, 330 West 42nd Street, New York, New York. In the area for the return address are the handwritten words "Airmail Special delivery."

DISSERTATION CONCERNING ALBERT OSBORN, BRUNO RICHARD HAUPTMANN, AND ROSEMONT ENTERPRISES, INC

When the imprisonment of Clifford Irving and his wife are considered, one simply *cannot* help but lean in the direction that the Osborns "were not the sharpest knives in the drawer." It appears that the Osborns did not just "get their goose cooked" – *it was burnt to a crisp!* However, this was not the first time that "The Old Man" (Albert Osborn) was suspected of being in alliance with the "dark side."

CHARLES LINDBERGH, ALBERT OSBORN, AND BRUNO RICHARD HAUPTMANN

Daddy Albert Osborn, along with his sons Paul and Russell, were discredited with their analysis of the Clifford Irving hoax documents, but at least Clifford didn't get sent to the electric chair because of it. Richard Bruno Hauptmann, who was alleged to have kidnapped Charles Lindbergh's son, was not so lucky.

Charles Lindbergh became an American celebrity when he flew his plane, the Spirit of St. Louis, from New York to France in 1927. This was the world's first solo, nonstop trans-Atlantic flight. Lindbergh found himself rocketed to fame as America's most venerated hero. Today, hundreds of tourists and businessmen and women make that flight every day. But in 1927, the flight was tantamount to a person getting into a rocket ship and flying round trip to Mars. "Dangerous" is an understatement for the chance taken by Lindberg, with the likelihood of him reaching his goal at probably less than 50 percent. Lindbergh became known as the "Lone Eagle." His name was in the news and on the lips of partygoers everywhere. The "Lindy Hop" dance style was named in his honor. Charles went on to even greater fame and fortune with several other notorious record-breaking accomplishments – some with his wife. But let's not get off tracks. (His is a fascinating story. If you want to know more about Charles Lindbergh, or what has been written about him, you can go to this website: www.thenewamerican.com/culture/history. For the purposes of this discussion, read "Item #7: The Lindbergh Baby Kidnapping Mystery.")

Charles Lindbergh married Anne Morrow, and in 1930 she gave birth to their first child, Charles Lindbergh, Jr. The media nicknamed the boy "the Eaglet" and there was much ado in the news about the boy during the two years of his life.

On March 1, 1932, 20-month-old Charles Lindbergh, Jr. was abducted from his bedroom on the Lindbergh estate. The kidnapper left behind a ransom note demanding $50,000 (a substantial sum in those days.) The Lindbergh's paid the ransom, but to no avail. The baby had been murdered and his body dumped in the woods only four miles from the Lindbergh home.

This was the "crime of the century" to most people. Charles Lindbergh was not only a celebrity in this country but had garnered fame worldwide for his airborne exploits. Charles and Anne were devastated by the incident. The tragedy changed the course of their lives and they never fully recovered.

BRUNO RICHARD HAUPMANN ENTERS THE PICTURE

A Google search will turn up much more on Hauptmann than you will find below. A summary of the facts is more than enough to make the point:

1. Serial numbers from the Lindbergh ransom money had been taken, but only a trickle of the bills ever turned up, mostly at banks outside Norman Schwarzkop's jurisdiction. (He's the fellow appointed as Chief Investigator in the Lindbergh case.)

2. A fellow named Bruno Richard Hauptmann used a $10.00 bill at a gas station that was from the ransom payment.

3. Police found approximately $14,000 more of the ransom money at Hauptmann's house.

4. A fellow named Isador Fisch had *also* lived in the Hauptmann house and had returned to Germany in December 1933, where he died from tuberculosis.

5. Hauptmann claimed that "the money was left at his house by Isador Fisch, with whom he had entered into several business ventures and that Fisch owed him $7,000." (Randolph Hearst, of Hearst Newspapers fame, claimed this to be a "Fisch Story.") Hauptmann's claim was that "upon discovery of the money, when he snooped into the shoe box left with him by Fisch, he decided to spend some of it."

6. Hauptmann had a prison record in Germany and had entered the United States as a stowaway. (This was true as times were harsh in post WWI Germany, and Hauptman was 19 years old at the time. Hauptmann admitted that he had committed some petty thievery for food and clothing, but had promised his mother before she died, that he would never do it again. (Hauptmann had no further criminal record.)

7. With Hauptmann's arrest, Norman Schwarzkopf believed he had an open and shut case.

8. Two eyewitnesses placed Richard Hauptmann near the Lindbergh residence around the time of the kidnapping. The above-mentioned H. Norman Schwarzkopf was a *political* appointee. Norman, prior to this, had been a department store floor walker. This job was his only criminal justice experience prior to being appointed to the prominent position of Superintendent of the New Jersey State Police.
   FBI Director Herbert Hoover offered the superior federal resources to Schwarzkopf, but Schwarzkopf refused Hoover, claiming that he "wanted to keep the police free from federal intervention." Schwarzkopf also refused to use a fellow named Ellis Parker, a famous detective who had solved more than 200 murder cases and had been recommended by the Governor. This time he refused because super-sleuth Ellis Parker "was not in his jurisdiction."

HAUPTMANN EVIDENCE COMES TO LIGHT

1. A fellow named Isador Fisch had, indeed, lived in the Hauptmann house and had entered business deals with Hauptmann which ended in Fisch owing Hauptmann money.

2. Fisch *did* return to Germany where he died from tuberculosis in 1933. His brother was to come from Germany to settle his estate.

3. The prosecution claimed that Hauptmann alone did the kidnapping, ransom exchange, and murder, brushing aside that the Bronx carpenter would be unlikely to know anything about the activity of the Lindbergh household or that the Lindbergh's would be out that evening.

4. Hauptmann was sentenced to death.

5. New Jersey's Republican Governor learned that there was much wrong with the case and gave Hauptmann a stay of execution.

6. Newspapers (especially the Hearst newspapers) became disgruntled with the stay of execution, having previously concluded that the existing evidence (trial by popular opinion) was sufficient. They called for Hauptmann's blood, claiming he was a "child murderer" – hence whipping their readers into frenzy. Hauptmann always went by his middle name "Richard," but the newspapers always referred to him by his first name "Bruno" as it sounded more ruthless.

7. Hearst newspapers offered to provide Richard's wife, Anna Hauptmann, with an attorney. This was a trap because the attorney, Edward Reilly, had stated from the beginning in confidence that "Bruno Hauptmann is guilty and should burn!"

8. Anna Hauptmann had little money and was caring for her own baby. Not knowing the mindset of attorney Reilly, or the dogged cynicism of Randolph Hearst, Anna accepted the offer.

9. Not a single fingerprint on the ransom notes, in the nursery, or on the entry ladder, linked Hauptman to the crime; however, this information was not released to the public.

10. Little more than $14,000 of the $50,000 ransom money was ever found.

11. Shoeprints found at the crime scene and in the cemetery where the ransom money was exchanged did not match Hauptmann's. This evidential material was *omitted* by the prosecution.

12. *In a sworn affidavit*, Hauptmann's superintendent claimed that Hauptmann had worked at the Majestic apartments in New York City until 5:00 pm on the day of the

kidnapping. Therefore, Hauptmann could not have been placed at the crime scene when the kidnapping took place. However, after being summoned into the New York City District Attorney's Office, the superintendent changed his story, claiming that he could no longer be "positive." Work records for that day vanished.

13. The two eyewitnesses that placed Hauptman at the crime-scene were discredited, although they had been paid well for their testimony. When Governor Hoffman interviewed the 87-year-old Amandus Hochmuth, he found him to be partially blind, admitting to prosecutors that he could not identify a flower vase ten feet away. The second witness, the illiterate Millard Whithed, was labeled a chronic liar by his neighbors. He initially denied to police seeing anything suspicious during or after the kidnapping – but came forward two years later, motivated by reward money.

14. After getting off work on the Tuesday of the kidnapping, Hauptmann had waited for his wife, who had worked late on her job at Frederickson's, a New York City bakery-café. This was normal for Hauptmann. In fact, he often walked the Frederickson's dog while waiting for his wife. Not only did the Frederickson's confirm that Hauptman had walked their dog on that night; but in the process of dog walking, Hauptmann had gotten into an argument about the dog's ownership with August Von-Henke, who had mistaken it for his own lost dog. A bakery customer, Louis Kiss, remembered the argument. Neither August nor Louis had any personal ties to Hauptmann and, therefore, had no reason to lie.

15. The day after Louis Kiss testified to what he had witnessed, New York City attorney Berko pressed him to change his testimony, both threating to arrest him and then offering him money. Kiss informed Berko that "he had told the truth in court and would not change his testimony for any price."

16. **After Hauptmann's arrest, the New York police gave samples of Hauptmann's writing to handwriting expert <u>Albert D. Osborn</u>, who *first* reported that the samples did *not* match the ransom notes. The police had forced Hauptmann to copy the ransom note's words dozens of times <u>exactly</u> as they had been written, "*with no allowances to correct words that had been misspelled.*" They then selected the copies most like the ransom notes. When Osborn learned that ransom money had been found in the Hauptmann house, he changed his testimony citing that, "the words Hauptmann had misspelled were exactly the same as those misspelled on the ransom notes." *The fact Hauptmann had been told to copy all the words exactly as they had been spelled and written fell by the wayside.***

17. The State paid eight handwriting experts over $39,000 to examine the ransom note copies Hauptmann had been told to write. That was a sizeable sum in those days, approximating $351,000.00 in today's Federal Reserve notes. The prosecution then used the testimonies which were most likely to incriminate Hauptmann. (Often, experts testify in favor of those who are paying their fees.) Hauptmann's wife could only afford one handwriting expert.

18. The above mentioned Isidor Fisch, who had lived with the Hauptmann's and who Hauptmann claimed had left the money in his house, had been a confidence man in many swindles. Fisch had even swindled Hauptmann in their joint ventures.

19. Isidor Fisch had tried to launder "hot money" *after* the Lindbergh ransom payment.

20. Fisch applied for a passport *the same day* the Lindbergh baby's body was found.

21. Hauptmann's friend, Hans Kloppenburg, saw Fisch give Hauptmann a box for safekeeping before his departure to Germany.

22. Prosecutor Wilentz warned Kloppenburg that "if you say on the witness chair, that you seen Fisch come in with that box, you'll be arrested right away." *Kloppenburg testified as to what he had seen anyway.*

23. As the jury deliberated, a mob surrounded the courthouse, chanting "Kill Hauptmann." Some of the jurors undoubtedly feared they would be victims of mob violence.

24. Hauptmann was told that if he would "confess his guilt that his sentence would be commuted to life imprisonment," he refused.

25. Hauptmann's spiritual adviser, Reverend John Matthiesen stated, "I have had fifteen very intimate and soul-searching conversations with Bruno Richard Hauptmann, and I am convinced that he tells the truth."

26. Hauptmann's attorney (Edward Reilly) spent only 40 minutes with Hauptmann's wife, Anna, before the trial.

27. The famous detective, Ellis Parker (mentioned above), confided to Governor Hoffman that Hauptmann "couldn't have written those ransom notes – not if his life depended on it."

28. Hauptmann died in the electric chair in 1936, declaring his innocence to the end.

29. Hauptmann's wife, Anna, spent the following 60 years attempting to garner support for her dead husband's vindication.

The evidential material favorable to Richard Hauptmann, against considerable political and financial odds, most certainly established more than just "a shadow of a doubt" in his defense.

Note: #9 above: As far back as 1932, latent fingerprints could be removed from paper, metal, and glass items and used as circumstantial evidence.

The fallout from the Lindbergh baby murder produced an extensive amount of crackpot activity and speculations:

1. Charles Augustus Lindbergh was an outstanding member of the America First Committee, which opposed the entry of the United States into WWII, although Lindbergh changed his opinion with the advent of Pearl Harbor. *Prior* to Pearl Harbor, the Lindbergh haters of the time tried to cast him as a "Nazi racial supremacist" who deliberately murdered his own son because the boy had two overlapping toes. Later they would also assert that Charles had the child's body cremated to destroy evidence. (How strange it is that there were those who would make such a claim at the time. "Nazi," in German, is a conjunction of the words *"National Socialism,"* and Lindbergh and his father were anything but.)

2. The child's nurse and pediatrician had viewed the body prior to the funeral, and an autopsy had also been performed. Careful records had been kept as to what they found.

3. A news reporter, with his photographer, had gained entry to the mortuary, forced open the casket, and photographed the child's remains. (Apparently it was necessary to undress the child's corpse to conduct the grisly and unlawful research.)

4. Realizing that their child would never escape exploitation, the Lindbergh's had the baby's remains cremated and scattered the ashes from an airplane.

A plausible, yet sinister, theory is that the Lindbergh kidnapping and murder was inspired by money and politics. In the speculation and facts to follow, we hear the faint ringing of contemporary bells.

Charles Lindbergh (the aviator) and his father, U. S. Congressman Charles August Lindbergh, were both adamantly opposed to entering WWII and bitterly fought against the Federal Reserve Act, which they prophesied "would only benefit a few bankers while plunging the average man into inflation and economic despair." (The current Federal Reserve dollar is now worth less than 8 percent of what the precious metal backed dollar was valued at in the 1930s and, with our current multi-trillion-dollar indebtedness, we can be assured its value will decline even further.) Consider the notes below.

1. Walter Liggett, speechwriter for Lindbergh Sr., was murdered in 1935. The case was never solved.

2. In 1936, Louisiana politician Huey Long, biggest reelection threat to Franklin D. Roosevelt, was assassinated.

3. Louis McFadden, the Federal Reserve's chief congressional critic, survived two attempts on his life before dying suddenly, also in 1936.

4. A credible threat to Roosevelt's reelection remained – Charles Lindbergh Jr. Although Lindbergh was constitutionally too young to run for the office, an exception could have been made, just as an exception was made for Roosevelt when he ran for a third term. If nothing else, Lindbergh's fame would have garnered tremendous support for *any* Republican candidate.

Besides, what must have been inside knowledge of the Lindbergh home and their plans for that night, much evidence suggests conspiracy. Several police officers attempted to reenact the Lindbergh abduction single-handedly, but none succeeded – not even in daylight and with a sturdier ladder. Ransom money continued to appear even after Hauptmann's arrest. Super-snoop Ellis Parker – considered to be New Jersey's best detective, independently found another suspect. But it was Ellis Parker who ended up in prison for seizing the suspect.

A book was written by Professor Alan Marlis, who taught for 35 years at City University of New York. Marlis puts forth the argument that it was James Warburg who was behind the Lindbergh baby's kidnapping. Warburg was a prominent banker and member of President Franklin D. Roosevelt's "brain trust." Warburg is best remembered for telling a Senate sub-committee in 1950, "We will have world government by conquest or consent." He was the son of Federal Reserve architect, Paul Warburg. (It's interesting to note, in these contemporary times, that the Federal Reserve is neither a "Reserve" nor a "U.S. Federal" entity. With the latest advent of that phony Iran Nuclear Deal and the giving away of trillions of our tax dollars to bankers with worldwide influence, Warburg may well have been correct in his prophesy those many years ago. World government, controlled by socialism, *may well be in our extremely near future*.) (Hopefully, this dire prophecy began to change as of January 20, 2017.)

Republican activities of the Lindbergh's, (in opposition to the Federal Reserve Act and the possibility of Charles Lindbergh running in the presidential election against Franklin Roosevelt) were brought to a halt by the kidnapping and heartbreaking murder of their son. **Note**: James Warburg took a two-month vacation in Europe in April of 1932, just after the kidnapping and ransom payment.

As the news-driven hatred of Hauptmann subsided and after many years, writers such as Anthony Scaduto and Ludovic Kennedy made convincing arguments that Hauptmann was innocent and railroaded into the electric chair.

So, we've come this far with a novel case wherein handwriting expert <u>Albert Osborn</u> testified in favor of those who had paid his bill back in 1936 and have arrived at the most probable conclusion that Albert testified (and got his sons to testify) in favor of McGraw-Hill and Clifford Irving in the 1970s for the same monetary reasons. Research has turned up an unexpected and stunning conclusion, but we will get into that later. What follows now (supported by information from the FBI files set forth above) is an insight into the shadiness of those who dishonored, betrayed, and embezzled, from the greatest US industrialists of the 20th century.

1. The book *Empire*, written by Donald Barlett and James Steele and published in 1979, has been credited as being *the most comprehensive book* on the family, life, and times of Howard Hughes. The material which these authors researched for their book – *and in such a short period of time* – can only be considered extraordinary, (*unless it was given to them* by someone who had previous access to this stored material and a vested interest in providing the information.) One of the most curious things is that **Rosemont Enterprises, Inc. is never mentioned even once in this 766-page book!** Monty Montrose is only mentioned in a fleeting line "…Howard told Raymond Holliday and Monty Montrose and the crew…" and also in the index "Montrose, M. E., 368," and that's all folks! *In the entire book, that is all! Why?* It's pertinent here to add that Barlett and Steele went to great lengths in *Empire* to maintain that "Hughes probably never employed a double to impersonate him." Once again, *why* was that so important to suggest? Consider the following.

   Thorough research has indicated that all cursive known documents written by Howard Hughes were "cleaned clean" from all Hughes domiciles and business locations wherein they may have resided prior to and after 1965; and that a great deal of money was spent to this end. However, there still must be some known documents somewhere that will eventually turn up. But for now, none have been found. (Refresh with Chapter VI as to cursive writing forgeries.) (It is entirely possible that *legitimate cursive document, written by Howard Hughes,* may eventually be discovered! Perhaps the publication of this book will bring those documents to light.

   As for now, the problem of a <u>true</u> cursive comparison of any legitimate documents written by Howard Hughes has been clandestinely solved by the Summa, Inc. pirates. The letter given to Charles by his friend Howard in 1964 Mexico <u>would never have compared with the forgeries used by Rosemont Enterprises.</u> Plain and simple, the documents used to prove fraud against Clifford Irving and Melvin Dummar were forgeries and <u>not authentic</u> in terms of Howard Hughes. This is not to say that Irving and Dummar did not conspire to defraud, but that all the exemplars used by Rosemont, Inc. against Irving and Dummar were questionable documents – *all of them!*

   Now, *is there still any great mystery* as to why there is but *one* sketchy known exemplar of H.H.'s cursive writing prior to 1965? *That one sketchy exemplar might also be considered questionable.* (Refresh with Chapter VI, exhibits 43 and 44 found in Federal Files.)

2. From *Empire* we learned all about the Clifford Irving hoax and the "Mormon Will" hoax, but absolutely *nothing* about Rosemont Enterprises? Rosemont was the legal arm, backed by the tremendous wealth of the Hughes empire, which could – and did – drag any writer or news source into court if they obtained any **letters,** documents, or photos, indigenous to Howard Hughes and failed to turn them over to Rosemont. Problems would also ensue if one were to write a short story or a book about Hughes. (Letters were the very first of the many things listed which Rosemont wanted to get its hands on – *letters*?) (Hughes gave Charles a letter, or perhaps a codicil, in *1964!*)

3. Only the surface has been scratched on the voluminous documents accumulated in federal files wherein Rosemont, Inc. was courtroom active. But just that small scratch is enough to make it obvious that there is a ***tremendous gap*** in the information regarding Rosemont, Inc. in the book *Empire*. Why? In an affidavit (Exhibit 81), which takes Clifford Irving and McGraw-Hill to task, Chester Davis comes forth with the information that ***he has been the "legal-beagle" for Rosemont since 1965***. Exhibits 64-D and 64-E more clearly describe Rosemont, Inc. 1965 is a gratuitous date indeed for Monty Montrose, Chester Davis, and others, who knowingly participated in the greatest rip-off of the 20th century.
   Note: Notary, mentioned in Exhibit 81 was Howard Eckersley, inside man for Summa Inc. This is *not* a known document.

4. Here repetition is required to bring home a point. It was discovered that Rosemont, Inc. ***was created*** in 1965 by Monty Montrose and Chester Davis (*allegedly* at the behest of Howard Hughes). Of the many documents accumulated, we needed but a few to establish Rosemont Enterprises, Inc. as a formidable force in the Clifford Irving hoax, the "Mormon Will" hoax and many other courtroom battles concerning Howard Hughes. How was the disregard and blatant omission of Rosemont, Inc., the date it was formed, and those who formed it, beneficial to the Howard Hughes hoax? It was later established in court that Rosemont's activities ***were not legal***. The Judge maintained, *"The people had a right to know."* It's far more than idle conjecture to maintain that the reason the year 1965 was kept in *low profile* by Rosemont and others for so many years is because *1965 is the year the real Howard Hughes died, and the great hoax began.* Those skilled in the art of "super-snoopery" would have come to this conclusion had they began their research and ferreted out the facts after 1965 and up until 1976 when evidence was still fresh.

5. The re-publication of *Empire* as *Howard Hughes: His Life and Madness* "appears two years after the *publication* of ***The Price of Their Souls: The Truth about Howard Hughes and Those Who Betrayed Him. Howard Hughes: His Life and Madness, is the same book as Empire.*** The change in the book's title serves two purposes: (1) to cement in the *pseudo-facts,* previously purveyed – that Howard Hughes ended his life as a deranged, drug addicted, reclusive hypochondriac – and (2) to discredit *The Price of Their Souls* in hopes that *no* investigation would re-open regarding Howard Hughes. It has been well established in this book, and previously in *The Price of Their Souls*, that it was shortly after 1965 that the Hughes empire began to fall into disarray. It is realistic to believe that some opportunists, or their offspring, who know the truth are still out there.

6. A straightforward fact is that virtually **all** the handwritten exemplars used by Rosemont, Inc., that were supposedly written by Howard Hughes, ***are not known exemplars.*** In any court of law these days, and/or in most courts of law in the 1960s and 1970s, few, if any, would recognize those Rosemont documents as known. ***The only explanation*** is that the use of these documents as evidence was backed by

substantial wealth and power wherein bribery and/or fear and intimidation were used as tools.

a. The only exception found, as to the misuse of these documents as evidence, was a hastily scribbled drink order on a waitress's notepad, kept as a souvenir by Barbara Thackery, a cocktail waitress. (You may refresh with L. Russell's explanation, as to known exemplars and his view of the Thackery note pad writings in Chapter VI.)

b. Keep in mind that ***absolutely none*** of the supposed Howard Hughes cursive exemplars used by Rosemont, Inc. **pre-date 1965.** It has been well documented that this was the year Rosemont, Inc. was created by Chester Davis, Maynard "Monty" Montrose, and *supposedly* Howard Hughes. (See Exhibits 64-D, 64-E, and 81.)

c. Why is it that *no* "H.H." cursive writings used by Rosemont, Inc. have been written prior to 1965? Howard must have written *some known documents* prior to 1965. Could it have been that someone was concerned that some "non-consequential person" might turn up with a cursive document <u>that had been written</u> by Hughes – a legitimate will or codicil perhaps? (No, *not* Melvin Dummar!) It's a given that <u>a real cursive exemplar</u> by Howard Hughes *would not have* matched up with the phony documents used by Rosemont, Inc. (See Chapter VI.) Had legitimate exemplars been used; the question would have arisen as to "why is there this dramatic change in Howard's handwriting after 1965? And who is this fellow forging all these questionable exemplars and claiming them to be documents written by Howard Hughes?" Now *that,* most certainly, would have blown the pirating of the Hughes estate and obliterated the thieves' cover!

It's well established that Daddy Osborn and his boys "went to the wall" with Clifford Irving and McGraw Hill in their quest to substantiate Clifford's claim to be the authorized biographer for Howard Hughes. Many publishers had waited in line for the lucrative profits, soon to be delivered, when the Rosemont, Inc. vs. McGraw-Hill and Clifford Irving dust settled. Oh yes! There was affidavit after affidavit and reams of cleverly worded documents as the Osbornes pointed out their expertise in the field, as well as the *alleged legitimacy* of the Irving documents and voice tapes. Other honorable and respectable experts also gave affidavits supporting Clifford Irving's claim, but alas, all in vain. It was a ***hoax***, and a hoax by any other name...

This chapter's objective was to shine a light on the real activities concerning Rosemont, Inc., (established by Monty Montrose, Chester Davis, and *allegedly* Howard Hughes in 1965.) Rosemont Enterprises, Inc. was a major player in the legal activities of Summa, Inc., the powerhouse of the Hughes empire. This has most *certainly* been established! Among other things that have come to light concerning Rosemont Enterprises, Inc., is that Rosemont, Inc. was *not* just overlooked or missed by Bartlett and Steele in their 766-page book *Empire* but ***was intentionally omitted!***

The Osborns' part, as cursive writing analysts favorable to McGraw-Hill and Clifford Irving against Rosemont, Inc. is a *typical* illustration of Rosemont's multi-faceted activities. Rosemont, Inc. was clearly and deeply involved in many legal battles concerning "Howard Hughes." Its primary purpose was to keep all legitimate personal information concerning Hughes closely guarded and out of the public eye. It has become convincingly apparent that the reason for conducting this sham was *not* to protect Hughes or the Hughes business networks, but to help create a clandestine vehicle for embezzling large sums of money from a dead man's empire under the guise of legitimacy. "Oh yes, Howard wants to buy up as many gold and silver mining claims in Nevada, as he can get his hands on. Oh yeah, Howard agreed to that and etc. Also, here is a letter he wrote concerning this, or that, or whatever."? That the cursive writings submitted, allegedly having been written by Howard Hughes, could <u>never</u> be considered *known exemplars* made little difference in those many courtroom clashes. There was example after example of bait/switch and bluff after bluff, <u>but no known exemplars</u> other than several Hughes signatures prior to 1965, which had been prolifically *forged* on other documents down through the years.

When the research began, it certainly appeared that the Osborns, and their skills as cursive writing analysts were barely reliable at best and bought and paid for at worst. Research has graphically pointed out that, in most contemporary attorneys' minds, Albert Osborn may have been considered criminal regarding Richard Hauptmann. So why not business as usual concerning Clifford Irving and McGraw-Hill? However, the *main objective* was to establish Rosemont, Inc. as a critical feature in keeping a mega-hoax perpetual. Yes, let us reiterate, "**a perpetual mega-hoax!**" Yes, a hoax masterfully crafted and ongoing until Chester Davis, Nadine Henley, Bill Gay, and Bob Maheu could bag up enough of the Hughes millions to keep them in platinum lifestyles – if, in their minds that was even possible. Their greed thrived for ten years, and it appears to have been insatiable.

They never gave up on the degradation of a long-dead Howard Hughes, which served to further their decadent ambitions, until busted out of power by Will Lummis. <u>It also appears that Will Lummis continued the ruse after taking control to further his own monetary desires.</u> It is so pathetically sad that one of the greatest industrialists this country has ever known – a provider of thousands upon thousands of jobs, a great wartime industrial protector of the United States, and a better man than most – would be so demeaned by *those degenerate life forms*, named above.

Prior to the information cited below, one might waver on the edge of becoming a Clifford Irving apologist. "How in the world could Clifford Irving believe he could get away with his hoax and obvious false claims concerning Hughes?" With information now accumulated, it is obvious that anything concerning Howard Hughes after 1965 was a hoax, but Clifford could have had no way to know this. So, the elephant in the room is, how could Irving possibly believe that he could pull off his scam? So much for the Osborn *team* as well. They were soundly discredited. When all the cards were on the table and the attempted swindle brought to light, the obvious truth was that *Clifford Irving and his accomplice, Richard Suskind, had never exchanged a single written or spoken word with Howard Hughes!* It was impossible, since they – and most others at the time – did not know that Hughes had been dead for seven years, give or take a few months.

In the end, Richard Suskind, Clifford Irving, and his wife, Edith, *all* admitted to the hoax. Clifford did time in the United States and his wife went to prison in Switzerland where she had set up a fictitious account in the name of H. R. Hughes (Helga R. Hughes) to cash the McGraw-Hill checks. Even more mysterious than Irving thinking he could get away with his hoax is, how could the Osborns have given sworn testimony in the courtroom, in front of God and everyone, **that the extensive letters,** supposedly written by Hughes to both Clifford Irving and *McGraw-Hill*, **were written by the same hand** *as all the <u>previous</u> letters supposedly written by Hughes.* These letters, in the possession of Rosemont, Inc., had been prolifically used in courtroom activity and in periodicals as being known Hughes documents on many occasions. **All had been written within a seven-year timespan** *after 1965.* In retrospect, and with a reasonable conviction that the Osborns had simply sold their *alleged* expertise to a wealthy bidder, *one begins to consider the improbable.*

Per the Hauptmann information above, one may certainly come to the opinion that Albert Osborn had used his knowledge of cursive writing to help send an innocent Richard Hauptmann to the electric chair. Was it a result of political pressure, for money, or both? I suppose we will never know. But what about Albert's sons who also attested as cursive writing analysts in the Clifford Irving scam? Any man who has a son will note an innate rebellious streak within them. (Most of us are aware of the same within ourselves in younger years.) So how did Daddy Albert get sons Russell and Paul to go along with what would later come to light as an obvious hoax? Those men signed their credibility away on several sworn affidavits (as per above) favorable to Irving and McGraw-Hill. What was their future after that? Was the money *that* good? What about Frank McCulloch (New York Bureau Chief of Time-Life News Service) and Ralph Graves (Managing Editor of *LIFE* magazine?) Both provided affidavits *in opposition* of Rosemont Enterprises, Inc. Upstanding and straightforward, these men would never intentionally risk injury to their reputations. Also, it is unthinkable that they would risk the reputation of the company that employed them. Was Clifford Irving *that good of a used car salesman?* Concerning all these fellows listed above, what phony evidence was so convincing that they felt obligated to swing into the Irving camp against Rosemont, Inc.? Would they intentionally risk their own livelihood along with the credibility and financial resources of their employers? *Something seemed very wrong!*

Fortunately for us, our super-sleuth "Russ" "had worn many hats" in his law enforcement career. "Cursive Writing Analyst" (at which he excelled) was one of the many. In the pursuit of thoroughness, *the Irving letters that the Osborns had analyzed for Clifford Irving and McGraw-Hill, were given to Russ together with documents used by Rosemont, Inc. Russ did a comparative analysis.* At the time, the thinking was to further portray the Osborns as the super-bad boys they appeared to be. It was believed that Ralph Graves, Frank McCulloch, McGraw-Hill, and others had unwittingly fallen into lockstep behind the Osborns, having been victimized by the excellent salesmanship of Clifford Irving and Richard Suskind. <u>**This does not now appear to be the case!**</u>

MORE PERTINENT INFORMATION FOUND, AND LETTERS ANALYZED

Cursive writings analysis by Laurence "Russ" Russell, his letter, and cursive letters are analyzed below. Those used by Rosemont Inc. and Clifford Irving, respectively, as supposedly known exemplars, and supposedly written by Howard Hughes.

HANDWRITING EXAMINATION CONDUCTED JULY 24, 2016 AT HENDERSON, NEVADA

At the request of Mr. Charles Clotfelter of Henderson, NV, I examined each of the (4) photocopied letters (see below listing) and a typewritten questionnaire with handwritten responses, with the purpose of providing a definitive opinion as to the authorship of each of those documents. Not having a sufficient quantity of *known* handwriting exemplars of Howard Hughes, makes it difficult to provide an opinion as to his definite authorship of the letters (listed below.) However, from those very limited handwritten exemplars, *believed* to have been written by Howard Hughes, I am able to state that it is my opinion that the real Howard Hughes did not author any of the letters or the questionnaire listed below. Who did author these letters? It is unknown at this time. However, through careful examination of the photocopied letters and questionnaire, I am able to state that the same person most probably authored each of these four letters and the handwritten responses found on the questionnaire. There is no more than one author involved. Only one unknown author is responsible for these letters (and questionnaire) which covered the years of approximately 1968 through 1972.

Russ L. Russell (Chief of Police - Retired)

Documents (Letters and Questionnaire,) questionable exemplars all; none known. #1 and #2, bogus by Clifford Irving's courtroom admission - examined:

1. Exhibits 102-A and B: Undated "Dear Mr. Irving - Exemplars" handwritten letter, two pages long, signed in the name of Howard R. Hughes.
2. Exhibits 103-A, B, C, and D: Handwritten letter, dated 11-17-71 "Exemplars addressed to Mr. Harold McGraw" (of McGraw Hill,) four pages in length, signed in the name of Howard R. Hughes.
3. Exhibits 104-A, B, and C: Undated "Dear Chester and Bill Exemplars" handwritten letter, three pages in length, signed in the name of "Howard R. Hughes."
4. Exhibits 105-A, B, and C: Handwritten letter, dated 3-16-68, addressed to "Bob." Exemplars, three pages in length, signed in the names of "Howard" and "H."
5. Exhibits 106-A and B: Two-page typed questionnaire Exemplar, completed in long hand, signed in the name of "Howard Hughes."

BOTTOM LINE HERE IS: *THE LETTERS SUBMITTED BY ROSEMONT ENTERPRISES, INC. AS HAVING BEEN WRITTEN BY HOWARD HUGHES, AND THOSE SUBMITTED BY CLIFFORD IRVING AS HAVING BEEN WRITTEN BY HOWARD HUGHES, WERE ALL WRITTEN BY THE SAME UNKNOWN AUTHOR.*

EXHIBIT 102-A

10 DEC 1970

Dear Mr. Irving:

Thank you for the gift of your book, which I thoroughly enjoyed reading. Your inscription was very thoughtful.

I find myself deeply in-terested in the fellow you have written about, despite a natural inclination to the contrary. I cannot help wondering what has happened to him.

I would hate to think what other biographers might have done to him, but it seems to me that you have portrayed your man with great consideration and sympathy, when it would have been tempting to do

1. Dear Mr. Irving letter concerning "Howard" & Clifford
1222257 – 0 -87 – HQ – 119739 – BULKY 19 pages 87 & 88

EXHIBIT 102-B

This has impressed me.
I do remember your
father and I was sorry
to learn of his passing.
Yours truly,

H. R. Hughes

EXHIBIT 103-A

2. Letter from "Hughes" to McGraw Hill – Concerning Clifford as his biographer
1222257 – 0 – 87 – HQ – 119739 – BULKY 19   pages 21 – 22 – 23 - & 29

11 - 17 - 71

NOV 22 1971
McGRAW-HILL BOOK CO.

Mr. Harold McGraw
McGraw Hill
New York, N.Y.

Dear Mr. McGraw -

The facts placed
before me, I find
astonishing. I do not
understand, in the
first place, why it is
not possible for your
publishing house in
possession of a legiti-
mate contract between
myself and Mr. Clifford
Irving and between your-
selves and Mr. Irving,
for the publication of
my autobiography, cannot
deal firmly and force-
fully with other
publishers who which
are asserting fraudulent
claims to the rights
which I have granted
to Mr. Irving and Mr.

EXHIBIT 103-B

Irving in Turin has granted to you, without my intervention.

I have said before, and I will say again, that this Mr. Post and Mr. Eaton in no way represent me and have no rights granted by me to sell articles or books purporting to be authorized or written by me. I have given no material whatsoever to these people and no documents, and any claim by them to the contrary is fraudulent and criminal and I am sure these people are employed by my enemies.

In the event that they or any publisher

EXHIBIT 103-C

should attempt to publish any material supposedly secured by me or authorized by me, and you can do nothing to prevent this through normal channels, I assume you - and I ask that you in turn will now assure them - that I will do all in my power, and take whatever legal steps are necessary to halt what I consider an outrage on my privacy and my painfully worked out agreement with you and Mr. Clifford Irving.

I have been made aware, although not fully to my satisfaction of McGraw Hills apparently embarrassing

EXHIBIT 103-D

very near future.
I have already given
my approval in
advance to Mr. Irving,
and I have the utmost
faith that he will
be faithful to my
wishes in this preparation
of the manuscript.

Most sincerely yours,

Howard R. Hughes

EXHIBIT 104-A

95-211845 PF KII

Dear Chester and Bill -

I do not understand why the problem of Maheu is not yet fully settled and why this bad publicity seems to continue, It could hurt our company's valuable properties in Nevada, and also the entire state.

I believe my company is one of the biggest employers (if not the biggest in the state, and surely what damages an entity employing this many Nevadans is bad for the state itself.)

You told me that, if I called Governor Laxalt and District Attorney George Franklin, it would put an end to this problem.

I made these calls, and I do not understand why this very damaging publicity should continue merely because the properly constituted board of directors of Hughes Tool Company decided, for reasons they considered just, to terminate all relationship with Maheu and Hooper.

3. Chester & Bill letter
122257 – 0 – 95 – HQ – 211845 – BULKY 84 pages 88 – 89 – 90

EXHIBIT 104-B

I asked you to take whatever action is necessary to accomplish the objectives briefly outlined above.

I ask you now please to inform the members of the board of Hughes Tool Company of my desires and feelings in respect to this matter.

It is not my wish to try to tell the board what action should be taken. That is their job. But it seems there has been some uncertainty as to where I stand, and I want this cleared up at once.

I do not support Maheu or Hooper in their defiance of the Hughes Tool Company Board of Directors, and I deeply desire all concerned to be fully aware of this immediately.

I ask you to do everything in your power to put an end to these problems, and further I ask you to obtain immediately a full accounting of any

EXHIBIT 104-C

and all funds and/or property to which Mr. Maheu may have had access.

As I have said, this matter has caused me the very gravest concern, and is damaging my company and all the loyal men and women associated with me in the very deepest and far-reaching way.

My sincere regards;

Howard R Hughes

EXHIBIT 105-A

Bob—

You ask my adice as a friend.

The only substantial loss involved here is the opportunity to tie up some of these properties for our benefit. However, this may not be lost.

We may perhaps be able to obtain an option on these properties if we work quickly enough tonight. You will need my assistance and I will work much more effectively if we have the hotel deal settled first. Why dont you see Moe and tell him everything this bastard Maier has done to us and how terribly upset you are about it. Sometimes a friend will do something out of sympathy he will not do for any other reason.

Why not tell Moe you are going to be simply imersed in the responsibility of trying to recapture the prior position of exclusivity which we previously enjoyed in this mining field. That this will be a full time job and so you are having one of Holliday's [illegible]

4. Bob Letter dated 03/16/68
1222257 – 0 – 95 – HQ – 211845 – BULKY 84 pages 96 - 97 - 9[illegible]

EXHIBIT 105-B

Then, this might lead to a situation where you could suggest adroitly to Moe that if we could wrap this up tonight. You would not have to turn the Stardust deal over to somebody else, and you would get the credit for closing the Stardust deal instead of the man from Houston.

You may be surprised, Bob, but many times a man like Moe will make concessions on a business deal like this for a friend's personal benefit — when he would never make the same concession because he is driven to it by bargaining.

I mean, for example, that I believe Moe would go further as a gesture of personal friendship to you than he ever would as the result of negotiating pressure brought by me. You see if I try to bargain Moe into a deal, his pride asserts itself and he says "never!" Whereas, as a favor and gesture of personal friendship to you when you are depressed by

EXHIBIT 105-C

...the treasury of a trusted employ who betrayed your trust, Moe might easily do what he would not do for me.

Anyway, please try,

Stoward

I urge you not to fire Meier until we discuss him just a little more. Let's please dispose of Moe and then I will give my full attention to Meier. I just simply have a one-channel mind, please forgive me,

Sf.

EXHIBIT 106-A

1. Is Chester Davis authorized to represent you in this McGraw-Hill matter without limitation, including obtaining all information from any bank?

*Yes. Also please con-
centrate on who re-
ceived the money*

2. Did you, in 1965, grant to Rosemont Enterprises, Inc. the sole and exclusive right to publish your life story?

#2 Yes

3. Did you at any time authorize McGraw-Hill or Clifford Irving or anyone other than Rosemont to publish your autobiography or biography or any material relating to you? (This does not relate to copyrighted magazine articles you permitted to be published prior to 1960)

*No. I would like to see
these forgeries*

4. I understand that Clifford Irving was born on November 5, 1930 and that his father before changing his name some time after 1930 was known as Jay Rafsky, a cartoonist who drew a panel entitled "Potsy" about policemen and firemen which appeared in Collier's magazine. Have you ever met or do you know a Clifford Irving, or did you ever talk to him, or did you ever communicate or correspond with him in any way or did you in any manner whatsoever otherwise collaborate with him or anyone else in the preparation of an autobiography or anything else to be published about you?

No. I do not know either.

5. Did you furnish Clifford Irving or anyone (other than Rosemont) with any material of any kind, including tape recordings, either directly or through others for the purpose of an autobiography or for the publication of anything about you?

Not at any time.

6. Did you sign or authorize the execution on your behalf of a contract with McGraw-Hill or Clifford Irving for the publication of anything by you or concerning you?

Same as above.

7. Did you receive or authorize anyone else to receive any money directly or indirectly from McGraw-Hill or Clifford Irving for the publication of anything by you or concerning you or for anything else?

No

8. When is the last time you personally endorsed a check for any reason?

*More than 10 years ago
Howard R. Hughes*

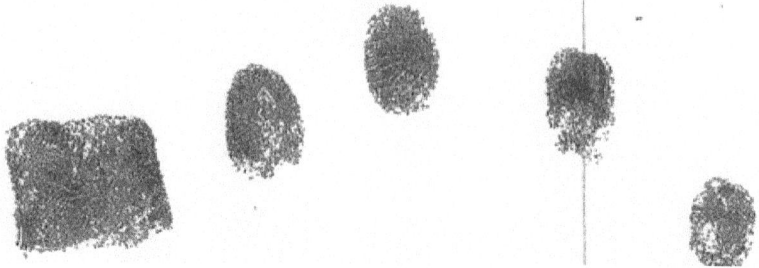

5. Denial of Clifford Irving as Hughes biographer written by "Hughes."
1222257 – 0 – 95 – HQ – 211845 – BULKY 84   pages 110 & 111

EXHIBIT 106-B

9. Did you ever give McGraw-Hill, Clifford Irving or anyone else instructions of any kind relating to the publication of anything concerning you?

Absolutely not

10. The original press release issued by McGraw-Hill states that the purported "autobiography" was substantially based on taping sessions with you over a period of many months during 1971. Other than what you may have done with respect to copyrighted articles which appeared prior to 1960, have you ever dictated, written or prepared any tapes, manuscripts or recordings relating to your life or to any incidents in your life for the purpose of the publication of any kind of biography or for any other purpose?

No

11. It has been suggested that someone may have had access to handwritten notes or memoranda or other communications in your handwriting or of tapes of conversations with you which could have become available to others. With the exception of tapes or other material in connection with the copyrighted articles that were published prior to 1960, the message to me and Bill Gay during the Maheu litigation and the letters you wrote last year to the Nevada State Gaming Commission, are you aware of the existence of any authentic material of the types described which could have become available?

None should be available

12. Did you ever start to write your autobiography or did you ever tell any of your assistants that you were writing an autobiography and ask any of them to deny it if questioned?

Absolutely not

Howard R. Hughes

241

EXHIBIT 107

Clifford Irving's affidavit concerning "H.H." tapes was found in Federal File 12222-0-87-HQ-119739-BULKY 19 (pages 233, 244, 245, and 255) and (pages 1, 12, 13, and 23, respectively, of the affidavit.) The entirety of the affidavit is not inclusive, only enough to bring home the point that the taping of a voice, all believed to be Howard Hughes, was brought in as evidence by Clifford Irving. Of course, it was not Hughes! (Begins with Exhibit 107, ends with 110). Irving admitted to the hoax and went to jail because of it.

SUPREME COURT OF THE STATE OF NEW YORK
COUNTY OF NEW YORK
- -X

ROSEMONT ENTERPRISES, INC.,   :   INDEX NO.

                    Plaintiff,   :   800/72

    -against-   :

McGRAW-HILL BOOK COMPANY, McGRAW-HILL   AFFIDAVIT
INC., TIME INCORPORATED, DELL PUBLISHING
COMPANY, INC., CLIFFORD IRVING and   :   IN
JOHN DOES I through III,
                                 OPPOSITION
                   Defendants.   :
- -X

STATE OF NEW YORK   )
COUNTY OF NEW YORK) ss:

          CLIFFORD IRVING, being duly sworn, deposes and says:

                I

   1.   DEFENDANT HEREIN:

     I am a Defendant in the above described action and make this affidavit in opposition to Plaintiff's motion for a Preliminary Injunction and an order granting Plaintiff leave to take depositions upon oral testimony.

   2.   CITIZENSHIP:

     I am a United States citizen, being born in New York, New York, on November 5, 1930.

   3.   FATHER:

     My father, the late Jay Irving (born Irving Joel Rafsky) was a cartoonist for Collier's Weekly and the Chicago Tribune-New York News

1. Clifford Irving has taping session with Howard Hughes.
1222257 – 0-87 – HQ – 119739 – BULKY 19 (Pages 233 – 245 - & 255 of Federal file)
(Pages 1-12-13- & 23 of affidavit) [Testimony of Taping is Article VII]

EXHIBIT 108

FBI FILE 12222-0-87-HQ-119739-BULKY 19—PAGE 244
Clifford Irving's affidavit concerning "Howard Hughes" tape-recording session.

in January and February of 1971, acknowledged to me, on the telephone and in person, that he had received both letters.

12.8 I wrote one more letter to Mr. Hughes on December 26, 1971, at the George Gordon Holmes address previously mentioned. However, in September of 1971, Mr. Hughes had advised me personally that this address was "no good any longer." He did not give me an alternate address and he has never given me a telephone number where I could reach him. I sent the December 26th letter anyway, because I thought it was certainly worth the effort to try and reach him, due to the unusual circumstances following McGraw-Hill's announcement of publication of our book. Photocopying facilities were available on Ibiza at the time and I made two copies of the letter, one of which I mailed to Shelton Fisher, President, McGraw-Hill Inc. Attached as Exhibit M.

VII

13. <u>MEETINGS WITH HOWARD HUGHES AND TAPING SESSIONS WITH HOWARD HUGHES:</u>

13.1 <u>February 13, 1971, Mexico:</u>

After several telephone calls from Mr. Hughes to me in Ibiza, Mr. Hughes arranged our first meeting in Oaxaca, Mexico. This took place on <u>February 13, 1971.</u> An emissary of Mr. Hughes, known to me only as <u>Pedro,</u> picked me up at the Hotel Victoria in Oaxac at approximately 7:00 A.M. and drove me to a mountaintop called <u>Monte Alban</u> where Mr. Hughes awaited me in a parked car. Mr. Hughe identified himself to me as Howard Hughes and was clearly recognizable to me as Howard R. Hughes by reason of prior photographs that I had

EXHIBIT 109

FBI FILE 12222-0-87-HQ-119739-BULKY 19—PAGE 245
Clifford Irving's affidavit concerning "Howard Hughes" tape-recording session.

with my father in the early 1940's which corroborated what my father had told me regarding those meetings.   Mr. Hughes and I spoke inter-mittently for between one and two hours and then arranged a meeting for the following day.

    13.2 February 14, 1971:

    On that following day, February 14, 1971, the man known to me as Pedro flew me by private plane to Juchitan airport on the isthmus of Mexico, and we then drove in a car to Salina Cruz, where I went for a swim. Mr. Hughes and I finally met in the early afternoon in a room in a hotel in Tehuantepec. Our discussion lasted intermittently for several hours, during which time Mr. Hughes repeatedly left the room and went elsewhere for periods of ten to twenty minutes. Mr. Hughes vanished at about 6:00 P.M. and I returned to Oaxaca and then the following morning to New York. The man known to me as Pedro gave me what appears to be a Polaroid photograph, taken of me by a Hughes aide as I descended from the plane at Mexico City Airport enroute from New York. This, it was explained to me, was for identification purpose and to insure that I was not accompanied by newsmen.

    13.3 March 4, 1971, Puerto Rico:

    Following Mr. Hughes' telephoned instructions, I flew on March 2, 1971 from Ibiza via Madrid to San Juan, Puerto Rico. I was met at the airport by an emissary of Mr. Hughes known to me only as Jorge, or George. This man took from me the draft copy of the Letter of Agreement dated March 4, 1971, between Mr. Hughes and myself that I had previously prepared in Ibiza, and told me to register at the El San Juan Hotel in San Juan, which I did. At approximately 4:00 A.M.

-13-

EXHIBIT 110

FBI FILE 12222-0-87-HQ-119739- BULKY 19 – (signature sheet)
Clifford Irving's affidavit concerning "Howard Hughes" tape-recording session.

by McGraw-Hill, Time Inc., myself and Mr. Hughes.

Clifford Irving

Sworn to before me this

_18_ day of January, 1972.

MARTIN S. ACKERMAN
Notary Public, State of New York
No. 31-5014605
Qualified in New York County
Commission Expires March 30, 1972

CC: White & Case
14 Wall Street
New York, New York 10005

Cravath Swaine & Moore
1 Chase Manhattan Plaza
New York, New York

CRITIQUE ON ABOVE EXHIBITS

Is it any wonder why McGraw Hill, Frank McCulloch, and others would believe Clifford Irving when the same voice on the recording Irving produced was the same voice they had previously heard during a conference call from the Bahamas? At that time, all believed it was the voice of Howard Hughes.

How in the world could all the letters and statements above have been written by the same hand (person) when we know for certain that the letters submitted by Clifford Irving were deemed to be forgeries? (He admitted to the forgeries. He and his wife went to prison because of the forgeries.)

It is preposterous to assume that Clifford went to prison because he wanted free room and board while he wrote his book *Hoax*. Oh yeah! He was "all in" on the biography hoax. But what did he know, in the *beginning,* that so emboldened him, his wife, and best friend Richard Suskind? And what did Irving know *later* as the spoof began to spin out of control?

By the way, the fingerprints at the bottom of the Irving denial documents must have been superimposed from legitimate prints taken off the Department of Defense records. (See Chapter VI, Exhibits 106-A and 106-B.) According to Russ, superimposing prints was an easy thing to do – even in the seventies. These appear to be terribly smudged prints anyway; and it is entirely probable, whether superimposed or intentionally smeared, that no lab tests of these prints were ever done. (Later analyses of these prints will deem them to be unreadable and, quite possibly, intentionally skewed).

Okay, nay-sayers, go to the Rosemont documents, expand them, print them out, and lay them side by side. Study them for a bit. Compare them to the Irving letters. And most probably, you also will conclude that the above letters (all of them) were indeed written by the same hand. A signature is easy to forge, *but whole letters?* No way!

So here we have it: (a) Hoax documents written by the same hand as Rosemont, Inc. documents, *supposedly* written by Howard Hughes earlier, but after 1965. (b) Clifford Irving's tape recordings of "Howard Hughes" with the same voice as was heard by Frank McCulloch, McGraw-Hill, and others in the Bahamian conference call (to prove the Irving hoax.) And now it comes to light that Albert, Paul, and Russell Osborn were on the up and up, which certainly explains why they were willing to give exhaustive affidavits as to the authenticity of the Irving documents. So, we have four cursive writing experts (inclusive of L. "Russ" Russell,) in agreement that the Rosemont, Inc. documents and the Clifford Irving *hoax* documents, were written by the same hand (person)!

Yes, let's give Albert Osborn (The Old Man) a pass here, together with his sons. They apparently did their jobs well. What did the Osborns say to the Press after the Irving hoax was exposed? Had they sensed the gravity of their peculiar situation? Taxes had to have been brutal on the Hughes estate. Was the government involved? Irving never testified as to *who* his forger was. Apparently, he was in a plea bargain situation where he wasn't obligated to do so. Did the Osborns bite the bullet and just fade away? Were they paid to keep their mouths shut? Were they threatened? There are still a lot of unanswered questions here. Perhaps more information will come to light soon, but for now it's imperative to get this book into print in hopes of getting more investigative help. (You will discover later that in Melvin Dummar's "Mormon Will Scam," he was not obligated to give up his forger either.)

So, what might be the real story concerning the Clifford Irving hoax? Once again let us consider – without a lot of replication – the following. In the beginning, Clifford had to have believed that he could pull off an elaborate Hughes hoax and get away with it. Clifford Irving was/is obviously intelligent. We cannot say any less about an author of his magnitude. He had to have been so confident he could pull off his scam that he was willing to risk his reputation and the financial wherewithal of McGraw-Hill and others who were unknowing participants. Irving must have believed somehow that he could make his claim believable to even the most skeptical of partisans and observers.

Clifford had to have had access to the forger – the same forger who had faked all the other phony documents supposedly written by Howard Hughes **after 1965.** Therefore, he had to have believed that his documents would be accepted as authentic since *they were written by the same hand as those documents in the possession of Rosemont Enterprises, Inc. and supposedly written by Howard Hughes!* Now, having said this, Clifford had to have supposed that (a) Hughes was alive and clandestinely wanted him to write his biography in the beginning, (b) that Hughes was dead and he had access to the forger who was a separate entity from the doppelganger "Hughes" in the Bahamas, (c) the voice Clifford Irving had on his tapes was the same voice that McCullock *presumed* he had heard in his earlier phone contact with pre-1965 Hughes and would be the same voice McCullock, McGraw-Hill, and the others heard in the conference call from the Bahamas, and (d) last, but not least, that the voice, *supposedly coming from the Bahamas, was probably coming from somewhere stateside.* (The news group did not call the Bahamas to talk to Hughes. Chester Davis set up the conference call and called the news group. At the time, all parties presumed that the voice they heard was coming out of the Bahamas!)

Now we can most certainly speculate, with near perfect accuracy, that it was a conspicuous discovery by Chester Davis – or one of the other original Hughes estate pirates – that tipped the scales in favor of Rosemont, Inc. Irving's wife was using the fictitious name of "H. R. Hughes" on a Swiss bank account to cash the McGraw-Hill checks. (Irving had McGraw-Hill make out the checks to H. R. Hughes, so they could be deposited to the phony Howard Hughes account!) Now, let us take it even further and say that the phony Swiss bank account was not smart. Why? Well, because there is a very strong possibility that Davis, Henley, and Gay found out about the phony account through an insider tip. Perhaps it was a banker friendly to Gay, Henley, and Davis that clandestinely broke protocol and informed the "dirty trio" that McGraw-Hill was giving Clifford Irving checks made out to H. R. Hughes and that they were being deposited to a Swiss bank where Gay, Henley, and Davis *already had* millions upon millions of stolen Hughes estate monies squirreled away! Oh yeah, there can be little doubt that they would know all about "the lay of the Swiss banking landscape." (An inside tip from a McGraw-Hill employee or a detective following the Irvings are also strong possibilities.)

WHO WAS THE FORGER?

How was Irving bated with a seemingly foolproof way to make a million with the promise of much more to be eventually deposited into the Irving coffers? Of course, a likely suspect would be Robert "Bob" Maheu. And how could "Bobbie Boy" convincingly pull it off? By causing Irving to believe, in the beginning, that Howard Hughes was alive and really wanted Irving to write his Biography. *Maheu may have temporarily gained access to the original forger* of Hughes's documents (strong-arm, bribery, or threat of exposure.) *After all Bobbie was supposedly Hughes's right-hand man after 1965 until he got fired by the Summa, Inc. trio. He was also the "go to" man in hiring Hughes impersonators early on.* A simple letter, under Maheu's guidance, which that forger would write, could be compared by Clifford Irving with numerous other phony documents. These would be documents that Rosemont, Inc. had used many times before in newspapers and various periodicals as known documents (which they were not.). Obviously, the documents Irving saw matched up perfectly, as they did for Russ. Throw in a few voice tapes on top of this; *and voila, the scam had the appearance of a foolproof scenario* – or so the Irving group must have believed at the time.

Let's back up a little and revisit Bob Maheu's fall from power in 1970. Maheu was definitely the tail that waged the Summa, Inc. dog *after 1965* up until 1970. However, he was out scammed by Gay, Henley, and Davis. (Refresh with Federal Documents, Exhibits 14-A, 15, and 16.) Bobbie was adjudged to be a less than honorable employee and the judge threw in with Gay, Henley, and Davis and got Maheu sacked. The instrument used was a phony cursive document, supposedly written and signed by "Hughes." Maheu could not divulge his knowledge of the "Hughes" imposter scams *without implicating himself!* (It is entirely possible that there was more than one forger – one for lengthy cursive letters, several for signatures, and now, with the advent of the Clifford Irving tapes, a vocal "Hughes" as well. Also let us not forget that visual "Hughes" was rarely seen. Never having to worry about finances, all the players had plenty of free time to practice. Keep in mind that the value of $1,000,000.00 in the 1970s is well worth $11,000,000.00 in today's inflated currency. At the rate monies were disappearing from the Hughes coffers between 1965 and 1976, the embezzling opportunists running the Hughes Empire were platinum plated. They could more than afford to keep and pay as many comrades as were needed for their swindle to look legitimate.

And, once more, let's regress a little and state that it's unlikely that "Hughes" moved from the Bahamas because he fell into paperwork disfavor with the Bahamian government. Charlie was there in 1964 and he knows better! First, "Bahamian Howard" was not the real Howard Hughes; and if he had been asked for fingerprints and various photos, the scam would have been revealed then and there. It was only after Bob Maheu got fired in 1970 that the "H.H." entourage began its mutable moves between Las Vegas, Nevada; London, England; Montreal, Canada; Nicaragua; Freeport, Bahamas; ending in Acapulco, Mexico. And It was only <u>after</u> the imposter "Hughes's" location in the Bahamas was reveled in the Clifford Irving scam, that Bob Maheu would send his men down to stir up Bahamian trouble. It was only then that the "Hughes" entourage would move to Acapulco, Mexico. It was an undisclosed location and only a select few would know of it. Bob Maheu was, once more, <u>not</u> one of the informed.

It's not prudent to believe that "H.H." liked a change in scenery every few months or so. He was always kept out of view and in his room anyway – sickly and likely "stoned" most of the time. (Go back to Chapter II and read Gordon Margulis's take on the wish of his boss in Vancouver, Canada). Also see Exhibits 179-D and E. The main objective, it appears, was to keep the imposter away from Maheu. The greatest fear of Bill Gay, Nadine Henley, and Chester Davis was that Maheu could, once more, get control of the visual imposter "Hughes," as well as the cursive "Hughes," and could thereby again gain control of the Hughes Empire. He might even get Davis, Gay, and Henley fired by convincing whoever the phony "Hughes" was, that the Maheu slate would be more lucrative than that of the Summa, Inc. trios. Whatever was happening – with or without Maheu – *it all fell apart when the phony "Hughes" account in Switzerland became known* and Irving and his accomplices were obligated to fess-up.

The quandary is simply this: we *know* that the <u>phony Rosemont, Inc. exemplars</u> matched up with the <u>phony Irving exemplars,</u> and *none of them* were <u>known</u> exemplars. The Irving/Maheu pact, <u>if</u> it existed, had to be well thought out before Irving and his family would have gotten on board. Benign in the beginning, it could have gotten edgy when challenged by Rosemont, Inc. – a development which may not have been anticipated because Irving and his accomplices were in the know about a long dead Hughes. The idea that Clifford Irving was threatened by Maheu is not too far out of line; in fact, it seems highly likely. Irving nearly died of fright when the phony Swiss bank account came into question. When the scam began to unravel, it's entirely possible that Maheu could have had a snuff film of Salvatore "Sam" Giancana being malevolently and slowly murdered and used this to threaten Irving and his family. (Sam was a "goodfella" friend of Maheu, whose expertise was money laundering and other criminal acts. He was directly tied to the Hughes Empire through Maheu *after* 1965.) In the beginning, Irving and his accomplices may have believed that Irving was chosen to be the *legitimate* biographer for Hughes. However, once up to their necks in the ploy, they were stuck fast as flies on flypaper and had to continue the ruse or suffer dire consequences at the hands of Maheu. Clifford Irving, his wife, and Son, as well as David Suskind, may well have become potential targets for Maheu; and Bobbie-Boy could have made it crystal clear that he would take decisive action should he become implicated in the Irving scam in any way. For these reasons, the Irving group may have taken the full rap when the sting unraveled, while Maheu, once more, *slithered* off into the sunset.

ANOTHER LIKELY SCENARIO

Considering there may have been at least *two* forgers between the years of 1965 and 1976 – one good at signatures and another good with both signatures and extensive documents – could Howard Eckersley have been one, or both? As you read through the Exhibits 111 through 116-B below, you will find that most of them were encountered above in Chapters IV and VI. In analyzing these documents, as a group, it became necessary to put "all the ducks in a row" so to speak. The intention is to bring home yet another specific observation with easy visual and minimal confusion and shine a light on Howard Eckersley. Eckersley was close to the phony "Hughes" during the crafting of *all* the questionable documents below.

Exhibits 111 and 112:
A great deal of suspicion is generated by a supposed "Hughes" passing through customs on the way back into the United States from Canada. On Exhibit 112, the location of prints is noted where the supposed "H.H." pressed down while signing the aircraft inspection report. (Refresh with Chapter IV) Howard Eckersley is on board with the scheme at the time.

Exhibit 113:
1. A supposed "Hughes" document giving Richard Gray vast power of attorney.

2. This document is notarized by Howard Eckersley. However, Eckersley is a Summa, Inc. insider and not an officer of the court or a law enforcement official; therefore, this power of attorney (POA) cannot be considered as a known document. (Very sloppy "Hughes" signature.)

Exhibits 114-A and 114-B:
1. Letter used by Chester Davis and Bill Gay to fire Bob Maheu. (Later deemed to be a forgery by FBI agent Appel. (Exhibit 16)

2. Another supposed document which has no *true* known document of Howard Hughes with which to compare it.

Exhibit 115:
1. First page of a letter that was believed to have been written by Howard Hughes to the publishing house of McGraw-Hill, insisting that Clifford Irving is in his employ as his biographer.

2. We know that this letter is a forgery because Clifford Irving admitted to the hoax. Both he and his wife went to prison for the attempted fraud – Clifford in

the U.S. and his wife in Switzerland. (However, in having this document analyzed, we found them to have been written by the same hand as many other *supposed* "Hughes" documents used by Rosemont, Inc. (Refresh with Chapter VI)

Exhibits 116-A and 116-B:

1. Rosemont, Inc., with its attorney Chester Davis, produced a questionable document wherein "Howard Hughes" denounces Clifford Irving as his biographer.

2. The questionnaire is not a known document since it had *not* been notarized by the court, or any officer of the court. It cannot be compared with any known documents written by Hughes because, to date, there have been no extensive true known documents written by Howard Hughes found that can be used for comparison.

3. Take note of the fingerprints on both pages of the letter. In a ploy to lend authenticity to a document which was not, and could not be, authorized by an officer of the court, it was not stated that the fingerprints on the documents were ever analyzed by a crime lab. It's a convincing assumption that the Hughes fingerprints have been underlined superimposed onto the sheets from *previous legitimate* Hughes prints taken *prior* to or in 1965. (Russ asserts that this was relatively easy to do, even in the 1970s)

    a. Notice of the *rolled thumbprint* on each sheet. It seems *unlikely* that any in the "Hughes" entourage would feel the need to do this or even know it to be standard procedure by a legitimate print specialist. One or two freshly inked un-smudged prints, had they been authentic, would have done the job. This attempt at legitimacy is *overdone*. (Full *superimposed* prints would have had to, as they did, include the rolled thumbprint – first superimposed, then intentionally smeared with fresh ink.)

    b. Legitimate fingerprints? Highly questionable; but it was all that was needed to push Clifford Irving and McGraw-Hill over the edge. (More on the comparison of these prints with "H.H." autopsy and legitimate Hughes prints later).

EXHIBIT 111

FBI FILE 1222257-95-HQ-179917-1—PAGE 15
Supposed Hughes Signature

FILE PAGE 15 EXEMPLAR 5

VI-RC-69   PRIVATE AIRCRAFT INSPECTION REPORT   AIR-4-IC

Plane No *N 123 H*   Make _____ Model _____

Nationality *USA*   Color *W & Gold*

Pilot *R. J. GERCEVICH*   License No. *1091371*

Address *1040 Euclid SANTA MONICA CALIF.*

Owner *HILTON HOTEL INC*

Address *720 S. Michigan Chicago, ILL.*

Departure from U. S. *SANTA MONICA* Date *8-28* Time *5:15 PM*

U. S. Arrival Time *1125* Last Foreign Port *VANCOUVER* Hour *0800*

Foreign Ports Visited _____

Time Inspection Requested _____

Inspector Travel Time _____ Waiting _____ Inspection _____

	Name of Passengers	Address	Citizenship	
1	*R. S. BROWN*	*Co Pilot*	*USA*	*SYLMAR CALIF.*
2	*L. F COLLIN*	*FLT ENG*	*USA*	*HAWTHORNE CALIF.*
3	*J. H. RICKARD*	*2063 N 220 E PROVO*	*U.S.A.*	
4	*L. B. MYLER*	*4897 S. NANISCA SH.*	*USA*	
5	*G. J. MARGULIS*	*4000 SAN JOAQUIN. LAS VEGAS*	*USA.*	
6	*Hunt*	*308 E ST. SH.*	*USA*	
7	*H. Hughes*	*GULF BP AUSTIN LAWN KAY DR*	*USA*	
8	*HOWARD ECKERSLEY*	*5422 Rt 56*	*USA*	
9				
10				

Pieces Baggage _____ Cargo _____ Yes _____ No _____

Interceptions: _____

Where Found _____

Origin _____

Inspector *CAL. HAR*   Service _____ Date _____
(1st Rev. - Jan. 1972)

D720928037 Q1 IH

252

EXHIBIT 112

FBI FILE 1222257-95-HQ-179917-1—PAGE 2
Supposed Hughes Fingerprints

FILE PAGE 2 EXEMPLAR 2

EXHIBIT 113

Supposed legitimate power of attorney notarized by a Summa, Inc. insider employees.

0107041
95-211845 PF KG

THE STATE OF NEVADA:

COUNTY OF CLARK:

KNOW ALL MEN BY THESE PRESENTS:

That I, HOWARD R. HUGHES, a resident of Las Vegas, Clark County, Nevada, do by these presents name, constitute and appoint RICHARD GRAY, of Houston, Harris County, Texas, my true and lawful agent and attorney-in-fact, and my said agent and attorney-in-fact shall be and is hereby authorized and empowered in my name and on my behalf, to the same extent and for all intents and purposes as if I were acting in person, to do and perform the following acts and deeds:

1. To prepare and file, or cause to be prepared and filed, in my name any, and all applications, affidavits, supporting schedules and other documents required, necessary, or proper in connection therewith, with the Nevada Gaming Commission, the Nevada Gaming Control Board and any and all governmental or regulatory agencies or authorities of the State of Nevada and any political subdivision thereof, for gaming licenses to be issued to me, the said Howard R. Hughes, in accordance with the laws of the State of Nevada, and regulations promulgated thereunder.

2. To apply for and obtain in my name, and to furnish or cause to be furnished any and all necessary information which may be required in connection therewith, any and all licenses, authorizations or permits to carry on a hotel and gaming business on premises known as the Desert Inn in Las Vegas, Clark County, Nevada.

IN WITNESS WHEREOF, I have hereunto set my hand this 24TH day of March, 1967.

Howard R. Hughes
Howard R. Hughes

WITNESSES:

Howard L. Eckersley
George R. Francom

MAR 24 1967
G.C.B. CARSON CITY

EXHIBIT 114-A

Questionable Exemplar
FBI FILE 12222-57-HQ-211845-BULKY-84—PAGE 88
Chester and Bill – letter. 1st sheet

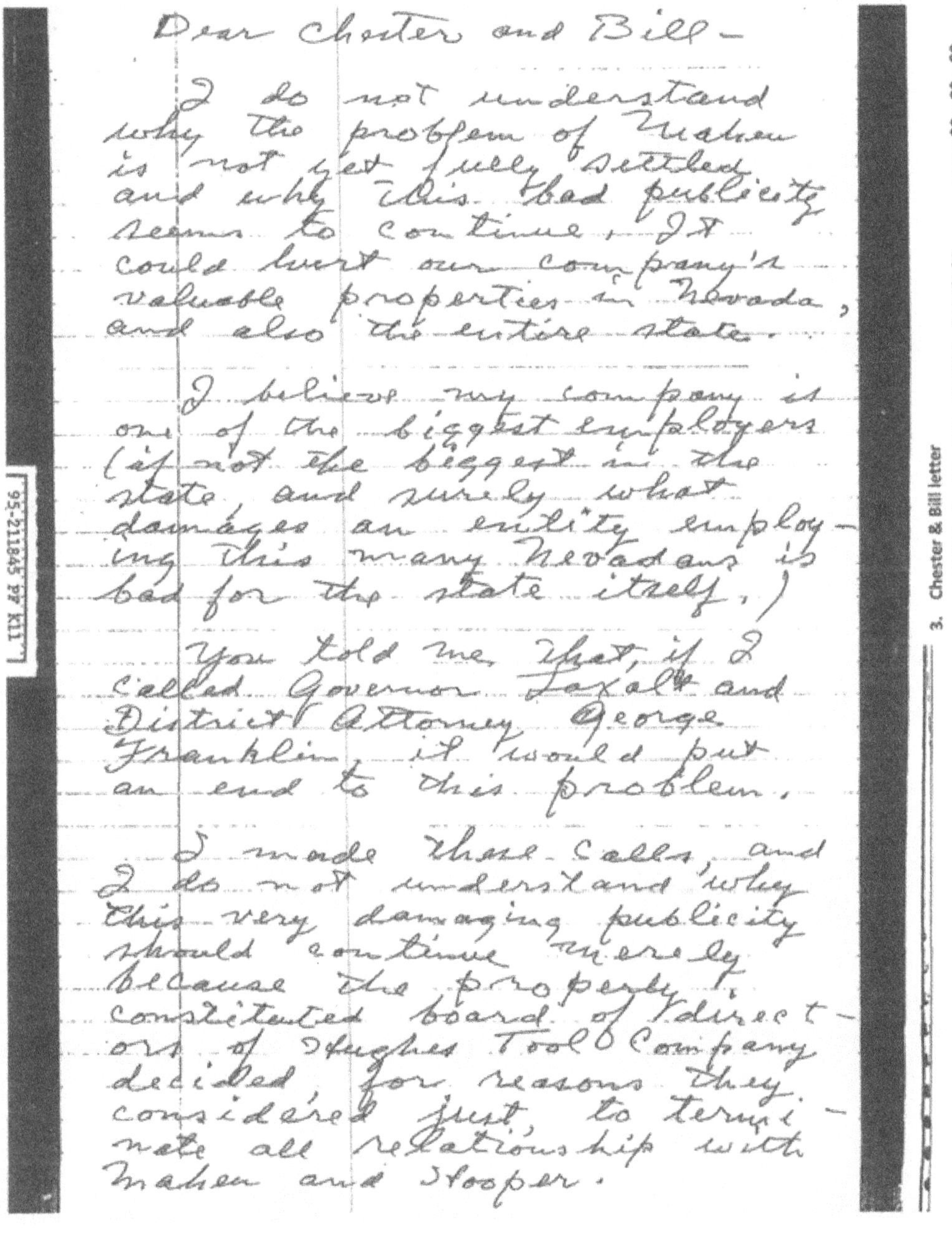

Dear Chester and Bill—

I do not understand why the problem of Maheu is not yet fully settled and why this bad publicity seems to continue. It could hurt our company's valuable properties in Nevada, and also the entire state.

I believe my company is one of the biggest employers (if not the biggest in the state and surely what damages an entity employing this many Nevadans is bad for the state itself.)

You told me that, if I called Governor Laxalt and District Attorney George Franklin, it would put an end to this problem.

I made these calls, and I do not understand why this very damaging publicity should continue merely because the properly constituted board of directors of Hughes Tool Company decided, for reasons they considered just, to terminate all relationship with Maheu and Hooper.

95-211845 PP KII

3. Chester & Bill letter
122257 – 0 – 95 – HQ – 211845 – BULKY 84 pages 88 – 89 – 90

EXHIBIT 114-B

Questionable Exemplar
FBI FILE 12222-57-HQ-211845-BULKY-84—PAGE 89
Chester and Bill – letter. 2nd Sheet

and all funds and/or
property to which Mr.
Maheu may have had
access.

As I have said, this
matter has caused me
the very gravest concern,
and is damaging my
company and all the loyal
men and women associated
with me in the very
deepest and far-reaching
way.

My sincere regards;

Howard R Hughes

EXHIBIT 115

Questionable Exemplar
FBI FILE 1222257-O-87-HQ-11739-BULKY-19—PAGE 21
Presented to McGraw/Hill by Clifford Irving

EXEMPLAR 4

11-17-7

NOV 22 1971
McGRAW-HILL BOOK CO.

Mr. Harold McGraw
McGraw Hill
New York, N.Y.

Dear Mr. McGraw -

The facts placed
before me, I find
astonishing. I do not
understand, in the
first place, why it is
not possible for your
publishing house in
possession of a legiti-
mate contract between
myself and Mr. Clifford
Irving and between your-
selves and Mr. Irving,
for the publication of
my autobiography, cannot
deal firmly and force-
fully with other
publishers who which
are asserting fraudulent
claims to the rights
which I have granted
to Mr. Irving and Mr.

EXHIBIT 116-A

FBI FILE 1222257-0-95-HQ-211845-BULKY-84—PAGE 110
1st Page Clifford Irving denial questionnaire – "H.H." cursive.

1. Is Chester Davis authorized to represent you in this McGraw-Hill matter without limitation, including obtaining all information from any bank?

Yes. Also please con- centrate on who re- ceived the money

2. Did you, in 1965, grant to Rosemont Enterprises, Inc. the sole and exclusive right to publish your life story?

#2 Yes

3. Did you at any time authorize McGraw-Hill or Clifford Irving or anyone other than Rosemont to publish your autobiography or biography or any material relating to you? (This does not relate to copyrighted magazine articles you permitted to be published prior to 1960)

No. I would like to see these forgeries

4. I understand that Clifford Irving was born on November 5, 1930 and that his father before changing his name some time after 1930 was known as Jay Rafsky, a cartoonist who drew a panel entitled "Potsy" about policemen and firemen which appeared in Collier's magazine. Have you ever met or do you know a Clifford Irving, or did you ever talk to him, or did you ever communicate or correspond with him in any way or did you in any manner whatsoever otherwise collaborate with him or anyone else in the preparation of an auto-biography or anything else to be published about you?

No. I do not know either.

5. Did you furnish Clifford Irving or anyone (other than Rosemont) with any material of any kind, including tape recordings, either directly or through others for the purpose of an autobiography or for the publication of anything about you?

Not at any time.

6. Did you sign or authorize the execution on your behalf of a contract with McGraw-Hill or Clifford Irving for the publication of anything by you or concerning you?

Same as above.

7. Did you receive or authorize anyone else to receive any money directly or indirectly from McGraw-Hill or Clifford Irving for the publication of anything by you or concerning you or for anything else?

No

8. When is the last time you personally endorsed a check for any reason?

More than 10 years ago
Howard R. Hughes

5. Denial of Clifford Irving as Hughes biographer written by "Hughes."
1222257 – 0 – 95 – HQ – 211845 – BULKY 84   pages 110 & 111

EXHIBIT 116-B

FBI FILE 1222257-0-95-HQ-211845-BULKY-84—PAGE 111
2nd Page Clifford Irving denial questionnaire-"H.H." cursive.

9. Did you ever give McGraw-Hill, Clifford Irving or anyone else instructions of any kind relating to the publication of anything concerning you?

Absolutely not

10. The original press release issued by McGraw-Hill states that the purported "autobiography" was substantially based on taping sessions with you over a period of many months during 1971. Other than what you may have done with respect to copyrighted articles which appeared prior to 1960, have you ever dictated, written or prepared any tapes, manuscripts or recordings relating to your life or to any incidents in your life for the purpose of the publication of any kind of biography or for any other purpose?

No

11. It has been suggested that someone may have had access to handwritten notes or memoranda or other communications in your handwriting or of tapes of conversations with you which could have become available to others. With the exception of tapes or other material in connection with the copyrighted articles that were published prior to 1960, the message to me and Bill Gay during the Maheu litigation and the letters you wrote last year to the Nevada State Gaming Commission, are you aware of the existence of any authentic material of the types described which could have become available?

None should be available

12. Did you ever start to write your autobiography or did you ever tell any of your assistants that you were writing an autobiography and ask any of them to deny it if questioned?

Absolutely not

Howard R. Hughes

A. Were all those "long script forgeries" and "phony signatures" done by Eckersley alone? Before and after 1965, "notary" Howard Eckersley <u>was</u> the inside Summa, Inc. man for Bob Maheu, Bill Gay, Nadine Henley, Chester Davis. He was one of the senior "Hughes" caretakers as well.

B. Did Howard Eckersley become disgruntled about senior caretaker John Holmes (the drug runner) getting bumped upstairs into the "big bucks?" This is about the time that Holmes became one of the executives on the Summa, Inc. board. Did Eckersley then jump ship, so to speak, deciding to wing it with Clifford Irving?

C. Could Eckersley have felt betrayed by Bill Gay, Chester Davis, and Nadine Henley? Did he decide it was time to get a bigger piece of the pie by searching out and throwing in with Irving?

D. Most certainly, if blackmail were afoot, Eckersley would have been holding all the cards.

E. Was Eckersley then offered a sweet deal he couldn't refuse by the Summa, Inc. board? A deal that got him to come back home? (Hence the Clifford Irving denial letter written in the same hand as all those other phony documents?) Was it when the phony Swiss bank account came into question that Eckersley decided to return to the devils he knew, or was "H.H." aide Clarence Albert Waldron the lengthy forger?

F. More evidence of forgery has turned up, but it was late in coming and, because it closely correlates with the "H.H." autopsy at Methodist Hospital, Houston (Chapter XII), it became pertinent to enter it as Exhibit 177. It now appears that "Hughes's" aide Clarence Albert Waldron may have been the writer of all those collective exemplars supposedly written by "Hughes." No doubt a prolific forger will eventually get caught over a ten-year period. This forgery scenario has been taken apart and put properly back together <u>later</u> in this book. Both Eckersley *and* Waldron had plenty of free time to practice and were paid extremely well. As to caring for the imposter "Hughes," they did little. Concern for the care of "Hughes" will be covered in more depth in Chapter XI.

Now that we've found that the Irving denial letter was *also* written by the same hand (Yes, the same person that wrote all the other phony documents – all except Dummar's phony "Mormon Will," of course), where do we go? Well, since we are now this deep into the biggest scam of the twentieth century, let us get into dead people and autopsies.

CHAPTER X

FIVE MEN DIRECTLY CONNECTED TO THE HUGHES EMPIRE DEAD 1975 TO 1976

First Paragraph Below Is an Excerpt from Previous Charles Clotfelter Book,
The Price of Their Souls

RESEARCH ON ATTORNEY L. RICHARD GRAY
(Date of Death May 7, 1975)

Attorney Richard Gray, partner in the law firm of Andrews, Kurth & Gray, represented "Hughes," after 1965 in many Las Vegas business deals. Gray was deep into Summa, Inc. activities in Nevada and had to know the truth about the scams perpetuated in the name of Howard Hughes. Gray died of a heart attack on May 7, 1975, while a passenger on a private plane. He was only forty-nine. [117] Did he know too much? Barlett and Steele in their book *Empire* didn't say, but it's likely that Gray had a traumatic experience during the flight that brought on his heart attack. It seems just a little too convenient. If the conspirators had already decided to kill the imposter "Hughes" in 1976 and were working toward that end, Gray may have known about it. Perhaps he suggested that he was deserving of a bigger piece of the Summa, Inc. money pie? Or, perhaps Gray just angered someone who liked to kill people – people who didn't agree with his politics, [118] or someone who didn't like paying interest on a $4 million-dollar loan? [119]

Of course, it's been a while now and there's quite a bit of water under the bridge, but it certainly seems that someone, or perhaps several others, were getting paid a lot of money to cover up information that could have clarified what took place between 1965 and 1976. In-depth searches in Nevada, New Mexico, and Houston, Texas, for any autopsy files, news articles, police reports, etc. have been done. Extraordinarily little turned up that would give a better understanding of Richard Gray's young demise. Below you will find several of the many letters of inquiry to various information sources, including the law firm of Andrews & Kurth. We did find out that there is an ongoing lawsuit between Andrews & Kurth L.L.C. and the surviving relatives of Attorney Gray. It seems that Gray had earned a lot of that "free-and-easy" "Hughes" money and, after his *young* death, his relatives wanted a taste of that. After all, it was Richard Gray who "earned" it. (We can be quite certain that Richard knew all about those worthless pieces of dirt holding Nevada together, including mining claims wherein hardly *any* rudimentary assays were taken. They were, in truth, little more than lizard habitats. However, the record shows that between the dates of 1965 and 1976, one of America's greatest and wealthiest twentieth century industrialists, "Howard Hughes," just couldn't get enough of those worthless pieces of dirt. Really?

Concerning Richard Gray, to date, Russ has been unable to get any information from the above law firm, and it's unlikely, aside from a lawsuit, that he will. When one considers Johnny Meier (Exhibits 212-A through 212-L), and how he was able to jump ship and end up *untouchable* in Canada. Bad boy Johnny absconding with millions in kickback money from those worthless properties and mining claims. And no one was the wiser? Don't you think Richard Gray, with his "Hughes" power of attorney, knew all about that?

Yes, that's right. A most interesting document was found in the FBI files (Exhibit 119-A) wherein Richard Gray was given power of attorney (1967) by "Hughes" to deal with the Gaming Control Board and any other regulatory agencies in Nevada. Oh-oh, Gray's power of attorney was notarized by Howard Eckersley and some guy named George? And what is wrong with that you might ask? Well, for one thing Eckersley and George, if George was even a real person, *were both inside men*! Richard Gray's POA document is *not* a *known* document.

Oh yeah, Richard was *well connected* to the Hughes empire in Nevada. It's hard to believe that he was "unknowingly" working for an *imposter* "Hughes." The real Hughes had always been a "hands-on" sort of fellow, *not a moron*. Don't you think the real Hughes would have demanded assays on those extensive mining claims if he intended to buy them? The real Hughes was a fellow *who knew* that a power of attorney can be a lethal instrument if inappropriately used. Attorney Gray could well have been "The man who knew too much." Below appears Russ's diligent letters of inquiry. Although Russ put forward a valiant effort to secure documentation on Gray, it appears the clean-up crew had been diligent as well. But we do have that questionable POA document from the FBI Files. (Included below, beneath Russ's letters of inquiry.)

EXHIBIT 117. #1

6/13/2014   RE: Assistance Needed from the Chron

Jack Sweeney
Chairman of the Houston Chronicle

Mr. Jack Sweeney:

I never intended to ask you assistance, but I am having a major problem
with the Chron, and am bringing such to your attention.

I have written to help@chron.com a total of three (3) times since April 2014
(this year). I have yet to receive any type of response, at all, from that desk.

I am trying to locate the obituary for a fairly famous Attorney in Houston,
named **J. Richard Gray** who died in a plane crash on 5/7/1975. Mr. Gray
had worked for the noteworthy law firm of Andrews, Kurth in Houston.
(as info - letters to that law firm have not received a response either).

The exact date of the obituary is unknown, but it should be in the vicinity of the death
date of 5/7/1975.

I am hopeful that a member of your staff can implore the "help" desk to respond
to my multiple emails. The Obituary is very important to me.

Thank you in advance for your response, time, and consideration.

Sincerely,

Laurence M. Russell
Henderson, NV
(Retired CA Rural Cities Chief of Police)

EXHIBIT 118. #2

Laurence M. Russell
P. O. Box 91263
Henderson, NV 89009-1263

June 12, 2014

Bob Jewell, Esq.
Managing Partner
Andrews Kurth L. L. P.
600 Travis Street, Suite 4200
Houston, TX 77002

      Re: Death & Obituary of Kurth Attorney L. Richard Gray

Dear Mr. Jewell:

Letters addressed to the Office Manager have not been responded to, and thus I ask your assistance.

I am trying to locate the obituary for a fairly famous Andrews Kurth attorney (in Houston) named **J. Richard Gray** (or possibly **Grey**) who died in a plane on 5/7/1975, possibly while flying over New Mexico. Mr. Gray had worked for your firm for quite a few years, and one of his clients was Howard R. Hughes of Las Vegas and Houston.

The exact date of the Obituary is unknown, but it should be in the vicinity of the death date of 5/7/1975. Research through the Houston Chronicle has not been successful.

I am hopeful that a member of your staff can assist me, through directing me to the Obituary, or providing a copy of same from your files. This Obituary is very important to my research.

Thank you in advance for your response, time, and consideration.

Sincerely,

Laurence M. Russell
Henderson, NV   (Retired CA Rural Cities Chief of Police)

EXHIBIT 119-A

Proxy below cannot be considered a *"known document."* It was not witnessed by an Officer of the Court or any law-enforcement Official. It was "good ol' boy" Howard Eckersley a "Summa, Inc." inside notary, who did the "trick." (Eckersley is now suspect.)

<u>Note</u>: Howard Eckersley's name, and George's 'whatever his last name is,' are thoroughly pressed on the document – Hughes's name is vague and sloppy. If Eckersley had signed both his and Hughes's name on the document, in a clean and concise manner, a forgery would have been obvious upon analyzing pressure points, pen lifts etc. Nevertheless, even with the sloppy signing of the Hughes name, both Eckersley and Hughes' signatures have similar characteristics.

THE STATE OF NEVADA:

COUNTY OF CLARK:

KNOW ALL MEN BY THESE PRESENTS:

That I, HOWARD R. HUGHES, a resident of Las Vegas, Clark County, Nevada, do by these presents name, constitute and appoint RICHARD GRAY, of Houston, Harris County, Texas, my true and lawful agent and attorney-in-fact, and my said agent and attorney-in-fact shall be and is hereby authorized and empowered in my name and on my behalf, to the same extent and for all intents and purposes as if I were acting in person, to do and perform the following acts and deeds:

1. To prepare and file, or cause to be prepared and filed, in my name any, and all applications, affidavits, supporting schedules and other documents required, necessary, or proper in connection therewith, with the Nevada Gaming Commission, the Nevada Gaming Control Board and any and all governmental or regulatory agencies or authorities of the State of Nevada and any political subdivision thereof, for gaming licenses to be issued to me, the said Howard R. Hughes, in accordance with the laws of the State of Nevada, and regulations promulgated thereunder.

2. To apply for and obtain in my name, and to furnish or cause to be furnished any and all necessary information which may be required in connection therewith, any and all licenses, authorizations or permits to carry on a hotel and gaming business on premises known as the Desert Inn in Las Vegas, Clark County, Nevada.

IN WITNESS WHEREOF, I have hereunto set my hand this 24TH day of March, 1967.

Howard R. Hughes

WITNESSES:

MAR 24 1967
G.C.B. CARSON CITY

RESEARCH ON ATTORNEY RAYMOND A. COOK

The following is a lead-in letter from Charles Clotfelter to Chief Russell as "Russ" began his research on Raymond Cook. Russ turned up documentation of a most unpleasant end for both Raymond and his wife Florence. Following the lead-in letter, you will find several letters of inquiry by Russ and the information he was, and was not, able to find.

EXHIBIT 119-B

Hello Russ,
Please Research the following:
RAYMOND A COOK (Attorney for Summa, Inc.)
(Date of Death August 9th, 1975)
Worked with the law firm of Andrews-Kurth-Campbell & Jones.

Cook was fired from Summa, Inc. early-on but rehired by Howard Hughes in 1961; filling the vacancy left by Noah Dietrich who was fired in 1957. (Noah Dietrich was fired after leading a failed coup to have the reclusive Howard Hughes declared incompetent and confined to an institution.) Dietrich tried to get Howard's personal Doctor Vern Mason in on the plot. (It was probably Mason, Howard's personal friend for many years, who "dropped the dime" on Dietrich.)

In 1961 Attorney Raymond Cook acted as liaison between Hughes and Northeast Airlines; he worked closely with Chester Davis on this project. Later, in 1965 after the death of Vern Mason, he became the director of the Howard Hughes Medical Institute in Miami, Fla. where several Hundreds of Millions of dollars were tied up and were tax write-offs for the Hughes Industries. Cook was an attorney and did not hold a Medical Degree. He was retired from this job for three or four years prior to his "unfortunate auto accident;" Bill Gay and Chester Davis took over the job, at the Hughes Institute, after Cook quit.

Cook gets his, together with wife Florence, on August 9th, 1975. The two of them just happened to be in an intersection when along comes a big ol' bus and neatly broadsides them. (Was it a stop-sign and not a stoplight, at that intersection?) So (Knock-um in the head, drive-um to a remote area, roll-um into the intersection, get up a full head of steam on that big ol' Bus and smash the hell out of their little ol' car.)

Location of wreck: Brenham Texas. Population in 2002 Atlas only 13,507; it stands to reason that in 1975 the population was considerably less and very thin in the outskirts.

Things to look for:
1. Were there any passengers on the bus?
2. Did the Bus Driver suffer any major injuries?
3. How many eyewitnesses?
4. Did the accident occur in a remote area?

Charles Clotfelter

EXHIBIT 120

Laurence M. Russell
P. O. Box 91263
Henderson, NV 89009-1263

July 18, 2014

Ms. Andrea Heigas
Head Librarian
Nancy Carol Roberts Memorial Library
200 W. Vulcan Street
Brenham, TX 77833

Re: **Commendation** for Library Employee Will Felder

Dear Ms. Heigas:

This letter outlines a matter of mutual concern.

I have been involved in an extensive research project the last two years, and had run into an obstacle when I attempted to locate information regarding a fatality traffic accident which occurred outside of Brenham in mid-1975. Requests sent to Police Departments, the Texas Rangers, and the Texas Dept. of Public Safety has not yielded any helpful information.

I then called the Brenham Banner newspaper and they referred me to your Library. In a telephone call three days ago, I asked help and assistance from Library employee Will Felder. With the scant information I provided, in less than 24 hours, Mr. Felder was able to identify the traffic fatalities (2) and information which will prove to be very helpful to my research. In addition, Mr. Felder also obtained a scanned copy of the newspaper article which outlined the traffic accident and emailed it to me – all in less than two days. Months of prior research yielded nothing; Mr. Felder obtained complete and thorough information in 48 hours.

I am very appreciative of Will Felder dedication to job duties, and his willingness to help inquiring minds. He truly is a fine representative of your Library, and displays all the tenets of true Customer Service.

I commend the work of Will Felder, and ask that you consider conveying my personal thanks and appreciation to him. He is a true asset to the Nancy Carol Roberts Memorial Library.

Sincerely,

Laurence M. Russell
Henderson, NV
(Retired CA Rural Cities Chief of Police)

EXHIBIT 121
North-West, out of Houston, Traveling on Highway 290 Texas, you will arrive at junction #36

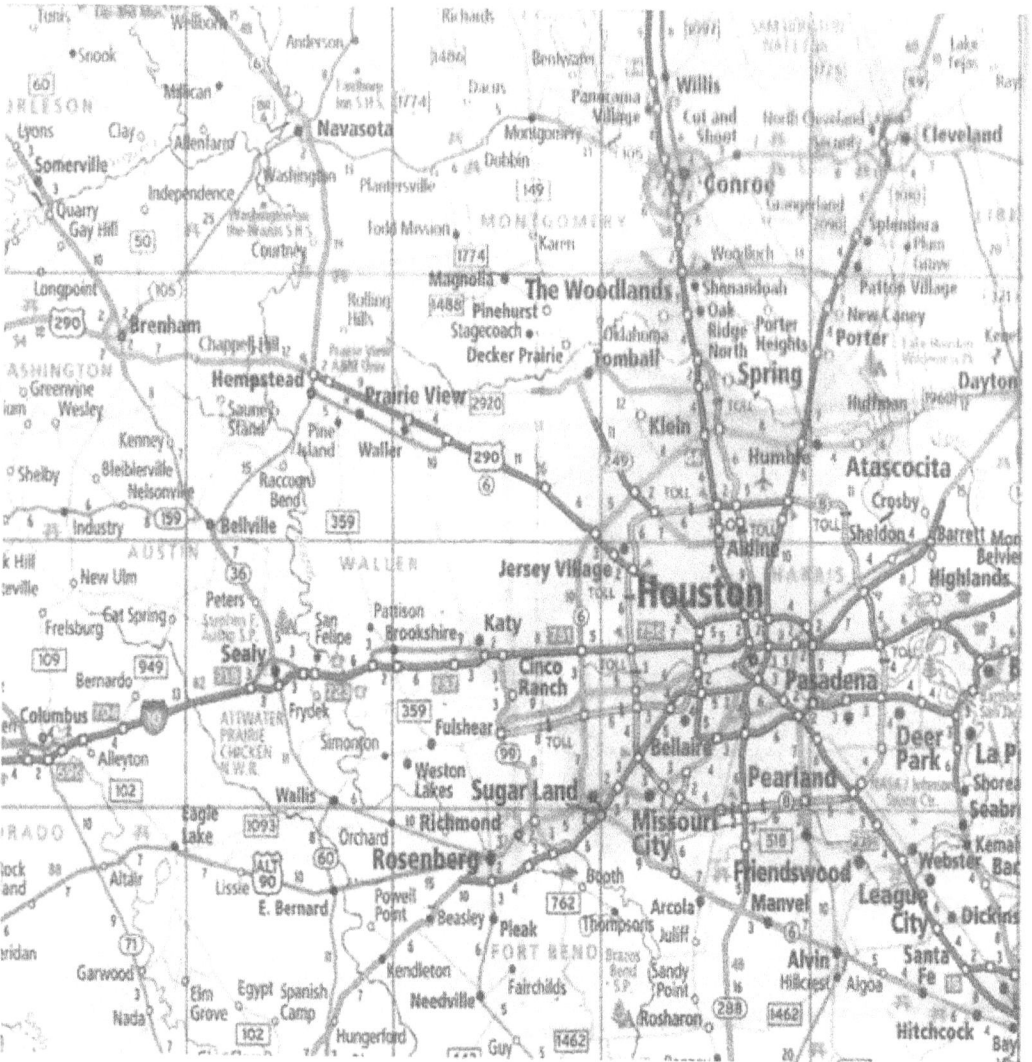

In the letter to Russ (Exhibit 119-B above), written before research into the demise of Cook was initiated, foul play was suspected, but became an intense possibility when the facts became clarified. To stage an "accident," it would need to be in an isolated area of rolling hills. The players would need to be few, and evidence would need to be disposed of as quickly as possible.

268

Documents below indicate what was and was not found:

A. No record of a city Police report, regarding the accident, was found.
B. No record with the Texas Highway Patrol had been kept.
C. A county Sheriff's report came up nil as well.
D. Autopsy report, if even done, could not to be found.

What was found:

E. The location as seen in Exhibit 121 above. <u>Chappell Hill</u> on 290 to the southeast of Brenham and <u>Gay Hill</u> on Highway 36 northwest of the city. This indicates the remoteness necessary for foul play to have been afoot, as suggested in the above letter to Russ (Exhibit 119-B) when he began his research.
F. No structures in the vicinity, except a Restaurant at the time. Whether it was open or closed or had visibility of the fatal intersection at the time is unknown. (Restaurant location - remote.)
G. Only two witnesses. (Few as predicted.)
H. Why would the Cooks be coming off the main Highway 290 on a feeder loop in the middle of nowhere anyway? They should have been traveling via Highway #290 heading back to their home in Houston, and not feeder highway #36, which would have landed them in Rosenberg. As per the news articles below, it was a stop sign, not a stoplight, where the feeder loop entered the intersection.
I. The witnesses were the bus driver, who broadsided the Cook vehicle, and his single passenger. *That is all – two –* few indeed, as predicted in Exhibit 119-B. Bus passenger's name was Jones and, like the name Smith, makes a good alias; driver's name is not mentioned.
J. The only fatalities were Raymond and his wife Florence. (As predicted in Exhibit 119-B.)
K. *The single bus passenger* was treated for a minor injury and released; the bus driver suffered *no* injuries. (As predicted in Exhibit 119-B.)
L. Had the bus been a Trailways, Greyhound, or school bus, it would have been a stretch to suspect a plot. However, this bus belonged to a secondhand outfit known as the Kerrville Bus Co. (as noted in the news article Exhibit 123 below). It would have been most interesting to have had more data as to what *type* of bus struck the Cook's vehicle. (Obviously, the front grill on that bus was heavy duty.) Where did it come from and where was it going *with its lone customer?* Unfortunately, all that information has been strategically wiped clean.

News articles below:

EXHIBIT 122

July 30, 2008

Andrews Kurth prevails in suit over Howard Hughes' cash

Andrews Kurth wasn't negligent by cutting a former partner who represented tycoon Howard Hughes out of a share of a $15 million contingent fee related to the firm's work for maternal heirs of Hughes' estate, a Houston jury decided on July 24. In a suit filed in state district court in 2007, the estates of former Andrews Kurth partner Raymond Cook (pictured) and his wife -- the couple died in an automobile accident in 1975 -- alleged the firm engaged in breach of fiduciary duty, fraud, misrepresentation, breach of contract, self-dealing and conversion by excluding them from a share in the contingent fee. But in a 10-2 verdict returned on July 24, jurors in 164th District Judge Martha Hill Jamison's court found AK's negligence, if any, did not cause injury to the estates, the firm did not fail to comply with its fiduciary duty to the Cook estates, did not fail to comply with its partnership agreement, and did not commit fraud against the Cook estates. The plaintiffs had alleged in *Cook v. Andrews Kurth* that they were entitled to a share of the $15 million contingent fee because the firm's partnership agreement provides a partner's estate with income for six years after the partner's death. Hughes died in 1976, and the firm entered into the contingent-fee agreement with the maternal heirs in 1977. But Andrews Kurth alleged the Cook estates weren't entitled to any of the contingent-fee money because it wasn't paid to the firm until 1984, which was nine years after Cook's death. Plaintiffs attorney Rick Harrison, a partner in Austin's Fritz, Byrne, Head & Harrison, could not be reached for immediate comment. Andrews Kurth defense attorney Murray Fogler says the firm's partners are "delighted" with the verdict. A hearing to enter judgment is scheduled for Sept. 8.
-- *Brenda Sapino Jeffreys*

EXHIBIT 123

A. No record of a city Police report regarding the accident was found.
B. No record with the Texas Highway Patrol had been kept.
C. A county Sheriff's report came up nil.
D. Autopsy report, if even done, could not to be found.
Had investigator Russell not turned up the news articles below, the Raymond Cook incident could never have been clarified. Absolutely all law enforcement particulars have been wiped clean.

Bus-Auto Crash Here Kills Houston Couple

Two Houston residents were dead on arrival at Bohne Memorial Hospital Saturday afternoon when the car they were driving struck a passenger bus at the intersection of Hwy. 36 S. and U.S. Hwy 290, near Willie's Steak House.

Ray A. Cook, 39, and wife Florence, of 1936 Sunset Blvd., Houston, were killed in the crash which occured at 3:25 p.m.

According to police, the bus, owned by the Kerrville Bus Co. was proceeding south on Hwy. 36 when the Cook car, stopped at a traffic control sign on Hwy. 290 E., entered the intersection in the path of the bus.

The front of the bus and the left side of the car collided.

The car was actually crossing Highway 36 from a loop feeder road.

It took officers considerable time to pry the door open on the Cooke vehicle after the impact with the bus.

Cook was said to be a Houston attorney

Elizabeth J. Jones, passenger of the bus, was treated for injuries at Bohne Memorial Hospital.

Brenham Man Drowns In Lake Sunday

Samuel Luera Sr., 25, of Brenham, drowned in Lake Somerville at 4:15 p.m. Sunday.

According to Chief Deputy Sheriff Elwood Goldberg, Luera fell overboard when the boat turned suddenly. Panic apparently caused the

Brenham School Officials To Attend TEA Meet

Representatives of the

EXHIBIT 124

WRECKED AUTO in which Mr. and Mrs. Ray Cook of Houston were killed Saturday afternoon when it collided with a Kerrville Bus do Highway 36 South and U.S. Highway 290 near Willie's Steak House as the Cook car attempted to cross Highway 36 from a loop feeder road. (Banner photo).

Funeral Service Slated For Couple Killed Her

Funeral services are slated for 3 p.m. Wednesday at St. Luke's Methodist Church in Houston for Mr. and Mrs. Raymond A. Cook who died in a car-bus collision here Saturday afternoon.

Dr. J. Kenneth Shamblin will officiate at the memorial services for the civic leaders, followed by a family graveside service.

Cook, 66, was vice-president of the Howard Hughes Medical Institute and a former board member of Trans World Airlines and Northeast Airlines.

A lawyer, he was a senior partner in the firm of Andrews, Kurth, Campbell and Jones. He was a Phi Beta Kappa graduate of Rice University and a graduate of the University of Texas Law School.

He was a member of the Alumni Board of Governors of Rice, and he and his wife were Rice Associates.

Mrs. Cook, 58, traced her family lineage to Mos Austin and Stephen F. Austi She was a Rice graduate, member of the Junior Leag of Houston and a member the Daughters of the Republ of Texas.

She went to Washington invite President Frankl Roosevelt to dedicate the S Jacinto Monument. She als was a founding member of t Houston Museum of Natur History.

The Cooks, of 1936 Suns Boulevard, were returnin from a board meeting of t Scott and White Memori Hospital in Temple. He ha been chairman of the board Amigos de las Americas.

The Cook car was stru broadside by the bus at t intersection of the U. S. 2 frontage road and Texas South when the Cook car faile to stop.

Survivors include fou children.

EXHIBIT 125-A

More on Raymond Cook:

Howard Hughes: The Legal Battle For Access to His Billions Continues

In 1976, Howard Hughes, the reclusive and eccentric billionaire, and at the time America's richest man, died. His handwritten will mysteriously appeared days later at a Morman Church. Under the will, the Morman Church was to receive $1.5 billion. Melvin Dummar, the gas station attendant who claimed to have found a disheveled Hughes lying in the Nevada desert and "saved his life," was to receive $156 million for his kindness.

The intestate heirs of Mr. Hughes suspected foul play. They hired the law firm of Andrews Kurth to contest the will. After a seven month trial, a Nevada court threw out the will (determined to be a forgery), and declared that Howard Hughes died intestate.

Andrews Kurth received millions of dollars for its representation of the Hughes heirs. One of its partners, Raymond Cook, died in 1976. His estate was settled through Southern National Bank of Texas.

Now 30 years later, the heirs of Cook's estate are suing Andrews Kurth for breach of its fiduciary duty to disclose to the estate and to CVK's client the existence of a contingent fee agreement between Andrews Kurth and Hughes' maternal heirs. The specific claim is that the Andrews Kurth partnership agreement provided to Cook's estate a percent of the firm's income generated within 5 years of Cook's death. The contingent fee agreement between the law firm and Hughes' heirs was entered into in 1977, within a year of Cook's death, although the millions earned by Andrews Kurth were not realized until more than 5 years after Cook died.

In the present suit, Cook's estate is now attempting to prove that Andrews Kurth kept the existence of the contingent fee agreement with the Hughes heirs hidden from Cook's estate (and from the Southern National Bank's involved trust officer, CVK's client) when that estate was settled in 1979. Recently, CVK partner Gene Buckle represented the trust officer in his deposition taken by the Texas lawyers for the Cook's heirs.

Breach of a claimed fiduciary duty to disclose salient facts by a law firm to its partner's estate can be far reaching, both in time and in scope, as the Cook estate case shows. For more information on this fascinating case, contact Gene Buckle at ebuckle@cvk-law.com.

Yet again, *another* attorney working for the same law firm as had Richard Gray (Andrews, Kurth, Campbell & Jones, LLP) meets an untimely death. (*Gray and Cook, within three months of each other*.) It can be said, with little doubt, Cook had inside and in-depth knowledge of the Hughes empire. Raymond must have gotten paid handsomely for the time he spent working for a supposed "Hughes" and undoubtedly left this world expecting to get paid considerably more – a percentage of that $15 million "Hughes" contingency fee litigating the "Mormon Will" scam. And what about his wife Florence? Well, they did not know what she knew and couldn't leave her hanging around stirring up suspicion. Looks like a "package deal." Whatduyathink?

Now let us put it together here as simply as possible. Two attorneys – both having worked for the same law-firm of Andrews, Kurth, Campbell & Jones – had *represented Hughes* and the Hughes empire in multi-million-dollar business deals after 1965, and both died untimely deaths within three months of each other? Russ, despite his most diligent efforts, was *unable* to find any police records, sheriff records, or autopsies on either Cook or Gray. It makes one wonder; do you – wonder?

So here we have the two "Hughes" attorneys (Richard Gray and Raymond Cook), together with Bob Maheu's mob connections Johnnie Rosselli and Sam Giancana, and "Acapulco Hughes," all meeting the Grim Reaper from 1975 to 1976. This really should have peaked someone's interest as all were, or had been, directly connected to the *inside workings of the Hughes empire* and all *five* deaths occurred within 14 months! There had been some speculation that Johnnie and Sam had been murdered by Cuba's Fidel Castro after their failed attempt to assassinate him. There's quite an extensive narrative in Empire as to just how Johnnie and Sam got on the wrong side of Castro; however, neither the CIA nor the FBI would admit to the plot. It seems likely that the Summa, Inc. trio – and Bob Maheu at an earlier time – had other uses for the money-laundering Giancana and hit-man Rosselli. Howard Hughes *never* had a *knowing* association with criminal types. All this "smoke and mirrors" appears to distract from the type of swamp fellow Bob Maheu was. The inference here is that Maheu was liked by Hughes. But anyone who researches this in any depth will find that Hughes *never* had a close association with Maheu prior to 1965. And it's quite possible that it was only Bill Gay, Nadene Henley, and Chester Davis who knew that Maheu was working for the Hughes Industries in a "snoop" capacity since it was Bill Gay who brought Maheu into the Hughes Industries.

It is shadowy that "goodfellas" Johnnie Rosselli and Sam Giancana died in Florida in 1975 back to back. However, we know these were murders because Johnny was found floating in a 50 gallon oil drum off Key Biscayne, Florida, and Sam had been killed torturously slow in his Florida home with numerous 22 caliber "slugs" pumped into him.

All four of the individuals mentioned above had obviously reaped tremendous wealth from the Hughes empire after 1965; and all four would have, or could have, wanted *more*. This may well have been in the minds of Bill Gay, Chester Davis, and Nadine Henley when they realized – or planned for – the clear possibility that

"Acapulco Hughes" down in Mexico would eventually die. A little more redundancy here: "Acapulco Hughes," had he lived to recuperate in a stateside hospital, would certainly have been the worst problem for the Hughes estate pirates. Legitimate fingerprints, blood type, perhaps words muttered in a drug-induced euphoria to the effect, "They've been trying to kill me!" ("Acapulco Hughes" makes the fourth man *down* in a 14-month period, closely followed by Johnnie Rosselli! There may have been more, but that's all that can be pointed out so far.) Both Johnnie Rosselli and Sam Giancana had done work for the Hughes Industries; having been brought on board by Maheu. They knew a lot about its operations prior to 1965 as well.

Dates of Death (D.O.D.):
D.O.D. 05-07-75: Richard Gray
D.O.D. 06-19-75: Salvatore "Sam" Giancana
D.O.D. 08-09-75: Raymond and Florence Cook
D.O.D. 04-05-76: "Howard Hughes"
D.O.D. 07-28-76: "Johnnie" Rosselli
All the above handily *dead* within 14 months!

Let's do a little speculation here, shall we? Although there is evidence that crimes have been committed, it's not known exactly how they had been plotted. In the brief speculative analysis below, keep in mind that at the time it was suspected that "Sam" Giancana and Johnnie Rosselli were killed by Cuban operatives friendly to Fidel Castro. *Supposedly,* Sam and Johnnie had plotted with the U.S. Government to assassinate Fidel. It was also purveyed, that Fidel was a vengeful and determined adversary who would go to great lengths to get even with those who would try to kill him. But then there were *many* who wished Castro less than well. So, what could be the reason for killing Johnnie and Sam <u>within a year of each other and so close to the death of "Acapulco Hughes"</u>? After all, Fidel was terribly busy with his socialist agenda, i.e. killing off any hint of free enterprise and any and all malcontents in Cuba. By 1975 all weaponry, handguns, etc. had been confiscated from private citizens and street crime was at an all-time low. The criminals were either dead or hard at work doing Castro's bidding. As it is in all socialist dictatorships, Cubans had little left to steal anyway. In effect Castro had turned Cuba into his own personal plantation. But then, just perhaps, it wasn't Castro who ordered Johnnie and Sam's back-to-back deaths? Castro took power in 1959; a lot of water had passed under the bridge by 1975. If it was Cuban operatives who "did" Johnnie and Sam, how were they able to get close enough to get those jobs done? Giancana lived in a Miami fortress, protected by bodyguards. Rosselli also had his own personal protection. It goes with the territory. It would take an amiable personal relationship, a large suitcase full of money, or both, to get close to these two "wise-guys."

When we consider that Rosselli and Giancana were tight with Maheu to launder money for the Summa, Inc. foursome, spy on adversaries, etc. and that Bob Maheu only reached his exulted position of "Hughes's Right-Hand Man" immediately after 1965, just what was it that gave Maheu the power to spend "Hughes's" money, at will, and hire dishonest others to supposedly do "Hughes's" business? Prior to 1965 Maheu had only been a subordinate to the Summa Staff; and being an ex-FBI agent, his main job was probably simply to do research. We will go deeper into Maheu probabilities later and how he was able to pull off this "tail-wagging-the-dog" charade, and what it was that eventually got him fired from the Hughes Industries. After firing Maheu, it was the remaining Summa, Inc. board of Henley, Davis, and Gay who held all the cards, as well as the Summa, Inc. purse strings. So, isn't it probable they would want, and be able to keep, contact and control of operatives such as Sam Giancana, Johnnie Rosselli, and the man who forged "Hughes" documents on request?

ONCE MORE LET'S DO A LITTLE PROBABLE SPECULATION

A. Richard Gray, an attorney and not a Doctor, knew a lot about the inside workings of Summa Inc. <u>After</u> Vern Mason, previous C.E.O. of the Howard Hughes Medical Institute conveniently dies, in 1965, Richard Gray fills-in as its C.E.O. In 1970 Gray calculates that things might be getting a little "dicey," he gets "cold feet." Perhaps Richard came across information which strongly links the previous C.E.O. Vern Mason with Howard Hughes and what Howard's true medical condition was *prior* to, and up to 1965. In any event he wants to get out of the "Summa, Inc. Club" and turns in his resignation. Things rock along until 1975 when things are about to change down in Acapulco Mexico – where an imposter "Hughes" is holed up. The phony "Hughes" is appallingly sick. Bill Gay, Nadine Henley, and Chester Davis, know that this "H.H." cannot be allowed to recuperate in a state-side Hospital or their grandiose "caper" will be uncovered. The Summa, Inc. tribunal see Gray as a lose end. He knows too much. Richard should have known that *you don't just quit "The Syndicate."* The Summa threesome hires Sam Giancana for the job and give him a generous suitcase full of money. Poor Richard ends up in a private plane somewhere over New Mexico with Giancana. A lethal dose of something is put into his drink, or perhaps they just dangle him from the plane, or both. Gray is only 49 years old, but it is too much for his heart; he has a heart attack and dies. Now it's Sam Giancana *who knows too much or perhaps wants too much* – Sam Giancana becomes another lose end.

B. Just prior the death of "Acapulco Hughes" Bill Gay, Nadine Henley, and Chester Davis call a little meeting and invite Johnnie Rosselli over. They have a plan to put a million and a half bucks in cold, clean cash on the table. The Tribunal already knows the mindset of "Hit Man" Johnnie. A million "bucks" in the 1970s was a "God-awful" amount of tax-free money. (Ten times greater than the buying power of today's federal reserve notes.)

   Then comes the pitch. "Listen Johnnie, we have a couple of jobs for you at $500,000 each; the two pigeons are Sam Giancana and Raymond Cook." The Tribunal than expounds on what no-good S.O.B.s Sam and Raymond are. They offer to sweeten the deal by another half million if Rosselli will take out Sam in a cruel and unusual manner.

There is a reason for this. The Trio want the murder to look like a *vengeful* killing. ("Now Johnnie, when you finish with Sam, we want you to take lots of photos.") At first Johnnie is a taken back by a hit on Giancana. After all, they had been partners in many shady deals, and Sam is a "Made Man" in the crime-syndicate. However, Johnnie is overwhelmed by this financial windfall at his fingertips, and he agrees to the deal.

So just how is Rosselli going to handle his dilemma? Plan #1: He touches bases with Giancana and pitches it that the U.S. Government wants to hire the two of them to "hit" the Cuban belligerent Fidel Castro. (This ploy has been suggested by the Summa, Inc. trio as being the best way for Rosselli to cover his tracks after the Giancana hit – it will look like the *Cubans* did it. Plan #2: Johnnie has a colleague who owes him a favor and works for a second-hand bus company in Texas. Bottom line, "doing" Raymond Cook is not going to be a problem, but Giancana is going to be a *big* problem! The big bosses in New York and Chicago would not take lightly to one of their own being "taken out."

Johnnie, among other things, is a con man and gives Giancana his "confidence." "Come-on Sam, we don't even have to do the job, we'll just take the money and say we tried." Giancana goes for it, and Rosselli suggests a day to firm up the plan. Johnnie insists that Sam be home alone – after all, this is government business. Rosselli explains their secrecy and that he will be handing over a large quantity of *government tax-free money*, so nobody, but nobody, can see or know about the transaction. "Now listen Sam, the quantity of cash I'm bringing to you is such that even your employees cannot be trusted." Sam gives his security the night off and rests assured that "Good-Fella" Rosselli will be there if a problem arises. Johnnie walks into the Giancana fortress free and clear. Now Johnnie has this neat little 22 caliber pistol and, instead of pulling money out of his briefcase, *Johnnie gets his gun.* One shot between the eyes knocks out Sam and he then becomes a "meat target" for Johnnie. Round after round is pumped into Giancana. When the job is finished, and the blood is oozing nicely, Johnnie takes his photos, creeps out of the Giancana fortress, and gets about taking care of Raymond Cook. (Cook scenario was described earlier in this chapter.)

C. Once Raymond Cook, Richard Gray, and Sam Giancana are out of the way and "Acapulco Hughes" has taken his last plane ride, all has gone well for the Summa Inc. trio. But there is still one last lose end – Johnnie Rosselli. Rosselli has already been paid a substantial amount for his services, but he will never spend much of it. After the death of "Acapulco Hughes," Chester Davis, Nadine Henley, and Bill Gay *clandestinely* forward the Giancana photos, covered with Rosselli's latent fingerprints to the "Mob Bosses" in New York and Chicago. *They then know who "hit" their man Giancana.* They are not happy. Perhaps they even see Rosselli as a threat to their own well-being. They catch Johnnie, put him into a fifty-gallon steel drum, and weld on the top. (Johnnie is probably alive during the process.) They knock holes in the drum, believing it will sink and stay down, and make final preparations to dump it off the Florida coast. Once out to sea, with Johnnie screaming for mercy, the boys open cold beers and admire their handy work. After exchanging a pun or two, one of the boys gives the perforated drum a push. It rolls overboard, and Johnnie sinks away into deep water. However, methane gas from Johnnie's decomposing corpse eventually brings the drum back to the surface where it is discovered by fishermen.

D. As of July 28, 1976, "Acapulco Hughes" has been dead for approximately three months, ensuring that he, as well as the four persons mentioned above, will *never* be a problem for the Summa, Inc. group. What went on with "Hughes" between the years of 1965 and 1976 will remain secreted away, excepting for a few of the well-paid Summa crew.

E. In Exhibit 125-B, we see how *well-connected* Robert Maheu was to organized crime. The Exhibit was taken from the book *Empire*, authored by Donald Barlett and James Steele. Whoever provided them with their information wanted to portray organized crime as an intriguing way "bad boys" could make a living. If our CIA or FBI depended on mobsters to carry out their bidding during those years, then shame on them and shame on the government agencies involved. But then perhaps, the below depiction, of the way things supposedly were, was meant to serve ulterior motives. Robert Maheu was a "bad boy" and most who knew of him, or associated with him, were aware of his sordid dealings. We can safely infer that Bobbie Boy and his employment by Summa, Inc. was unknown to Howard Hughes. Whatever activities Maheu indulged in regarding the Hughes, Corp. may have only been known to Bill Gay (the fellow who hired him), Nadine Henley, and Chester Davis.

Let's look at this from a different perspective. Maheu was a spendthrift. Billie, Nadine, and Chester had no control over his lavish spending as long as he was considered "Hughes's right-hand man" (as depicted earlier). They managed to get rid of him with a phony cursive document, but not without a battle. Robert Maheu lost complete control of Summa, Inc. when Gay, Henley, and Davis *clandestinely* spirited the "visual Hughes" out of Nevada and hid him in a location unknown to Maheu. But even though "Hughes" was out of Maheu's reach, Bobbie was still pretty much of a "loose cannon." Without control of the phony "Hughes" and the phony "cursive Hughes," Maheu was dead in the water, with no hope of regaining control of the Hughes Industries. When Will Lummis was assigned as <u>executor</u> of the Hughes Industries, perhaps it was time to "let the cat out of the bag?" Hence the information below in Exhibit 125-B.

Maheu knew everything about both the real and the phony "Hughes's" and the operations of Summa, Inc. after 1965. If Will Lummis (appointed Chairman of the Summa Corporation in 1976) had gotten himself into the kind of trouble that needed a plea-bargain to get out of, he could always have pointed to what had gotten Maheu fired in 1970 and the unsavory criminal characters Maheu associated himself with. "Bob Maheu cannot be believed, cannot be trusted, and was behind *all* distasteful activity concerning Hughes!"

EXHIBIT 125-B

Howard Hughes never associated himself with gangsters or misfits. The CIA never admitted to a plot to kill Castro, and the FBI knew nothing about the supposed conspiracy either? But Bill Gay, Nadine Henley, and Chester Davis must have known that Maheu was "connected" and a "made man." Hence the speculative drift of supposed benevolent activities between the CIA, the FBI, Robert Maheu, and his organized crime connections. The following is taken from the book *Empire*.

Capone, Frank Costello, Charles (Lucky) Luciano, Charlie Fischetti, Louis (Little New York) Campagna, Benjamin (Bugsy) Siegel, Anthony (Big Tuna) Accardo, Paul (The Waiter) Ricca, Frank (The Enforcer) Nitti, and Meyer Lansky.

It was precisely these associations that led Rosselli and the ex-FBI agent Maheu to form an alliance back in 1960. At the time, Maheu was on a leave of absence from Hughes, freelancing for the Central Intelligence Agency, as he occasionally did whenever the CIA had an especially sensitive mission in which it "didn't want to have an agency person or a government person get caught."[25] In this case, the mission was the assassination of Cuban premier Fidel Castro.

The CIA had retained Maheu to serve as a go-between, and early in September of 1960 he met with Rosselli in the Brown Derby Restaurant in Beverly Hills and offered him a $150,000 contract to kill Castro. Rosselli accepted, and later that month the two men flew to Miami to lay the groundwork for Castro's removal. Rosselli, using the cover name John Rawlston, started screening Cuban candidates to carry out the work. Not long after, Rosselli introduced Maheu to two of his associates, a "Sam Gold," who he said would serve as a "backup man," and "Joe," who would "serve as a courier to Cuba and make arrangements there."[26] Sam Gold turned out to be Salvatore Giancana, of the Chicago crime syndicate. Joe was Santo Trafficante, the organized-crime boss in Cuba before Fidel Castro came to power.

From the very beginning Maheu had trouble with Giancana, whose mind was not on his work. The mobster was obsessed with a notion that his girlfriend, Phyllis McGuire of the singing McGuire Sisters, was having an affair with comedian Dan Rowan in Las Vegas. To allay Giancana's suspicions and keep him in Miami, Maheu arranged to have an electronic eavesdropping device installed in Rowan's room.

With the CIA's blessing, Maheu gave $1,000 of the agency's money to a Florida private detective to plant the bug. But after doing so, the detective unwisely left his monitoring equipment unattended in a nearby hotel room where it was discovered by a maid. The maid reported her find to local authorities. The detective was arrested, and he implicated Maheu before Rosselli could post bond.

The FBI, completely unaware of the Castro assassination plot, launched an investigation. When FBI agents questioned Maheu, he was vague, telling them only that the wiretap was placed in connection with a project "on behalf of the CIA relative to anti-Castro activities."[27] At the same time, Sheffield Edwards, the CIA's director of security, sought

CHAPTER XI
METHODIST HOSPITAL AUTOPSY OF
"H.H." CORPSE - HOUSTON, TEXAS
PART 1

EXHIBTS OF HOWARD R. HUGHES'S PAST INJURIES SUSTAINED IN
XF-11 TEST-FLIGHT-CRASH INTO BEVERLY HILLS, CA. IN 1946

ALSO, EXHIBITS OF "H.H." AUTOPSY REPORT DONE:
METHODIST HOSPITAL, HOUSTON, TEXAS IN 1976

A note of interest here is that upon the arrival of the "Hughes" corpse in Houston, Texas, Hughes's Aunt, Annette Lummis, was at first against any fingerprinting or photographs of any kind. The Hughes organization and its medical team were against it as well; they *didn't even want an autopsy performed and wanted the body to be immediately cremated.* * Upon discovering that this was not a lawful procedure and that an autopsy *must be performed*, she changed tracks but wanted the body cremated immediately after the autopsy. Upon learning that the legalities preceding <u>any</u> cremation would require that an even more <u>in-depth</u> autopsy be performed, Annette once more changed her mind and allowed a standard autopsy. With both of Howard's parents having been buried in the Hughes family plot *without* having been cremated, one cannot help but wonder what all the fuss was about? Below is the evidence which reveals many good reasons for Annette Lummis's and the "Hughes" camp's concern:

<u>Note</u>: We do know that Dr. Vern Mason was Hughes's personal friend and C.E.O. of the Hughes Medical Institute in Miami. What is not common knowledge is that Dr. Mason was immediately cremated only <u>two days</u> after *his* death. No ceremony for his friends, no autopsy, and no history of family survivors? (Exhibit 65-B above.) My goodness, how convenient that was for Rosemont Enterprises, Inc. (See Chapter IX.)

Russ, upon visiting the Hughes family plot at the Glenwood Cemetery in Houston, Texas, discovered that someone had the entire site poured with concrete <u>after</u> "H.H.'s" interment in 1976. ("Acapulco Hughes" had already been placed in a heavy duty *1,000 -pound sealed* coffin, which was then lowered, with great difficulty, into a *heavy-duty stainless-steel vault* and covered with six to eight feet of dirt. As to who had the site poured with concrete *there is no record?* ** (Exhibit 126 below.) Now, why would anyone want to do that? Let us consider that a distant relative of Dr. Frankenstein may have been lurking about in Houston desirous of fresh body parts. No? Well maybe a nearby medical school had been stealing corpses out of the Glenwood Cemetery and this was a preventive measure? Well okay, let's consider the most obvious reason: could it be possible that there were those who were doing everything in their power, at the time, to make sure that no one would be able to lift off the *true* fingerprints of that "H.H." corpse back in the time when it would have been possible? (DNA print technology was not the developed science in those years as it is today.)

*Exhibits 130-D-Bottom Page, to 130 E-Top Page.

**Exhibits 126-A, 126-B and 130-H. It would have taken *more than a novice* to break through that concrete cover, dig through all that dirt, open that sealed stainless-steel vault, and, lastly, open that *thousand-pound sealed casket* containing the corpse. Doesn't the pouring of all that concrete over the entire gravesite seem a bit overly zealous, if not paranoid? Could it have been of grave concern to the "Hughes" relatives and caretakers that someone might gain access to the "H.H." corpse for identification purposes? Think of all the calculation which took place in the short time allotted – from the time the corpse arrived in Houston and soon thereafter (two days) when it was planted in the Glenwood Cemetery. (Literally out of the Autopsy and into the ground.) It's easy to believe that Anette and Will Lummis (the "Hughes" relatives) knew they would be burying a corpse long before it and the "Hughes saviors," arrived in Houston.

But, currently, what has become *most* obvious is that the parasites on the Hughes fortune have made a <u>grave</u> error. *The objective now is to make a strong enough argument to exhume the imposter.* Chapter by chapter it's becoming quite clear that the fellow they flew up from Mexico, who was in his final hours, could not be allowed the remotest chance to live! Eventually there would have been "legitimate" fingerprints taken, among other things, and the hoax would have been revealed. What would have happened if "Acapulco Hughes" talked to the nurses and doctors under the influence of various medications or decided to make a death-bed confession? The death in flight of "Acapulco Hughes" has all the appearances of a homicide. When will law-enforcement wake up and realize that Howard Hughes was dead in 1965? Will this book stimulate enough interest to get out the jackhammers? Perhaps, but for the time being, motive will continue to be established, and *yes*, this book leans heavily in the direction of several homicides, especially concerning a "Hughes" flown up from Mexico! All for the most compelling motives in the history of the world: wealth and power. (Note: Lee Harvey Oswald's body was exhumed in 1981, so why not a phony "Hughes?")

As mentioned earlier (Fingerprints, Chapter V), when Russ went looking for the "H.H." autopsy report in the Harris County Coroner's Office, it was no surprise that it had gone missing. (The Methodist Hospital Autopsy Report was destroyed as well? See letters in Exhibits 131-A and 131-B.)

Following the Hughes Family Plot photos below, we dig into a copy of the "Hughes" autopsy report, which good sleuth Russ found in the possession of a Dr. Forrest Tennant in West Covina, California. Dr. Tennant had been contracted to do an analysis of the drugs administered to "Hughes" prior to his death in 1976. Dr. Wilbur Thain, Dr. Chaffin, and caretaker John Holmes were the providers and, *it most certainly appears* that they gave massive doses of codeine solution to a comatose "H.H." The codeine found in the "H.H." corpse autopsied at Methodist Hospital, Houston, was enough to kill a bear!

Mexican physician Dr. Montemayor Martinez had been called to the Acapulco Princess Hotel and got a first-hand view of the disgracefully emaciated wreck of a man reputed to be Howard Hughes. Extremely upset with what he witnessed, he strongly questioned why the fellow he was viewing "had not been in a hospital weeks ago." He later testified that: "*In my opinion, he* (the fellow he viewed) *died of a disease called neglect. When a patient becomes unconscious you put him in a hospital!"*
(Exhibits 130-E bottom paragraphs and top of page 130-F)

EXHIBIT 126-A

Hughes Family Plot poured with concrete after 1976.

283

EXHIBIT 126-B

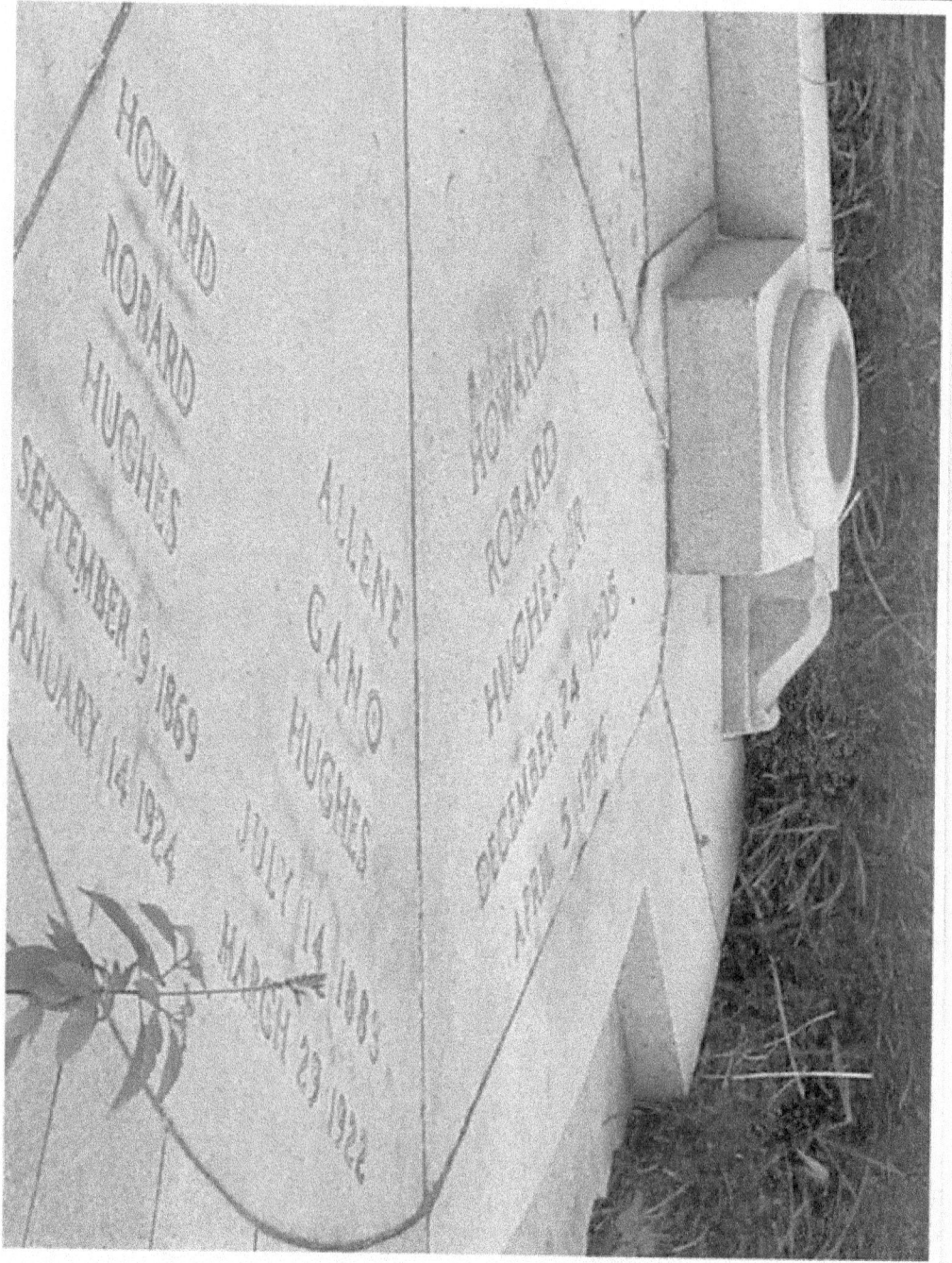

EXHIBIT 127-A
"Dr. Wilbur Thain's Trial"

684   EMPIRE

THAIN: On any given day, no, sir.

ATTORNEY: The only thing you can do and the only thing you have recorded in that record is what you were delivering?

THAIN: That's correct.

ATTORNEY: As a matter of fact, you weren't even there most of the time those drugs were being administered, were you?

THAIN: I was not there in his presence at any time that he was administering them.

ATTORNEY: And you gave this quantity to an addict or a person you knew at least had been an addict of the same drug that you were giving him. Is that right?

THAIN: I was not present at the time or had knowledge of the time he was taking these excessive amounts. As to whether he was an addict or not, I don't know, sir.

ATTORNEY: In your medical judgment, sir, you know that a person cannot take those quantities of codeine without becoming addicted, don't you?

THAIN: I'll have to say yes to avoid getting into an argument with you, but it is an argumentative problem, sir.[165]

Thain said he never discussed the amount of codeine and other drugs he was giving to Hughes with the other three doctors, Crane, Lawrence Chaffin, and Homer Clark. In fact, Thain acknowledged, they had no idea of the "amount of drugs" he was giving Hughes.[166] Thain said he obtained the codeine directly from a New York pharmaceutical house and did not write prescriptions for the drug, but that he "did not know" that "under the laws of the State of Utah that it's illegal for a physician to directly dispense any controlled substance [codeine] without a prescription."[167]

On September 21, 1978, after a one-week trial, the jury found Thain innocent.

Intriguing questions remain about Howard Hughes's death. Hughes died with an exceptionally high level of codeine in his body. The *Philadelphia Inquirer*, which obtained a copy of the then secret autopsy report, disclosed in June of 1977 that an analysis made by the newspaper of the toxicological results included in the autopsy showed that Hughes "had a potentially lethal amount of narcotics in his body" when he died.[168] The autopsy report listed the codeine level in his blood as 1.96 micrograms per milliliter of blood and described it as "only minimum amounts."[169] In truth, the 1.96 figure was considerably above the

EXHIBIT 127-B

1.4-microgram level found in the bodies of persons known to have died of codeine poisoning.*

During Thain's trial, Dr. Forest S. Tennant, Jr., assistant professor of public health at the UCLA School of Public Health and executive director of Community Health Projects, one of California's largest drug-abuse treatment programs, testified that based on his study of the autopsy report he concluded that Hughes had taken "anywhere from 5 to 9 grains" of codeine before his death.[170]

Other medical authorities say it is difficult to pinpoint the precise amount of codeine that Hughes may have taken, and that it could well have exceeded twenty grains. But far more significantly, Dr. Tennant testified, and pharmacologists and pathologists agree, the codeine in Hughes's body "was taken within 6 to 8 hours of death."†[171]

That was an astonishing finding, one totally ignored by federal prosecutors at Thain's trial. Hughes had been unconscious for nearly twenty-four hours before he died, according to testimony given in other legal proceedings by Dr. Chaffin and aides who were with him.‡ In other

---

* On October 27, 1976, when Dr. Jack L. Titus, the pathologist who performed the autopsy, testified in a deposition in connection with the administration of Hughes's estate, he described the codeine levels cited in the autopsy report as "compatible with therapeutic usage." Two years later, at Dr. Thain's trial, Titus acknowledged that his previous statements were "in error" because he had misinterpreted milligrams for micrograms. Thus the level of codeine was 1,000 times greater than he originally thought.

† Codeine is a fast-acting drug which reaches a peak level in the bloodstream within one to two hours after it is administered. About one-half to two-thirds of a dose of codeine appears in the urine within six hours, and excretion is virtually complete in twenty-four hours.

‡ Dr. Thain, who had received an employment contract and a lifetime consulting agreement from Summa Corporation in 1975, providing him with an annual salary of $60,000 for serving as one of Hughes's physicians, testified that from February until April 5, 1976, the date of Hughes's death, he saw the industrialist on only three occasions. He said he had his last conversation with Hughes toward the "end of February." Next, he said, "I saw him while he was sleeping, but not to talk to him, about the oh, middle of March, 17th or 18th." He did not see Hughes again, he said, until the morning of April 5, when he arrived at the Acapulco Princess about 8 A.M. At that time, he testified, he found Hughes "in a coma, rather flaccid. He was having seizures, multiple seizures. His pupils were dilated and fixed. His blood pressure had been stabilized in and around 100–120. His pulse wasn't too bad. He had been unconscious, I understood, since the night before. He really looked moribund, the type of person—he just looked like he was ready to die."

EXHIBIT 128-A

Excerpts from Albert B. Gerber's Book: *Bashful Billionaire,* Copyright 1967
List of Injuries Sustained by Howard Hughes in XF-11 Crash 1946

'70   *Bashful Billionaire*

mediately burst into flames, destroying both itself and the house at 808 North Whittier Drive.

Luckily for Hughes he hit the ground still in the fuselage with the plastic cockpit canopy gone. With his last remaining strength he forced himself out of the burning plane and collapsed. Two men saw him: Marine Sergeant William Lloyd Durkan and Captain James Guston quickly reached his side to pull him to safety. Hughes was still conscious and Sergeant Durkan asked him, "Is there anyone else in the plane?"

Instead of replying to that question Hughes asked, "Did anyone get hurt in the crash?" When they indicated that they did not believe that any person had been hurt he seemed to sigh and sag with relief.

An ambulance from the Beverly Hills Emergency Hospital arrived and took him on a stretcher to that institution. Half an hour after his arrival he was moved, still on the same stretcher, to the Good Samaritan Hospital, where he was examined by Dr. Verne R. Mason who then issued the first bulletin on Hughes' condition:

> Fracture of the left clavicle.
> Fracture of the posterior portion of the upper nine ribs on the left side.
> Fracture of the first two ribs on the right side.
> Possible fracture of the nose.
> A large laceration of the scalp on the left side.
> Extensive second and third degree burns of the left hand.
> A large second degree burn of the lower part of the left chest extending from the nipple line to the medial scapular line.
> A large second degree burn of the left buttock.
> Numerous cuts, bruises and abrasions of both arms and both legs, numerous small cuts about the face.

A later report said:

"In the early morning of July 8, 1946, hemorrhage occurred into the left pleural space, and this was followed by an effusion into the chest. This pleural space was tapped and 3400 cc. of bloody liquid was removed at three tappings. The hemoglobin content of this fluid was 18% and it is probable that 650 cc. of hemorrhage took place into the chest."

Hughes' friends and associates held no hope for his recovery. Odekirk, who had been flying the A-20 in order to

EXHIBIT 128-B

better observe the test flight, took the room next to Hughes in the hospital and spent the long, sleepless night peering anxiously into the injured man's room. Reporters and movie actresses, top executives and military officials flocked to the hospital to wait for news. The first medical bulletin gave him only an outside chance to live.

At dawn Hughes regained consciousness and demanded a pencil and paper so that he could write out what he believed to be the cause of the crash.

By the second day he had reported that he thought the crash was caused by some malfunction of the right propeller.

On the third day, annoyed by his inability to move or be moved without suffering excruciating pain, he sent for Odekirk and ordered construction of a special bed he had designed, made of separate rubber squares, each square operating with an individual motor. The completed design resembled today's full-power automobile seat—each square could go up or down and turn in either direction—tilt or rake. This enabled Hughes, by operating the controlling push-buttons, to rearrange his position with a minimum of pain.

The hospital was deluged with flowers, telegrams, baskets of fruit and numerous visitors, who descended upon it in full cry. The casual observer might well have concluded that the institution harbored a world leader or at least a princely member of a major royal house. The President of the United States, Harry S Truman, wired, "I am watching eagerly all the reports concerning you. I feel sure you will win the fight. With every good wish."

On the fourth day Hughes asked for his good luck charm —a battered felt hat that he wore on all test flights, races, and other potentially dangerous occasions. Policeman E. R. Davis found it in the wrecked cockpit, dirty and water-soaked but miraculously unburned, and Hughes welcomed it as an auspicious omen.

Many Hollywood stars came to the hospital or called regularly: Lana Turner, Katherine Hepburn, Ginger Rogers, Ava Gardner, Linda Darnell, Cary Grant and Errol Flynn were among those who figuratively haunted his bedside, although none could pass the guarded hospital door.

After a week of continued improvement Hughes suddenly suffered a relapse. He had just dictated his belief as to the cause of the accident. Then he rallied and recovered.

Despite the crash, the government accepted delivery of the FX-11 on January 14, 1947. From the viewpoint of Hughes

EXHIBIT 129-A

Excerpt from Bartlett and Steele's Book: *Empire* Howard Hughes put his feet onto the instrument panel with knees up to chest, XF-11 Crash 1946

126   E M P I R E

ing to break completely loose from the airplane any landing gear door which might have jammed into a broadside position. I could not see anything which was holding the plane back, yet it felt as if some giant had the right wing of the airplane in his hand and was pushing it back and down.[14]

Hughes increased power on both engines, cut it back, then increased it only on the right engine. Nothing worked. He was still losing altitude. Looking past the cockpit, he thought of bailing out, but feared he was already too low and also felt he still "might be able to correct the situation."[15] By making major adjustments to ailerons, rudder, and spoilers, he was able to keep the plane level. But nothing slowed the loss of altitude. From five thousand feet just east of Hughes Aircraft, he was at twenty-five hundred feet when he passed over Washington Boulevard, two thousand at Venice Boulevard, and at less than one thousand when he crossed Pico Boulevard on a northwesterly course that was taking him into the heart of Beverly Hills. The plane was making a terrible racket when it crossed Wilshire, and dropped to less than five hundred feet when it groaned over Santa Monica Boulevard. Again, Hughes put the landing gear down, hoping to shake the problem loose. There was no change.

Planting his feet high on the instrument panel, Hughes braced himself for the inevitable. Below were the luxurious grounds, swimming pools, and homes of Beverly Hills, into one of which he was about to crash. Soon he saw the one—a large two-story house with a peaked roof, just a block shy of the grounds of the Los Angeles Country Club. Knowing that he would never clear the roof, Hughes fought to keep the XF-11's nose high to "flare" the ship into the roof and avoid a nose-down crackup.[16]

With a deafening noise, the right engine and landing gear crashed into the second floor of the house, at 803 North Linden Drive. The impact sent the plane yawing to the right, with the right wing slicing into the house and garage next door, at 805 North Linden. As the plane turned sharply right it hurtled sideways through the air, shearing off a utility pole, then bounced and skidded through an alley before finally coming to rest in a heap between two houses at 808 and 810 North Whittier Drive. A fire broke out, engulfing the wreckage and one of the houses.

A few houses away, marine Sergeant William Lloyd Durkin was relaxing with friends after dinner when he heard the whine of a low-flying airplane in distress. Seconds later, after a thunderous crash, he raced outside and saw wreckage down the street. As he ran toward it there

EXHIBIT 129-B

Excerpt from Bartlett and Steele's Book: *Empire*
List of Injuries Sustained by Howard Hughes in XF-11 Crash 1946

THE SENATE INVESTIGATION   127

was an explosion, and flames shot up in an orange glow. Just as Durkin got to the plane, the pilot crawled out of the cockpit and collapsed on a burning wing. Scrambling into the blaze, Durkin grabbed the man, pulled him from the fire, smothered his burning clothes, and called for help. Several hours later he heard on the radio that the man he had pulled from the wreckage was Howard Hughes.[*]

No one else was injured. The house at 808 North Whittier burned to the ground, but the owner, Lieutenant Colonel Charles A. Meyer, was in Europe serving as an interpreter at the Nuremberg war trials.

The crash nearly killed Hughes, however. At Good Samaritan Hospital, doctors grimly determined the extent of his injuries. His chest was crushed. He suffered fractures of seven ribs on the left side, two on the right, a fracture of the left clavicle, a possible fracture of the nose, a large laceration of the scalp, extensive second- and third-degree burns on the left hand, a second-degree burn on the lower part of the left chest, a second-degree burn on the left buttock, cuts, bruises, and abrasions on his arms and legs, and many small cuts on his face. His left lung had collapsed and his right was also injured. His heart had been pushed to one side of his chest cavity. He was in severe shock. No one in the emergency room thought he would live through the night.

The two doctors in charge of the medical team attending Hughes were well acquainted with the patient. Verne R. Mason, an internist whose patients included many Hollywood stars, and Lawrence Chaffin, a surgeon for the Santa Fe Railroad's hospital in Los Angeles, had each treated Hughes for about fifteen years. As they inserted a tube in his crushed chest to drain fluid accumulating in the lungs, the doctors told Hughes, who had remained conscious throughout his ordeal, that he might not live. To relieve the pain and make bearable what all of them were certain would be his last few hours, Mason gave him injections of morphine.

Get-well messages, including one from President Harry S Truman, deluged the hospital. Although seemingly on his deathbed, Hughes refused to see most of his friends who hurried to the hospital. The only people he allowed through the armed guard outside his door were sev-

[*] Hughes rewarded Durkin for saving his life with a $200-a-month stipend. Later, in a lawsuit for damages which he filed against Hamilton-Standard, the manufacturer of the XF-11's propellers, Hughes listed the monthly reward payments to Durkin, as well as the airfare costs of flying Durkin's parents from Pittsburgh to Los Angeles, as among the expenses he wanted to recover from the company as a result of the crash.

EXHIBIT 130-A

Following Exhibits from Richard Hack's Book: *Hughes*
(Pages 12, 13, 14, 15, 16, 17, 18, 19.)
"Death by Neglect"

1 2   Hughes

however, Bowen offered to place calls to the Department of Immigration and Naturalization Service to expedite the clearance of the critically-ill patient. Bowen was told that the identification number on the side of the blue-striped, white Lear jet was N–855W. What he was not told, however, was that the airplane had yet to even leave the ground in Acapulco.

By the time the jet finally left Mexico at 11 a.m. with two pilots, two doctors, one aide and Hughes on board, Bowen already had sent his administrative assistant Edward McLellan to Houston Intercontinental to alert customs officials there of Hughes' pending arrival. As was typical of the magic that the mere mention of the name Howard Hughes evoked, the customs officials agreed to arrange to meet the plane on the runway, a breach of accepted procedure, in an effort to expedite the patient's transfer to the Methodist ambulance.

For over two hours, McIntosh's team was assembled and waiting. For what seemed like an interminable length of time, and in medical terms it was, much of Houston's Methodist Hospital was placed on hold. Despite Bowen's efforts to maintain secrecy, the rumor that a "famous patient" was about to be admitted soon began to make the rounds of the various floors. From obstetrics to cardiology, guesses ranged from Elizabeth Taylor to President Gerald R. Ford. As testament to Bowen's clampdown, no one thought of Howard R. Hughes.

Just before 1 p.m., the Methodist Hospital doctors, administrators, and nurses drove to the airport in two cars and one ambulance, keeping in contact using a CB radio and walkie-talkies. Conversation during the 30-minute ride centered on anything but the elusive billionaire, until just before the trio of vehicles pulled up to an airport security car waiting at a side entrance. Only then was Hughes' name brought up, and only to discuss personnel assignments one final time. Drs. McIntosh and Berglund were to enter the plane to examine the patient, while the remaining doctors and nurses were to stay on the runway awaiting further instructions.

Edward McLellan had cleared the medics' approach through airport supervisor Paul Porter, and had done his job well. The coterie of man-power and equipment was waved onto the runway and appeared prepared for any development—except perhaps the one that eventually materialized.

At 2 p.m., the Lear jet carrying Howard Hughes descended into the smog-filled skies of Houston Intercontinental Airport and was directed onto a side gateway where the doctors and ambulance were waiting with customs officer Marie Denton. For Dr. McIntosh, this was a moment of prideful exhilaration. His plan was working flawlessly; and as he approached the jet's opening door, he tightened his grip on his medical bag and silently prayed.

EXHIBIT 130-B

Death by Neglect   1 3

McIntosh was met at the door by Dr. Wilbur Thain who matter-of-factly announced, "I lost the beat just a few minutes ago. He's gone."

McIntosh was astounded. In the course of the morning, he had gone from beginning a typical day at the hospital, to arranging for medical care for a comatose billionaire, to now suddenly dealing with a corpse. Not willing to believe the inevitable, he offered to try resuscitation. All the equipment, after all, was in place. "It's no use," Thain countered, repeating, "he's gone, he's gone."

When the gurney carrying Hughes' body was removed from the jet, customs officer Marie Denton commented that Hughes appeared to be "like an old emaciated man. Well, really, I couldn't even tell that it was a man from the side view. I only saw a profile, and went by his birth certificate."

What struck ambulance driver Jay Dixon as strange was the mood of those now standing around as the body of the late billionaire was covered and loaded for transport to the hospital. "There was some laughter at one point. It seemed out of place," he said. The customs official agreed, adding that no one, including Hughes' doctors or his aide, seemed unduly upset or distraught.

Perhaps the most stunned was pilot Roger Sutton. He was not even told that Hughes had died until the plane had landed. "I was shocked and saddened," he said. "I've never had a passenger die before."

Fifty minutes after Howard Hughes' jet had landed in Houston, his body arrived at the morgue dock of Methodist Hospital. The clouds that had obscured much of the sky had parted only minutes before. Dr. Jack Titus felt the sun on his arms as he waited for ambulance attendants Jay Dixon and Len Stom to unload the stretcher on which Hughes lay, still shrouded in the bright yellow blanket. It fell to pathologist Titus to make the initial external examination of the body as soon as it was delivered to the morgue.

"I found an elderly white male," Titus reported, "with gray hair, somewhat thinned, and a gray beard. The body appeared remarkable, emaciated and dehydrated. The estimated length of the body was about 6' 2". A plastic intravenous catheter was present in the left antecubital fossa[1] and the left arm was taped to a towel-covered board. The eyes were open and the pupils dilated and fixed. Although there were contractures of moderate degree of the knees, it should be noted that there was not evidence of rigor mortis in any of the skeletal muscles of the body. Based upon the information that the body came from the cabin of an airplane at appropriate environmental temperatures, was transported immediate-

---

1. The area of the arm in front of the elbow, typically used to draw blood.

EXHIBIT 130-C

ly by an ambulance, and this examination done essentially immediately upon arrival of the body at The Methodist Hospital morgue, it is my firm opinion that death occurred less than three hours prior to the time of my examination," Titus concluded, thus confirming Thain's timing of Hughes' death just prior to landing.

After the initial examination, Hughes' body was placed in a body cooler within the morgue, and autopsy technician Ray Henderson and a hospital security guard were left to maintain the integrity of the corpse. With the body secured, hospital president Ted Bowen faced an entirely different set of crises: containing the media circus that would inevitably follow any announcement of Hughes' death, and determining exactly why and how Hughes had died. Both challenges came with their own set of legal restrictions, and a new and very powerful variable: the next of kin.

Annette Gano Lummis, the 85-year-old sister of Hughes' mother, was the recluse's closest known living relative. Equally as important, she was intensely private and avoided any hint of spectacle during her long and distinguished life in Houston. When she was notified of Hughes' death by the hospital, she asked her son William to make the funeral arrangements. Her only instruction: that there be no autopsy of the body of her nephew. It was a request that put her in direct conflict with Houston's medical examiner, Dr. Joseph Jachimczyk, who was about to be brought into the unfolding drama.

After clearing customs, Drs. Thain and Chaffin plus John Holmes were brought to Methodist Hospital where they assembled in Bowen's office with Drs. McIntosh and Berglund to recount the events leading up to their arrival in Houston. During that meeting, Thain announced that Hughes died at 1:27 p.m. According to Chaffin, the plane had just passed over Brownsville, the Texas border town across the Rio Grande from Matamoros, Mexico. "He died in Texas," Chaffin repeated, in case any seated in Bowen's office had missed the point. Of more concern at the moment to Bowen was the fact that neither Chaffin nor Thain were licensed to practice medicine in Texas, necessitating a call to the coroner's office and the formal involvement of Joseph Jachimczyk.

While Dr. Titus took responsibility for notifying Jachimczyk, Bowen grappled with his other growing problem. The media had begun receiving bits and pieces of the story, and a half-dozen journalists had appeared at the hospital and an equal number of photographers were attempting to gain entry to the morgue. CBS had already assembled a news team on the scene, anchored by Terry Drinkwater. CBS interrupted its regular feed to broadcast the news of Hughes' death. They were unable, however, to confirm the cause.

In an effort to keep the news media at bay, Bowen decided to issue an official press release worded to relate what was now common knowledge

EXHIBIT 130-D

while avoiding what all were eagerly seeking to learn: what had killed the mysterious Mr. Hughes and what did he look like when he died?

At 5:30 p.m., administrative assistant Larry Mathis read the following press release:

> At 9:00 a.m. today, The Methodist Hospital was notified that Mr. Howard R. Hughes was to be flown to Houston from Acapulco for medical treatment at The Methodist Hospital. At approximately 2:00 pm today, a Lear jet arrived at Houston Intercontinental Airport carrying the body of Howard Hughes. Mr. Hughes was accompanied by two physicians and one administrative aide. A physician who accompanied Mr. Hughes informed The Methodist Hospital that Mr. Hughes had expired about 1:27 p.m. en route from Acapulco to Houston. The body was brought to The Methodist Hospital. Further questions will be answered by Mr. Arelo Sederberg[4] in Los Angeles.

In making the announcement and accepting no questions, Mathis managed to elude more than he revealed, and only heightened the efforts of the media to uncover relevant data. Drs. Thain and Chaffin were followed back to their rooms at the Warwick Hotel, where Hughes executive Bill Gay had also registered. The home of Annette Lummis was photographed, and attempts were made to interview the elderly woman, who was horrified at the prospect of publicity. Additional guards were placed outside the morgue in addition to the continual surveillance adjacent to the cooler holding Hughes' body. And the Houston medical examiner called a meeting of those involved, including William Lummis, for 8 p.m. that evening.

Dr. Joseph Jachimczyk had a comfortable working relationship with Drs. McIntosh and Titus, and wanted to cooperate with the hospital to minimize discomfort for the family while at the same time satisfying Texas law. Legally, he could have demanded control of the case and the body, performed a complete autopsy, and arrived at his own educated conclusions as to the cause of death. Instead, he agreed to allow the hospital to take charge of Hughes' autopsy, that Lummis was convinced was required, particularly in light of the fact that Hughes' nephew insisted that the billionaire had wanted to be cremated.

Positive identification of the body was proving to be another stumbling block, both legally and with Aunt Annette. The Hughes next-of-kin was against any fingerprinting or photographs of any kind. Given the condition of the deceased eccentric, it stood to reason that the Hughes organization and his medical team were opposed to it as well. Dr.

---

4. Arelo Sederberg worked for the public relations firm of Carl Byoir & Associates who had represented Hughes for nearly 50 years.

EXHIBIT 130-E

Jachimczyk, however, was not to be so easily outmaneuvered, and for that matter, neither was the FBI, who wanted some definitive proof that the body that had now been in the cooler of the hospital morgue for over four hours was indeed that of Howard Robard Hughes. Drs. Thain and Chaffin were ready to swear that it was, and had already signed documents to attest to that fact So too did long-time Hughes aide John Holmes.

By the following morning, when the group met for a second time in the office of Ted Bowen, the issue was still undecided. Helping to push for privacy, Annette Lummis had decided that cremation was no longer necessary, despite Hughes' previously revealed wishes. Predictably, it was Drs. Thain and Chaffin who seemed most concerned about the potential leak of any autopsy photos to the press.

"My immediate thought," Chaffin said, "is that (columnist) Jack Anderson would go to any lengths to get photographs of the body of Howard Hughes."

"That's why we are using security," countered Titus.

"They'd go to any means—pay any amount of money to get those photographs," repeated Chaffin.

"Unless it is absolutely necessary, positively mandatory, let's don't take the photographs," emphasized Thain. "Safes are not safe at all with these people. We've been through this with people like Anderson and Greenspun.[5]" After all, he reasoned, the Lummises were no longer pressing for cremation, which was the initial reason that photographs were mentioned.

"There are hazards to having him buried," Chaffin thought out loud. "Someone could dig him up."

"The *National Enquirer* would pay $100,000 to get pictures," Thain said. "They may pay up to $250,000!" he added for drama.

The desperation in Thain's voice hid a motive that had little to do with money. Thain and Chaffin were both concerned about their reputations should details of Hughes' actual condition at the time of death be elaborated in the press. Accompanying photographs would be ultimate proof to reinforce what Dr. Montemayor was then stating publicly in Mexico.

As Hughes' doctors were meeting in Houston, Dr. Montemayor was testifying in Acapulco, explaining his theory that Howard Hughes died an unnecessary death. "In my opinion, he died of a disease called neglect," Montemayor stated after describing how he came to treat Hughes the previous Saturday. "The man needed to be in a hospital . . . weeks ago," he later told attorneys. "Dr. Chaffin and Dr. Thain told me that

---

5. Hank Greenspun, publisher of the *Las Vegas Sun* newspaper.

The Howard Hughes Hoax

EXHIBIT 130-F

their patient rejected medical help. When a patient becomes unconscious, you put him in a hospital."

At Methodist Hospital, the media coverage continued to expand.
News trucks were parked along the edge of the visitor parking lot in
spaces that had been assigned by the administrative offices. Coffee,
donuts, and orange juice were made available to journalists who had been
given a working-press area in the hospital's north conference room. By
1:00 p.m., however, they had all made their way to the basement morgue
where Hughes' autopsy was starting.

Dr. Malcolm McGavran, pathology's chief prosector,[6] began the
autopsy by fingerprinting the corpse now known as N–76–92, while
administrative assistants, Mike Williamson and Gary Cottongim, kept a
running account of events as required by law. Dr. McGavran was assisted
by Dr. Titus, senior pathologist Dr. Roberto Bayardo, and autopsy technician Ray Henderson. Medical examiner Jachimczyk and his assistant,
Dr. Ethel Erickson, were occupied at the time in an animated discussion
with Drs. Thain and Chaffin, who were still concerned about photographs being taken of the body. They had been informed that Mathis
Pittman, Methodist Hospital's pathology photographer, was waiting to
enter the autopsy room under police guard.

Pittman, in fact, was upstairs at that moment in the administration
offices, having camouflaged his photographic equipment under sheets on
a stretcher. It was the autopsy room itself that was under police protection at this point, with Houston Police Officer E.C. Tyler on duty in the
autopsy anteroom with Len Stom. Chief Martin of the Houston Fire
Department ambulance division arrived at the anteroom in time to hold
the door for David Workman and Buster Fontenot, Methodist Hospital
x-ray technicians, who entered the now-crowded autopsy room with Dr.
Henry McIntosh, Ted Bowen and hospital vice-president Ted Gilbreath.

The strong halogen lamp bathed the room in harsh white light that
only added to the surrealistic theater taking place. Howard Hughes, who
had spent his life trying to escape medical examination of any sort, was
now being scrutinized by eight doctors, two hospital administrators, two
assistants, and three technicians. To this mix was added yet another player:
Dr. Oscar Maldonado, an oral surgeon, who had been called to examine
the deceased's teeth.

While Jachimczyk ultimately came to the decision to prohibit photographs of the body, he also rejected the initial set of fingerprints that
were taken as being insufficient for the purpose of identification, and
called his fingerprint expert, Horace Tucker, into the mounting drama.
With Tucker's help, water was injected under the skin of Hughes' shriv-

---

6. A prosector is a physician or biologist skilled in dissection.

EXHIBIT 130-G

eled fingers in order to plump them up enough to produce a valid set of prints.

With the pressure off of Drs. Thain and Chaffin regarding potentially damaging photographs, their mood lightened to the point that Chaffin asked for help in changing some Mexican pesos into American dollars (a runner was eventually sent to the bank across the street from the hospital), and Thain joked about the lushness of Acapulco and the poor timing of Hughes' death. Thain, it seemed, had enjoyed his few months on the Mexican Riviera.

As McGavran, Titus and Bayardo removed the various body parts, they were weighed with the resulting figures then posted on a blackboard: heart 340, liver 1180, right lung 300, left lung 390, spleen 170, right kidney 90, left kidney 110. All weights were listed in grams.[7]

The routine business of identifying the cause of death took on more subtle tones as McGavran and Jachimczyk huddled, comparing written notes and repeatedly looking at the kidneys. "Chronic malnephritis," "renal failure," "renal death" were suggested as contributing factors before Titus joined the discussion and a formal decision was made.

At 4:00 p.m., the undertakers from the George H. Lewis & Son Funeral Home removed the body from the morgue and placed it in their hearse parked at the morgue dock. At the same moment, reporters and photographers were listening as Larry Mathis introduced Ted Bowen, who waited before approaching the microphone until he was certain that the body was well on its way. "The preliminary autopsy findings demonstrated that Mr. Hughes died of chronic renal disease." He offered no further elaboration. It was left to McIntosh to explain. "Renal means kidney, two of them. Chronic means a long time. And failure means that they don't work so well."

In answering questions from the gathered newsmen, Joseph Jachimczyk said that there was nothing unusual about the death of the reclusive billionaire. "As far as I am concerned, it's an ordinary death. It's an extraordinary individual involved, perhaps, but the death is like any other death."

What Jachimczyk, McIntosh and Bowen failed to mention was that Hughes' weight had fallen to ninety-three pounds. His parchment-like skin, that had been denied sunlight for over thirty-five years, hung from his bones which were clearly visible without any protective layer of fat. X-rays indicated that five hypodermic needles were broken off in his upper arms. His forearms, biceps and groin area were filled with track marks from continued injections of drugs. His body oozed fluid from

---

7. Normal weights for such organs are heart 112 grams, liver 1456, right lung 400, left lung 406, spleen 180, right kidney 112, and left kidney 112.

EXHIBIT 130-H

Excerpt from Richard Hack's Book: *Hughes*

Death by Neglect   1 9

open bed sores, his left temple had a severed, bloodied tumor, and his left shoulder was dislocated. The level of codeine in Hughes' body was five times a lethal dose. And his teeth were so loose that merely examining them caused them to fall out of his gums and into his throat.

This strangest of executives who died a "normal death" was buried the next day at Glenwood Cemetery next to his father and mother. For all his efforts at privacy during his life, no effort was made to keep the press away from the funeral. In fact, Annette Lummis seemed to be surprised to find thirty reporters at the gravesite. She was joined for the short eight-minute service by her family, plus Thain, Chaffin and Holmes, none of whom she had ever met.

The Very Rev. Robert T. Gibson, dean of Houston's Christ Cathedral where Lummis was a member, performed the service, reading from the Episcopal Book of Common Prayer. "We brought nothing into this world, and it is certain we can carry nothing out. The Lord gave, and the Lord hath taken away."

As the family sat on gray folding chairs under a faded red awning protecting the gravesite, there were no tears for their famous relative. They showed no emotion, for indeed he was a stranger to them. At 8:05 a.m., fifteen minutes after they had arrived, the family silently retreated to their cars and drove away into the early morning traffic.

Cemetery workers lowered Hughes' 1000-pound coffin into a stainless steel vault, and the bier mechanism strained and creaked under the unusual load. As they locked the vault lid and proceeded to fill the grave with dirt, only a handful of reporters remained. In another five minutes, the gravesite was deserted. Five tall, narrow and empty trumpet urns stood as silent sentries, bordered by bamboo shrubs and a chain-link fence along the Buffalo Bayou. Finally, Howard Hughes had found the peace that had evaded him for much of his existence, back in the very town where he was born. But not even in death would the mystery that swirled around his life abate. If anything, as executors attempted to settle his estate by examining his life, his saga took on a new and even stranger reality.

EXHIBIT 131-A

L. "Russ Russell's Enquiry to Methodist Hospital Houston, Texas "Is Your Howard Hughes Autopsy File Also Missing?"

Laurence M. Russell
P. O. Box 91263
Henderson, NV 89009

August 20, 2016

Dr. Marc L. Boom, President & CEO
Houston Methodist Hospital – Texas Medical Center   PERSONAL
6565 Fannin Street
Houston, TX 77030

      Re; Autopsy of Howard R. Hughes

Dear Dr. Boom:

I am hopeful of your response to an important question. First a little background.

The corpse of Howard Hughes was brought to Methodist Hospital on April 5, 1975 (flown from from Mexico, but allegedly the death occurred over Texas while enroute). Methodist was asked to perform the Autopsy on the corpse.

The full Autopsy report was provided to the Harris County Coroner's (Medical Examiner) office following the Autopsy completion.

Checking with the Harris County Medical Examiner's office, I was told that the Autopsy report has been _"missing"_ since sometime in the year 2000.

I only write to you at this time to ask one question: Is there a copy of the Howard Hughes Autopsy report on file at Methodist Hospital, or is it also "missing?"

As info, I already possess a copy of the Autopsy report, as provided by a Doctor who testified in a Federal Court trial in Salt Lake City, UT in 1976 (approx..). I do not wish a copy of any report which your Hospital may have in file. I only wish to find out if your Hospital still has a copy of that Autopsy Report.

I know you are very busy; perhaps a member of your Executive Staff may research this matter and respond via my email address?

Thank you in advance for your time and consideration.

Laurence M. Russell ("Russ")
(Retired CA Rural Cities Chief of Police)

EXHIBIT 131-B

Russ was correct – The Methodist Hospital no longer has the "High Profile" Howard Hughes Autopsy File – They threw it away?

HOUSTON
Methodist
LEADING MEDICINE

Ramon M. Cantu
Executive Vice President
Chief Legal Officer
Strategic and Business Development Officer

Legal Services
6565 Fannin, Dunn 200
Houston, Texas 77030
713-441-4182
Fax: 713-790-7092
E-mail: mcantu@houstonmethodist.org
houstonmethodist.org

September 22, 2016

Laurence M. Russell
P.O. Box 91263
Henderson, NV 89009

Re: Medical Records of Howard Hughes

Mr. Russell,

Dr. Boom forwarded your letter to me inquiring whether The Methodist Hospital has a copy of Mr. Hughes' autopsy report. Per our policy, The Methodist Hospital does not retain medical records back to this period of time, and we do not appear to have retained a copy of this report.

Very truly yours,

Ramon M. Cantu
Executive Vice President
Chief Legal Officer

RMC:jlp

cc: Marc L. Boom, M.D.

EXHIBIT 132

000
AUTOPSY REVIEW OF HOWARD R. HUGHES (PAGE 1 OF 15)

September 10, 1978

MEDICAL REVIEW OF
HOWARD R. HUGHES

by

Forest S. Tennant, Jr., M.D., Dr.P.H.
Community Health Projects, Inc.
336½ South Glendora Avenue
West Covina, California   91790
(213) 919-5807

and

Assistant Professor
Division of Epidemiology
UCLA School of Public Health
UCLA Center for Health Sciences
Los Angeles, California   90024

Prepared For:

Gary E. Elliott
Special Agent
United States Department of Justice
Drug Enforcement Administration
Los Angeles World Trade Center, Suite 800
350 S. Figueroa Street
Los Angeles, California 90071
(213) 688-2650

and

Max Wheeler
Assistant United States Attorney
350 S. Main Street
Salt Lake City, Utah 84101

EXHIBIT 133

000

AUTOPSY REVIEW OF HOWARD R. HUGHES (PAGE 2 OF 15)

INDEX FOR CASE-REVIEW

OF HOWARD R. HUGHES (HRH)

EXHIBIT 134

000

AUTOPSY REVIEW OF HOWARD R. HUGHES (PAGE 3 OF 15) 1.

I. INTRODUCTION

In June, 1978, I was requested by Special Agent, Gary Elliott, and Assistant U.S. Attorney, Max Wheeler, to be a United States Government consultant involving alleged illegal and inappropriate prescribing and administering of narcotics by Wilbur S. Thain, M.D. for the deceased, Howard R. Hughes (HRH). The essence of this report and any public testimony or information that I may give is based on my review of materials and information supplied to me by Mr. Elliott and my knowledge of the various aspects of narcotic use and abuse.

This short report contains some scientific, medical, and legal references to help substantiate the opinions given here.

II. REVIEW MATERIALS, FINDINGS AND INTERPRETATION

Listed here are the review materials made available to me. Of considerable medical and legal importance is that HRH's physicians kept no medical records on HRH.

A. Letter from Gary Elliott to Forest Tennant, M.D.

1. Findings

Codeine Phosphate, Empirin-Codeine[R], and Valium[R] were supplied to HRH between August, 1974, and April, 1976. Between August 6, 1974, and December 13, 1975, Dr. Wilbur Thain ordered and received 5,500 dosage units of Codeine Phosphate. (Were 60 mg. or 1 gr. injectable tablets). A total of 2,000 dosage units of 1 gr. Codeine Phosphate were ordered for HRH between December 19, 1975, and HRH's death on April 7, 1976.

2. Calculation to Determine if Enough Codeine Prescribed to Maintain Addiction

Given here is a simple mathematic calculation to determine if HRH was prescribed enough Codeine Phosphate between August 6, 1974, and December 13, 1975.

EXHIBIT 135

Continued from page 289

Continued from page 289

000

AUTOPSY REVIEW OF HOWARD R. HUGHES (PAGE 4 OF 15)   2.

Total Codeine Dose of 5500 Grains   =   11.16 Grains (670 mg) per day
493 days between 8/6/74 and 12/13/75

Total Codeine Dose of 2000 Grains   =   18.35 Grains (1101 mg) per day
109 days between 12/19/75 and 4/7/76

3. Interpretation

The amount of Codeine Phosphate prescribed by Dr. W. Thain to HRH during this period is more than enough to maintain physical addiction.[1-7] A daily codeine dose of 500 to 800 mg. is similar to the dosages consumed by codeine addicts who seek treatment.[8] The doses of codeine prescribed to and consumed by HRH could only be done by a person who had consumed codeine on a chronic basis and developed tolerance to it. Here are general guidelines concerning codeine:

a. Usual prescribed pain-relieving dose   30-60 mg. every 4-6 hours[3,6]

b. Toxic dose in non-tolerant person   Over 200-300 mg. in single dose[3,7]

c. Death dose in non-tolerant person   Over 500-800 mg. in single dose[7]

B. Death Certificate of HRH

Death Date April 7, 1976 - Age 70

Immediate Cause: Chronic Renal Failure due to: Chronic Interstitial Nephritis with Papillary Necrosis

C. Finger Prints of HRH - no pertinent information to Case-Review

D. Birth Certificate of HRH

Born December 24, 1905

E. Statements of Identification by Wilbur S. Thain, M.D., Lawrence Chaffin, M.D., and John Morrison Holmes. No significant information regards Case-Review.

F. Authorization for Autopsy by Annette G. Lummis (aunt of HRH), by William R. Lummis (son of Annette G. Lummis). No significant information regards Case-Review.

EXHIBIT 136

000

AUTOPSY REVIEW OF HOWARD R. HUGHES (PAGE 5 OF 15)

3.

G. Toxicologic Examination of HRH at Death

Blood, urine, and other body fluids were taken from HRH at the time of autopsy.

1. Findings

Alcohol = Negative (Cerebrospinal fluid)

Barbiturates = Negative (Blood)

Acetylsalicylic Acid = Negative (Blood)

Drug Screen = Negative (Blood, Urine, Liver, and Stomach contents)

Phenacetin - Negative (Blood, Urine, Liver, and Stomach contents)

Narcotics

0.196 mg. % Codeine (Blood)

4.8 mg. % Codeine (Bile)

6.6 mg. % Codeine (Urine)

0.7 mg. % Codeine (Liver)

2.2 mg. % Codeine (Stomach contents)

2. Calculation to Determine Dose of Codeine Taken by HRH before Death

a. 42 Kilograms (Weight of HRH at death)

x .09 (Blood volume is 8.5 -9.0 % of body weight)

3.78 Liters or 3780 ml.

b. $\frac{.196 \text{ mg. Codeine in HRH blood}}{100 \text{ ml.}} = \frac{X}{3780 \text{ ml.}}$ Approximate amount of Codeine consumed in blood volume

X (Approximate amount) = 7.41 mg. Minimal amount of Codeine consumed in 4-6 hours before death

3. Interpretation

The amount of codeine found in the blood of HRH at death is very compatible with tolerance and addiction to codeine. It also corre- lates reasonably well with known amounts prescribed to him. Codeine is one of the fastest acting and most rapidly metabolized narcotics,

EXHIBIT 137

and it remains in the blood stream for only 4 to 6 hours after consumption. Since higher levels of codeine were found in the bile and urine than in the blood,[2,5,7] it is likely that HRH consumed his last codeine 2 to 6 hours before death. Since HRH was tolerant to codeine, a blood level many times higher than the level found here would be required to produce death.

H. Laboratory Studies on HRH

Blood was drawn in Acapulco about 48 hours before death when HRH's aides and physicians realized that he was seriously ill. This blood was apparently available for testing at Methodist Hospital in Houston.

1. Findings

	Blood Taken 2 Days Before Death	Blood Taken Immediately After Death
Blood Urea Nitrogen (Normal 8-24 mg/dl)	47 mg dl	60 mg dl
Creatinine (Normal .5 - 1.5 mg/dl)	1.4 mg dl	2.0 mg dl

2. Interpretation

The pertinent blood studies indicate renal failure (e.g. "uremic poisoning"), and they are compatible with finding that there was atrophic kidneys due to long-term phenacetin (Empirin[R]) abuse.

I. Autopsy Report from Methodist Hospital, Houston, Texas, April, 1976

1. General Appearance at Death

a. Weight - 42 kilograms (87 pounds)

b. Height - 185 cm. (72.7 inches)

c. Elderly appearance

d. Gray hair, thinned and gray beard

e. No bed sores

2. Major Diagnoses

a. Granular atrophy of kidneys with necrosis of most renal papillae due to phenacetin abuse (found in Empirin-Codeine[R])

EXHIBIT 138

   b. Adeno fibromatoses hyperplasia of prostate with partial urethral obstruction

   c. Moderate urethral stricture

   d. Renal failure

   e. Emaciation and dehydration

3. Accessory Diagnoses

   a. Fibrotic apical scars both lungs and old, fibrotic left pleural adhesions (history of old left thoracic injury)

   b. Metallic pin left hip from repair of prior fracture

   c. Contusion of left shoulder

   d. Chronic peptic gastric ulcer

   e. Single focus of 60% atherosclerotic narrowing of mid left descending coronary artery

   f. Focal complex atherosclerotic lesions of aorta

   g. Adenoma (2 cm) right lobe of thyroid

   h. Single left vertebral artery

   i. Moderate dilatation occipital portions of lateral cerebral ventricles

   j. Ulcerated nodule of scalp (cystic adenocarcinoma)

   k. Multiple needle punctures and ecchymoses forearms - fresh

   l. Moderate contractures (15-20° flexion) of both knees (history of not walking for about 3 years since fracture of hip)

   m. Osteoporosis

   n. Diverticulosis of colon

   o. Dental caries - severe - evidence of neglect

X-Ray of Arms of HRH

A remarkable x-ray of HRH's arms reveal four broken, imbedded needle points (about ½ inch each) in the subcutaneous tissues of the right arm.

EXHIBIT 139

AUTOPSY REVIEW OF HOWARD R. HUGHES (PAGE 8 OF 15)

One needle point is imbedded in the left arm. Superficial veins are calcified as a result of venous infections, inflammation, and/or intravenous injection of insoluble materials. This is frequently found with the injection of non-narcotic compounds like those found in Empirin[R].9-11

Memorandum from HRH to Staff Regarding Medical Prescriptions - Date: October 2, 1958

This memoranda gives very detailed instructions to staff on how to secure and process prescriptions including triplicate (narcotic) prescriptions. These instructions do not impress me as being flexible enough to obtain sufficient quantities of narcotics (e.g. codeine or other) to be addicted, although the memorandum displays a knowledge of procedures to obtain narcotics. They do appear to be compatible with intermittent misuse, over-medication, and abuse of drugs.

Log of HRH's Activities Kept by Aides between Oct. 31, 1971, and July 1, 1973.

1. **Content**

    This detailed log was kept by HRH's aides and records the specific time of each day that HRH engaged in various activities, including the following:

    a.- Used bathroom

    b. Ate

    c. Watched films or television

    d. Sat in chair, reading

    e. Took drugs and type of drug

    f. Transacted business

    g. Left hotel

2. **Major Activities and Drug Use**

    Several points relevant to the medical and drug history of HRH are found in this log. These points are summarized:

EXHIBIT 140

UUU

AUTOPSY REVIEW OF HOWARD R. HUGHES (PAGE 9 OF 15)

a. Diet consisted mostly of chicken but HRH ate regularly.

b. HRH was apparently very constipated since he took as many as 20-25 laxative (Surfax^R) capsules in one dose.

c. Was regular user of diazepam (Valium^R), 10 mg., and HRH's aides usually referred to them in the log as BB's ("Blue Bomber" since they are a blue tablet). HRH would often consume 4 or 5 (40-50 mg.) at a time, usually to sleep. Some days he consumed as many as 9 (90 mg.) Valium^R which indicates considerable tolerance, long-term previous consumption, and possibly physical addiction.

d. Codeine was consumed on an irregular basis, but in very large doses. It was usually consumed as Empirin #4 (60 mg. of codeine with aspirin 227 mg.; phenacetin 162 mg.; and caffeine 32 mg.). On many days during this period he consumed, in one dose, 10 or 12 Empirin^R which is 600 to 720 mg. One notation indicates he consumed 25 Empirin (1500 mg.) in one dose. These doses indicate tremendous tolerance and considerable previous consumption of narcotics since single doses of about 800 mg. are often fatal in the normal human. It is not possible to determine from this log if HRH was physically addicted to codeine since most days during this period do not indicate codeine use.

e. Beginning on June 14, 1972, there are notations that HRH engaged in the "Big E." This usually occurred in the bathroom which suggests that the "Big E" was an enema.

EXHIBIT 141

vvv

AUTOPSY REVIEW OF HOWARD R. HUGHES (PAGE 10 OF 15)

f. The log indicates that HRH could mentally function well at least intermittently during this period of time. HRH transacted some business, including stock sales, leases, and tax decisions. He met with President Somoza of Nicaragua on March 13, 1972.

On at least one occasion he left his hotel to fly a plane. He frequently read newspapers. The log also recounts the famous telephone interview on January 7, 1972, regarding the infamous and fraudulent Clifford Irving biography and later signings with McGraw-Hill and affidavits for the New York Supreme Court. He made several trips and stayed in numerous locations, including Managua, Miami, Vancouver, and England.

3. Medical Notes

There are numerous medical notes of which the meaning of some are unclear to me.

Note	My Interpretation
1. Aides changed bandages on 2 occasions, and at least 2 falls, including 1 from toilet stool.	Possible skin infections at site of injections and/or from falls. Occasional falls would be expected with his high doses of sedatives and narcotics.
2. Same spoon always used for medicine.	No record of liquid medication, so I assume this was spoon used to dissolve codeine in water for self-administration.
3. Complained of frequent chilliness and sensitiveness to temperature change.	Chills are frequent when blood levels of a narcotic such as codeine drop. Could also possibly be related to progressive renal failure (e.g. "uremic poisoning") or individual trait.
4. Dr. Clark visited only one time. No other recorded physician visits, lab tests, or medical records. No mention of how medications obtained.	Highly unusual to have so much prescription medication and only one physician visit.

EXHIBIT 142

000

AUTOPSY REVIEW OF HOWARD R. HUGHES (PAGE 11 OF 15)

5. Hair, beard and nails occasionally trimmed by aides. No mention of tooth brushing.	Partially explains poor dental condition noted at death.
6. Complained of "illness" only one time. No recorded complaints of pain.	Cause unknown. Possibly narcotic withdrawal, minor infection, or progression of uremia.
7. Concealment of medication habit indicated only one time when HRH instructed aides not to empty trash in bathroom until permission given. No mention of syringes.	May have been effort to conceal intravenous drug use, other medication habit, or even unrelated to drugs.
8. Unusual obsessions and habits only indicated in requests for Kleenexes and special preparation of bedding. No hallucinations or delusions.	Habits appeared peculiar or "eccentric" but no real evidence of a psychotic or severe mental disorder.

M. Personal Communication with Gary Elliott, Special Agent, regarding HRH's Medical and Drug History

Special Agent, Gary Elliott, diligently obtained considerable information regarding pertinent facts concerning the medical and drug history about HRH. He obtained this additional information from interviews with:

> HRH's physicians
>
> HRH's aides

Pertinent points are:

1. HRH was in a widely-publicized plane crash in 1946. He was administered large amounts of morphine* while in the hospital, but it is unknown if he became addicted.

2. HRH began using Empirin[R]-Codeine after leaving the hospital, but the precise amounts and frequency of use are unknown. It is unknown if HRH was ever addicted to codeine prior to 1970's.

3. HRH sustained a fall in London in 1973 (Log's last date is 7/1/73) which fractured his hip and required a metal pin for repair. HRH never walked again.

*Morphine is a narcotic pain reliever very closely related to codeine. When taken internally, codeine partially converts to morphine.

EXHIBIT 143

000
AUTOPSY REVIEW OF HOWARD R. HUGHES (PAGE 12 OF 15)

IV. LEGAL ASPECTS OF CASE

The legal question in this case is whether narcotics were illegally supplied to HRH by Dr. Wilbur Thain.

A. Facts Bearing on Case

1. Codeine and Empirin-Codeine are narcotics whose control and distribution are regulated by the "Federal Comprehensive Drug Abuse Prevention and Control Act of 1970. (Title 21, United States Code). Plain codeine is listed under this Act as a Schedule II drug, and Empirin-Codeine[R] a Schedule III drug. Schedule II drugs have a high potential for abuse and may lead to dependence, but have an accepted medical use with restrictions in the United States.

2. The Law clearly states that if a Schedule II drug is dispensed to a person by a practitioner other than a pharmacist and in other than an emergency situation, it shall be prescribed on a triplicate prescription. The use of the drug must be for an accepted medical use which in the case of codeine is only for pain.

3. In the case of HRH the following did not occur:

    a. No prescription orders or written instructions were kept since no medical records were maintained;

    b. No triplicate prescriptions with HRH's name on them were filed;

    c. No good faith medical examination was done and results recorded to establish a need for the medical use of codeine.

    d. Codeine was intravenously used by HRH, and this is not a currently accepted use for codeine.

B. Personal Opinion

It is my personal opinion, based on knowledge of narcotic law and current medical practice, that Dr. Wilbur Thain violated Section 841 of the 1970 Federal Drug Abuse Act.

EXHIBIT 144

000
AUTOPSY REVIEW OF HOWARD R. HUGHES (PAGE 13 OF 15)

CHRONOLOGICAL HEALTH HISTORY

Based on review of the facts available to me, I summarize HRH's health and drug history as follows:

Date	Age in Years	Event
1946	41	Plane accident with severe injuries. Exposed to high doses of the narcotic, morphine.
1947-1958	42-53	Intermittent overuse of Empirin[R] (codeine, aspirin, phenacetin, caffeine) and possibly other drugs.
1958	53	HRH gives detailed instructions to staff to insure that prescription drugs are available in quantities large enough to misuse, over-medicate, and abuse. Addiction not evident.
1958-1971	53-66	Increasing misuse and abuse of prescription medications, particularly Empirin[R] medications. Health and work function not significantly impaired. Intermittent addiction and probably some intravenous use of drugs. Kidneys probably starting to degenerate from phenacetin in Empirin[R]. 12,13
1971-1973	66-68	Severe, intermittent abuse of codeine, Valium[R], and Empirin. Probably some intravenous abuse. Occasional falls due to Valium[R] abuse. Able to intermittently function with work at reasonably high level and even fly an airplane. Kidneys continue to deteriorate. Constipated due to narcotics. Poor dental care.
1973	68	Fell and sustained fractured hip requiring a metal pin for repair. Fall probably result of drug abuse.
1974-1976	68-70	Continuous intravenous abuse of codeine and probably Empirin[R]. Drugs supplied illegally by physicians. Unable to walk due to hip problem and develops leg contractures. Work, hygiene, diet, and dental care deteriorate. Progressive renal failure and uremic poisoning.
April 7, 1976	70	Dies from kidney failure due to chronic phenacetin (found in Empirin[R]) abuse. Autopsy shows brain and heart in good condition for age, so HRH could have lived much longer and in better health had he not misused drugs.

EXHIBIT 145

000
AUTOPSY REVIEW OF HOWARD R. HUGHES (PAGE 14 OF 15)

IV. LEGAL ASPECTS OF CASE

The legal question in this case is whether narcotics were illegally supplied to HRH by Dr. Wilbur Thain.

A. Facts Bearing on Case

1. Codeine and Empirin-Codeine are narcotics whose control and distribution are regulated by the "Federal Comprehensive Drug Abuse Prevention and Control Act of 1970. (Title 21, United States Code). Plain codeine is listed under this Act as a Schedule II drug, and Empirin-Codeine^R a Schedule III drug. Schedule II drugs have a high potential for abuse and may lead to dependence, but have an accepted medical use with restrictions in the United States.

2. The Law clearly states that if a Schedule II drug is dispensed to a person by a practitioner other than a pharmacist and in other than an emergency situation, it shall be prescribed on a triplicate prescription. The use of the drug must be for an accepted medical use which in the case of codeine is only for pain.

3. In the case of HRH the following did not occur:

   a. No prescription orders or written instructions were kept since no medical records were maintained;

   b. No triplicate prescriptions with HRH's name on them were filed;

   c. No good faith medical examination was done and results recorded to establish a need for the medical use of codeine.

   d. Codeine was intravenously used by HRH, and this is not a currently accepted use for codeine.

B. Personal Opinion

It is my personal opinion, based on knowledge of narcotic law and current medical practice, that Dr. Wilbur Thain violated Section 841 of the 1970 Federal Drug Abuse Act.

EXHIBIT 146

000
AUTOPSY REVIEW OF HOWARD R. HUGHES (PAGE 15 OF 15)

V. REFERENCES

1. Tennant FS Jr.: Development of Addiction to Prescribed Narcotics. Calif Soc for Treatment of Alcoholism and Other Drug Dependencies 3:3, 1978.

2. Himmelsbach CK: Studies of Certain Addiction Characteristics of (a) Dihydro-morphine ("Paramorphan"), (b) Dihydrodesoxymorphine-D ("Desomorphine"), (c) Dihydrodesoxycodeine-C ("Desocodeine)", and (d) Methyldihydromorphinone ("Metopon"). J Pharmacol Exp Ther 67:239-249, 1939.

3. Seevers MH and Pfeiffer CC: A Study of the Analgesia, Subjective Depression, and Euphoria Produced by Morphine, Heroin, Dilaudid and Codeine in the Normal Human Subject. J Pharmacol Exp Ther 56:166-187, 1936.

4. Lasagna L and Beecher HK: The Analgesic Effectiveness of Codeine and Meperidine (Demerol). J Pharmacol Exp Ther 112:306, 1954.

5. Himmelsbach CK and Andrews HL: Studies on Codeine Addiction. II. Studies of Physical Dependence on Codeine. Public Health Rep Suppl 158:11-17, 1940 .

6. Kay DC, Gorodetzky CW and Martin WR: Comparative Effects of Codeine and Morphine in Man. J Pharmacol Exp Ther 156:101-106, 1967.

7. Jaffee JH and Martin WR: Narcotic Analgesics and Antagonists: The Pharmacologic Basis of Therapeutics (Goodman CS and Gilman A eds) The MacMillan Co., New York, New York, 1975, pp 245-284.

8. Tennant FS Jr: Outpatient Treatment and Outcome of Prescription Drug Abuse (In Press).

9. Shuster MM, Lewin MC: Needle Tracks in Narcotic Addicts. New York St J Med 68:3129-3134, 1968.

10. Young AW, Rosenberg FR: Cutaneous Stigmas of Heroin Addiction. Arch Derm 104:80-86, 1971.

11. Tennant FS Jr: Complications of Propoxyphene Abuse. Arch Intern Med 132:191-194, 1973.

12. Murray T and Goldberg M: Chronic Interstitial Nephritis: Etiologic Factors. Ann Intern Med 82:453-459, 1975.

13. Nordenfelt D: Deaths from Renal Failure in Abusers of Phenacetin Containing Drugs. Acta Med Scand 191:11-16, 1972.

EXHIBIT 147

THE METHODIST HOSPITAL TEXAS MEDICAL CENTER
6516 BERTNER • HOUSTON, TEXAS 77025 • (713) 790-3311 • CABLE: METHHOSP

DEPARTMENT OF PATHOLOGY

Dr. Jack L. Titus dictating notes for the record on the case of Mr. Howard R. Hughes.

Shortly after 9:00 AM on Monday, April 5, 1976, Dr. Henry McIntosh and Mr. Ted Bowen informed me confidentially that Mr. Howard R. Hughes was to arrive at The Methodist Hospital shortly after noon on that date in a critically ill state. Reportedly he was being transferred to The Methodist Hospital from Acapulco, Mexico. I was asked to arrange the most marked confidentiality of any and all laboratory work related to his case and, at the same time, expedite any and all laboratory work because of his critical illness. Appropriate arrangements were made for that aspect of his hospitalization. The patient was to be admitted under the pseudonym of John T. Conover.

Subsequently at approximately 2:00 PM on Monday, April 5, 1976 I received a call from Mr. Ted Bowen who had just been informed that the hospital conveyance and the physician who had gone to meet the plane bringing Mr. Hughes to Houston had found that he had died in route. The body was being transported to The Methodist Hospital morgue until appropriate arrangements, particularly from the legal standpoint, as well as from the family standpoint, could be made.

At 2:50 PM on Monday, April 5, 1976 Mr. Ted Bowen and I were at the morgue dock of The Methodist Hospital when a Methodist Hospital ambulance arrived. Dr. Robert Berglund, Chief Medical Resident, a hospital nurse, Mr. Jay Dixon and Mr. Len Stom accompanied the body of an elderly white male. These individuals stated that this was the body of the man known as Mr. John T. Conover, who was stated to be Mr. Howard Hughes.

Under our supervision (that is, Mr. Ted Bowen and myself) the body was moved to the morgue of The Methodist Hospital. At 3:00 PM on Monday, April 5, 1976, in The Methodist Hospital morgue, I performed a brief external examination of the body reported to be that of Mr. Howard Hughes. The findings were those of an elderly white male with gray hair, somewhat thinned, and a gray beard. The body appeared remarkably emaciate and dehydrated. The estimated length of the body would be about 6'2". A plastic intrav catheter was present in the left antecubital fossa and the left arm was taped to a towe covered board. The body had been covered with a yellow blanket. The eyes were open an the pupils dilated and fixed. Although there were contractures of moderate degree of the knees, it should be noted that there was no evidence of rigor mortis in any of the skeletal muscles of the body. Likewise, there was no evidence of livor mortis. Based upon the information that the body came from the cabin of an airplane at appropriate

EXHIBIT 148

AUTOPSY REVIEW OF HOWARD R. HUGHES (PAGE 2 OF 4)

environmental temperatures, was transported immediately by an ambulance at appro-priate environmental temperatures, and this examination done essentially immediately upon arrival of the body at The Methodist Hospital morgue, it is my firm opinion that death occurred less than three hours prior to the time of my examination. Other physicians present at the time of this brief initial examination included Doctors Malcolr H. McGavran, Robert Berglund, Roberto J. Bayardo, and Henry D. McIntosh. Other observers were Mr. Ted Bowen, Mr. Larry Mathis and Mr. Ray Henderson, the latter most being an autopsy technician of the Pathology Service of The Methodist Hospital. The opinion as to the preliminary estimate as to death having occurred less than three hours prior to the examination at 3:00 PM on April 5, 1976 was concurred in by Doctors McGavran and Bayardo, the other two pathologists present.

Pending notification of next of kin, the arrival at the hospital of the attending physiciar who accompanied Mr. Hughes to Houston, and assessment of the legal aspects of the situation, the body was placed in a body cooler in the morgue of The Methodist Hospital. Security measures were arranged for to be maintained continously throughout the remainder of the day with Mr. Ray Henderson, Autopsy Technician, in constant attendar a designated administrator of The Methodist Hospital in constant attendance, and a security officer of The Methodist Hospital in constant attendance.

At approximately 3:15 to 3:30 PM on April 5, 1976 I met in Mr. Bowen's office along with other physicians and administrators of The Methodist Hospital with the individuals that had accompanied Mr. Hughes to Houston. These included Dr. Lawrence Chaffin, Dr. Wilbur Thain and Mr. John Holmes. In our preliminary interview, from a medical stand-point the salient features, in my opinion, of Mr. Hughes' medical history included the following:

1. An extraordinary reluctance to permit the usual medical evaluations.
2. A history of a fracture of the left hip in August, 1973 which was repaired surgically in London, England.
3. Some propensity to self-medicate with a variety of proprietary medications, including aspirin and phenacitin containing compounds.
4. Regarding the apparent final illness, Drs. Chaffin and Thain reported that from their limited knowledge, Mr. Hughes had been reported to them as not having been eating nor drinking well for approximately the last three weeks.

In addition, he apparently had increasing malaise. Over the past two or three days of life, particularly the past 24-36 hours, he developed some confusion. Somewhat suddenl and unexpectedly on Sunday evening, April 4, he developed a shock-like state for which he was treated with intravenous fluids. In recognition of the apparent sudden worsening of his condition, the decision was made to transfer him to Houston for further care as soon as arrangements could be made. Dr. Chaffin, Dr. Thain and Mr. Holmes told us that in his seriously ill state, apparently nearly comatose, he was put in a private jet with the aforementioned three gentlemen in attendance and transferred to Houston.

EXHIBIT 149

During most of the flight from Acapulco, Mexico to Houston his condition remained essentially unchanged; that is, unresponsive with intravenous fluids running and oxygen being administered. Sometime after the plane had passed Brownsville, Texas there was progressive loss of all vital signs so that at the time of beginning let down in Houston, all vital signs had ceased. Dr. Thain noted the time to be 1:27 PM, CST. Subsequent events are as described in the foregoing paragraphs with the transportation of the body to The Methodist Hospital and our observations upon arrival there.

Having determined from the foregoing that (1) this patient, reported to be Mr. Howard Hughes, had died in Texas; (2) that the plane bearing his body had landed in the jurisdiction of the Harris County Medical Examiner; (3) that death had occurred at approximately 1:30 PM, CST on April 5, 1976; and (4) that no physician licensed in Texas was in attendance prior to death, it was clear that the Medical Examiner for Harris County must be contacted. Therefore at 4:00 PM I was able to reach Dr. Ethel Erickson, Deputy Medical Examiner of Harris County as Dr. Joseph Jachimczyk, Medical Examiner for Harris County was at that moment out of the city. I explained the entirety of the situation to Dr. Erickson. I indicated to Dr. Erickson that the attending physicians were present and in addition, contact had been made with the next of kin, Mrs. F. Lummis of Houston, who is an aunt of Mr. Hughes. Her son, Mr. Will Lummis, an attorney in Houston, representing his mother with power of attorney for his mother, came to the hospital to handle the immediate funeral arrangements. After discussion among all the parties concerned and further discussions with Dr. Erickson, at about 8:00 PM on April 5, 1976 Dr. Jachimczyk, who had returned to town, and Dr. Erickson met with Mr. Lummis, Dr. Thain, Mr. Holmes, Mr. Larry Mathis and me. Dr. Jachimczyk indicated the necessity for an autopsy. As a courtesy to the family of Mr. Hughes and to the Hughes interests, he indicated that if an appropriate autopsy permit were given by the next of kin, and, if the Pathology Department of The Methodist Hospital were willing to perform a complete autopsy and thereafter, complete a proper death certificate, the Medical Examiner's office would consider that the legal requirements of the situation were satisfied. Parenthetically, it may be noted that this is the usual and customary practice for Houston patients who are DOA at Houston hospitals. After these consultations, Mr. Will Lummis indicated he would discuss the question of an autopsy further with his mother, but was certain that he could return the next morning, that is, Tuesday, April 6, 1976, to sign an autopsy permit which would authorize pathologists at The Methodist Hospital to conduct a complete autopsy on the body reported to be Mr. Howard Hughes.

On Tuesday morning, April 6, 1976, Mr. Lummis signed the usual Methodist Hospital autopsy permit form which was duely witnessed. Hospital legal counsel agreed it was appropriate permission. Dr. Jachimczyk was informed that a proper autopsy permit had been obtained and that a complete autopsy would begin at about 1:00 PM on Tuesday, April 6, 1976. The autopsy would be carried out by myself in concert with Doctors Malcolm McGavran and Roberto Bayardo. Dr. Jachimczyk and Dr. Erickson were invited to be present as knowledgeable colleagues whose expertise was deemed appropriate. In addition, as is usually the case, the attending physicians, Drs. Thain, Chaffin, and McIntosh, were asked to attend.

EXHIBIT 150

For the File   0001

Page Four   AUTOPSY REVIEW OF HOWARD R. HUGHES (PAGE 4 OF 4)

Arrangements were made to obtain specific identification by usual methodologies includin
finger printing, total body x-rays, and preparation of a dental chart. Following these
arrangements in view of a valid autopsy permission signed by the appropriate next of kin,
arrangements for clear identification of the individual to be autopsied, and appropriate
consultation with the Harris County Medical Examiner's office, the autopsy described
in the protocol that follows was done. The autopsy number assigned to this case is
N-76-92.

This concludes the notes preliminary to the formal autopsy protocol and report on
case N-76-92, Mr. Howard Hughes. The time is 5:00 PM, April 6, 1976, when this
record is dictated from notes made over the past 24 hours or so.

Jack L. Titus, M.D., Ph.D.
Chief, Pathology Service
The Methodist Hospital

EXHIBIT 151

Dental Findings

0002

AUTOPSY REVIEW OF HOWARD R. HUGHES (PAGE 1 OF 1)

THE METHODIST HOSPITAL TEXAS MEDICAL CENTER
6516 BERTNER • HOUSTON, TEXAS 77025 • (713) 790-3311 • CABLE: METHHOSP

Dr. Oscar Maldonado dictating the findings of a dental examination performed on a
70 year old caucasian male identified as the body of Howard R. Hughes, whom had
apparently died about 24 hours prior to this examination.

The dental examination was done at The Methodist Hospital in the morgue on
April 6, 1976 at approximately 2:30 PM in the presence of several witnesses
including Doctors J.L. Titus, M.H. McGavran, R. Bayardo, H.D. McIntosh, W.
Thain, L. Chaffin, J. Jachimczyk, E. Erickson, and Mr. Ted Bowen.

The dental findings are as follows:

Mr. Hughes' teeth were in a poor condition of neglect. He had a generalized condition of a chronic periodontal disease with inflammation and hypertrophy of
his gum tissue. He also had large areas of tartar deposits around his lower
anterior teeth. Most of his upper and lower anterior teeth were loose due to
the peridontal disease with bone resorpcion.

He had only two missing teeth – his lower left central tooth and lower left second
molar. The remainder of his teeth, in addition to periodontal disease, were
badly decayed. His upper right lateral and cuspid teeth were completely destroyed
by decay and only the root portions of those teeth could be identified. The upper
right first bicuspid and third molar had large decay in the cervical portion of
these teeth. In his upper left cuspid and first bicuspid there was decay around the
cervical area of these teeth. On his lower right second molar there was a large
decay involving the nerve portion of this tooth.

He had several gold fillings in the occlusal aspect of his upper right first and second
molars, upper left first, second and third molars, lower right first and second
molars, and lower left first molar. These fillings appeared to be gold inlays or
maybe some were gold foils. They were in good condition with no recurrent decay.

The x-rays seen of his face, PA and lateral views, were not very satisfactory. They
were unremarkable, except the gold metallic fillings already described, as well as
the multiple decayed teeth and a large bone lesion on his lower right jaw around the
second molar area, secondary to the extensive decay; perhaps an abcess or a granu-
loma. No other bone pathology could be identified by x-rays.

The examination was completed at 3:00 PM, April 6, 1976.

Oscar Maldonado, D.D.S.

OM/bjs

EXHIBIT 152

0003

AUTOPSY REVIEW OF HOWARD R. HUGHES (PAGE 1 OF 5)

THE METHODIST HOSPITAL TEXAS MEDICAL CENTER
6516 BERTNER • HOUSTON, TEXAS 77025 • (713) 790-3311 • CABLE: METHHOSP

AUTOPSY PROTOCOL

N-76-92
Howard R. Hughes
70 years old
Male caucasian

EXTERNAL EXAMINATION

The body is that of an aged, cachectic, caucasian male weighing 42 kilograms and measuring 185 cm. The skin "tents" when elevated. The hair and beard are grey. The sclera are clear, the corneas have arcus senilis bilaterally, the irides are brown, the pupils are RR and E at 4 mm. The auditory canals are clear. A 2.2 cm oval, centrally ulcerated, nodule is present on the left parietal scalp. The hair surrounding this has been trimmed. The oral cavity and pharynx are clear. The teeth are carious (see attached dental report). The trachea is midline. The thyroid is not palpable.

The left supra and infraclavicular fossae as well as the left shoulder and upper arm and posterior axillary fold are modestly swollen, edematous, and discolored a bluish-grey. A left acromio-clavicular separation is palpable with overriding of the clavicle. The remaining skin of the anterior chest is unremarkable. Multiple recent needle punctures and recent ecchymoses are present on both forearms. The abdomen is scaphoid. The penis is circumcised; urethral meatus is small measuring 4 mm. The testes are intrascrotal. The groins and perineum are without lesions. The anus is patent and without lesions.

A 17 cm linear scar is present on the left hip from the level of the pubic symphysis distally. The remainder of the thighs and legs show bilateral 15-20° flexion contractures of the knees. A metallic pin in the left hip is demonstrated by radiologic examination.

Examination of the back shows a distinct dorsal scoliosis with the curvature to the right, and depressed white scars overlying the left mid scapula and running laterally and inferiorly to the mid axillary line at the level of the costal margin. Six, 1.5-2.5 c superficial centrally crusted ulcers of the skin over the sacrum and adjacent iliosac areas are present.

EXHIBIT 153

0003

AUTOPSY REVIEW OF HOWARD R. HUGHES (PAGE 2 OF 5)

THE METHODIST HOSPITAL TEXAS MEDICAL CENTER
6516 BERTNER • HOUSTON, TEXAS 77025 • (713) 790-3311 • CABLE: METHHOSP

AUTOPSY PROTOCOL   Page Two
N-76-92
Howard R. Hughes, Jr.

INTERNAL EXAMINATION

Subcutaneous adipose tissue is scant to absent and 2 mm in thickness over the mid
abdomen.

The diaphragms are both at the level of the 6th interspace. The right pleural cavity
contains 30 ml of serous fluid, the left 20 ml of like fluid and the pericardium 50 ml
of clear serous fluid. The peritoneum is dry. All organs are normally situated. The
left pleural cavity is partially obliterated by fibrous adhesions.

Heart

The heart weighs 340 grams. The right and left ventricular thickness are 10 mm and
3 mm respectively. The tricuspid, pulmonic, mitral and aortic rings measure 13.5,
8.7, 12.4 and 9.2 cm. The mitral ring is focally calcified medially. No valvular
lesions save fenestrations are noted. No epicardial, myocardial or endocardial lesions
are noted. The left coronary artery is dominant. Mild to focally moderate coronary
atherosclerosis is present with a single focus of 60% luminal narrowing in the mid
portion of the left anterior descending artery.

Vessels

The aorta is minimally involved by nonulcerated athromatous plaques in the ascending
arch and descending portions. The abdominal aorta distal to the renal vessels shows
4 ulcerated plaques with attached fibrinous thrombi. The great vessels of the neck
and abdominal branches arise in their usual anatomic positions. The renal arteries
are patent and show minimal atherosclerosis. The pulmonary arteries are patent and
without evidence of thromboemboli. The inferior vena cava, renal and hepatic veins
are patent and without lesions. The portal and splenic veins are grossly normal.

Lungs

The right lung weighs 300 grams and the left lung 390 grams. Save for the previously
described fibrous adhesions and bilateral fibrous apical scars, no lesions are found.
The tracheobronchial tree and larynx are without lesions.

Liver

The liver weighs 1180 grams and is grossly of normal appearance. Multiple transections
show no lesions. The bile ducts and gallbladder are without lesions.

EXHIBIT 154

AUTOPSY REVIEW OF HOWARD R. HUGHES (PAGE 3 OF 5)

THE METHODIST HOSPITAL TEXAS MEDICAL CENTER
6516 BERTNER • HOUSTON, TEXAS 77025 • (713) 790-3311 • CABLE: METHHOSP

AUTOPSY PROTOCOL   Page Four
N-76-92
Howard R. Hughes, Jr.

Urinary Bladder

The urinary bladder is filled with approximately 250 ml of cloudy yellow urine. The wall is trabeculated. No mucosal abnormalities are noted. The ureteral orifices are not dilated.

Esophagus

No abnormalities.

Stomach

A linear, 2 x 0.5 cm, chronic peptic ulcer is present on the lesser curvature of the stomach at the incisura.

Duodenum and Small Bowel

No abnormalities.

Large Intestine

Sigmoid diviticula are present. No mucosal or mural lesions are noted.

Bones

The vertebral bodies are moderately osteoporotic as are the ribs and sternum.

Brain and Spinal Cord

The dura is intact and no evidences of epidural or subdural hematomas, recent or remote, are found. The brain weighs 1540 grams. The cortical surfaces show no lesions. The basilar cerebral vessels are with usual anatomic distribution with the exception that only one vertebral artery is present, situated on the left. No aneurysms are noted at any of the bifurcations. Athromatous involvement is minimal. No evidences of cingulate, uncal or cerebellar tonsillar huniation is present.

EXHIBIT 155

0003

AUTOPSY REVIEW OF HOWARD R. HUGHES (PAGE 4 OF 5)

THE METHODIST HOSPITAL TEXAS MEDICAL CENTER
i516 BERTNER • HOUSTON, TEXAS 77025 • (713) 790-3311 • CABLE: METHHOSP

AUTOPSY PROTOCOL   Page Six
N-76-92
Howard R. Hughes, Jr.

MICROSCOPIC EXAMINATION

The salient abnormalities corroborating and extending the gross findings are:

Kidneys

The renal papillae are shrunken and fibrotic showing extensive loss of collecting
tubules with residual peritubular hyalinization and both interstitial and intratubular
deposits of urates and calcium. No active acute inflammatory process is present
and no frank recent necrosis is found. The arcuate and interlobular arteries show
modest to marked fibrous subintimal thickening. Extensive zones of obsolete, totally
fibrotic glomeruli and scarring are present with mild to modest lymphoid interstitial
inflammatory infiltrate. Acute pyelonephritis is not present.

Prostate

Nodular hyperplasia, predominantly adenomatous is present. A microfocus of well
differentiated adenocarcinoma is also present.

Urinary Bladder

Mild chronic cystitis is present.

Pancreas

Mild centilobular ductal dilatation with retained secretion is present.

Bone Marrow

The marrow is minimally hypoplastic. The vertebral bodies evidence modest osteoporosis. Evidences of osteitis fibrosa are not found.

Skin

The lesion of the left parietal scalp is an eccrine adenoidcystic adenocarcinoma
(cylindroma).

EXHIBIT 156

0003

AUTOPSY REVIEW OF HOWARD R. HUGHES (PAGE 5 OF 5)

THE METHODIST HOSPITAL TEXAS MEDICAL CENTER
6516 BERTNER • HOUSTON, TEXAS 77025 • (713) 790-3311 • CABLE: METHHOSP

AUTOPSY PROTOCOL   Page Seven
N-76-92
Howard R. Hughes, Jr.

Thyroid

The nodule in the left lower pole is a follicular adenoma.

Stomach

The ulcer is chronic with fibrous replacement of part of the muscularis.

Lungs

The apical scars are without evidence of active inflammatory or granulomatous component. The remainder of the samples show no evidence of pneumonia or passive congestion.

Sections of the heart, liver, adrenals, brain, pituitary, bone marrow, spleen show no abnormalities.

Malcolm H. McGavran, M.D.
Chief, Anatomic Pathology

Jack L. Titus, M.D., Ph.D.
Chief, Pathology Service

EXHIBIT 157

0004

AUTOPSY REVIEW OF HOWARD R. HUGHES (PAGE 1 OF 1)

Lungs

The right lung weighs 300 grams and the left lung 390 grams. Save for the previousl
described fibrous adhesions and bilateral fibrous apical scars, no lesions are found.
The tracheobronchial tree and larynx are without lesions.

Liver

The liver weighs 1180 grams and is grossly of normal appearance. Multiple transecti
show no lesions. The bile ducts and gallbladder are without lesions.

"I was sick and ye visited me."—MATT. 25:36

Bilateral pulmonary apical fibrous scars
Fibrous pleural adhesions, left (history of hemothorax following crashing injury, 30 years)
Follicular adenoma of the thyroid
Nodular hyperplasia of the prostate
Dilitation and trabeculation of the urinary bladder
Moderate stricture urethral meatus
Eccrine adenoidcystic adenocarcinoma, left scalp
Lipoma, left upper arm
Contusion of the left shoulder with acromioclavicular separation
Scoliosis of the dorsal spine
Osteoporosis, moderate
Scars of the left back (history of crashing injury, remote)
Diverticulosis of the colon
Emaciation and dehydration

COMMENT

The anatomic findings combined with the history of prolonged use of phenacitin containing
analgesics establish the renal lesion as analgesic nephropathy (see Burry, A.F., Nephron
5:185-201, 1967). The recent, two day premortem and the postmortem chemical analyses
document impaired renal function. The toxocologic studies show only minimum amounts of
codine and salicylate.

Jack L. Titus, M.D., Ph.D.
Chief, Pathology Service
Prosector-Pathologist

HOWARD R. HUGHES, JR.

IPS 289 7/73

EXHIBIT 158-A

0005
AUTOPSY REVIEW OF "HOWARD R. HUGHES"

THE METHODIST HOSPITAL TEXAS MEDICAL CENTER
6516 BERTNER • HOUSTON, TEXAS 77025 • (713) 790-3311 • CABLE: METHHOSP

DEPARTMENT OF PATHOLOGY

April 7, 1976

Henry D. McIntosh, M.D.
6516 Bertner
Houston, Texas 77030

Dear Doctor McIntosh:

The following are the preliminary anatomic diagnoses on Howard R. Hughes, autopsy number N-76-92. Mr. Hughes reportedly died at 1:27 PM CST on April 5, 1976 and was dead on arrival at The Methodist Hospital at 2:50 PM CST, April 5, 1976. The autopsy was performed on April 6, 1976, beginning at 1:30 PM.

Cause of Death:
    Chronic renal failure due to chronic interstitial nephritis with papillary necrosis.

Major Diagnoses:
    1. Granular atrophy of kidneys (total weight 200 grams) with necrosis most of renal papillae.
    2. Adenofibromatous hyperplasia prostate with prominent median bar partially obstructing urethra.
    3. Moderate stricture urethral meatus.
    4. Renal failure.
    5. Emaciation and dehydration.
    6. Generalized osteoporosis.

Additional Findings:
    1. Fibrotic apical scars both lungs and old, fibrotic left pleural adhesions (history of prior left thoracic injury).
    2. Metallic pin left hip from repair of prior fracture.
    3. Separation left acromio-clavicular joint with edema and hematoma left shoulder.
    4. Chronic peptic gastric ulcer at incisura angularis.
    5. Single focus of grade 3 atherosclerotic narrowing (60% luminal narrowing) in mid left anterior descending coronary artery; focal calcification medial aspect mitral valve annulus.
    6. Focal complex atherosclerotic lesions aorta (grade 2 atherosclerotic disease).
    7. Adenoma (2 cm.) right lobe of thyroid.
    8. Single left vertebral artery.
    9. Moderate dilatation occipital portions of lateral cerebral ventricles.
    10. Cylindroma left parietal scalp.
    11. Multiple needle punctures and ecchymoses forearms.

EXHIBIT 158-B

FROM JAMES PHELAN'S BOOK HOWARD HUGHES: THE HIDDEN YEARS

112   **Howard Hughes: The Hidden Years**

dinner for the boss." The chefs spent most of the day preparing it. When it was ready, Margulis put it on a serving cart, wheeled it to the elevator, and took it up to the abandoned penthouse.

"Dinner for the boss," he told the guard, as he pushed the cart through the partition door. The dinner was consumed by two functionaries. The same day, Chuck Waldron came in and changed all the locks on the ninth floor to make certain the secret of Hughes's flight was preserved as long as possible.

While Margulis went through the motions of serving meals for the vanished Hughes, Stewart and three others—Eric Bundy, Norm Love, and Fred Jayka—cleaned up the billionaire's little bedroom.

"It was—well, pretty awful," says Stewart. "There hadn't been a maid in the room for four years, and it had never been vacuumed or dusted." The memory is plainly distasteful to Stewart and he is reluctant to talk about it.

Stewart's job was to dispose of Hughes's empty bottles of pain-killing drugs. They had been stacked on a wide shelf in the bedroom closet, and when Stewart opened the door he was astonished at the sight.

"There must have been a hundred of them," he says. "I didn't count them, but they were stacked on top of each other, and they almost filled the shelf space."

Stewart's first instructions were to put them in a gunnysack, smash them with a hammer, and bury the sack of broken bottles at some remote spot far out in the desert. Then his instructions were changed. He was told to pack the bottles in boxes and deliver them to the Romaine headquarters.

"I had my wife drive me from Las Vegas to Los Angeles," Stewart says. "I turned over the empty bottles to the Romaine staff. I don't know why they wanted them, and I didn't ask."

The three functionaries had to deal with an even darker Hughes secret. For years he had had the habit of urinating into a wide-mouthed Mason jar while reclining on his lounge chair. His kidneys were malfunctioning long before they failed in Acapulco and precipitated his death. Relieving himself took hours, and he was too weak to sit all that time in the bathroom. Instead of being

EXHIBIT 158-C

FROM JAMES PHELAN'S BOOK HOWARD HUGHES: THE HIDDEN YEARS

emptied, the jars had been capped and stacked in a corner of his little bedroom. The employees had to get rid of a three-year supply of Hughes's urine and then wash and destroy the jars. One aide kept interrupting the job to go off into an adjoining bathroom and retch.

When they were finished, and Stewart had removed the empty drug bottles, the Desert Inn housekeeping crew came in for the final cleanup. They took the old draperies, and some of the sheets and towels, and burned them; the room had to be deodorized.

A few of the house-cleaning staff whispered stories to their closest friends—with warnings never to speak a word about what they were told. They told others, with the same warning. Rumors spread that there was something dreadfully wrong with the billionaire who owned the Desert Inn and much of Las Vegas.

But there was already such a confusion of myths about Hughes that many who heard this new story passed it off as another fabrication.

Maheu heard these rumors soon after he learned that Hughes had been taken out of the Desert Inn, but before he was told he was fired. He already knew there was something wrong with Hughes, but he didn't know the details. When Hughes had left Boston to come out to Las Vegas in 1966, Maheu knew that two aides had to stay behind and clean up his bedroom at the Copley-Plaza Hotel there. The new stories propelled him to the wrong conclusion. He assumed that Hughes had totally ceased to function and that others were acting in his stead.

When he was told a week later that Hughes had fired him, Maheu didn't believe it. There was logic in his reasoning and in his conclusion that someone other than Hughes had issued the order.

"The last time I had talked to him," Maheu says, "there was no inkling that I was out of favor. He had assured me repeatedly that I was to be with him the rest of his life, and warned me not to let the Romaine-Houston people drive a wedge between us. I had a half-dozen projects in the works for him.

"And finally, I had been hired by Hughes as his chief executive officer, and if I was to be fired, Hughes was the man to do it.

"All it would have taken was a single phone call from him. If

EXHIBIT 158-D

BACK DUST COVER FROM JAMES PHELAN'S BOOK
HOWARD HUGHES: THE HIDDEN YEARS.
"HUGHES" AIDES, GORDON MARGULIS AND MELL STEWART,
TWO OF PHELAN'S INFORMATION SOURCES

JAMES PHELAN has been described by The New York Times' Pulitzer Prize-winner Wallace Turner as "one of the best investigative reporters of his generation." At sixty-four Mr. Phelan's track record for the big story is a long one. Former Governor Edmund (Pat) Brown credits his re-election in 1962, when he defeated Richard Nixon, to Phelan's article in The Reporter magazine on the Hughes-Nixon loan. Reporting for the Saturday Evening Post, Phelan was the first journalist to show that former District Attorney James Garrison had no case against Clay Shaw when Garrison accused Shaw of conspiring to kill President Kennedy.

For over twenty years James Phelan has been following the career of Howard Hughes and has written about him in numerous publications, including the Saturday Evening Post, Paris Match, Playboy and The New York Times. Mr. Phelan now lives in Long Beach, California.

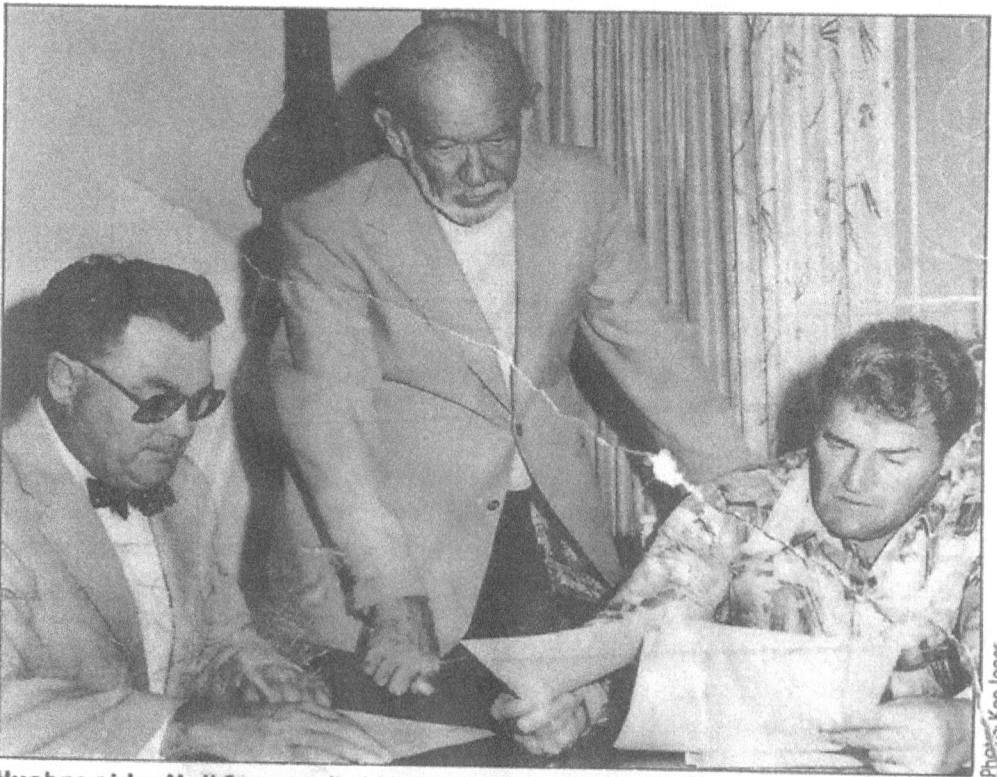

Hughes aides Mell Stewart (left) and Gordon Margulis (right) with James Phelan

EXHIBIT 159

. Dr. Henry D. McIntosh

0005

AUTOPSY REVIEW OF HOWARD R. HUGHES (PAGE 2 OF 2)

Toxicologic and histologic studies are in progress. As soon as these studies are completed, the final autopsy report will be available.

Sincerely yours,

Jack L. Titus

Jack L. Titus, M.D., Ph.D.
Chief, Pathology Service
The Methodist Hospital

JLT/bjs
cc: Wilbur S. Thain, M.D.
Lawrence Chaffin, M.D.

EXHIBIT 160

0006   1976

Ext. 671 (Day
Ext. 212 (Nig.

AUTOPSY REVIEW OF HOWARD R. HUGHES (PAGE 1 OF 3)

OFFICE OF THE MEDICAL EXAMINER
OF HARRIS COUNTY

HARRIS COUNTY COURT HOUSE
HOUSTON, TEXAS 77002

April 10, 1976

TOXICOLOGICAL EXAMINATION

RE: Howard R. Hughes

CASE NUMBER: N-76-92

LABORATORY RESULTS

Alcohol = Negative (Cerebrospinal Fluid)
Barbiturates = Negative (Blood)
Acetylsalicylic acid = Negative (Blood)
Drug Screen = Negative (Blood, Urine, Liver and
    Stomach Contents)
Phenacetin = Negative (Blood, Urine, Liver and
    Stomach Contents)
Narcotics = 0.196 mg. % Codeine (Blood)
    4.8 mg. % Codeine (Bile)
    6.6 mg. % Codeine (Urine)
    0.7 mg. % Codeine (Liver)
    2.2 mg. % Codeine (Stomach Contents)
Blood Group = "A"

Joseph A. Jachimczyk, M. D., J. D.
Chief Medical Examiner

Larry D. Hobbs
Assistant Toxicologist

EXHIBIT 161

0006

AUTOPSY REVIEW OF HOWARD R. HUGHES (PAGE 2 OF 3)

IRCA
CALCM
GLUC
BUN
CREA
CL

5.5
9.1
44.
60.0
2.0
85.

N-76-92
J. L. Titus

Normals:
gluc ±20 less than serum
protein 15-25 (cisternal)
calcium ±5
-76-92 J. L. Titus

EXHIBIT 162

0006
AUTOPSY REVIEW OF HOWARD R. HUGHES (PAGE 3 OF 3)

J. L. Titus, M.D.

410-URINALYSIS - LAB 3

ROOM NO.
DATE

LAB 3

ROUTINE ADMISSION URINALYSIS (ADULT)	20980
ROUTINE ADMISSION URINALYSIS (PEDIATRIC)	20981
ROUTINE URINALYSIS	20978
O.B. ADMISSION	20962
T&A ADMISSION	20835

TEST & NORMAL RANGE	X	CODE	RESULT	TEST	X	CODE	RESULT
ROUTINE PHYSICAL & CHEMICAL EXAMINATION	✓	[illegible]		KETONES: NEG		[illegible]	NEG
COLOR & DESCRIPTION yel		[illegible]	Cl	MICROSCOPIC EXAM		[illegible]	
SPECIFIC GRAVITY 1.001-1.030		[illegible]	1.018	RBC/HPF			35-40
OSMOLALITY 250-1200 mOSM		[illegible]		WBC/HPF			2-4 — Hyaline Cast 15-20 (HPF)
pH 5.5-7.0		[illegible]	6.0	MUCUS			mod
PROTEIN LESS THAN 10 MGM%		[illegible]	10 MGM%	EPITHELIAL CELLS			light
GLUCOSE NEG		[illegible]	NEG	Spermatozoa		PRESENT	
OCCULT BLOOD FT TR		[illegible]	NEG	Bact		light	DATE, TIME & INITIAL

N76-92

All reports of copies given to Dr. McGlavran — Patty

J. L. Titus, M.D.

410-BLOOD CHEMISTRY

ROOM NO.
DATE

LAB 14

ELECTROLYTES (NA, K, CL, & CO2)-BUN-CREATININE
ELECTROLYTES
ARTERIAL GASES pH, pCO2, PO2, O2-SAT
BUN CREATININE
REMARKS:

THE METHODIST HOSPITAL HOUSTON, TEXAS

TEST & NORMAL RANGE	X	CODE	RESULT	TEST & NORMAL RANGE	X	CODE	RESULT
CO_2 24-31 mM/L		[illegible]		BUN 8-24 mg/dl	✓	[illegible]	60
Cl 96-106 mEq/L	✓	[illegible]	85	CREATININE 0.5-1.5 mg/dl	✓	[illegible]	2.0
Na 135-148 mEq/L	✓	[illegible]	108	URIC ACID MALE 4.5-9 ? /dl FEMALE 3-7.5 mg/dl	✓	[illegible]	5.5
K 3.5-5.0 mEq/L	✓	[illegible]	23.4	SUGAR (GLUCOSE) 65-110 mg/dl	✓	[illegible]	44
pH 7.35-7.45		[illegible]		CALCIUM 9.0-10.5 mg/dl	X	[illegible]	9.1
pCO_2 35-45 mm Hg		[illegible]		PHOSPHORUS 2.5-4.5 mg/dl		[illegible]	
pO_2 60-90 mm Hg		[illegible]		MAGNESIUM 1.7-2.8 mg/dl		[illegible]	
O_2-SAT. 93-97%		[illegible]		PLASMA HEMOGLOBIN 0-20 mg/dl		[illegible]	

DATE, TIME & INITIAL Am 4-6-76 4:30

267 Spinal fluid - for Dr. N

performed 4/9/76
Spec. of 4/6/76

410-BLOOD CHEMISTRY

ROOM NO.
DATE 4/9/76

LAB 14

ELECTROLYTES (NA, K, CL, & CO2)-BUN-CREATININE
ELECTROLYTES
ARTERIAL GASES pH, pCO2, PO2, O2 SAT
BUN CREATININE
REMARKS:

TEST & NORMAL RANGE	X	CODE	RESULT	TEST & NORMAL RANGE	X	CODE	RESULT
CO_2 24-31 mM/L		[illegible]	8	BUN 8-24 mg/dl 15-25		[illegible]	47
Cl 96-106 mEq/L 120 mEq		[illegible]	99	CREATININE 0.5-1.5 mg/dl		[illegible]	1.4
Na 135-148 mEq/L 140-155		[illegible]	114	URIC ACID MALE 4.5-9 ? /dl FEMALE 3-7.5 mg/dl		[illegible]	
K 3.5-5.0 mEq/L 2-3		[illegible]	24.4	SUGAR (GLUCOSE) 65-110 mg/dl		[illegible]	

A 76-92

EXHIBIT 163

AUTOPSY REVIEW OF HOWARD R. HUGHES (PAGE 1 OF 3)

8 April 1976

TO WHOM IT MAY CONCERN:

I, Jack L. Titus, M.D., did physically participate in and observe the fingerprinting of the corpse, reportedly the body of Howard Robard Hughes that arrived D.O.A. at The Methodist Hospital on Monday, 5 April 1976. This fingerprinting was done at the time of the autopsy on April 6, 1976. Mr. Horace Tucker, Dr. Joseph Jachimczyk, and Mr. Ray Henderson participated in the fingerprinting, and Mr. Tucker actually took the finger prints.

Three sets of fingerprints were made, dated, and the time indicated. retained one set for the autopsy records of The Methodist Hospital and si one set. Two sets of fingerprints were given to Dr. Joseph Jachimczyk; portedly one set is for his file and one set is to be sent to the FBI.

I observed Mr. Tucker to sign each of the three sets of fingerprints.

The individuals named above are: Jack L. Titus, Chief of Pathology, The Methodist Hospital; Mr. Horace Tucker, an employee of the Harris County Medical Examiner's office; Dr. Joseph Jachimczyk, Chief Medical Examiner, Harris County; and Mr. Ray Henderson, Autopsy Technician, The Methodist Hospital.

Jack L. Titus

Jack L. Titus, M.D.
Chief of Pathology
The Methodist Hospital

ATTEST:

Ted Bowen

Ted Bowen
President, The Methodist Hospital

Michael V. Williamson

Michael V. Williamson
Vice President, The Methodist Hospital

STATE OF TEXAS

COUNTY OF HARRIS

SUBSCRIBED AND SWORN before me this 8th day of April, 1

Carolyn J. Wilburn

CAROLYN J. WILBURN

EXHIBIT 164

0007

AUTOPSY REVIEW OF HOWARD R. HUGHES (PAGE 2 OF 3)

J. L. Titus
4-6-76

4/13/76
opened & resealed
J. L. Titus

EXHIBIT 165

0007
AUTOPSY REVIEW OF HOWARD R. HUGHES (PAGE 3 OF 3)

JACK L. TITUS, M. D., Ph.D.
THE METHODIST HOSPITAL TEXAS MEDICAL CENTER
DEPARTMENT OF PATHOLOGY
6516 BERTNER • HOUSTON, TEXAS 77030

N-76-92
Mr. Howard Hughes' body
finger prints taken on 4/6/76 at approx.
3:00 p.m. by Mr. Vance Tucker.

J. L. Titus, M.D.

EXHIBIT 166

THE METHODIST HOSPITAL TEXAS MEDICAL CENTER
6516 BERTNER • HOUSTON, TEXAS 77025 • (713) 790-3311 • CABLE: METHHOSP

0008

AUTOPSY REVIEW OF HOWARD R. HUGHES (PAGE 1 OF 5)

June 11, 1976
10:50 AM

For the Record:

This morning I met with Mr. Will Lummis concerning the autopsy report on Howard R. Hughes, N-76-92. I gave Mr. Lummis copies of all documents in our files, specifically including the following:

1. My personal notes on the events leading up to the autopsy of Howard R. Hughes which were dictated on April 6, 1976.

2. A copy of the final autopsy report including the complete protocol, the microscopic examination and dental examination.

3. Copies of statements of identification by Doctors Thain, Chaffin, and Mr. Holmes.

4. Copies of statements concerning the fingerprinting prepared for the FBI and IRS on April 8 and April 13, 1976 respectively.

5. Copy of report of FBI fingerprint identification dated April 9, 1976 addressed to Dr. Joseph A. Jachimczyk.

These are the only copies of these documents that have been made by my office.

Jack L. Titus, M.D., Ph.D.
Chief, Pathology Service

JLT/bjs

338

EXHIBIT 167

THE METHODIST HOSPITAL

0008

AUTOPSY REVIEW OF HOWARD R. HUGHES (PAGE 2 OF 5)

AUTHORIZATION FOR AUTOPSY

DATE: *April 6, 197*

TIME: *10* 30 A. ~~P.~~

I (we) hereby consent and grant permission to the physicians and surgeons of The Met dist Hospital for a complete postmortem examination, including the removal and reten tion or use for scientific or ~~therapeutic~~ purposes of such organs, tissues, and parts, ~~including the eyes~~ as the physicians and surgeons in attendance at The Methodist Hospit of Houston may deem desirable on the body of *Howard R. Hughes*

(Please write in name of deceased)

Restrictions *none*

(Please write in any restrictions. If no restrictions, write "none".)

Annette E. Lummis — *Aunt* *Houston, Texas*

Signature of relative (next-of-kin) *by Wm. R. Lummis, Attorney-in-Fact*

Signature of relative _____ Relationship _____ Address _____

Signature of relative _____ Relationship _____ Address _____

Witness: *Jack L Titus, M.D.* Relationship *none*

Witness: _____ Relationship *none*

Date of Death *April 5, 1976* Time of Death *Reportedly approx*

If no autopsy permit is obtained, give reasons why: _____
(To be filled in by Attending Physician or House Officer)

Comment *at 4:00 P.M. on 4/5/76, Dr. E. Erickson, Med. Exami. Office called, subsequent discussions with Dr. Jachimczyk author pathologists of Methodist Hospital to do autopsy*

Date of Autopsy *April 6, 1976* Time started _____ Completed _____

Admitting Office notified of completion of autopsy at _____ _____

Hour Date

339

EXHIBIT 168

0008

AUTOPSY REVIEW OF HOWARD R. HUGHES (PAGE 3 OF 5)

THE METHODIST HOSPITAL TEXAS MEDICAL CENTER
6516 BERTNER • HOUSTON, TEXAS 77025 • (713) 790-3311 • CABLE: METHHOSP

13 April 1976

This statement was prepared at the request of Mr. William J. Kurak, Special Agent, Internal Revenue Service, Intelligence Division, Houston, Texas.

The original was given to Mr. Kurak, Special Agent, Internal Revenue Service, Houston, Texas; and a copy is retained for the records of The Methodist Hospital.

Ted Bowen
Ted Bowen
President, The Methodist Hospits

Jack L. Titus
Jack L. Titus, M.D.
Chief of Pathology
The Methodist Hospital

EXHIBIT 169

THE METHODIST HOSPITAL TEXAS MEDICAL CENTER

0008

AUTOPSY REVIEW OF HOWARD R. HUGHES (PAGE 4 OF 5)

TO WHOM IT MAY CONCERN:

I, Jack L. Titus, M.D., Chief of Pathology at The Methodist Hospital, made a sworn statement dated April 8, 1976, concerning the taking of finger-prints by Mr. Horace Tucker on April 6, 1976, from a corpse, reportedly the body of Howard Robard Hughes.

I am making this statement to expand upon and clarify paragraph two of the above described statement (a photocopy of that statement is attached).

Three complete sets of fingerprints were made from the corpse by Mr. Horace Tucker. The prints were dated and the time indicated. Mr. Tucker, Dr. Joseph Jachimczyk, and I examined the three sets of prints, and I took one set which I signed. To the best of my recollection, this is the only set that I signed. The set signed by me was made a part of the autopsy records of The Methodist Hospital.

The other two complete sets of fingerprints were taken by Mr. Tucker and Dr. Jachimczyk with the understanding that one set would be delivered to the FBI and one set retained by the Harris County Medical Examiner's office.

Jack L. Titus, M.D.
Chief of Pathology
The Methodist Hospital

ATTEST:

Ted Bowen
President, The Methodist Hospital

Larry L. Mathis, Vice President
The Methodist Hospital

STATE OF TEXAS

COUNTY OF HARRIS

SUBSCRIBED AND SWORN before me this 13th day of April, 1976.

EXHIBIT 170

0008

AUTOPSY REVIEW OF HOWARD R. HUGHES (PAGE 5 OF 5)

THE METHODIST HOSPITAL TEXAS MEDICAL CENTER

6516 BERTNER • HOUSTON, TEXAS 77025 • (713) 790-3311 • CABLE: METHHOSP

8 April 1976

This statement was prepared at the request of Mr. Robert Russ Franck, Special Agent in charge of the Federal Bureau of Investigation, Houston, Texas.

The original was given to Mr. R. W. Suter, Special Agent, Federal Bureau of Investigation, Houston, Texas; and a copy is retained for the records of The Methodist Hospital.

Ted Bowen

Ted Bowen
President, The Methodist Hospital

Jack L. Titus

Jack L. Titus, M.D.
Chief of Pathology
The Methodist Hospital

EXHIBIT 171

BLOOD – ATTACHMENT (page 1)
CHART ILLISTRATING "BLOOD TYPES" ALSO "BLOOD GROUPS"
Ease or Difficulty in Obtaining Donors of various types of blood.

/14/2014

New Health Guide
New Health Guide for Your Everyday Health.

Home   Skin Problems   Healthy Diet   Miscellaneous   Digestive Disorders   Breast Cancer   More...

Categories
- Skin Problems
- Healthy Diet
- Miscellaneous
- Digestive Disorders
- Breast Cancer
- Blood Health
- Drugs & Supplements
- Pregnancy
- Drugs
- Women's Health
- Hair
- Neurology
- Baby Health
- Pain Management
- Oral Health
- Breastfeeding
- Giving Birth
- Weight Loss
- Health Benefits
- Celebrities with Disability
- Healthy Beauty
- Exercise & Fitness
- Fertility
- Orthopedics
- Dental Health
- Sex & Pregnancy
- Muscle Health
- Healthy Tips
- Ear-Nose-Throat
- Allergies

VIEW ALL...

Similar Topics

Blood Being Too Thin
Functions of Blood
AB Positive Blood Type
How to Increase
Hemoglobin?
Low Protein in Blood

Same Category

Normal Creatinine Levels

Blood Type Chart

Blood type is classified according to the presence or absence of substances inherited from one's parents, called inherited antigenic substances. The International Society of Blood Transfusion (ISBT) recognizes 32 human blood group systems. The most important are ABO (it determines blood type - A, B, AB and O) and the RhD antigen that denotes the +/- status of the blood type (for example, A- or O+). Here lists some useful blood type charts based on ABO and RhD blood system.

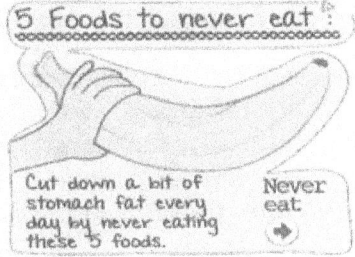

Blood Type Transfusion Chart

Your blood contains antibodies and antigens, or natural defenses against foreign substances. Antigens (protein molecules), are found on the surface of red blood cells. Your blood also contains plasma, in which antibodies are found. Antibodies and antigens recognize any foreign substance in your body, and act to destroy the foreign substance.

Blood types are classified according to the ABO system:

- A: contains A antigens and anti-B antibodies.
- B: contains B antigens and anti-A antibodies.
- AB: contains both A and B antigens but no antibodies.
- O: contains no antigens, but contains both anti-A and anti-B antibodies.

Blood Type	% of Population	Can Give Blood to	Can Receive Blood from	Chance of Finding a Compatible Donor
A+	34.3%	A+, AB+	A+, A-, O+, O-	80% (4 out of 5)
A-	5.7%	A+, A-, AB+, AB-	A-, O-	13% (1 out of 8)
B+	8.6%	B+, AB+	B+, B-, O+, O-	60% (3 out of 5)
B-	1.7%	B+, B-, AB+, AB-	B-, O-	9% (1 out of 12)
AB+	4.3%	AB+	Universal recipient (can receive all blood types)	100%
AB-	0.7%	AB+, AB-	AB-, A-, B-, O-	14% (1 out of 7)
O+	38.5%	O+, A+, B+, AB+	O+, O-	50% (1 out of 2)

http://www.newhealthguide.org/Blood-Type-Chart.html

343

EXHIBIT 172

Blood Attachment Page 2 of 5

566

two or three occasions from the late 1930s until 1950, when Dr. Mason had not been available Dr. Crane treated Hughes, and in December of 1961 Hughes became Crane's full-time patient. "From then on," he said, "I made house calls on a fairly regular basis at his request."⁴⁷ With the move to Nassau in November of 1970, the demands on Dr. Crane became more persistent:

For the first nine months I was on twenty-four hour call . . . with the exception of a total of approximately ten days at home during that period. I would see him subject to his call, and somewhere in there I asked for and received relief on rotation. The first one was Dr. Clark. . . . When that rotational program started, I spent six weeks on twenty-four hour call and was relieved for two weeks by Dr. Clark, and then returned for another six-week period myself. During the time that I was there I saw him whenever he would call. . . . It might be once a day, or I might spend a month there and not be called at all. But I better be around and available.⁴⁸

Throughout the last fifteen years of Hughes's life, Dr. Crane saw him more often than any other physician. Yet in all those years, he never conducted "a complete physical examination" of Hughes.⁴⁹

Dr. Homer Hone Clark was the pathologist. Born November 23, 1921, at Provo, Utah, Dr. Clark graduated from Brigham Young University in 1943 and the George Washington University School of Medicine in 1948. In 1954 he joined the pathology department at Latter-day Saints Hospital in Salt Lake City. Dr. Clark's younger brother, Rand Hone Clark, was a Romaine Street graduate who had become an assistant to Bill Gay, working out of the Summa executive offices in Encino. In 1969, when Hughes needed a blood transfusion, a sample of his blood was sent to Dr. Clark in Salt Lake City. The physician matched it and shipped blood supplies to Las Vegas for the transfusion. Although he did not see Hughes in 1969, Dr. Clark performed a series of laboratory tests on blood specimens attributed to Hughes, measuring the white blood cell count, hemoglobin, and hematocrit. When Hughes was moved to Nassau, Dr. Clark, a Mormon like his brother, was asked to become a permanent member of the Hughes medical staff. In 1971 he began rotating shifts with Dr. Crane. An outgoing, loquacious man given to malapropisms and lapsed syntax, Dr. Clark described his duties:

EXHIBIT 173

XF-11 Crash (Finding Blood for Hughes, Page. 3 of 5) Note: "Hands Seared to the Bone."

with incredible incompetence for so experienced a pilot. He lost his head, and instead of landing at once at Culver City Airport, began banking steeply inland, as far as Beverly Hills, looking for a golf course on which to land. But it wasn't 1936 and he wasn't flying the H-1 or H-2. He careened; his right wing again pulled down sharply. Out of control, agonized and ashamed and even a little afraid, he began to plunge.

He saw the streets of Beverly Hills rushing up to him. It was too late to cut down the engines or to cut them out, advisable procedures in such an emergency; it was too late to bail out. All he could do was hang onto the wheel to try to avoid crashing nose-first. He pancaked through a roof on North Linden Drive, slicing it off like the top of a cake.

He ripped across the street at 200 miles an hour, his left wing slashing through the master bedroom of a second house, owned by actress Rosemary De Camp, covering it with debris and shattered glass. The right wing snapped off and the tip killed a neighbor's dog. Hughes, with a series of tearing, smashing sounds, crashed the XF-11 to rest in the tangled eucalyptus trees of Whittier Drive.

As the gas tanks threatened to explode, Hughes stood up like a blazing scarecrow, his hair and clothes on fire, hanging onto his hat. He forced open the Plexiglas cockpit cover, searing both hands to the bone. He staggered onto the right wing stub and into the arms of a marine, Sergeant Bill Durkin. Seconds later, as Durkin dragged him clear, the plane exploded. "Was anyone else in there?" Durkin asked. "No," Hughes replied through blackened lips. "I was alone."

He sat on the grass, holding his head and moaning. The pain was too intense to bear; it seemed his body had turned to charcoal. People stood around staring. Nobody so much as brought a glass of water. A fireman turned up and did nothing; he didn't even aim a hose at the stricken man.

Durkin thrust the spectators aside, burst into the house of actor Dennis O'Keefe, and called the paramedics. They managed to get Hughes into a stretcher, though every time they touched him he could not hold back the screams. The ride to the Beverly Hills Emergency Hospital was a horrifying ordeal. Every traffic stop or bump in the road had him crying out and clawing at the glass. He aged twenty years on the journey.

When he was carried into the hospital shouting his name, a

The Howard Hughes Hoax

EXHIBIT 174

XF-11 Crash (Finding Blood for Hughes, Page. 4 of 5) Note: <u>Splintered Ribs</u> + Other Injuries

HOWARD HUGHES: THE SECRET LIFE ◆ 125

white-clad attendant appeared and told him he couldn't stay there. All doctors were off duty on a Sunday. The richest man in America had to be carted off to Cedars of Lebanon, on the eastern side of town, a time-consuming journey even on a Sunday.

When he got to Cedars someone asked him to fill in a form absolving the hospital of blame if he should die. Glenn Odekirk had managed to find him and almost killed the official who presented the form. For hours, neither Dr. Lawrence Chaffin nor Dr. Verne Mason, his personal physicians, could be located. At last, Chaffin turned up.

He found Hughes barely conscious by now and in a severe state of shock. Almost incoherently, Hughes murmured that he hoped nobody would blame him for the accident; that something infernal had happened to the plane. Chaffin acted promptly. He ordered a blood transfusion. But, first, Hughes's blood had to be tested. Only one sample of his blood type could be found for a transfusion. Chaffin told the nurses to dress the burns on the left arm, left chest, and left leg. Nine of the left ribs were fractured, and three of the right. The area where the ribs attached to the breastbone was splintered like matchwood, as were the left clavicle and the sixth and seventh cervical vertebrae. The left side of his chest was filled with blood. He had such severe bleeding of the esophagus that he couldn't swallow for days. His heart shifted to the right, and the right heart wall was contused. He was bruised and lacerated from head to foot, and, it seemed, the bleeding would never stop.

He was given intravenous feeding and morphine and was told he might not survive. His burned hands could not even be guided over the signature space on a will. Indeed, he was in no condition to make one.

As soon as the news hit the radio, an extraordinary array of past and present lovers or friends besieged the hospital, which became a scene that very few fashionable parties could match. The all-star cast of visitors included Cary Grant, Tyrone Power, Linda Darnell, Gene Tierney, and Richard Cromwell; of these, Hughes admitted to his room only Cary Grant. Noah Dietrich was out of town; Glenn Odekirk moved into an adjoining room and was in devoted attendance for days. Johnny Meyer was not allowed in. When his aunt Annette and her husband, Dr. Frederick Lummis, flew in from Houston, Hughes hurt them by saying he didn't want to see them. He didn't intend to wound them: he just didn't want them to see him in

346

EXHIBIT 175

BLOOD – ATTACHMENT (PAGE 5 of 5)
PATURNITY LAWSUIT AGAINST HOWARD HUGHES, JR.
JUDGE ORDERS BLOOD TESTS TO DETERMINE VALIDITY OF CLAIM
Results: Howard Hughes had no children.

When Howard Hughes (the reclusive multimillionaire) died, he left no legitimate heirs. Soon, however, a long succession of people claiming to be his children began to appear. A young man claiming to be Howard Hughes's child sued for a share of the estate. The judge ordered blood tests to determine the validity of the claim. Howard Hughes had blood type B, the mother of the young man had blood type A, and the young man himself had type O blood.

a. If you were the judge, how would you rule? b. Use the Punnett Square below to explain probability of question 5. (3x3 punnett) . If the mother is type AB and the father is type O, what possible blood type(s) might their children be? a. b. Use the Punnett Square below to explain probability of question 6. (3x3 punnett)

WHO WAS THAT FELLOW THEY BURIED IN HOUSTON?

Having viewed Exhibits 127-A thru 131-B above, keep in mind the clear fiasco illuminated in Chapter V, wherein one can only concur that: if the fingerprints of a supposed "Hughes" were <u>not</u> clandestinely switch at some point, what *else* could possibly have been going on with such *flagrant* bungling of the fingerprinting process? The naïve acceptance of these fingerprints as legitimate also leaves many questions unanswered, as do the other Exhibits (above) concerning the "H.H." autopsy review.

Exhibits 127-A and 127-B:

TAKEN FROM DONALD BARLETT AND JAMES STEELE'S BOOK *EMPIRE*
These Exhibits clarify the necessity for Dr. Forest Tennant to have the copy of a Methodist Hospital autopsy file of the corpse who, at the time, most people believed to be that of Howard R. Hughes Jr.

Exhibits 128-A and 128-B:

TAKEN FROM ALBERT B. GERBER'S BOOK *BASHFUL BILLIONAIRE*
Howard Hughes's Injuries from XF-11 plane crash in 1946.
This detailed report is reasonably exact. Most probably Mr. Gerber was writing his book in 1965; the copyright is 1967. The propaganda about a neurotic, drug addicted, reclusive "Howard Hughes," had not yet begun to circulate.

In his research (Chapter V), Russ mentions the disappearance of the *entire* original Harris County Autopsy File for "Howard Hughes," which had *supposedly* been safeguarded in Houston, Texas. (Note: Exhibits 131-A and 131-B.) Someone didn't just take copies of the file – *it appears they stole the entire file!* At this point, the average detective would probably have quit, but Russ persevered. This development only served to make him more aggressive in his research. Russ, with great difficulty, turns up a copy of the "H.H." autopsy file, which may have been the only one left in existence. In Exhibit 132, "Autopsy Review," We see that a Dr. Tennant had been called in during the trial of Dr. Wilbur Thain ("Hughes's" personal physician and brother-in-law to Summa, Inc. CEO, Bill Gay.) There was suspicion at the time that "Hughes" had been administered lethal doses of codeine which attributed to his death. With the understanding that Barlett and Steele's Book *Empire,* or the same book under a different title *Howard Hughes: His Life and Madness*, <u>has many inaccuracies in the years after 1965</u>, pages from their book, nevertheless, were used as a comparison reference in the 1946 XF-11 crash injuries of Howard Hughes. These earlier literary accounts are widely associated with news sources at the time, and they are about 95 percent in agreement with each other. However, there was a tremendous amount of information at the time which should have appeared, but did not, in the book *Empire*.

REASONING FOR THE USE OF *EMPIRE'S* INFORMATION

In 1976, the year that "Hughes" *supposedly* died, the battle was raging between Annette and William Lummis and the Summa Board of Directors Bill Gay, Nadine Henley, Chester Davis, soap salesman John Holmes, and others for control of the H.H. empire. Doctor Wilbur Thain was in with this clique, attempting to retain control; Annette and Will Lummis were after all of them. The information in Exhibits 127-A and 127-B, which was *allowed* to appear in *Empire*, is accurate. However, the death of a supposed "Hughes" due to drug overdoses (Exhibits 127-A and 127-B) is not the main thrust of this chapter. We will get into that later in Chapter XII.

Autopsy Review of "H.H." Exhibit 143: Legal Aspects of Case B – Opinion: Dr. Forrest Tennant gives his knowledgeable findings concerning Dr. Thain. (Dr. Tennant's personal experience and research sources are thorough.) The questions needing answers about drugs and the Houston Methodist Hospital corpse establish the necessity for Dr. Tennant to have the "H.H." autopsy report. A well-founded conclusion was rendered which *did not* prove favorable for Dr. Thain.

In this chapter (Part 1 of the Methodist Hospital autopsy of "Howard Hughes") you will find news and hospital reports concerning injuries sustained by Howard Hughes when he crashed his XF-11 prototype plane into Beverly Hills, California, in 1946. In the following Chapter XII, Part 2 of the Methodist Hospital autopsy of "Howard Hughes", you will find comparisons and critiques of what was visibly evident in the autopsied corpse at Methodist Hospital in Houston, Texas, in 1976.

Exhibits 128-A and 128-B
    FROM ALBERT GERBER'S BOOK *BASHFUL BILLIONAIRE*
    Howard Hughes's Injuries from Xf-11 Plane Crash In 1946.
    In Agreement With:

Exhibits 129-A and 129-B
    FROM BARLETT AND STEELE'S BOOK *EMPIRE*

Exhibits 130-A through 130-H
    EXCERPTS FROM RICHARD HACK'S BOOK *HUGHES*:
    THE PRIVATE DIARIES, MEMOS AND LETTERS.

Concerning the excerpts from Richard Hack's book *HUGHES*, it can be truly said that the book was well researched and well written. Richard Hack had obviously found a source, with feet on the ground, during the Methodist Hospital autopsy of "H.H." in 1976. Exacting and enlightening, it appears that there were numerous noteworthy observations that went unrecorded by many. Mr. Hack is a renowned investigative journalist with a great many credits to his name. We certainly thank Richard for his revelations of important data concerning "Hughes," which further leads us to believe that there were attempts made during the "H.H" autopsy procedure to obscure the obvious.

Richard has recorded that the disposition of the "Hughes" caretakers Holmes and Drs. Thain and Chaffin was anything but sad at the loss of "Hughes." Ambulance driver Jay Dickson observed the mood around the body of "Hughes" and was a bit taken-back by what he heard as the body was taken off the plane and loaded for transport to Methodist Hospital. Mr. Hack's take: "There was laughter, at one point; it seemed a bit out of place." Richard goes on to point out that the most stunned person involved in the transport of the "Hughes" corpse, was the pilot Rodger Sutton. Rodger stated, "I was shocked and saddened; I never had a passenger die before." Well, it was probably more than just *not knowing* of his passenger's demise that had him concerned. FAA Regulations in 1976 were quite specific in that if, by chance, a passenger aboard *any plane* is near death, or presumed to have died in transport, "the pilot is obligated to land his plane at the closest available airport," which in this case, would have been Brownsville, Texas. Brownsville had several Hospitals in 1976; one, Valley Regional, was new, having finished construction in 1975. Therefore, it had state-of-the-art personnel and equipment. The reasoning for the FAA Regulation is obvious: a passenger who is close to death or *thought* to have died, may still have a chance to be saved with the medical equipment and wherewithal found in a hospital. When taking into consideration the dire circumstances of "H.H." while in the air over Mexico, the pilot should have been notified of the situation. He then would have radioed the nearby Brownsville airport; the airport in turn, would have notified a nearby hospital and an ambulance would have been waiting.

A question arises from the information in Exhibit 130-C. *When "Hughes" died between Acapulco and Houston, how in the world did Dr. Thain, aide Holmes, and Dr. Chaffin know the plane was over the Brownsville border town in a Leer Jet traveling 500 miles per hour, unless they had asked the pilot about their airborne location?* Pilot Sutton would pass over several more available airports as the plane made its way to Houston. But according to Sutton, he had not known of the on-board death until the jet landed. Nobody told him anything, and he was focused on flying the plane. Why had the "Hughes" caretakers been secretive of the facts until the plane had touched down in Houston?

In his book *Hughes,* Richard Hack also points out that, "Dr. Thain had joked about the lushness of Acapulco and the poor timing of 'Hughes's' death. Thain, it seems, had enjoyed his few months on the Mexican Riviera." (See Exhibit 130-G, Paragraph 1.) What comes to mind here is, if Dr. Thain had been in Acapulco for this length of time, he had to have known how terribly sick "Hughes" was. He should have dropped by from time to time to look in on the fellow who was paying him the big bucks. So why, in God's name, did Thain not put the man in a hospital earlier? Was it just coincidence that he happened to be in Acapulco on a two-month vacation preceding the death of "Hughes," or had he known all along that he would soon be dealing with a corpse? Thain had even flown to the Bahamas while "Hughes" was dying in Mexico. There seems to be a discrepancy regarding Thain's travel. In his book *Hughes,* Richard Hack maintains that Dr. Wilbur Thain had been on the "Mexican Riviera" for several months *prior* to the death of "Hughes" and had indicated his enjoyment of his vacation. (See Exhibit 130-G, also

Paragraph 1.) Yet in the book *Empire* (Exhibit 127-B), Thain maintains that he had seen "Hughes" "on only three occasions in 1976." The first was "toward the end of February," then the "middle of March 17th or 18th," and then on "the morning of April 5" when he found "H.H." "in a coma, rather flaccid." To have a clear understanding of Dr. Thain (Bill Gay's brother-in-law) and the big bucks he was getting paid for a little part-time work, see Exhibit 127-B, bottom where it reports that Dr. Thain was being paid $60,000.00. That kind of money in the seventies was *substantial*, Summa, Inc. had even continued to pay him after the burial of the "Hughes" corpse in Houston and throughout 1978 during the time of his trial. That "Hughes" had massive quantities of codeine still in him when they did the autopsy is more than strange when one considers that, as per Dr. Wilbur and the aides, "Hughes had been unconscious since the night before." *That* certainly removes any doubt that the man could have done it to himself! Once codeine is in the system, *half of it dissipates within six to eight hours, but the Methodist Hospital corpse was still loaded with the stuff upon arrival in Houston.*

Let's take these strange happenings concerning Drs. Thain, Chaffin, and caretaker Holmes to a conclusion:

A. See Exhibit 130-A. At approximately 2:15 p.m. on April 5, the jet carrying the corpse of "H.R.H." touches down in Houston.

B. See Exhibit 130-D. Drs. Thain and Chaffin were followed back to their rooms at the Warwick Hotel by reporters *soon* after.

C. Consider also, regarding Exhibit-130-D, Bill Gay (Summa, Inc. C.E.O. and man with his fingers on the purse strings.) never cared about "Hughes's" medical problems, and there's *no record of him ever having visited his boss anywhere for ten or more years.* He had to have known about the broken hip in London and various other maladies affecting "Hughes" down through the years. After all he and Nadine Henley were the ones channeling the money to pay for various "Hughes" aides' wages, hotels, and medical expenses. But Gay was "Billy on the Spot," in Houston, when the "Acapulco Hughes" corpse arrived at Methodist Hospital. Gay had registered earlier at the Warwick Hotel and had remained in waiting for Thain, Chaffin, and Holmes.

D. These were the good ol' days of *no cellphones.* Bill Gay could not have been informed by any of the "Hughes" caretakers from the plane before it landed in Houston. Plus, the plane's pilot didn't know that "Hughes" had died until the plane touched down in Houston. So Gay would have to have been informed about the Houston-bound "Hughes," *before* the plane left the tarmac in Mexico. Why was this *particular* bout of sickness so important to Bill Gay? Had he known that *this time* "Hughes" would arrive dead in Houston?

E. "Hughes" was extremely sick but, as far as anybody knew, and according to aide

Holmes and Drs. Chaffin and Thain, "Hughes" died over Brownsville, Texas at 1:27 p.m. Central Standard Time (CST). According to Exhibit 130-B, they agreed that pilot Sutton had not learned of the "Hughes" death until the plane landed at 2:15 p.m. CST. (In the sky over Houston at 2:10 p.m. and stopped on the tarmac at approximately 2:15 p.m. See Exhibit 130-A

F. This is a good place to point out a small discrepancy. In Exhibit 130-B (first two lines), Dr. McIntosh (Methodist Hospital) was met at the door of the plane by Dr. Thain who matter-of-factly announced, "I lost the beat just a few minutes ago, he's gone." In the following paragraph, *McIntosh offers resuscitation*, citing that "all the instrumentation is available." *Thain counters with "it's no use, he's gone, he's gone."* The time elements concerning "Hughes's" death do not correlate. It is strange that no one picked up on this. The "elephant in the room" is, did this "Hughes" die over Brownsville at 1:27 p.m., as per aide Holmes and Drs. Chaffin and Thain (Exhibit 130-C) or was he losing vital signs over Brownsville (Exhibit 149) and die on approach to Houston? It appears that Chaffin, Holmes, and Thain didn't get their stories straight. What we do know is that Chaffin and Holmes were adamant about "Hughes" having died over Brownsville and not in Mexico's airspace. (See Exhibit 130-C).

G. All key personnel *had known* of "Hughes's" sickness for a long time. But Summa, Inc. C.E.O. Bill Gay *never* went to Mexico – or anywhere else "Hughes" might have been – to visit his boss, and the Doctors, who were all on handsome retainers, rarely visited, until he was on his death bed. Apparently, *no one cared enough* to put this "Hughes" in a State-side hospital earlier.

H. The "H.H." corpse arrived on the ground in Houston at approximately 2:15 p.m.; it was probably around 2:45 p.m. before either Thain or Chaffin could possibly have called Bill Gay to notify him of "Hughes's" death. Yet Billy Gay, out there in California, had somehow managed to jump on a plane and check into the Warwick Hotel before Thain, Chaffin, and Holmes? And how had Gay known *beforehand* that they would be meeting at the Warwick Hotel? (Exhibit 130-D.)

I. Now, having laid out the facts, is it too much to presume that "Hughes" was dead in Mexico and that either Thain or Chaffin had called Bill Gay to tell him of this event? Or had they called Bill Gay when "Hughes" was still alive in Mexico, to tell him that the big moment had arrived and that there would be no live "Hughes" delivered to the Methodist Hospital in Houston? But then if doctors Thain and Chaffin had to meet Bill in Houston *at the Warwick Hotel*, is it any wonder why they never had time to stop in Brownsville with a dying "H.H."? Or did Bill Gay know "Hughes" had died in Acapulco?

J. One may wonder as well, did Anette and Will Lummis know ahead of time that the "H.H." corpse would be arriving in Houston? It had to take a while to find a *huge stainless steel vault, dig a hole big enough to put it in, locate a thousand-pound sealable casket in which to place the "H.H." corpse, and schedule a bier mechanism strong enough to carry it all.* Yet they did it all within two days? Oh! Almost forgot about that slab of concrete poured over the entire Hughes family plot. (Exhibits 126-B and 130-H)

K. Let us also take into consideration Exhibit 174. Dr. Chaffin had been at Cedars Hospital, California, in 1946 when Hughes crashed his XF-11 into Beverly Hills. He was <u>also</u> present during the "H.H." autopsy in 1976 at Methodist Hospital (Exhibit 149), having been invited in by Dr. Titus. Dr. Chaffin must have known about those splintered ribs and damage to their attaching breastplate. According to medical sources, this type of injury would have been <u>glaringly evident</u> in an autopsy 30 years later. (Exhibit 174) However, Dr. Titus, the autopsy lead, noted only that the corpse's "ribs were moderately osteoporotic." Did Dr. Titus not see anything relating to the severe rib or breastplate injury? *Was the aftermath of this obvious 1946 injury not noted because it wasn't there?* Okay, there you have *that!*

Let us get on the rest of the story.

Exhibits 131-A and 131-B:
RUSS WAS CORRECT. THE HOUSTON METHODIST HOSPITAL NO LONGER HAS THE "HIGH-PROFILE" HOWARD HUGHES AUTOPSY FILE. WHAT DID THEY DO WITH IT? THROW IT AWAY?

CLARITY OF A CRITICAL POINT PER EXHIBIT 134, PAGE 3 OF 15:
"Between August 6, 1974, and December 13, 1975, Dr. Wilbur Thain ordered and received 5,500 dosage units of Codeine Phosphate." These "were 60 mg. or 1 gr. injectable tablets." * "A total of 2,000 dosage units of Codeine Phosphate were ordered for H.R.H. between December 19, 1975, and H.R.H.'s death on April 5, 1976." Half of a dose of codeine dissipates from the body in six to eight hours and is completely gone from the system in 24. (Others say less time is needed for complete elimination.)
*<u>**Note:**</u> Injectable tablets must *first* be dissolved into solution.

Exhibits 127-A, BOTTOM PARAGRAPH, AND 127-B, TOP TWO LINES:
Here we learn that "H.R.H." had lethal amounts of codeine in his body when he died. Also, that the 1.96 micrograms per milliliter of blood in "H.R.H." "was considerably *above* the 1.4-microgram level found in the bodies of persons known to have died of codeine poisoning."

Exhibit 127-B, * PARAGRAPH 4.:
On October 27, 1976 (Dr. Thain's trial), Dr. Jack Titus, autopsy pathologist of "H.R.H." corpse at Methodist Hospital, Texas acknowledges that his previous statement on "normal therapeutic dose" was in error; he had "misinterpreted milligrams for micrograms,"

hence the level of codeine in the "H.R.H." corpse was <u>1,000 times greater!</u>

Dr. Forest Tennant, pathologist, concludes that "Hughes" <u>had taken</u> "5 to 9 grains" of codeine prior to his death on April 5, 1976. Other medical authorities say it was difficult to determine and *could well have exceeded 20 grains.* Pharmacologists and pathologists agreed that the codeine in the "H.R.H." corpse "was taken within 6 to 8 hours of death." (The elephant in the room *here* is, "How could this very sick and crippled "Hughes" get out of his bed, dissolve numerous codeine phosphate capsules into solution, load the solution into syringes, and inject himself – all during the time he was comatose or in a coma?" *No!* This "Hughes" <u>did not take</u> these massive injections; <u>he was given</u> these extreme dosages by others!)

Dr. Thain had stated that he arrived at the Acapulco Princess on the morning of April 5 at "about 8 A.M. and found "Hughes" "in a comma, rather flaccid. He was having seizures, multiple seizures." He also stated that he understood that "H.H." "had been unconscious … since the night before." Let's do the math: *16 hours, plus eventually loading "H.R.H." into the plane in Acapulco and being in the air over Brownsville, Texas, at 1:27 p.m. Central Standard Time, equals 21 hours?*

QUESTIONS RAISED BY THE ABOVE DOCUMENTATION:

A. 2,000 dosage units of codeine phosphate (injectable tablets) were ordered by Dr. Thain between August 6, 1974, and December 13, 1975; and an additional amount of 2,000 dosage units of 1 grain codeine phosphate tablets were ordered for "H.R.H." between December 19, 1975, and "H.R.H.'s" death April 5, 1976. * Did the "Caretakers" plan on giving "H.H." a bath in the stuff, or were they storing it up with a plan in mind?
   * The April 7, 1976 death of "H.R.H." in Exhibit 134 is incorrect – date of this "H.H.'s" death is April 5, 1976. "H.H." was buried on April 7.

B. The <u>1976</u> quantity of codeine in the Methodist Hospital corpse was extremely high during the autopsy of "H.R.H." but later was determined to be <u>1,000 times greater</u> as per testimony of Dr. Titus, at Dr. Thain's trial, in 1978. Was renal failure *really* what finished off "H.R.H.?"Another thing to consider is that, if renal failure was the culprit, why had this "H.H." *not* been taken *earlier* to the Hughes Medical Institute in Miami, Florida? At H.M.I.M. there were state-of-the-art blood cleansing machines available – *and Hughes owned the place!*

   1. Was it *not* Dr. Titus who opened and resealed the envelope containing the "H.R.H." corpse's fingerprints delivered to the federal agent for analysist?

   2. Is it *probable* to presume that Dr. Titus, the "Lead Pathologist" in the "H.R.H." autopsy, had knowingly skewed the autopsy findings?

3. If there are *addicts who have a tolerance to codeine and yet died from codeine poisoning at 1.4 micrograms per millimeter of blood* and the "H.R.H." corpse at Methodist Hospital in 1976 was originally thought to contained *1.9 micrograms per millimeter of blood,* is this not *a tad* unusual? (Add to that Dr. Titus's testimony at Dr. Wilber Thain's trial where he indicates that the dosage was considerably more.)

4. At Dr. Thain's trial two years later, Dr. Titus admitted, under oath, that he had mistaken milligrams for micrograms and that the codeine present in the "H.R.H." corpse was *1,000 times greater.* Is this not more than suspicious? *
   (1,000 x 1.9 = … well, you do the math.) *
   *(Exhibit 127-B, Paragraph 4) Yes this is repetitive, which leads to the below:

5. With the possibility of first-degree murder on the table, could Dr. Titus have gotten cold feet?

C. The autopsy report stated there were *"multiple recent needle punctures"* in the forearms of "H.R.H." (Exhibit 152) Were these deliberately done by his caretakers to insinuate that "H.R.H." had loaded *himself* with the massive amounts of codeine? (Exhibit 138, Item k.) This would have been difficult for a crippled man who had lain "unturned" in bed for so long that he had multiple bedsores. (As per Dr. Victor Montemayor. (See Exhibit-178-A.)

D. "H.R.H." had been unconscious for 21 or more hours; but *"5 to 9 grains,"* or more (others said it could have been 20 grains) had been dissolved and injected "within 6 to 8 hours" prior to his death on April 5, 1976. Who were the only ones that could have dissolved the codeine tablets and injected them into "H.H.?" Once again, as stated in Exhibit 127-B, it was later determined to be a greater amount. Note: "Hughes had not walked for three years after getting his hip broken in London, so how could *he* have overdosed himself? (See Exhibit-142.)

SIMPLIFICATION OF THE ABOVE EVIDENCE:
(Codeine in the "H.H." Corpse at Methodist Hospital, Houston, and attributing factors correlated.)

A. When the Mexican Doctor Montemayor was called to the Acapulco Princess Hotel to view and advise on "H.H.," he was absolutely amazed at what he found. (Exhibit 178-A) "H.H." was comatose and dehydrated. Montemayor recommended the *immediate application of intravenous fluids.* He then noted the multiple signs of kidney failure and that "Hughes's" body had numerous bed sores. Also, Dr. Montemayor was informed by Dr. Chaffin and aide Clarence Waldron that "Hughes" had been unconscious since the night before. Dr. Montemayor's immediate reply was, "When a man becomes unconscious you put him in a Hospital." Waldron's reply: "Hughes was difficult to deal with."

B. When the "H.H." corpse arrived at Methodist Hospital; the receiving hospital doctors immediately noticed *dehydration*. Doctor Montemayor had noted dehydration earlier that day in Mexico and recommended a drip-feed be installed, but this was on April 5. (Exhibit 178-B) However, Drs. Thain and Chaffin claimed that "Hughes" had gone into shock on April 4 and was treated with intravenous fluids. (Exhibit 148) Could it be that neither Drs. Chaffin nor Thain had the good sense to have this procedure performed earlier then Dr. Montemayor's suggestion and then decided to lie about it? Even though the "H.H." corpse arrived in Houston with "a drip-feed needle in its arm, strapped to a board with a towel cushion," was the drip-feed ever used? What is apparent, is that this "Hughes" had consumed no fluids for quite a while, either by mouth or drip, hence the noted dehydration at Methodist Hospital. It certainly appears that Dr. Montemayor's suggestion was not acted upon at the time, or afterwards for that matter. Was this intentional by the "Hughes care team" to keep the toxins concentrated in his system – a quicker kill so to speak?

C. Dr. Titus, Pathologist and Lead Autopsy physician, fails to make note of bedsores on the corpse, which had been previously noted by Dr. Montemayor in Mexico. (Exhibit 178-A)

D. In the autopsy files, "fresh," i.e. current and numerous, needle-tracks and ecchymosis (a discoloration/bruising of the skin) in the forearms of the corpse are noted.

E. In 1976, autopsy physician Dr. Titus maintains that codeine concentration in the "H.H." corpse "is within normal therapeutic limits."

F. In 1978, at Dr. Wilbur Thain's trial, Dr. Titus changes his story and says that "the codeine concentration, in the 'H.H.' corpse, was 1,000 times greater than he had originally calculated."

G. Taking "F" above into consideration, there can be no doubt that the Methodist Hospital "H.H." corpse *did* contain lethal dosages of codeine!

H. Codeine for "Hughes" was delivered in massive quantities and in tablet form, which were first dissolved into solution prior to injection.

I. Hence, giving the above,
   1. This "H.H." had not walked for three years before he died.

   2. He had developed "many bedsores" because he was too sick to turn himself in bed from time to time. Obviously, none of the aides available had the consideration to do it for him?

3. He had been unconscious 20 to 21 hours, or possibly longer, prior to leaving Mexico.
4. How did this terribly sick "H.H." rise-up, dissolve massive quantities of codeine tablets into liquid form, and inject them in his forearms and veins with lethal dosages of the drug six to eight hours prior to his arrival, as a corpse, at Methodist Hospital, Houston?
a. Considering #2, medical personnel say that it may take one to two weeks of being immobile to develop "multiple bedsores." This "H.H." could not walk, he couldn't sit up in bed, he had been unconscious for a considerable amount of time, and yet he overdoses himself?

5. When finally arriving on the scene, Doctors Chaffin and Thain had to have known that this "H.H." was suffering from kidney failure. They had to be able to read the obvious medical signs, just as the Mexican Doctor Victor Montemayor and the "H.H." corpse receiving doctors, at Methodist Hospital, had when they off-loaded the corpse from the plane

.

6. If this "H.H." had been flown to Howard Hughes Medical Institute in Miami, when kidney problems were first noted, could he have been saved? (Howard Hughes Medical Institute in Miami was privy to the latest technology in kidney machines – all purchased on Hughes-grant money?)

7. If Dr. Thain had immediately loaded "H.H." into his plane at 8:30 a.m. when he arrived at the Acapulco Princess and then flown him to H.H.M.I. or a Brownsville Hospital *instead of doing two hours of document shredding first*, could the fellow have been saved? (The "H.H." jet did not leave the Acapulco tarmac until 10:30 a.m.) Wouldn't it have been a good idea for Dr. Thain to have left his party in the Bahamas a few hours earlier as well? (See Exhibit 179-A.)

8. Was it kidney failure *only* that killed "H.H." or was it a combination of bad kidneys, dehydration, starvation, neglect, and the poisonous, concentrated, lethal, amount of codeine that had been injected into his body?

9. The "whys" of these above travesties has been clearly revealed in previously compiled evidence, as well as in what follows below.

10. Now that we have *overly clarified* this drug fiasco of an imposter "H.H." corpse flown into Houston, Texas on April 5th, 1975. After pointing out multiple irregularities, numerous times, of caretakers who were anything but, how could this have been anything in the end but a slow, cruel, torturous, death of an imposter "Hughes"?

EXHIBITS 132 THROUGH 170 (ABOVE) ARE COPIES OF METHODIST HOSPITAL HOUSTON, TEXAS AUTOPSY FILES OF AN IMPOSTER "HUGHES"

CHAPTER XII
PART 2

METHODIST HOSPITAL AUTOPSY OF "HUGHES" CORPSE HOUSTON, TEXAS. PARDON THE RECOUNTING OF THE ABOVE EXEMPLARS – THE PURPOSE IS TO FIX FIRMLY AND EXACTLY WHERE THE INFORMATION, USED BELOW, CAN BE FOUND. NOW, LET'S GET INTO THE MEAT, BONES, AND BLOOD OF THE MATTER.

Here in Chapter XII we break out the facts and clarify the information in the above Exhibits. Clear observations will show that there are many square pegs not fitting into round holes and vice versa.

KNOWN INJURIES TO HOWARD HUGHES SUSTAINED ON JULY 7, 1946, XF-11 TEST PLANE CRASH.

BROKEN BONES: As evidenced in Exhibit 128-A occurring July 7, 1946:
   a. "Fracture of the left Clavicle."
   b. "Fracture of the posterior portion of the upper nine ribs on the left side."
   c. "Fracture of the first two ribs on the right side."
   d. "Possible fracture of the nose."

BROKEN BONES: As evidenced in Exhibit 129-B occurring July 7, 1946:
   a. "His chest was crushed."
   b. "He suffered fractures of seven ribs on the left side."
   c. "Two ribs on the right."
   d. "Possible fracture of the nose."

BROKEN BONES: As evidenced in Exhibit 174 occurring July 7, 1946:
   a. "Nine of the left ribs were fractured, and three of the right."
   b. "The areas where the ribs attached to the breastbone were splintered like matchwood as were the *left clavicle* and the sixth and seventh cervical vertebrae."
Note: Okay, somebody lost count of the fractured ribs on the man's left side (Exhibit 129-B), however, there are numerous other graphic accounts substantiating that Howard Hughes was severely "busted up" when he crashed his XF-11 plane prototype.

METHODIST HOSPITAL, HOUSTON <u>AUTOPSY 1976</u>

BROKEN BONES BELOW: As evidenced in "Hughes" 1976 autopsy report at Methodist Hospital, Houston, Texas.

Exhibit 138, page 7 of 15, #3. Accessory Diagnoses b.
   "Metallic pin left hip from repair of prior fracture"

Exhibit 154, page 3 of 5 Bones
   "The vertebral bodies are moderately osteoporotic as are the ribs and sternum."

Exhibit 158-A, page 1 of 2, "Additional Findings" item #3.
   "Separation left acromia-clavicular <u>joint</u> with edema and hematoma left shoulder. *"
   Unusual: This is a contemporary injury, no indication *here* of that 1946 *splintered Clavicle*. (See Exhibits 128-A and 129-B). Also see (Exhibit 174).

Exhibit 158-A, Additional findings, item #1, page 1 of 2.
   "Fibrotic apical** scars both lungs*** and old, fibrotic left pleural adhesions, history of prior left thoracic injury."

* Reference is to the clavicle *joint* <u>only</u>; no history of *busted* clavicle indicated here. Edema is "swelling" and "hematoma" is a localized mass of "extravasated" blood. (Extravasate: "To exude from or pass out of a vessel.") This injury appears to have happened *soon before* the 1976 autopsy *while "H.H." was in the tender loving care of John Holmes, Clarence Waldron, and other senior aides.* There is <u>no</u> indication of a previously broken (splintered) clavicle having mended over many years, i.e. calcification, irregular mending of bone, etc.
  ** Apical: "upper part" of lung as opposed to "basil," bottom.
***<u>Note</u>: "Fibrotic apical scars both lungs." Impact to *the top* <u>back</u> of an individual can, and perhaps did, damage the *apical* lungs of this corpse. In the 1976 autopsy report, there is a scar noted on the Methodist Hospital's corpse's back, although not explicit as to where, it was most probably the *upper* back.

METHODIST HOSPITAL, HOUSTON <u>AUTOPSY 1976</u>
SUMMATION OF COMPARATIVE EVIDENCE ON BROKEN BONES:

As evidenced in Exhibit 150, page 4 of 4, we know that "total body x-rays" <u>were taken</u>. That's how they found the "repair of fracture and metallic pin in the left hip." The left hip fracture happened when caretakers dropped "H.H." in the restroom in London 1973. This bone break *does not count* as a comparison, as <u>it was not</u> a break that occurred in 1946 when Howard Hughes crashed the XF-11.

In Exhibit 154, page 3 of 5, Bones, we learned that "<u>The vertebral bodies are moderately osteoporotic as are the ribs and sternum.</u>" At this point ***nothing else is indicated***, although it is known that Howard Hughes had <u>nine</u> ribs busted on his *left* side and three on the *right in 1946*. This being the case, it was reasoned that various rib fractures, unevenness of healing, and damage to where they connected to the sternum, * would be evident along with the moderate osteoporosis.

* Sternum: A long flat bone articulating with the cartilages of the first seven ribs (frontal) <u>and the clavicle.</u>

Revisiting Exhibit 128-A, we learn that not only was the "anterior" (frontal) of those nine-ribs on the left side of Hughes's body severely damaged, but also the "posterior" (rearmost) portion of those same ribs were damaged. Obviously, the <u>vertebrae</u> at the back of those nine-ribs were damaged as well, which would explain the eventual vertebrae deterioration which caused Howard's upper torso to sway and fold downward in the way Charles saw him in 1964.

In Exhibit 174 we learned that "Where the ribs attached to the breastbone they were splintered like matchwood, <u>as were the left clavicle and the sixth and seventh vertebrae.</u>" Several Doctors have been consulted as to this bone damage being evident 30 years later in an autopsy – the replies were "yes" and "absolutely."

But then, in Exhibit 158-A, <u>additional findings</u>, item #1, page 1 of 2, *almost as if an afterthought*, they find "Fibrotic *apical* scars both lungs and old, fibrotic left pleural adhesions, history of prior left thoracic** injury." (Apical "top-most" left-lung scarring caused with damage to left thoracic portion of back. This <u>would not</u> be damage as found in Exhibit 128-A, i.e. <u>posterior and anterior</u> areas of the Hughes's nine ribs on the left side of his torso. Also, Dr. Titus was non-specific as to exactly which vertebra had been damaged. (Exhibit 158-A)
** Thorax: Ribs, sternum, scapula, vertebrae, etc.

It is no longer speculation regarding what went on with fingerprints in Chapter V. We have the documentation. But let us include a briefing and a little deeper analysis of that fiasco here from "Russ" Russell. It fits in well with the above Exhibits here in the Autopsy Chapter:

> On April 6, 2015, some 39 years after the alleged death of Howard Hughes, both the Houston Chronicle and a local TV station there featured a brief article in which they discussed the fact that the FBI had been assigned the responsibility of taking the fingerprints of the Houston corpse to Washington, DC for confirmation that the body was that of Howard Hughes.
>
> As I learned of these print and TV articles, I instantly thought back to discussions that Charlie and I had several months earlier, in which we were reviewing paperwork found within the Houston Methodist Hospital Autopsy file. We turned up many real problems with the 1976 handling of the "H.H." corpse fingerprints.
>
> Identifying a corpse, by name, as mentioned earlier in this book, is the #1 requirement of an Autopsy procedure, and should receive the upmost integrity in the handling of corpse fingerprints. As mentioned earlier, two different people, working for the Houston Methodist Hospital, took fingerprints from the "H.H." corpse, at two different times (and days). The second set of fingerprints, the following day, were put on "strips of paper" and neither an approved FBI fingerprint card, or a "Corner's Card" were utilized. In addition, at some stage a set of these "strips of paper" were put in an envelope and signed by someone on the reverse side. Later, as the evidence shows, that envelope was opened, before transmission to the traveling FBI Agent, and later closed. (See Exhibits 163, 164, and 165)
>
> In Police work, we have the nationwide term called "Chain of Custody." This procedure ensures that evidence is signed for, from the minute of acquisition through final handling, either at Court, or by a Judge. There was absolutely NO "Chain of Custody" in the handling of the Houston corpse fingerprints. None. That is, until the FBI Agent received it and transported it, personally, to the FBI Crime Laboratory in Washington, DC. Even then, we do not know who the actual transporting FBI Agent was that signed for it, or if he even *did* sign for it? We still do not even know exactly what fingerprints were received by the Crime Laboratory. The sanctity of the process was completely ignored, which made it extremely easy to substitute other fingerprints for those supposedly transported to the FBI Crime Laboratory.

Russ L. Russell (Chief of police Retired)

SO ABOVE WE HAVE A SITUATION WHEREIN THERE WAS ABSOLUTELY NO CHAIN OF CUSTODY IN THE HANDLING OF THE SUPPOSED "HUGHES" FINGERPRINTS AT METHODIST HOSPITAL AND MANY OTHER IRREGULARTIES CONCERNING "PRINTS" BACK IN CHAPTER V.

IN CHAPTER VI WE HAVE SEEN <u>QUESTIONABLE</u> EXEMPLARS BANTERED ABOUT IN THE COURTROOM BY ROSEMONT, INC. AS IF THEY WERE <u>KNOWN</u> EXEMPLARS.

THEREFORE, IT SHOULD COME AS NO SURPRISE THAT MANY THINGS ARE AMISS IN THIS AUTOPSY CHAPTER AS WELL.

The "H.H." corpse, autopsied at Methodist Hospital, had a mishap which damaged its thorax, per Dr. Jack Titus. (Exhibit 158-A) But who is to say it occurred in the XF-11 crash in 1946? Dr. Titus eluded to this supposition when he indicated the damage was due to "a History of crashing remote". However, Dr. Titus is extremely vague and non-specific as to exactly which vertebrae had been damaged. Knowing that no previous Howard Hughes X-rays were used for comparison in the Methodist Hospital "H.H." autopsy, this is understandable – if one's intentions were to obscure the findings.

The *Methodist Hospital corpse did have a scar on its back, which was not indicative of Howard Hughes and Hughes had a severe burn on his buttock, left chest, and left hand, which did not appear on the Methodist Hospital corpse.* A practical supposition could be made that the damage to the Methodist Hospital "H.H." corpse's thorax could have happened in an auto accident or fall. (There was no indication by Dr. Jack Titus that the thorax damage was minor or all encompassing; his observation was <u>vague,</u> to say the least.) Dr. Titus is simply referring to the left side upper-vertebral bodies of the thorax; he noticed nothing unusual when viewing the left clavicle, sternum, posterior, or anterior parts of any ribs or where they attached to the vertebrae or breastbone. Also, there was no indication of the severity of the thoracic injury by Dr. Titus, i.e. *exactly which* vertebrae had been damaged or to what degree. Could it be possible that Drs. Thain and Chaffin *forgot* which vertebral bodies had been damaged in the XF-11 crash? Could it also be possible that Dr. Titus was *vague* because it might be obvious later that the damage to the Methodist Hospital corpse would *not* match up with damage done to Howard Hughes in previous 1946 X-rays?

"Apical" *topmost* scarring on the lungs seems to have occurred from a blow specific to the Methodist Hospital corpse's *upper* back. However, as evidenced in Exhibits 128-A and 129-B, Hughes had substantial damage to his thoracic cage, heart, lungs and his sixth and seventh cervical vertebrae. (Exhibit 174) In the autopsy, Dr. Titus (Exhibit 154) is *unspecific* regarding thoracic damage in that Methodist Hospital corpse. Do you suppose the damage done to those sixth and seventh cervical vertebrae of Howard Hughes mentioned in Exhibit 174 went unnoticed because it wasn't there? But then again, *Drs. Wilbur Thain and Lawrence Chaffin were both present during the "H.H." autopsy* by special invitation by Dr. Jack Titus. Were there simply "too many cooks in the kitchen" for those boys to skate around or had they failed to do their homework? (Drs. Chaffin and Thain invited into "H.H." autopsy by Dr. Titus, Exhibit 149.)

The scar on the Methodist Hospital corpse's left top back area strongly suggests that it could have been incurred from an auto mishap, a construction mishap, or any number of other accidents that could have caused the damage.

In any event, would not damage to someone's left thorax (non-specific in autopsy) be visibly evident 30 years after the fact? And what about damage to the rib cage and splintered ribs (Exhibit 174) where they attach to the sternum body? *** And how about the posterior parts of those same ribs where they attached to the vertebrae? Could they all miraculously heal *without some indication of ever having been damaged*? Isn't it strange that these Hughes injuries were not mentioned in the autopsy?

***When Dr. Titus looked at the vertebrae, ribs, and sternum of the Methodist Hospital corpse, he noted *only* that "the vertebral bodies were moderately osteoporotic as are the ribs and sternum."

Hughes's left clavicle had also been *splintered like matchwood* together with those sixth and seventh cervical vertebrae (Exhibit 174). How could this obvious damage go <u>unnoticed</u> by Dr. Titus? "Planting his feet high on the instrument panel, Hughes braced himself for the inevitable." (Exhibit 129-A) The impact from the XF-11 crash was so forceful that <u>Hughes's chest was crushed,</u> eleven ribs were fractured and, where they attached to the sternum, they were splintered like matchwood. His left clavicle was busted, and his heart was pushed to the far side of his chest cavity."

LACERATIONS, CUTS AND BURNS, SUSTAINED BY HOWARD HUGHES:
As evidenced in Exhibits 128-A, 129-B, and 173, of which many would leave scars upon healing.
XF–11 Test Plane crash July 7, 1946:
    a. "Large laceration of the scalp on the left side."
    b. "Extensive second and <u>third degree burns on the left hand.</u>"
    c. "A large second degree burn on the lower part of the left chest extending from the nipple line to the medial scapular line."
    d. "A large second degree burn on the left buttock."
    e. "Numerous cuts, bruises, burns, and abrasions of both arms and both legs."
    f. "Numerous small cuts about the face."

LACERATIONS, CUTS AND BURNS, SUSTAINED BY HOWARD HUGHES:
As evidenced in Exhibits 128-A, 129-B, and 173, many of which would leave scars upon healing.
XF-11 Plane crash July 7, 1946:
    a. "A <u>large</u> laceration of the scalp."
    b. "Extensive second and <u>third-degree burns</u> on the left hand."
    c. "He forced open the plexiglass cover, searing both hands to the bone":
    d. "A second degree burn on the left buttock."
    e. "Cuts, bruises, and abrasions on his arms and legs."
    f. "Many small cuts on his face."

METHODIST HOSPITAL, HOUSTON, <u>AUTOPSY 1976</u>
SCARRING FROM LACERATIONS, CUTS AND BURNS OF "H.H.,"
As evidenced in the autopsy report at Methodist Hospital, Houston – April 1976:

Exhibit 152, 0003, page 1 of 5

"The left supra and infraclavicular fossae as well as the left shoulder and upper arm and posterior axillary fold are modestly swollen, edematous, and discolored a bluish-gray. A left acromia-clavicular separation is palpable with overriding of the clavicle. *The remaining skin of the anterior chest is unremarkable.*" *

* We've already been here in "Broken Bones," but that "the remaining skin of the anterior chest is "unremarkable" seems a bit strange when one considers the burn evidence indicated in Exhibits 128-A, 129-B, 1946 XF-11 Crash. As illustrated in these Exhibits, there was a substantial second-degree burn of the lower part of the left chest extending from the *nipple line* to the *medial scapular line.*" In such a large, wrap-around sensitive area as described, it is a given that scar tissue could form and be evident 30 years later or, at the very least, skin discoloration would be noticeable. (This burn scar was quite large.) **Notes:** a. Medial: "Center of" b. Scapular: "A large triangular flattened bone lying over the back ribs."

Exhibit 155, 0003, page 4 of 5

"The lesion of the left parietal scalp is eccrine adenoid cystic adenocarcinoma (cylindroma.)

Exhibit 152, 0003, page 1 of 5

"A 2.2 cm oval, centrally ulcerated, nodule is present on the left partial scalp. The hair surrounding this has been trimmed."

Exhibit 157, 0004, page 1 of 1

"Eccrine adenoid-cystic adenocarcinoma, left scalp" (same as above.)

"Lipoma, left upper arm."

"Scars of the left back (history of crashing, remote)"

SUMATION OF COMPARATIVE EVIDENCE ON SCARS, CUTS AND BURNS:

Once again, the Methodist Hospital is as remarkably *shallow* regarding scars, cuts, and burns as it was with broken bones. In Exhibit 157, 0004, page 1 of 1, we see where the Methodist Hospital autopsy attributes "a scar on the left back to a history of crashing," calling it "remote" and *alluding* to the Hughes XF-11 crash in1946. However, according to Exhibits 128-A and 129-B, there was "a second degree burn on the left buttock" of Hughes after the XF-11 crash. But (a) There is no mention of buttock burn, scarring, or skin discoloration on the corpse in the Methodist Hospital autopsy report 1976, and (b) there is no mention of a scar on the "left back" of Howard Hughes in Exhibits 128-A and 129-B that refer to the XF-11 crash. What about that "third-degree" * burn on his left hand as evidenced in Exhibits 128-A and 129-B - XF-11 Crash. *That would leave a nasty scar*, and what about the mention in Exhibit 173, XF-11 Crash of "hands seared to the bone"? There is nothing in the 1976 Methodist Hospital autopsy to indicate this obvious tissue damage. In Exhibit 174, we find that "Hughes's hands were so badly burned that he could not sign a will." This is most interesting since (a) Hughes must have asked for a will to be made up and brought to him, and (b) when he found himself on the brink of death, he believed a will to be appropriate. (We will go into more depth on wills and the myth that Hughes died intestate (without a will) in Chapter XIV. In any event, the massive scarring of Hughes's hands is never mentioned in the Methodist Hospitals autopsy report. However, they were quite explicit, numerous times, on the contemporary "ecchymosis & embedded needles" on the Methodist Hospital corpse's forearms. (Exhibit 138, 000, page 7 of 15, #3-k and various other Exhibits.)

If you return to Exhibits 128-A, 129-B, and 174 and read the complete litany of cuts and burns sustained in the XF-11 crash, you would come to the conclusion that many of the injuries would leave obvious scars. There is no logical explanation as to why all these items are missing in the 1976 Methodist Hospital autopsy if, indeed, the corpse at Methodist Hospital was that of Howard Hughes. Also, there was a scar over the right eyebrow of Hughes and a scar on his right leg as well; and no, these do not appear in the Methodist Hospital autopsy file, even though they were used as "identity scars" by the FBI in the application for Hughes's 1942 pilot's license? (Exhibit 3) Now, where do you suppose *those* scars went to? But, a tiny (less than one-inch oval tumor) on the corpse's left scalp is noticed not just once but several times in the Methodist Hospital's autopsy?

*Third degree burn: epidermis, fat, muscle and, often as not, *tendons* are destroyed.

There's a lot of focus on the left scalp of "H.H." in the 1976 Methodist Hospital autopsy report; so, let's take a hard look at that. And *yes*, there was a "large laceration of the left scalp" sustained by Hughes in the 1946 crash, as referenced in Exhibits 128-A, 129-B and 174.

AS REFERENCED IN THE METHODIST HOSPITAL 1976 AUTOPSY REPORT:
"The lesion of the left parietal scalp is eccrine, adenoid, cystic, adenocarcinoma (cylindroma.)" Wow! Now that is a *huge* identity for a *tiny*, less than *one inch* in size skin blemish.

a. Lesion: "A wound or injury."

b. Eccrine: "Denoting the flow of sweat" or blood.

c. Adenoid: "Gland like: of glandular in appearance."

d. Cystic: "Relating to a cyst."

e. Cyst: "An abnormal sac containing gas, fluid or a semisolid material"

f. Adenocarcinoma: "A malignant neoplasm of epithelial cells in glandular or gland like pattern."

g. Cylindroma: "A round tumor – may form from ducts or glands."

In analyzing the <u>head</u> injury of the corpse that is *supposed* to be Howard Hughes at the Methodist Hospital in 1976, I think we can safely say that:

a. It was round.

b. It had a cystic tumor at its center or was a tumor in its entirety.

c. The small cyst was filled with blood, lymph, or both.

d. It was a wound that developed or occurred <u>recent</u> to the 1976 Methodist Hospital autopsy.

e. It may have occurred when caretakers dropped this "H.H." in the toilet while they were in London, England, in 1973 or later.

f. Someone had taken pains to trim the hair from around this small wound to make it <u>more visible</u>? This was noticed by Dr. Titus, the Physician performing the autopsy and <u>had not been trimmed</u> during the autopsy procedure. (Exhibit 152, 003, page 1 of 5)

g. It was only 2.2 cm in diameter (2.2 centimeters = less than 1 inch.)

h. It was *not* <u>a 30-year-old skin blemish</u> that would develop from a "<u>large scalp laceration,</u>" as depicted in Exhibits 128-A and 129-B, XF-11 Crash. And we should note here that the hair on the head of the corpse autopsied at Methodist Hospital was "gray and <u>somewhat</u> <u>thinned.</u>" (Exhibit 147, 001, page 1, bottom paragraph) This being the case, if they could find a small 2.2-centimeter cystic tumor on the scalp, wouldn't they also have noticed residual scarring from the *large laceration* Howard Hughes received in the 1946 XF-11 plane crash?

SOFT TISSUE INJURIES HOWARD HUGHES SUSTAINED ON JULY 7, 1946 XF-11 CRASH:

DAMAGE TO HEART AND LUNGS: As evidenced in Exhibits 128-A, 129-B and 174. Occurring in XF-11 Test Plane crash July 7, 1946:

    a. "Hemorrhage occurred into the left pleural space."

    b. "Effusion into the chest"

    c. "3400 cc. of bloody liquid was removed at three tappings."

    d. "Hemoglobin content of this fluid was 18%."

    e. "It is probable that 650 cc. of hemorrhage took place into the chest."

DAMAGE TO HEART AND LUNGS: As evidenced in Exhibits 128-A, 129-B and 174. Occurring in XF-11 Test Plane crash July 7, 1946:

    a. "His chest was crushed."

    b. "His left lung had collapsed, and his right was also injured."

    c. "His heart had been pushed to the far side of his chest cavity."

DAMAGE TO HEART AND LUNGS: As evidenced in Exhibit 174. Occurring in XF-11 Test Plane crash July 7, 1946:
> a. "His heart shifted to the right."
> b. "The right heart wall was contused."

EXAMINATION OF HEART AND LUNGS: As evidenced in "H.H." 1976 autopsy at Methodist Hospital Houston, Texas:
Exhibit 153, 0003, page 2 of 5
> a. "All organs were normally situated."
> b. 60% luminal narrowing (fat) – mid portion of left anterior descending artery.

Exhibit 156, 0003, page 5 of 5
> a. Lungs: "The apical scars are without evidence of active inflammatory or granulomatous component. The remainders of the samples show no evidence of pneumonia or passive congestion."
> b. Heart: "Sections of the heart show no abnormalities."

Exhibit 158-A, ,0005, page 1 of 2
> a. Additional findings:
> > 1. Fibrotic apical scars both lungs and old, fibrotic left pleural adhesions (history of prior left thoracic injury. *)

*   **Note**: thoracic injury is left unspecific by Dr. Titus.

SUMATION OF COMPARATIVE EVIDENCE ON HEART AND LUNGS:

Once again, like broken bones and scars, it is evident that the Methodist Hospital autopsy simply does not correlate with internal damage as depicted in the 1946 XF-11 crash of Howard Hughes. Let us start with the Methodist Hospital consensus that, "All organs were normally situated." However, according to Exhibits 128-A, 129-B and 174, when Hughes crashed the XF-11, "his heart had been *slammed* over to the far side of his chest cavity; and according to Exhibit 174, "his right heart wall had been contused."* Taking this into consideration, did his heart, over the next 30 years, creep back over and nestle exactly where it was supposed to be with nothing evidential to indicate it had been displaced or contused (i.e., badly bruised)? Well, in truth there's not much that holds the heart in place; it just hangs in there, from birth to death, faithfully doing its job. However, and often as not, when a heart receives a resounding slam that moves it to the far side of a chest cavity, there may be scar tissue generated on the heart's *arteries* from stressfully stretching and, if the heart is severely contused, scar tissue may be evident there as well. They went to a lot of trouble at Methodist Hospital to "section" the heart. ** Yet they found nothing abnormal there? They found *no* residual scar tissue, which would indicate that the arteries had been stretched, or that the right heart wall had been contused? However, in their *close* observations of heart and arteries, they did notice 60 percent luminal narrowing (fat) in the mid-portion of the left anterior descending artery (Exhibit 153), but in the heart arteries, no indication of scarring from stretching? In the F-11 crash, Hughes's left lung had *collapsed,* and the right lung had been injured as well, per Exhibits 128-A and others. The obvious slam Howard's lungs received would likely leave massive *scarring on both lungs.* When a lung has collapsed, and then eventually re-inflated, scarring would appear most prominently in the area facing the impact. This, in the case of Hughes, would be the frontal area of the lungs behind those 12 busted ribs. Hughes had braced himself by putting his feet on the plane's control panel and placing his knees on his chest – hence broken ribs and damaged lungs and heart "as his plane slammed into the well-made houses of Beverly Hills." In Exhibit 158-A, Autopsy Review, Dr. Jack Titus writes about "apical scars" he found while examining the thoracic trunk – in other words, the back-top area of the lungs. This type of apical lung scarring appearing in the Methodist Hospital, Houston, corpse can occur with an impact to the top back. Hence, the same impact that damaged the Methodist Hospital corpse's left-side thoracic column (see Exhibit 138, Autopsy Review, page 7, #3. a.) is left non-specific by Dr. Titus. In viewing the osteoporotic ribs and sternum, Dr. Titus maintains in Exhibit 153, Autopsy Review, that "All organs were normally situated." Obviously, he saw no scarring until he got into the *back top thoracic column* area of the Methodist Hospital corpse; and *these* lung scars appear *only* in the *upper* "apical"*** area of the lungs; most probably noticed when the lungs were lifted out for weighing; hence "additional findings." Left, *undefined*, thoracic damage was also considered in "additional findings" in both Exhibits 138 and 158-A.

* This was in Dr. Vern Mason's report to the press in 1946 after the crash.
** "Section:" Cut into thin strips for microscopic examination.
*** "Apical": Uppermost or Top as opposed to "Basal" Lower area or Bottom.

A GROUPING OF CONTEMPORARY OBSERVATIONS, PRIOR TO, DURING, AND AFTER THE 1976 METHODIST HOSPITAL AUTOPSY:

Exhibit 137, 000, page 6 of 15, H. 2. Interpretation: (e.g. "uremic poisoning")

Exhibit 138, 000, page 7 of 15, d. and e. (Renal failure – Emaciation and Dehydration.")

Exhibit 138, 000, page 7 of 15, #3. Accessory Diagnosis - c." ("Contusion of left shoulder")

Exhibit 138, 000, page 7 of 15, #3. Accessory Diagnosis - k." ("Multiple needle punctures and Ecchymosis forearms – FRESH")

Exhibit 138, 000, page 7 of 15, #3. Accessory Diagnosis – Osteoporosis

Exhibit-138, 000, page 7 of 15, #3. Accessory Diagnosis - o. ("Dental caries – severe –Evidence of neglect")

Exhibit 138, 000, page 7 of 15, J. <u>X-Ray of Arms of "H.H."</u>
("A remarkable x-ray of "H. H's" arms reveal four broken, embedded needle-points [about ½ inch each] in the subcutaneous tissues of the right arm")

Exhibit 139, 000, page 8 of 15, – Nasty stuff on imbedded needles, vein calcification, etc.

Exhibit 140, 000, page 9 of 15, d. "It is not possible to determine from log if "H.H." was physically addicted to codeine since most days during this period do not indicate codeine use" (???)
Note: The above seems strange. This "H.H." injected, and was injected, with so much junk over the years that his veins had calcified. How then could he *not* had been an addict to some degree? The "H.H." corpse at Methodist Hospital was *loaded* with codeine. An *attempted* inference seems to be that this "H.H.' loaded himself up on a binge? (Unlikely when one considers the dissolving of the tablets, the loading of syringes numerous times, and the massive amounts of codeine injected.) This "H.H." had been *comatose when Thain gave him an injection at 8:00 a.m. on the day he died.* Now – what about the *tremendous quantity* of codeine found in that Methodist Hospital "H.H." corpse which had been taken *"within 2 to 6 hours prior to death?"* How was it even possible that this "H.H." could have dosed himself when the "H.H." corpse at Methodist Hospital "<u>had been unconscious for twenty or more</u> hours *before* death?" (Exhibit 127-B, bottom of page.)

Exhibit 141, 000, page 10 of 15, #3. Medical Notes, Note 1. "Aides changed bandages on 2 occasions, and at least 2 two falls* including 1 from toilet stool." Note 4. "Dr. Clark visited only one time. No other recorded physician visits. No mention of how medications obtained." (Part 2 of 4.) Dr. Forest Tennant at Dr. Wilbur Thain's trial stated, "Highly unusual to have so much prescription medication and only <u>one</u> physician visit."
*   Exhibit 141 above: "At least two falls" how about *many* falls? This "H.H." had not walked for three years prior to his death; these injuries had to have happened from his being dropped by his aides *many times.* A bang on his head, a dislocated left shoulder, a broken hip, a scar on his back, busted apical vertebrae etc.?

Exhibit-142, 000, page 11 of 15, Pertinent Points from M.3. "H.R.H. sustained a fall in London in 1973 (Log's last date 07/01/73) which fractured his hip and required a metal pin for repair. "H.H." never walked again."

Exhibit-143, 000 page 12 of 15, Page Bottom. Opinion as per Dr. Tennant:
"It is my personal opinion, based on knowledge of narcotic law and current medical practice, that *Dr. Thain violated Section 841 of the 1970 Federal Drug Abuse Act."*

Exhibit-144, 000 page 13 of 15. "April 7, 1976 at Age 70, "H.H." dies from kidney failure." (April 7 as date of death is incorrect in the autopsy report. He died April 5.

The autopsy began with the taking of fingerprints on April 5, which were discarded and taken a second time the next day. The autopsy was finished on April 7, 1976, at Methodist Hospital, Houston.)

1. Drugs supplied illegally by Physicians.
2. Unable to walk due to hip problems and leg contractions.
3. Progressive renal failure and uremic poisoning.
4. Heart in good condition?

Exhibit 148, 0001, Autopsy Review of "Howard R. Hughes," page 2 of 4, As per Dr. Jack Titus: (two sentences down from page top.) "It is my firm opinion that death occurred less than three hours prior to the time of my examination."

Exhibit 148, 0001, page 2 of 4, bottom of page: Regarding the apparent final illness, Drs. Wilbur Thain and Lawrence Chaffin reported that, "from their limited knowledge, Mr. Hughes had been reported to them as not having been eating or drinking well for approximately the last three weeks. In addition, he apparently had increasing malaise over the past two or three days of life, particularly in the past 24-36 hours, he developed some confusion. Somewhat sudden and unexpectedly on Sunday evening, April 4, he developed a shock-like state for which he was treated with intravenous fluids. In recognition of the sudden worsening of his condition, the decision was made to transfer him to Houston for further care as soon as arrangements could be made. Drs. Thain, Chaffin and Mr. Holmes, told us that in his seriously ill state, apparently comatose, he was put into his private jet." (Emphasis added.)

It's highly *improbable* that "Hughes" was treated with intravenous fluids on April 4 as stated by Drs. Thain and Chaffin, as they were *conveniently oblivious* to this need prior to Dr. Victor Montemayor's suggestion on April 5 when he examined "Hughes" at the Acapulco Princess Hotel. The "H.H." Methodist Hospital corpse was noted to be "severely dehydrated upon being removed from the plane, and later as well, during the autopsy." It's unlikely that "Acapulco H.H." had had a drink of water for a considerable length of time, or had any intravenous fluids other than codeine solution, administered at any time recent to his death, thereby concentrating the poison toxins and chemicals awash in his body. "Hughes" was transported to Houston in his private jet which the "caretakers" said had been adapted for the transport. But Dr. Thain had arrived in a medical transport plane from his party in the Bahamas. Why was *that* plane, which was already adapted, not used to fly "Hughes" sooner to any hospital? Was it used as a decoy while they illegally spirited "Hughes" out of Mexico in his private jet without a legitimate flight plan or a legal Mexican visa?

Exhibit 149, Autopsy Review of "Howard R. Hughes," page 3 of 4. "Dr. Jachimczyk was informed that a proper autopsy permit had been obtained and that a complete autopsy would begin at about 1:00 PM on Tuesday April 6, 1976," In concert with Dr. Jachimczyk were Doctors Malcom McGavran, Roberto Bayardo, Lawrence Chaffin, Wilbur Thain, and Macintosh.

ANALYSIS OF ABOVE EXHIBIT INFORMATION (CONTEMPORARY TO 1976) CONCERNING THE METHODIST HOSPITAL AUTOPSY OF THE "HUGHES" CORPSE:

We will give this separate attention because of the absurdity in believing that this <u>6 foot 2 inch, 87 pound</u> "H.H." was a tough dictator who ruled over his caretakers and doctors with an iron fist, preparing and "self-injecting" tremendous amounts of codeine phosphate, *without the help* of his caretakers. Suspicious and appalling, why was there not a single "H.H." caretaker or doctor willing to speak up and act when this "H.H." was starving and drug-abusing himself into *oblivion*. (*If* indeed, he *was* doing this to himself.) His "caretakers" were not even concerned enough to turn him in bed from time to time to prevent bed sores! Their job was to affirm and act upon the obvious, and the man obviously had been needing professional medical care for at least a year in the more controlled environment of a stateside hospital!

"Acapulco Hughes" was terribly sick from renal failure, among other things, and together with a drug overdose, died from it. It is highly unlikely that the real Howard Hughes would willingly want to be kept in Mexico suffering from renal failure (of which there were many indicators) while he <u>owned</u> a hospital in Miami, Florida, that specialized in kidney treatment and had the latest technology in kidney machines for cleansing the blood! Miami is less than 4 hours from Acapulco, Mexico, by Jet. Had his alleged "care-team" not been so *careless*, this "H.H." could have been cared for in complete secrecy by a team of specialists at the Howard Hughes Miami Medical Institute, had that been his wish. <u>He *owned* the place!</u> (Well, the real Hughes did anyway.)

There are many medical "tells" to indicate kidney failure (renal failure) *long before* it becomes fatal: cloudy urine, frequent urination, edema, lethargy, loss of appetite, and, of course a standard blood test would readily indicate something was amiss. (And *yes*, they did blood tests in Acapulco, Mexico, in 1976.) One of the more amazing things here is that *this* "H.H." had more than four doctors on retainer. However, Dr. Wilbur Thain had been the only doctor to make two previous visits to Acapulco and Dr. Lawrence Chaffin only went down on the one occasion when "Acapulco H.H." was dying. Any, or all, of them could have been flown in by jet in a matter of hours *much earlier in the man's illness*. After all, weren't they being paid the big-buck retainers? It certainly appears to even the naivest, that the aides and doctors did little concerning the man's health, and everything to order and ship in massive quantities of drugs so that – with their help – he would abuse them!? It comes to mind that this "H.H." may not even have been a consenting victim!

It now appears entirely possible, with what we have learned, that "Acapulco H.H." could have been pumped-up with narcotics against his wishes for no other reason than to keep him quiet in his misery.

With the evidence *provided above*, <u>it's difficult to believe</u> that neglect was *all* that was going on with "Acapulco Hughes."

This is probably a good place to consider some of the information in Exhibits 158-B and 158-C, pages 112 and 113 of James Phelan's book *Howard Hughes: The Hidden*

Years. These are straightforward and correct in their content. Were you to go to the library and check out Mr. Phelan's book, you would find a large glossy photo on the book's back dust cover. In this photo, Mr. Phelan is going over source materials with Mell Stewart and Gordon Margulis, which will appear in his book. So, the information given by these two "H.H." aides is factual, enlightening, and totally believable. It is believable that at that time both Stewart and Margulis honestly thought the fellow they worked for after 1965 was Howard Hughes. However, there are some problematic conditions that appear in these two Exhibits: Why with an <u>overload</u> of "H.H." aides, didn't any of them clean up that disgusting "H.H." abode atop the Desert Inn from 1965 to 1970? Maids never saw the inside of the Desert Inn penthouse until its final cleaning, and this was after four years of "H.H." living in squalor together with his aides. What the hell were Chuck Waldron, Erick Bundy, Norm Love, Fred Jayka, Mell Stewart, and Gordon Margulis getting paid for anyway? And what was the need for all these aides who did so extraordinarily little work? Was the strategy of the Summa, Inc. pirates simply: "Look at it this way Chester, with all these "H.H." aides on the payroll, who's going to question that the fellow they are supposedly caring for is the real Hughes? Only a couple of the aides know the truth and they, together with the phony Hughes, *are our boys*!" "Yeah, I see what you mean Billy, ya got-ta hand it to our phony 'Hughes,' he's one damn good actor. As for the aides, we are paying them six times the going rate for unskilled labor. They'll keep their mouths shut for that kind of money."

The filth this "H.H." was compelled to live in at the Desert Inn, Las Vegas, is unfathomable. It's completely understandable why Mell Steward would be "reluctant to talk about it." Had this "H.H." been the iron-fisted tyrant that all those aides and doctors portrayed him as, he would simply have told them *outright*: "Okay you guys, get to work and clean up this dump or hit the road!" Remember the good ol' days with Howard Hughes, his establishment of the Howard Hughes Medical Institute, his concern with cleanliness, his well-documented refusal to shake hands? This "refusal to shake hands" was not a glitch in the mentality of Howard Hughes as it was often portrayed as being. Instead it was a belief that is as valid today as it was earlier for Hughes: "Shaking hands *is* the best way in the world to transmit disease." *A man like this does not live in filth!*

But let us get to one of the important aspects found in the above Exhibits. And yes, the point is emphasized in this book several times. When this "H.H." was living in the Desert Inn penthouse, Las Vegas, he had kidney problems (renal problems) early on, per Exhibits above. These kidney problems were severe and yet *not once in ten years,* did the "Hughes" entourage <u>ever</u> take him to the Howard Hughes Medical Institute, Miami (Hughes's own Hospital) where the latest technology in renal treatment was available, and where he could have been treated under another name, if he chose. *Where were* all those doctors who were getting paid the BIG-BUCKS to look in on him from time to time and take care of "Hughes's" medical needs? They certainly had no problem with sending him an abundance of drugs, extensively used to "jack-him-up," sight unseen!

Let us continue. Consider this: The autopsy referenced above in Exhibit 138, "000" page 7 of 15, e. noted "Emaciation and <u>dehydration</u>." Also, Exhibit 147, page bottom states, "The body appeared remarkably emaciated and <u>dehydrated</u>." Also, Exhibits 130-F and 130-G, page bottom and page top state, "With Tuckers help, water was injected under the skin of Hughes's shriveled fingers in order to plump them up enough to produce a valid set of prints." (Which, according to the autopsy record from Methodist Hospital found in this exposé, they never did.) Yet, in Autopsy Exhibit 148, bottom, "Somewhat suddenly and unexpectedly on Sunday evening, April 4, he developed a shock-like state for which he was treated with *intravenous fluids.*" Well, if this had truly been the case, and a simple glucose-saline drip feed had been administered to this "H.H.," why would Dr. Montemayor Martinez make the suggestion the next day when he visited "H.H." in Acapulco (Exhibit 178-B), that "Intravenous fluids should be administered because the patient appeared to be dehydrated and suffering kidney failure"? Why are there numerous observations of the Methodist Hospital corpse being so dehydrated that it could be noticed by the naked eye? It was never noted by Dr. Malcolm McGavran that there was a problem with the first set of prints taken. Also, Dr. McGavran must have taken the "H.H." corpse's fingerprints, <u>later rejected</u>, *on a fingerprint card and not on strips of paper.* (See Exhibit 130-F). Did the good doctor use the <u>last</u> print card available in the Methodist Hospital or did the Coroner's Office not have a single coroner fingerprint card in stock? (Refer back to Chapter V with any questions.)

It should be obvious by now, that any *real* doctor or caretaker, blind in one eye and unable to see out of the other, <u>would have known </u>that something was terribly amiss with this 6 foot 2 inch, <u>87 pound</u> fellow – *at least several months before he died.* This "H.H" was totally "bananas," as his caretakers would often have us believe, hiding out in various corners of the globe for fear of being seen. They would often leak various news tidbits of how he urinated in wide-mouth jars, storing them in a corner of his residence, or insisted on being "disheveled," letting his fingernails and hair grow to unsightly lengths. "Hughes" never kept a secretary on hand after 1965 that could type out his business deals or wishes, but insisted on writing everything cursively? (None of the *many* aides hired by Summa, Inc, could type, none had nursing credentials, and yet they were giving the man injections and enemas in abundance?) How much of a battle could this extremely sick, emaciated old man have put up if they had moved him, even against his desires, into a proper stateside medical facility?

When the Mexican Doctor Victor Montemayor Martinez was called in to view and advise on this living bag of skin and bones, he was absolutely dismayed at what he witnessed! See Exhibit 130-E and read the two paragraphs at the bottom starting with, "The desperation in Thain's voice ..." and finish on Exhibit 130-F, top two sentences. There is more. Go to Exhibit 176 and read the description of the neglect that eventually lead to the death flight of "Hughes." But let's take this scenario to the next step:

A. In Exhibit 130-B, when Hughes's Leer Jet, carrying the "H.H." corpse landed in Houston, Texas, and the lead receiving doctor, Dr. McIntosh, was informed that his patient had died in flight "a few minutes ago," his first instinct was to try resuscitation. As noted, in the above Exhibit, all the equipment was in place for this procedure. But Dr. Thain would have none of this and excitedly countered this protocol with, "It's no use, he's gone, he's gone." Could Thain have known that this "H.H." corpse had been dead for a considerable length of time <u>prior</u> to "over Brownsville"? (Exhibit 130-C)

B. Later, in Exhibit 130-E, the "H.H." Doctors Thain and Chaffin are concerned about leaks to the press. They were supposedly concerned that their reputations might suffer should the press go with "in-depth coverage" of the corpse. Was this idea a "smoke screen" for their real concern? When one takes in *all* the information, including the autopsy report, nothing could be more apparent than that this "H.H." was poorly taken care of at best, or *criminally drugged and abused at worst!* What becomes obvious is that Doctors Thain and Chaffin may well have been concerned that, with more eyes on the Methodist Hospital "H.H." corpse, more questions would have been asked, hence increasing the risk of others learning that the Methodist Hospital corpse <u>had not</u> died a normal death. <u>What *else* could have been discovered is the focus of this book.</u>

C. In Exhibit 130-G, above we find Dr. Thain in jovial spirits, joking and commenting on the lushness of Acapulco, the poor timing of the "H.H." death, and his enjoyment of the Mexican Riviera. He has seen his patient once during his vacation, According to one account, Thain arrives at the Acapulco Princess Hotel the morning of April 5, *after his party in the Bahamas was over*, and finds "H.H." in a coma. The aids tell Thain that "Hughes" had been unconscious since the night before. (That was when Thain was first called.) (Exhibit 127-B)

D. In Chapter XIII, Russ gives us an in-depth understanding as to how wrong the Justice System can sometimes go with high-profile well-funded individuals. But for now, let us "cherry-pick" his information to make our point. (Reference information directory found in Chapter XIII.

 1. August 1974, Dr. Thain agrees to provide narcotics to "Howard Hughes." He is awarded a $300,000 five-year contract with Summa, Inc. as "medical adviser and consultant," plus executive benefits. (That is a lot of money, back in the seventies, easily $3 million in today's currency – and this was only part-time work.) He will only see his patient three times: March 17, March 18 (per his account), and April 5, 1976, to earn his fare. (But hey, he's *Bill Gay's brother-in-law,* and Bill Gay is C.E.O of Hughes Corp., with fingers on the purse strings.)

 a) Per Exhibit 127-B, Thain claimed it was on his April 5 visit that "He found 'Hughes' in a comma, and that *'Hughes' had been unconscious since the night before."* (This is attested to Dr. Chaffin and caretaker Holmes.)

b) If (a) is true, who pumped "H.H." up with the mega doses of codeine, discovered to still be present in the corpse when it arrived at Methodist Hospital?

c) Drug specialist Dr. Tennant claims that the codeine in the Methodist Hospital corpse had been put there no more than "2 to 6 hours prior to death." (See Exhibit 137.)

2. 5,500 grains were delivered to "H.H." caretakers August 6, 1974 through December 13, 1975. Additional 2,000 grains were delivered to "H.H." caretakers through April 5, 1976.

3. "Howard Hughes" dies on April 5, 1976.

DAILY CODEINE DOSAGES ADMINISTERED TO "HUGHES" 08/O6/74 THRU 04/05/76:

TOTAL CODEINE DOSE OF 5,500 GRAINS = 11.16 GRAINS (*670 MG*) PER DAY
493 DAYS 08/O6/74 THROUGH 12/13/75
TOTAL CODEINE DOSE OF 2,000 GRAINS = 18.35 GRAINS (*1,101 MG*) PER DAY
109 DAYS 12/19/75 THROUGH 04/05/76

GENERAL PRESCRIBED DOSE: 30 TO 60 MG EVERY 4 TO 6 HOURS

TOXIC DOSE: 200 TO 300 MG PER DAY

However, what must be kept in mind here is the estimated dosages of codeine attributed to the Methodist Hospital "H.H" corpse were 1,000 times greater then what was originally calculated, according to lead Methodist Hospital pathologist Dr. Titus at Dr. Thain's trial.

THE CONTENT OF CODEINE FOUND IN THE METHODIST HOSPITAL "H.H." CORPSE GREATLY EXCEEDED THE DEATH DOSE OF 500 TO 800 MG.

Dr. Wilbur Thain loaded up the caretakers with codeine phosphate for "H.H." in the four months prior to his April 5, 1976 death!

4. In the autopsy at Methodist Hospital Houston, the doctors discover that the "H.H." 87-pound, 6-foot 2-inch corpse is laden with "death dosages" of codeine. (More clarification in Exhibits 136 and 137.)
Note: Half of a therapeutic dose of codeine will exit the system in six to eight hours and will completely dissipate in 12.

5. "Hughes dies over Brownsville, Texas, at 1:27 PM," according to Drs. Thain and Chaffin. The autopsy report in Exhibit 147 says the Hughes jet arrived in the air, over Houston at approximately 2:00 PM.

a) However, Leer Jets in the seventies had a cruising speed of 520 miles per hour. Therefore, it would have taken *40 minutes* to fly the 300 aeronautical miles from Brownsville to Houston and not the 33 minutes as indicated above. Okay, 2:00 p.m. was an estimate, and there is only a seven or eight-minute differentiation. However, here we should factor in the jet's landing time plus the time for the doctors to reach the plane and begin to off-load the "H.H." corpse. They were in a hurry so let us allow 10 minutes to land and 10 minutes to begin the retrieval of the corpse. Therefore, it would have been a total of 57 or 60 minutes *after* Brownsville <u>before</u> Dr. Thain could have spoken to Dr. McIntosh. Dr. Thain's first statement was, "I lost the heart-beat a few minutes ago." Dr. McIntosh immediately offers resuscitation. But Dr. Thain maintains that, "It's no use, he's gone, he's gone," as stated in Exhibit 130-B. However, later Drs. Thain and Chaffin and aide Holmes stated, that "H.H." had died over Brownsville at 1:27 p.m.

b) So, the "H.H." caretakers maintained that "H.H." "had died over Brownsville at 1:27 PM." But how could they have known that "Hughes" had died over Brownsville unless they had asked the plane's pilot where they were? But they *did not* ask the pilot their location when "H.H." died. Pilot Sutton was shocked at the discovery when he landed the plane in Houston to the news that "H.H." had died during the flight. Plus, the pilot may not even have known *when* they were over or near Brownsville – the jet was traveling over 500 miles per hour.

c) Federal Aeronautic Procedure *in the seventies* was that a pilot must put down his aircraft, at the closest available airport when notified that a passenger has died. The reasoning here is that a near death passenger could be saved if the pilot has radioed ahead for a waiting ambulance. Procedure, or no procedure, both Drs. Thain and Chaffin were supposedly intelligent men and were *doctors*! They had to have realized that a hospital would have equipment for resuscitation. Why in the world did they not just fly "H.H." to the Hughes Medical Institute in Miami Florida *earlier*, where they had state-of-the-art kidney machines? The Mexican Doctor Montemayor had already observed, and Thain and Chaffin should have known much earlier as well that the man's kidneys were not functioning properly. One cannot help but question the real motives of Drs. Chaffin and Thain. Did they really want to *save* this "H.H.?"

d) Let us do some supposing here. Suppose that you and a fellow doctor were being paid big bucks to take care of the wealthiest man in America. You obviously either liked your employer or, at the very least, liked the benefits and the money. You are a doctor, so you are not going to just *give away* your skills. It took you a lot of effort and suffering to achieve your lofty position. Okay, maybe you *do not* like your employer, but you and your compadre want to keep getting paid. Your employer has been extremely sick and suddenly takes a turn for the worst. You load him into his Leer Jet and head for Houston, where you know he will be well cared for. As you are approaching Brownsville, Texas, you note that your boss's pulse is erratic, and his breathing labored. You *know* this because *you are in an emergency situation* and it is what you've been trained for. You know that the quicker you can get your patient to a hospital the better his chance of surviving. You quickly consult with your fellow physician. "He's deteriorating rapidly, should we tell the pilot to put down in Brownsville or fly on to Houston?" If you really wanted to save your employer, what would be *your* decision? (It's a no-brainer; and yes, there was a well-equipped new hospital in Brownsville, Texas, in 1976. Instead, they flew over several other cities with hospitals on their way to Houston. But then let us consider this, if you had been either Drs. Thain or Chaffin, wouldn't your *original* destination have been Miami or Brownsville from the "git-go" if you genuinely wanted to save your patient? How about scheduling a flight and a hospital when the fellow first became unconscious? The Mexican Dr. Montemayor suggested this when he first laid eyes on "H.H.," and it is probably what any *real doctor* would have done if *they truly wanted to save this patient.*

e) Upon receiving the "Hughes" corpse at Methodist Hospital, the Houston doctors determined that the corpse had been dead for "no more than three (3) hours." This is normally deduced by taking a measurement of heat still in the body (liver/rectal) and then, taking in all pertinent factors, extrapolate the approximate time of death. Once again, this procedure *does not appear* in the Methodist Hospital, Houston, autopsy. (Also, the cornea of the eye begins to cloud over thirty minutes after death and is, of course, progressive.)

f) The above information raises several questions. Did Drs. Thain and Chaffin really want this "H.H." to live; or had they made sure early on that this "H.H." would not live to recuperate in a Brownsville, Miami, Houston, or any other hospital? Also, as was pointed out earlier, did this "H.H." die over Brownsville or did he die on approach to Houston. It appears that Dr. Thain could not make up his mind which lie to go with.

(Thank you, seasoned pilot, Captain Jean-Luke, for the aeronautical information (a) through (c) above.)

AUTOPSY EXHIBITS (ABOVE) BEGIN WITH "000" AND END WITH "0008"
(Various pages)

Exhibit 138 – 000 - page 7 of 15, <u>Accessory Diagnosis</u> "k. Multiple needle punctures and ecchymosis forearms – FRESH." (Emphasis added.) <u>Note</u>: "Ecchymosis" is, according to medical dictionaries, the escape of blood into the tissues from ruptured blood vessels. "Fresh" means current, multiple, many.

Exhibit 138 – 000 - page 7 of 15, "<u>X-Ray of Arms HRH:</u>
A remarkable x-ray of HRH's arms reveals four broken, embedded needle points (about ½ inch each) in the subcutaneous tissues of the right arm."

Exhibit 140 – 000 - page 9 of 15, "The HRH medical log."
"It is not possible to determine from this log if H.R.H. was physically addicted to codeine since most days during this period do not indicate codeine use." *

According to Thain, Chaffin and Holmes, this "H.H." had been direly confused for 24 to 36 hours. (That's what *they* said, but could it have been considerably longer?) The confusion eventually developed into an eight-hour shock-like state. In Exhibit 127-A, start with "Intriguing questions," excerpt from book *Empire*, bottom paragraph, and read through Exhibit 127-B. Could it not be possible that this "H.H." suffered many, if not all, these nasty needle wounds *immediately prior* to, or *during*, his flight from Acapulco to Houston? Or that the man was dead before the plane left the tarmac in Mexico? Apology for the redundancy here, but it seems *unlikely* that this extremely sick and crippled fellow could have dissolved the codeine-phosphate tablets, loaded the syringes, and, unassisted, injected massive doses of codeine** into himself. This fellow was direly confused and later comatose for a considerable length of time *prior* to his death flight to Houston. An addict will try to enter a vein rather than randomly jab the needle directly into muscle tissues. Are we "off a cliff" here with the suggestion that <u>this "H.H." had considerable help</u> with those numerous injections, especially in his forearms *immediately prior to his death,* and if so, *why?* It seems Dr. Thain, Dr. Chaffin, and caretaker Holmes were very *busy*. We know that the poor fellow presumed to be Hughes arrived dead in Houston with enough codeine in him *to kill a horse!* See Exhibit 127-B, mid-page of the *Empire* excerpt and start with, "On October 27, 1976 Dr. Jack L. Titus ...." etc.) Amazing, simply *amazing*, that Dr. Titus, the lead physician heading up the "Hughes" autopsy, had not the intelligence to know the difference between milligrams and micrograms. This "H.H." simply had to have been pumped up with massive amounts of codeine six to eight hours prior to his death <u>while he was unconscious!"</u>

* If "H.H." *was not* addicted to codeine, what was the purpose of Doctors Thain and Chaffin and caretaker Holmes stocking massive quantities of the stuff. (He took other painkillers as well; hence all those medicine bottles left at the Desert Inn Penthouse upon his departure from that location. These are the bottles that had to be gathered up and delivered to the Summa, Inc. group on Romaine Street in Los Angeles.)

** Codeine phosphate was the form of codeine which Dr. Thain ordered, <u>in enormous amounts, patient unseen,</u> for this "H.H."

***Exhibit 136 and 137 – 000 - pages 5 and 6 of 15, Codeine "is one of the fastest acting and most rapidly metabolized narcotics; it remains in the blood stream for <u>only</u> 4 to 6 hours after consumption. Since higher levels of codeine were found in the bile and urine than in the blood, it is likely that <u>"HRH" consumed his last codeine 2 to 6 hours before death.</u>" (Yes, we are aware that in this same paragraph they have claimed that "H.H." was tolerant to codeine" and that "a blood level many times higher than the level found would be required to produce death." However, *this* was the prognosis *prior* to Dr. Thain's trial, where Dr. Titus admitted to having mistaken milligrams for micrograms. That means <u>the level of codeine in the corpse of this "H.H." had been 1,000 times greater!</u>" (Exhibit 127-B, mid-page.) Also indicated on the same page, "That was an astonishing finding… Hughes had been unconscious for nearly 24 hours before he died." *Therefore, once again, the massive dosages of codeine had to have been pumped into him while he was unconscious!* Let's plug an interesting perspective in here. Going back two years earlier, we find that Dr. Thain had taken over the "Hughes" drug treatment job from Dr. Crain. Apparently, Crain, seeing the writing on the wall, had gotten "cold feet." You will soon be reading Russ's take on the Dr. Crain, Holmes, and Dr. Thain, court cases wherein Dr. Thain had been awarded a $300,000 contract to provide "Hughes" with mega dosses of codeine phosphate from 1974 until April of 1976. And while we are about it, what were Drs. Chaffin and Thain and aide Holmes doing in those hours in between when "H.H." was visited by Dr. Montemayor Martinez and when they finally loaded him into his last plane ride?

Note: Exhibit 134 Findings: "Between August 1974 and April 1976 Dr. Thain ordered 5,500 dosage units of Codeine Phosphate," and between December 19, 1975 and "H.H.'s" death on April 5, 1976, an additional 2,000 dosage units were ordered. Now that's what one could call "*preparedness*." (It could have been more, but that is what they admitted to.) Could those boys have been looking forward to April 1976?

A FORENSIC LOOK INTO THE MOUTH OF "ACAPULCO HUGHES"

Review Exhibit-130-H, top of page for a more graphic description.
Review Exhibit 151 – 0002 - page 1 of 1, "Dental caries…severe…evidence of neglect."

Oscar Maldonado, D.D.S. investigated the mouth of the Methodist Hospital "H.H." corpse, because this is what a forensic dentist eventually does; but he may well have been in near disbelief after looking at the 1976 dental x-rays of this popular billionaire.

Many people go to Mexico for dental work in hopes of, and often finding, a better deal. It can safely be presumed that there were dentists in Acapulco in the 1970s that could have done quite a good job. So here we have a fellow who *supposedly* liked to get numb from codeine, because this is about all that codeine does (codeine does not pack the same thrill as morphine or heroin). So, what could possibly have been the problem of getting his teeth cleaned and fixed periodically? Obviously, the fellow could well afford dental care and *was not afraid of needles.*

This "H.H." must have concerned himself with his teeth at one time; he did have several gold fillings. Rotting teeth can be very painful unless, of course, his caretakers kept him constantly boosted with sundry painkillers. (According to Webster, caries means progressive destruction of gum tissues, bone, and severe tooth decay.) No dentists in Mexico? No way to fly "H.H." back to the states, incognito, for dental work? Of course, his teeth were rotting away in England, Canada, and the Bahamas, but it's safe to presume that they had dentists there as well? Self-imposed poor dental hygiene on behalf of "Acapulco Hughes?" Was he a prisoner? Even prisoners here in the United States get far better dental care then this fellow received.
Note: What is the first thing a dentist does prior to getting *any* dental work done? Well, of course, it is X-rays. So, the speculative question here is, "Were the Summa, Inc. pirates afraid of leaving behind a dental record which could be traced or compared with those of the real Howard Hughes?"

BLOOD:

There were tremendous difficulties in obtaining a history of blood type on Howard Hughes. The corpse autopsied at Methodist Hospital had blood type A. (See Exhibit-160, page 1 of 3.) Dr. Titus did not specify as to positive or negative, it was just A, which makes sense; they weren't going to give the corpse a transfusion. The most difficult, and often impossible information to obtain is that which resides in medical records. Medical records are closely guarded by the medical institutions wherein they reside. Fear of lawsuits drives the concern. The release of medical records can occur only when requested by the individual to whom they apply or, if subpoenaed, in a lawsuit. The information gathered, however, seems to indicate that the blood type of the real Hughes *was not* A.

a. Exhibit 171, Blood – Attachment page 1, B Negative (B-) is the most difficult of <u>all</u> blood types for which to find a donor. (Nine percent chance or 1 in 12; and donor must be B- or O-.)

b. Exhibit 172, Blood – Attachment page 2. "H.H." needed a blood transfusion in 1969 (Reason not stated.)

1. Sample of "H.H.'s" blood is sent to a Dr. Homer Clark in Salt Lake City, Utah.

2. <u>Dr. Clark performed laboratory tests on blood specimens *attributed* to "Hughes."</u>

3. "Hughes's" blood is matched and sent to Las Vegas, Nevada. (Exhibit 172)

4. 1971 "H.H." goes to the Bahamas. Dr. Clark is asked to become a permanent member of the "Hughes" medical staff. (Hence another doctor invited into a well-paid, do nothing job – he *never* goes down to Acapulco to see a sickly "Hughes," nor does he ever go to any of the other many locations where "Hughes" resided in the last years of his life.) Why was he asked into such a cushy, do nothing, job? Drs. Clark, Thain, and Chaffin were on expensive retainers, but were oh-so-difficult to find when "H.H." was rotting away in Mexico and needed them most. Could it be possible that Doctor Clark may have stumbled upon something when he was testing "blood types attributed to Hughes?" (Exhibit 172) clearly states that Clark "performed <u>a series</u> of laboratory tests on blood specimens <u>attributed</u> to Hughes." Therefore, he had legal authority to research historic medical situations (plane crashes, etc.) where the real Hughes needed transfusions. For Dr. Clark to be sure he was on the right track, it is obvious *he would not* use a single source. No doctor at that time or now would have wanted to take the slightest chance of killing one of the world's wealthiest industrialists by giving him the wrong blood type. This would have been – and would be now – "a quick end to a budding career." Persons with type A positive blood, have an 80 percent chance of quickly finding a donor or (four out of five) and a person having type A negative blood is a relatively easy match at 13 percent or (one out of eight) type A, positive or negative, can be readily found in any hospital blood bank – even in "primitive" 1969 Las Vegas, Nevada; and yet it was necessary to search Salt Lake City, Utah for a match?
Note: In all the Hughes literature searched, Dr. Homer Clark is never mentioned as having traveled to visit "Hughes" at anyplace, or at any time.

c. Exhibit 174:

1. Howard Hughes crashes his XF-11, prototype, plane into Beverly Hills, California.

2. Doctors Vern Mason and Laurence Chaffin cannot be immediately located.

3. Dr. Chaffin is first to be found and, upon being summoned to the Hospital, realizes that Hughes is going to need a blood transfusion. (Blood type not stated.)

4. Hughes's blood is tested and <u>only one sample of his type could be found</u>? This is the well populated Los Angeles area of California?

d. Exhibit 175 - Blood – Attachment page 5:

1. In this attachment, when the statement is made, "When Howard Hughes (the reclusive multimillionaire) died," they are referring to the year 1976, not knowing it was 1965.

2. Here the Judge, in a paternity lawsuit against the Hughes estate, orders blood tests to determine the validity of a mother's claim that Hughes had fathered her son. (The blood type of the mother was A and her son was type O.)

3. The court, having "subpoena" power <u>apparently</u> gets the Hughes blood type from the medical records of the XF-11 Beverly Hills, 1946 crash, which <u>establishes the blood type as B</u> (positive or negative not noted in article). (Exhibit 175)

4. Apparently records from Methodist Hospital, Houston, which indicate that the corpse of "H.H." had blood type A, *were not* accessed. Did the Lummis's stonewall the Judge's staff with a formality? Was Methodist Hospital in Houston in fear of giving out the "H.H." corpse's blood type because there might then be many Hughes paternity lawsuits instigated, wherein they could get legally involved? Did Annette Lummis prohibit any release of autopsy information because she knew the true blood type of Howard R. Hughes Jr. had been B negative, and the "Hughes" Methodist Hospital corpse had blood type A? She could have done this knowing she and son Will might be fraudulently exposed. Did the Judge's staff simply subpoena other *known* information on Hughes's blood rather than "take her on"? Could the Judge have been bribed and told to get Hughes's blood-type from the XF-11 crash? Oh yes, this has happened many times with personal relationships; please do not be naive. It should be remembered that Anette and Will Lummis did not even want the corpse flown up from Mexico, photographed, fingerprinted, or autopsied! But she *did* want the corpse to be immediately cremated. (Exhibit 130-D and 130-E) The Lummis

family was quite wealthy; Annett's son Will was a prodigious Houston attorney, and they were accustomed to getting things *their* way. Nevertheless:

5. Had the blood, subpoenaed by the Judge been type A (as indicated in the Methodist Hospital Houston autopsy of "H.H."), the mother may well have won her case.

6. <u>The mother loses the case.</u>

7. <u>Howard Hughes died intestate; he had no children.</u>

8. Indications are that the blood type of the *real* Howard Hughes had been type B negative. (See Exhibit 175, Blood Attachment.)

WHAT WAS HAPPINING IN MEXICO WITH "ACAPULCO HUGHES?"

Let's build a scenario of high probability. (a) Let us take into consideration the means of one of the world's wealthiest men. (b) Let us also consider what is now known about the "H.H." autopsy investigation, cursive writing, fingerprinting, etc. And (c) let us plug in the probability of the incredible evil, which avarice can produce, when vast amounts of ill-gotten power and wealth are to be had. (We mean <u>many</u> millions here, at a time when a silver dollar was worth the same as a paper dollar and a million bucks were truly *a million bucks!*) In the minds of criminals, or their accomplices, there need be but three conditions in play to commit a crime: Motive (money), Method (embezzlement), and Opportunity (<u>a manipulated imposter</u> who all, but few, believed to be the billionaire Howard Hughes.)

In the last few months of life for "Acapulco Hughes," it appears that the only care given to this 6-foot 2-inch, 87-pound miserable wretch of man, was little or no care at all. Now wouldn't, or shouldn't, Doctors Wilbur Thain and Lawrence Chaffin have wanted to keep those lucrative retainers coming in every month? What about caretakers John Holmes, Clarence Waldron, Eric Bundy, and Clyde Crow, wouldn't they have wanted to stay on that "H.H." lucrative payroll? Wouldn't all of them have wanted for the fellow, in their charge, to cling to life for as long as possible? Well, no, not if "the fix" was already in. John Holmes, for instance, was already promised a chair on the board of Summa, Inc., powerhouse of the Hughes empire. Johnnie knew what was going on and may have well covered his ass insulating himself from the whim, fancy, or repercussions of Bill Gay, Nadine Henley, and Chester Davis. They could not just kill him, so they invited him into the fold. Primarily Holmes had become the "darling boy" because of what he had done for the cause, what he knew, and what he was willing to do. Dr. Thain (brother in law to Bill Gay, Summa, Inc. C.E.O.) gets lucrative promises for all the same reasons. Dr. Chaffin, as well. What seems obvious is that the

"Hughes" aides and doctors listed above, couldn't have cared a "rats-ass" *less* for this miserable "H.H." (It appears that Gordon Margulis was out of the picture by this time.) All the others had been impatiently waiting, like spiders, to get on with their lucrative lifestyles. The "fix," with embezzled millions, had *been in* long ago; the only thing in their way was a *sick and miserable 6-foot-2-inch, 87-pound drug addict.* (Why law enforcement in those years, or soon after, did not suspect a hoax and follow the money-trail, remains a shameful mystery.)

Information was leaked many times by those few individuals in close contact with this "H.H." Often he was alluded to as being a cold-hearted dictator who constantly demanded and got what he wanted. If he wanted drugs, he got drugs; if he did not eat, none dared confront him with the necessity. Obvious also, he was unable to walk for three years, was let fall, or was dropped many times, and his caretakers did little to prevent this. Oh, those poor, beleaguered doctors and caretakers, who had to kowtow to this neurotic reclusive "H.H." *at every turn, whim, or fancy.* Most probably, that's not exactly what was going on down in Old Mexico and prior locations. By now, to be sure, most readers of this book have reached many of the same conclusions. When one thinks of the carelessness of the many "Hughes" caretakers and how numerous they were, one is a bit mystified as to how so many could be in on the plot. Well, let's look at it this way, how many generally honorable souls could be led down the dark path with the offer of a million or more dollars (one million in the seventies is worth ten million in today's inflated currency). One can be assured that half of that amount would be almost anyone's price! But even this was small change when one considers that *the original Hughes estate pirates set out to steal hundreds of millions of those 1965 to 1976 dollars.*

The whole scenario of a wealthy, iron-fisted and drug-addicted, despot, who had absolutely no concern for his health, and had absolute dictatorial control over his caretakers, is not supported by the evidence that has turned up! Go to Exhibits 179 D and E and view Gordon Margulis's take on what went down in Canada when he and Mell Stewart were a part of the caretaker team. Also, it was Romaine St. headquarters that instructed Mell Stewart, when the "Hughes" entourage vacated the Desert Inn in Las Vegas, to "gather all the glass bottles in the Desert Inn Penthouse, put them in a gunny sack, smash them with a hammer and bury them in the desert." (Exhibits 158 B and C) This decree was later rescinded, and Mell was then told to "put them into a box and bring them to Romaine Street headquarters, Los Angeles." It was the senior caretakers who ran the show and called the shots in Canada and offshore in other countries (Exhibits 179 D and E); *but* they got their marching-orders from Romaine Street headquarters in Los Angeles. One of those senior caretakers was John Holmes. That's right, John Holmes, the drug courier who was overseeing subordinate aide Beebe Myler when he dropped "H.H." in a London toilet and broke the man's hip, the same John Holmes who a supposed grateful "H.H." put on the Summa, Inc. Board of Directors, pending his demise" – *Summa, Inc. the powerhouse of the entire Hughes empire!*

It should be entered here that the good deed done by "Acapulco H.H." for John Holmes was quite exceptional. "Hughes" <u>supposedly</u> died intestate, leaving no golden parachutes for *any* of his Summa, Inc. employees; and yes, this was inclusive of the big "kahunas" Bill Gay, Nadine Henley, and Chester Davis. But Johnnie gets a lucrative position on the Summa, Inc. Board of Directors, supposedly at the behest of "Hughes"? Strange also is that a neglected Hughes would give *massive* salary and benefit *increases* to his top-echelon personnel and his numerous aides after 1965.

What becomes obvious is that this derelict "H.H." who all, but those few in the know, believed to be the real Hughes, should have been put into a decent hospital or facility years before his demise. Even after getting his hip broken in London (<u>he never walked again for the three years up until he died in April of 1976),</u> this "Hughes" was not to find a safe haven, and "*Why not?*," you may ask. This was supposedly the billionaire Howard Hughes. It certainly seems reasonable that if seclusion and anonymity were desired in a decent stateside facility, it could have been arranged and purchased at what would be considered a reasonable price by this wealthy industrialist. It's not that he couldn't have afforded better care—he was the wealthiest man in America, <u>and</u> he even *owned* a Hospital in Florida!

WHO WAS CARING FOR THE 2ND WEALTHIEST MAN IN THE WORLD?

Let's start off this piece with a question: How strange was it that this "H.H." had many caretakers on duty when he became severely ill, totally incapacitated, and near death, and none of them seemed concerned that their employer was dying of neglect? Many "Hughes" caretakers were there but were they just hanging out? Okay, Chuck Waldron and one-time soap salesman John Holmes, were on the job; but what was everybody else doing? How much care was needed for a starving, bedridden, dehydrated, drug-addict, who was seldom turned to prevent bed sores? (Maids *never* came in to clean the Acapulco Princess Penthouse. Living conditions there must had to have been squalid, much like they had been at the Desert Inn, Las Vegas.) Apparently, it was no big deal that this "H.H.," who was under Holmes' care, had been dropped on numerous occasions? And then there was the incompetent Dr. Chaffin who, when showing up late on the scene at the "H.H." suite of the Acapulco Princess Hotel, had no clue of what to do for his half-dead patient? Dr. Chaffin calls in Doctor Montemayor Martinez for some advice? Of course, the advice was given in absolute dismay: "*Get this man into a stateside hospital immediately!*" But apparently this suggestion was not taken in earnest because Chaffin, perhaps now in fear, had one of the aides contact Dr. Thain who was at a party in the Bahamas. (Exhibit 179-A) Thain was having such a good time at his party that he didn't leave right away but, it seems obvious, he must have assured Dr. Chaffin that he would be there "after the party" and not to worry about his 6 foot 2 inch, 87 pound comatose charge. When Thain eventually arrived many hours later, he immediately entered the <u>file</u> room, of the "H.H." Acapulco Princess Hotel suite and began shredding documents.* When satisfied with the *shredding*, he entered the room where the comatose "H.H." lay and administered several injections (or more?) which he maintained would "take a while to work."

Apparently, the injections worked well (depending on how you looked at it) and there were many other injections that came either before the plane left the tarmac in Mexico or in route. (See ecchymosis above in autopsy report.) In any event, "Acapulco H.H." arrived *dead* in Houston, Texas, with numerous needle wounds in his forearms. Large doses of codeine had to have been injected intravenously** as well. *The "H.H" corpse was awash in the stuff*. Doctors Thain and Chaffin and aide Holmes probably had to finish up the job in the air, because they had to get themselves and "Hughes" out-of-town quickly. Dr. Montemayor Martinez was stirring up a fuss with the Acapulco press and it would not have been long before the Acapulco police would get curious about the happenings at the Acapulco Princess Hotel – which they did. (Exhibits 130-E, bottom, and 130-F, top) Dr. Thain made a big deal about "H.H" having *died over Brownsville, Texas*. (Exhibit 130-C) He, and nefarious others, *knew* that if it became common knowledge that the fellow died on the ground in – or over – Mexico, then Mexico would have taken precedent with the autopsy and investigations; and a substantial award would have been *more* than expected. Evidence gathered in Mexico would have undoubtedly been a disaster for the entire "H.H." "care" team They would have lost control. The Summa, Inc. team of Gay, Henley, and Davis would probably have had to begin packing for their island hideaways in the Caymans.

*Exhibit 179-C: While Dr. Thain was busily shredding documents instead of giving immediate care to his dying patient, Doctor Montemayor Martinez was thinking about press reports because of his visit to the "H.H." suite in the Acapulco Princess. Therefore, the number one imperative for Drs. Thain and Chaffin and aide Holmes were to get this half, or completely dead, "H.H." off the ground in Mexico and on his way to Houston. (The plane's pilot only learned of his high-profile passenger's death when the plane landed in Houston. (See Exhibit 130-B), fourth paragraph down, "Perhaps the most stunned ...."

**Could it be possible that aide John Holmes, without ready knowledge of intravenous injections, had started the forearm injections early on when "H.H." lost consciousness? It then could have been presumed later that this "H.H." had dosed *himself* up. However, this could have been naivety on behalf of Holmes in a ploy to make it look like this "H.H." had done himself in. Upon Dr. Chaffin, and later Thain, entering the picture, the overdose procedure certainly would have become more sophisticated. (In the autopsy, Dr. Titus's original statement regarding his analysis of the volume of codeine in the "H.H." corpse was that "the amount was in keeping with therapeutic dosages." However, it was eventually discovered that Dr. Titus had been off by a margin of 1,000! This was revealed two years later at Dr. Thain's Trial.) Go to Exhibit 127-B, starting with "on October 27, 1976 ..."

So now the case has been made, and it is considerably more than astute speculation when we ask, "Who was that corpse flown up from Mexico in 1976?" It seems quite evident that over the years, <u>this</u> "H.H." eventually became addicted to and controlled by drugs and fear, later to become sickly and crippled in a surreal world unable to escape his tormentors. No longer a man of his own volition, he existed only to further the ambitions of those who would profit handsomely from this momentous charade. When it became apparent that he needed care in a controlled facility, the cat was about to escape the bag. The ruse would have eventually become apparent. Therefore, what was to be done? What would any embezzling group of common cold-hearted, maggot-minded criminals have done?

EXHIBIT 176
A VERY DISTURBED MEXICAN DOCTOR SEES WHAT HAS BEEN HAPPINING TO ONE OF THE WORLD'S WEALTHIEST MEN - HE CALLED IT LIKE HE SAW IT.

Mexican doctor saw no hope for Hughes

By KERNAN TURNER

ACAPULCO, Mexico (AP) — On the day he died, Howard Hughes weighed only about 80 pounds, his hair and beard were long and stringy, and his body was pitted with bedsores, a Mexican doctor who attended him reports.

Hughes was unconscious, dehydrated, had a head infection and was suffering from kidney failure, Dr. Victor Manuel Montemayor Martinez said in a signed declaration given to the Mexican attorney general's office.

The doctor said that after examining Hughes he did not expect the billionaire to live more than a few hours.

Hughes was taken from his penthouse at the Acapulco Princess Hotel and flown by private plane to Houston on April 5. He was dead when the plane landed.

Federal Judge Antonio Uribe Garcia made Montemayor's statement available to newsmen Tuesday along with those from others questioned during a police investigation into Hughes' death.

Montemayor's declaration said:

He was called to the 20th-floor penthouse about 5 a.m. April 5 and found Hughes "half naked with only bedsheets covering his body, ... very pale, with his right eye open, the left not so much but about half open, breathing in pants, slowly, in a state of complete unconsciousness."

His eyes showed little reaction to light, and his neck and face twitched.

Hughes' hair was long, thin and gray, his beard stringy and dark chestnut in color. There were numerous bedsores on the body.

Aides said an open sore on the left side of Hughes' head was the result of a benign tumor that had been aggravated by a blow received in a fall. One of Hughes' aides told the court Hughes suffered the fall in The Bahamas before he came to Acapulco Feb. 10.

Montemayor said Eric Iverson Bundy of Hughes' staff appeared to be in charge and that there were also two American doctors and a bodyguard in the room. When the Mexican expressed surprise that Hughes had been kept in the hotel in such condition, they told him Hughes was hard to deal with and did not want to go to a hospital.

An ambulance arrived about 8:15 a.m., the doctor said, and the driver reported they left for the airport at 10:30 a.m. The driver, C. Jaime Quevedo, said he saw his passenger's head as he was lifted into the plane and he was "unconscious, not moving." He added that he was "not able to say whether the person they were transferring was alive or dead."

Bundy, 71, said in a statement filed with the court that he had worked for Hughes for 34 years, the last eight as his private secretary. He said he called Dr. Montemayor when he realized Hughes was gravely ill and that Hughes was breathing when he was put in the ambulance.

Another private secretary who was present, C.A. Waldron of Sun Valley, Calif., said in his statement that the decision to take Hughes to Houston was made by Dr. Wilbur Thain, 50, of Logan, Utah, one of the two American doctors present.

Dr. Thain accompanied Hughes on the flight. Waldron said that before the departure none of the doctors "checked to see if the patient had died or was still in a deep coma."

Waldron was cleared Tuesday of a charge that he had forged Hughes' signature on the recluse's tourist card when he arrived from The Bahamas. Judge Uribe Garcia ruled there was no evidence to sustain the charge.

The Courier-News   Wednesday, April 14, 1976   C-1

news

EXHIBIT 177
MORE EVIDENCE OF FORGED DOCUMENTS.
HAS THE FORGER OF ALL THOSE QUESTIONABLE EXEMPLARS,
IN THE POSSESSION OF ROSEMONT, INC., BEEN FOUND

The New York Times   https://nyti.ms/1Pub2aG

ARCHIVES 1976

Aide Is Released

SPECIAL TO THE NEW YORK TIMES APRIL 14, 1976

MEXICO CITY, APRIL 13 — A Mexican Federal Judge unexpectedly dropped today all charges against an aide to the late Howard R. Hughes who had been arrested and accused of falsifying the – billionaire's signature In Acapulco two months ago.

The aide, Clarence Albert Waldron, a 41-year-old executive of Mr. Hughes's Summa Corporation, recovered $400 that had been posted as bond last night and immediately left Acapulco for Los Angeles.

After studying the charges and evidence for almost 72 hours, Federal Judge Antonio Uribe Garcia concluded on the basis of a technicality that there were insufficient "elements" to prove that Mr. Waldon had forged the signature on Mr. Hughes' tourist card when the latter entered Mexico Feb. 11.

Mr. Waldron was one of three aides who stayed behind in Acapulco after Hughes was rushed to Houston on April 5 in a vain attempt to save his life.

The three aides were detained in the Acapulco Princess Hotel, Mr. Hughes' home during his final eight weeks. After an extensive interrogation by the Federal police, Mr. Waldron was charged Saturday with falsification of immigration documents. The two other aides, Eric Bundy and Clyde Crow, were released.

Over the weekend, Mr. Waldron was held in Acapulco's municipal jail pending court appearance yesterday at which time he was freed on bail.

EXHIBIT 178-A

𝕿𝖍𝖊 𝕹𝖊𝖜 𝖄𝖔𝖗𝖐 𝕿𝖎𝖒𝖊𝖘   https://nyti.ms/1HjKMyl

ARCHIVES | 1976

DOCTOR RECOUNTS HUGHES'S LAST DAY

SPECIAL TO THE NEW YORK TIMES   APRIL 14, 1976

ACAPULCO, Mexico, April 13 (AP) — A Mexican doctor who visited Howard R. Hughes shortly before he died last week described the billionaire recluse as unconscious, dehydrated, al. flicted with a head infection and suffering kidney failure.

The description of Mr. Hughes's condition was contained in a signed declaration taken from Dr. Victor 'Manuel Montemayor Martinez by the Mexican Attorney General's of fice and made available to newsmen today.

Federal Judge Antonio Uribe Garcia made Dr. Montemayor's declaration available, along with statements taken from other witnesses questioned by the police.

The doctor's declaration included these observations:

He was called to the 20thfloor penthouse of the Acapulco Princess Hotel at about 5 A.M. April 5 and found Mr. Hughes "half naked with only bedsheets covering his body," which had many bedsores.

The patient had thin, long gray hair and a stringy, chestnut-colored beard that also was long. He weighed only about 80 pounds.

Mr. Hughes was "very pale, with his right eye open, the left not so much but about half open, breathing in pants, slowly, in a state of complete -unconsciousness." His eyes showed little reaction to light and his neck and face were twitching.

There was an open sore on the left side of his head, which Hughes aides was the result of a benign tumor that had been aggravated by a blow received in a fall.

A court declaration by one of his aides yesterday said Mr. Hughes suffered the fall in the Bahamas before flying to Acapulco Feb. 10.

EXHIBIT 178-B

Dr. Montemayor said he was met at the hotel by Eric Iveison Bundy, a Hughes aide who appeared to be in charge, and there were two American doctors and a bodyguard also in the room.

Dr. Montemayor examined Mr. Hughes for two hours and suggested that intravenous liquids be administered because the patient appeared to be dehydrated and suffering kidney failure.

When he said it was strange that Mr. Hughes should be kept in a hotel in such condition, the aides told him Mr. Hughes was hard to deal with and did not want to be in a hospital

An ambulance arrived to take Mr. Hugh-es to his plane at the Acapulco airport at about 8:15 A.M., the doctor said.

Party Identified

Court documents, including copies of tourist visas, identified those who accompanied Mr. Hughes to Houston in a Lear jet as Lawrence Chaffin, 83 years old, of 132 N. Hudson Ave. (no city given); John Mor-1 rison Holmes, 60, of Los An-j geles, and Dr. Wilbur Sutton Thain, 50, of 1856 N. 1200 East, Logan, Utah.

Mr. Hughes's address on his tourist card was Box 2438,1 Bahamas.

Those aboard the plane said that Mr. Hughes died at 1:27 P.M. that day while the jet was over south Texas.

A federal police report filed with the court said Dr. Montemayor was "the only person outside the [Hughes] group who saw the invalid."

In the court statement made by Mr. Bundy, 71, he said he had worked for Mr. Hughes for 34 years, the last eight as private secretary. It said he had called Dr. Montemayor when he realized Mr. Hughes was gravely ill.

Mr. Bundy's statement declared that Mr. Hughes was breathing when he entered the ambulance on a stretcher "covered with a white sheet."

C. Jaime Quevedo, the ambulance driver, signed a statement saying he and another ambulance attendant waited at the hotel employees' entrance from about 8:30 A.M. to 10:30 A.M. April 5 before rushing a man to a private plane.

It said Mr. Quevedo saw the man's head as he was lifted into the plane at the airport and the patient was "unconscious, not moving." It added that Mr. Quevedo was "not able to say whether the person they were transferring was alive or dead."

Another declaration included in the court papers was signed by Clarence Albert Waldron, Hughes employee since 1956 and private secretary since 1966.

EXHIBIT 178-C

Mr. Waldron, who was detained last Thursday by the police, was cleared by the court today of a charge that ha had forged Mr. Hughes's signature on a tourist visa. Mr. Waldron had been released yesterday, and Judge Uribe Garcia ruled later there was not evidence to sustain the charge.

A reporter asked Mr. Waldron where he was going and he replied, "back to God's country."

Mr. Waldron's signed statement to the federal police said Dr. Thain had decided to trans. ter Mr. Hughes to Houston. It said that before Mr. Hughes's departure no doctors "checked to see if the patient had died or was still inn deep coma.""

EXHIBIT 179-A
EMPIRE PROLOUGE XXII

a little milk, but that was all. Dr. Norman Crane, one of two personal physicians then on duty in the penthouse, went in to see him a few times, but other than recommending that Hughes should eat and drink more, there was no treatment. Growing steadily weaker, Hughes spent his days sleeping or lingering in a semiconscious state. In his rare wakeful moments, he was confused, disoriented, and often incoherent.

Jack Real, a Hughes executive and one of Hughes's oldest associates, later said that he put in a telephone call to Logan, Utah, for Dr. Wilbur Thain, the physician who had overall responsibility for Hughes's medical care. As Real recalled the conversation:

"I don't want to play doctor, Wilbur, but your patient is dying," Real said.

"Well, goddamn it, you are playing doctor and mind your own business," Dr. Thain said.

"Wilbur, you need to get here," Real repeated.

"I've got a party in the Bahamas and I'll come over after that," Dr. Thain said.[9]

Hughes's decline was making all of them uneasy. They had wondered for years what would happen when he sank to this stage. Putting him in a hospital was not an appealing option, but in the past they had at least been close to good hospitals. Now they were hundreds of miles from one, and without an airplane. The organization had airplanes all over the world, yet none had been sent to Mexico. But whatever was done with the old man would not be decided by the men in the penthouse. They knew this was a decision for Los Angeles.

When Francom came on to relieve John Holmes at 4 P.M. Saturday afternoon, April 3, 1976, Hughes was delirious. He spoke very slowly, each word a struggle, and put together the words only made gibberish. Hughes was trying to tell Francom something, but he could not make out what it was. Something about an insurance policy.[10] Hughes kept repeating, "insurance policy, insurance policy." Francom's inability to understand frustrated the old man, and he called Holmes back into the bedroom. Then, as both stood next to the bed, Hughes launched into the same disjointed monologue, saying over and over something about an insurance policy. Holmes also failed to understand; he and Francom stared uncomprehendingly at each other as the old man mumbled on.

The doctors drew a blood sample from him that afternoon. They usu-

EXHIBIT 179-B
EMPIRE PROLOGUE XXIV

shift, Francom told him that the old man was worse. During his shift, Francom had anxiously summoned another of Hughes's personal physicians, Dr. Lawrence Chaffin, to the bedroom. Waldron looked in. Hughes was propped up in bed unconscious, his face and neck twitching uncontrollably. Dr. Chaffin sat at his bedside. Sometime after midnight Chaffin came out of the bedroom and asked Francom and Waldron to summon Dr. Thain to Acapulco at once.[16] There was another flurry of telephone calls to Los Angeles. Thain was tracked down by phone an hour later. A small, private air ambulance had been hired from a Fort Lauderdale company. The plane would pick up Thain in a few hours and bring him to Mexico.

At dawn on Monday, April 5, Thain had not yet arrived, so Chaffin put in a hurried call to an Acapulco doctor, asking him to come to the Princess Hotel to examine a patient who was very ill.[17] Dr. Victor Manuel Montemayor responded quickly, and by 5:45 A.M. he had ascended in the service elevator of the Princess to the penthouse and made his way first into Room 2008, then Room 2010, and finally Room 2012, the bedroom.

The man lying in the hospital bed appeared to be suffering from a seizure. When Dr. Montemayor pulled back the sheet to begin his examination, he was appalled at the body underneath, a long skeleton clad in wrinkled, wasted flesh. The sick man was tall, over six feet, but he weighed less than a hundred pounds. A tumor gaped open on the left side of his scalp. His forearms were splotchy with black, blue, and yellow marks. His left shoulder was bruised and swollen. Bedsores covered his back. Needle tracks ran up and down both arms and thighs. What Dr. Montemayor could not see was that enough codeine circulated inside the body to kill an ordinary man.

As he took the man's blood pressure, felt his pulse, and listened to his heart, Dr. Montemayor could not understand why this patient was not in a hospital. Money could not be the reason. This was the most expensive suite in the most expensive hotel in Acapulco, yet this man was starving, dying of neglect like a beggar. The seizure, Montemayor soon diagnosed, was caused in part by the failure of the brain to receive enough blood—a condition made worse because the patient's head was raised. After making his tests, Dr. Montemayor concluded that the man was suffering from severe dehydration and should be given oxygen and intravenous fluids immediately.[18]

Dr. Montemayor looked up from the bed and asked the two doctors why the man was not in a hospital. They answered that he was a very

EXHIBIT 179-C
EMPIRE PROLOGUE XXV

difficult patient who did not like hospitals. Looking down at the helpless, unconscious wreck before him, Dr. Montemayor was puzzled by the explanation.

"This man should be in a good hospital," Montemayor told Chaffin. "As a friend, I'm telling you, don't stay here in Mexico to find a hospital. Take him back to the States."[19] Packing his bag to leave, Montemayor took one last look at the old man on the bed, concluding that although seriously ill, the man need not die if he were taken immediately to a hospital and given proper care.[20]

In the office next to the bedroom, word came in—Los Angeles had decided. Hughes was to be taken to a hospital. Several locations had been considered: Salt Lake City, Miami, the Bahamas, even London. In the end, they had settled on Houston. The plane bringing Dr. Thain to Mexico was to carry Hughes back to the city of his birth, and the city he had avoided since the deaths of his parents fifty years before. One of the men in the office telephoned the Manzanaris Funeral Parlor in Acapulco and ordered an ambulance.

It was after 7 A.M. that Monday morning before Dr. Thain finally arrived. Instead of going immediately to see Hughes, Real said Dr. Thain moved into the office next to the bedroom and began rummaging through the filing cabinets, pulling out papers that had flowed between Acapulco and Los Angeles, feeding them into a shredder.[21] To Jack Real, it seemed that Thain spent two hours destroying documents before he went in to examine Hughes.[22] Then he wrote a prescription and asked one of the men to have it filled. When the medicine arrived a few minutes later, Thain used it to give Hughes several injections.[23] As he was giving him the shots, he mentioned to the others in the bedroom that sometimes it took a while for the medicine to produce a reaction. As the minutes ticked by, Hughes showed no change. He lay in a trancelike state, oblivious to everything around him, breathing with great difficulty.

At 10:30, the men began preparing to take him to the plane. The hotel security chief was alerted to make the service elevator available and to clear the ground floor near the elevator doors of onlookers. An aide left for the airport to make sure the airplane was in the proper location and ready. Another went in search of carts sturdy enough to handle the oxygen tanks and other medical equipment.

At 11 A.M. they lifted Hughes out of bed, placed him on a stretcher, and carried him down the hall to the elevator, which took them straight to the lobby. The doors opened and they quickly carried him through a

EXHIBIT 179-D

Excerpt taken from James Phelan's Book: *Howard Hughes: The Hidden Years.*

The jet landed at Vancouver in the early daylight hours, in a heavy rain. This time the advance work had been done properly. Canadian officials were waiting to check the party into the country without intruding upon its principal. "We had nothing to ask," said one official stiffly. "We were aware of his identity, and of the fact that he and his colleagues were self-supporting and not likely to become charges of the welfare services."

Hughes was transferred from the plane to a waiting car in a wheelchair and driven to a rear entrance of the Bayshore Inn, overlooking the Vancouver harbor.

"In spite of the miserable weather, the boss was in an upbeat mood," said Margulis. "When we got to the hotel, I started to get the wheelchair out of the car trunk.

"He said, 'Don't bother. I'm going to walk in.'

"With Francom on one side of him and me on the other, he just *walked* into the hotel like anybody else. Took his time, too.

"In the foyer there was a middle-aged lady, and over at one side a fellow cleaning the windows," Margulis said. "Normally that would have thrown him into a panic, but he just stopped and looked around."

"This is pretty nice," Hughes said.

One of the aides told Margulis, "Get the wheelchair and get him moving."

"I told him to ease off and let the boss look around a little bit."

When they took Hughes up the elevator to the suite they had picked out for him, Hughes went over to the window and looked out, instead of scuttling into his bedroom.

"The aides had picked the big middle room for The Office," Margulis said. "The boss gazed out the window awhile and watched a seaplane landing in the harbor. He said he liked the view.

"The aides didn't like that one bit," said Margulis. "They told me to get him away from the window and into his bedroom.

"Then something happened that really frosted me. The boss said he liked the big room and the view and said it would make a nice sitting room for him. He hadn't had a sitting room for years, and he'd always had the windows taped and never looked out.

EXHIBIT 179-E

Excerpt taken From James Phelan's Book: *Howard Hughes: The Hidden Years.*

"They warned him that somebody could fly past the sitting room in a helicopter and shoot his picture with a telephoto lens. 'Here's *your* room,' they told him, and took him into another little blacked-out bedroom, with the draperies all taped down tight. He just went along with them, and they had him back in his cave again. After a while he got into bed, and called for a movie, and everything was just the way it had been for years."

But to the outside world, the fiction was cultivated that Hughes was moving out of isolation. In April, Eckersley told a Vancouver reporter that Hughes would shortly be releasing the contemporary photographs he had promised. A Hughes publicist said that the picture-taking project was moving ahead, that three photographers were under consideration for the historic portrait, and that one fine day soon the public would be shown a photograph of the invisible man.

A year later there were still no pictures. No official photograph of Hughes was ever released.

Among those curious about what Hughes looked like were some people high in the inner circle. They included Kay Glenn, the operative executive for the entourage.

In 1971 *Look* magazine ran an article about Hughes and put an artist's concept of the billionaire on its cover. It showed him with long hair down his back like a hippie.

Kay Glenn bought a copy of *Look,* and later questioned Margulis.

"That sketch of Hughes," he said. "Is that how he looks?" It was a tribute to the efficiency of the Secrecy Machine that even its overseer didn't know what the billionaire looked like.

Margulis says that the sketch was a remarkably accurate portrait. "But I didn't think it was any of Kay Glenn's business, so I told him hell, no. That turned out to be a good answer. When the boss got barbered in Nicaragua, he *didn't* look like the *Look* sketch."

Glenn finally got a look at his employer in Vancouver.

"Glenn was waiting at the hotel when we arrived," Margulis said. "He'd done some of the advance work there. When we came in from the airport, he was at the door when we brought the boss in.

DR. VICTOR MOTEMAYOR MARTINEZ AND CHUCK WALDRON EXHIBITS AND THEIR IMPLICATIONS

NUGGETS OF KNOWLEDGE (ABOUT MEXICO) WORTHY OF REMEMBRANCE

It was about the turn of the century, 1997 or 1998, in Las Vegas, Nevada, and Charles had been called for jury duty on a real-estate issue. Charles was working "graveyard shift" driving a Taxi. He was two years into this very tough and tiresome 12-hour nightly job, and the last thing on his wish list was to be involved in a court case. It was a *first* for Charles – to be called for jury duty. But he would go, take the cut in pay, and do his patriotic chore. He might even learn something from the process, which he did. There were many vacancies and when the names of persons summoned for jury duty were called, they observed a measure of despondency in the attending judge. Charlie remembered the well-spoken tutorial given. The judge reached into his pocket and removed his wallet, laid it on the podium before him, and began his dissertation, "I am always disappointed in the number of jury summons which go un-answered when we need citizens on a jury to fulfill their obligation to their fellow Americans. My family and myself immigrated here from Mexico when I was very young. My father, a good and honorable man, explained to me early on that the reasons America had grown so strong and offered so much to its citizens was because of its Constitution and Bill of Rights, which are supported by a fair and reasonable Judicial System. Those of you summoned and willing to participate in our Justice System, are fine and upstanding persons. But the laws which govern America could be so much fairer if more of its citizens would be willing to participate in its well-founded and honorable constitutional judicial institutions." The judge then picked up his wallet, which lay before him on the podium, and held it up for all to see. This is what he said. "The one statement of my father which inspired me to first become an attorney and later a judge, was simply this. *'Son, the only Bills of Rights one will find in Mexico, and most other Countries, are the bills he has in his wallet.'"*

Dovetailing into the above tutorial, Charles remembered a more personal episode concerning Mexico, which happened to his brother Ronald. Their military family lived in San Diego, California. When Ron was only 12 years old, he decided one day to "get away from it all" and take a solo trip into Old Mexico. He was no stranger to Mexico, since his father had taken both him and Charles "south of the border: on several fishing trips. Waiting for a young boy's father to return from overseas seems like an eternity for a "military brat," so why wait? Ron got up early one morning during summer vacation and rolled up a blanket with his single shot .22 rifle and a box of ammo in the middle, perhaps with rabbits in mind. He also took along a handline, hooks, and sinkers for fishing, if he could find some suitable rocks along the Mexican shoreline. After making himself several peanut butter sandwiches, Ron headed out the door. Walking to the nearby highway, he began hitching his way toward Mexico. Ron got to Mexico, but instantly wished he hadn't. He was arrested by Mexican police for smuggling weaponry and ammunition into the country. Instead of sending Ron back home, he was tossed into a small cell of the Tijuana jail with drunks and hard-core hombres that were despondent, sick, and belligerent. Ron was totally miserable among the smell and squalor of that dreadful cage, but what could he do? After several awful days, the police allowed him to make a phone call home to his obviously distraught mother. To get her son out of jail would cost his mother $200.00 cash, back in a time when this was more than a reasonable month's pay. The boy's rifle, ammo, and blanket were confiscated as well. Ron had vomited a lot and hadn't eaten anything for nearly three days. He was a thin boy to begin with but lost 15 pounds during his ordeal. Ron was sick with dysentery for several weeks thereafter as well. The lessons to be learned here are: *If* an infraction of Mexican law can be construed as a major violation, it will be; Mexico is *never* forgiving. If you haven't the immediate satisfactory finances available to buy your way out, the Mexican police and its judicial system will definitely have suggestions on how to get the financial help *they* require from your relatives, friends, or both and, most generally, it will be whatever *the federales* feel the market will bear.

If there should be any, having read this dissertations, believe that this couldn't possibly be the case with our friends south of the border, the cold, hard, truth would be revealed were you to go down there and check it out. You might even make an obscene gesture to a most modest officer of Mexican law just to see what will happen. You may rest assured that after a few days in one of *their* jails, on a diet of tortillas and beans, you will be most willing to comply with their desires. You may also be assured that your compliance *will not be cheap!*

Keeping the above two incidents in mind, let's investigate the activities of one Clarence "Chuck" Waldron, a senior aide in the "Hughes" entourage, arrested by the Mexican police and jailed for forging "Howard Hughes's" signature on a tourist visa.

Things began to come apart when a Mexican doctor (Dr. Victor Montemayor Martinez) is called in to view an incredibly sick, 6-foot-2-inch, bag of skin and bones. He is absolutely amazed at what he finds and is perhaps mystified as to why he has been called in—as there is already one doctor from the United States present and one soon to arrive from his party in the Bahamas. The comatose man he finds is, supposedly, none other than the famous reclusive billionaire Howard Hughes! The full extent of what he finds after a two-hour examination becomes clear in Exhibit 178 A. His reaction to what he finds seems to be beyond the comprehension of the two "Hughes" personal doctors, Thain and Chaffin, who appear relatively unconcerned and unknowledgeable. Dr. Montemayor points out the signs of the man's renal failure and dehydration (among the many other things wrong with the picture) and suggests an immediate intravenous drip-feed. He also strongly suggests that they get the man to a stateside hospital, as quickly as possible, because he believes the man can still be saved. (One cannot help but wonder where Doctors Thain and Chaffin went to school? However, their pretended ignorance now seems to have served a sinister objective.)

As is evident in Exhibit 178 B, Dr. Montemayor is still on the premises of the

Acapulco Princess Hotel as he knows that "about 8:15 AM an ambulance arrives to take Hughes to his plane at an airport nearby." However, the ambulance must wait until 10:30 a.m. before rushing the man to his private plane. What do you suppose Thain, Chaffin, and Holmes could have been doing during that two-hour and fifteen-minute window? At first, Dr. Montemayor is probably thinking that the "Hughes" entourage was arranging a flight plan and talking to customs, but then has second thoughts when no custom agents show up at the Princess Hotel. Mystified, Dr. Montemayor decides to go to the Acapulco police, the local newspaper, or both. But it is too late. "Hughes," Chaffin, Thain, and Holmes are now in-flight and on their way to Houston. But aides Clarence Waldron, Clyde Crow, and Eric Bundy do not get out fast enough and are detained by the Mexican police.

Clyde Crow and Eric Bundy could probably have been declared suspects "guilty through association" according to Mexican law but are released, never having to post bail. However, this is not the case with Clarence Waldron; the police eventually throw him into lock-up. The Mexican Federal Police have done their research and *yes*, they did have a cursive writing analyst, most probably quite good at it, in Mexico City. The determination was made that the "Howard Hughes" signature had been *forged* on his visa document. The cursive analysts had legitimate, original, inked signatures of Howard Hughes in their databanks. Howard Hughes had visited Mexico many times in the past for business reasons or rest and relaxation and had signed tourist visas and other documents on those occasions. They also had a current, freshly inked signature of Clarence Waldron from *his* tourist visa; pen lifts and other traits which matched up with the supposed "Hughes" signature on both his and "Hughes's" visa.

Let's break from the above scenario and take a hard look at Chuck and when he first became one of the Summa, Inc. "Darling Boys." At the time, his claim was that "he had been brought on board Summa, Inc. by Howard Hughes himself." According to Waldron, the information, regarding his employment came to him via senior aide John Holmes. (Remember Holmes, the drug-courier?) Information below is taken from his book *The Mysterious Howard Hughes Revealed*. Oh yes, Chuckie wrote a book, although it might have been better for his legacy if he had not.

Early on, *but after 1965*, Waldron's first major job for Summa, Inc. was to take a trip to the Bahamas. This would be arranged with Jack Hooper, a close associate of Robert Maheu. (We also know Robert Maheu and his close *mob* connections with "hit man" Johnnie Rosselli and the "money laundering" Sam Giancana.) Maheu was the tail wagging the Summa, Inc. dog at the time. (An interesting note here is that it's now 1967 and "Howard Hughes" has supposedly been squirreled away in dark rooms with his aides for a year or so, supposedly using various cursive documents with which to direct his companies.) Do you see this as unusual for the world's second wealthiest man? Hughes had stayed out of sight from 1957 to 1965 and communicated with the heads of his various companies via telephone and facsimile. All was financially well with the Hughes Industries *until after* 1965, when his companies – suddenly and unexpectedly – began to lose millions on practically a daily basis. Okay, having said that, let's get back on point.

A fellow named Lee Murrin, "Hughes's personal secretary," cuts a check in the amount of $180,000, (which had the buying power of $1,620,000 in today's inflated currency). The check is then given to "Darling Boy" Chuck Waldron with the instructions to take it to the bank and convert it to cash. (This is in September and October of 1967.) Was the check made out to cash or Chuck Waldron? (That is a mystery. Chuckie does not say in his book.) In any event, Chuck walks out of the bank with $180,000.00 in Benjamins –and not even one bodyguard accompanies him. (Exhibit 182 below.) Waldron then heads for Nassau, in the Bahamas, to pay for suites leased by Hughes in 1957. So here we have that crazy, reclusive, drug-addict "Hughes" now thinking it's time to pay the bill on some resort rooms leased, but left unoccupied since 1957? That seems unusual. Hughes was *never* known to be a "spendthrift" sort of fellow. On the contrary, he was thought to be quite frugal for many years before 1965. So, let's extrapolate it out: 10 years x 12 months = 120 months at approximately 30 days each month = 3,600 days x $50 dollars a day = $180,000.00. The extrapolation has indicated that Hughes was willing to pay $50.00 a day for one large suite, or two smaller suites at $25.00 a day, for ten years and never use the suites? Wow, that guy was *really crazy*; a simple phone call to the hotel a few weeks into 1957 would have saved a lot of cash. That was big money in the 1950s and 60s to be needlessly paying out for hotel suites from 1957 to 1967 – and never used? It's not like Hughes couldn't have had one of his secretaries to call the Emerald Beach Hotel *anytime* and, with a little extra "grease," gotten any suite he wanted at just about any time of the year? But then maybe Waldron's story is not exactly what was happening in 1967.

If one believes that just because Howard Hughes was wealthy that he was a spendthrift who didn't concern himself with a measly $180,000.00 in unused hotel suites, return to Exhibit 129-B and read the bottom caption. Therein Hughes not only figures into his lawsuit against Hamilton-Standard the stipend he has awarded Sargent William Durkin (the Marine who pulled him from the XF-11 crash) but has also entered the airfare costs of flying Durkin's parents from Pittsburg to Los Angeles. *When Howard Hughes was alive, he always knew where his money was going!*

Charlie, the fellow who knew Howard Hughes in 1964, had actually stayed at the Emerald Beach Hotel in Nassau in 1964, and does not recollect any part of Howard's conversation that pertained to the Emerald Beach Hotel. He probably would have remembered, had Howard ever mentioned it. In their conversations together, Howard must have known that Charlie had arrived in Mexico after leaving Nassau several months earlier. But, nevertheless, let's get back on track.

Chuck Waldron boards his plane at Los Angeles International Airport (L.A.X.) without declaring the $180,000.00 in cash, even though the Federal requirement in those years was to *declare all cash $10,000.00 and above* that was being taken out of the country. He arrives in Nassau, slips past their customs as well, and takes a cab to the hotel to pay 10 years' worth of unoccupied, but well dusted, hotel rooms. Did Chuck get a receipt for his transaction for "Hughes" when he paid the bill? Would the Internal Revenue Service have believed it if he had; after all he slipped out of the country with

$170,000.00 above the legal transport limit? And why didn't Lee Murrin just cut a check, payable to the Emerald Beach Hotel? After all, according to Waldron himself, Bob Case, the Assistant Hotel Manager had asked Waldron "How are you going to pay for it, by check?" (Exhibit 182) That would have been so much safer; if the check had been lost, it could not have been cashed without approval. But to lose $180,000.00 cash – *now, that would have been a problem!*

Let's bring back Charlie and his recollection of happenings in the Bahamas in 1964. There were a lot of peculiarities going on with the Nassau banks, too many for such a small 8- by 12-mile island. At the time, the influential Bahamians were pushing hard for independence from Great Brittan so they could more easily take care of their wealthy customers who had a *lot* of money there. These were the type of customers who lived abroad and wanted to make *huge* deposits, with minimal questions asked.

Just think of how happy all that money would have made Chuck Waldron. What if he had opened one of those clandestine Nassau bank accounts that only *he* could access and, if so, what would Chuckie be willing to do when the "Marker" was called in by Billy, Chester, Bobby and Nadine-a-ling? When "Hughes" left his Desert Inn Penthouse in 1970 he supposedly opted not to stay at the Emerald Beach Hotel but found the Britannia Beach Hotel more to his liking. The guess here is that he really didn't like the Emerald Beach Hotel after all. And as for the $180,000.00, "easy come, easy go?" Not likely.

After getting dropped a few times in Nassau (a bang on the head, a dislocated shoulder), "Hughes" decides to take "a hop, skip, and a jump" over to Acapulco, Mexico, on February 12, 1976. Oh, by the way, he had no valid Bahamian visa at that time and no passport either. But he did have a serious developing case of renal failure, from which he *supposedly* died 56 days later. So why not just a "hop" over to the Howard Hughes Medical Institute in Miami, Florida? Oh yes, H.H.M.I. had all the latest in kidney machines for cleansing the blood and all the medical knowledge available at the time. *Kidney disease had to have been obvious and detectable 55 days earlier.* But we've been there already, let's get back to happenings after February 12 up to April 5, 1976.

The private jet carrying "Hughes" and several of his aides flies into an Acapulco airport. Its passengers disembark and are escorted to the Acapulco Princess Hotel by Mexican immigration authorities. The authorities do not have an opportunity to talk with "Hughes," because he had been taken away immediately by wheelchair, disappearing into to one of his traditional dark, small, rooms. There are still several visas needing to be signed, two by the attending aides and one by "Howard Hughes." But this does not happen; and after patiently waiting around for a considerable amount of time, the immigration authorities leave the visas on a table. When they return later to retrieve the cards, they find them to have finally been signed. Immigration authorities had not been present during the signing of the cards.

Chuck Waldron leaves for a short stay in Los Angeles but is contacted four days later by Mexican Immigrations. The signature on "Hughes's" visa is not the same as

Hughes's known signatures on file from Howard Hughes's previous stays in Mexico.

Chuck Waldron returns to Acapulco, but no more is said by the authorities concerning the forged "Hughes" visa *until* April 5, 1976 when a dead or dying "Hughes" was quickly loaded into a private jet and spirited off to Houston. The Mexican authorities were not informed of the "Hughes" departure, no flight plan had been made, and they are left with only a signed visa card which, in retrospect, they realize has been forged. However, they <u>do</u> manage to catch Chuck Waldron, Clyde Bundy, and Eric Crow, who did not manage to leave the country quickly enough. (Were the aides left behind to clean up as much traceable evidence as possible – just as they had done at the Desert Inn in Las Vegas?)

In Waldron's book *The Mysterious Howard Hughes Revealed*, Waldron paints himself as a kindly aide who only wants to take good care of his boss, the notorious Howard Hughes. He maintained that when Doctor Montemayor visited the "Hughes" Princess Suite, that the doctor had told him, "Without telling my government (that I told you to do so,) get this man to the best hospital in the United States." (Exhibit 183) But in reality, that was not all Dr. Montemayor had to say about that miserable wreck of a neglected man he had found in the Princess Hotel. (Exhibits 176, 178-A, 179-B) Sooner, rather than later, Dr. Montemayor was telling his story to the Acapulco news media and, most probably, the Mexican police as well. Let us take it apart and look more closely at the evidence:

A) April 5, 1976: Dr. Montemayor visited the terribly sick and neglected man in the Acapulco Princess Hotel. He believes this man to be the reclusive billionaire Howard Hughes.

B) April 5, 1976: A dead or near dead "Hughes," without a valid visa, passport, or Mexican flight plan is clandestinely spirited out of Mexico.

C) April 5, 1976: A fellow believed to be "Howard Hughes" dies in flight to Houston, Texas.

D) April 7, 1976: Mexican police return to the Princess Hotel and find that Chuck Waldron, Clyde Bundy, and Eric Crow are still there. They take them into custody.

E) Mexican authorities had gotten a cursive analysis of the "Hughes" visa back from Mexico City. They release Clyde Bundy and Eric Crow, but <u>hold</u> Waldron. Waldron's signature had the same characteristics as those in the "Hughes" signature on the forged visa.

  1. According to insinuations by Chuck Waldron (in his book), he was rudely held hostage for whatever gain the Mexican police could milk out of him. Had this been the whole story, would not they also have held Crow and Bundy as accomplices and tripled their proceeds? Or could it have been that when the

cursive analysts in Mexico City, finished their comparisons of the Crow, Bundy, and Waldron signatures, it was Waldron *only* who came up as the forger?

F) Things began to go badly for Waldron. (Exhibits 176, 178-A, 179-B) The police asked questions that were based on information they could only have gotten from Dr. Montemayor *after* he had visited "Hughes" at the Princess Hotel.
1. Dr. Montemayor recalls that the fellow he had examined at the Princess had a long stringy, chestnut colored beard. (Exhibit 178-A) Could this have been because there was food and filth trapped in the beard? Could the aides have washed "Hughes" up a little prior to hustling him off to Houston? A chestnut colored beard is not noted in the Methodist Hospital's autopsy report. If they had taken time to shave and bathe him, wouldn't it have been more prudent to get him quickly into a hospital and take care of his bath later? Were they perhaps finishing up some last-minute injected medication?

G) In Exhibit 185, we find that Waldron gets a call off to the Summa, Inc. foursome in Los Angeles via Humberto Banos. Time to loosen the purse strings.

H) Exhibit 178-A: Federal Judge Antonio Uribe Garcia releases Dr. Victor Montemayor's signed declaration to the newspapers. Dr. Victor's declaration encompasses what he had found at the Princess Hotel.

I) Judge Garcia then studies the evidence against Waldron for 72 hours (until the price was right?) and then determines, *based on a technicality,* that Waldron was innocent.

J) Judge Garcia gives Waldron back his $400.00 bail money, and even goes so far as to say, "Chuck Waldron is a very honest man."

K) Chuckie thanks the nice judge and maintains that, "when you are telling the truth you don't have to remember what you said:"
1. I did not sign Hughes's visa card.
2. *No!* I did not sign that visa card.
3. Hughes signed his *own* visa card.
4. *I swear to God* that I did not sign Hughes's visa card!
5. Etc. etc. etc. etc.....

L) Waldron puts a little entry in his book "Not everyone in Acapulco, though, was happy with the findings. (Exhibit 187-A) Perhaps that little entry was not a good idea either?

EXHIBIT 180

Sometimes, after more than a reasonable period of time had passed, the assignee would naturally conclude that Mr. Hughes no longer wanted or needed them, and they would be inclined to return to their normal duties. One of the fears of these employees was that if they decided not to wait—that would undoubtedly be the time that Hughes would call for them. In fact, this happened a number of times.

It was as if he had radar and could tell when the patience of a standby person had reached its limits. Then it was that he would activate their "standby" status.

The inside joke among his loyal employees was that the initials H. R. H. stood for "Howard Radar Hughes!"

"This scared the hell out of Paul!"

Initially, Howard Hughes' determination to invest in Las Vegas came from his personal experiences in that growing city. Two items in a news article in the *New York Times*, January 14, 1968, give some insight into the possible reasons that Hughes would be so successful in obtaining numerous holdings in Nevada.

Apparently Nevada's Governor Paul Laxalt was called to Washington, D.C. where he was introduced to a large amount of information gathered by the Federal Bureau of Investigation. This information had to do with the extent of the underworld's control of various casinos in Nevada.

"This scared the hell out of Paul! It made him anxious to help Hughes buy these places." It was hoped that Hughes' purchases would help wipe out the image of Nevada's gambling being controlled by the "underworld."

Mr. Parry Thomas, who was at that time President of the Bank of Las Vegas, advanced the second reason for Hughes' decision for going to Nevada. He felt that the fact that Nevada had no State

EXHIBIT 181

Income or Inheritance Taxes had had some influence on Hughes' decision to move there. According to Hughes' theory: "There are very few places in America where I can afford to be caught dead." (1)

The January 1 telephone message from Howard Hughes to Chuck Waldron came through one of his aides, John Holmes. Hughes wanted Chuck to take a trip to the Bahamas. He was to accompany Jack Hooper, a close associate of Robert Maheu, who at the time was head of Hughes' security operations in Nevada, and John Egginwyler. They were to look for hotel space at the Britannia Beach Hotel for Hughes and his staff. This would be in anticipation of a relocation to the Bahamas from the Desert Inn Hotel in Las Vegas.

Hughes was no stranger to the Bahaman Islands as he had been there before. There was one unusual aspect about the request, however. The expectation was that when Hughes returned to the Bahaman Islands, he would stay at the Emerald Beach Hotel where Hughes had stayed during the summer and fall of 1957. Hughes liked it there, and when he left the island, he continued renting his rooms, thinking he would like to return sometime.

Paying for Unoccupied Hotel Rooms

Chuck had been there before, too. He explained that in September and October of 1967, he had been directed to go to the Bahamas to pay for the continuation of the unoccupied rooms. There didn't seem to be any logical reason that Hughes would want the reservations to be continued. It had been ten years since he had been there, and he had not returned to use his rooms once! Even his aides, who returned occasionally to pay the hotel bill, would not use their boss's leased rooms.

Nevertheless, Hughes had not authorized the termination of the rent/lease arrangement with the hotel; therefore, the hotel was justifiably deserving of receiving the rent money.

EXHIBIT 182

This particular time, Chuck was assigned the duty of paying the ongoing hotel bill. Hughes' personal secretary, Lee Murrin, tendered a check to Chuck with instructions to have it converted to cash at the nearby South Hollywood Branch of the Bank of America. At the time this bank was located on the corner of Hermosa and Santa Maria Boulevard, diagonally across the street from the Sam Goldwyn Studios.

Taking the check and an empty briefcase to the bank with him, Chuck cashed the check and stuffed his briefcase full of $100 bills. They had been counted and wrapped in bundles of $10,000.00 each. He walked out of the bank with nearly $180,000.00 in currency with which he would pay the rent that had accumulated on Hughes' empty rooms at the Emerald Beach Hotel.

Bob Case, the assistant manager of the hotel, met Chuck at the airport when he arrived in the Bahamas. Back at the hotel and in his office, the two discussed a few particulars about the hotel in general and Hughes' reserved rooms in particular. Bob Case made a determined effort to assure Chuck that Hughes' request for confidence about his arrangements had been maintained. Chuck was emphatically assured that not many of the hotel personnel even knew of the arrangement that Hughes had with the hotel, but that those who knew did not talk about it to others.

The assistant manager told Chuck that a maid was still dusting the rooms once a week and that the Emerald Beach Hotel would welcome a visit from their distinguished client whenever he desired to return.

When Bob Case finally got around to conducting the business of receiving their payment, he asked, "How are you going to pay for it? By check?"

Chuck smiled and replied, "No! With cash!" He then opened his briefcase, exposing the $180,000 in $100 bills.

A slightly surprised Bob Case, concerned about other peoples' ability to visually see the transaction within the room, moved

EXHIBIT 183

doctors that when a person is in a coma, if their eyelids remain partially open, the eyes could become very dry and irritated. So, under their direction, Chuck obtained eye drops and placed the fluid in Hughes' eyes on a regular basis in order to keep them moist.

A local Mexican doctor, Dr. Victor Manuel Montemayor Martinez, was also called in for consultation on Howard Hughes' condition.

The aides also wanted Dr. Martinez to help them determine which of the available local medical services would be best for treating Hughes' condition. His opinion coincided with Hughes' doctors' evaluation concerning the current and emerging serious nature of Hughes' health. As for the local medical facilities, he recommended that, "Without telling my government (that I told you to do so), get this man to the best hospital you can in the United States!"

Chuck receives a call that Hughes had died!

Back-up preparations were already being made for such a transfer. The small Lear Jet that had been dispatched to bring Dr. Thane to Acapulco was now being prepared for Hughes' return trip to the United States.

Chuck assisted John Holmes, Dr. Larry Chaffin, Dr. Wilbur Thain, and other company personnel, in preparing Hughes for the ambulance that had been provided by the "Manzanarez Agency."
He was then driven to the "Plan De Los Amates Airport" for the flight to the United States. The Lear Jet was an executive aircraft and was not designed to accommodate stretchers and medical patients.

In order to remedy this problem, Chuck quickly organized a space for Hughes, utilizing three passenger seats for the placement of his stretcher. Gordon Margulis then helped Chuck lift Hughes onto the plane and secure him for the flight to the United States. John Holmes, Dr. Chaffin, and Dr. Thain would accompany Hughes to the States.

EXHIBIT 184

A time or two during the questioning they suggested to Chuck, "Just say you did!"

"The implication of this request seemed to be that if I would just say that I did it, all of this interrogation would end, and I could be on my way."

They kept asking him about the various physical items and some of the conditions that they had seen in Howard Hughes' room. Then they had another whole list of questions:

Hughes' age?

His Health?

Had he had been ill long?

Why did you suddenly have to call a Mexican doctor?

Why did you wait so long to get the doctors up there?

Why did you wait until noon to decide to fly him out?

Who was it that ordered the ambulance?

When they asked him if there was anyone else who had seen or could verify that Hughes was not dead when he left the country, Chuck told them, "The ambulance driver and the attendant."

Gertz replied, "Well, those are *your* people.   Is there somebody else?"

Chuck replied, "No!"

Next, they questioned him about the cars that they used to transport Hughes to the plane and who was in them.   They admonished Chuck, "Now, make sure you get this right!"

Chuck answered this question, and then went on to explain how he and another associate had loaded Hughes aboard the plane on a stretcher.

Their argumentative reply was, "Well, you know he left illegally because we didn't get his tourist card."

Mr. Rodriguez asked Chuck the question several times, "How was it that you knew that Hughes was alive when he left?"

His answer each time was, "He was breathing, and you could see his chest moving up and down. His limbs were not moving, but

EXHIBIT 185

he was breathing, which was apparent from observing the oxygen equipment attached to him."

"Who could verify that he was living?"

Chuck responded, "The doctors and the pilots."

Once the interrogation was over for the day, Chuck was taken back downstairs to join Eric Bundy and Clyde Crow. The three were pleased to note that the people at the hotel had been considerate enough to send some prepared meals over for them. However, the meals had been placed on the table earlier, and Mr. Rodriguez and some of the others associated with him had eaten them during the interrogation.

At no time up to this point in their interrogation were any of the three told of their legal rights, nor were they permitted to make any telephone calls. The only visible outside support they had was the presence of the hotel's "Chief of Security," who had stayed there with them all day, and their driver, who was there until about 8:00 P.M.

Humberto Banos, who had helped Chuck earlier, had tried unsuccessfully to get back into the building to see them. Finally which took a little bravery on his part, he found a way to get in. Chuck asked him to call Kay Glenn in Los Angeles and notify him of their predicament. This he did, and after that, no one there would tell the three of them anything. So they remained uncertain as to what was going to happen to them for the rest of the night. Eventually, they were placed in separate rooms and had guards assigned to watch each of them.

Again Chuck was confronted with his unearned reputation of being the professionally trained, personal bodyguard for Hughes. Whenever Chuck would make a move in his room, whether it was to get a cup of water from the sink or to make a move toward the lavatory, a triplicate "mirror movement" of security officers moved with him.

Whenever this happened, Chuck would have to halt his forward movement and try to explain to them what it was that he was

EXHIBIT 186

The judge would then take the summary, and the materials into his chamber for final review.

"Tell Mr. Waldron that he is a very honest man!"

Members of the press were there also and took pictures of the same statements and documents that the judge had in his possession. After reading and reviewing the statements and interviews related to the case, the judge sent word out to Chuck by way of his assistant. "Tell Mr. Waldron that he is a very honest man."

Evidently he had been quite impressed with the consistency and accuracy with which Chuck had responded to all of the questions during the interrogations.

Therefore, the judge's decision was that Chuck Waldron was "Not Guilty, …and, therefore, free to go."

Chuck asked the legal assistant to "Thank the judge for me." He also added another part to his message sent back to the judge in regard to the judge's statement about Chuck's honesty. He said, "If you tell the truth, you don't have to remember what it was that you said before."

The police captain and members of the police force who had guarded him came to him and apologetically explained that they were glad for him. They said that in guarding him as they did and in taking him to prison, they were just doing their job. Chuck assured them that "he understood."

The final communication with the judge had been a much more pleasant experience than those he had had with others prior to this. The papers he was handed had sufficient legal terminology to tell the story of his detention, but the only thing that interested Chuck was the summary at the end of the letter. It stated:

EXHIBIT 187-A

"Because of the statements and findings, IT IS RESOLVED: FIRST, - Being the 14th hour of the day the 13 of April of nineteen hundred and seventy-six, for the lack of evidence for prosecution, a writ of liberty is issued in favor of CLARENCE ALBERT WALDRON, as related to the crime of forgery of documents, ..."
CITIZEN CHIEF OF LOCAL IMMIGRATIONS, THIS CITY.

Acapulco, Guerrero, 13th of April 1976

District Judge in the State,
Attorney, Antonio Uribe Garcia.

cc. To Clarence Albert Waldron, as his ticket to liberty.
This City.

Mr. Jaffe and Chuck left Acapulco that afternoon, April 13, 1976, and arrived in Los Angeles at about 8:15 P.M.

Not everyone in Acapulco, though, was happy with the findings! "The Mexican Federal Prosecutor, Manuel Rodriguez Delgadillo, said the case had been appealed to the 2nd Circuit Court in Toluca, capital of the State of Mexico."(3)

EXHIBIT 187-B

This is probably a good place to include this Exhibit. It gives light to the tremendous amounts of money, clandestinely "ripped out" of the Hughes Companies after 1965. It will be referred to in the following (Chapter XII.) Strangely no one ever knew where the money had gone.

THE FIGHT FOR THE FORTUNE   677

and chief executive officer of Summa Corporation, Lummis had engineered a striking turnaround on the part of the Hughes holding company. After Davis, Holmes, and Myler had been dismissed from the Summa board, Lummis fired Davis as the company's chief counsel, and shortly thereafter Bill Gay resigned. Under Lummis's tight management, the years of multimillion-dollar losses at Summa ended and the company appeared to be well on its way to recording multimillion-dollar profits.

In June of 1978, Lummis filed a complaint in the New Castle County Chancery Court in Wilmington, Delaware, asking the court to appoint him trustee of the Howard Hughes Medical Institute—now run by Gay and Davis. The institute's articles of incorporation provided that it was to be controlled by a single trustee. That, naturally, was Howard Hughes. The articles of incorporation also provided that only Hughes could appoint a successor trustee. He never did. Lummis contended that as the administrator of the Hughes Estate, and therefore the legal representative of Hughes, he should be named trustee by the Delaware court. The Delaware attorney-general's office joined in this action, requesting the court to appoint, if not Lummis, then some other qualified individual or institution, as trustee, and require the medical institute to account to the court for its activities. Whatever the outcome of the twin legal proceedings, it is certain that the tide of litigation that engulfed Hughes while he was alive will not recede for many years after his death.

Indeed, the estate had inherited some sixty civil lawsuits that were pending against Hughes or his companies when he died.* The two

* As part of his own investigation to determine what role, if any, Hughes may have played in defending against the various legal actions brought against him, Lummis, on the recommendation of Dean, retained a prominent psychologist to assess Hughes's mental condition, with particular emphasis on the last years of his life. The psychologist was Dr. Raymond D. Fowler, Jr., professor and chairman of the Department of Psychology at the University of Alabama and the developer of the most widely used computerized system of personality test interpretation in the country, a system employed by more than a thousand mental health agencies and institutions and one-third of the psychiatrists in private practice. A slight, soft-spoken, skilled interrogator with a capacity for eliciting critical information from the most reluctant witnesses, Dr. Fowler spent months interviewing and reinterviewing those who worked for Hughes, and examining Hughes's voluminous private papers, in an effort to put together a psychiatric profile of the nation's best-known recluse. By the end of 1978, Dr. Fowler had concluded that Hughes's condition in his last years "resembled that of a chronic psychotic patient in the very worst

Waldron Case Review
As per "Russ" Russell:
Justice occasionally comes with a price tag, as we learn below.

Clarence "Chuck" Waldron was one of several aides of Howard Hughes. By his own account, he waited on, and stood by Howard Hughes at every geographical location for more than 10 years, including Hughes's stints in the Bahamas and Mexico. Again, by his own account, we learn that one of his major duties (among other duties) was to prepare and arrange papers for Howard Hughes to sign, a job normally given to a secretary or other type of aide.

With regards to Mexico, the man identified as Howard Hughes by three aides, arrived in Acapulco on/about February 4, 1976. Early in the morning, he arrived by private plane, accompanied by anywhere from 3-10 aides, with an origin of the Bahamas. Some of the aides traveled on the plane with him, while others took commercial flights from Los Angeles, where Summa, Inc. headquarters was originally located.

Learning of his pending arrival, Mexican Immigration Authorities met his plane and talked with the accompanying aides. These authorities facilitated Hughes travel to the Acapulco Princess Hotel and stood by as they awaited completion of the required Tourist Visas. The authorities never had the opportunity to meet or talk personally with the Howard Hughes fellow, and instead left his unsigned Tourist Visa on a table in his hotel room, along with two other Visas that needed to be signed by aides.

Somehow, and at some-time, the Tourist Visas were all signed. There were two for "aides," and one specifically for Howard Hughes. The Immigration authorities returned later in the day and collected the "signed" Tourist Visas. That was the last that anyone referred to the Visas until four days later.

Four days after their arrival in Acapulco, "Chuck" Waldron returned to Los Angeles for several days of "time off." During his time in Los Angeles, he received a telephone call from Mexican Immigration Authorities asking him if he knew anything about the Howard Hughes Tourist Visa card, and that the signature on the card did not match known handwriting of Howard Hughes which was in their existing files. Waldron denied knowing anything at all about the signing of the Howard Hughes Tourist Card.

On March 25, 1976 Waldron returned to Acapulco from Los Angeles. Nothing else transpired after he received that Immigration authorities call while he was in Los Angeles.

So, Hughes had arrived in Acapulco on February 4th, Waldron left on/about February 8th or 9th (to Los Angeles), and returned to Acapulco on March 25th. It wasn't until April 5th or 6th that the Visa subject came up again, some 60+ days after "Hughes's" arrival in Acapulco. On April 5/6, the Mexican Federal Police arrived at the Princess Hotel, inquiring about the death of Howard Hughes. Hughes allegedly had died while aboard a private jet which was transporting him to Houston. The death allegedly occurred somewhere over Brownsville, TX according to doctors on board the plane.

Two days later (April 7ᵗʰ) the Mexican police returned to the Princess Hotel. As Waldron was preparing to leave, the Mexican police took Waldron and two other aides into "informal" custody, transporting them to see Chief of Police Gertz of the Federal Police. Chief Gertz brought up the subject of the Hughes Tourist Visa Card but allowed the three individuals to leave at the conclusion of that interview.

The next day proved the most decisive day for Waldron, as the Mexican police received a formal handwriting examination report (from their Handwriting Expert in Mexico City), which declared that Waldron had forged the name of Howard Hughes on his Tourist Visa Card. Again, Chief Gertz called in Waldron to his office, and advised Waldron of the Handwriting report. Waldron denied knowing anything about the forgery. At that time, Waldron submitted a written statement in which he denied the forgery.

It was about that time that Waldron, and aides Evie Bundy and Clyde Crow were taken into custody. The next day Waldron put in a phone call to the Mexican Attorney General, asking him to investigate the matter. Later that morning, the Attorney General put out an order to release Bundy and Crow and continue to hold Waldron in custody. Instead of leaving, Bundy and Crow decided to stay with Waldron. A few minutes later, Waldron was transported to a local prison and charged with "Forgery" on April 12ᵗʰ, Waldron was transported to the courthouse, made a brief appearance, and then was returned to the Prison. Later in that day, Waldron was released on "bail" from the local Prison. The next day (13ᵗʰ), Waldron had to return to the courthouse to complete some paperwork. It was at that time that the judge interviewed Waldron. After that interview, suddenly without any previous discussion, the judge declared that Waldron was an "honest man," declaring him "not guilty" and free to go.

This announcement took the Federal prosecutor, and the Mexican police, by complete surprise, and they were not happy ("irate" would be a better description). They had an Expert's report that Waldron had forged the Hughes Tourist Visa card and were expecting their day in Court.

Immediately the Federal Prosecutor appealed the judge's ruling to the 2ⁿᵈ Circuit Court in Toluca, Mexico, and awaited their opinion.

However, later that day (13ᵗʰ), Waldron took advantage of the judge's ruling, and left Acapulco via plane. He never returned to Acapulco.

Justice comes at a cost in Mexico – throughout Mexico that is. There is little doubt that someone got to the judge and provided an incentive to acquire and issue his "innocent" ruling in the "Forgery" case. Ironic indeed, as on the night of April 5ᵗʰ, somehow the alleged body of a medical patient, going by the name of Howard Hughes, was spirited away in a private plane, without Federal authorities permitting the exit, and with knowledge that the original Mexican Tourist Visa was forged.

Little is known of Waldron's activities (or employment) after the (alleged) Hughes death in the airplane over Brownsville, TX from Acapulco. There are several indications that Waldron moved to Las Vegas, NV. During the Federal

Civil Court case, filed by Summa, Inc. against Summa executives, several aides to Hughes, Doctors treating him, and Waldron's attorney, told the Court that Waldron was a "house painter" in Las Vegas.

One reference source wrote that Waldron became a full-time painting contractor, while other references recalled that Waldron became a Board Member on at least two Homeowner Associations (HOA's) in Las Vegas. Additionally, the NV Secretary of State has advised that Waldron was one of a few General Partners in a real estate investment firm known as Tioga Pines Limited Partnership, in Las Vegas, NV, until his death in 1996 after which his wife, Colleen, took his place.

Although Waldron first started working for the Summa Corporation in March of 1957, it was not until 1974 that Waldron received his first official "Employment Contract." As noted within that Contract, (see Exhibits 215-A-B-C and D,) Waldron (and others) were compensated extremely well while working for Summa. As an "aide," Waldron's 1974 salary was $ 60,000 a year, an incredible amount, concerning his alternating duties as one of 6 or 7 "aides" to Howard Hughes. Other "aides" were earning $ 65,000 a year and up. This salary did not include bonuses, compensation for un-used sick and vacation time, and yearly salary increases. $60,000 in salary compensation in 1974 would have a value of approximately $600,000 a year in 2019.

Previously noted, a major event in Waldron's life started in 1979, just 3 short years after the alleged death of Howard R. Hughes. On January 24, 1979, the Summa Corporation, along with William R. Lummis (Co-Special Administrator of the Estate of Howard R. Hughes), and the First National Bank of Nevada (an additional Co-Special Administrator of the Hughes estate), filed a Federal Civil Law Suit in the State of Nevada, against Waldron (and several others), charging that each of them took advantage of Howard Hughes and through a series of self-dealing schemes and conspiracies, they wrongly converted assets of Hughes to their own use, thereby breaching their respective fiduciary duties to Hughes, resulting in damages in excess of $50 Million dollars.

Joining Waldron as defendants (respondents) were aides known as Levar Myler, John Morrison Holmes, Howard Eckersley, James Rickard, and George Francom Jr. Additionally, executives of Summa, known as Frank Gay, Chester Davis, and Kay Gibbons, were also named as defendants (respondents). And finally, not left out from this Civil action were doctors Wilbur Thain, Norman Cranc, and Homer Clark. It is interesting to note that some other aides, and personal doctors of Howard Hughes, were not named in this Civil action. Other Summa Corporation employees, such as Nadine Henley Marshall, were not included in the initial filing of this civil action, but later were added to the list of defendants (respondents).

Reviewing individual pages of this 6,000+ page civil action, disclosed several noteworthy allegations. A) Holiday pay and special bonuses were paid to Summa Corporation employees, and some executives, effective November 1973; b) certain Summa Corporation employees and executives were listed on Nevada Gaming Licenses for various Casinos owned and operated by the

Summa Corporation; c) Dr. Wilbur Thain had a "pet project" known as the "Executive Health Spa" located inside the Desert Inn Hotel (in Las Vegas); d) At some point, after November 1973, without the knowledge of Howard Hughes, Summa Corporation moved their administrative offices to Las Vegas, NV from Los Angeles; e) all employees submitted Requests for Reimbursement to Summa, Corp. Administrative offices, relative to expenses they had each allegedly incurred, and they were promptly reimbursed (by check); f) Long-term employment and consulting contracts had been authorized (since the early 1970's) for all the aides and doctors named in this civil action.

And, as it turned out, Summa, Inc.'s violation of the Employment Contracts led to the partial downfall of the Federal Civil Court case. With little regard to the wording of each Contract, Summa, Inc. terminated each of the employee defendants (respondents) immediately following the filing of the Federal Court case, completely disregarding contract wording which outlined employee termination procedures and compensation. None of the defendants (respondents) received any compensation following that 1979 termination date (except some Attorneys were compensated for their paperwork which they filed in support of the defendants – Waldron, as one, receiving $ 3,500 for his Attorney's work.

A critical court ruling led to the final downfall of the Federal Civil Court case. The Federal Civil Court case had been filed in Las Vegas, NV. Almost all the 13+ defendants (respondents) had filed Affidavits in which they said that they had not conducted any activities (as described in the Court filing) in Las Vegas, and their visits there did not constitute Summa Corporation activities. Each defendant (respondent) denied committing any conspiratorial act within the Nevada Court's jurisdiction. After careful and very lengthy Court hearings, the Court ruled in favor of the defendants and upheld their position that they had not committed conspiratorial acts, during 1974 – 1979, within the jurisdiction of the Nevada Federal Court. The Federal Court Case was dismissed (1981) with no compensation due to either the Summa Corporation or any of the defendants (respondents).

Puzzling to me is the fact that, instead of a Federal Criminal case, William Lummis, on behalf of the Summa Corporation, chose to file a Civil case against the 13+ defendants (respondents). The criminal case could have involved embezzlement, conspiracy, forgery, gaming violations, use of the RICO statute, and other possible Federal crimes. It appears that Summa was looking to obtain monetary compensation rather than punitive actions against the defendants (respondents).

(In Federal Court cases, "defendants" is the actual term used in criminal cases – as persons charged with a crime. In civil court cases, "respondents" is the term used for people charged with violation of civil statutes. Very frequently, "defendants" is the term applied to those charged in Civil Court with a violation, rather than the designation "respondents," which is the correct term).

L "Russ" Russell

Viewing Russ's analogy in another light, it appears that Will Lummis *did not want* to get into a "pissing match" in Federal court, which would involve embezzlement, conspiracy, forgery, etc. To be successful at that level could have meant prison time. Someone might turn "State's Evidence" to lessen their stay and the "cat would have been out of the bag." Real investigations would ensue, the death of a supposed "Hughes" would have been looked at differently, *and heads would have rolled!* It appears that a "no loss no gain show" was all any of the parties wanted. Could this have been agreed upon beforehand? "Well, we did go to court and we did do this and that, and we did give it our best shot." Of the many things Will Lummis may have been, *he was no dummy!* He had to have known that Federal court would have been his best option, if he truly wanted to win, and he chose *not* to use it.

As for Chuck Waldron, Clyde Crow, and Evie Bundy being left behind while Drs. Thain, Chaffin, and Holmes made good their escape, what could they have been doing at the Acapulco Princess that required them to take the risk? Was it the same destruction of evidence that occurred at the Desert Inn Las Vegas, Nevada? They had to have known that the Mexican Doctor Montemayor could show up at any moment with the federales. So, what was it that so compelled them to take the risk?

No! – this fellow in Acapulco was *no* iron-fisted psychotic, suicidal, despot of whim and fancy, a tyrant to whom his employees bowed and trembled. When one considers the autopsy analyses above and reads the exemplars above and below, the only logical presumption is that this miserable wretch of man was subjected to horrific abuse and then simply thrown away when his usefulness expired. This "Hughes" could not even be taken to a dentist during his tenure for fear of a dental record being left behind! He certainly could not have been given *any chance* to recuperate in a controlled environment with decent medical care; this would have revealed what and who he really was and the purpose he had served! And to Will Lummis and his psychiatric pursuits to further label "Acapulco Hughes" as the real Hughes who was hopelessly drug addicted and psychotic (Exhibit 187 B-above), we say, "*Sorry* Will, it just doesn't work anymore."

Hey Will, after the half-hearted tries wherein you didn't really want to expose the Hughes empire pirates for murder one, embezzlement, etc., how much of the stolen money did you get back from the Old Summa, Inc. team? Will, you've been found out! So, the Old Summa, Inc. pirates did a little suing on their own, did they? (You scratch my back and I'll scratch yours?)

So much for the fiasco in Mexico concerning the last few days of "Acapulco Hughes." Let's move on to the activities of Drs. Thain, Chaffin, Aide Holmes, and others, who "supposedly" had the best interests of "H.H." in mind.

CHAPTER XIII

Court Activity of Drs. Thain, Crane, and Chaffin, and Caretaker Holmes:

The courtroom activity concerning Doctor's Thain, Chaffin, and Crane and caretaker Holmes, was skewed enough so that they could escaped with probation only, despite strong evidence that reveals them complicit in providing an overdose of drugs that helped kill – or did kill – the fellow they flew up from Mexico. They were indicted but managed to rig the system in their favor. However, Russ has turned up the information on *how* they did it. His report follows.

L. "RUSS" RUSSELL
How Two Doctors Scammed the Justice Department

Easily the most elaborate medical scheme ever devised, two seemingly distant medical Doctors acted in concert to divert attention from a pharmaceutical prescription scheme, as outlined below:

The background, for what would later become a scheme, started in the mid 1950's when Dr. Norman F. Crane began to write prescriptions for the famous Industrialist Howard Hughes. Howard Hughes had been in a devastating plane crash years earlier; therefore, needed these drugs to ease the persistent and lingering pain from his numerous injuries. The prescriptions were written for the regulated drugs Empirin Codeine and Codeine Phosphate, both either Schedule II or III drugs as regulated by the drug enforcement arm of the U.S. Justice Department. While in the hospital, recuperating from his catastrophic XF-11 test plane crash into Beverly Hills, Hughes's personal friend and confident, Doctor Vern Mason and he, decided on the types of drugs, listed above. This was believed to be a reasonable means to subvert the use of Morphine and its addictive side effects. The prescriptions were initially written in the name of Howard Hughes but later in the name of John Holmes. Holmes would take the signed prescription forms to one of his pharmacies (usually in Los Angeles) and have the prescriptions filled, after which he would personally deliver to "Howard Hughes," regardless of where "Hughes" was temporarily residing. When one considers the research that has now been done, it is reasonable to doubt the person using these drugs, after 1965, was the real Howard Hughes. Nevertheless, the drugs continued to flow and be used. At various times, the "Hughes" individual was residing in Las Vegas, the Country of Mexico, various European cities, or one or more of the Caribbean

Islands. As the scheme progressed, the prescriptions would be written in the names of other individuals, who had been aides earlier then 1965, to Howard Hughes, but regardless of prescription name, they were still submitted and then picked up, by the "Hughes" caretaker John Holmes, in ever increasing quantities; as the above listed "opioids" can and did become addictive.

The Indictment, as issued on March 6, 1978 in Las Vegas, NV, charged both Dr. Crane and John Holmes, both of Los Angeles, with one count of violating Title 21 of the US Code, Section 846, Conspiracy to illegally distribute Schedule II and III drugs to the individual called "Howard Hughes."

The Indictment further charged that specifically between 1966 and 1970, Dr. Crane wrote the prescriptions in either Holmes or other names, and Holmes would have the prescriptions filled in Los Angeles, after which time he would pick up the drugs and transport them to Las Vegas where an individual using the name of "Howard Hughes" was residing in the Desert Inn Hotel/Casino. Dr. Wilber Thain eventually set up a transaction with a wholesale drug provider where he could get greater quantities of the drugs with less difficulty.

The Indictment further charged that:
1. Dr. Crane and John Holmes conspired to distribute the above noted Schedule II and III drugs to "Howard Hughes:"
2. The specific period of time, this scheme was conducted, was between 1966 and 1970.
3. Dr. Crane would write the prescriptions and Holmes would have the prescriptions filled, most usually at a Los Angeles Pharmacy.
4. At the outset of this illegal activity, Dr. Crane wrote the prescriptions in Holmes name alone, but gradually Dr. Crane started writing the prescriptions in other person's names, mostly aides or employees of "Howard Hughes;"
5. Regardless of to whom the prescription was written, Holmes, alone, was responsible for picking up the drugs from the pharmacy.
6. After picking up the drugs, Holmes would transport the Codeine from the Los Angeles pharmacy initially to Las Vegas, where he would give the Codeine to "Howard Hughes" who was then residing at the Desert Inn Hotel.
7. A total of at least 480 prescriptions of Empirin-Codeine and or Codeine Phosphate were written (by Dr. Crane) filled and provided to the individual "Howard Hughes," by John Holmes.

Dr. Crane and John Holmes pled "not guilty" to the Indictment, and the Federal case was initially scheduled for trial (in Las Vegas) for June 6, 1978. Several actions took place after that plea. The plea was later changed to "nolo contendre," and with Dr. Crane's promise to cooperate with the Federal Prosecutor in the case against Dr. Wilbur Thain, the two of them (Crane and Holmes) received one year of "probation," with their prison sentence suspended.

Scheme No. 2 (The unlawful procurement of drugs to be sent to "Hughes" in Mexico) actually took place from August 1974 through April 1976 in the State of Utah and picked up surreptitiously right after Scheme No. 1. Although Federal prosecutors had complete knowledge of each individual scheme being conducted in their geographical areas, at no time did both prosecutors "apparently" consider the intertwining of the schemes. This lack of consideration (of conspiratorial conduct) may have been the reason that Dr. Wilbur Thain (further discussed below) was found "not guilty" after a jury trial in Ogden, UT.

Dr. Wilbur Sutton Thain was indicted on June 6, 1978 in Salt Lake City, UT. The Indictment charged him (alone) with a violation of Title 21, United States Code, Section 846 (a)(1) = "possessing, distributing, and dispensing codeine phosphate at six-week intervals to Howard Hughes, without a legitimate medical purpose." Dr. Thain pled "not guilty" to the Indictment, and after a few continuances, a trial took place (in Ogden, UT) on September 21, 1978.

During the trial, several facts came out:
1. Until his alleged death, Howard Hughes was President of the Summa Corporation, based in Los Angeles, but with an office in Las Vegas.
2. As the selected doctor for Howard Hughes, Dr. Thain was paid by the Summa Corporation from March 1, 1975 through his 1978 Federal Trial.
3. Dr. Thain's contract with the Summa Corporation stipulated that he was to be paid for all services that he performed on behalf of the Summa Corporation.
4. Dr. Thain had a 5-year contract with the Summa Corporation as a "medical advisor and consultant." This contract paid him some $60,000 a year, plus Executive bonuses and other fringe benefits.
5. Evidence was shown that a total of 5,500 dosages of codeine phosphate had been delivered to "Howard Hughes" by Dr. Thain.
6. The codeine phosphate prescribed was in tablet form which was later dissolved into an injectable solution for "H.H.'s" use.
7. Dr. Thain utilized drug stores in Logan, UT and Rockville Center, New York for pickup of the prescribed drugs.
8. Unlike the Dr. Crane case, Dr. Thain did not have a "courier" to deliver the prescriptions or pick up the drugs for him. John Holmes had performed this task for Dr. Crane.
9. On a 6-week plan, Dr. Thain personally delivered the drugs to Howard Hughes in Freeport, the Bahamas, and Acapulco, Mexico.
10. The delivered drugs were packaged such that "six weekly batches were dispensed to Howard Hughes for his personal injection."

With no independent knowledge, beyond reviewing each of these Federal Court cases, I thought to myself "Why wasn't a conspiracy charge filed against each of the doctors, for their obvious planning of the entire scheme to illegally provide drugs to the individual they knew as "Howard Hughes"? Weren't the Federal prosecutors aware of their planning? Could the planning have been as obvious to them as to me? And then I read a 1978 article listed in the Chicago Tribune. (Very interesting considering no other newspaper or source possessing their knowledge.) The Tribune wrote that:

> It was Dr. Crane's co-operation with DEA Agents which led to the Indictment of Dr. Thain (exactly three months later). Dr. Crane admitted his providing drugs to Howard Hughes, but he ended that relationship in April 1974. In August 1974, Dr. Thain agreed to provide

narcotics to Howard Hughes (I note that it was March 1975 that the Summa Corporation, of which Howard Hughes was president, gave Dr. Thain a 5-year contract, for his services, at the rate of $300,000 (minimum) plus some additional executive benefits.)

With "Howard Hughes" (his double) dead in April 1976, the Federal cases suffered due to their inability to subpoena "Hughes" and obtain his testimony (about drug use) both before the impaneled Grand Juries and the Federal Court trials of each of these Doctors, the same Doctors who were present with him, as he was flown from Mexico to the US, and *allegedly* died during the airplane ride.

In 1979 Dr. Thain was interviewed by Dennis Breo of both the American Medical News and People Magazine. Dr. Thain was quoted as saying "Hughes took codeine but was not addicted to it." (despite the **480** doses (of Empirin Codeine and Codeine Phosphate) delivered to him by John Holmes between 1966 and 1974 (as outlined in the Federal Indictment of Crane and Holmes), and **5,500** doses handed out to him by Dr. Thain between August 1974 and April 1975, and, as well, an additional **2,000** doses between December 19, 1975 and April 5, 1976 (as outlined in the Indictment of Dr. Thain). Dr. Thain insisted that Aspirin was the real culprit which led to the death of the person, going by the name of Howard Hughes – not the exorbitant amount of Codeine being provided to him by Dr. Thain.

Sources/References for Crane/Thain Article

1. US v. Norman Crane and John Holmes, Federal District Court Case # 78-00022-01, Las Vegas, NV.
2. US v. Wilbur Sutton Thain, Federal District Court Case # NCR-78-21, Northern Division, District of Utah.
3. People Magazine, July 30, 1979. Dennis Breo interview of Dr. Wilbur Thain.
4. Salt Lake Tribune, June 7/8, 1978 article taken from the Chicago Tribune. – involves Summa Corporation, Dr. Thain, and Dr. Crane.
5. Deseret News (Paper) – June 7, 1978 – Indictment of Dr. Wilbur Thain.
6. Chicago Tribune, June 7, 1978 – Indictment of Dr. Wilbur Thain. (Section 1, page 3)

L. Russ Russell

THE FIRST NATIONAL BANK OF NEVADA
AS ORIGINAL DIRECTOR OF THE HUGHES ESTATE:

Well, so much for "skate-board enthusiasts" Drs. Thain and Crane and aide Holmes. But let's take time here to investigate another interesting development. We have always known that Will Lummis had been *appointed*, by judicial decree, as the co-director of Summa, Inc., which we also know was the powerhouse in control of the Hughes empire.* What we *didn't* know is with whom Annette and Will Lummis shared this responsibility; it was never common knowledge. Now we know that it was the First National Bank of Nevada, and we will pursue this a bit further in Chapter XIII. (The first executive director of the Hughes Estate was the First National Bank of Nevada. The questions concerning this strange fact is *how* and *why*?) Will and Annette Lummis, as co-directors, were *later* additions.

Perhaps you might ask, "Could it be that the Mormon Church holds the original, or a copy, of Hughes's *holographic* will?? Well for one thing, Melvin Dummar was intent on clandestinely squirreling a copy of that phony "Mormon Will" into the Church offices and the envelope which contained it was addressed to David O. McKay (Church Prophet at the time). So, let's speculate that early on Howard *liked* Mormons; they were sincere, clean and respectful. Bill Gay, a Mormon among others, rose to a predominant position in the Hughes empire. If Howard liked Mormons in the beginning, *why* would he leave his Mormon lieutenants *without* golden parachutes when he knew the "Grim Reaper" waited in the wings? One could say that he was a stingy sort of fellow, crazy perhaps, who conspired to take it with him to the grave? But how could this make any sense if he simply gave away $180,000.00 for hotel rooms in the Bahamas which he never used? (Neither scenario is correct.) Could it have been that, toward the end of his life (in 1965 *not* 1976), he knew his lieutenants for what they had *degenerated* into. In consideration of evidence uncovered, it's entirely feasible that Howard Hughes *did* leave a holographic will created prior to 1965. It can also be supposed that, after his death, it was deliberately hidden or destroyed by the Hughes estate pirates and that it was a will wherein his corrupted lieutenants were omitted. He had to have believed that this prior to 1965 legitimate holographic will, "binding as a band of steel," would in the end accomplish his wishes. Considering the way Charles saw him in 1964, it is apparent that Hughes simply wanted to remain obscure and *did not want the world to know of his pathetically twisted physiology*. It was a sad situation that would have garnered world media events. He did *not* want to spend his final years with photos circulating of his wretched physique and the pity of the masses. He would remain undercover until the end; but *he would* entrust the Fathers of the Mormon Church (The Council of the Twelve led by David O. McKay at the time) to carry out his final will and testament. Yes, there is/was a will; *it is/was a holographic will* with a *codicil* attachment. When Hughes really died in 1965, the L.D.S.* Church would need to keep things on the hush-hush, so there would not be numerous contenders. Naturally, they would parcel out a few million to the distant relatives of Hughes, but it's more than just a hunch that the Mormon Church is holding a holographic will naming the *legitimate* beneficiaries of the Hughes estate.

*Note: Mormon Church and L.D.S. are both identities for The Church of Jesus Christ of Latter-day Saints.

CHAPTER XIV

MELVIN DUMMAR AND
THE "MORMON WILL" SCAM
(Or perhaps it should be called the "*Moron* Will" scam.)

Melvin Dummar was the fellow who received notoriety with his claim to be a beneficiary of Howard Hughes. The story goes that Melvin had stopped his pick-up truck in the desert near Tonopah, Nevada, in January 1968 to "make a little rain" and finds a derelict "Howard Hughes" crawling around in the dirt. Melvin gets "Howard" on his feet and drives him to Las Vegas. "Hughes" supposedly includes Melvin in his last *holographic will* for saving his life. This document of behest became known as "The Mormon Will." Of course, Melvin never collected because it was a phony document. Every *thinking* person *knew* it was a phony document, and yet Melvin *did no jail time* as a conspirator. No, not a single day; ever wonder why? (Documents below will bring to light one of the most ridiculous forgeries and scams ever encountered by the FBI.) Melvin and his attorneys took another run at it in November 2006 in Salt Lake City, Utah; but Melvin got jinxed by Judge Bruce Jenkins who threw it out.

The preliminary information can be found in Chapter II. But we have substantially more documentation now, *and suspicions are confirmed!*

Noah Dietrick had been an attorney of Hughes early in the 1950s but was fired by Howard in 1958. However, his name appeared in the "Mormon Will" as the will's executor (spelled execut*er* [sic] by the will's forger.) When ol' Noah was informed of this supposed nicety, he promptly provided Dummar with attorneys and funds. "It's his handwriting and his signature. It's not just similar, it's the real thing," but of course it *really* wasn't. His assertion certainly engenders wonderment as to just how much money Noah might have filched during *his* employment with Hughes.

It appears that in their attempts to discredit Special Agent James E. Lile, Melvin's attorneys made unpardonable mistakes in the ensuing depositions; they asked questions for which *they* did not know the answers. Agent Lile could then clearly indicate his most astute credentials and accomplishments. Lile was, without doubt, the best man for proving a handwritten hoax. (All the pages of Agent Lile's deposition are *not* listed below – only the pertinent ones since it was in an extensive FBI file.)

Most information is taken directly from FBI files:

EXHIBIT 188

FBI FILE 95-HQ-211845-Bulky7—PAGE 2

RALPH KERRY, C.S.R.
COURT REPORTER – DEPOSITIONS
1830 WEST EIGHTH STREET
LOS ANGELES, CALIFORNIA 90057
381-6635

James E. Lile, Special Agent
Federal Bureau of Investigation
Ninth and Pennsylvania Avenue N.W.
Washington, D.C. 20535

Re: Estate of Howard R. Hughes, Jr.

Dear Mr. Lile:

Enclosed herewith is your deposition, taken July 3, 1977. After reading it, please sign it on the signature line on page 189 before a Notary Public, having your signature notarized.

If you wish to make any changes in any of your answers, you may do so with pen and ink, initialing each change. Then return the deposition to me promptly for filing with the court.

Yours truly,
Ralph Kerry

Encl.
cc Harold Phoden, Esq.

EXHIBIT 189

FBI FILE 95-HQ-211845-Bulky76—PAGE 18
Pertinent Lines 10 through 28.

RALPH KERRY. C.S.R. & ASSOCIATES

Deposition page 15

1   introduce that three-page will and the inner envelope, front
2   and back, as an exhibit?
3   I'm handing you a document. If you will review this
4   document and tell me whether this is – and it's a Xerox –
5   of the inner envelope and the three-page will that you reviewed.
6   A   Yes, this appears to be a copy of the one will and
7   envelope I examined.
8   MR. BLUMENFELD: Okay, let's mark that as Exhibit Lile
9   3-a   through e.
10   Q   BY MR. BLUMENFELD: Mr. Lile, do you have any other
11   specialties other than the ones you have indicated, other than
12   with regard to the questioned documents?
13   A.   I specialize in the examination of photocopies and
14   photocopying machines.   I've published articles in technical
15   journals on the topic.   I additionally have a particular
16   specialty in the examination of printing – that is, mechanical
17   printing processes and printing material.
18   Q   Any other specialties?
19   Those are the major fields.
20   Q   How long have you been with the Federal Bureau of
21   Investigation?
22   A   For more than 16 years.
23   Q   And would you tell us briefly, during these 16
24   years, what you did with the Federal Bureau of Investigation?
25   A   Yes, I originally served in a clerical capacity
26   when I was very young after high school.   Later, after I
27   attended classes at George Washington University, I qualified
28   for the position of technician in the laboratory.   I served as

EXHIBIT 190

FBI FILE 95-HQ-211845-Bulky76—PAGE 19
Pertinent Lines 1 through 28.

RALPH KERRY. C. S. R. & ASSOCIATES

Deposition Page 16

1   technician in the laboratory a few years. Thereafter, upon
2   completion of my education, I entered the FBI Academy for
3   special training.
4   Q   Approximately what period of time?
5   A   We're talking about 1958 through 1966
6   Q   And in 1966 you entered the FBI?
7   A   As a special agent, yes. Prior to that time, I
8   had been a non-agent employee technician myself.
9   After becoming a special agent, I served approximately
10   three years as a field investigator special agent.
11   Q   Doing what?
12   A   Various type of criminal investigations and other
13   responsibilities usually assigned to the field.
14   Q   What years?
15   A   1966 through '69. In early 1969 I returned to
16   Washington to the FBI laboratory on a full-time basis.
17   Q   In 1969 what did you do at that time?
18   A   At that time I studied; I worked under the guidance
19   And supervision of experienced examiners; I have read
20   extensively, I attended classes, conducted experiments, both
21   of the classic variety in the questioned document field and did
22   original research.
23   Q   During this period from 1969 forward, while you
24   were studying, did that include all areas of your expertise so
25   That you focused in any particular area initially?
26   A   That included all areas – initially covered all
27   areas of questioned documents and included a Master of Science
28   Degree from George Washington University in forensic science.

EXHIBIT 191

FBI FILE 95-HQ-211845-Bulky76—PAGE 20
Pertinent lines 1 through 11.

RALPH KERRY. C. S. R. & ASSOCIATES

Deposition page 17

1. Q   When did that occur, your Master of Science in ---
2. A   I believe in 1973, that I obtained the Master of
3. Science Degree.
4. Q   And have you been called upon to testify in any
5. trial in connection with questioned documents?
6. A   A large number of times, yes.
7. Q   In what area have you testified?   Would it be in
8. any of these special areas of expertise you have mentioned or
9. just generally in all areas?
10. A   As a practical matter, it has been in all areas but,
11. a numerical majority have involved handwriting.
12. Q   I see.   Have you also been called to photograph any
13. crime scenes at any time?
14. A   No, I have not.
15. Q   You're not a photographer?
16. A   No, I am not.   I have received very basic photo-
17. graphic training, some basic chemistry of photography but
18. Do not consider myself a photographer, not a professional.
19. Q   You conducted tests on the physical evidence with respect
20. to the inner envelope and the three-page will, which we
21. have labeled Exhibit Lile 3-a through e; is that correct?
22. A   That's correct.
23. Q   Now, with respect to just the envelope, the inner
24. envelope, what test did you conduct on that envelope, other
25. than the handwriting?
26. A   Other the handwriting, any tests that I
27. conducted were limited to non-destructive tests.   The under-
28. standing at that time I received the evidence was that my

In (Exhibits 194 and 195, below) consideration is given to the sloppiness of the "Mormon Will" and Agent James Lile is questioned extensively on this. Excerpts from Allen Gerber's book clarify the matter. (Exhibits 192 and 193) It's pertinent to point out that Allen was, most likely, writing his book prior to 1965. (Gerber's copyright is 1967) Should you, by chance, happen to read his book, you will find his observation of Hughes in a completely different light from the toxic propaganda circulated later by the Summa, Inc. pirates between 1965 to 1976; propaganda ridiculous and adverse, to keep the curious at bay.

EXHIBIT 192

From Allen Gerber's book, Bashful Billionaire, page 288.
Research shows that when it came to letters typed out by his secretaries, Howard Hughes was meticulous and exacting. He was as hard on himself as he was on others when it came to excellence.

On those occasions when Hughes actually visited his Romaine Street office his primary purpose would be to dictate some specific business contract or letter that he wanted to do personally. This act was accompanied by an elaborate ritual. First, he insisted on having two different typists prepare the identical letter. Second he dictated directly to the typists, not trusting to the transcription skills of stenographers. When the typists were ready to start, he personally adjusted the typewriters so the margins of the letters would come out where he wanted them to be.

Hughes is a perfectionist who will not tolerate an erasure or even a smudge. He might dictate half a letter, then change his mind about a word and require the typist to start over on fresh stationery.

The selection of the secretaries who would work in the beige building perhaps involved more screening and more investigation than the CIA uses for its agents. The amount of intelligence material compiled on a secretary was unlimited, primarily because Hughes wanted to be absolutely certain there would be no leaks from his headquarters.

After they were selected, secretaries received unusual instructions. They were not permitted to wear nail polish or perfume. Make-up had to be kept to a minimum and, although lipstick was not prohibited, all other cosmetics were strongly discouraged.

Each girl worked alone in her private office so that no one could know what anyone else was doing. Great emphasis was placed on the following instructions to each employee: No one is permitted to receive personal phone calls at work. Away from the job it is strictly forbidden to talk to anyone about the work or about the employer or supervisor.

Hughes' personal typists led a fairly easy life. Primarily they were required to remain on call at any hour of the day or night. Other secretaries were available as substitutes if needed, but typists had to record in advance the fact that they were

EXHIBIT 193

EMPIRE

When one reviews the testimony in Exhibit 192 concerning the meticulousness of Howard Hughes, one cannot help but to believe that: a) the real Howard Hughes never wrote that *slovenly* "Mormon Will," (b) that Eckersley had been truthful as to what he said about a Hughes Holographic will, and (c) Barlett and Steele had *base reasons* for stating: "Howard probably never wrote a holographic Will."

THE LAST YEAR   629

"He did say that in those days he was in and out of the house. It was written at the gray house behind the tenth green of the Bel Air Country Club. He said he gave it a lot of thought. He'd think about it, come home at night, rough draft a few things. In other words, it took a great deal of time. He mentioned a couple of months."[68]

In a memorandum to Howard Eckersley, Hughes was more explicit:

It was carefully written seated at a desk, and complying to all the rules governing such wills (such as no other typed or printed material on any of the pages). And to illustrate the extremity with which I complied, I did not even use paper with lines, such as this. It was all done under the supervision of my personal attorney Neil McCarthy, and I assure you no detail was overlooked.[69]

Hughes said he was so meticulous in writing the will that "I am assured it is binding as a band of steel."[70]

Despite these convincing accounts, Hughes probably never composed a holographic will. At the time he described the holographic will to Eckersley, he also confided that Eckersley was one of its beneficiaries. "You as well as other members of my staff were identified by description rather than by name," he said.[71] That would have been impossible. Hughes lived at the "gray house," where he said he wrote the will, more than a decade before he formed the personal staff of which Eckersley was a member.

There was, however, another will—a document that Hughes never discussed. This was the will so often revised by Hughes and retyped by Nadine Henley in 1947. On Hughes's orders, the draft will had been placed in a bank safe-deposit box in Hollywood, where it remained until 1974 when Miss Henley, on her own initiative, moved it to a safe in Romaine Street. Hughes had never signed the will. Those senior Hughes executives who knew of it also knew that it was not valid.

Against this background, John Holmes was given the delicate assignment of raising the subject of his employer's last will and testament. Following a suggestion by Miss Henley, Holmes first asked if Hughes might not think it wise to update his will. This brought forth the familiar rambling story of his holographic will written at the "gray house." Holmes next pursued the matter by memorandum: "Chester Davis, Seymour Mintz, Mickey West, Lee Murrin, Nadine Henley, Bill Gay have no knowledge of the existence of your will. Even Raymond Holliday said that if you had a will it would have been so old that Noah Dietrich would have been probably the administrator and chief

433

EXHIBIT 194

FBI FILE 95-HQ-211845-Bulky76—PAGE 25
Pertinent lines 11 through 23.

RALPH KERRY. C. S. R. & ASSOCIATES

Deposition Page 22

1   date is obliterated
2   Q   And how about the postage meter number?
3   A   Same is true of the postage meter number; in some
4   instances, portions of the numbers are visible, but we could not
5   make a determination as to what the exact numbers were.
6   Q   Did you try to determine whether those numbers
7   were actual numbers used by Pitney Bowes?
8   A   No. In conversation with Mr. Greenhalgh, he
9   advised me he had already attempted to do that and he himself
10 had been in contact with Pitney Bowes, so I did not do it.
11 Q   Now, getting back to this erasure on the word Las;
12   how did you determine it was an erasure?
13 A   It's very noticeable, particularly when oblique
14 lighting is placed parallel to the surface of the paper.   In
15 this instance, the fiber fractures; the disturbances, are very
16 noticeable.
17 Q   Could you determine whether the erasure was on the
18 paper before the words were put on or the words themselves were
19 erased?   Is that possible to –
20 A   There are faint traces of previous ink writings in
21 those areas, giving an appearance that previous ink writings – that
22 is, one letter, portion of a letter - - had been erased and then
23 written over again.
24 Q   Now, with respect to the stains on the will itself,
25 did you make any analysis of the stains?
26 A   Well, the first simple analysis was to give a test
27 to see if there was any noticeable odor of solvent. Some will
28 have an odor and will stay for quite a while, particularly if

In observation of the lines below we realize that Agent James Lile was no 'lightweight' when it came to the analysis of phony documents; he told it the way he saw it and, being a fellow of good character and education, it's highly unlikely that he would jeopardize his career by being dishonorable or inconsistent.

EXHIBIT 195

FBI FILE 95-HQ-211845-Bulky76—PAGE 44
Pertinent lines 16 through 25.

Note: Howard Eckersley or Chuck Waldron could have written this memo for "H.H." line 8-9 below. *It is not a known document.*

RALPH KERRY. C. S. R. & ASSOCIATES

Deposition Page 41

1   agency except duly constituted law enforcement agencies and in
2   any matters except criminal, unless the United States govern-
3   ment is a party at issue.
4   Q   BY MR. BLUMENFELD; I see.   That's right; you did
5   so advise me.
6   A   Yes.
7   Q   But now, with that in mind, would that also include,
8   in your opinion, making an analysis of the Eckersley memo at
9   the present time?
10   A   Under the circumstances, yes, it would.
11   Q   And it would be independent of the amount of time
12   available?
13   A   Well, the amount of time available or the equipment
14   necessary would be a completely different set of issues and
15   considerations.
16   Q   All right.   You prepared a report on your analysis,
17   your handwriting analysis of the three-page will?
18   A   That's correct.
19   Q   And what was your conclusion?
20   A   That the three-page will and the inner envelope,
21   that is, the writings on them, were not prepared by Howard R.
22   Hughes, but that instead those writings represent a very poor
23   attempt to copy or simulate the writings of Howard R. Hughes;
24   and that no determination could be made as to who the actual
25   author was.

Note: It is an irregularity (line 21, 22 and 23) on behalf of Agent Lile to infer that any documents used by Rosemont, Inc., to disprove the "Mormon Will," were known documents, none of them are.

Below the Dummar attorney is hopeful that that the sloppiness and ignorance contained in the "Mormon Will" can be attributed to illness, drugs, or both; but Agent Lile is steadfast in his assessment that the will is a forgery.

EXHIBIT 196

FBI FILE 95-HQ-211845-Bulky76—PAGE 52
Pertinent lines 1 through 20

RALPH KERRY.   C. S. R. & ASSOCIATES

1   A   I don't think it would be -- -- always be possible to
2   tell whether the person was suffering from a particular illness
3   by examining the writings, no.
4   Q   Let me rephrase it: Is it possible you could be
5   looking at the questioned document and comparing it to an
6   exemplar and reach a conclusion that a different person wrote
7   the questioned document, but yet it may have been the same
8   person suffering from some of these diseases or illnesses to
9   affect his handwriting?
10   A   No. I don't think an examination of that type would
11   result in a conclusive erroneous report.   I would say more
12   Likely it would result in an inconclusive finding because,
13   again, from experience, some handwriting characteristics in
14   common will stay in that person's writings regardless of the
15   effects and influences on him.   I've seen this many times and
16   most papers written bear this out.   There will be some changes
17   --- perhaps a lot of changes -- but there will still be many
18   strong similarities in those writings so a positive, erroneous,
19   non—identification is highly unlikely.   I myself do not believe
20   I could be involved in something of that type, no.
21   Q   Do you think it's possible for two experts in the
22   same field as the questioned documents field to reach opposite
23   conclusions on a particular questioned document?
24   MR. LILIENSTERN: I'll object to the question as being
25   too general and calling for speculation on the part of the
26   witness.
27   Q   BY MR. BLUMENFELD: That's fine; you may answer
28   A   This has occurred on many occasions.   Yes, there is

Agent James Lile has given an in-depth account as to why the "Mormon Will" is a *forged* document. Dummar and his accomplices had tried to forge the document from previous documents they had found, believing these to be the true writings of Howard Hughes. But once again there was a huge problem because all the exemplars, they had procured were *questionable exemplars, not known exemplars,* and *all* were written after 1965. For an in-depth explanation, return to Chapter V.

All the exemplars used by James Lile, to prove the Will a forgery, *were* *questionable* *documents.* (Chester and Bill letters, *Life Magazine* etc. were all written *after* 1965.) What needs to be kept in mind is that Agent Lile is pointing out all the irregularities and characteristics of forged letters, wills, and memos. So *even if* the later than 1965 documents used by Agent Lile had been legitimate *known* exemplars (which we *now* know they were not), he would still have recognized the Mormon Will as a forgery.

EXHIBIT 197

FBI FILE 95-HQ-211845-Bulky76—PAGE 53
Pertinent lines 4 through 27

RALPH KERRY. C. S. R. & ASSOCIATES

Deposition page 50

1   Q   Each one would have reached a conclusive opinion
2   on the questioned documents?
3   A   For various reasons, yes, that is correct.
4   Q   Now, Mr. Lile, tell us each and every factor upon
5   which you based your conclusion that Howard R. Hughes did not
6   write the will?
7   A   First of all, my examination of the questioned
8   writings revealed every and all of the classic characteristics
9   that are found in copied, or simulated, writings. There were very
10   blunt beginning and ending strokes; the absence of smooth,
11   tapering lines, no free flowing even quality, whatsoever to the
12   writings; irregularities in the curving strokes; pen lifts in
13   totally illogical places; retouches in the letters in totally
14   illogical places; the poor quality of connecting strokes
15   between letters. All of these things are the classic
16   characteristics of copied, or simulated, forgeries and they are
17   all present in these writings. This, in itself, led me to the
18   conclusion that these writings are not the normal writings of
19   whoever prepared them.
20   In examining the writings of Howard R. Hughes, the
21   exemplar writings, I found these same basic letter formations
22   in the Hughes writings but found the Hughes writings were
23   typical, normal, free flowing, smooth handwriting, did not
24   demonstrate that collection of characteristics which I have
25   been taught, and verified myself to be present in copied or
26   simulated writings. Additionally, I found letter formations
27   present in the letters of the will that were foreign to the

EXHIBIT 198

FBI FILE 95-HQ-211845-Bulky76—PAGE 54
Pertinent lines 1 through 15

RALPH KERRY. C. S. R. & ASSOCIATES

Deposition page 51

1   writings of Howard R. Hughes, as shown in the exemplars. I
2   found that certain letters, particularly letters which did not
3   appear in the Life Magazine photograph of the "Chester and Bill"
4   letter, those letters varied greatest in formation from the
5   writings of Howard Hughes, an indication that the person
6   preparing, or the persons preparing, the will did not have at
7   their disposal writings as a model that contained all of the
8   letters that were used in the will -- -- primarily capital letters,
9   upper case letters.
10   There was a combination of differences noted in the
11 writings when compared to the exemplar writings of Hughes and
12 the classic characteristics of copied or simulated writings that
13 led me to the conclusion, first of all, that those writings are
14 attempts -- -- poor attempts -- -- to copy or simulate the writings
15 of Howard R. Hughes and were not prepared by Howard R. Hughes.
16 Q   Now, as I understand your earlier testimony, you
17 Indicated that originally you had a photocopy of the three-page
18 will; is that correct?
19 A   Yes, that's correct.
20 Q   And you examined that document?
21 A   No, I looked at it.
22 Q   You looked at it. Did you reach a conclusion at
23 that time as to whether the document was written by Howard R.
24 Hughes?
25 A   I did not even go into in-depth examination at that
26 time. I waited for the original document.
27 Q   I understand that, but did you reach a tentative
28 conclusion at that time?

EXHIBIT 199

FBI FILE 95-HQ-211845-Bulky76—PAGE 103
Pertinent lines 12 through 28.

In the Lile deposition, pages 100 and 101 below, the attorneys attempt to attribute the sloppiness and ignorance in the "Mormon Will" due to kidney failure – but it just doesn't work. Agent Lile clearly explains that this <u>could not</u> be the case.

RALPH KERRY. C. S. R. & ASSOCIATES

Deposition Page 100

1   results back from Pitney Bowes and they were as I described them

2   before. He, thereafter, followed them up by sending a letter

3   to me at my office, and, attached to it, was a letter he had

4   received from Pitney Bowes concerning the results of their

5   examinations of the photographs and the results were, in summary, as I

6   said before.

7   I glanced at the letter, saw it was the same type

8   Information -- -- never read the whole thing. I stuck it in my

9   File.

10   MR. MENCHETTI; I wanted you to be aware that letter did

11   exist.

12   Q   BY MR. BLUMENFELD: Mr. Lile, are you aware of what

13   renal failure is, insufficiency Kidney failure, kidney

14   insufficiency?

15   A   I'm not real familiar; I've heard the term.

16   Q   Would you know whether or not it has any effect on

17   A person's handwriting if someone has that?

18   A   I never heard or learned anything specifically

19   along those lines. No, I wouldn't --

20   Q   Did you give any consideration to the possibility

21   that the writer of the will was ill?

22   A   I had anticipated, prior to receiving the original

23   document, that some attempt might have been made, if this will were not

24   genuine, to duplicate the writings of an elderly and infirm

25   person or that it might be the result, that is, the reason to

26   examine the original document, might reveal they were the writings of

27   someone very ill, very infirm, or elderly. I was aware of that.

28   At the time I received it, I did expect something along those

EXHIBIT 200

FBI FILE 95-HQ-211845-Bulky76—PAGE 104
Pertinent lines1 through 28

RALPH KERRY. C. S. R. & ASSOCIATES

Deposition Page 102

1   lines one way or the other. The results of my examination,
2   however, discounted that.
3   Q   I'm not sure I understand you. Did you say you
4   anticipated, prior to receiving the will, that someone could
5   claim that or it could exist?
6   A   No, to backtrack just a little bit. There had been
7   so much publicity, of course, as to the purported poor state
8   of health of Mr. Hughes in his later years that I anticipated
9   that the will, if it were legitimate, might show some places
10   of someone very ill or someone very elderly, or if not legitimate,
11   might show the traces of someone trying to make it so appear.
12   I had this in mind at the time. However, in examining, I
13   found it did not have any of these elderly, tremulous type
14   formations in the writings I have been led to believe are
15   present in the writings of persons in poor health or very old.
16   Instead, it had the poor-line quality, the wavering's, rather
17   then the actual tremor of the hand, all the classical signs of
18   a simulated or copied forgery.
19   Q   You stated just now you did not have the signs that
20   you were led to believe would be indicated by someone who is
21   ill or aged; is that what you said?
22   A   As a result of my readings, and based upon the
23   cases I have examined involving the writings of elderly persons,
24   based on my experiences, perhaps is a better term.
25   Q   I thought you indicated earlier that there is no
26   condition that would change the basic characteristics of some-
27   one's writing?
28   A   That's true; the basic characteristics will still

EXHIBIT 201

FBI FILE 95-HQ-211845-Bulky76—PAGE 115
Pertinent lines 11 through 28.

The attorneys continue to ask questions as to Agent Lile's expertise: These mistakes further weaken their argument as to document's authenticity. Maybe it's not nice to form opinions about attorneys, but perhaps a standing rule in depositions and courtrooms should be that, <u>if you are setting a trap,</u> *never ask a question to which you do not know the answer.*

RALPH KERRY. C. S. R. & ASSOCIATES

Deposition Page 112

1   A   Yes, I had original documents. I had no complaint
2   about the reproduction.
3   Q   And with respect to any conversation you may have
4   had with Mr. Shaneyfelt, did that in any manner influence the
5   opinion and conclusion which you have expressed in your report
6   and you have expressed on the record for us today?
7   A   Absolutely not.
8   Q   Did you form your conclusion independent of the
9   judgment of others, including Mr. Shaneyfelt?
10   A   Yes, I did.
11   Q   Mr. Blumenfeld touched on your background just a
12   bit. I'd like to ask you a few more questions, Mr. Lile.
13   what is the nature of your formal educational
14   attainment?
15   A   I have a Bachelor of Arts degree from the University
16   of Northern Colorado and a Master of Science in forensic
17   science from George Washington University, Washington, D.C.
18   I have attended classes at the Institute of Paper Chemistry in
19   Appleton, Wisconsin, which is the largest specialized paper
20   production and examination facility in the world. I Have
21   attended classes, lectures at various other institutions and
22   at various meetings of professionals around the country.
23   Q   All right, sir, and what field did you receive
24   your undergraduate work in?
25   A   I had my major in history and minor in English.
26   Q   And the degree which you described for us, that is,
27   the Master of Science, forensic science, how long a period of
28   study is that, if one pursues it on a full-time basis?

EXHIBIT 202

FBI FILE 95-HQ-211845-Bulky76—PAGE 116
Pertinent lines 1 through 28

RALPH KERRY. C. S. R. & ASSOCIATES

Deposition Page 113

1. A   On full-time basis, I believe it's a two-year
2. program. I attended on a part-time basis, and it required
3. three years.
4. Q   Mr. Lile, are you a member of any professional
5. Societies in the field of questioned documents examination?
6. A   Yes, I am.
7. Q   Will you tell us what societies in which you hold
8. membership are?
9. A   Member of the American Academy of Forensic
10. Science Questioned Documents Section.
11. Q   You mentioned earlier what I would characterize a
12. regional or local group of document examiners, I believe?
13. A   Yes, these are loose-knit organizations to which
14. there is no actual membership involved. They are almost social,
15. fraternal-type groups, where periodically the document
16. examiners in particular geographical areas will assemble for
17. luncheon and have speakers and shop talk a little bit. I've
18. attended numerous of those.
19. Q   With respect to your experience in the FBI
20. laboratory, could you give us -- -- and I'm sure this is going to
21. be a very broad range of examples of types of documents you
22. have been called upon to examine in your work.
23. A   It's a very wide range. It ranges from things as
24. mundane as bad checks to documents in major type cases, such
25. as kidnap, ransom notes. In between you would have all types
26. of frauds and forgeries, embezzlements of various types, not
27. only involving handwriting, but typewriting, paper, photocopying;
28. worked extensively in cases involving counterfeiting of

EXHIBIT 203

FBI FILE 95-HQ-211845-Bulky76—PAGE 117
Lile Deposition page 114. Lines 1 through 28

RALPH KERRY. C. S. R. & ASSOCIATES

114

1 securities, stocks and bonds. I've worked ~~almost exclusively~~ *most extensively* yet

2 *of any* in the laboratory in matters of photocopying machines and

3 photocopiers. I would say about as wide a range as the entire

4 range of questioned documents is and at some time examiners

5 will receive documents on it.

6   Q   Did you tell us earlier that you began working

7 again as a special agent, that is, you returned to the

8 laboratory, in the capacity of a special agent in 1969?

9   A   In 1969, in February of 1969, yes.

10   Q   Since that time to the present date, Mr. Lile,

11 what percentage of your working time have you devoted to the

12 examination of questioned documents?

13   A   It's a full-time job.

14   Q   With respect to your conversation with Mr. Blumen-

15 feld, did that concern the merits or anything concerning your

16 conclusion and opinion or was that solely devoted to the

17 mechanics of your coming out for the deposition?

18   A   As I recall, it was limited to the mechanics of

19 him arranging for my transportation and him arranging for the

20 official permission for me to travel here. He did mention he

21 was particularly interested in the opening and the resealing

22 of the so-called inner envelope rather than the remainder of

23 the examinations; and, to the best of my recollection, that was

24 pretty much the complete conversations.

25   Q   All right, sir, I believe you mentioned earlier --

26 he inquired whether it would be possible for you to review

27 additional exemplars to be provided to you?

28   A   Yes, I guess that was a subsequent telephone call,

EXHIBIT 204-A

FBI FILE 95-HQ-211845-Bulky76—Page 183
Pertinent lines 14 through 28

RALPH KERRY. C. S. R. & ASSOCIATES

Deposition Page 180

1   so that, when the flap is later sealed, again, unless the
2   person who is doing the resealing is extremely meticulous and
3   careful, they will not perfectly align the flap with the
4   previous glue line but, again, that glue line doesn't always
5   remain. Sometimes it does not ooze out from under the flap page.
6   Sometimes the original adhesive was to wet. Perhaps the
7   steaming was so wet it washed it off the surface of the page.
8   There are several possible explanations, which is why I
9   mentioned the presence of the glue line can be significant, but
10   the absence of it isn't necessarily of any significance.
11   Q   So, it's of no significance whatsoever one way or
12   the other?
13   A   One way or the other; that's true.
14   Q   Now, Mr. Menchetti asked you a couple questions
15   with respect to the quality of the forgery and you indicated
16   you felt it was one of the poorest forgeries you had ever
17   examined in your career?
18   A   Very poor.
19   Q   If we were to take a scale of forgery only from one
20   to ten, where would you place it, if you can?
21   A   Very, very hypothetical, and I don't feel I can
22   give you an answer under the circumstances. It's just poorly
23   done. That's all I can say.
24   Q   Lct' say your experience in forgery, forgetting a
25   hypothetical; in your experience of quality of forgeries, would
26   you say this is the worst you have ever seen?
27   A   Wouldn't say it's the worst. I would say it's one
28   of the poorer ones. I don't know how better to describe them.

EXHIBIT 204-B

FBI FILE 95-HQ-211845-Bulky76—PAGE 18
Pertinent lines 1 through 17

RALPH KERRY. C. S. R. & ASSOCIATES

Deposition Page 181

1   Q   you said it was done by a person unskilled. What
2   did you mean by that?
3   A   Some persons, in my experience in examining
4   questioned documents, have become very skillful in forging.
5   The average person is not skilled. I'm not meaning to imply
6   this person lacks any manual dexterity whatsoever; merely that
7   this person has not practiced the craft sufficiently long to
8   develop skills enough to try to pull off something like that.
9   Q   Could you determine anything else about the writer
10   of the will, other than the fact he was unskilled and an
11   unskilled forger?
12   A   As a matter of fact, I couldn't even state with any
13   certainty there was one writer involved in the preparation of
14   the will.
15   Q   So, the answer to that question is you can't tell?
16   A   Can't tell. I cannot tell anything except who did
17   not prepare it.
18   Q   Mr. Menchetti asked you if you discussed your
19   findings with Mr. Stangel. Now, who was the first one between
20   you and Mr. Stangel, that is, to conduct the examination?
21   A   Myself.
22   Q   And when the report came in, did Mr. Stangel -- -- and
23   the questions from the Attorney General -- -- did Mr. Stangel know
24   he was going to be the backup examiner?
25   A   At that time, no, he did not.
26   Q   When did he first find out?
27   A   Can't give you a specific date. It was at or about
28   the time Mr. Gillham was transferred.

EXHIBIT 205-A

FROM FEDERAL FILES – PHOTO'S OF THE "MORMON WILL"
ACTUAL DOCUMENTS BELOW: THE ENVELOPE

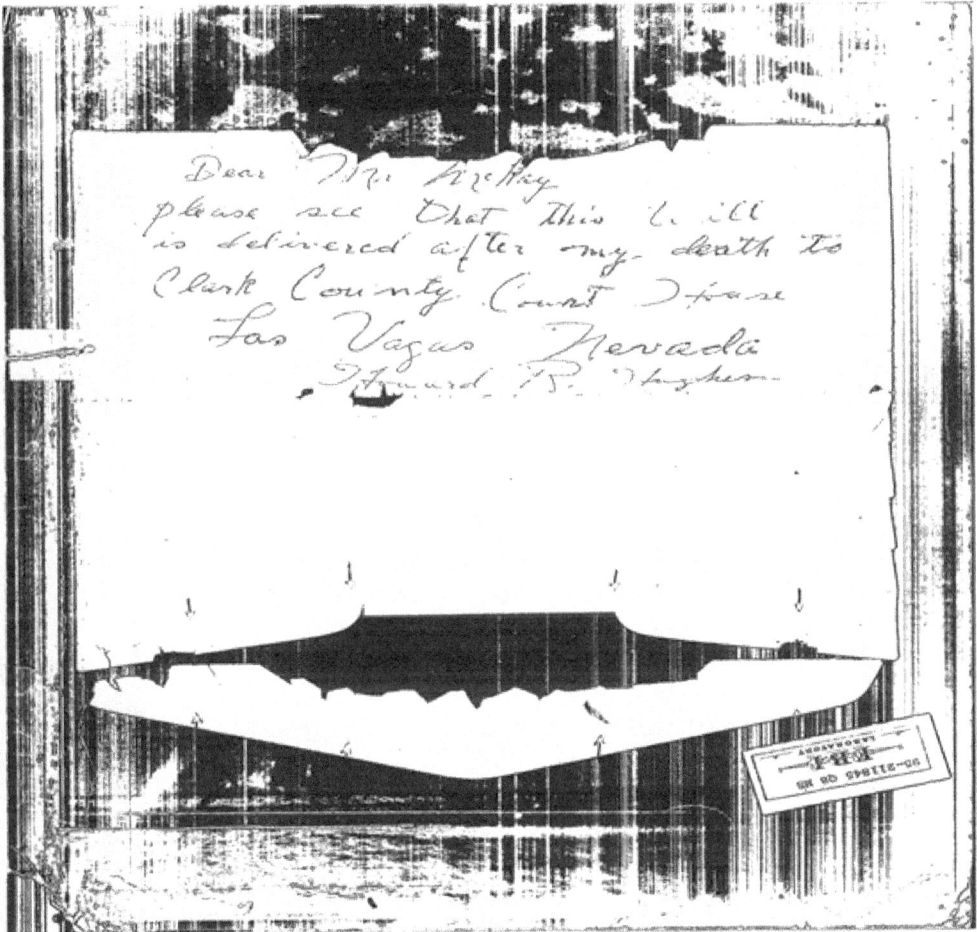

EXHIBIT 205-B
PAGE 1

Last Will and Testament

I Howard R. Hughes Stein of
sound and disposing mind and
memory, not acting under duress,
fraud or the undue influence
of any person whomsoever,
and being a resident of Las Vegas
Nevada. declare that this
is to be my last Will
and revoke all other Wills
previously made by me —

After my death my estate
is to be devided as follows —

first: one forth of all my assets to go to Hughes Med-
ical Institute of Miami —

second: one eight of assets
to be devided among
The University of Texas —
Rice Institute of Technology
of Houston —
the University of Nevada
and The University of Calif.
Howard R. Hughes
— page one —

EXHIBIT 205-C
PAGE 2

third: one sixteenth to Church
of Jesus Christ of Latter-day
Saints — David O. Makay-Pre

Forth: one sixteenth to establish a home for Orphan
Cildren —

Fifth: one sixteenth of assets
to go to Boy Scouts
of America.

sixth: one sixteenth to be
ifevided among Jean Peters of
Los Angeles and Ella Rice
of Houston —

seventh: one sixteenth of assets
to William R. Lommis of
Houston, Texas —

eighth: one sixteenth to go
to Melvin Du Mar of
Gabbs Nevada —

Howard R Hughes

— page two —

EXHIBIT 205-D
PAGE 3

ninth: one sixteenth to be
devided amoung my
personal aids at the time
of my death-

tenth: one sixteenth to be
used as school scholarship
fund for entire Country-

the spruce goose is to be given
to the City of Long Beach, Calif-

the remainder of My
estate is to be devided among
the key men of the company's
I own at the time of my
death.

I appoint Noah Dietrich
as the executer of this will-

signed the 19 day of
March 1968

Howard R. Hughes

-page three-

95-211845 Q11 MS
FBI

CRITIQUE ON FEDERAL AGENT JAMES LILE'S DEPOSITIONS:

Agent James Lile gave an in-depth account of why the "Mormon Will" is a *forged* document. Dummar and his accomplices had tried to forge the will from previous documents they found, believing these to be the true writings of Howard Hughes. But once again there was a problem – all the exemplars they had procured were questionable exemplars, *not* known exemplars, and *all* were written *after* 1965. See details in Chapter VI.

All the exemplars used by James Lile to prove the will a forgery were *questionable documents;* (Chester and Bill letters, *Life Magazine*, etc. were all written *after* 1965.) What needs to be kept in mind is that Agent Lile is pointing out all the irregularities and characteristics of forged letters, wills, and memos. So then, even *if* the post-1965 documents used by Agent Lile had been legitimate known exemplars (which we now know they were not), he would *still* have recognized the Mormon Will as a forgery.

Clearly, in Exhibits 204-A and B, Agent Lile maintains that he is "unable to make a determination as to *who* wrote the Mormon Will." Keep in mind that he was comparing it with documentation that Howard Hughes *supposedly* had written, the Chester and Bill letters, Dear Bob, etc. These writings are bad documents as far as authenticity goes; no officer of the law gave witness to or saw Hughes write any of them; therefore, they can only be deemed questionable exemplars at best. *If* they could have found an extensive known exemplar, actually written by Howard Hughes, with which to compare them, then – and only then – would they have had the true exemplars that might have been deemed collective exemplars. Therefore, *all documents used were, and are, questionable.* Consequently, when Lile maintains, "can't tell, cannot tell anything except who did not prepare it." (See lines 15, 16, and 17 in Exhibit 204-B.) What he is in effect saying is that the same person who wrote the "Mormon Will" was not the same person who wrote the collective exemplars he used for comparison. *He should not have indicated* that the comparison exemplars he used were "Hughes known exemplars." This is a serious mistake on behalf of Agent Lile, as he should have graphically pointed out that all the exemplars he used for comparison to the "Mormon Will" were not known exemplars, but simply questionable exemplars and that there was *no proof* that Howard Hughes had written *any* of them. Agent Lile should not have presumed that the exemplars, hc used for comparison had been written by Howard Hughes!

"THE MORMON WILL TEXT"

Let's take a hard look at "the last Will and Testament of Howard R. Hughes Jr." according to Melvin Dummar and his co-conspirators. The original phony holographic will discussed above has been converted to typescript below and numerically designated for easy reading and location.

[Sic] which follows each error, means the typescript was copied exactly from the holographic "Mormon Will." All errors are exactly as they appeared.

EXHIBIT 205-E ---- ON THE ENVELOPE

1	**Dear Mr. McKay**
2	**Please see that this will**
3	**Is delivered after my death to**
4	**Clark County Court House**
5	**Las Vegas Nevada**
6	**Howard R. Hughes**

EXHIBIT 205-F ----THE WILL

1	**Last Will and Testament**
2	**I, Howard R. Hughes, being of sound mind and disposing mind and memory,**
3	**not acting under duress, fraud or the undue influence of any person whomever, and**
4	**being a resident of Las Vegas Nevada, declare that this is to be my last Will and**
5	**revolt [sic] all other wills previously made by me –**
6	**After my death, my estate is to be devided [sic] as follows –**
7	**First: one-forth [sic] of all my assets to go to Hughes Medical Institute of Miami –**
8	**Second: one-eight [sic] of assets to be devided [sic] among the University of Texas**
9	**– Rice Institute of Technology of Houston – the University of Nevada – and the**
10	**University of Calif.**
11	**Third: one-sixteenth to Church of Jesus Christ of Latter-day Saints - David O. McKay Pre.**
12	**Forth [sic]: one-sixteenth to establish a home for Orphan Children [sic] –**
13	**Fifth: one-sixteenth of assets to go to Boy Scouts of America.**
14	**Sixth: one-sixteenth to be devided [sic] among Jean Peters of Los Angeles and Ella Rice of Houston –**
15	**Seventh: one-sixteenth of assets to William R. Lommis [sic] of Houston, Texas –**
16	**Eight; one-sixteenth to go to Melvin DuMar [sic] of Gabbs, Nevada –**
17	**Ninth: one-sixteenth to be devided [sic] among my personal aids at the time of my death**
18	**Tenth: one-sixteenth to be used as a school scholarship fund for entire country –**
19	**the spruce goose is to be given to the City of Long Beach, Calif.**
20	**The remainder of my estate is to be devided [sic] among key men of the**
21	**company's [sic] I own at the time of my death.**
22	**I appoint Noah Dietrich as the executer [sic] of this will –**
23	**Signed the 19 [sic] day of March 1968**
24	**Howard R. Hughes**

DUMMAR NOTES:

The Dummar scam would have us believe that sick ol' drug addicted Hughes would write a sloppy holographic will, a will that contained numerous misspelled words, poor grammar, and basic ignorance as to how to spell his aunt Annette and nephew Will's last name (Lommis instead of Lummis). Had Howard *actually* written that sad excuse of a will his mother would have turned over in her grave, especially after spending all that money to send him to the best college preparatory schools. "Oh Howard!" She would have thought. "How could you possibly write such a terribly messy will with which to give away a billion-dollar estate – an estate that took you a lifetime to build?!" (Howard Hughes was born on Christmas Eve 1905. Had he actually lived until 1976, when he *supposedly* died, he would only have been 71 years old. Therefore Hughes, even *if* he had been in the derelict, drug-addicted condition the *parasites* in his empire inferred he was, he still *could not* have written that pathetic "Mormon Will." Eight years earlier, he was only 63 years old! Also, Howard never called the seaplane he built, and spent millions of his own money on, Spruce Goose. Its name was The Hercules, and none dared call it Spruce Goose, at least not in his presence. (Review Exhibit 192 where Howard Hughes is exacting, neat, and precise in his writings.)

To revisit a previous thought, why would Dummar and his accomplices concoct a holographic will when a common typed will, notarized by an old, perhaps now dead, judge or notary could have been more easily fabricated? A *typed* will would have been so much tidier and comprehensive, don't you think? A single forged Howard Hughes signature and several initials would have been so much easier than *creating a whole forged holographic will!*

Reason: The forgers somehow knew that a genuine holographic [handwritten] will existed, and this existing will *must be superseded* for their deception to succeed. To bring home the point with a bit of repetition: Being that Howard Hughes was predisposed to *cursive wills:* "My will, will be as binding as a steel belt," hence his existing will *must be superseded by yet another cursive will. Yes, a cursive will is the strongest type of will.* Unfortunately for them, the fraudsters could only try to copy written material which Hughes had supposedly written after 1965. However, and unfortunately for them, there has been no *authentic*, extensive documentation before or after 1965 that has come to light. It can certainly be supposed that the L.D.S. Church knew Dummar's claim to be fraudulent since they possibly had, and may still have, the *neat and carefully written* legitimate Hughes will. It can also be supposed that the Church could not come out in the open after 1965 when Hughes died to say they were custodians of a legitimate Hughes will. There would have been an avalanche of claims, perennially springing up, on the Hughes estate. Although they may have known of Hughes's poor health and his impending death, they may not have known exactly when he died. The first L.D.S. custodians of Howard's true will may have waited patiently for a cursive codicil to

453

turn up. They may have been notified that Howard Hughes gave a codicil to a fellow named Charles in 1964 Mexico but were unaware it had been stolen. The information might have been leaked by someone in the know, either within the Mormon Church or perhaps by one of Howard's corrupt lieutenants who had been contacted for advice by the Church. How else could Dummar's story *parallel so closely* what happened to Charles in Mexico in 1964? For example, the road-side meetings, Howard's statement to Charles, "I hope I spelled your name right," the misspelling of Dummar's name as "DuMar" in the "Mormon Will." It's a given that the bogus will pirates *knew how* to spell Melvin's last name and intentionally misspelled it. The bandits *had to have been* privy to inside knowledge found within a codicil, the same document which Charles once held. The reality is that Melvin Dummar sought out the L.D.S. Church offices, into which he had covertly delivered the phony will, and then lied under oath that he had done so. *If* the will *had been legitimate*, why didn't Dummar simply take the will openly and directly to the Mormon Church Offices? Or why did he *not* notify a member of the "Mormon Council of 12" or whoever was the Prophet at the time; after all it *was* addressed to David O. McKay. Even an investigative reporter would have been a good option – those guys and gals are always ready for a Pulitzer. Why not deliver it directly to the Summa, Inc. group? Did he know they were a den of thieves? And, if he knew them for what they were, who told him?

Perhaps as time went by, the process of exploiting the Hughes vast wealth began – investments, payments to co-executors, etc. Those involved in the conspiracy probably hoped the codicil bearer would never appear. *But he (Charles Clotfelter) discovered who he was* and made known to the world the existence of the codicil when he published his book, *The Price Of their Souls,* in 2011. Charles sent a copy of the book to the movers and shakers of the L.D.S. Church as well as the current Prophet.

Dummar lied numerous times under oath (his deposition follows); but when confronted with the fact that his latent palm print was on the envelope, he changed his story and said that he *had* steamed open the envelope and read its contents. So, after lying, he then confessed that he knew himself to be one of the will's beneficiaries. He also lied under oath saying he did *not* deliver the document to the offices of the Mormon Church, but later confessed that he had. (It appears that throughout Dummar's life, he was never to be the sharpest blade in the drawer. In all probability, he was looking over the shoulder of the forger whose intelligence he mistakenly believed to be greater than his own; hence he knew the phony will's contents from the beginning.)

EXHIBIT 206

This Portion of Dummar's Deposition Can Be Found On Page 660 Of Donald Barlett And James Steele's Book *Empire*

Melvin Dummar's courtroom deposition proceedings in November of 1976 wherein he blatantly lies eleven times when questioned under oath:

1	LAWYER:	When was the first time you saw a copy of that purported will?
2	DUMMAR:	It was in April at the end of April and a news reporter from Salt
3		Lake City … brought a copy of it up and gave it to me.
4	LAWYER:	Prior to that time, you had never seen a copy of that will?
5	DUMMAR:	No, I hadn't.
6	LAWYER:	Have you ever seen the original of it?
7	DUMMAR:	No.
8	LAWYER:	Let me talk to you straightaway, Mr. Dummar, at the outset, did
9		you write that will?
10	DUMMAR:	No.
11	LAWYER:	Did you have anything to do with the writing of it?
12	DUMMAR:	No.
13	LAWYER:	Did you write either of the envelopes and the messages, the
14		message on either of the envelopes or the note which was
15		included in the will?
16	DUMMAR:	No.
17	LAWYER:	Did you have anything to do with writing those notes or those
18		envelopes?
19	DUMMAR:	No.
20	LAWYER:	Did you have any of those documents in your possession at any
21		time?
22	DUMMAR:	No.
23	LAWYER:	Do you as of today, Mr. Dummar, have any idea how this
24		purported will ended up on the desk of one of the Mormon
25		Church employees on the 25th floor of the church office building
26		headquarters?
27	DUMMAR:	No.
28	LAWYER:	You had nothing to do with getting the will there?
29	DUMMAR:	No.
30	LAWYER:	Have you ever had your hand on this outside envelope?
31	DUMMAR:	No.

Is there any mystery as to why Dummar never passed a legitimate polygraph test? Don't you think it strange that not a single latent fingerprint *from anyone* appeared anywhere on the envelope or on the will itself? *But when caught later in his lie, Dummar admitted to having held and read the will.*

Dummar must have been a party to the scam. He and his accomplice probably wore gloves when helping to prepare or handle the phony document. Dummar simply made the mistake of pressing his palm on the exterior of the envelope at some point. Could it be when he nervously slid the envelope into the Mormon Church office's paperwork? He probably had some knowledge of latent fingerprints – and might even have cut the tips off gloves to use over his fingers when handling the envelope in the Church offices – but never thought about latent *palm prints*. Law enforcement was well aware of the benefits of *latent palm prints* even in those years.

Okay, we know that Dummar's accomplice didn't know how to spell *divide,* and was consistent in this error several times; used "eight" when it should have been *eighth;* and used "forth" when it should have used *fourth.* Aside from these and other errors, a most glaring mistake was that they spelled Howard's nephew's last name "Lommis," when the correct spelling is Lummis. Howard was a well-educated man. His parents had sent him to college preparatory schools, and most college-preparatory schools in those years used college texts, as Howard must also have done. It's highly unlikely Howard would have made such blatant misspelling errors. Hughes was an astute fellow of letters, how else could he have built his billion-dollar empire? But one thing is for certain – *Howard would never have forgotten how to spell his aunt and nephew's last name!*

What can be viewed as the worst blunder in the "Mormon Will" was when they decided to plug in Noah Dietrich as the "executer" [sic] (correct spelling executor) of the will. Well, of course Noah was delighted with this concept and paid for the attorneys to help out in Dummar's defense. Noah: "Oh yeah, that's Howard's writing, that's him alright." But of course, it never was – it was wrong in four major ways:

1. Howard was dead in 1965.
2. The "Mormon Will" was supposedly written in 1968.
3. Howard called his plane the Hercules and never referred to it as the Spruce Goose.
4. Howard *fired* Dietrich in March 1957 when Dietrich had led a failed coup d'état to have Howard declared mentally incompetent and confined to a mental institution. Dietrich tried to get Howard's personal physician and friend Vern Mason in on the deal, but it backfired. Mason undoubtedly went straight to Hughes with the ploy. Mason would never have *sold out* Hughes (see Exhibit 65) and Hughes would never have named Dietrich as the executor of his Estate! There were other things wrong with the "Mormon Will" but the four above are glaringly *wrong.*

In Exhibits 207-A and B of the Lile deposition, the attorneys and agent Lile hash out the longevity of latent fingerprints on documents as well as the impressions left by writing on paper when the ink may have disappeared over time. This is the second time that fault is found with Agent Lile. The first time was the presumption of known exemplar comparisons, when they were not. (See Chapter VI Exemplar Exhibits 45, 56, 47, etc. and Chapter V Fingerprint Exhibits 30, 31-A, and 31-B.) On page 171 of the Lile Deposition, Agent Lile gives a lame assessment regarding fingerprints. However, this is excusable, since agent Lile was a cursive writing expert not a "print man." Although he points out that latent prints have longevity, he was unable to give instances of longevity over many years. (Here, reiterated, is that the *only* print of any kind appearing on the "Mormon Will" was on the envelope which enclosed the will, and it was Dummar's palm print. The supposition here is that the attorneys wanted Lile to say that Hughes's latent prints could have disappeared over the eight-year period from when "H.H." had supposedly written the will and when it fell into the possession of Dummar or that prints could have been cooked off when the document was steamed open by Dummar. Dummar claimed to have done this when he confessed to having lied under oath. When caught in his lie, he then claimed to have accessed the contents of the envelope addressed to David O. McKay. Although Lile attests to longevity of latent prints (below,) he could not specify any particular case wherein they had survived for a substantial period of time. Having researched this, the research indicates that *Hughes's latent prints should have been all over that will if he had indeed written it, and where were Dummar's prints if he had not worn gloves in handling the will previously when he read it, or when he handled it upon depositing it into the church offices?* The fellow who delivered the document to Dummar left no prints. Dummar who recanted and said he had recently "steamed the letter open and read its contents" left no fingerprints on the envelope or on the interior three pages of the will. Whoever forged the "Mormon Will," if not Melvin, left no prints. But, most *glaringly*, none of Hughes's prints were found! So, let's get *real here* – the FBI processed the "Mormon Will" for latent fingerprints. (Perhaps they found an L.D.S. office clerks' fingerprints, but no others; there is no documentation of this.) However, they did find Dummar's latent *palm* print. This is when Dummar recanted and admitted to handling the documents and confessed to all the other lies he had told!

Note #1: Melvin steaming open the envelope would not cause any, and certainly not all, of the latent prints on its interior to disappear. He claimed to have steamed *only the seal* of the envelope, opened the envelope, handled all three pages, and then resealed it. It's clear that there should have been many of *his* latent fingerprints on the three pages and on the envelope as well had he not worn gloves. (Refresh with Chapter V.) So, at the risk of overly emphasizing the obvious – Melvin Dummar knew the con was on! (Okay – there is duplication galore in the above analysis making it *abundantly* clear that the "Mormon Will" was a phony and that "Magic" Melvin was thoroughly involved in the scam.)

Note #2: They found Dummar's *palm print on the envelope* that contained the three pages of the "Mormon Will," but no fingerprints. There can be little doubt that the FBI Forensic Lab processed the entire phony document and its envelope for additional fingerprints and palm prints and, owing to the <u>lack of any other finger or palm prints,</u> it is obvious that all the makers and handlers of the phony will wore gloves to conceal their identities. A direct quote from our supper-sleuth L. Russ Russell: "The way I, and most cursive analysts would see it, is that it's virtually impossible for anyone to cursively write a two or more-page document without leaving behind latent palm or fingerprints *unless they wore gloves."*

Below we delve further into Federal Agent Lile's deposition. It's quite clear that many curious things took place during the Melvin Dummar trial. More curious is how many people bought into the travesty. It was bad enough that Dummar was a phony and all the legal beagles knew what he was, but what really boggles the mind is that numerous questionable – and only questionable – documents would be used to discredit Dummar's claim.

EXHIBIT 207-A

Agent Lile's analysis of the "Mormon Will"
FBI FILE 95-HQ-211845-Bulky76—PAGE 174

RALPH KERRY. C. S. R. & ASSOCIATES

Deposition Page 171

1   A   They can, yes, sir.

2   Q   Over a period?

3   A   Humidity in particular can cause them to fade.

4   Q   How about time?

5   Time, there are variables involved, time,

6   presence or absence of humidity, storage of the document,

7   whether protected or not. For instance, a folded document,

8   protected within pages of a book on a shelf in a library will

9   last and maintain some characteristics for many, many years,

10   including fingerprints.

11   Q   How many years?

12   A   Well, again, there are too many variables involved.

13   I could not give you a specific time frame.

14   Q   Is it possible indented writings could disappear

15   after two, three months?

16   A   Under some circumstances, yes, I think it's

17   possible.

18   Q   You indicated also that fingerprints would also

19   be maintained over a period of time?

20   A   In some instances, I said it's possible that even

21   fingerprints could be retained.

22   Q   Let's deal with fingerprints for a moment. Are you

23   saying that fingerprints can be retained on a document more

24   than five years?

25   MR. MENCHETTI: Objection as being out of the scope of

26   expertise of the witness.

27   MR. BLUMENFELD: I think the witness has testified he

28   believed that fingerprints can in fact be retained over a period

EXHIBIT 207-B

Agent Lile's analysis of the "Mormon Will"
FBI FILE 95-HQ-211845-Bulky76—PAGE 175

RALPH KERRY. C. S. R. & ASSOCIATES

Deposition Page 172

1   of time -- -- after a period of time.
2   THE WITNESS: I stated in the protection of a document
3   that, in regard to protecting a document, I have heard in
4   discussions with our latent fingerprint people even finger—
5   prints on occasion have been found in protected documents for
6   a fairly long period of time. I don't recall the exact time
7   frame they were discussing. This is not from my own experience
8   and my own expertise.
9   Q   You have no knowledge?
10   A   No, I don't
11   Q   Now, just to clarify a point: We look at a document of
12   more than one page, and we see the absence of the indented writing?
13   All we can say is there is an absence of the indented writing?
14   A   That's exactly right.
15   Q   Nothing else?
16   A   I would say that, yes.
17   Q   Now, I believe Mr. Freese asked you if you looked
18   inside the inner envelope to see whether there were any marks
19   of any kind in the inner envelope. You said you didn't know;
20   Is that correct?
21   A   I said I didn't have anything in my notes which
22   would indicate one way or the other but, again, knowing the way
23   I work and the way I keep notes, I write things of significance.
24   If there is nothing significant there, I frequently will make
25   no notes whatsoever, because I know what my procedures are.
26   Q   But you don't recall? You have no memory of ever
27   looking inside the envelope to check?
28   A   I honestly have no clear recollection of looking

Charles R. Clotfelter

EXHIBIT 208

HOWARD HUGHES AND THE MORMON CHURCH CONNECTION
Lead-in Document to <u>Original</u> Administrator of Howard Hughes Estate:
(First National Bank of Nevada)

Under the common law of Texas as well as that of California, a decedent has only one domicile for death tax purposes. California v. Texas, 437 U.S. at 603, 98 S. Ct. at 3109 (Stewart, J., concurring); see Texas v. Florida, 306 U.S. at 408, 59 S. Ct. at 568. Because "neither Texas nor California is or will become a party to the proceedings in the other's courts, neither will be bound by an adverse determination of domicile in the other's forum." California v. Texas, 437 U.S. at 603, 98 S. Ct. at 3109. Lummis seeks only a determination that will bind both sets of taxing officials[14] and will thus preserve the estate's assets from either total or near-total depletion. Such a determination, rather than impeding the states in enforcing their laws, would effectively implement their rules that death taxes may be imposed only by a state in which a decedent is domiciled at his death and that a decedent may have only one domicile. The equitable bill in the nature of interpleader, codified in section 1335, enables Lummis to obtain a binding domicile determination from a federal tribunal. We hold that the district court has jurisdiction over Lummis' suit; thus we reverse its dismissal order.

REVERSED AND REMANDED.

District Judge of the Southern District of Alabama, sitting by designation

The Internal Revenue Service estimated that the estate was worth approximately $465,000,000. The California inheritance tax referee valued the estate at $1,106,345,516. The administrators, by contrast, asserted that its value was $166,800,000

The Texas courts appointed William Rice Lummis and Annette Gano Lummis, Hughes' aunt and Lummis' mother, as temporary co-administrators. Annette Gano Lummis died and her powers vested in Lummis. In Delaware and Louisiana, Lummis was appointed administrator. Richard Gano was appointed administrator in California. The First National Bank of Nevada was originally appointed administrator in Nevada, but Lummis was subsequently named co-administrator

Each state seeks to tax the estate's tangible assets located within its borders and all of its intangible property

Chapter II notes that Charles Clotfelter and Melvin Dummar's information about "road-side meetings with Howard Hughes" are amazingly similar in their content. Also, that Melvin Dummar categorically lied 12 times under oath and never passed a legitimate polygraph (lie detector) test. As it was written on the envelope of the "Mormon Will," the second courier (supposedly Dummar) was to see that the designated letter, i.e. "will," was to be delivered to "David O. McKay" who, in turn, was to deliver it to the Clark County Courthouse in Las Vegas, Nevada. Exhibit 208 above indicates that it was the First National Bank of <u>Nevada</u> which was the <u>original Administrator</u> of the Hughes estate. Only *later* did Will Lummis step into the picture. <u>So, who was it, and what document was it, that made the *first* designation</u>? There is no doubt that the so called "Mormon Will" was a forgery! However, when one considers the in-depth knowledge of the "Mormon Will's" forgers, the elephants in the room are:

1. *When* did they get the details for their scam?
2. *Where* did they get them from?
3. *What necessitated* that the "Mormon Will" be holographic?
4. Why was Melvin Dummar not held accountable for lying numerous times in the courtroom?
5. Why did the Judge **not** press Dummar as to who his accomplices were?
6. Why was Melvin Dummar never jailed? And, last but not least, how was it possible for Dummar and his attorneys to be *so brazen* as to try to litigate the scam, once again, in the Utah Courtroom of Judge Bruce Jenkins in 2006?

The answer is amazingly simple, there *is* a legitimate Howard Hughes will (with a codicil attachment). It can only be that one, or all, of the six parties below, know where it is and, for obvious reasons, remain silent on the issue:

1. Melvin Dummar and his accomplice. (Dummar now deceased as of 2019)
2. The First National Bank of Nevada. (No Longer in the State of Nevada.)
3. The Mormon Church.
4. Will Lummis.
5. The old Summa, Inc. entourage.

What about that "stumbling dance" with fingerprints in Chapter V? There can be little doubt that a huge portion of the Hughes estate was siphoned off in taxes. When one considers the above rationale, it can be understood why Dummar was not prosecuted for "one of the worst attempts to forge a will ever investigated by the F.B.I.!" <u>Had he been prosecuted and threatened with 24 years of imprisonment, he would have undoubtedly plea-bargained for a lighter sentence</u>! The results would have been **catastrophic;** eventually all the scam artists, who had a part in bilking the Hughes estate, would have skipped off to parts unknown with their embezzled millions and the phony "Hughes" in the Greenwood Cemetery in Houston, would definitely have been dug up to be properly fingerprinted!

Reflecting once again (yes, more duplication) for complete clarity, did sick ol' Howard don gloves to write his last will and testament, i.e. "The Mormon Will"? None of his fingerprints appeared on the document. A suggestive argument in the Agent Lile deposition above was that perhaps Howard's latent prints did not survive because the will had lain about for eight years until discovered by some Good Samaritan and clandestinely delivered to Melvin Dummar. So why didn't the delivery boy who supposedly gave the document to Dummar leave any latent prints on the document's envelope? And what about Dummar's latent palm print? After lying about it, he confessed that he had steamed open the envelope and read its contents. Also, the forger who actually wrote the document left no prints on the will's envelope *or* on the three pages of the will. *A latent Hughes print was never found;* in fact, not a single latent fingerprint of Dummar's was found on the entire document or its envelope. *But Melvin Dummar's palm print was?* It was such a pity that in the above deposition, Agent Lile could only state: "latent prints have a history of longevity." Had he known and cited that latent fingerprints were used by the Nazi Hunters after WWII; the question would have been clearly answered. ("Nazi" is an abbreviation, in German, of Hitler's "National Socialist Party.") Nazi prints had been taken off various documents and used in courtrooms *forty to fifty years – or longer – after WWII.* (Refresh with Chapter V, Exhibits 30, 31-A and 31-B.)

Even though Melvin Dummar blatantly lied numerous times from the onset of the investigation, it was never proven that he had written the will himself. Of course, it's still a mystery as to who his accomplice or accomplices were. Why is that?

Questions: There were other phony Hughes wills submitted, many typed, but why was it that Dummar's so called "Mormon Will" ended up being bandied about in the courtroom at tremendous public expense? Why was it that Dummar never did any time for his obvious attempt to defraud the Hughes estate of millions of dollars? And, while we are focused on one of the poorest attempts to defraud in the history of the FBI, why did Dummar and his accomplices believe they could be successful at taking yet another run at the money in the Utah court of Judge Jenkins in November of 2006? Yes, as stated above, they went at it again, but wanted it done in Salt Lake City, Utah - *not* Las Vegas, Nevada where they experienced their first failure; but alas, Judge Bruce Jenkins threw it out. Did Dummar believe he had an ace in the hole because they could then subpoena Bill Gay and various members of the L.D.S. hierarchy to prove the existence of a previous Hughes holographic will? **It was foolish of Dummar to proceed, because had he been successful, the documents he copied for his *forged* "Mormon Will" were not *known* exemplars; they also were bogus! Hence had Bill Gay or members of the Mormon hierarchy produced a *legitimate* Howard Hughes will, it still would not have matched up with the phony will or the questionable exemplars the Mormon Will forgers attempted to create it from!** Or was it just a ploy to get a million or two out of Bill Gay or Will Lummis, who may have feared the revelation that the real Howard Hughes had died in 1965? If so, the bluff did not work!

Note: Let's take a simplified look at what went down with Melvin Dummar and the other fraudsters. Keep in mind that Dummar was under oath in the courtroom when he blatantly lied numerous times. Later he admitted to numerous lies, and yet was never convicted of perjury:

1. Melvin claimed he had never seen the "Mormon Will" until it was brought to his little gas station by a Salt Lake City reporter. Later he admits to *that* lie and said that he *had* seen it earlier when it was delivered to his gas station by a, yet to be identified, "Good Samaritan."

2. Melvin maintained that he had nothing to do with shuffling the will into correspondence mail on the 25th floor of the Mormon Church Offices. But when confronted with the fact that his latent palm print was found on the envelope containing the will, he changed his story and admitted that *he did* deposit the will in the Mormon Church Offices.

3. In the courtroom, and once more under oath, he claimed that he had not opened the Will's envelope when it was delivered to him by the "Good Samaritan," and had not known its contents. Later he changed this story to say that he had "steamed open the envelope, read its contents, and then resealed it" and thereby *knew* it had named him as a beneficiary of the Hughes estate to the tune of $150 million.

4. If Melvin opened the envelope containing the "Mormon Will," to which he later confessed, and resealed it after reading its three-page contents; *why was not a single latent fingerprint of his*, found on the envelope or on its three pages? It had obviously been fully processed for latent prints by the FBI, or how would they have found Dummar's latent palm print? It's obvious that if Melvin was so innocent and naïve and did not know of the attempted fraud, why would he wear gloves when handling the envelope and the three pages of the will? Also obvious is that it was simply a foolish mistake that Melvin left his palm print on the envelope, and even more foolish for Melvin to think that a latent palm print could not be used as an identity factor. He had been careful not to touch the envelope with his fingers, or those prints would also have been on the envelope together with his palm print.

5. Dummar lied a minimum of 11 times in the courtroom while under oath!

6. FBI Agent Lile stated several times in his deposition, and under oath, that the "Mormon Will" was one of the *worst* fraud attempts that he had ever born witness to.

7. However, the most glaring part of the so called "Mormon Will" is that not a single latent fingerprint of Howard Hughes was found anywhere on the envelope or on the will's three pages. (Refresh with fingerprints in Chapter V.) This brings up the question, "**If** said document was authentic, why would a *supposedly* enfeebled and sick Howard Hughes don gloves to write his last will and testament?" Now that all the evidence indicates that Hughes did not write that so-called "Mormon Will," what about the forger who did? Quite obviously the forger also wore gloves as he/she left no prints!

Dummar would have everyone believe that it was some type of a *grand conspiracy* to beat him out of his rightful $150 million. But every thinking person, abreast of the facts, knew the truth, as was obvious from the magnitude of evidence listed above. But Melvin didn't fair too badly. He wrote a book, which brought him some ready cash and even got royalties from a movie *Melvin and Howard*, that was inspired by his book. You have to hand it to Dummar – he was a party to one of the sloppiest, worst-case forgeries in the history of the FBI, he lied like a rug, and yet came out of the courtroom smelling like a rose. What did he know that protected him then, or even now? Could it have been that he was privy to information completely known to only a few insiders – information concerning the *true* holographic will of Howard Hughes? Are state and federal government agencies also involved in some way?

Given the above federal documentation concerning Dummar, and the news clipping below from the FBI Los Angeles files concerning Martha Jo Graves and Harold W. Mallet – who were convicted of forging another Howard Hughes will – does *anyone* have a better explanation?* A single relevant lie in a court of law is *perjury*, unlawful, and punishable under the law, *even if one later admits to the lie.* Martha Stewart, television personality, author, businesswoman, went to jail for it. Although she was innocent of a crime; and Michael Flynn, former National Security Advisor to President Donald Trump, got into some profoundly serious trouble for a single lie, although he had committed no crime. Martha-Jo and Harold Mallet (Exhibit 209-A) found out the hard way that lying to a judge has serious consequences. Now what do you suppose Melvin Dummar would have done had the judge told him: "*Listen here Melvin*, by our research and your own omission, you have perjured yourself a minimum of 11 *distinct* times in my courtroom. You have lied to the FBI as well; so, if you don't, or can't, tell us who your accomplices are, I'm going to give you two years for each offence!" Do you think Melvin would have caved? Under similar circumstances, wouldn't you? So why didn't anyone hold Melvin's feet to the legal fire? What else was going on? Bad boy Magic Melvin – fraudster and liar – skated right out of the courtroom to enrich himself later with a book and a movie of how he was so poorly abused. (The above exposé points to a situation where had the judge thrown Melvin in jail, he may have turned state's evidence and told the court where he had obtained the hoax material; and all would have been exposed.

Simply put, there is a legitimate Howard Hughes holographic will somewhere, with an 85 percent probability that it resides within the confines or the Mormon Church Archives. And Melvin Dummar *knew* of it and the contents of its attached codicil as well! Hence the reason for his attempt to clandestinely squirrel that phony "will" into the Church offices, where it would soon be discovered by an L.D.S. employee. There is obviously great wealth and powerful crony politics at play to keep this truth concealed, keeping the greatest hoax of the twentieth century perpetual.

EXHIBIT 209-A

***(04-16-84 News clip from FBI Los Angeles files below.)**

FD-350 (Rev. 12-5-78)   ·(Mount Clipping In Space Below)

3-year sentence for forging will of Howard Hughes

A 54-year-old woman was sentenced Friday to three years in state prison for forging a document and passing it off as the will of the late billionaire Howard Hughes.

Martha Jo Graves received the prison term after pleading guilty to one count of conspiracy to commit forgery and theft and one count of perjury in connection with the fraudulent will case.

Deputy District Attorney Mitchel J. Harris said Graves was the formulator of the phony will bequeating a portion of Hughes' estate, valued at between $166 million to $1.1 billion, to a mining company in which she became controlling stockholder.

A co-defendant in the case, Harold W. Mallet of Canyon Country, pleaded guilty to similar charges and was placed on four years probation and fined $5,000.

Mallet, an Aspen Airlines executive, only signed his name as a witness to the document, while Graves was the key figure in the case, Harris said.

The authentic Hughes will has never been found. Hughes died April 5, 1976.

Since the reclusive aviator's death, Harris said, about 50 documents purporting to be Hughes' will have been presented in California, Texas and Nevada but all the documents have been determined to be forgeries.

Graves was a secretary for Earl Hightower, an oil and gas industry attorney who died in a 1974 plane crash. After the lawyer's death, Graves claimed she found the phony document among Hightower's personal effects in 1981.

The four-page document dated July 24, 1960 was described as a "cut and paste job" by experts who examined it for its authenticity, Harris said.
— JEFF SNYDER

(Indicate page, name of newspaper, city and state.)

Date: 4-14-84 SAT.
Edition: DAILY NEWS

Title:

Character:
or
Classification:
Submitting Office:

15B-24486-15

SEARCHED_____ INDEXED_____
SERIALIZED_____ FILED_____

APR 16 1984

FBI—LOS ANGELES

EXHIBIT 209-B

Las Vegas Sun

May 14, 1976 SUN ● A9

Hughes wills probe considered

Las Vegas (AP)—Authorities said yesterday a criminal investigation is being considered into a rash of wills, all purportedly written by the late billionaire, Howard R. Hughes, which have been filed here.

The district attorney, George Holt, said yesterday his office is "looking very carefully" at the recent wills, and an investigation into possible forgery, fraud or perjury is under consideration.

"At this time we don't have any investigation," Mr. Holt said, but after the filing of four wills here, including three this week, "we're looking at it very seriously now."

Later, Mr. Holt issued a news release stating his office would "vigorously prosecute criminally any such person or combination of persons" who fraudulently claim heirship.

Mr. Holt pointed out 1- to 10-year prison sentences are possible for persons found guilty of such felonies as forgery, fraud or perjury.

Mr. Hughes left a fortune estimated between $1.5 billion and $2.5 billion.

WHERE IS THE WILL?

Please excuse the redundancy below, but the intention is to completely bring to light what once seemed like an unlikely probability.

Answer: Unless it has been destroyed, it is convincing that there is a legitimate Howard Hughes holographic (handwritten) last will and testament in the archives of the Mormon Church in Salt Lake City, Utah. Therefore, we can safely suppose that the Dummar "Mormon Will" scammers wanted to subpoena some, if not all, of the council of twelve, and perhaps even the current prophet himself to testify in the courtroom of Judge Bruce Jenkins, in 2006. *This phony ploy could actually have established the existence of a legitimate Hughes holographic will,* but it would have done the Dummar fraudsters little good. True Howard Hughes documents <u>would not</u> have matched up with those of the "Mormon Will" forgers, or the collective exemplars use by Rosemont, Inc. for that matter. (Back to Chapters VI and IX.) It's well established that the collective exemplars themselves were forgeries. If Hughes's legitimate will still exists, it's highly probable that there is a legitimate codicil attachment with it. (Howard never did anything halfway; when he made a commitment, he kept it.) This codicil would specify to whom he chose to bequeath shares of his estate. (Perhaps for Charles it would be a college education or property for Jean Peters his last wife.) It would have been there during David O. McKay's term as L.D.S. president in 1965, and it should still be there to this day. A most probable scenario is that the Mormon Church is a beneficiary because at the time Howard felt them to be upstanding and honorable men who would steadfastly honor his last will and testament. It is plausible that if the person designated in the codicil does not make an appearance – due to causes natural or unusual – the Mormon Church will receive a greater reward. Oh yes, Hughes co-executor Will Lummis bought out many distant Hughes relatives that may have collected upon final distribution of the Hughes estate; hence ending up with a large chunk of the enchilada on his end; but this was probably not all the beneficiary monies that would be available from the Hughes estate.

All the evidence presented so far in this book clearly indicates that Howard Hughes knew what his lieutenants had become. When Bill Gay, Chester Davis, and Nadine Henley realized that Howard would never come out of his self-imposed exile under any circumstances, they became pigs at the trough of greed, power, and self-indulgence. For these reasons Howard, aware that he was soon to die, would never *willingly* leave them a penny of his estate. By 1965 his corrupted lieutenants must have already stolen millions from the Hughes empire. Howard would have believed that their larceny would be cut short upon his death. Howard Hughes was obviously a reasonable and rational man. Had his chief lieutenants continued to be honorable and decent individuals, he would assuredly have rewarded them handsomely. But alas, no golden parachutes for those rotten apples. His disdain for Rufus and Annette Lummis, who burned him off years earlier in his youth, is well documented. (Rufus, his uncle, wanted to control the inheritance of young Howard and was angry when he could not achieve that goal; and Aunt Annette cut young Howard out of her will early on because he wouldn't do what she wanted.) That any of the Lummis progeny would somehow be endearing to Hughes is highly unlikely as well. Until 1965, Howard made great strides in just about every project he undertook; of course, it was his love of aeronautics wherein he would excel.

After 1954, when his appalling disability was gradually becoming more obvious, those he had handpicked earlier to participate in his massive achievements, like sharks, began to smell blood. They began to sense his inability to live his life as a normal man. They may never have known fully of his terribly bent physiology, but eventually they would know that he would never come out of his reclusive lifestyle under any circumstances. Secure in this knowledge, they began to clandestinely pillage the financial empire he had created; *however, Howard knew of their covert ambitions!* His trust and faith, in all who he had once supposed honorable, was destroyed. He would not willingly leave his corrupted lieutenants any gratuities upon his departure from this world. Is it then so difficult to believe that Howard would leave a portion of his estate to the custodians of his will – his estranged wife Jean Peters, whom he loved and had kept her part in a marriage deal, or a young man traveling in Mexico he had rescued, liked, and felt had promise?

It is disgusting to any reasonably decent person to realize the depths to which Howard's *once* trusted lieutenants would sink as they gorged themselves on wealth not rightfully theirs. Thank you, L. "Russ" Russell for helping to balance the scales. With Russ's knowledge and experience, it has been possible to bring to light and share this accurate and enlightening portrayal of the real Howard Hughes. A light has been cast into the darkness. Hopefully, the truth, within this book, will set Howard's spirit free.

EXHIBIT 209-C

California's Prestige Magazine
PALM SPRINGS LIFE

ERSE YOURSELF DURING BNP

Howard Hughes
More Than Just a Tourist. . .

SITE STAFF / AUGUST 17, 2010 /
PSL AND VILLAGER (HTTPS://WWW.PALMSPRINGSLIFE.COM/CATEGORY/PSL-AND-VILLAGER/) /
LEAVE A COMMENT (HTTPS://WWW.PALMSPRINGSLIFE.COM/HOWARD-HUGHES/#RESPOND)

Howard Hughes and Ida Lupino bask in the sun on Palm Canyon Drive during April 1935 visit to Palm Springs.
Palm Springs Life Archives

Be the first to get latest updates and exclusive content from Palm Springs Life straight to your email inbox.

Stay Updated

EXHIBIT 209-D

Article Found In Palm Springs Life August 17, 2010

Howard Hughes was a frequent visitor to the Palm Springs area for more than 30 years beginning around 1925. He stayed in a leased house or suites at the Racquet Club or Ingleside Inn, usually in the company of a young Hollywood starlet.

"One time he rented a house and painted all the windows black," recalls Noah Dietrich. "He didn't play golf in Palm Springs, but he made plays for a lot of actresses and he went out on the town a lot."

Ida Lupino, Ava Gardner and Elizabeth Taylor were among the actresses the billionaire squired in the desert. Hughes frequently flew one of his own planes to the resort. In the late 1920s he began a routine of early morning flights from Los Angeles over the high desert east of the San Gabriel Mountains to Palm Springs, then west to the coast and back to Los Angeles.

One of Hughes' last flights to Palm Springs occurred in 1956 when his passenger was Florida Gov. LeRoy Collins, with whom the industrialist was discussing plans to build a medical institute.

The trip was typical of many Hughes made to negotiate business deals away from his offices and staff in Los Angeles.

His 1948 purchase of RKO followed four months of secret talks with studio owner Floyd Odlum at Odlum's ranch near Indio. Hughes and Odlum's wife, the late aviatrix Jacqueline Cochran, had been friendly rivals for air speed records in the 1930s.

Hughes sometimes came to Palm Springs under an assumed name, hiding out in hotel rooms while his business associates and the public remained in the dark about his whereabouts. He was so adept at dropping out of sight, a late summer 1944 clandestine trip to Palm Springs was not discovered by Noah Dietrich or other close associates until after Hughes' death.

In 1976 a Hughes Aircraft mechanic disclosed that he and the boss had spent several months flying between Palm Springs, Las Vegas and Reno, using phony names at hotels and doing no work.

Hughes' many visits to the Ingleside Inn were recorded on file cards by, then-owner Ruth Hardy. A card dated Oct. 12, 1946, noted Hughes had checked into Room 301 under the name Earl Martyn and Ava Gardner had checked into Room 102 as Mrs. Clark. Hughes paid $40 cash per night for both rooms.

Where There's a Will, There's a Way...

Howard Hughes wrote at least six wills between 1925 and 1950, but signed only the versions composed in 1925, 1928 and 1938, according to court records and recollections of his associates.

Unsigned wills were prepared in 1944 and 1950. Noah Dietrich remembers, "I was with Howard when he made out his will in 1950 at the office in Los Angeles. I helped him draw up that will and I advised him to handwrite it so it couldn't be forged."

Dietrich was named executor of the Hughes' estate in the 1928 and 1938 signed wills and in the 1944 and 1950 unsigned wills, creating fears among Hughes' executives in 1975 — the year before the billionaire's death — that Dietrich would end up administering the empire.

When reading the above magazine article, one can certainly say that "gossip sells." So, Howard Hughes had several female friends, what is so terribly wrong with that? None of the gossip about Hughes that has been found in researching this case indicates that the ladies found him to be less than a perfect gentleman. If he had the windows in a cottage painted black to prevent some snoopy reporter from obtaining personal photos, what's wrong with that? And didn't Hughes have a right to a personal life aside from business? Is a fellow to be found wanting because he didn't always tell everyone where he was going and how long he would be gone? *After all, he was his own boss!* Let's get on with things considerably more important than what Howard did with his free time.

In Exhibit 209-C and D, it appears that Howard Hughes had written *many* wills, some having been entered into court records and others not markedly noted. Noah Dietrick maintains that he was with Hughes when he made out his will in 1950 and that it was he who advised Hughes to "handwrite it so it couldn't be forged." It's difficult to believe that *traitor* Noah can be believed, after trying to sabotage "Hughes" in an attempt to have him confined to a mental institution. So, let us rely on Exhibit 193, where it states that Neil McCarthy, Hughes's personal secretary and attorney, made the holographic will suggestion and, perhaps at the time, did think of Howard Eckersley as a faithful and upstanding employee, but let's speculate even further:

1. According to Noah Dietrick, who Hughes fired in 1958, "the Hughes 1950 Will was cursive, and it is the last Will written by Hughes." So, the question here is: if Howard would go to all the trouble of writing a cursive will, why would he not sign it? It's curious that these early cursive documents were not found and used by Rosemont, Inc.? They were the ones who had access to all previous files concerning Hughes. Russ couldn't find *any*; were they also destroyed by Rosemont, Inc. or the Summa, Inc. groups?

2. Noah Dietrick threw in with Melvin Dummar on the "Mormon Will" scam. He would want all to believe that he could correctly recognize Hughes's handwriting since he was named in the phony Mormon Will as its executor. "That's his handwriting all right, not just a copy, it's the real thing." But the "Mormon Will" was a con, Melvin Dummar was a con man and a liar, and so was Noah. Noah and Melvin had to crawl back under their respective rocks when Judge Jenkins threw the case out of his courtroom in 2008, Salt Lake City, Utah. (As per Exemplars from the CIVIL DOCKET CASE #: 1:06-cv-00066-BSJ Melvin Dummar Plaintiff – William Rice Lummis Defendant. "Mormon Will.") Additionally, Howard Hughes probably did not need Dietrick to tell him that a cursive will is the strongest kind of will, Hughes already knew this. (See Exhibit 193.) Another odd thing that comes to mind is, if Howard Hughes went to all the trouble to "*hand write* and *sign* a will in 1938," where is it now?

3. If "Howard Hughes wrote *at least six wills between 1925 and 1950* (Exhibit 209-D)

but signed only the versions composed in 1925, 1928, and 1938;" as viewed in <u>court records</u> and recollections of his associates, it becomes obvious that Hughes knew what a legitimate will was, and was a prolific writer of wills as well. Also, let's take into consideration that if a legitimate will was drafted in 1938 and signed by Hughes, would not *that will* be the one to use as dispute in a court of law, had arguments been legitimate, in those many "Hughes" will cases? A simple forensic comparison, of such documents, would have produced a true cursive comparison and, most probably have produced Hughes latent fingerprints as well. Therefore, such a will could, most certainly, have been considered binding. How convenient it is for fraudulent parties to escape when judges *fail to see the circumstantial evidence available through forensic latent fingerprints and cursive writings*? (Refer to Chapter V for longevity of latent prints and Chapter VI forensic cursive writing analysis.)

4. Does it not seem *extremely unlikely* that a fellow who would write no less than <u>six wills</u>, between 1925 and 1950, would die intestate in 1976? How many wills *have* you written in the last twenty-five years?

5. According to the above *Palm Springs Life* news article, Howard Hughes did write a will in 1938 and, "according to court records and recollections of his associates," it was the last will he wrote and signed, plus, it was *holographic*. Apparently, and according to Exhibit 209-D, it was necessary to display it in a courtroom setting. But to date Russ, has been unable to locate it. (Eighty years ago – wow!) Had Russ been able to find the 1938 will, that document would have *still* been binding in 1976 when "Hughes" supposedly died. Wherever could that will have gone? It certainly appears that Rosemont, Inc. or Summa, Inc. found it, before 1976, and destroyed it?

6. In Exhibit 174, we find that *"Hughes's hands were so severely burned,* from the XF-11 crash into Beverly Hills, *that he could not sign a will."* This is most interesting because: (a) Hughes must have asked for a will to be made up and brought to him, and (b) when he found himself on the brink of death, *he believed a will to be appropriate.*

Below exemplars were gotten from the Civil Docket For Case #: 1:06-cv-00066-BSJ Melvin Dummar Plaintiff – William Rice Lummis Defendant. "Mormon Will."

Keep in mind that the case cited below is based on a phony will. It appears that "<u>restricted documents</u>" came to light and were mentioned in several instances. (Exhibits 210-E and 210-F) Shortly after a thorough review of these (secret) documents, Judge Jenkins denied the motion Melvin and his cohorts had filed, throwing it out of his courtroom. (Exhibit 210-D, #74 below.) Now, what do you suppose those restricted documents could have contained, and why are they restricted? (Despite Russ' best efforts, and his FOIA request, the restricted documents have not been released to him to date.)

EXHIBIT 210-A

CLOSED,PROSE

US District Court Electronic Case Filing System
District of Utah (Northern)
CIVIL DOCKET FOR CASE #: 1:06–cv–00066–BSJ

Dummar v. Lummis et al
Assigned to: Judge Bruce S. Jenkins
Case in other court: Tenth, 07-04062
             Tenth Circuit Court, 07-04185
Cause: 18:1964 Racketeering (RICO) Act

Date Filed: 06/12/2006
Date Terminated: 01/08/2007
Jury Demand: Plaintiff
Nature of Suit: 370 Other Fraud
Jurisdiction: Diversity

Plaintiff

Melvin Dummar

represented by **Knute A. Rife**
RIFE LAW OFFICE
PO BOX 2941
SALT LAKE CITY, UT 84110
(801)809-9986
Email: karife@rifelegal.com
LEAD ATTORNEY
ATTORNEY TO BE NOTICED

Stuart L. Stein
THE STEIN LAW FIRM
CITY PLACE STE 2200
2155 LOUISIANA BLVD NE
ALBUQUERQUE, NM 87110
(505)889-0100
Email: info@steinlawfirm.com
LEAD ATTORNEY
ATTORNEY TO BE NOTICED

V.

Defendant

William Rice Lummis
also known as
William Frank Lummis

represented by **Gordon L. Roberts**
PARSONS BEHLE & LATIMER
201 S MAIN ST STE 1800
PO BOX 45898
SALT LAKE CITY, UT 84145-0898
(801)532-1234
Email: ecf@parsonsbehle.com
LEAD ATTORNEY
ATTORNEY TO BE NOTICED

James T. Blanch
PARSONS BEHLE & LATIMER
201 S MAIN ST STE 1800
PO BOX 45898
SALT LAKE CITY, UT 84145-0898
(801)532-1234

EXHIBIT 210-B

Email: ecf@parsonsbehle.com
ATTORNEY TO BE NOTICED

Nicole G. Farrell
PARSONS BEHLE & LATIMER
201 S MAIN ST STE 1800
PO BOX 45898
SALT LAKE CITY, UT 84145-0898
(801)532-1234
Email: ecf@parsonsbehle.com
ATTORNEY TO BE NOTICED

Randy L. Dryer
PARSONS BEHLE & LATIMER
201 S MAIN ST STE 1800
PO BOX 45898
SALT LAKE CITY, UT 84145-0898
(801)532-1234
Email: ecf@parsonsbehle.com
ATTORNEY TO BE NOTICED

Defendant

Frank William Gay   represented by   **Eric K. Schnibbe**
MAGLEBY CATAXINOS &
GREENWOOD
170 S MAIN ST STE 1100
SALT LAKE CITY, UT 84101
(801)359-9000
Email: schnibbe@mcgiplaw.com
LEAD ATTORNEY
ATTORNEY TO BE NOTICED

Peggy A. Tomsic
MAGLEBY CATAXINOS &
GREENWOOD
170 S MAIN ST STE 1100
SALT LAKE CITY, UT 84101
(801)359-9000
Email: tomsic@mcgiplaw.com
LEAD ATTORNEY
ATTORNEY TO BE NOTICED

Date Filed	#	Docket Text
06/12/2006	1	COMPLAINT against William Rice Lummis, Frank William Gay (Filing fee $ 350, receipt number 4681011476), filed by Melvin Dummar. Assigned to Judge Bruce S. Jenkins (jtj,) (Entered: 06/12/2006)
06/21/2006	2	NOTICE OF INELIGIBLE ATTORNEY -Attorney Stuart L. Stein, for Plaintiff Melvin Dummar, has been notified that he/she is not a member in good standing and can not practice before this court. Plaintiff's address has been added. (jwt,) (Entered: 06/21/2006)
06/21/2006	12	**RESTRICTED DOCUMENT** SUMMONS Returned Executed by Melvin Dummar (jmr) (Entered: 07/06/2006)

EXHIBIT 210-C

10/24/2006	30	MOTION to Strike 27 Memorandum in Opposition to Motion, *Exhibits Attached Thereto* filed by Defendant Frank William Gay. (Schnibbe, Eric) (Entered: 10/24/2006)
10/24/2006	31	MEMORANDUM in Support re 30 MOTION to Strike 27 Memorandum in Opposition to Motion, *Exhibits Attached Thereto* filed by Defendant Frank William Gay. (Attachments: # 1 Exhibit 1)(Schnibbe, Eric) (Entered: 10/24/2006)
10/25/2006	32	**NOTICE OF HEARING ON MOTION** re: 30 MOTION to Strike 27 Memorandum in Opposition to Motion, *Exhibits Attached Thereto*: Motion Hearing set for 11/2/2006 01:30 PM in Room 420 before Judge Bruce S. Jenkins. (kms) (Entered: 10/25/2006)
10/25/2006	33	ORDER granting 29 Motion for Leave to File Memorandum in Support of F.W. Gay's Motion to Strike Exhibits to Plaintiff's Memorandum Opposing Defendants' Motions to Dismiss. Signed by Judge Bruce S. Jenkins on 10/24/06.(jwt,) (Entered: 10/26/2006)
10/27/2006	34	NOTICE of Appearance by James T. Blanch on behalf of William Rice Lummis (Blanch, James) (Entered: 10/27/2006)
10/27/2006	35	Defendant's MOTION for Joinder re 30 MOTION to Strike 27 Memorandum in Opposition to Motion, *Exhibits Attached Thereto* filed by Defendant William Rice Lummis. (Blanch, James) (Entered: 10/27/2006)
10/27/2006	36	REPLY to Response to Motion re 17 Defendant's MOTION to Dismiss *First Amended Complaint* filed by Defendant William Rice Lummis. (Blanch, James) (Entered: 10/27/2006)
10/27/2006	37	MOTION for Leave to File Excess Pages filed by Defendant Frank William Gay. (Attachments: # 1 Text of Proposed Order)(Schnibbe, Eric) (Entered: 10/27/2006)
10/27/2006	38	REPLY to Response to Motion re 19 MOTION to Dismiss *First Amended Complaint and All Claims Alleged Against Him With Prejudice* filed by Defendant Frank William Gay. (Attachments: # 1)(Tomsic, Peggy) (Entered: 10/27/2006)
10/30/2006	39	ORDER granting 37 Motion for Leave to File Reply Memorandum in Support of F.W. Gay's Motion to Dismiss first Amended COmplaint and All Claims Alleged Against Him Therein as an Overlength Memorandum. Signed by Judge Bruce S. Jenkins on 10/30/06. (jwt,) (Entered: 11/01/2006)
11/01/2006	40	MEMORANDUM in Opposition re 30 MOTION to Strike 27 Memorandum in Opposition to Motion, *Exhibits Attached Thereto* filed by Plaintiff Melvin Dummar. (jwt,) (Entered: 11/01/2006)
11/02/2006	41	Minute Entry for proceedings held before Judge Bruce S. Jenkins : Motion Hearing held on 11/2/2006.Argument & discussion heard. Crt recesses 2:38 PM, reconvenes 2:53 PM. Argument & discussion heard. Crt rules:- Reserves (takes under advisement), motion to dismiss. re 30 MOTION to Strike 27 Memorandum in Opposition to Motion, *Exhibits Attached Thereto* filed by Frank William Gay,, 21 MOTION For the Court to Take Judicial Notice of Adjudicative Facts re 19 MOTION to Dismiss *First Amended Complaint and All Claims Alleged Against Him With Prejudice* filed by Frank William Gay,, 19 MOTION to Dismiss *First Amended Complaint and All Claims Alleged Against Him With Prejudice* filed by Frank William Gay,. Attorney for Plaintiff: Knute A. Rife, Stuart L. Stein, pro hac vice, Eric Hoffland, pro hac vice, Attorney for Defendant Randy L. Dryer, James T. Blanch, Eric K. Schnibbe, Peggy A. Tomsic. Court Reporter: Mindi Powers.(Time Start: 1:33 PM, Time End: 4:45 PM, Room 420.) (mrw,) (Entered: 11/20/2006)
01/08/2007	42	**RESTRICTED DOCUMENT** TRANSCRIPT of Proceedings held on 11/02/06 before Judge Bruce S. Jenkins. Court Reporter: Mindi Powers, RPR. Tape Number: 110705MP. (jwt) (Entered: 01/08/2007)

EXHIBIT 210-D

		07-4062 re 54 Notice of Appeal. (jmr) (Entered: 05/31/2007)
05/31/2007	74	Minute Entry for proceedings held before Judge Bruce S. Jenkins : Motion Hearing held on 5/31/2007 re 56 Plaintiff's MOTION Depositions Pending Appeal re 54 Notice of Appeal filed by Melvin Dummar. Argument & discussion heard. Crt rules:- Denies, motion to perpetuate.Mr. Dryer to prepare & submit order.Attorney for Plaintiff: Knute A. Rife, Stuart L. Stein, Attorney for Defendant Randy L. Dryer, Peggy A. Tomsic. Court Reporter: Mindi Monson.(Time Start: 1:40 PM, Time End: 2:26 PM, Room 420.) (mrw) (Entered: 06/11/2007)
06/22/2007	75	ORDER re 74 Motion Hearing. Follows oral order of 5/31/07.Signed by Judge Bruce S. Jenkins on 6/22/07. (jwt) (Entered: 06/22/2007)
08/07/2007	76	**RESTRICTED DOCUMENT** TRANSCRIPT of Proceedings held on May 31, 2007-Motion Hearing before Judge Bruce S. Jenkins. Court Reporter: Mindi Powers, RPR. (jmr) (Entered: 08/07/2007)
09/07/2007	77	Correspondence from The Tenth Circuit to counsel re: petition for extraordinary writ of mandamus docketed and assigned case number 07-4185. (jmr) (Entered: 09/11/2007)
09/10/2007	78	Correspondence-cc: from Stuart Stein entitled Proof of Service on Hon. Bruce S. Jenkins. (jmr) (Entered: 09/11/2007)
09/24/2007	79	Order of USCA as to 77 filed by Melvin Dummar. According to the USCA the The Petition for Writ of Mandamus or Such Writ the Court Deems Appropriate Under its All Writs Authority is of the USDC for the Dist of UT is DENIED. Petitioner's request for oral argument is DENIED as moot. (Attachments: # 1 Cover Letter)(jmr) (Entered: 10/02/2007)
10/23/2008	80	MANDATE of USCA-Tenth Circuit as to 54 Notice of Appeal(07-4062) filed by Melvin Dummar. According to the USCA the judgment of the USDC for the Dist of UT is AFFIRMED. Mr. Dummars motion to dismiss the appeal and remand for additional trial proceedings is DENIED. Finally, the Tenth Circuit sees nothing improper in the representations of the Gays to this court in their motion for substitution, so Mr. Dummars motions to strike the joint brief and oral argument of Defendants and for a stay are DENIED. Mr. Dummars motion for extension of time to reply to Defendants supplement to their response is GRANTED. Mr. Dummars reply shall be filed as of the date received, July 14, 2008 Judgment included with mandate: Yes. (Attachments: # 1 Judgment, # 2 Mandate Cover Letter)(jmr) (Entered: 10/23/2008)
10/29/2008	81	ORDER of USCA-Supplement to Mandate 80 from the Tenth Circuit as to 54 Notice of Appeal(07-4062) filed by Melvin Dummar. Order filed by Clerk of the Court granting in part and denying in part the bill of costs. Appellees are awarded claimed costs of $118.90. The amounts claimed for copying motions and responses are denied. The request for costs of hearing transcripts is properly taxed in the district court. (jmr) (Additional attachment(s) added on 10/29/2008: # 1 Cover Letter to Supplement of Mandate) (jmr). (Entered: 10/29/2008)
10/29/2008	82	ORDER of USCA 10th Circuit/Supplement to the Mandate as to 54 Notice of Appeal filed by Melvin Dummar. Appellees are awarded their claimed costs in the amount of $118.90. For further details, see order. (Attachments: # 1 Supplement to Mandate)(ce) (Entered: 10/30/2008)

PACER Service Center
Transaction Receipt

EXHIBIT 210-E

Russ L. Russell
P. O. Box 91263
Henderson, NV 89009

March 21, 2018

Honorable Judge James C. Mahan
Federal District Court – Southern District of Nevada
333 S. Las Vegas Boulevard –
Las Vegas, NV 89101

      Re: Request for Consideration to Release Restricted Document

Dear Honorable Judge Mahan:

I seek your assistance in a matter of mutual concern.

My associate and I are looking into the various attempts to defraud and victimize the Mormon Church by NV resident Melvin Dummar.

In that regard, we are looking into the various Federal law suits filed by Melvin Dummar in multiple jurisdictions. One lawsuit, heard in your Court (cv-00610-JCM-PAL) was disposed of on 12/26/2007. During review of all potential evidentiary documents, we found a Court Docket referral to a "*Restricted Document*" (see attached). When visiting the Federal Court Clerk yesterday, I was told that I could only review this "*Restricted Document*" with your Honor's authorization.

I understand the sanctity of a "*Restricted Document*," and understand your latitude in releasing same. I only ask if it would be possible for you to give me authorization to either/both review the Restricted Document(s), and obtain a copy of said document?

I thank you, in advance, for your consideration in this matter of mutual concern.

Sincerely,

Russ L. Russell
(Retired CA rural cities Chief of Police,
and former U. S. Postal Inspector in SF)

EXHIBIT 210-F

Russ L. Russell
P. O. Box 91263
Henderson, NV 89009

March 22, 2018

Honorable Judge Bruce Jenkins
Federal District Court – District of Utah
351 South West Temple, Room 1100
Salt Lake City, Utah 84101

    Re: Request for Consideration to Release Restricted Document

Dear Honorable Judge Jenkins:

I seek your assistance in a matter of mutual concern.

My associate and I are looking into the various attempts to defraud and victimize the Mormon Church by NV resident Melvin Dummar.

In that regard, we are looking into the various Federal law suits filed by Melvin Dummar in multiple jurisdictions. A Federal lawsuits, heard in your Court *(06-cv-00066-BSJ,)* was disposed of on 1/8/2007. During review of all potential evidentiary documents, we found Court Dockets with referral to a *"Restricted Document"* (see attached). When visiting the Federal Court Clerk yesterday, I was told that I could only review this *"Restricted Document"* with your Honor's authorization.

I understand the sanctity of a *"Restricted Document,"* and understand your latitude in releasing same. I only ask if it would be possible for you to give me authorization to either/both review Document #s 12, 42, & 76, , and obtain a copy of said document?

I thank you, in advance, for your consideration in this matter of mutual concern.

Sincerely,

Russ L. Russell
(Retired CA rural cities Chief of Police,
and former U. S. Postal Inspector in SF)

EXHIBIT 211

The New York Times   https://nyti.ms/1H74x6Z

ARCHIVES | 1979

Ex-Hughes Aides Accused of Plot

SPECIAL TO THE NEW YORK TIMES   JAN. 25, 1979

LAS VEGAS, Nev., Jan. 24 — Howard R. Hughes's former aides, doctors and top executives siphoned at least $50 million from his vast financial holdings by manipulating and isolating the drug-addicted industrialist in the last years of his life, according to a lawsuit filed Nevada District Court today.

Special to The New York Times

Defendants accused of the conspiracy include Frank William Gay. former president of the Summa Corporation, Chester Davis, a New York lawyer, three doctors who had treated Mr. Hughes, and seven personal aides.

The suit contended that Mr. Hughes's environment, health and business dealings were out of his control when the 70year-old multimillionaire died on April 5, 1976, while being flown from seclusion in Acapulco, Mexico, to Houston because his employees took advantage of his reclusive nature and drug usage and "breached their fiduciary duty to Huges."

The suit was filed here by Samuel Lionel, a Las Vegas lawyer, on behalf of the First National Bank of Nevada, William Lummis, a cousin of Mr. Hughes, the Summa Corporation, Hughes Airwest and Hughes Properties Inc. First National Bank is the co-special administrator of the Hughes estate, along with Mr. Lummis.

Besides Mr. Gay and Mr. Davis, the defendants are seven former Hughes aides — Kay Glenn, Levar Myler, John Holmes Jr., Clarence Waldron, Howard Eckersley, James Rickard and George Francom — and Dr. Wilbur Tham, Dr. Homer Clark and Dr. Norman Crane.

The lawsuit accused the defendants of siphoning at least $50 million from Summa through a senes of self-dealing schemes and of funneling the money into inflated employment and consulting contracts.

HOW TO DRAW UP A PHONY WILL
OR
HOW MUCH DUMMAR CAN YA GET?

There can be no confusion as to why Dummar and his cohorts realized their best shot at having the phony "Mormon Will" viewed as a legitimate document was because they *knew* Howard Hughes had written an earlier underline cursive will. Therefore, their *phony* will must supersede Howard's previous legitimate will and *cursive* was the key. A major irony here is that all those letters in the possession of Rosemont Enterprises, Inc. *are not legitimate known exemplars!* How could they have been, Hughes was dead in 1965? The questionable exemplars, bandied about as *known* documents by Rosemont, Inc. could not be compared with any known document Hughes wrote *before* or after 1965. Reason tells us that Hughes knew how to write well and had to have written some legitimately noted documents or letters prior to 1965. (Charles had held one in his hand in 1964.) But so far, no others have been found. If they had been, they were probably quickly destroyed by the Rosemont, Inc. document clean-up crew. The only *single thing* they had for comparison as a known item was Howard's signature – a signature which is easily found and had been forged many times on numerous documents! But the Dummar dummies went to the library and found documents which they, and numerous others, mistakenly presumed to have been written by Hughes. *They then did a miserable job of forgery from those documents,* which we now know *were* also *forgeries.* (Graphically illustrated in Chapter VI.)

Yes, much of the logic and research above and below is repetitious, but consider this, had these interrelated things, researched and cited, *not* been reasonably and conspicuously connected in this book, the light may never have been cast upon the true legacy of Howard R. Hughes, Jr.

A. A kind-hearted fellow named Howard helps a young man named Charles out of a dire situation in the most southern part of Mexico in 1964. Charles was extremely sick with amoebic dysentery. (History has it, that the Spanish conquistadors lost a substantial number of men to this specific illness.)

B. Howard gives Charles a ride in his van – a two-day journey – to the more northern town of Oaxaca where Charles could board a north-bound train, returning him to the United States.

C. Howard and Charles stop the night of the first day at a small motel. Howard allows Charles to sleep in his van for the night; but would only allow this if Charles promised "not to go through his personal things." He then explains that he would invite Charles into the motel room except "there was no place for him to sleep."

Charles assumes that there was only one bed in the room and that it had been especially adapted to Howard's unfortunate deformity. A logical conclusion, as Howard had driven directly up to the front of the motel room, had a key, and did not check in with the motel's office. It never crossed Charles's mind, at the time, that Howard may have owned the place; but what *did* seem logical is that Howard probably made the round trip south often, for whatever reason, and this motel had been often used by him.

D. By the time they had stopped at the motel, a bond of trust had developed between Howard and Charlie or Howard would never have allowed Charles to sleep in his van, considering the items he must have had in it. Also, the letter Howard wrote and placed in Charles' backpack as he slept, had to have been written with pen and stationery already in the motel room: Charles had not seen Howard take these items from the van and into the motel room with him.

E. The year was late 1964.

THE YEARS 1964 AND 1965 ... AND THOSE FEW YEARS THEREAFTER

1. In late **1964** a young man named Charles is helped out of a precarious situation in the bottom of old Mexico. The fellow who helps Charles and gives him a ride in his van is only known to Charles as Howard. Charles's benefactor is terribly deformed, and Charles is taken aback by this at first. Eventually Charles realizes that his benefactor is a clear-thinking rational fellow. Howard helps Charlie get to a train station farther north where the trains run on regular schedules. During their two-day journey north, Howard and Charles become friends. On the first day, Howard confides in Charles that **"the doctors have given me only eight months to live."**

    The night of the first day Howard allows Charles to sleep in his van if Charles will promise "not to go through any of his personal things." Charles promises. During the evening Charles sleeps the sleep of the "near dead," having been sick for nearly three weeks. While Charles is sleeping in Howard's van, Howard puts a letter in his backpack. Howard refers to the letter the next day and adds, "It won't mean much to you now, but will later, so don't lose it."

2. In Exhibits 42-D and 42-E, we learn that in the early **1960s** Hughes can only be contacted through Raymond M. Holliday, Executive Vice-President of Hughes ToolCo, Inc., Inc. in Houston, Texas. All calls for Hughes are screened by a Mrs. Betty Patrick. Mrs. Patrick then calls Raymond and delivers the communiqué. When Hughes calls Raymond Holliday for an update, Raymond delivers the information to Hughes, who decides what action to take on its content. The Hughes responses are then channeled back through Holliday, then to Mrs. Patrick, who in turn delivers the information back to its originator.

    The objective here is to "keep an eye on the ball." Apparently, when Holliday is abruptly replaced in his communications with Howard Hughes *after* **1965**, Holliday becomes suspicious, especially when Robert Maheu ends up **in 1965**, as "Hughes's right-hand man." Hughes never talks to Raymond after **1965,** of course with good reason, *he can't*. Hughes is dead. Holliday is mystified as to why Hughes never called him to explain about Maheu. By 1970, Holliday is getting very apprehensive about the Summa, Inc. acrobatics. He forwards a report that shows Hughes's Nevada properties have lost $3.2 million in 1969 and is on track to lose $13 to $14 million in 1970 "Considering that Hughes had invested more than $150 million in Nevada alone since 1967, the figures were most depressing." (Exhibit 42-G) At the bottom of this same Exhibit, it's maintained that Maheu's activities "could hardly be equated with thievery" … "nor could Maheu be held accountable." *Well, yes, he could have been held accountable! And yes, he was a thief!* Unless you adhere to the belief that it was that drug addicted, reclusive, hypochondriac, Howard Hughes who was doing all that stupid footwork. If you revisit Exhibit 116-A, Item #8, you will see that in the Irving denial letter, "Hughes" claims *not* to have *personally* signed a check for more than 10 years.

Raymond Holliday has been a personal friend and trusted Hughes employee for many years and beginning in the early 1960's, it certainly appears that he was held in <u>higher</u> esteem then Bill Gay, Nadine Henley, or Chester Davis. Holliday knows his status with the real Howard Hughes. Hughes will only talk to him via telephone, excluding all others. Holliday knows that Hughes would never abruptly cut off communications without a personal explanation. If the after **1965** "vocal Hughes" were to attempt communications with Holliday, Holliday would have *immediately* known the "con was on." The <u>real</u> Hughes and Holliday had many in-depth conversations and Holliday would have quickly caught on to the act of a phony vocal or visual "Hughes." When the phony "Hughes" jumps back to Managua, Nicaragua, from Canada, Raymond Holliday decides he'll fly down and meet personally with "Hughes" but is turned away <u>for a third time</u>. (Exhibit 42-H) Of course he's turned away, and it's obvious why. Holliday would know in a heartbeat that the fellow masquerading as "Hughes" was a phony and the cat would have been out-of-the-bag! He suspects the Summa, Inc. crew of "ripping-off" the Hughes Corporations and quits shortly thereafter. (See Exhibit 18-A: FILE PAGE 107, FEDERAL FILES 1222257-0-62-HQ-99801.)

Maheu gave a sliver of the Raymond Holliday information to the FBI after he was fired from Summa, Inc. It seems his hope at that time was that he would be able to weasel his way back into the inner circle with a possible threat of an exposure of Chester Davis, Bill Gay, Robert Maheu, and Nadine Henley. The bluff that did not work. "Bobbie Boy" didn't press the issue further for fear that the federal boys might turn up *too much* information and expose the Hughes scam – a con where, in the beginning, he was complicit. Even when the cursive letter to fire him, supposedly written by Hughes, is determined by the FBI to be a forgery, Maheu begins to pull back on his accusations. (Exhibits 15, 16, 17, and 18-A.) This was brought to light by federal cursive analyst Agent Charles Appel. But Agent Appel took it a step further and *also* finds a "Howard Hughes" forged signature in **1964** or **1965** (most likely **1965**). Maheu must then back off. He can't take the chance of pushing the issue for fear the total scam would be uncovered. (See bottom of Exhibit 16, Federal File.)

3. Dr. Vern Mason is the man Howard Hughes claimed saved his life after the tragic XF-11 crash into Beverly Hills. Dr. Mason became a personal friend of Howard Hughes early on. When Hughes builds the Howard Hughes Medical Institute, in Miami, Florida, he names Dr. Mason as its C.E.O., a job Mason retains until abruptly dying in **1965.** He is cremated two days later, without an autopsy and without a ceremony. (Exhibit 65-A)

4. In **1965**, Rosemont Enterprises, Inc. is set up by Chester Davis with "Monty" Montrose as Director/Treasurer and Chester Davis as its attorney. The purpose of this quasi-legal corporation is to claim and control all **letters,** photos, and biographical materials of "Howard Hughes." (See Exhibit 81 from Federal Files.) None of this appears in the Hughes documentary *Empire*.

5. In reading these dissertations, the important thing to keep in mind is that "Howard Hughes" supposedly becomes a derelict *only after* **1965.** Out of sight after 1954, he still ran his <u>profitable</u> companies from afar via telephone and facsimile, wherein Raymond Holliday of Hughes ToolCo, Inc. played a key role. Holliday had always done a good job for his employer and friend Howard Hughes. Raymond was named with Hughes in the multi-million-dollar TWA lawsuit, which eventually was an enormous win for the Hughes Industries.

6. All Rosemont Enterprise, Inc. documents, supposedly written by Hughes and used in courtroom activity, **were written after 1965.** They were acclaimed as known exemplars, but in truth were only questionable exemplars. (See Chapter VI.)

7. After **1965** "Hughes" keeps no secretaries and *none of his many aides know how to type.* All business documents are written cursively.

8. Salvatore "Sam" Giancana (money launderer for the mob) and Johnnie Roselli (hitman), both "Goodfella" friends of Bob Maheu, are brought on board with Summa, Inc. in **1965**

9. In **1965** "Hughes" moves to Las Vegas, Nevada, and begins to make ridiculous acquisitions. He purchases numerous empty mining claims in which no precious metals were to be found and thousands upon thousands of acres of worthless desert where no one could see the potential. "Bagman" John Herbert Meier skips off to Canada with <u>millions</u> in kick-back money from the worthless mining claims and other worthless acquisitions. Never extradited, he gets away clean. Perhaps the Summa group didn't go after him because he knew too much. In 1978 a federal

district judge in Utah orders Meier to pay $7.9 million to the Hughes organization. He never does; it was all just a show.

10. "Hughes" is never taken to *his* hospital, the Howard Hughes Medical Center in Miami, Florida, even though "Hughes's" kidney problems are known as far back as **1965** when he resided in the Desert Inn Penthouse in Las Vegas, Nevada. (H.M.I.M. has the latest in dialysis equipment and is known for its technology and treatment of renal problems.)

11. In **1967** Jean Peters separates from Hughes in an out-of-court agreement. At the time, no alimony or other monies were known. Clearly, she, *like Raymond Holliday,* no longer hears from Hughes. The Summa, Inc. crew shuffles in the paperwork and non-disclosure agreements; "Hughes" need not be present. The con was on, and the Summa, Inc. bandits were gearing-up for the greatest heist of the twentieth century. Jean never knew the danger she had been in. In **1970** Jean Peters threatens a formal divorce from Howard Hughes as a way to get what had previously been promised. Its plausible Jean knows the real Hughes is dead. However, once again, Jean and Howard never appear in court together. It appears that, in that previous separation agreement, a settlement of sorts *had* been agreed upon. Jean was to get the French chateau up on Mulholland Drive and a stipend for life. However, Jean is stonewalled on the stipend by Summa, Inc. *She obviously collected a lump sum* in 1970 as all went quiet. "Hughes" never did appear in court and, once again, all paperwork is handled by Summa, Inc. via Chester Davis. (Exhibit 13, from Federal Files)

12. Hughes Industries <u>loses</u> multi-millions of dollars for ten years after **1965.**

a. When Will Lummis is appointed C.E.O. of Summa, Inc. in 1976, the Hughes companies once again began to <u>make</u> millions. The financial hemorrhaging of the Hughes Corporation was *shallowly* researched by Will Lummis (relative and attorney appointed by the probate judge as co-administrator of the Hughes estate). Except for John Meier, it *never* came to light as to *how the evaporation of other millions* had taken place. It was simply explained away as poor management and overpayment to employees by a supposed derelict "Howard Hughes." (See Exhibit 187-B.)

b. To research the vanishing of millions when Bill Gay, Nadene Henley, Chester Davis, and Robert Maheu were running the show, would have shed light on the con. However, if Will Lummis were to remain in the appointed Summa, Inc. seat of power and enrich himself as Summa, Inc. C.E.O., he would have to let the shenanigans of Billie, Nadene, Bobbie, and Chester remain hidden. (Yes, "Acapulco Hughes" was a phony.) If a phony "Hughes" were to come to light, the lawsuits would have *never* ended. And what if one of the con artists were to plea-bargain and turn state's evidence to get a lighter sentence? Also, let's consider what would have happened if a <u>true holographic will</u>, written by Howard Hughes *prior to* **1965,** were to be discovered? Anything could have happened with <u>Murder One</u> on the table! (Murder One would have been that starved, dehydrated, and drugged "Acapulco Hughes" they flew up from Mexico in 1976) Lawsuits, after 1976, were filed by Will Lummis and The First National Bank of Nevada, against Bill Gay, Chester Davis, Nadine Henley, and various "Hughes" aides and they, in turn, filed lawsuits against Will Lummis and The First National Bank. But as for settlements, it seemed to be just for show or a bluff. Only a few thousand dollars were paid out by parties involved.

13. Frank McCullough, New York Bureau Chief of Time-Life News, claimed to have spoken to Howard Hughes many times between the years 1958 to 1962 and in 1964 and 1965 **but not after 1965.** (See Exhibit 75.)

14. **None** of the "Howard Hughes" exemplars, supposedly written by Hughes and used so prolifically by Rosemont, Inc. in various courtroom activities, precede **1965** and **none** of them **are true known exemplars.**

15. **1966** Dr. Norman Crane and aide John Holmes begin their drug scheme and, together with Dr. Wilber Thain end up eventually scamming the Justice Department. (Chapter XIII. Read Russ's analysis.)

16. Chuck Waldron had been brought on board Summa, Inc. after 1954 but quickly rises to "Hughes" Senior Aide and Private Secretary status *after* **1966.** Most unusual as Waldron *was not* a registered nurse, *didn't type,* and had no secretarial skills.

17. **1967** Waldron leaves with $180,000.00: (Exhibits 181 and 182). Chuck Waldron is among the "maids in waiting" for "Hughes," at whim or fancy, to be select one as a cash currier of $180,000.00 (Exhibit 181) to pay a ten-year-old suite bill at the Emerald Beach Hotel in the Bahamas. Keeping in mind that $15,000.00 a year, in the 1960s, was darn good wage for menial work. Chuck was not a nurse, couldn't type, was useless in cleaning up the residences of "Hughes's" Desert Inn Penthouse. And yet "Howard Hughes" decides to risk sending Chuck out of the country with $180,000 in cold-clean cash? But perhaps it was Chuck's writing skills that so impressed "Hughes" i.e., Mexico customs documents, Dear Bob letter, Clifford Irving denial letter, etc. – all *questionable* documents.

18. **1967** Richard Gray gets a "Hughes" Power of Attorney, *notarized by "inside man" Howard Eckersley,* to handle "Hughes" Nevada operations. (Metal-less mines, worthless desert properties, etc.)

19. In **1967** Allen Gerber publishes his Book *Bashful Billionaire*, which is a kinder and more realistic view of who and what Howard Hughes really was. The research material for his book mostly precedes **1965.**

20. **1967** Robert "Bob" Maheu has an epiphany concerning gold and silver mining in Nevada. He knows little about the mining industry but somehow convinces "Howard Hughes" that this will be a tremendous money maker and lays out his plans. "Hughes" *supposedly* embraces the idea, and the plot is hatched.

"THE GREAT HEAVY METAL MONEY MAKER"
(Translation: The Bleeding Wealth Scam)

Howard Hughes made billions in numerous investments prior to 1965, at one point becoming the wealthiest man in America. Hughes was no man's fool prior to 1965; however, after 1965 he *supposedly* became a foolish, drug addicted, reclusive hypochondriac. For ten years, after 1965, "Hughes" could only be accessed by his lackadaisical caretakers and a couple of very stupid doctors. Is there anyone reading this book that still believes it was Howard Hughes who made those numerous, foolish, and absurd decisions between 1965 and 1976? Well, for you doubters, let us see if we can flush any lingering reservations out of your minds in the text that follows.

Robert "Bob" Maheu gets the ball rolling after *supposedly* convincing "Howard Hughes" that there's big money to be made mining gold and silver in Nevada. Of course, "Bobbie" knows nothing about the mining industry, but he talks it over with Bill Gay, Nadine Henley, and Chester Davis – the other "top dogs" on the Summa, Inc. board of directors. They then come to a unanimous decision; it looks like an excellent way wherein they *can all prosper*. None of the above directors have had any previous knowledge about mining, but Bob Maheu says, "Howard's sold on the idea let's gofer it."

1. Bob Maheu *supposedly* doesn't like a fellow by the name of John Meier. "Johnnie" had worked at Hughes Dynamics, a company which had been set up and seeded with Hughes's money; all done by Summa, Inc. C.E.O. Bill Gay, but unknown by Hughes. How Gay was able to do this is a mystery. (Exhibits 212-B and C)

2. All employees working at Hughes Dynamics had believed that Johnnie had *several* doctorate degrees and he was addressed as "Dr. Meier." However, as it turned out, the "good doctor" had little more than a high-school education. (Exhibit 212-C)

3. Hughes Dynamics "folds," *supposedly* because "Hughes" found out about it and shut off the money supply. (Exhibit 212-A) However, it does seem strange that the company's dissolution was because it lacked cash flow from the "Hughes coffers." If the company had been making money earlier than **1965** when "Hughes" supposedly found out about it; it seems the real Hughes would probably have either kept it or sold it to get his money back. So, it does appear that the company was a liability. (Exhibit 212-A) Where the money went is unknown, but what *is known* is that Bill Gay was not fired for his secretive embezzlement indiscretion and never paid back any of the "Hughes" monies he seeded Hughes Dynamics with. It shouldn't seem odd that Hughes didn't take any action against Bill Gay for stealing, as Hughes was dead in 1965.

4. But Bill Gay sees something in Johnnie Meier (knowing full well what Meier is) and presses Bob Maheu to give the "doctor" a job. (Exhibit 212-B) Billy cites Meier's "two doctorate degrees" and assures Maheu that "Johnnie is a man we can work with." But Meier, as you are soon to see, has other talents. He knows nothing about mining, but low and behold, he ends up working closely with Maheu to buy worthless California and Nevada mining claims.

5. It's now **1968** and John Meier is the go-to man for the buying of worthless mining properties for "Hughes." (Exhibit 212-E, bottom) Maheu has apparently "kicked back" somewhere doing what he does best – dipping into the Summa, Inc. coffers and spending Hughes's money. Meier enlists help from other men who have a few mining properties of their own. They come to realize they have a friend in Johnnie Meier. Among these new cohorts are Jack Cleveland, Leonard Traynor, and Dennis Hill – men skilled in acquiring worthless mining claims cheaply and selling them at huge profits, through Meier to "Howard Hughes." Some properties sold to "Hughes" were not even owned by the sellers, and the real owners had to fight for the return of what was rightfully theirs. (Exhibit 212-H at page bottom)

6. A most interesting note here is that the First National Bank of Nevada was somehow involved in the designs of Bobby Maheu and Johnnie Meier as evidenced by the above-mentioned Leonard Traynor and Dennis Hill. Both Leonard and Dennis had opened accounts at the (now defunct) First National Bank of Nevada in November of 1968, depositing large "Hughes"/Summa, Inc. checks. Another item of interest here, is that it was none other than the First National Bank of Nevada which was named as the first administrator, and later co-administrator, with Will and Anette Lummis of the Hughes estate in 1976. Was there a particular reason this bank had been selected prior to naming Will and Anette Lummis to their posts as co-executors? Had Howard Hughes crafted a document prior to 1965 naming the bank to the administrative post upon his demise? Or was it simply that Will Lummis knew that Bob Maheu, John Meier, Bill Gay, Nadine Henley, and Chester Davis had used First National Bank of Nevada for nefarious reasons and that it would be easy for him to do the same? Okay, enough speculation for now, let's get on with the rest of the sting.

7. So, on and on it went for several years as John Meier bought thousands of acres of land *with worthless mining claims _for which assays had never been taken_*. All the while, *real miners* in the Silver State of Nevada who knew the industry well, found it odd that Hughes was not investing in legitimate claims. (Exhibit 212-F)

8. $950,000.00 was siphoned out of the "Hughes" accounts to build a mill to process the hoard of "Hughes" ore soon to be mined. (Remember a million dollars in the sixties was a considerable amount of cash. A one-ounce silver dollar could be bought for one paper dollar and an ounce of gold could still be purchased for forty of those same paper dollars; todays markets are approximately $22.00 for an ounce

of silver and $1,800.00 for an ounce of gold.) A small mill was eventually built near Tonopah, Nevada, but closed shortly thereafter as a non-profit entity.

9. "Johnnie" Herbert Meier eventually skips off to Canada with embezzled millions leaving Maheu, Gay, Henely, and Davis holding an empty bag. Meanwhile *thinking* people are wondering what "Hughes" is going to do with all those worthless pieces of dirt?

10. So now Johnnie's on the run, but often returns to the United States for nefarious purposes:

    a. He sets up a tax-exempt non-profit enterprise in New Mexico and writes bad checks.

    b. He "hangs out" in New Mexico, using aliases for a while until the scams get too hot.

    c. He finds ways to sell off his assets in the United States so he can make a clean break.

    d. He's caught in Point Roberts, just inside the United States, in 1973 and 1974, is indicted by a Grand-Jury but jumps bail on a $100,000 cash bond and goes back to Canada.

    e. Steps back into New Mexico from time to time and creates aliases which he uses for phony companies and stock transfers.

    f. Alfred Netter, an affiliate of John Meier, is murdered in the Beverly Hilton Hotel in Beverly Hills, California. He was stabbed numerous times. The hotel suite was a bloody mess. It was apparent Alfred had tried desperately to escape his fate. He had been at the Beverly Hilton for a business meeting with John Meier. Cash from Alfred's "key man" insurance policy of $400,000.00 is later deposited to John Meier's account in Switzerland.

    g. In 1978 a U.S. District Judge in Utah orders Johnnie to pay $7.9 million to the Hughes corporations. Of course, he never does.

    h. It seems strange that while Meier was busy embezzling his millions, the "Hughes" trolls (Maheu, Gay, Henley and Davis), apparently not getting paid (on the books) millions for their supervisory obligations, were oblivious to Meier's self-enrichment. Were they *not* the ones viewing the payments for all those worthless mining claims? Or was it that crazy, drug-addicted, reclusive, derelict, "Hughes" himself, keeping the books, writing the checks, and doing all that negotiating? (In the Clifford Irving disclaimer, Exhibit 106-A, "Hughes" claims not to have signed his name to a check in ten years.) None of the Summa, Inc. four ever knew exactly how much Meir had embezzled, but a conservative estimate was $20 million. (Current value, in Federal Reserve notes, $180 million.) One can't help but wonder just how many ways Johnnie may have had to "split the take?" In all probability he would have to had come up with a substantial amount from time to time *to keep the Summa, Inc. imps quiet.* But then *other* Summa, Inc. millions were also vanishing at the same time, which must have kept the Summa, Inc. boys – and one girl – busy. A tiny piece of the evaporating "Hughes" wealth can be viewed at the bottom of Exhibit 42-F.

11. And now we come to the most amazing aspect of all – the "embezzlement sting" of the Hughes Corporations:

a. The First National Bank of Nevada, the bank instrumental in gaining deposits and negotiating Summa, Inc. monies for the above Meier-Maheu deceptions, is somehow designated as the first administrator <u>and later</u> co-administrator of the Hughes estate after "Hughes" dies in 1976. The other two co-administrators, that the Probate Judge *later names* are <u>Anette and Will Lummis.</u> (Exhibit 211)

b. Obviously Will Lummis could only have been one of two things – very stupid or very crafty. He had to have figured out what Maheu, Meier, Traynor, Cleveland and Hill, had done between 1965 and 1976 concerning bogus mining claims. Claims that Maheu, Gay, Henley, and Davis knew all along had gone down with Johnnie Meier. So, was Will Lummis somehow instrumental in getting the judge to appoint the First National Bank of Nevada as the first administrator of the Hughes estate, or was something (or someone) else involved that influenced the bank's appointment? Had Lummis found an institution he could work with – as did Maheu, Meier, Gay, Henely, and Davis? Had there been vast amounts of Hughes money in the bank's coffers? And, if so, who were the bank's major stockholders and where are they now? (See Exhibit 211)

c. And last, but not least, do probate judges shop around with various banks in order to designate one, most likely, to be the <u>first</u> administrator of an estate? Why was it <u>not</u> Will and Annette Lummis named as the Hughes estate administrators *from the beginning?* Did Will Lummis become *clairvoyant* and make the arrangements early-on? Did Will Lummus know beforehand that the phony "Hughes" would be dead in 1976?

LET THE BUYER BEWARE
SPECULATION

When a confidence man, which is where the word "con" comes from, works his deception on his victim, his dialogue has a greater margin of truthful words then deceptive ones. He literally *gives you his confidence*! For example, at a cocktail party where numerous wealthy persons have congregated, you chance to meet an amiable fellow who takes you under his wing. He points out several people at the party who he claims to have made wealthy through various stock investments and then introduces himself as Johnathan Goodlife, a Stock Advising Partner working for the brokerage firm of Goodlife, Gold, & Rich. A jovial chat and a few cocktails later, Mr. Goodlife appears to be the kind of friend a fellow would want to handle his portfolio, especially when one of the fellows Mr. Goodlife pointed out earlier comes over to profusely thank him for the tremendous job done in his personal enrichment.

The next day you do a little research and sure enough, there exists the stock brokerage firm of Goodlife, Gold, & Rich. You call, and the firm's receptionist informs you that "Mr. Goodlife is not taking any new clients, but that she will have one of the other agents help you when he is free." She then offers to schedule you an appointment. But you want to talk to Mr. Goodlife himself and you call the personal cell number on the card Goodlife gave you at last night's party. Mr. Goodlife comes on the line, in the middle of his golf game, and is a bit miffed *until* he realizes who you are. You later invest $40,000.00 cash with Mr. Goodlife in the hopes of doubling your wealth within two months; of course, he gives you a receipt for the money. You're excited! However, you sadly find out two months later that, although the stock brokerage firm of Goodlife, Gold, & Rich does exist and is a legitimate entity, and a Mr. Goodlife is a legitimate partner in the firm, the Mr. Goodlife you met at the party two months earlier had stolen Goodlife's identity for the evening. His two "clients" at the party were part of the con, and your 40 grand is forever gone!

So, given the above dissertations concerning the estimated rip-off of $20 million from the Hughes coffers for worthless mining claims, it appears that this sting was too huge to sweep under the rug. Donald Barlett and James Steele *could not* leave it out of their documentary *Empire*, as they did (1) Rosemont, Inc. and Monty Montrose and Chester Davis's part in the firm and (2) the "smashing of the glass medicine containers" and "bury them far out in the desert," etc. after "Hughes" was moved out of the Desert Inn penthouse. For Barlett and Steele to leave out this much-publicized mining swindle would have left too much of a vacuum in their book and cause a loss of credibility. Barlett and Steele chose to put most of the information available in the John Meier swindle in their book. This information can be readily checked through various news sources after 1965 and into the 1970s with about 90 percent accuracy.

We have used pages (below) from *Empire* as Exhibits to further support our case. However, if you believe this wealth-bleeding scam was the solo brainchild of John Meier, you would be wrong. Or if you would believe that Bob Maheu, Bill Gay, Nadine

Henley, or Chester Davis were innocent or that it was that foolish, drug addicted, psychotic, recluse "Hughes" who was calling the shots, you would also be wrong. The final line in Exhibit 212-K below states, "the great gold-and silver-mining swindle could not have been carried out without the cooperation of someone in the Hughes hierarchy, someone in a key position until the day Howard Hughes died." These were not words generated by Barlett and Steele and put into the book *Empire* because of their own investigation. These were the thoughts of many in the various media outlets at the time. This $20-million, *or more*, swindle was obvious duplicity, and *it had to be included in Empire.* To even the shallowest of intellects, the most obvious scenario is simply this: It was not just **"someone"** in the Hughes hierarchy who was complicit, **they all were** – all, that is, except for the real Howard Hughes. He was dead in **1965** before the greatest con of the twentieth century was instigated! And you can bet your bottom-dollar that $20 million was only the tip of the iceberg compared to the *hundreds of millions ripped-off from the Hughes Estate between 1965 and 1976!* (Please keep in mind here that even the *estimated* and conservative $20 million in the 1970s would be worth $200 million in today's inflated currency.) The bandits got away with much more than that.

What has been extensively outlined above can be likened to phony professional wrestlers who strut about in the ring showing off their massive bodies and huge egos, but once on the mat they whisper in each other's ear, "Now I'll bite your arm and you jump up and kick me." Half of the crowd screams indignations while the other half cheers; but in the end when the make-believe show is over, nobody really got hurt – and next week it will be the loser who will be deemed worthy to take home the championship belt – and the money keeps pouring in.

And that's the Summa, Inc. charade! It was far more than huge indiscretions, massive theft, and intense courtroom dramas. It was also the horrid torturing of a phony "Hughes" and death of this frail human being through obvious drug overdoses and neglect. There were also the strange deaths of others as described in Chapter X. The irony is that no one gave back the stolen money, no one went to prison, and, in the end, all the players got to keep their pilfered ill-gotten wealth. And why was this you may ask? Consider this, should <u>one</u> of the persons culpable in these scams been sentenced to extended imprisonment, he/she would likely have turned state's evidence to receive a lighter sentence. And the rest of the maggots would have been flushed down the garbage disposal with the rotten meat! But how could any crime this massive go un-detected and un-punished you may ask? The answer is as simple as it is realistic – when hundreds of millions of dollars are in the hands of criminals, it's easy to take full advantage of corrupt attorneys, bent judges and, in the end, turn a facade into a work of art! Does a picture speak a thousand words? See photo of "Slick Johnnie" John Meier. (Exhibit 212-L) You will find more information on "Doctor" Meier in the following Exhibits. Who knew? **They all knew!!!**

EXHIBIT 212-A

to guess Hughes's intentions. Even so, optimism bloomed in Virginia City. Gold and silver dug out of the Comstock had helped to finance the Civil War for the North, lifted California out of a severe depression, provided capital for the building of San Francisco, and seeded family fortunes for men like George Hearst, the father of newspaper publisher William Randolph Hearst. But little of the wealth had remained in Virginia City, and few of the people. Where once more than thirty thousand had lived in the 1800s, there was now a town of only two thousand people, many of them engaged in the tourist business. A revival of the mining industry would mean a revival of Virginia City.

There were, to be sure, skeptics. A state mine inspector questioned whether Hughes could ever profitably mine gold and silver claims. Other mining engineers doubted that "any commercially practical breakthrough in mining" could be applied in the area.[12] It was naturally assumed that the eccentric industrialist had a masterplan for reopening the state's long-abandoned gold and silver mines, a plan based on inside information and unique expertise not available to anyone else. That was the way Hughes did business. Everyone knew it.

Hughes had assigned full responsibility for securing gold and silver claims to John Herbert Meier, a thirty-four-year-old Long Island native and former life insurance company manager. A big, genial man who was six-foot three and weighed 205 pounds, Meier had an engaging manner and shared Maheu's facility for moving comfortably within political, business, and social circles. But he was an odd choice to head a multimillion-dollar mining program. Most recently he had worked in electronic data processing. His mining experience was nil and, moreover, Maheu had just recommended to Hughes that Meier be fired for continuing indiscretions, the latest being his premature release of information to the media about Hughes's mining plans. Instead, Hughes told Maheu not to fire "this bastard Meier,"[13] and two weeks later, Hughes, curiously, placed Meier in charge of mining.

Meier had come to Las Vegas on a strong recommendation from Bill Gay. Before Nevada, he had worked as a $17,500-a-year assistant in marketing management at Hughes Dynamics, an obscure subsidiary of the Hughes Tool Company in Los Angeles. Hughes Dynamics, which sold a computerized management-information service and later branched out into computerized credit reporting, had been "formed without [Hughes's] knowledge" by Gay.[14] When Hughes subsequently learned that $9.5 million of his money had flowed into the struggling company,

EXHIBIT 212-B

he ordered it closed.* It was at that point, according to Maheu, that Gay took a keen interest in Meier's future welfare, asking Maheu if he could find a place for the young man on Maheu's payroll. Gay spoke highly of Meier's background, averring that he "had been employed by Hughes Aircraft, that he had two doctorates, that he [Gay] had brought him over to Hughes Dynamics."[15] There had been some suggestion, by Gay or one of his associates, that "Meier's wife was dying of cancer and that he was in dire financial straits."[16]

Maheu obliged, and Meier's first assignment was to evaluate investment opportunities for Maheu himself. Soon thereafter, Meier went to work full time persuading the Atomic Energy Commission to abandon its underground nuclear tests in Nevada. With the new job came a new title—"scientific adviser to the Hughes Tool Company," and frequent trips to Washington, where he met with government officials and politicians.[17] It was Meier's behavior on these trips that first provoked Maheu's displeasure. Wherever he went, it seemed, Meier regaled politicians and even fellow Hughes employees with stories about his intimate relationship with his boss. When he described himself as the "right-hand man" of Howard Hughes, everyone was impressed.[18] Not many visitors to Washington could tell of personal experiences with Hughes.

In an organization where the only constant was secrecy, no executive could be sure with whom Hughes was, or was not, meeting or talking. It was safest to assume that anyone who claimed to have had lunch with Hughes really had—or at the very least that he had had, say, a telephone conversation and was embroidering it. After all, what other Hughes lieutenant would question the assertion and thereby admit that he himself was not so favored in the Desert Inn penthouse? Least of all Maheu, who never once met his employer.

Meier's stories, however, eventually proved embarrassing to Maheu. After Nixon entered the White House, Maheu, working through his own political channels, secured a promise that the president would either call Hughes or send Secretary of State Henry A. Kissinger to meet with Hughes to explain the administration's position on underground testing.

* Robert Maheu has testified that Hughes learned about the existence of Hughes Dynamics quite by accident. The company was making arrangements to share the top floor of a Los Angeles office building with a fashionable restaurant. "Jean [Peters] had gone there for lunch" one day, Maheu said, and the maitre d' or one of the captains "happened to mention how pleased they were . . . that her husband was going to occupy the balance of the top floor, whereupon she went home and told him about it and he blew his top. . . . That is what he told me."

EXHIBIT 212-C

But then he was thwarted by Hughes's reclusiveness. Despite the urgency of the subject, Hughes was not prepared to deal with any strangers, whether in person or on the telephone, whether the president or the secretary of state. So Maheu could not follow through on the White House promise. But with Meier running around Washington recounting tales of his luncheons with "the old man," Maheu found "it very difficult for us to explain to Dr. Kissinger and the President of the United States that they could not talk to Mr. Hughes."[19]

Meier, of course, had never lunched with Hughes. He had never met Hughes. He had never talked with Hughes on the telephone. All his reports to Hughes were channeled through Maheu or one of the five aides in the Desert Inn penthouse. Finally, "Dr. Meier," as he had been known at Hughes Dynamics, had apparently never earned one doctorate, let alone two. According to a loan application Meier submitted to a bank, he had a high school diploma and some technical training in the United States Army. Nonetheless, Meier began 1968 as the Hughes organization's ambassador without portfolio to Nevada's mining towns, seeking out gold and silver claims.

A PARADE OF PROSPECTORS

The Virginia City properties were just the beginning. Two weeks after the quarter-million-dollar purchase of the Comstock claims, Maheu forwarded a memorandum to Hughes touting another acquisition: "We obtained an option from Mr. and Mrs. Denny Hill last month on 240 acres of mining property including seven patented mines for $240,000. The estimated value of this property is $2 million. It is primarily composed of zinc, lead and silver at Goodsprings in Clark County. . . ."[20]

To convince Hughes of the true value of the Hill claims, if such convincing was necessary, Maheu noted that two wealthy Texans, the Murchison brothers (John Dabney and Clinton William, Jr., whose fortunes also flowed out of their father's oil business) were ready to pounce on the property if Hughes did not exercise his option. "The man representing the Murchison interests from Texas is in town waiting to give them a firm offer if we turn this down," Maheu reported. "The Murchison people do not know that we have an option on this property."[21]

Three months later, on July 18, 1968, Maheu sent along to the Desert Inn command post two more memoranda enthusiastically summarizing the potential of more mining properties on offer to Hughes: "Approximately $150 million worth of silver, lead, zinc, gold and copper

EXHIBIT 212-D

Leonard Traynor, a deputy state mine inspector, was another close friend of Cleveland and an acquaintance of Hill. Cleveland arranged for Traynor to sell Hughes sixty mining claims for $250,000. It is unclear how much, if any, of Traynor's $250,000 found its way back to Cleveland. Both men have since died. But on November 4, 1968, Traynor and Dennis Hill opened a joint savings account at the First National Bank in Las Vegas and deposited a cashier's check for $77,539. The check represented part of the proceeds from the sale of Traynor's claims to Hughes.

Then there were the thirty-six mining properties in Mineral County that Hughes purchased on Maheu's recommendation for $276,500 from Basic Industries, Inc. According to a stock-ownership certificate for Basic Industries, dated February 21, 1968, "all of the issued and outstanding stock" of the company was owned by Jack Cleveland.[26]

As for the two claims that Hughes bought for $35,000 from the Atlas International Corporation, the president of the company and a major stockholder was Hill. Another substantial stockholder was Cleveland.

All in all, 1968 was a good year for prospector Cleveland. Of the nearly $4 million paid by Howard Hughes for one series of mining properties, Cleveland owned, had an interest in, or received "commissions" on the sale of more than half. And 1969 started out every bit as well.

Cleveland and his company, Basic Industries, now became something more than just sellers of gold and silver mines. Cleveland, in fact, was serving as a mining consultant to John Meier, who was serving as a mining consultant to Hughes. There was even talk that Basic Industries would act as a managing agent for Hughes's growing inventory of claims. During May and June of 1969, Cleveland's company established an office in the central Nevada mining town of Tonopah and collected $99,186.33 more from Hughes for miscellaneous services.

By this time, Basic Industries had taken on a new employee and stockholder, John Herbert Meier.

Mrs. Jean Beckers, who worked as Cleveland's private secretary in 1968 and part of 1969, was unable to remember precisely how much Cleveland and his company paid Meier. But she did recall that Meier was paid by check. Sometimes the checks were drawn on an account in a northern Nevada bank, and sometimes Mrs. Beckers wrote the checks at Cleveland's office in Las Vegas. Her memory was hazy on amounts, although she "would guess they would be more in the thousands than in the hundreds."[27]

EXHIBIT 212-E

And what services was Meier performing for Basic Industries in exchange for the payments?

"I really don't know what you would call his services," mused Mrs. Beckers. "I really don't know."[28]

Whatever his services, "Dr. Meier" was being paid by Hughes to buy mining properties at the same time he was being paid by a company that was selling mining properties to Hughes.

A PIG IN A POKE?

As 1968 gave way to 1969, Meier continued to press for the acquisition of additional mining claims. On January 9, 1969, he put together a three-page report for Maheu outlining proposals to develop Hughes's properties:

Hughes Nevada Operations has now acquired approximately one-half of the area of Tonopah mining, some in Nye County and some in Esmeralda. This consists of approximately 80 percent of the known silver reserves in this area.

I am recommending the establishment of an exploration headquarters for a milling facility to mill on a custom basis and for a metallurgical testing program. This would include a modern assay office. . . . This program would be a preliminary to a larger milling facility established in the center of the known reserves as determined by the exploration program. . . .[29]

The one-year price tag on the milling operation was $950,000, but there were complications. Remembering Hughes's pathological concern about federal income taxes, Meier pointed out,

One of the prime advantages of mining for silver is that the mined silver can be stored without having to pay income tax on it as a profit. Continuous mining expenses can be incurred and until the silver is actually disposed of, no credit need be taken for the silver mined. It should be stored in the mines. Thus a considerable loss can be sustained prior to having to pay income taxes on the silver mined.[30]

And last, but not least, the Hughes mining chief proposed that "during 1969 we acquire additional mining properties, after we have carefully evaluated them, as we have done in the past four months."[31]

By now, there seemed no need to wait for an answer from either Maheu or Hughes. In the time before and after the report to Maheu, Meier continued to negotiate for more gold and silver mines. In one of those transactions, Traynor, the deputy state mine inspector, sold seven

EXHIBIT 212-F

more claims to Hughes for $200,000. The sale was noteworthy for two reasons: first, deeds filed in the Virginia City courthouse showed that Traynor had bought the claims just one day before he sold them; second, the claims were situated on rocky sagebrush land surrounding the old Occidental Mine outside Virginia City. The Occidental was one of those mines which even during the great gold rush of 1860–1880 was most unprofitable. Miners and investors had poured a lot more money into it than they had taken out.

Once again, the natives speculated as to Hughes's plan. One perplexed Storey County official observed, "Old timers here can't figure out what the deal is. There's other property might be more productive he could've gotten."[32] When Traynor was asked whether he had sold any other properties to Las Vegas's biggest gambler, he declined to discuss the matter, but said he saw no conflict between his position as a state mine inspector responsible for enforcing Nevada mining laws and his position as a private investor selling mines to Hughes. "I wanted to make some money for myself and help mining in the state," Traynor said. "I read up on the history of Virginia City and checked out the mine some time back. Hughes might do some good for mining in this state. They are a good legitimate operation. Look what they did for gambling. . . . Hughes might be the best thing this state has ever had for mining."[33]

Traynor also took exception to the criticism leveled at Hughes by some miners who contended that he could not be serious about mining because of the scattered location of his claims and who charged that his free spending was driving up prices on all properties. These people, said Traynor, "can't see the forest for the trees. The Hughes people are serious about this. They are not just playing around. They didn't just buy a pig in a poke. They studied this."[34]

Jack Cleveland, who had already sold Hughes more than $1 million in mining properties, was equally enthusiastic. "The theory is that a major part of the silver is still there in those mines," Cleveland maintained. "We have 400–500 percent better methods of mining than they had in the boom days of those mines. The only advantage they had was cheaper labor."[35]

For one who once said too much, Meier now said very little; he just continued to buy claims. In January, Cleveland's Basic Industries sold sixty-eight claims in Churchill County to Hughes for $340,000; Dennis Hill sold four more claims in Esmeralda County for $280,000; and Hill and Cleveland's Atlas International sold twelve claims in Nye County

EXHIBIT 212-G

by the merger of West Toledo Mines Company and the American Mining Company, two other companies in which Hatsis had an interest.*

Hatsis delivered the mining information requested by Meier in August of 1968, and sometime thereafter the two talked by telephone. An ebullient Meier, saying that he had discussed Hatsis and his Toledo Mining Company "with Howard Hughes personally," reported that Hughes not only was interested but was "greatly impressed with [Hatsis] because he was a man from a modest background and a small coal-mining town in the State of Utah, who had made it on his own."[63]

A series of conferences followed, often late at night, during which Meier would refer to some approval from the "penthouse" or "the old man." He said Hughes wanted to buy from Hatsis, but only if Hatsis would deal with an intermediary, one Everd B. Van Walsum, an accountant and representative of a Netherlands company known as Maatschappij–Intermovie N.V. The Dutchman, confided Meier, "was internationally connected with Howard Hughes personally" and it was "the personal desire and direction of Howard Hughes" that Hatsis should work only with him.[64]

Hatsis was ready. He advised Meier that his Toledo Mining Company already owned a number of claims in Nevada and Utah that "might be sold to the Hughes organization."[65] Meier responded that Hughes was most interested. This intense interest by Hughes ignored a report filed just weeks before with the Securities and Exchange Commission in Washington, listing the various Toledo Mining Company claims and offering this assessment of them:

There are no known commercially mineable ore bodies on any of the claims in which [the company] has an interest or which [the company] owns, and [the company] has no present plans for exploration on these properties.[66]

No one in the Hughes organization seemed concerned that a lot of money might soon be laid out for worthless claims. The game went on. In December of 1968, Meier told Hatsis that Hughes was ready to buy mining properties known as the Rattler group for $300,000. That transaction and the sale of other Toledo Mining Company claims for $330,000 were completed within two months. In April of 1969, Meier interrupted Hatsis's game on a Salt Lake City golf course with an urgent

* The vice-president of the new Toledo Mining Company was J. Bracken Lee, the mayor of Salt Lake City and a former Republican governor of Utah, who gained some notoriety in the mid-1950s when, to demonstrate his opposition to the American foreign aid program, he refused to pay his federal income taxes.

EXHIBIT 212-H

and Trust Company in Salt Lake City. Escrow and attorney's fees amounting to $13,023.98 were paid by the bank, which then issued a check for the balance of $1,386,976.02 made payable to Globe Mineral.

The president of Globe Mineral endorsed the check back to Continental Bank, and the bank in turn issued a cashier's check in the amount of $1,386,976.02. The check was made payable to none other than Maatschappij—Intermovie N.V., the Netherlands company represented by Everd B. Van Walsum.

This was the last of a series of deals in which nearly $5 million from the sale of mining claims to Hughes was moved through a string of foreign corporations and trusts and bank accounts in the Bahamas and Liechtenstein, and finally to a secret numbered account in Switzerland.

Everd B. Van Walsum, of course, had never met Hughes. He had never spoken with him, and he most assuredly was not "internationally connected" with Hughes, as Meier had assured Anthony Hatsis.

Rather, Everd B. Van Walsum was working for John Herbert Meier.

In a little less than two years, Meier had overseen a Hughes payout of $20 million for more than two thousand mining claims scattered across the deserts and mountains of Nevada and California. What were they worth?

Meier had estimated to Maheu, and Maheu had reported to Hughes, figures adding up to hundreds of millions of dollars. But a consulting geologist who studied the Hughes properties in the Belmont Mining District in Nye County, Nevada, concluded that "105 of the 112 claims involved had no value in terms of recognizable mineral deposits." He recommended that "they be dropped from ownership rolls."[78] In the Morey Mining District in Nye County, a geologic study "found that no metallic mineralization occurs anywhere on the property." The 104 Hughes claims were described as "worthless as mining prospects."[79] In the Red Hills Mining District in White Pine County, a geologic examination disclosed that sixty-five of eighty-five Hughes mining claims "lack metallic mineralization and can be considered worthless as mining properties."[80]

Not only had Hughes paid dearly for gold and silver properties that contained no gold or silver, some of the claims he paid for were not even owned by the sellers. In one instance, Hughes was obliged to pull up his claim stakes when the real owners of the property complained. Some claims, to be sure, did have recoverable mineral deposits. A mod-

EXHIBIT 212-I

452   E M P I R E

est mill was constructed at Tonopah, but the mining operation never made any money and the mill was closed several months after Hughes died in an effort to conserve the assets of his estate.

And what of "Dr. Meier"? In December of 1969, a month after leaving the Hughes organization, Meier was hired by Anthony Hatsis in Salt Lake City to serve "as a special adviser and consultant" to the president of the Toledo Mining Company.[81] His fee was fixed at $6,000 a month and he was granted an option to buy 300,000 shares of stock in the Toledo Mining Company.

That same month, Meier, true to his press release, created his Nevada Environmental Foundation, a tax-exempt, nonprofit organization "to provide research, education, information, publications, conferences and scientific knowledge for the practical solution to problems encountered in a comprehensive inventory of the degradation of our ecological environment in the United States."[82] It was an imposing charter, but the foundation eventually became best known for an incident involving a prominent California ecologist who was invited to deliver a speech in Reno at the foundation's expense. Believing that the Nevada Environmental Foundation was supported by Hughes, the ecologist was perplexed when the check he received from the foundation bounced. Meier then drifted on to New Mexico, where in 1972 he mounted a desultory and unsuccessful campaign for the Democratic party's nomination for the United States Senate.

At that time Meier still owned his home in Las Vegas. But in July of 1972, he sold it, moved his family to Vancouver, and applied for permanent residence in Canada.[83] Later in the year, Meier also sold two apartments he owned in Hermosa Beach, California, apparently liquidating the last of his holdings in the United States.

His decision to relocate and sell off his properties was a fortunate one, for in 1973 and 1974 Meier was indicted by a federal grand jury in Las Vegas for income-tax evasion. He was accused of failing to report some $2.5 million in income, mostly money that IRS agents said he had pocketed in the Hughes mining transactions.

Meier subsequently was arrested while visiting Point Roberts, just inside the United States border and not far from his suburban Vancouver home. Government attorneys, sensing that he would not show up for trial, requested bail of $100,000, which Meier promptly posted in cash. He then returned to his home in Canada. As feared, Meier did not appear for trial; his bail was forfeited and a bench warrant was issued for

EXHIBIT 212-J

his arrest, with new bail to be set at $500,000.* Through it all, Meier maintained his innocence, claiming to be the victim of a conspiracy by the Internal Revenue Service, the Central Intelligence Agency, the Justice Department, and the White House.

After he left the United States, Meier continued to wheel and deal, working on a complex series of financial transactions involving stock transfers and, once again, mining claims, this time in New Mexico. Sometimes using aliases, Meier was connected to a string of corporations, mostly dummy companies, but the real business action centered around a company called Transcontinental Video Corporation, a New Mexico corporation.

Late in 1974, Alfred Netter of Vancouver, an associate of Meier's in Transcontinental Video, flew to Los Angeles. On Tuesday, November 26, Netter, forty-four years old, Israeli-born, who stood five feet, seven inches, weighed 155 pounds, and wore a black toupee checked into the Beverly Hilton Hotel in Beverly Hills. What happened during the next few days is uncertain. But on Friday, November 29, Netter called Meier and the two discussed "business."[84] About eleven o'clock that night, a waiter brought dinner for two to Netter's room. At 2:25 P.M. the following day, when a hotel maid entered the room, she found Netter, wearing only a pair of shorts, lying on the floor. There was blood on the twin beds, blood on the floor between the beds, blood on the lamp, blood on the clothes closet, and blood on the bathroom sink. There was a stab wound on Netter's head, four stab wounds in his chest, two in his back, two on the right forearm, and multiple perforations of the heart, liver, and lungs.[85] Someone had carved up John Meier's partner. After Netter was murdered, the London Life Insurance Company paid $400,000 on a "key-man" life insurance policy that had been issued to Netter as an officer of Transcontinental. In time, according to law-enforcement authorities, the $400,000 found its way to a Meier account in Switzerland.[86] The murder remains unsolved.

By 1978, Meier, still carefully avoiding the United States, was deeply involved in a business deal with the king of Tonga, a string of some one

---

* Because income-tax evasion is not an extraditable offense, Meier cannot be brought to trial unless he returns voluntarily to the United States. He continues to live comfortably in Delta, British Columbia. Jack Cleveland, who sold the first mining claims to Hughes and who worked closely with Meier in the mining venture, also was indicted on federal income-tax evasion charges and also fled to Canada. He died on November 9, 1973, at Vancouver, British Columbia, at the age of sixty-four.

EXHIBIT 212-K

the civil lawsuit brought by the Hughes organization against him. But when Meier was brought before an Australian magistrate, he was promptly released after he produced his passport identifying him as a Tongan diplomat.

As one Tongan official philosophically lamented, "If he did it to Howard Hughes he could do it to us. The world is full of stupid people."[92]

One question, however, persists: How was it possible for Hughes, the businessman always so suspicious of others, to spend $20 million for gold and silver mines that, for the most part, had no value?

Perhaps the most likely explanation, and one never pursued by either the Hughes organization or by any law-enforcement agency, was the most obvious. It also was the most embarrassing, and far-reaching in its legal ramifications. Simply stated, it was this: the great gold- and silver-mining swindle could not have been carried out without the cooperation of someone in the Hughes hierarchy, someone in a key position until the day Howard Hughes died.

EXHIBIT 212-L
This photo can be found in the book Empire who got it from United Press International.

John H. Meier, who
oversaw the acquisition
of millions of dollars in
worthless mining claims
for Hughes and later
fled to Canada.
*United Press
International*

There are not enough words to thoroughly describe those who set out to destroy the legacy of the man known a Howard Robard Hughes, Jr. With malevolent premeditation they couched their plans of grandiose wealth and power. It is now clear what Bill Gay, Chester Davis, Robert Maheu, Monty Montrose, and others had become in their cold-hearted pursuit. There may be some who read this book and say, "Well Hell, I would have joined the team for *that* kind of money!" Should you be one of those types, be careful what you wish for. It's a dangerous path should you choose it, as it was for others cited in this text. Did the Devil make them do it? The answer to that is probably no. Good and evil dwells within us all, it's simply a matter of which you choose to serve, and to what height or depth you are willing rise or descend.

Russ and Charlie have had many conversations concerning fingerprints.

1. How could that Methodist Hospital fingerprinting fiasco go so wrong?

2. During the Clifford Irving – Rosemont dispute, why did neither party suggest that documents, supposedly written by Howard Hughes, be tested for latent fingerprints?

    a. Were those terribly smudged Hughes fingerprints on the Clifford Irving denial letter really put there by Howard Hughes? Were they processed by a crime lab to make certain that they were actual, freshly inked Hughes prints, or superimposed prints smudged? You would think that McGraw-Hill would have insisted on that, especially for the money they were spending. However, they did not. Wow, what a dynamic bluff! McGraw-Hill didn't know until the end that Irving was running a hoax; and the very last thing they would suspect was that Rosemont, Inc. _also_ was involved in a massive multi-million-dollar hoax!

    b. There's no evidence that the Irving letters were processed for latent prints.

    c. Rosemont, Inc. _would never have suggested_ that the cursive letters Irving produced be sent to a crime lab. Why? It's obvious that Rosemont would have been required to do the same with their questionable documents, and that would have been a full-blown disaster. A sure disaster for both the Irving and the Rosemont camps. Oh, my goodness, no legitimate Hughes prints on any summitted documents, no legitimately *known* cursive documents presented!?

3. And no, the gaming commission in Las Vegas, Nevada, never got any acceptable prints from Howard Hughes. But in their analysis, they did get some *questionable* prints. According to Federal crime lab analysis: "We should have absolutely nothing to do with this." (Exhibit 9)

4. "Identification Division cannot guarantee in any manner that the record furnished to the Gaming Authorities positively concerned Howard R. Hughes." (See Exhibit-10, Federal Files.)

5. In their analysis of latent prints, Canadian Customs could not find even a partial print attributed to Hughes on a document he had supposedly signed. "The latent prints are not identical with the fingerprints of Howard Robard Hughes, born December 24, 1905, in Houston, Texas." (See Exhibit 8, Federal Files.) The prints had been noted and isolated by customs of the fellow who pressed down on the document and supposedly signed the name "Howard Hughes," but whose prints and who's signature was it really? The lab results were baffling; a determination could not be made.

6. "Fingerprint card furnished to the gaming authorities could not be positively identified as that of Howard R. Hughes?" (See Exhibit 11.)

EXHIBIT 213

This Exhibit was a latecomer from Russ, an item he had difficulty finding. Perhaps it should be moved into Chapter V for more clarity there; however, it well serves it's purpose here as well. You will find reference to it in the fingerprint chapter. (Confidential redactions on card.)

According to Russ, "This Exhibit is a copy of <u>a real Coroner's fingerprint card</u> as submitted by a California enforcement agency in 1987. Coroners offices, contract Medical Examiners, Pathologists, and Hospitals which perform autopsies per contract with local Sheriff's Departments, usually used this 10-print FBI style fingerprint card to take fingerprints from a deceased person. Note that all the descriptive information on the deceased individual is annotated on the fingerprint card." <u>This is the same type of Coroner's card used earlier in 1976 as well, but was not used in the "Hughes" autopsy done at Methodist Hospital, Houston, Texas</u>.

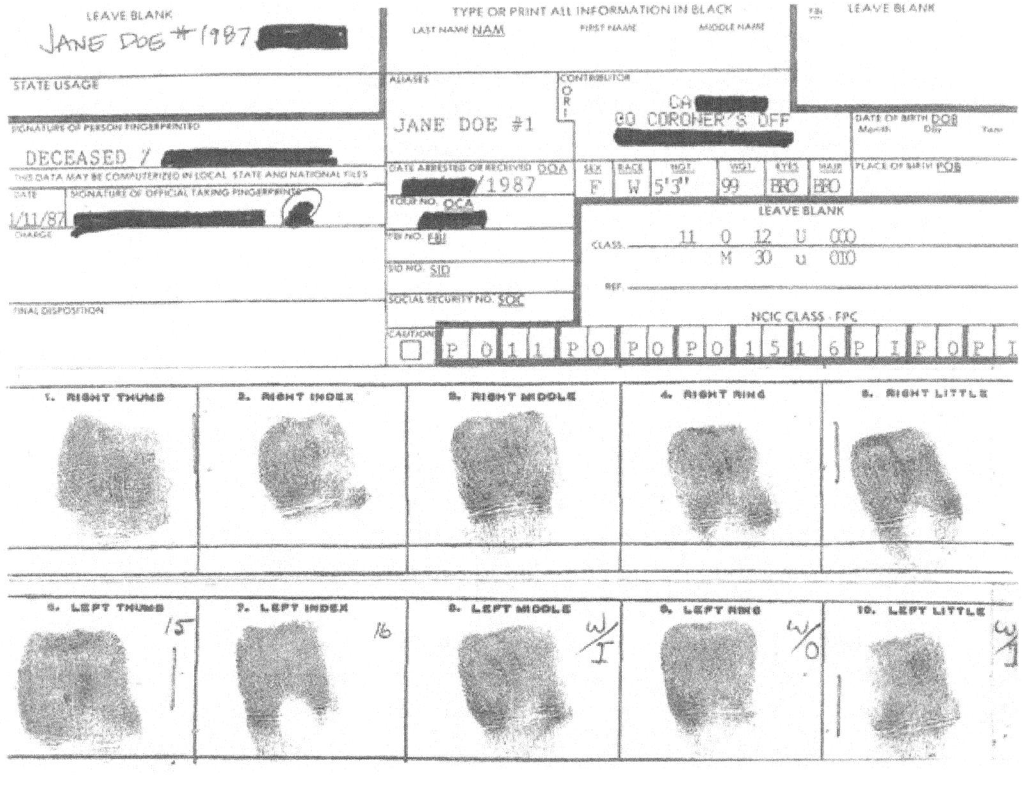

9/24/2018   San_Mateo_County_Jane_Doe_fingerprint_chart.jpg (1594×1247)

The above Coroners fingerprint card should have been used at Methodist Hospital in 1976, but as you saw in the Chapter V Exhibits, it was not! And yes, this card was used *throughout* the United States in 1976.

Research done in Chapter V is incriminating; however, it leaves open two major questions: a) Why did the FBI drop the ball on so many occasions, and b) why were those many cursive documents, supposedly written by "Howard Hughes," *never* processed for the existence of latent prints!?

Below you will find *Russ's final dissertation on latent fingerprints.* Not only will you be enlightened by the knowledge learn, you will be amazed at the tools used by law enforcement to catch criminals.

THE CAPTURE OF THE SWEET-TOOTH BOMBER
As per L. "Russ" Russell:

Fingerprints have always been a real interest of mine. And as part of my career, I've been fortunate to "make" several cases through the identification of fingerprints. Fingerprints developed on questioned documents; fingerprints developed on credit card receipts; fingerprints developed on extortion letters; fingerprints developed on a gas station bathroom stall, fingerprints developed on the external wrapping of mailed packages which contained narcotics or Internationally smuggled restricted items.

However, the one case I played a part in, back in 1976, merits more discussion than any of the above. On January 10, 1976, suspicious small packages were mailed to the houses of four San Francisco Board of Supervisors members. Fortunately, one member viewed the suspicious parcel and its wrapping and called the San Francisco Bomb Squad. It turned out that the parcels each contained a See's candy box, outfitted with ½ stick of dynamite and hard candies to act as shrapnel. That Board member called each of the other members, and fortunately no one had attempted to open the parcels, each designed to explode when the brown paper wrapping was disturbed. At one house, children were throwing the box around like a football until the telephone call came in.

Once disabled by the San Francisco Police Bomb Squad, each of the bombs were turned over to Postal Inspectors for investigation. A significant part of the investigation involved sending the parcels to the U.S. Postal Inspector Crime Laboratories in both South San Francisco and Washington, D.C. The local Laboratory processed the packages for fingerprints, while the D.C. Laboratory followed up assessing each of the component parts of the bombs.

I played a lessor part of the investigation. My job was to try to learn where the See's candy boxes had come from. This involved a study of the internal portion of each candy box bomb, and a visit to the See's Candy factory in San Bruno, CA. After these duties, I learned that the boxes had been brand new, and had never been used to store candy for resale. I was one of about 10-15 Inspectors assigned to the bomb investigation.

Meanwhile, the local Laboratory processed each candy box for latent fingerprints. As I recall, and remember viewing, only one exceedingly small piece of brown paper wrapping contained a segment of a fingerprint. The segment was approximately 1/4 the size of a dime. One-fourth. Incredible small but there were enough "points" for an Examiner to eventually, make a suspect identification. However, not enough "points" to develop a specific suspect using then-known fingerprint comparison machines, but enough "points" of identification to allow an Examiner to make a favorable comparison against other known suspect fingerprints.

No suspects were developed through normal investigative procedures, and the case remained "dormant" for several years.

Then, in November 1980, something occurred outside of Santa Cruz, CA which led to the identification of one of the candy box bomb makers. I was in the last days of my Postal Inspector career. I was sitting in a San Jose, CA office, when I received a telephone call on the 3rd of November 1980, almost 5 years since the candy box bombs were received by the San Francisco Board of Supervisors members.

A 31-year old wealthy woman, named Maureen Minton, had been murdered on September 19, 1979, and her live-in boyfriend, Ronald Huffman, age 40, was charged with her axe murder. In connection with his arrest, Huffman was fingerprinted. I do not recall who made the identification, but several months later (in early 1980), it was learned that the very small segment of brown wrapping paper on one of the candy box bombs, which contained the fraction of a fingerprint, was positively identified as belonging to Ronald Huffman.

Case partially solved, and all because of a single fingerprint segment, no larger than a 1/4 of a dime.

Over the years, I've learned that, for a variety of reasons, 3% of the public do not leave fingerprints on anything they touch; 3% of the public can lie and successfully pass a Polygraph test; and that 3% of the public can be accused of shooting a weapon because of chemicals found on their skin, when they haven't even touched a gun. However, for those that leave fingerprints on paper items, it has been found that they'll continue to leave fingerprints on subsequent paper items, unless they have taken means to hide their fingerprints.

L "Russ" Russell

EXHIBIT 214-A

CASE NO. A185995
DEPARTMENT NO. X
DOCKET NO. K

IN THE EIGHTH JUDICIAL DISTRICT OF THE STATE OF NEVADA

IN AND FOR THE COUNTY OF CLARK

FIRST NATIONAL BANK OF NEVADA,   )
Nevada Co-Special Administrator   )
of the Estate of Howard Robard   )
Hughes, Jr. (Deceased), WILLIAM   )
R. LUMMIS, Nevada Co-Special   )
Administrator of the Estate of   )
Howard Robard Hughes, Jr. (De-   )
ceased), and Texas Temporary   )
Co-Administrator of the Estate   )
of Howard Robard Hughes, Jr.   )
(Deceased); SUMMA CORPORATION,   )
HUGHES AIR CORP., d/b/a/ HUGHES   )
AIRWEST; and HUGHES PROPERTIES,   )
INC.,   )
)
                Plaintiffs,   )
)
           vs.   )
)
FRANK WILLIAM GAY, CHESTER C.   )
DAVIS, NADINE HENLEY MARSHALL,   )
DAVIS & Cox, a Partnership,   )
MAXWELL E. COX, HOWARD M. JAFFE,   )
D. MARTIN COOK, KAY GIBBONS   )
GLENN, LEVAR BEEBE MYLER, JOHN   )
MORRISON HOLMES, JR., CLARENCE   )
ALBERT WALDRON, HOWARD LORENZO   )
ECKERSLEY, JAMES H. RICKARD,   )
WILBUR SUTTON THAIN, M.D.,   )   A F F I D A V I T
JOHN DOES ONE THROUGH SIX, AJAX   )
CORPORATIONS ONE THROUGH SIX,   )
AND ABLE & BAKER PARTNERSHIPS   )
ONE THROUGH SIX,   )
)
                Defendants.   )
_____)

STATE OF NEVADA   )
)SS
COUNTY OF CLARK   )

        GARY LEWIS RAY, having been duly sworn, states as follows

        1. I was first employed by Hughes Productions in June

1968. I worked the summer as an airplane guard at Clover Field,

Santa Monica, California. I went away to college that fall and

returned to work at Hughes Productions in June of 1969. I started

as an airplane guard at Clover Field and later became a driver

EXHIBIT 214-B

1 working out of the Romaine Street office. I continued my employ-
2 ment there until I graduated from college in June of 1971. Imme-
3 diately upon graduation I was transferred to the Summa security
4 office in Encino, California. Currently I am the manager of phy-
5 sical security for the corporate office of Summa Corporation in
6 Las Vegas, Nevada.
7   2. I have personal knowledge of the matters stated in
8 this affidavit and, if called as a witness, I could and would test-
9 ify competently thereto.
10   3. Sometime in May of 1971, after Howard R. Hughes had
11 left Nevada in November 1970, Kay Glenn directed Jan Johnson (an-
12 other Summa driver) and me to go to Las Vegas to clear the remain-
13 ing items from Howard R. Hughes' penthouse suite at the Desert Inn
14 and to bring what was there to the Romaine Street office in Los
15 Angeles, California.
16   4. Jan and I flew to Las Vegas. In Las Vegas we rented
17 an eighteen-foot enclosed truck.
18   5. We had received instructions from Mr. Glenn that this
19 was a "hush hush" project and that we were to pack the items we
20 found and return them to Romaine Street.
21   6. We met Jim Golden and he let us into the Desert Inn
22 penthouse suite. We found and boxed the following items, among many
23 others: numerous syringes, dozens of them; ampoules of some kind of
24 medication, such as sterile water or dextrose; bottles of dextrose,
25 saline solution, etc; several cabinets such as one would find in a
26 doctor's office; porcelain trays, stainless steel trays; dozens of
27 bottles of medication; various types of pills and the like--enough
28 bottles to fill a good-sized box, 24x24x20; numerous empty medicine
29 bottles and empty clear bottles the size of canning jars; medical
30 instruments and instruments which appeared to be surgical instru-
31 ments; an operating or examination table; a large lamp such as used
32 in an operating or examination room; centrifuge and sterilization

-2-

EXHIBIT 214-C

1 units; and dozens of quart jars of urine. I remember no labels or
2 dates on the jars containing urine.
3   7. We transported these boxed items to Romaine Street in
4 Los Angeles, California as instructed by Mr. Glenn, and placed them
5 in the back part of the building.
6   8. I know that these items remained there for a relative-
7 ly short period of time and then I noticed these things were no
8 longer where we had placed them.
9   9. After I was transferred to the security office in En-
10 cino, California, I installed physical security equipment at vari-
11 ous locations where Mr. Hughes stayed. In the summer of 1971 I
12 traveled to Nassau, Bahamas, for this purpose. I found that Mr.
13 Hughes would sleep at any hour of the day or night. I heard, on
14 many occasions, the aides say that Hughes would sleep as long as
15 eighteen to twenty hours at a time. My observations confirmed this
16 because I had to schedule my working time around Hughes' sleeping
17 and waking hours. I would be there to do something, such as work-
18 ing on Mr. Hughes' sound equipment, television or security equip-
19 ment in his bedroom, outside his bedroom or near his bedroom, and
20 would have to wait until Mr. Hughes went to sleep or until he
21 awakened, depending on what and where the work was.
22   10. In Freeport, Bahamas, after 1974, after I had gotten
23 to know Mr. Hughes' personal aides and was more accepted by them,
24 Chuck Waldron and Howard Eckersley commented to me in casual con-
25 versations on Hughes' forgetfulness, saying that he couldn't or
26 wouldn't remember one day the very things he had been told the
27 previous day.
28   11. When Hughes first moved to Nicaragua, to the eighth
29 floor of the Intercontinental Hotel in February of 1972, one morn-
30 ing an elevator apparently malfunctioned and opened to the eighth
31 floor permitting a group of reporters access to the floor. Mr.
32 Hughes was down the hall asleep in a room to the right, with the

-3-

EXHIBIT 214-D

1 door open. We were able to convince the reporters--as they stood
2 five feet from Hughes' door--that we knew nothing of Hughes and
3 that we had merely rented some of the rooms on that floor. The
4 aides, including John Holmes, afterwards were terribly upset and
5 explicitly insisted that no news of this incident be passed on to
6 Bill Gay or Chester Davis.
7   12. I observed that Hughes depended on the aides for his
8 food, medical attention he received and incoming and outgoing mes-
9 sages. The placement of furniture in Hughes' bedroom was deter-
10 mined by the aides prior to his arrival. This happened in Nicar-
11 agua, Freeport and Acapulco. Hughes' bed was placed in such a
12 manner so he would not face the door to the aides' office. Waldron
13 and Eckersley told me this was done so Hughes could not see them
14 moving about in the adjoining room. Waldron and Eckersley said
15 Hughes would prefer to be able to see into the adjoining room.
16   13. On the occasions I saw Mr. Hughes, his hair was
17 quite long and unkempt. On some occasions, his beard and hair were
18 trimmed. Such an occasion was when he met Turner Shelton, U.S.
19 Ambassador to Nicaragua, and Mr. Somoza, president of that country.
20   14. I also know from observations and from my conversa-
21 tions with the aides to Mr. Hughes that, so far as the aides were
22 concerned, Jack Real was definitely "on the outside". Jack Real
23 was not allowed into the "inner office" area except when invited.
24   15. I did observe that locks were changed more than once
25 after 1974, while Mr. Hughes was at the Xanadu Hotel in Freeport.

GARY LEWIS RAY

Subscribed and sworn to before me
this 21th day of March , 1980.

Notary Public

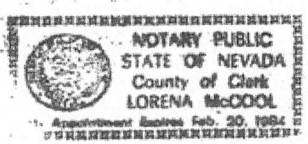

NOTARY PUBLIC
STATE OF NEVADA
County of Clark
LORENA McCOOL
Appointment Expires Feb. 20, 1984

-4-

EXHIBIT 215-A

SUMMA EMPLOYMENT AGREEMENTS   FEBRUARY 20, 1980

Name	Date Executed	Term Of Employment	Duties	Compensation	Expenses	Disclosure Of Information
Henley	7/23/74	1/1/74 – 12/31/75	Sr. Vice President & member of Board of Directors; subject to other positions; entire business time devoted to Summa; duties of comparable importance; may engage in non-conflicting activities; automobile, facilities & stenographic help available; not to compete with Summa.	$79,500 per year, bonuses & sickleave & vacation pay; salary changes according to Consumer Price Index.	Reasonable expenses, including entertainment & travel.	Employee shall not disclose names of Summa' customers or associates.
Glenn	7/15/74	1/1/74 – 12/31/79	Managing Director; all else same as Henley.	$70,000 per year; all else same as Henley.	Same as Henley.	Same as Henley.
Thain	3/1/75	3/1/75 – 2/28/80	Medical advisor & consultant; all else same as Henley.	$60,000 per year; all else same as Henley.	Same as Henley.	Not to disclose Summa's customers or parties which Summa associates with Not at any time to disclose confidential records nor publish nor write any material embarrassing or harmful to Summa; not to make records available to anyone who may disseminate it to public unless authorized by the Board of Dir.

514

EXHIBIT 215-B

SUMMA EMPLOYMENT AGREEMENTS   FEBRUARY 20, 1980

Name	Vacations	Disability	Termination Of Employment	Waiver Not To Be Inferred	Death	Non-Assign-ability	Agreement Binding On Summa Successor
Henley	With pay according to seniority date.	Compensation paid during illness or incapacity. After six months compensation will be reduced.	Agreement may be terminated for reasonable cause, e.g., conduct, discrediting Summa, violation of policies, disclosure of confidential information, failure to perform duties.	Waiver not to be inferred; failure to insist upon observance of any term does not constitute waiver.	If employee dies prior to termination of employment, spouse or beneficiary will receive 66 2/3% of monthly salary from time of death until the month in which agreement ends.	Agreement or benefits of agreement may not be assigned. Any assignments will be null & void.	Any successor of Summa must honor agreement.
Glenn	Same as Henley.	Same as Henley.	Same as Henley.	Same as Henley.	Same as Henley.	Same as Henley.	Same as Henley
Thain	"	"	"	"	"	"	"

515

EXHIBIT 215-C

SUMMA EMPLOYMENT AGREEMENTS   FEBRUARY 20, 1980

Name	Date Executed	Term of Employment	Duties	Compensation	Expenses	Disclosure of Information
Francom	12/30/76	1/1/74 – 12/31/76	Staff executive; entire business time devoted to Summa; assigned to duties of comparable importance; personal activities not to conflict with Summa; automobile & stenographic help & necessary facilities available.	$65,000 per year; bonuses & sickleave & vacation; increase subject to Consumer Price Index.	Reasonable, e.g. travel & entertainment.	Not to disclose names of Summa's customers or associates.
Holmes	7/15/74	1/1/74 – 12/31/78	Staff executive & member of Board of Directors; all else same as Francom.	$68,500 per year; all else same as Francom.	Same as Francom.	Same as Francom.
Waldron	7/15/74	1/1/74 – 12/31/80	Same as Francom.	$60,000 per year; all else same as Francom.	Same as Francom.	Same as Francom.
Rickard	7/15/74	1/1/74 – 12/31/79	Same as Francom.	$51,500 per year; all else same as Francom.	Same as Francom.	Same as Francom.
Eckersley	4/11/74	1/1/74 – 12/31/78	Same as Francom.	$65,000 per year; all else same as Francom.	Same as Francom.	Same as Francom.
Myler	7/31/74	1/1/74 – 12/31/76	Same as Francom.	$68,500 per year; same as Francom.	Same as Francom.	Same as Francom.

EXHIBIT 215-D

SUMMA EMPLOYMENT AGREEMENTS   FEBRUARY 20, 1980

Name	Vacations	Disability	Termination Of Employment	Waiver Not To Be Inferred	Death	Non-Assignability	Agreement Binding On Summa Successor
Francom	With pay according to seniority policies.	Compensation paid during incapacity; after 6 mos. compensation will be reduced.	Terminated for reasonable cause, e.g. failure to perform or disclosure of information.	Failure of either party to insist upon performance does not constitute waiver of contract.	Beneficiary will receive 66 2/3% of employee's monthly payment for the term of employment. Benefits will be reduced to extent of surviving spouse benefits under retirement plan.	Except for beneficiary, no one will receive rights or benefits of agreement.	Successor of Summa shall honor agreement
Holmes	Same as Francom.	Same as Francom.	Same as Francom.	Same as Francom.	Same as Francom	Same as Francom.	Same as Francom
Waldron	"	"	"	"	"	"	"
Rickard	"	"	"	"	"	"	"
Eckersley	"	"	"	"	"	"	"
Myler	"	"	"	"	"	"	"

517

EXHIBIT 216-A

In creating a rubber stamp for a CEO of a major company for use on multiple important documents, the item is generally crafted from an original signature which has been extensively practiced and carefully signed; hence the neatness and even flowing of the signature below. This stamp signature appears to have been created before the label "Summa, Inc." came into play.

The Howard Hughes Corporation

Howard Hughes

Type	Public
Traded as	NYSE: HHC (https://www.nyse.com/quote/XNYS:HHC)
Industry	Real Estate, Development
Founded	1913
Headquarters	Dallas, Texas United States
Revenue	US$1.06 billion[1] (2018)
Operating income	US$106.8 million[1] (2018)
Net income	US$57.7 million[1] (2018)
Total assets	US$7.36 billion[2] (2018)
Total equity	US$3.24 billion[2] (2018)
Number of employees	1,400[3] (2018)

EXHIBIT 216-B

The rubber-stamp signature for Howard Hughes, which appears in the above Exhibit, was clipped out and expanded. It was then pertinent to go to an original *known* signature of Howard Hughes: The known signature used is the one found on his fingerprint card when he applied for his pilot license with the National Defense Program. (June 25, 1942, see Exhibit 36.) The signature was clipped out and also expanded, the two signatures were then closely compared.

What becomes apparent below is that these two signatures appear to have been written by the same hand. No, they are not going to look *exactly* the same, as one was carefully practiced and neatly written (a bit ornate) because it was to be stamped onto numerous important documents. The bottom signature was written hurriedly, in the way one would sign a one-time signature on a check, or a document going to the IRS. These types of signatures are historically chaotic.

The telling similarities between the two signatures below is that the slant of the right side of the "H" is the same in both. The "H" connects to the top of the "o" in the same way in which the top of the "o" connects to the top of the "w." The "w" rounds off in a smooth and precise manner. The top of the "w" heads toward the top of the "a" in both, and finally, the way in which the back of the "a" bows downward and then swings into the "r" is the same.

Hence the neat and well-done stamp-signature falls somewhere between a known and a collective exemplar. This degree of carefulness and neatness in the stamp-signature is what Charles remembered when he momentarily glanced at the letter Howard had placed in his backpack in 1964 Mexico; it was neat and orderly.

**The Howard Hughes
Corporation**

Howard Hughes

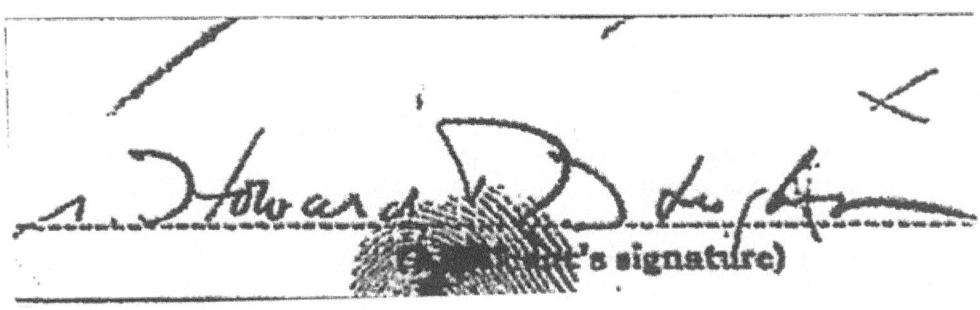

Howard D. Hughes

(s signature)

THE SWINDLE ON ITS SURFACE
The Tip of a Large Iceberg.

Finance statistics approximation: Buying power of $50,000.00 between the years 1965 and 1976 had the equivalency of $350,000.00 in todays inflated currency. These are Government statistics and are not based on the value of gold or silver which, of course, is substantially more.

Russ was able to get some information on the pay scales of the old Summa, Inc. syndicate, although not all the benefits are shown in Exhibits 215-A, B, C, and D above. One need not be a brain surgeon to see something terribly wrong with the information in these Exhibits. Can you imagine a bean counter or even an aide without basic skills in nursing or secretarial work getting paid $557,000 or even $455,000 per year in these days? The crew was then cemented in with contracts providing them with expense accounts, retirement benefits, medical insurance for themselves and family, etc. The litany of benefits for keeping their mouths shut and doing next to nothing were substantial for those years. Let's look forward to the day when we find out how much that same crew was earning prior to 1965. Knowing how much Nadine Henley was earning, can you imagine how much Bill Gay and Chester Davis were bringing in? We know that Robert Maheu was paying himself a cool half million per year, plus perks from 1965 to 1970. The information above came to light when Will Lummis and the First National Bank of Nevada decided to sue the old Summa, Inc. management team. They wanted to get back some of the 50 million or so dollars that had been syphoned off the Hughes Industries. ($50 million was probably a very shallow estimate of monies that went missing in the ten-year span between 1965 and 1976, but this is what they felt they could prove and possibly get without stirring up too much mud.) However, the old Summa group then decided to do a little suing themselves. Keeping in mind that both parties knew that the real Howard Hughes had been dead since 1965, there was no serious attempt to expose any fraudulent or criminal activity that would require jail time. Had Will Lummis done *this, as per Russ's comments above and below*, it's entirely possible that some weak-kneed soul who felt they couldn't do the time, might have turned state's evidence in exchange for probation. And, of course, with the possibility of murder one (the imposter Hughes) on the table…. Hence the mystification in "Russ" Russell's comment below excerpted from his critique above (Waldron Case Review).

> **"Puzzling to me is the fact that, instead of a Federal Criminal case, William Lummis, on behalf of the Summa Corporation, chose to file a civil case against the 13+ defendants (respondents). The criminal case could have involved embezzlement, conspiracy, forgery, gaming violations, use of the RICO (Racketeer Influenced and Corrupt Organization Act), and other possible Federal crimes. It appears that Summa, Inc. was looking to obtain monetary compensation rather than punitive actions against the defendants (respondents)."**
>
> **L "Russ" Russell**

WE NOW KNOW WHO HOWARD ROBARD HUGHES, JR. REALLY WAS AND WHAT TRANSPIRED AFTER 1965

We have come to the end of our literary journey. Now you know the real Howard Robard Hughes Jr. Not only did he do great things to enhance the human condition, he was quite a decent fellow as well. You may ask, "A decent fellow? Really?" To that there is only one answer, a resounding "Yes!" Perfection is not to be found in *any* of us, but Howard was a better man than most. It's a sure bet there will be those who wish to believe the rumors about Hughes prior to, and even after, 1965. "Oh, Hughes said this, and Hughes did that." And some of it may be true; however, what was once believed about things the man said and did after 1965, is pure fabrication.

All of us have done or said things we wish we could undo or unsay. These are *our* secrets, and we carry them with us day by day, and into the nights, for as long as we live. We often find justifications for those unsavory activities and find ways to live with them. But we know that, should we divulge these hidden deeds to others, they would view us in an unfavorable light; the unsavory deeds remain hidden within us. And then there are the foolish ones who believe that because no one knows of their distasteful activities, they are free to condemn others at whim or fancy for the slightest offence. Then come those most decadent among us, lesser humans, who know full well that what they have done is wrong, yet they take delight in their shadiest deeds. Above all things, their singular objectives are the pursuit of power and wealth. They laugh at those with principles and take advantage to profit from the diligence and intelligence of others at every opportunity. These sub-humans have been vividly portrayed in the chapters above, and rightly so. There was no bridge of morality left unburned and no beneficial lie left untold in their quest to plunder the Hughes estate – one of the world's greatest fortunes ever to be amassed by a brilliant, decent, and honorable man.

Howard contributed greatly to the aeronautical technology millions of people enjoy to this day as they visit loved ones and conduct business worldwide. In building military weaponry to help keep our enemies at bay for these many years, we can thank Howard for his ingenious contributions.

Much of the content above could have been delved into more deeply. Why it wasn't is simple. We wanted to bring you the most significant and relevant evidence from our research and analysis of the voluminous factual material we uncovered so that you could make your own deductions from this new light shed upon the life of Howard R. Hughes, Jr. Perhaps the repetition was a bit overdone sometimes; however, it was intended for clarification and to better instill the facts in your memory. With the compilation of all this research, there can be little doubt as to what happened to the Hughes Industries between the years of 1965 and 1976.

Will the greatest hoax of the twentieth century be fully brought into the light with the advent of this book? Will those of criminal intent with their massive ill-gotten wealth pounce and cry foul on this book's contents? Time will tell. However, any fallout will be anything but dull; and you, having read this book, are in on the ground floor.

Many years, and a great deal of personal time and finances, have been spent in the compilation of this work. As a result, the world will finally know the real Howard R. Hughes. The man was a prodigy and one of the greatest industrialists of the twentieth century. At long last all can see the truth. This book brings into the light the shadiest lies ever told to berate a decent man – lies that followed Howard into and beyond the grave.

The famous quote, *"No good deed goes unpunished,"* applies to what happened to Howard R. Hughes. Lies and degradation have shaped his legacy for these many years – and most glaringly after 1965. Our focus should be on the many contributions he made to industry, aeronautics, and his fellow man. This book has given you a better and more realistic view of this great American luminary. It's probable to say that if the majority of those having read this book – and now knowing the truth about Hughes – had the opportunity to spend two uninterrupted days with him as Charles did, they would have liked him. Howard was a fellow who would be willing to help if you were truly in need, a characteristic witnessed by Charles and many of Howard's employees and friends down through the productive years of his life.

The human condition is in dire need of prodigies such as Howard Hughes. They are needed every bit as much now as they were needed and celebrated throughout human history. Let us not be so foolish as to shovel Howard Hughes off into the dustbin of history; he was one of the all-time greats.

Rest in Peace Howard.

APPENDICES

APPENDIX A
REFERENCE BOOKS

A well recommended book *The Worst Hard Time* by **Timothy Eagan.** Although Eagan's book had nothing in it concerning Howard Hughes, information was used to clarify an experience, pertaining to the childhood of Charlie in *The Price of Their Souls.* This was Charles's first book where Howard Hughes played a key role. Exacting dates and instances of the great Dust Bowl era prior to and into the 1940s was needed. The two runaways, Charlie, and his friend, found themselves on a beach in Southern California. There they met an older fellow who told them a sad, but interesting story about his family's life of tribulation in the 1940s. Being just a kid in the early 1950s, Charlie could recall much of the story; however, accurate details were needed to bring this experience to life. Timothy Eagan's book is excellent in its portrayal of the great Dust Bowl areas of Texas and Oklahoma. The book is professionally written, and its accuracy and lucid documentation leaves one with the feeling that in his research, Mr. Eagan's heart was touched by those trapped in the squalor of one of nature's nastiest reprisals.

A main source of information researched was in a Hughes documentary written by **Donald L. Barlett and James B. Steele.** The book *Empire* was published by W. W. Norton & Company. The documentary is 766 pages in extent, including the Index. It's a bit of a mystery as to why the FBI, the CIA, or even local law enforcement didn't look more intensely at the information gathered by these two talented sleuths. Their research was exemplary, although it did appear that Donald and James often focused on hearsay and derogatory stories about Hughes far too often. It's as if they wanted to cast Hughes in a darker light whenever possible. Another mystery is why researchers such as Barlett and Steele could have been taken in by the gossip coming out of Romaine Street Headquarters in Los Angeles, California, and the Desert Inn Hotel in Las Vegas, Nevada, *after* 1965. Barlett and Steele had to have suspected, from time to time, that something was seriously wrong with the picture. On the other hand, having been misled with erroneous information and having put so much time and effort into their work, it's not expected that they will take lightly to the truth. However, their book was used because *many* of their sources are extensive, factual, and truthful – except for what they wrote about Howard Hughes between the years of 1965 to 1976. Here they were *totally misled and/or intentionally misleading.* Exactly how Donald and James came up with all their pre-1965 information, in such a short time is questionable.

Concerning background work done on Frank William Gay, Nadine Henley, Chester Davis, Robert Maheu, John Herbert Meier, Melvin Dummar, and various other pirates out to steal the gold from a dead man's teeth, Barlett and Steele appear to be pretty much on target, although they either looked the other way or did not fully comprehend the darker sides of these individuals. One is easily led to believe that had Barlett and Steele more thoroughly examined the material they had so laboriously gathered, they would have sensed a conspiracy. Perhaps they did, but perhaps the audacity of such a grandiose ploy simply didn't fit into their belief system. *But then, could there have been another side and purpose for their book?*

The first edition of *Empire* was published in 1979, less than three years after a fellow most believed to be Howard R. Hughes Jr. died and was buried in Houston, Texas. If you are not familiar with the publishing business during those years, the speed with which *Empire* was published – from inception to its finality – had to have been a record-setter. The information gathered on Howard Hughes and his family was *voluminous*. Then there was the chore of correlation, graphics, editing, typesetting, printing, binding, and last, but certainly not least, getting the book promoted and into the bookstores. Barlett and Steele must have garnered a lot of support from someone or somewhere. Financial shortfall becomes evident in most authors' lives. Also, one needs to take into consideration that less than six percent of books written during those years made it into print, and even fewer made a profit. However, this book must have returned reasonable proceeds as evidenced by a newer edition of this same book. It appears to be unabridged except for its name. This second edition was released in 2004, but the title had been changed to *Howard Hughes: His Life and Madness*. It appears that use of the key word *"madness"* in the title is intended to garner increased sales or drive home an opinion. All the information cited in *Empire* can be found in this re-titled edition; however, the pagination does not match. If you choose to research cited information, you must go to the library and check out the *first* edition *Empire*.

In the Endnotes, references to information that can be found in Barlett and Steele's book is designated using "B&S" and the page number. Page numbers for information excerpted from Barlett and Steele's book in Exhibits within the text of this book can be found in the Exhibit Index (Appendix C) following Endnotes below.

A book written by **James Phelan**, ***Howard Hughes: The Hidden Years*** and published by Random House was also a valuable resource. It was unusual, at first, that Mr. Phelan had discovered important information about Howard Hughes that had gone unacknowledged by Barlett and Steele. More information was expected from Barlett and Steele's book concerning Mell Stewart and Gordon Margulis. (Margulis is not mentioned even once in *Empire*.) Stewart and Margulis were personal aides to "Howard Hughes" both before and after 1965. It was strange and a bit troublesome that certain items of testimony by Mell and Gordon were not mentioned in *Empire*.

Mr. Phelan appears to have been diligent in his research. In the endnotes, Mr. Phelan's information is indicated using "J.P." and the page number in his book. Page numbers for information excerpted from James Phelan's book in Exhibits within the text of this book can be found in the Exhibit Index (Appendix C) following Endnotes below.

Also, reference is made to a book written by **Albert B. Gerber** entitled ***Bashful Billionaire*** and published by Dell. Once again information found in Gerber's book was not acknowledged in Barlett and Steele's book *Empire*. Mr. Gerber's book provides a more straightforward and happier portrayal of Howard Hughes. It appears that Mr. Gerber did his own research with little or no help from others. In the Endnotes, information from Mr. Gerber's book is designated with "A.G." and the page number. Page numbers for Exhibits from Albert Gerber's book can be found in the Exhibit Index (Appendix C) following Endnotes below.

An information source, which does not appear in my previous book, *The Price of Their Souls,* is ***Hughes***, written by **Richard Hack**. Perhaps there is no need to direct you to the library on this book. We have extracted the pertinent pages that support our case and collaborate with other Exhibits used to substantiate the authenticity of our investigation. However, this book is also well written and would be an interesting read for anyone interested in the life and times of Howard Hughes. Page numbers for exhibits excerpted from Richard Hack's book, within the text of this book, can be found in the Exhibit Index (Appendix C) following Endnotes below.

Howard Hughes: The Secret Life, written by **Charles Higham** contains, without doubt, the most graphic description of Howard Hughes's injuries after his XF-11 crash into Beverly Hills. Where the above writers were content with what the news media had to say, it's apparent that Mr. Higham got his information directly from an eyewitness source and an inside hospital source as well. Although much of what Mr. Higham wrote parallels the news media reports, he went into more detail on injuries sustained by Hughes. Page numbers for exhibits excerpted from Charles Higham's book, found within the text of this book, can be found in the Exhibit Index (Appendix C) following Endnotes below.

It is unfortunate that the above-noted authors did not more extensively question the possibility that the real Howard Hughes could have died earlier than 1976. However, the greatest hoax of the twentieth century *could only* have been perpetuated with the combined use of grandiosity, audacity, and the practically *unlimited ill-gotten wealth* of its perpetrators. These, indeed, were the tools used by the unscrupulous individuals mentioned in this book who mislead all but a few and sidetracked concerns that fraud and embezzlement had been afoot from 1965 to 1976. Perhaps the main reason for the above noted authors' naiveté was simply this: unlike Charles, *they had not known when the Great Hoax began.*

Investigator L. "Russ" Russell, Chief of Police (Retired), supplied copious information through his research and commentaries. As highlighted in Chapter III, his skills and diligence substantially reinforced the narrative and exposés of this documentary. Quite simply, this book has a greater level of authority because of his contributions.

Basic Galleys were sent out requesting analysis of the book's contents prior to final editing.

The responses from those skilled in the medical arts, legal arts and law enforcement were strikingly reinforcing with their level of support and validation. Several of their commentaries can be seen in the review section of this book. We are profoundly grateful for these comments and suggestions which helped to improve and efficiently convey this book's informative intentions.

APPENDIX B
ENDNOTES

1. *Empire*, Barlett and Steele, page 659
2. *Empire*, Barlett and Steele, pages 654-659
3. *Empire*, Barlett and Steele, pages 656-657
4. *Empire*, Barlett and Steele, page 657
5. *Empire*, Barlett and Steele, pages 628-629
6. *Empire*, Barlett and Steele, page 629
7. *Bashful Billionaire*, Albert B. Gerber, page 288
8. *Empire*, Barlett and Steele, page 674
9. *Howard Hughes*, James Phelan, page 131
10. *Empire*, Barlett and Steele, pages 159-161
11. *Bashful Billionaire* Albert B. Gerber, pages 258-259
12. *Bashful Billionaire*, Albert B. Gerber, page 145
13. *Empire*, Barlett and Steele, page 513
14. *Empire*, Barlett and Steele, pages 511-516
15. *Bashful Billionaire*, Albert B.Gerber, page 259 last paragraph
16. *Bashful Billionaire*, Albert B. Gerber, pages 15 and 73
17. *Bashful Billionaire*, Albert B. Gerber, pages 208-209
18. *Bashful Billionaire*, Albert B. Gerber, pages 294-295
19. *Empire*, Barlett and Steele, page 31
20. *Empire*, Barlett and Steele, pages 31-32
21. *Bashful Billionaire*, Albert B. Gerber, page 96
22. *Bashful Billionaire*, Albert B. Gerber, page 178 (Brewster wire-tapping is not mentioned in *Empire*.)
23. *Empire*, Barlett and Steele, pages 137-139, 142-143
24. *Bashful Billionaire*, Albert B. Gerber, page 287
25. *Empire*, Barlett and Steele, page 55
26. *Empire*, Barlett and Steele, page 61
27. *Empire*, Barlett and Steele, pages 66-67
28. *Empire*, Barlett and Steele, page 72 just above the large footnote
29. *Bashful Billionaire,* Albert B. Gerber, pages 152, 154
30. *Empire,* Barlett and Steele, page 72
31. *Bashful Billionaire,* Albert B. Gerber, page 153 and *Empire,* Barlett and Steele, pages 78-79
32. *Empire,* Barlett and Steele, page 82 and *Bashful Billionaire,* Albert B. Gerber, page 157
33. *Empire,* Barlett and Steele, page 203
34. *Empire,* Barlett and Steele, page 279
35. *Empire,* Barlett and Steele, pages 608, 670
36. *Empire,* Barlett and Steele, page 308
37. *Empire,* Barlett and Steele, pages 289, 304, 310, 427-30, 432-37, 516-519
38. *Empire,* Barlett and Steele, page 450-453
39. *Empire,* Barlett and Steele, pages 311,450
40. *Empire,* Barlett and Steele, page 429 at bottom
41. *Howard Hughes*, James Phelan, pages 52, 53
42. *Howard Hughes*, James Phelan, pages 112, 113
43. *Empire,* Barlett and Steele, pages 591 and 593 – 594
44. *Howard Hughes*, James Phelan, page 64
45. *Empire,* Barlett and Steele, page 308
46. *Empire,* Barlett and Steele, pages 309-310
47. *Empire,* Barlett and Steele, page 310; and *Bashful Billionaire,* Albert B. Gerber, page 208
48. *Empire,* Barlett and Steele, page 169 also see one of two last photos of H.H. between pages 262 and 263, top caption
49. *Bashful Billionaire,* Albert B. Gerber, pages 208-209
50. *Howard Hughes* James Phelan, page 66
51. *Empire,* Barlett and Steele, page 343

52. *Empire,* Barlett and Steele, pages 336-337

53. *Empire,* Barlett and Steele, pages 475-476

54. *Empire,* Barlett and Steele, pages 429, 446, 450, 451

55. *Empire,* Barlett and Steele, page 429

56. *Empire,* Barlett and Steele, page 450

57. *Empire,* Barlett and Steele, page 431

58. *Empire,* Barlett and Steele, pages 450-455

59. *Empire,* Barlett and Steele, explicitly page 455

60. *Howard Hughes*, James Phelan, pages 107, 113

61. *Empire,* Barlett and Steele, page 299

62. *Empire,* Barlett and Steele, page 224

63. *Empire,* Barlett and Steele, pages 124-126

64. *Empire,* Barlett and Steele, page 133

65. *Bashful Billionaire,* Albert B. Gerber, pages 21-22

66. *Howard Hughes*, James Phelan, page 55

67. *Bashful Billionaire,* Albert B. Gerber, page 259

68. *Bashful Billionaire,* Albert B. Gerber, pages 271-273, 346

69. *Bashful Billionaire,* Albert B. Gerber, pages 307

70. *Howard Hughes*, James Phelan, page xiii Foreword

71. *Bashful Billionaire,* Albert B. Gerber, pages 317, 321

72. *Bashful Billionaire,* Albert B. Gerber, pages 321-322

73. *Empire,* Barlett and Steele, page 368

74. *Empire,* Barlett and Steele, page 760

75. *Empire,* Barlett and Steele, page 276

76. *Empire,* Barlett and Steele, page 279

77. *Empire,* Barlett and Steele, pages 262,263, also on last page

78. *Howard Hughes*, James Phelan, pages 147, 159

79. *Howard Hughes*, James Phelan, page 16

80. *Empire,* Barlett and Steele, Prologue, pages xxiv-xxv

81. *Empire,* Barlett and Steele, page 685, just above the large footnote

82. *Empire,* Barlett and Steele, Prologue, pages xxiv-xxv

83. *Empire,* Barlett and Steele, Preface, page xii

84. *Howard Hughes*, James Phelan, page 19, top

85. *Howard Hughes*, James Phelan, pages 19-20; also, *Empire,* Barlett and Steele, page 686

86. *Empire,* Barlett and Steele, page 685

87. *Empire,* Barlett and Steele, page 685 also

88. *Howard Hughes*, James Phelan, page 149

89. *Howard Hughes*, James Phelan, page 9

90. *Howard Hughes*, James Phelan, pages 107, 130-142

91. *Empire,* Barlett and Steele, various hotel photos between pages 478, 479

92. *Empire,* Barlett and Steele, page 529

93. *Empire,* Barlett and Steele, page 529

94. *Empire,* Barlett and Steele, Prologue, page xxvi

95. *Empire,* Barlett and Steele, pages 272-273

96. *Bashful Billionaire,* Albert B. Gerber, page 250

97. *Empire,* Barlett and Steele, page 529

98. *Howard Hughes*, James Phelan, page 178

99. *Empire,* Barlett and Steele, page 289

100. *Empire,* Barlett and Steele, pages 291-292 at bottom and *Howard Hughes*, James Phelan, pages 51-52

101. *Empire,* Barlett and Steele, page 516, bottom

102. *Howard Hughes*, James Phelan, Foreward, page xiii

103. *Empire,* Barlett and Steele, page 629

104. *Empire,* Barlett and Steele, pages 31-32

105. *Empire,* Barlett and Steele, page 55

106. *Empire,* Barlett and Steele, pages 669-670

107. *Empire,* Barlett and Steele, Prologue, page xxii, page xxv – Death in Mexico

108. *Empire,* Barlett and Steele, Prologue, page xxv – Death in Mexico

109. *Empire,* Barlett and Steele, Prologue, page xxvi – Death in Mexico

110. *Empire,* Barlett and Steele, photos between pages 622 and 623 (third in series)

111. *Empire,* Barlett and Steele, Prologue, page xxvi – Death in Mexico

112. *Empire,* Barlett and Steele, page 682, footnote

113. *Empire,* Barlett and Steele, pages 300-302

114. *Bashful Billionaire,* Albert B. Gerber, page 315

115. *Empire,* Barlett and Steele, page 674

116. *Empire,* Barlett and Steele, page 224

117. *Empire,* Barlett and Steele, page 646

118. *Empire,* Barlett and Steele, page 310 and *Bashful Billionaire,* Albert B. Gerber, page 208

119. *Empire,* Barlett and Steele, page 309

120. *Empire,* Barlett and Steele, page 646, bottom

121. *Empire,* Barlett and Steele, page 674

122. *Empire,* Barlett and Steele, pages 291-292, bottom and *Howard Hughes*, James Phelan, pages 51-52

123. *Empire,* Barlett and Steele, page 291

124. *Empire,* Barlett and Steele, pages 626-627

125. *Empire,* Barlett and Steele, between pages 622 and 623, third page of photos

126. *Empire,* Barlett and Steele, page 685

127. *Empire,* Barlett and Steele, page 642

128. *Empire,* Barlett and Steele, page 685

129. *Empire,* Barlett and Steele, page 642

130. *Empire,* Barlett and Steele, page 299

131. *Empirc,* Barlett and Steele, page 669-671

132. Empire, Barlett and Steele, page 677

133. Empire, Barlett and Steele, page 686

134. Empire, Barlett and Steele, pages 129-130

135. Empire, Barlett and Steele, page 627

136. Empire, Barlett and Steele, page 627

137. Empire, Barlett and Steele, pages 222-223

138. Bashful Billionaire, Albert B. Gerber, page 346

139. Bashful Billionaire, Albert B. Gerber, pages 346-347

140. Bashful Billionaire, Albert B. Gerber, page 347

141. Bashful Billionaire, Albert B. Gerber, page 347 also

142. Bashful Billionaire, Albert B. Gerber, page 348

143. Bashful Billionaire, Albert B. Gerber, page 348

144. Bashful Billionaire, Albert B. Gerber, page 348

145. Empire, Barlett and Steele, pages 128-129

146. Bashful Billionaire, Albert B. Gerber, page 347

147. Bashful Billionaire, Albert B. Gerber, page 71

148. Empire, Barlett and Steele, page 687 bottom, page 678 top

APPENDIX C
EXHIBIT INDEX

APPENDIX C
EXHIBIT INDEX
Continued

APPENDIX C
EXHIBIT INDEX
Continued

CHAPTER V

APPENDIX C
EXHIBIT INDEX
Continued

APPENDIX C
EXHIBIT INDEX
Continued

APPENDIX C
EXHIBIT INDEX
Continued

APPENDIX C
EXHIBIT INDEX
Continued

APPENDIX C
EXHIBIT INDEX
Continued

APPENDIX C
EXHIBIT
Continued

Page 185—EXHIBIT 72: PAGE 29—FBI FILE:1222257-0-87-HQ-119739-bulky-19
"H.H." cursive letter (page 4 of 4), complete with bogus signature. Pages 24 to 28 non-inclusive as drift is obvious.

Page 186—EXHIBIT 73: PAGE 31—FBI FILE:1222257-0-87-HQ-119739-bulky-19
Frank McCulloch (New York Bureau Chief, Time-Life News Service) weighs in with an affidavit in opposition to Rosemont Enterprises, Inc. for a preliminary injunction to stop Clifford Irving, McGraw-Hill Book Co. and others.

Page 187—EXHIBIT 74: PAGE 32—FBI FILE:1222257-0-87-HQ-119739-bulky-19
Frank McCulloch believes Clifford Irving. He believes Hughes is trying to renege on the deal. Also believes he talked to "Hughes" in 1971.

Page 188—EXHIBIT 75: PAGE 33—FBI FILE:1222257-0-87-HQ-119739-bulky-19
Frank McCulloch, has telephone conversations with Howard Hughes between the years of 1958 and 1962. Conference call in 1971 set up by Chester Davis. McCulloch claimed to have spoken with Hughes in 1964 and 1965. Frank claimed that he had not spoken to Hughes after 1965 up until Dec. 1971: "Hughes's voice fades in and out." Frank is not 100% sure he's talking to Hughes.

Page 189—EXHIBIT 76: PAGE 34—FBI FILE:1222257-0-87-HQ-119739-bulky-19
Frank McCulloch believes that "he may have been listening to the voice of Howard Hughes in 1971, but that the connection was "bad" and "the voice tended to fade in and out," he's uncertain.

Page 190—EXHIBIT 77: PAGE 35—FBI FILE:1222257-0-87-HQ-119739-bulky-19
The Osborns enter the picture. Frank McCulloch has read Irving's 400-page manuscript and believes it to be authentic. "Bahamian Hughes" claims that documents on file with the Nevada Gaming Board, as well as the "Chester and Bill letter" are authentic; *none of them are.*

Page 191—EXHIBIT 78: PAGE 36—FBI FILE:1222257-0-87-HQ-119739-bulky-19
Irving has convinced Frank McCulloch that the H.H. manuscript is authentic. Frank has entered an opinion that is not correct.

Page 192—EXHIBIT 79: PAGE 53—FBI FILE:1222257-0-87-HQ-119739-bulky-19
Chester Davis threatens McGraw-Hill Book Co.

Page 193—EXHIBIT 80: PAGE 54—FBI FILE:1222257-0-87-HQ-119739-bulky-19
Here Chester Davis has Presumed too much – as Frank McCulloch eventually *did believe* the Irving manuscript to be authentic.

Page 194—EXHIBIT 81: PAGE 55—FBI FILE:1222257-0-87-HQ-119739-bulky-19
Critical Exhibit. Per Chester Davis, "Since 1965 Rosemont Inc. has held exclusive rights to Mr. Hughes's life story."

APPENDIX C
EXHIBIT INDEX
Continued

APPENDIX C
EXHIBIT INDEX
Continued

APPENDIX C
EXHIBIT INDEX
Continued

APPENDIX C
EXHIBIT INDEX
Continued

CHAPTER X

APPENDIX C
EXHIBIT INDEX
Continued

APPENDIX C
EXHIBIT INDEX
Continued

Page 290—EXHIBIT 129-B: Excerpt from Bartlett and Steele's book, *Empire.*
List of Injuries Sustained by Howard Hughes in XF-11 Crash in 1946. Burns, bones, cuts, etc.

1. * Lawsuit against Hamilton Standard for faulty propeller includes stipend for Durkin (the marine who pulled Hughes from the XF-11 wreck) as well as the cost of flying Durkin's parents from Pittsburg to Los Angeles.

Page 291—EXHIBIT 130-A: Excerpt from Richard Hack's book, *Hughes.*
Chapter "Death by Neglect" in which "Hughes" corpse lands in Houston, Texas, airport. Dr. McIntosh, Methodist Hospital, meets the plane.

Page 292—EXHIBIT 130-B: Excerpt from Richard Hack's book, *Hughes.*
"H.H." jet arrives in Houston, Texas. Dr. Thain states, "I lost the beat just a few minutes ago. He's gone." Dr. McIntosh wants to try resuscitation. "It's no use," Thain countered, repeating "He's gone, he's gone." Pilot Roger Sutton not told of the death until the plane landed. "I was shocked and saddened." The body appeared <u>remarkably emaciated and</u> <u>dehydrated.</u>

Page 293—EXHIBIT 130-C: Excerpt from Richard Hack's book, *Hughes.*
"H.H." Doctors Thain and Chaffin and aide Holmes maintain that "H.H." had died over Brownsville, Texas, at 1:27 p.m. <u>Above statement is in conflict with Exhibit 130-B</u> where Dr. Thain maintained that "I lost the beat just a few minutes ago;" upon the jet's arrival with the "H.H." corpse in Houston.

Page 294—EXHIBIT 130-D: Excerpt from Richard Hack's book *Hughes.*
Drs. Thain and Chaffin were followed back to the Warwick Hotel by reporters <u>where Hughes Executive Bill Gay had also registered.</u> Hughes's nephew <u>Will Lummis continues to insist that the body be cremated</u>. Neither Will nor Annette Lummis can bridge the legal gap. They had been against any fingerprinting or photos of the "H.H." corpse, insisting on immediate cremation.

Page 295—EXHIBIT 130-E: Excerpt from Richard Hack's book, *Hughes.*
1. Drs. Thain and Chaffin and aide Holmes sign documents maintaining that the corpse was that of Howard Hughes.
2. "Hughes's" Aunt Annette and the "Hughes" entourage cremation idea had its legal implications; neither Will nor, Annette Lummis could bridge the legal gap. They had been against any fingerprinting or photos of the "H.H." corpse, insisting on immediate cremation.
3. The bid for cremation by the Lummises and the "H.H." "caretakers" is lost. That "H.H." wished cremation was only supposition and here-say.
4. Dr. Montemayor (Mexican doctor) testifies that "H.H." had died an unnecessary death. "In my opinion he died of a disease called neglect."

Page 296—EXHIBIT 130-F: Excerpt from Richard Hack's book, *Hughes.*
Mexican Doctor Montemayor maintains that "when a patient becomes unconscious you put him in a Hospital." Original set of "H.H." fingerprints are rejected.

APPENDIX C
EXHIBIT INDEX
Continued

APPENDIX C
EXHIBIT INDEX
Continued

APPENDIX C
EXHIBIT INDEX
Continued

APPENDIX C
EXHIBIT INDEX
Continued

APPENDIX C
EXHIBIT INDEX
Continued

Page 326—EXHIBIT 157: AUTOPSY REVIEW OF HOWARD R. HUGHES

1. The right lung weighs 300 grams and the left lung 390 grams. Save for the previously described fibrous adhesions and bilateral fibrous apical scars, no lesions are found. The tracheobronchial tree and larynx are without lesions.
2. Eccrine adenoideystic adenocarcinoma, left scalp.
3. Separation left acromio-clavicular joint with edema and hematoma left shoulder, lipoma.
4. Scars of the left back (history of crashing injury, remote)

Page 327—EXHIBIT 158-A: AUTOPSY REVIEW OF HOWARD R. HUGHES

Additional Findings:
1. Chronic renal failure.
2. Emaciation and dehydration.
3. Generalized osteoporosis.
4. Fibrotic apical scars both lungs and old, fibrotic left pleural adhesions (history of left thoracic injury)
5. Separation left acromio-clavicular joint with edema and hematoma left shoulder.
6. Single left vertebral artery.
7. Cylindroma left parietal scalp.
8. Needle punctures / ecchymoses forearms.

Page 328—EXHIBIT 158-B: PAGE 112 FROM JAMES PHELAN'S BOOK *"HOWARD HUGHES: THE HIDDEN YEARS"*.

James Phelan is getting information for his book from both Margulis and Stewart. (This info. comes straight "from the horse's mouth," so to speak.)
1. "Hughes" leaves Desert Inn Penthouse, L.V.
2. Chuck Waldron changes all locks on 9th floor.
3. Eric Bundy, Norm Love, and Fred Jayka clean up "Hughes's" *little* bedroom.
4. The *little* bedroom hadn't been vacuumed or dusted for 4 years; no maid had entered. Aide Mell Stewart is reluctant to talk about it.
5. Stewart's job was to dispose of "Hughes's" empty bottles of pain-killing drugs. According to Mell Stewart: "there must have been hundreds of them."
   a. First instructions from Romain Street headquarters: "Put them in a gunnysack, smash them with a hammer, and bury the sack of broken bottles at some remote spot far out in the Desert."
   B. First instructions are negated, and Mell is instructed "to pack the bottles in boxes and deliver them to Romaine headquarters."
   c. Per Stewart: "I had my wife drive me from Las Vegas to Los Angeles. I turned over the empty bottles to the Romaine staff. I don't know why they wanted them, and I didn't ask."
   d. "Hughes" prone to urinating into wide-mouth Mason Jars.

APPENDIX C
EXHIBIT INDEX
Continued

APPENDIX C
EXHIBIT INDEX
Continued

APPENDIX C
EXHIBIT INDEX
Continued

APPENDIX C
EXHIBIT INDEX
Continued

Page 397—EXHIBIT 179-D: continued.
4. "Hughes" looks around the foyer and says, "This is pretty nice."
5. A senior aide tells Margulis, "Get the wheelchair and get him moving."
6. Margulis: "I told him to ease off and let the boss look around a little bit."
7. Once in the hotel suite, Hughes goes over to the window and looks out instead of scuttling off to his bedroom; he likes the view.
8. Senior aides pick the large middle room with a large picture-window for their office.
9. "Hughes" gazed out the window for a while watching a seaplane land in the harbor.
10. Margulis: "The Senior aides didn't like that one bit. They told me to get him away from the window and into his bedroom."
11. Senior aides mention "previous panic attacks" by "Hughes." Obviously, a ploy the imposter learned early on as part of the show. Hence the imposter and aide Margulis comply and "H.H." is hustled away to his darkened, dingy room.

Page 398—EXHIBIT 179-E: The real bosses were the aides, *not* "Hughes." According to Margulis: The senior aides are obviously calling the shots. "Hughes" is warned by the senior aides, that "somebody could fly past the sitting room in a helicopter and take his picture with a telephoto lens. Perhaps it didn't occur to the senior aides – the real people in charge – that the "Boss" could have grown a beard and worn a hat, or perhaps some dark glasses would have helped to conceal "Hughes's" identity. Is that what was *really* going on, or was it simply, "*Get back* in that dingy little room or I'm gonna slap ya!?"

Page 406—EXHIBIT 180: Clarence Waldron's book: *The Mysterious Howard Hughes Revealed* Governor Paul Laxalt wants to help fight organized crime in Las Vegas. He invites the Hughes group into the state and goes all out to inspire "Hughes" to purchase price-inflated properties, hotels with casinos, and worthless mining claims.

Page 407—EXHIBIT 181: Clarence Waldron's book: *The Mysterious Howard Hughes Revealed*.
1. Clarence "Chuck" Waldron, in 1967, is elevated to the job of "Hughes's" personal secretary. Chuck has no skills in this category and doesn't even know how to type. But John Holmes (the drug runner) informs Chuck that "Hughes" wants to put him in this elevated secretarial position and has a <u>special job</u> for him. (We'll see this in later Exhibits.)
2. The "Hughes" entourage wants to look for space at the Britannia Beach Hotel in the Bahamas, <u>not the Emerald Beach Hotel where he had *supposedly* stayed in 1957.</u>
3. With the mention of Jack Hooper, the inference is that Maheu knew all about this pending move. He didn't. Maheu was soon to be fired and "Hughes" would be secreted away where Bob Maheu could not interfere with the ongoing Summa Inc. activities.
4. Hughes had rented hotel rooms at the Emerald Beach Hotel in the Fall of <u>1957</u> (according to Waldron) and had continued to rent these empty rooms up until the Fall of <u>1967</u> (10 years).
5. "Hughes," at whim or fancy, decides to pay his ten-year accumulative hotel bill.

APPENDIX C
EXHIBIT INDEX
Continued

APPENDIX C
EXHIBIT INDEX
Continued

APPENDIX C
EXHIBIT INDEX
Continued

Page 433—EXHIBIT 193: Continued, From Barlett and Steele's book, *Empire*.
3.   Barlett and Steele had *base* reasons for stating, "Howard probably never wrote a holographic will."
<u>Note:</u> *If* Eckersley had lied about the holographic will by Hughes, he would need to be well versed in will procedure. It was Neil McCarthy, Hughes's personal attorney, who supervised Hughes in the writing of holographic wills, *not* Noah Dietrick. Eckersley, although discredited by Barlett and Steele in the book *Empire*, appears to be credible in this instance; where else would he get the information allowing him to wax proficient in the writing of holographic wills?

<u>NOTE:</u> On the Agent Lile deposition, pages 100 and 101 below, the attorneys attempt to attribute the sloppiness and ignorance in the "Mormon Will" to kidney failure – but it just doesn't work. Agent Lile clearly explains that this <u>could not</u> be the case.

APPENDIX C
EXHIBIT INDEX
Continued

APPENDIX C
EXHIBIT INDEX
Continued

APPENDIX C
EXHIBIT INDEX
Continued

APPENDIX C
EXHIBIT INDEX
Continued

APPENDIX C
EXHIBIT INDEX
Continued

Page 503—EXHIBIT 212-K: *Empire,* page 455.
1. How was it possible for "Hughes" to spend $20 million for worthless gold and silver mines?
   a) Opinion: Cooperation by someone in a key position of the "Hughes" hierarchy.
   b) Current Opinion: For ten years *many* in key positions of the Hughes Hierarchy feasted like maggots on a dead man's corpse.

Page 504—EXHIBIT 212-L: *Empire* and United Press International Photo of "Doctor" Johnnie.
1. OMG, it's Meier, a snail with human characteristics.

Page 507—EXHIBIT 213:
Per Russ: "This Exhibit is a copy of <u>a real Coroner's fingerprint card</u> as submitted by a California enforcement agency in 1987. Coroners offices, contract Medical Examiners, Pathologists, and Hospitals which perform autopsies, per contract with local Sheriff's Departments, usually use this 10-print FBI style fingerprint card to take fingerprints from deceased persons and all descriptive information is annotated on the card. Note: this is the same type card used earlier in 1976 as well."

Page 510—EXHIBIT 214-A:
1. Co-Special Administrator First National Bank of Nevada, together with Will Lummis, file suit against Frank William Gay, Chester C. Davis, Nadine Henley Marshall, John Morrison Holmes, Clarence Albert Waldron, Howard Lorenzo Eckersley, Dr. Wilbur Sutton Thain, and others. Their hope is to retrieve $50 million of the monies embezzled from the Howard Hughes estate.
2. This Exhibit is the lead-in page to an affidavit given by previous Summa Inc. employee Gary Lewis Ray describing what he and Jan Johnson found when they were part of the clean-up crew sent to the "Hughes" Desert Inn Penthouse in May of 1971. The "Hughes" enterouge had vacated the premises in November of 1970 – 5 months earlier.

Page 511—EXHIBIT 214-B:
1. Ray and Jan are instructed to clear *the remaining items* from the "Hughes" penthouse.
2. They are then instructed to bring these items to the Romain Street office in Las Angeles.
3. Instructions received from senior aide Kay Glenn are, "This is to be a "Hush-Hush" operation."
4. Gary Ray and Jan Johnson rent an eighteen foot enclosed truck in Las Vegas.
5. They are let into the "H.H." penthouse by a Jim Golden.
6. They find numerous syringes, ampoules of some kind of medication, bottles of dextrose and saline solution, etc.
7. Also found are several cabinets such as one would find in a doctor's office; porcelain trays, stainless steel trays; dozens of bottles of medication, various types of pills (enough to fill a 24x24x20 box).
8. Numerous empty clear bottles the size of canning jars.
9. Medical instruments and instruments which appeared to be surgical instruments, an operating or examination table; a large lamp such as used in an operating or examination room; centrifuge and sterilization units.

APPENDIX C
EXHIBIT INDEX
Continued

Page 512—EXHIBIT 214-C:

1. Ray and Jan find dozens of quart jars of urine without dates or labels.
2. They are instructed by Kay Glenn, to transport items to Romaine Street, Los Angeles, California, and place them in the back part of the building.
3. Per Gary Ray, "I know that these items remained there for a relatively short period of time and then I noticed these items were no longer where I placed them."
4. Per Ray, "In the summer of 1971 I traveled to Nassau, Bahamas. I found that Mr. Hughes would sleep at any hour of the day or night for as long a 18 or 24 per day."

Page 513—EXHIBIT 214-D:

1. Incident of near exposure after which Gary Ray is told that "no news of this incident is to be passed on to Bill Gay or Chester Davis."
2. The placement of furniture in "Hughes's" room is determined by the aides prior to his arrival. Waldron and Eckersley are the aides instrumental in furniture placement.
3. "Hughes" meets with the Ambassador to Nicaragua and President Somoza. (However, as we learned earlier, Hughes's friend and trusted C.E.O. of Hughes ToolCo, Inc., Raymond Holliday, is turned away *for the third time*?)
4. Aide Jack Real is an outsider, no office access.

Page 514—EXHIBIT 215-A:

1. 7/23/74 Nadine Henley goes under contract, $79,500 per year plus bonuses, sick leave and vacation pay. Salary changes according to Consumer Price Index.
   a. Expense account includes entertainment and travel.
   b. Employee shall not disclose names of Summa customers or associates.
2. 7/15/74 Kay Glenn goes under contract for $70,000 per year as Managing Director. All else same as Henley.
3. 3/1/75 Dr. Wilbur Thain goes under contract for $60,000 per year (work is only part time.)
   a. Expense account same as Henley.
   b. Disclosure of information: Not to disclose Summa's customers or parties which Summa associates with. Not at any time to disclose confidential records or publish or write any material embarrassing or harmful to Summa; not to make records available to anyone who may disseminate them to the public unless authorized by the Board of Directors.

Page 515—EXHIBIT 215-B:

1. Per Nadine Henley's contract:
   a. Vacations with pay according to seniority date.
   b. Disability: Compensation paid during illness or incapacity. After six months compensation will be reduced.
   c. Termination of Employment: Agreement may be terminated for reasonable cause, e.g. conduct discrediting Summa, violation of policies, disclosure of confidential information, or failure to preform duties.
2. Per Kay Glenn's contract: Same as Henley.
3. Dr. Wilbur Thain's contract: Same as Henley.

APPENDIX C
EXHIBIT INDEX
Continued

Page 516—EXHIBIT 215-C:

1. 12/30/76 George Francom Jr. goes under contract as Staff Executive; $65,000 per year plus bonuses, sick leave, expense account travel expenses, and vacation pay. Increase subject to Consumer Price Index.

   a. Disclosure: Not to disclose names of Summa customers or associates.

2. 7/15/74 John Holmes goes under contract as Staff Executive and Member of the Board of Directors at $68,500 per year. All else same as Francom.

3. 7/15/74 Charles Waldron goes under contract for $60,000 per year; all else same as Francom.

4. 7/15/74 James Rickard goes under contract for $51,500 per year. All else same as Francom.

5. 4/11/74 Howard Eckersley goes under contract for $65,000 per year. All else same as Francom.

6. 7/31/74 Levar Beebe Myler goes under contract for $68,500 per year. All else same as Francom.

Page 517—EXHIBIT 215-D:

1. 1. Per George Francom's contract:

   a. Vacations: With pay according to seniority policies.

   b. Disability: Compensation paid during incapacity; after 6 months compensation will be reduced.

   c. Termination of Employment: Terminated for reasonable cause, e.g. failure to perform or disclosure of information.

   d. Death: Beneficiary receives 66 percent of employee's monthly payment for the term of employment. Benefits will be reduced to extent of surviving spouse benefits under retirement plan.

2. Holmes, Waldron, Rickard, Eckersley, and Myler, same as Francom.

Page 518—EXHIBIT 216-A:

1. A signature stamp created for multiple documents and used extensively for the Howard Hughes Corp.

Page 519—EXHIBIT 216-B:

1. Stamp-signature is expanded and compared with a known document (expanded) and signed by Howard Hughes. (NDP, Exhibit 36)

2. Both signatures appear to have been done by the same hand – one is more ornate.

www.ingramcontent.com/pod-product-compliance
Lightning Source LLC
Chambersburg PA
CBHW061831260326

41914CB00005B/958